Gift of

Helen L. Lieghley

Sept. 1932

NAPOLEON

Napoleon went forth to seek Virtue, but, since she was not to be found, he got Power.—GOETHE.

NAPOLEON

By

EMIL LUDWIG

Translated by

EDEN *and* CEDAR PAUL

NEW YORK
BONI & LIVERIGHT
1926

First Printing, December, 1926
Second Printing, January, 1927
Third Printing, January, 1927
Fourth Printing, March, 1927
Fifth Printing, May, 1927
Sixth Printing, July, 1927
Seventh Printing, September, 1927
Eighth Printing, November, 1927
Ninth Printing, December, 1927
Tenth Printing, December, 1927
Eleventh Printing, January, 1928

PRINTED IN THE U. S. A. BY
QUINN & BODEN COMPANY, INC.
RAHWAY, N. J.

To

ELGA LUDWIG

Moscia. Summer 1924

TABLE OF CONTENTS

PAGE

List of Illustrations ix

Chronological Table xi

BOOK ONE

The Island 3

BOOK TWO

The Torrent 55

BOOK THREE

The River 165

BOOK FOUR

The Sea 357

BOOK FIVE

The Rock 545

Envoy 679

Author's Acknowledgments 683

Index 685

LIST OF ILLUSTRATIONS

FACING PAGE

Buonaparte in 1783. The first known portrait, drawn by his fellow-countryman Pontornini. Musée Nationale, Versailles 4

General Bonaparte in 1797. After a painting by Jean Guérin. Bibliothèque Nationale, Paris 36
(From the "Corpus Imaginum" of the Photographic Society, Charlottenburg.)

General Bonaparte in 1796. Engraving from the Kircheisen Collection 68

General Bonaparte. Unfinished portrait by Jacques Louis David. From the collection of the Duke of Bassano . . 100
(Photograph by Braun, Paris and Dornach.)

General Bonaparte in 1797. Drawing by Wocher in Basle. Town Library, Basle 140

General Bonaparte in 1798, during the voyage to Egypt. Sketch by André Dutertre 156

Bonaparte as First Consul. Painting by Girodet. Musée Nationale, Versailles 196
(Photograph in the Kircheisen Collection.)

Bonaparte as First Consul. Pencil sketch by J. D. A. Ingres. Germain Bapst Collection 228
(Photograph in the Kircheisen Collection.)

Bonaparte in 1802, as First Consul. Engraving by Alexandre Tardieu. After a drawing by Jean Baptiste Isabey . . 260

Bonaparte as First Consul. Painting by J. D. A. Ingres. Musée de Liége 292
(Photograph by Braun, Paris and Dornach.)

The Coronation. Detail from the picture by Jacques Louis David. Louvre, Paris 324
(Photograph in the Kircheisen Collection.)

Napoleon as Emperor. Painting by Vigneux. Count Primoli Collection 356
(From the "Corpus Imaginum" of the Photographic Society, Charlottenburg.)

FACING PAGE

Napoleon as Emperor. Bust by Houdon, Musée de Dijon . 388
(Photograph by J. E. Bulloz, Paris.)

The Emperor's profile. Sketched during Mass in the Tuileries. Germain Bapst Collection 420
(Photograph in the Kircheisen Collection.)

Napoleon as Emperor in 1809. Woodcut from a medal by J. P. Droz 452

Napoleon as Emperor. Engraving by Bourgeois, after a painting by Jacques Louis David 484
(From the "Corpus Imaginum" of the Photographic Society, Charlottenburg.)

Napoleon as Emperor in 1814. Painting by Horace Vernet. Tate Gallery, London 516
(From the "Corpus Imaginum" of the Photographic Society, Charlottenburg.)

Napoleon as Emperor in 1815. Engraving by Robert Lefèvre, after a painting by Muneret 548

Napoleon as Emperor in 1815. Woodcut, after a medal . . 580

Napoleon at St. Helena. Watercolour painting, probably by a Japanese, with a marginal inscription in Chinese ideographs concerning the owner. Broadley Collection . . 612

Death mask of Napoleon. By Dr. Antommarchi . . . 644

CHRONOLOGICAL TABLE

BOOK ONE

1769. August 15th, Napoleon born.
1779. At School in Brienne.
1784. At the military academy.
1785. Sub-lieutenant of artillery.
1789. To Corsica.
1791. April, lieutenant in Valence.
October, to Corsica.
1792. Putsch in Ajaccio. Banishment.
1793. Captain. Siege of Toulon.
1794. February, brigadier general.
August, arrested.
1795. June, at the Ministry for War.
October, suppression of the Paris rising.
Commander of the Army of the Interior.
1796. March 2nd, Commander of the Army of Italy.
March 6th, married to Joséphine Beauharnais.

BOOK TWO

1796-7. Battles of Millesimo, Castiglione, Arcola.
Rivoli, Mantua.
1797. At the castle of Montebello.
Peace of Campo Formio.
1798. In Paris till May.
May 19th, embarcation for Egypt.
Battle of the Pyramids.
1799. Jaffa, Acre, Aboukir.
October 7th, landing in France.
November 9th, coup d'état of the eighteenth Brumaire.
December 24th, First Consul.

BOOK THREE

1800. June 14th, battle of Marengo.
December 24th, attempted assassination.
1801. Peace of Lunéville.
Concordat with Pius VII.
1802. Peace with England.
Consul for life. Legion of Honour.

1804. March 21st, duke of Enghien shot.
May 18th, assumption of imperial title.
December 2nd, coronation.
1805. October, Trafalgar.
November, Vienna taken.
December 2nd, battle of Austerlitz.
Peace of Pressburg.
1806. Confederation of the Rhine. Joseph, King of Naples.
Louis, King of Holland.
October 14th, battle of Jena.
Berlin. Continental System.
1807. Battles of Preussisch-Eylau and Friedland.
June 7th, treaty of Tilsit.
Jerome, King of Westphalia.
1808. Rome. Madrid. Nayonne. Joseph, King of Spain. Murat, King of Naples.
1809. Excommunication. Battles of Aspern-Essling, Wagram, and Vienna.
1810. January, divorce.
April, married to Marie Louise.
1811. March 20th, birth of his son.

BOOK FOUR

1812. Battles of Smolensk, Borodino, Vittoria, Moscow.
December, return to Paris.
1813. April, battles of Lützen and Bautzen.
July, battle of Dresden.
October 16th to 18th, battle of Leipzig.
1814. Battles of Brienne, La Rothière, Champaubert, Montereau, Bas-sur-Aube, Laon, Arcis-sur-Aube.
April 6th, abdication in Fontainebleau.
April 20th, embarcation for Elba.
1815. February 26th, sails from Elba.
March 13th, outlawed.
March 20th, Paris.
June, battles of Ligny and Waterloo.
June 23rd, second abdication.
July 13th, letter to the prince regent.
July 31st, declared a prisoner.

BOOK FIVE

1815. October 17th, arrival in St. Helena.
1821. May 5th, death.

BOOK ONE

THE ISLAND

The story of Napoleon produces on me an impression like that produced by the Revelation of Saint John the Divine. We all feel there must be something more in it, but we do not know what.—GOETHE.

I

A YOUNG woman is sitting in a tent. Wrapped in a shawl, she is suckling her baby, and listening to a distant rumbling and roaring. Are they still shooting, though night has fallen? Maybe it is only the sound of one of those autumn thunderstorms whose echoes reverberate from the mountains; or perhaps it is nothing more than the murmur from the surrounding forest of pines and evergreen oaks, where foxes and wild swine have their lairs. She looks like a gipsy, sitting there with her white breast half covered by the shawl, brooding within the murky tent, uncertain what the fate of the day may have been. Now she hears the sound of hoof-beats. Is it he? He promised to come; but it is a long way from the fighting line, and the mists are rising.

The flap of the tent is thrown open, letting in a breath of night air. A man enters. An officer in a coloured tunic and wearing a plumed head-dress; a slim fellow, nimble of movement; a young patrician, in the middle twenties. He greets the woman ardently. Springing to her feet, she gives the nursling to her maid. Wine is brought. Taking the kerchief from her head, she stands before him, showing chestnut ringlets astray on a smooth, white brow. An eager question is on her well-shaped lips. Add to the picture that she has a long chin, a sign of energy; that her aquiline nose is thrown into relief by the firelight; and that on her hip there gleams the dagger which in this mountain land she never lays aside. We see a lovely amazon, daughter of an ancient race, sprung from men of action and resolution. The woman's forebears, like the man's, have for centuries been leaders and warriors; first across the water in Italy, and then in this craggy island.

But now, when all have gathered together against the hated

enemy, have joined forces in the attempt to drive out the French, here, in the wildest part of the mountains, whither the brave girl of nineteen has followed the husband fighting for their fatherland; who, now, could recognise in her the brilliant patrician, the magnet of all eyes? Here, nothing but pride and courage show that she is of noble birth.

The man, full of life and vigour, ever in movement, tells her all his news. The enemy has been beaten, driven back towards the coast. There is no escape. Envoys have been sent to Paoli.

"There will be a truce to-morrow. Letizia, we are winning! Corsica will be free!"

Every Corsican longs for many children. It is a land where an affront is instantly avenged by a dagger thrust; where the vendetta is sacred; where family feuds last from decade to decade and from century to century. The man before us wants many children, to ensure that his race shall persist; and the woman has learned from mother and grandmother that children are tokens of honour. She had become a mother at fifteen; but the baby she has just been nursing was her first boy.

The thought of freedom glows afresh, for the officer is adjutant to Paoli, the leader of the people.

"No longer shall our children be the slaves of France!"

II

With the coming of spring, despondency prevails. The enemy has landed reinforcements; the children of the island take up arms once more; again the young wife accompanies her husband to the war; this time she carries a child beneath her heart, the child conceived during the storms of the previous autumn.

"Often, in search of news, I would steal forth from our mountain nook to the battle-field; I heard the bullets whistling, but I put my trust in Our Lady"—so she would tell the story in later years.

In May, the Corsicans were defeated. There was a terrible

Buonaparte in 1783. The first known portrait, drawn by his fellow-countryman Pontornini. Musée Nationale, Versailles.

retreat through the dense forests and the rugged mountains. Among the multitude of men and the few women, rode Letizia, big with child, carrying her one-year-old boy in her arms, seated on a mule. They reached the coast safely. In June the defeated Paoli, accompanied by a few hundred of his faithful followers, had to flee to Italy. In July Paoli's adjutant, Letizia's husband, with other envoys, capitulated to the conqueror. The insular pride was humbled. But in August his wife brought the avenger into the world.

She named him Napolione.

This woman, who during the campaign had played the heroine and had shown a man's courage, must now, in the great house by the seashore, become a prudent and thrifty housewife. Her young husband, fanciful by temperament, lived more on plans than on income. For years his energies were mainly devoted to the great lawsuit concerning his inheritance. As a student in Pisa, where among his fellows he was known as Count Buonaparte, he had lived well but learned little. After the birth of his second son, he cut his studies short. How was he to make a living? In troublous times, a man of the world takes the world as it is; comes to terms with the conqueror; all the more since the French, in order to secure their footing in the island, are inclined to show favour to the Corsican nobility.

Soon he becomes assessor in the new lawcourts; superintendent of a nursery in which the king of France, eager to turn the new possessions to account, wishes to grow mulberries; and when the distinguished marshal comes to stay, no expense must be spared. There are still flocks of sheep in the hills and vineyards along the coast; his brother, archdeacon at the cathedral, is well-to-do; and his wife's half brother, another priest, a merchant's son, is skilled in worldly affairs.

By the time his proud and beautiful wife has reached her thirties, five boys and three girls have been born to her. This is well accordant to the notions of the islanders, for whom rivalries and vendettas are supreme virtues. But the rearing of eight children is a costly matter; so, day by day, the youngsters hear their parents talking about money. At length, however, the father finds a way out of his difficulties. Accompanied by his two eldest sons, now ten and eleven years of age, he sails to France, and journeys from Toulon to Versailles.

He brings recommendations from the marshal in Corsica. The Buonapartes' Italian title of nobility is confirmed by the Herald's College in Paris. To the Corsican official who has been loyal for a decade, King Louis makes a grant of two thousand francs. The two sons and one of the daughters are given scholarships in the Nobles' Schools. One son is to be a priest; the other, an officer.

III

A taciturn boy, small, shy, and lonely, sits reading in a corner of the garden. It is his own plot in the school garden at Brienne, and he has made a fence round it. Really, only a third of the enclosure is his own, for he has fenced in the plots of neighbours on either side. They may come in too; but woe to any one else who disturbs his privacy! He rushes furiously at the intruder. A little while ago, when the boys had had a fireworks' display, two of his schoolmates, who had been slightly burned, had run away to his garden for refuge. He had driven them out, flourishing a hoe at them.

No punishment will bring him to reason in this matter. The masters shake their heads and let him go his own way.

"The youngster is made of granite," says one of them, "but there is a volcano inside."

No one may touch this little kingdom of his in the garden, though part of it is usurped. He has an ardent feeling for his own independence. Writing to his father, he says: "I would rather be the first among the workmen in a factory than the last among the artists in the Academy." Did he get the idea out of Plutarch? Certainly he has an enthusiasm for that author, the lives of the great men as sketched by Plutarch, especially the Roman heroes. Of these, he is always dreaming. No one tells us that he ever saw this boy laugh.

To his schoolfellows he seems half a savage, or at best a queer foreigner. He knows scarcely a word of French, and has little inclination to learn the language of the foe. What a tiny little chap he is, and what a ridiculous name! His coat is too long. No pocket-money, nothing to spend, and yet he claims to be of noble birth! The scions of the French nobility laugh. Who cares about Corsican noblemen?

"If you Corsicans are such brave fellows, why did you let yourselves be beaten by our unconquerable troops?"

"We were one to ten," the lad angrily exclaims. "You just wait till I'm grown up, and I will pay you Frenchmen out!"

"Your father is nothing more than a sergeant, after all!"

An outburst of wrath from the boy, who challenges his tormentor. The young Napoleon is "kept in." He writes to his father: "I am tired of explaining my poverty; of having to endure the mockery of these foreign boys, whose only superiority is in respect of money, for in nobility of feeling they are far beneath me. Must I really humble myself before these purse-proud fellows?" The answer from the island is: "We have no money. You must stay where you are."

He stays five years; and, just as his revolutionary feeling is intensified by every slight, so does his self-confidence grow proportionally with the growth of his contempt for his fellows. The masters, indeed, monks one and all, have a good opinion of him, although he does not make much headway except in mathematics, history, and geography—subjects which appeal to a precise mind, a seeing eye, and also to the bitterness of spirit characteristic of one who belongs to a conquered race.

For always his thoughts turn back to his native island. In secret, he is angry with his father for having come to terms with the French. He has made up his own mind. He will get all he can out of the king at whose cost he now pursues his studies, so that in due time he may use the knowledge against his patron. He has a presentiment that some day he will set Corsica free. As yet all the lad of fourteen can do is to pore over books about his homeland, for he who would make history must first study history. He devours, too, all that Voltaire, Rousseau, and the great king of Prussia shortly before his death, have written on behalf of the liberation of Corsica.

Such a boy as this—solitary, suspicious, questing and rebellious, brooding rancorously over vast designs—what is he likely to become? Precociously thoughtful; endowed with a knowledge of men that is beyond his years. When Joseph, his elder brother, wishes to abandon the priestly career and to adopt the profession of arms, the youngster writes of him: "1. He lacks courage to brave the perils of the battle-field.—He will be a good garrison officer: well-grown and handsome, quick-witted and therefore inclined to pay frivolous compliments, with his talents he will always make a good impression in society. But in battle? 2. 'Tis too late to make a change. He might have got a rich benefice, and what an advantage that would have been to the family! 3. What branch of the service will he enter? The navy? (a) He knows nothing of mathematics; (b) his health could never endure life at sea. He is too light-minded for the sustained work that will be needed if he is to be an artillery officer." These are the reflections of a fifteen-year-old observer, who sees in himself the qualities that his brother lacks; and it is a perfect description of Joseph, who was, indeed, his father's son.

From this same father, Napoleon had inherited versatility and a vigorous imagination; from his mother came pride, courage, and accuracy; from both was derived his strong family feeling.

IV

"Only the sword-belt belongs to France; the edge is my own," thinks the youth, as he first buckles on his sword. At sixteen he has become a sub-lieutenant—and he will don uniform a good many more times before he dies. He has qualified for this rank by a year in the Paris Cadets' School, where he spent his time as he had spent it at Brienne, poring over books. A lad of Spartan tastes, he finds the prodigal expenditure of the sprigs of the French nobility (by whom he is utterly outshone) extremely distasteful. Since, however, nature sets him, even more than most young men, in the centre of his own world, he makes a virtue of necessity, and pens a memorial to the effect that luxurious living is unsuitable for budding soldiers. He must not get into debt, for he knows how poor they are at home. Now, when his father dies, the family affection of this Italian becomes intensified. Though little more than a boy, he begins to save money in order to help his mother.

After his examination, passed with fair credit, his superiors wrote of him: "Reserved and diligent, he prefers study to any kind of conversation, and nourishes his mind upon good authors. . . . He is taciturn, with a love for solitude; is moody, overbearing, and extremely egotistical. Though he speaks little, his answers are decisive and to the point, and he excels in argument. Much self-love, and overweening ambition."

Clad in his new uniform, the little sub-lieutenant goes to join his regiment at Valence, compelled by his poverty to walk a great part of the way. Three impulses stir his youthful heart: to despise and make use of his fellow-creatures, most of whom are empty-headed and pretentious; to extricate himself from the clutches of poverty; to learn much in order that he may rule others. The means and the goal are one. He is to be a leader in the struggle on the island, and then to make himself master of Corsica.

How dull life is in this garrison town! Of course, a young man should learn to dance, should taste the pleasures of lively society. He tries this, but soon abandons the attempt, for his teeming pride makes him want to hide his poverty. However, any one who holds converse with members of the burgher class, lawyers and shopkeepers, hears strange talk, gets wind of things that the young viscounts in Paris never dream of. Is it really true? Has the spirit of Voltaire's and Montesquieu's, and Raynal's writings actually climbed down so soon, to stalk among the provincial petty bourgeois? Is the movement which these prophets were conjuring up now seriously afoot? Can it be that the revolution is at hand?

Books clamour it abroad. Reading is free as breathing; and when a man has read all the books in the lending library, he can spare a franc or two now and again to buy a new book. True, the youth lodges in a café, and the clicking of the billiard balls in the next room is tiresome. But it would be still more tiresome to move. In personal habits, he is conservative.

What about his sentiments? Judge for yourselves. Like every young man of his generation, he is keenly interested in the State and society. There he sits in the room next the billiard-room; pale, lonely, in a hot and stuffy atmosphere. While his comrades, after their short hours of duty, scatter to seek distraction in gaming or the pursuit of women, the impoverished lieutenant bends over his books, reading with sure instinct about the things (and those only) that will be of use to him in days to come: artillery, its principles and its history; the art of siege; Plato's *Republic;* the constitution of the Persian, the Athenian, the Spartan State; the history of England; the campaigns of Frederick the Great; French finances; the Tartars and the Turks, their manners and customs, and the topography of their countries; the history of Egypt and the history of Carthage; descriptions of India; English accounts of contemporary France: Mirabeau, Buffon, and Machiavelli; the history and the constitution of Switzerland; the history and constitution of

China, India, the Inca State; the history of the nobility and the story of patrician misdeeds; astronomy, geology, and meteorology; the laws of the growth of population; statistics of mortality.

He did not simply flutter the pages of his books, but was an attentive reader. There is extant a whole series of copy-books containing Napoleon's notes, penned in an almost illegible handwriting. The contents of these, reprinted, occupies four hundred pages. Here we find a map of the Saxon heptarchy with a list of the kings for three centuries; item, the varieties of foot-race in ancient Crete; item, lists of the Hellenic fortresses in Asia Minor; item, the dates of twenty-seven caliphs, with a note of the strength of their cavalry, and an account of the misconduct of their wives.

Especially frequent are memoranda concerning Egypt and India, including even the measurements of the Great Pyramid and a catalogue of Brahminical sects. He copies a passage from Raynal: "In view of the position of Egypt, lying betwixt two seas, and in fact betwixt the East and the West, Alexander the Great conceived the design of establishing the capital of his world-wide empire in that country, and of making Egypt the centre of world commerce. This most enlightened of the conquerors had realised that if there was any practicable way of amalgamating his conquests into one consolidated State, it was by this use of Egypt, created as a point of union between Africa, Asia, and Europe." Thirty years later, he still had the words by heart. He had read them so often.

At this date, too, he begins original composition, drafting more than a dozen essays and projects: the placing of artillery; suicide; monarchical authority; the inequality of men; and Corsica, above all, Corsica—each were the topics. Rousseau, the most popular author of those days, is pulverised by Napoleon's realism. The young officer is epitomising Rousseau's views on the origin of the human race (in the *Discours sur l'origine et les fondements de l'inégalité parmi les hommes*), but abruptly he breaks off the epitome with the comment: "I don't believe a word of this." Then come a couple of pages filled with his own counterstatement. Human beings were not, to begin with, solitary; nor were they nomadic. They were happy, and lived apart, because they were not numerous enough to be forced into close contact. When the population grew more thick upon the ground, "then imagination came forth from the cave in which for so long it had been prisoned: self-confidence, passion, and pride reared their heads; there arose ambitious men with pale features, who took control of affairs, and mastered the multicoloured young popinjays, the Lotharios and lady-killers."

Do not we already hear him rattling his chains, in the dark cavern where he himself is prisoned with his titanic imagination? Do not we see the fancy portrait of the young author, pale of visage, full of hatred for the brilliant lady-killers who are his messmates?

Away from these fellows, who are Frenchmen! His gaze is still fixed upon his native isle, and it is to the advantage of Corsica that he twists the new sociological outlooks. We read in one of the essays: "How absurd to declare that divine laws forbid us to shake off a usurper's yoke! Were that so, then every regicide who has clambered into the vacant throne would be under God's protection, whereas in case of failure he would have lost his head. With how much better right, then, can a people drive out a usurping prince! Does not this speak for Corsicans? . . . Thus we can shake off the yoke of France, just as we shook off the yoke of Genoa. Amen."

Meanwhile, the fledgling genius wished to try its wings, and this urge led Napoleon to draft a novel on Corsica, and also some short stories. All were animated by hatred of France, but none of them were ever finished. Still he was learning his trade, spurred on by poverty, passion, and sentiment. Imagination rules the world, but cannons are the instrument whereby imagination realises its purposes. "I have no refuge but my work. I only change my linen once a week. Since I was ill, I have slept very little. . . . I eat only once a day."

He studies ordnance and munitions of war, always thinking in figures, so that every one says that he is a born mathematician. Now, side by side with the drafts of works of imagination, he draws up specifications of all the localities in the island where he would place batteries, dig trenches, station troops—if he had but the power! Beneath the network of poetical thoughts with which he has covered the island, he spreads over his maps a second network, wherein crosses denote big guns. Maps, maps! In his room beside the noisy café, he restudies everything conceivable, copies whole speeches out of the report of the parliamentary proceedings at Westminster, and sketches the remotest parts of the earth. At the end of the last of his copy-books, the final entry runs: "St. Helena, a small island in the Atlantic Ocean. English colony."

At this juncture he received a letter from his mother. Her powerful patron, the marshal, was dead; the house had lost its main prop; the mulberry orchard was no longer to be a means of livelihood; Joseph had no paid occupation; could the second son give any help? Shortly after this appeal reached him, he went home on furlough. Are we to consider him an unacknowledged conqueror, returning to the island of his plans and dreams? Read what he wrote in his diary:

"Always alone, though in the midst of men, I go back home that I may give myself up to my lonely dreams and to the waves of my melancholy. Whither, now, do my gloomy thoughts tend? Towards death. Yet I stand on the threshold of life, and may reasonably expect to draw breath for many, many years. For the last six or seven years I have been far away from my country. How great the joy—to see my own people once more!—What demon, then, is it that tempts me to self-destruction?—Since misfortune dogs my footsteps, and nothing gives me pleasure, why should I go on bearing a life in which, for me, everything goes awry?—What a tragedy in the homeland? My fellow-countrymen, in chains, kiss the hand that beats them.—Proud, buoyed up by a sense of his own worth, so lived of yore the happy Corsican, giving his days to the service of the State, and spending his nights in the arms of his beloved wife—the nights which nature and affection made divine for him. With the disappearance of freedom, those happy times have vanished like a dream. Frenchmen, not only have you stolen from us our greatest good, but now you are corrupting our morals! That is how I see my country, and yet I am powerless to help. Are there not reasons enough for quitting a world in which I must glorify those whom I hate?—If it were but the life of one individual which stood between us and our liberties, I should not be slow to act.—Life has become a burden to me, I have no enjoyment, nothing but pain,—and because I cannot live after my own fashion, everything is loathsome to me."

V

After a year spent in Corsica, a year rendered gloomy by money troubles and family cares, he was still in this mood of despair when his furlough expired. He returned not to Valence, but to Auxonne. What did the change matter?

But, at last, recognition comes. His new general, who sees that this subaltern of nineteen is well informed, puts into his hands the task of carrying out some works upon the parade ground. "Difficult calculations are involved; and so, for the last ten days, I have been busied from morning till night at the head of two hundred men. This unusual preferment has given some of my superiors a spite against me. They are furious that so important a job should have been taken out of their hands and given to a lieutenant."

The old depression recurs. Promotion will be desperately slow, and when he becomes a captain he will be retired on half-pay. He will return home, to be despised because he is a pensioner of the French. At long last, he will be buried in his native soil. Of that privilege, at least, the French cannot rob him! Were they, then, nothing but froth, the dreams of liberty revealed in the books he had read? If mighty France herself was unable to shake off the yoke of the nobility, to rid herself of venality and nepotism, how was poor little Corsica to shake off the French tyranny?

The young author fills his diary with new schemes. He would have had to pay heavily for it if the book had fallen into the hands of his superiors. "Draft for a memorial concerning monarchical authority. Set forth details as to the usurped power which kings enjoy to-day in the twelve monarchies of Europe. There are few of them who have not merited dethronement." Thus does he vent his spleen in the faithful diary; whilst in public on every royal birthday, dressed in gala uniform, he must join in the cry: Long live the king!

Another year of his youth is spent in the dull routine of such service, while Napoleon holds his peace and waits, dividing his energies between imaginative writing and mathematics.

The year of destiny has opened. Into the most out-of-the-way regions of the slumbering province comes the presage of the trumpets that are about to sound. We are in the month of June 1789. The melancholy lieutenant feels that the day of vengeance draws near. Is the arrogance of those who have so long humiliated him, to bring destruction upon their own heads? May it not be that the call of the myriads is also the battle-cry of the island? He takes his *Letters on Corsica;* sends them to his admired exemplar Paoli, in exile; and writes: "General! I came into the world when my country was perishing. My cradle was surrounded by men with the death-rattle in their throats, and by those whom despair had driven to tears. . . . With them, hope vanished. Slavery was the reward of our subjugation. To justify themselves, the traitors have heaped calumnies upon you. . . . When I read this, my blood boiled, and I resolved to scatter the mists. Now I shall blacken with the brush of shame all who have betrayed the common cause. . . . If I lived in the capital, I should find other means. . . . Owing to my youth, this undertaking may be fruitless; but I shall be helped by my passion for truth, my love for my country, and my enthusiasm. If you, General, will encourage in this work a young man whose coming into the world you saw, I shall gain confidence. . . . My mother, Madame Letizia, has charged me to remind you of the old days in Corte."

We notice a new tone, a symphony of new tones: the soaring emotion of the epoch; the gesture of the tyrannicide; the whole equipment of scintillating words, not an uprush of feeling (as in the pages of his diary), but deliberately chosen with an eye to their effect. Only one thing is alarmingly original, quite peculiar to the writer: the decisive "I" at the opening of the letter, this "I" as a great thesis, fronting the world. Immeasurable self-confidence is breaking a trail; for now the drum-taps of a new era are sounding; an era which will give the palm, not to birth but to action, thus sweeping away the only hindrance that has hitherto been insuperable. An unprecedented claim is voiced, a claim which henceforward will never cease to be heard. But at the close of the letter, with a courteous turn of phrase, he slips back into the familiar, implying that he looks to Paoli for protection. What adroitness, what good manners, we find in all the letters of this adolescent, who in person is still rough and enigmatical!

Paoli, the survival from an earlier day, is annoyed by such arrogance, and answers with civil irony that young people should not try to write history.

Four weeks after the sending of the letter, young people begin to write history, for the first time in the eighteenth century. They storm the Bastille; the great signal has been given; and France leaps to arms. Even in the garrison town of our young lieutenant, the masses riot and loot, until the propertied classes join forces with the troops. Buonaparte is at his post with his battery in the streets, and helps to shoot down the people. This is the first time he has fired a gun in real earnest. He acts under orders from the king's officers; but there can be no doubt that he acts whole-heartedly against the mob, which he despises no less than he despises the nobility.

In the depths of his soul, he regards this as nothing more than a dispute among foreigners. What does he care about Frenchmen who raise their hands against other Frenchmen? His brain is fired by a single thought: "Corsica's hour has come!" Madness or enthusiasm, an ideal or merely a catchword? What matter? Let us carry the message to our island. Apply for leave; and, in the turmoil of the new movement, be the first to reach home!

VI

Lieutenant Buonaparte landed on his island like a prophet carrying a new doctrine to a foreign coast. He was the first to bring the red cockade; to promise liberty, equality, and fraternity. Was not this a race of free mountaineers, who of old had been self-governing, but for twenty years had groaned under the heel of the oppressor—a conqueror who ruled through the instrumentality of the nobles and the Church, but did not understand the people?

What did it matter to the young Jacobin that until yesterday he had lived upon his patrician birth, that solely because of his rank he had been educated at the king's cost? What was the king to him? At length the peoples were to be free to rule themselves. If the new France, just awakened, had proclaimed the right of self-government, Corsica, which the old France had loaded with chains, must proclaim its own freedom. Citizens, the hour has struck! To arms! Let every one wear the red cockade of the new era; let us form a National Guard, as they have done in Paris! Let us wrest the means of power from the king's troops. I am an artillerist, and I will be your leader!

Twenty years of age, pale of countenance, with cold, blue-grey eyes, but with a mouth full of glowing phrases, such is the aspect of young Buonaparte as he hastens through the streets of Ajaccio. Every one in the little town knows him, and he is followed by a growing number of persons, some eager for liberty, and others in search of a change of any kind. To the crowd in the square, he seems a man bringing passionate hopes; his figure is that of a tribune of the people. In this half-oriental atmosphere, and among these quarrelsome families (so he says later), "a man soon learns to study the human heart."

But there is a set-back. No reinforcements come from the mountains; and, when the regular troops put in an appearance, they scatter the revolutionists. Within a few hours, all have been disarmed, though, for prudence, no arrests are made. This is a further source of disillusionment. He is not even a martyr, but only a would-be popular leader who has been defeated; his position borders on the ludicrous. Yet the fever is still burning in his veins, and at all costs he must do something to cool himself. A statement of grievances to the National Assembly in Paris! First of all, in the florid style of the day, an ode to the new freedom, and then a spate of complaints and adjurations. To the gallows with the king's servants! Arm the citizens of the island!—A committee promptly joins him in signing the document.

Weeks of waiting. What answer will come from Paris? Here is the courier at last. The island is to be a French province, having the same rights as the other provinces; in accordance with Mirabeau's proposal, Paoli and all the champions of liberty are free to return home. The lieutenant is taken aback. A province? In spite of the new ideas, and indeed because of them, the Corsicans are to remain Frenchmen? A strange form of liberty! But there, already, is the procession, headed by the authorities, on its way to the cathedral, where the decree from Paris is to receive a blessing. Buonaparte is prompt to seize the rope which all are seizing. He pens fiery manifestoes to his fellow-citizens, seeks supporters in the new political club, and engineers his elder brother's election to the town council. Meanwhile he continues to work at his history of Corsica, and reads to his mother choice passages of what he is writing.

"Can this be the great Paoli?" That is the question Buonaparte asks himself, when, after twenty years' exile, the hero of his youthful enthusiasms returns amid popular acclamations. "His talk and his appearance are so humdrum, so politic, so unsoldierly." But it was expedient to keep on good terms with Paoli, for he was to be the commander of the National Guard. In the mountains, the young artillery officer was for some time closely associated with the man who had been his father's chief just before his own coming into the world.

When they were sitting together or riding together—the tried veteran and the darkly aspiring young Corsican,—the latter would eagerly expound to the former his plans for an armed rising, and even for the forcible severance of the island from the new France. On these occasions, Paoli would look at Buonaparte with mingled pride and alarm. He could not but feel that the author of the *Letters on Corsica* really had a claim upon him. But the young fellow had the devil in his body; and (which was worse) in his brain, for in the man's brain was the image of the world throne in solitary splendour. Shaking his head, Paoli would exclaim:

"There is nothing modern about you, Napolione. You come from the age of Plutarch!"

For the first time in his life young Napoleon felt that he was understood. The Roman heroes of Plutarch were alone adequate to his aspirations. Paoli was the first to recognise the Roman in Buonaparte.

At length he has a phrase upon which his self-esteem

can luxuriate. Now, from his country retreat, when at Paoli's instigation he writes a manifesto, the superscription penned by his fevered imagination runs as follows: "23rd day of January in the 2nd year, from my study at Midilli." Ridiculous or sublime? However this may be, as soon as he has issued the dictatorial pronunciamento the young man has to hasten back to his military duties in France, for his furlough, though renewed again and again, has finally expired. Is he to sacrifice this last firm standing-ground? To what end? Why should he stay in the island any longer? The first place is occupied!

VII

"I am in a peasant's hut writing to you, after a long talk with the good folk. . . . It is four in the afternoon; the weather is fresh but mild; I thoroughly enjoyed walking. No snow yet, but there is snow in the air—Everywhere I have found the peasants staunch; . . . they are all ready to die for the constitution—The women are royalists almost without exception. No wonder for that, seeing that Liberty is fairer than they, and eclipses them. In Dauphiné, the priests have taken the oath of fealty to the constitution; they laugh at the bishops. —'Good society,' as it is called (three out of four are aristocrats), affects admiration for the British constitution. It is true that Peretti threatened Mirabeau with a dagger. This is little to our credit. The Patriotic Society must make Mirabeau a present of our national costume: biretta, vest, knee-breeches and hose, cartridge pouch, stiletto, pistol, and musket. It will certainly have a good effect."

Everything in this letter to Napoleon's maternal uncle, the abbé Joseph Fesch, bears witness to observation and calculation, the elements upon which the politician's influence is based: the weather, the State, travelling on foot, the conciliation of a man in high position, men's motives—all have been the objects of careful consideration. Vanity and avarice, these are the weaknesses to which an appeal can be successfully directed. We see deep into his soul when, in a bluntly-worded letter dating from those weeks, he arraigns an opponent thus: "Your study of human nature has taught you the price of every man's enthusiasm; for you, the difference between people's characters was summed up in a few gold pieces more or less!"

Gold pieces! Where were they to be had? Louis, the brother of thirteen, had come back to France with him. When Lieutenant Buonaparte (he had the full rank now) and his brother got back to Valence, they had no more between them than eighty-five francs, to provide for food, clothing, and the boy's education. They had to brush their own clothes.

Money! Not for enjoyment (he despises trivial pleasures), but to help him make his way in the world! Lyons Academy has offered a prize for an essay. Twelve hundred francs; one could for that sum equip half Corsica with weapons. "What truths and sentiments is it most important to inculcate upon men for their happiness?" The lieutenant smiles. The subject suits him very well. First of all, so to say, he leaves his card on the academicians who have chosen the theme. They are disciples of Rousseau. Our essayist opens by extolling the joys of nature, friendship, ardent idleness—three things which he neither knew nor prized. Suddenly the argument takes a political turn, against kings, and on behalf of the universalisation of the free enjoyment of possessions and rights. Then comes a sinister tone, as if the writer were contemplating in a mirror his own image as the pallid student of a few years before: "The ambitious man, pale of countenance, laughing sardonically, plays with crime, and intrigue is his chosen instrument. . . . If, at length, he gets his hand on the rudder of power, he soon wearies of the adulation of the crowd. . . . Men of great ambition have sought happiness, and have found fame."

Sublime forebodings, worthy of any of the characters in Plutarch. Soon the author expresses himself more plainly.

His ideal is Sparta; courage and strength are the outstanding virtues. A Spartan moved through life as a man moves in the plenitude of his powers. "He was happy because he lived in accordance with his nature. Only the strong man is good; the weakling is evil." Another presage glows in the following utterance: "Men who are truly great are like meteors: they shine and consume themselves, that they may lighten the darkness of the earth."

This was too much for the Lyons Academy, which declared the essay "unworthy of commendation." A fresh disappointment! The effort had brought neither money nor renown. With indefatigable assiduity, none the less, he resumes work on his Corsican novel, and pens a dialogue on love.

What? Does this word, too, shed its lustre into the youth's sombre mind? Are we to have an outpouring in the Rousseauist vein? Hearken to the words of our lieutenant, now twenty-two years of age: "I, too, was in love once, and learned enough of it to despise definitions, which only confuse the issue. I deny its justification; nay, more, I regard it as injurious to society and destructive to the happiness of the individual. Men could bless heaven if they were quit of it."

Fanfares interrupt these political and social musings, fanfares from Paris! Louis XVI, attempting to escape, had been caught at Varennes and brought back. The people had triumphed, and the revolutionary movement was intensified. On the second anniversary of the taking of the Bastille, the Red lieutenant proposed a toast to the patriots. From the island came to him sounds of confusion, the heart-beats of anarchy—for during these wild years the ripples of turbulence spread from Paris in widening circles, to reach distant shores. In Corsica, too, civil war is imminent. Back there, for a second venture!

VIII

Now the lieutenant has to play the part of Coriolanus. Catch voices, catch men; for, since the people have come into power, it is necessary to cultivate popularity. Archdeacon Lucien Buonaparte has chosen this convenient hour for dying, and the family is in easier circumstances. Mother's brother Fesch, another cleric, has been prevailed upon to join the Jacobin Club. Joseph can influence opinion in the town council. Is there any other man in the island competent to direct a battery? Of course the leader of the National Guard would have the real power in his hands. But suppose one should fail to secure election?

This time his furlough lasts only till the new year. Better be careful! He writes to his commanding officer: "Urgent circumstances have forced me to outstay my leave. But I have nothing to reproach myself with: more sacred duties, tenderer obligations, are my excuse." He hopes that he will not be cashiered. No answer! Well, he must take the risk.

Now comes the election of the commandant of the National Guard. Kinsmen everywhere, but that does not suffice. His mother keeps open house for party friends; often sympathisers from the hills have to be put up for the night; this is the way to catch votes. "At that time," writes a comrade, "he would for a season be taciturn and reflective; then he would be genial once more, pleasant to all comers, conversationally inclined, prepared to visit any one who might be of use, and doing his utmost to win adherents." When the commissaries come, he has one of them forcibly detained in his house; and he arranges that the supporters of a rival shall have a thrashing. This is a Corsican election! But when the palpitating day draws to a close, Napoleon has gained his end. He is second in command, with the rank of lieutenant colonel.

Shall he seize the opportunity, this Italian, of sending in his papers in France? Shall he leave the French service? Better be careful, still! From the memoirs of great commanders he has learned that it is always wise to leave a line of retreat open. "In this difficult posture of affairs," he writes to Valence, "a good Corsican's post of honour is in his native country. That is why my own folk keep me from returning to France. Since, however, I am not one to compromise where duty is concerned, I had it in mind to resign my commission." But, far from sending in his papers, he asks for arrears of pay, and actually speaks of France as "your nation." In answer, he is cashiered by the French military authorities.

Thus he has become a soldier of fortune more speedily than he had wished. He is without firm standing-ground; his only rights are the revolutionary rights of a National Guardsman, the member of a force which may go to pieces directly a reverse is sustained. Hic Rhodus! He must take advantage of the latent civil war between the townsfolk of Ajaccio and the Guard; must fan the flames, so that, amid the general confusion, he may assume the role of saviour! Is not the citadel, now occupied by the king's regular forces, a standing menace? Did not Frederick and Cæsar always begin by storming citadels? Seize the commander of the regulars, drive out this well-born booby, and thus, at one stroke, free the island! France, now involved in wars, will be unable to reconquer Corsica. The liberator will become a popular hero, and old Paoli will be no more than a legend.

On Easter Sunday, 1792, an open struggle occurred. Was the National Guard provocative; were the townsfolk playing double? Who began the affray? An everlasting problem! This much is certain, that Buonaparte, at the head of his battalion, tried to seize the fortress. But the garrison was not to be intimidated. Guns were trained on his men, and he had to withdraw. A complaint against the young officer was lodged in Paris; he was accused of armed rebellion, and a trial for high treason was impending. His exculpatory phrases deceived no one. Paoli, who had from the outset been somewhat alarmed at the zeal of his turbulent fellow-islander, hastened to proclaim his own loyalty to France, and to cashier the son of his old friend.

"If you turn against me, Paoli, I will turn against you," thought Buonaparte. "You had better be careful what you are about! To Paris, post-haste. Not for nothing is there a revolution there!"

Through the streets of the French capital, these hot summer days, strolls our adventurer, for whom everything has gone awry. He has neither money nor position. In France, he is a lieutenant, but regarded more or less as a deserter; in Corsica, he is a cashiered lieutenant colonel. The gravest charges are likely to be brought against him, and to-morrow he may be actually starving. The Jacobins are his last hope, and he joins Robespierre's faction, for nothing can save him but the fall of the dynasty. To him, the complete break up of the old order has become essential.

Life in Paris is costly. He pawns his watch, and, in spite of this, gets into debt—a thing he has hitherto been sedulous to avoid. Fifteen francs due to a wine-dealer! He proposes to his friend Bourrienne that the pair shall become house-agents. Does he envy those who sit in high places? No, he merely despises them. "Any one who sees at short range all that is going on, must admit that the peoples are hardly worth wooing for their favours. Here, human beings are perhaps even more base and calumniatory.—Enthusiasm is merely enthusiasm, and the French nation is outworn. No one seeks anything but his own advantage, and every one tries to push his way into the first rank.—Ambition undermines everything. To lead a quiet life, for oneself and one's family, that is the only lot worth having, with a fixed income of four or five thousand francs—if imagination would but cease to torment one, would quiet down!"

Woe to him who is thus plagued by a lively imagination! What colossal possibilities may be cooling in this Parisian cauldron, may arise out of the chaos of this titanic time! Being an

Italian, a foreigner, he can contemplate with equanimity the destinies of these Frenchmen, and, as a cold-blooded adventurer, can seek to turn their fortunes to his own account. The Jacobins are already coming to the front.

When the sansculottes storm the Tuileries, Buonaparte is among the onlookers. What are the thoughts of the man under the harrow? "Thank God, we are free once more." But what does the army officer say? "I saw soldiers threatened by civilians, and was terribly shocked.—Had the king shown himself on horseback, he would have gained the victory; such was the mood that morning." A few days earlier, when the king had been masquerading in the red cap of liberty, Napoleon had written: "What a fool! Why didn't he use grape-shot? If a few hundred of the mob had been shot down, the others would have run away!"

Still, his main feeling was one of liberation. His opponents had been overthrown. The day after the storming of the Tuileries, he wrote to his uncle: "You needn't worry about your nephews. They will know how to look after themselves." The new government does the handsome thing by Napoleon. Not merely is the deserter taken back into the service, but he is promptly raised to the rank of captain. He has, however, no inclination to hasten to his regiment. What does it matter to him that the king of Prussia is on the Moselle? What does he care about the wars of France? "I am a Corsican! Back to the island!"

IX

Is it possible? Has not the fresh wind from the sea, has not even the pure breeze from the mountains, been able to dispel that partisan spirit into which, everywhere, the struggle of ideas tends to degenerate? Calumny, corruption, anarchy: these are the forms which the strife has assumed in the island. Saliceti, the Corsican delegate to the Convention in Paris, is

Paoli's mortal enemy, and is therefore friendly to the Buonapartes now that they have turned against Paoli. The Jacobin Club in Ajaccio is divided, but revolutionary feeling is in the ascendant; and Paoli, the only honest man in the island, is stigmatised as a traitor because he is a moderate.

Who holds the reins of power? Every one and no one. Mutual suspicion is ripe, for in Paris the guillotine has been set up, the king has passed by that red road, and no one knows who will be the ruler there to-morrow. In Corsica, all go armed, and not the mountaineers alone; but orders from the coastland break unavailingly against the crags of the interior. Every one, here, is his own king; every one, his own avenger. Can there be a better field for this adventurer, who has nothing more to lose? He makes a third attempt to become master of the island.

Brother Joseph, Brother Lucien, and Uncle Fesch, all have adherents, but Napoleon is the first to gather the scattered forces. He has the confidence of the deputy, who needs a skilled artillerist to help him in the next faction fight. For the same reason, the Club is inclined to court his favour. Might it not be a good move to accuse Paoli of treason against France? We know that he has been influenced by his twenty years' enjoyment of British hospitality, and is it not in his mind to sell us to England? If Lucien were to go to Marseilles, and whisper the suspicion in the commissary's ears, Saliceti would soon be shouting it in the Convention. A little island like Corsica is a hotbed of intrigue. Since public life is controlled by two or three families, family life becomes merged in public life.

Ere long the Convention sends representatives to Corsica. Officers are appointed and dismissed without Paoli's leave or advice. Buonaparte, now a captain in the French service, regains in the island his position as commander. Before this, his abilities and the affection of his soldiers have enabled him to usurp the command once more, and the official appointment is no more than an endorsement of an accomplished fact. His chances are improving.

Then comes a terrible order from Paris. Paoli is to be arrested. But his opponents have overreached themselves. The hearts of the islanders warm towards the veteran hero. All rally to his support, and he defies the order.

Young Buonaparte is at a loss. Always he has had his ear at the heart of the people, not in the spirit of a lover, but in the investigatory mood of a physician. He tries to gain time, seeks a middle course, publicly proclaims himself on the side of the maligned Paoli; but also explains that he is a supporter of the sagacious Convention. Yet the Convention mistrusts this supporter, and now issues a warrant for his arrest also. Paoli likewise suspects him of wanting to have a foot in both camps. In a Paolist manifesto we read: "Since the brothers Buonaparte have supported the slander, and have sided with the commission, it would be beneath the dignity of the Corsican nation to have anything more to do with them. Enough to abandon them to remorse and public execration."

The enemies of the family raided the Buonaparte mansion, looted the place, and would have made short work of the inmates had not these already taken refuge with the commission.

Perhaps Buonaparte had wanted events to take this course. He had given the authorities in Paris plain proof that he was a staunch revolutionist. Certainly, they were now ready to show their trust in him. He, who a year before had led the Corsican volunteers against the French governmental artillery, was now made commander of this same artillery against the Corsican volunteers. Big guns! True, the others occupy the best positions, but at length he has power, ample power, with orders to protect the coast. Now then, Paoli, for our last duel!

But the old man, enjoying the full tide of popular favour, has also the best of it as a soldier. He holds the citadel. When Napoleon, acting this time as a Frenchman, makes his second attempt to storm that stronghold, he succeeds no better than before. A last endeavour is made to take the fortress from the islands. It is fruitless!

There is no longer a place for him and his in Corsica. They are banished by popular decree, and declared outlaws. The mother, so proud of her descent; her two sons, her two daughters, and her brother—all have been rendered shelterless by Napoleon's unsuccessful attack on Paoli. They must escape from the island at a few hours' notice. Through the silent woods, in whose recesses twenty-four years earlier she had found safety from the French, Letizia has now to flee towards the coast under the protection of the French. All her possessions are in the hands of her enemies. Nothing is left to her beyond the clothes she wears.

The artillery officer, twenty-three years of age, stands on the deck of the sailing ship that is bearing him to Toulon. Throughout the long June evening, he watches the coast recede; every cape, every ridge, is familiar to him. Thrice he has tried to conquer the island, as its liberator. Now he has been driven out by the Corsicans as a Frenchman. He is full of rage and of a thirst for revenge. The victories of France will strengthen him, and in days to come he will, after all, be master of Corsica!

But as he sails westward, and as the French coast draws near, our adventurer enjoys the sense of freedom that comes to him who is everywhere at home. Such is the happy lot of the man who has no country.

X

"How shabby their dresses are!" thinks Letizia Buonaparte, when her two half-grown girls come home from the market with their poor purchases. The refugees are living on the fourth floor of a confiscated house in Marseilles (the owner, a nobleman, has been guillotined). The mother is in the early forties. The three children with her are earning bread for the family as best they can; the two youngest are still in Corsica, cared for by relatives. Since the Buonapartes are "persecuted patriots," they receive a part of their rations from the commandant. Letizia, who is proud as ever, makes no complaints.

Soon Napoleon, who is travelling, has the chance of putting some lucrative opportunities in his brother's way, affairs connected with the supply of munitions of war. Maternal Uncle Fesch lays aside the priestly habit and becomes a man of business, in the silk trade. Then Joseph, who is of fashionable exterior, resembling his father in appearance, and, as the eldest, following the father's example in styling himself Count Buonaparte,—wins the hand of one of the two heiresses of a Marseilles silk merchant. Napoleon entertains thoughts of marrying his sister-in-law Désirée, the late silk merchant's other daughter.

He is on the move throughout this summer; now at Nice, with his regiment; now on the Rhone; now at Toulon. All the time, his soldier's eyes are on the look out; his artillerist's brain is noting the actual and the potential fortifications along this strip of coast. Soon he will make good use of the knowledge now acquired. Meanwhile he writes political dialogues. One of them in conversational form, appears as a pamphlet, printed at the public expense.

In this conversation, the manufacturer is of a familiar type. The well-to-do folk of Toulon, like their brethren in Marseilles, are, in fact, under Robespierre's rule, afraid of losing their heads or even their property. Concern for their money-bags tends to make them ever more solicitous for the welfare of the sometime royal house, now in exile. At length, in the hope of saving their capital, they call the enemies of France to their aid, handing over the remnants of the navy to the English, who in return promise them protection.

This is a fearful blow for the young republic. On all fronts, France is at grips with the forces of reaction. Belgium has been lost; the Spaniards are advancing over the mountains; in

Vendée, the Bourbon cause is gaining ground. Then comes the crowning disaster of Toulon. The republic calls up its last man for active service, enlists women, transforms the whole of France into an armed camp. Experts are doubly welcome.

Before Toulon, preparations are being made to drive out the English. As to how this is to be done, the Convention leaves that to the commander of the forces, originally a painter of pictures, in whom revolutionary enthusiasm is to make up for the lack of technical knowledge of the art of war.

Then it came to pass that young Captain Buonaparte, returning from Avignon whither he had been sent for a consignment of gunpowder, paid a visit to his fellow-countryman Saliceti, who introduced the young artillerist to the painter-general. After dinner, the dilettantes went for a stroll, and happened upon a 24-pounder, several miles from the sea. They began to boast of all that the gun would do. The expert assured them that, in its present position, it would be useless. He fired four shots to show them that the sea was quite out of range. Dumbfounded, they kept Buonaparte at Toulon, and set him to work.

"At last, one end of the rope is in my hands. Grip and hold fast!" thinks the lonely man with the strong will. With amazing activity, our captain has heavy guns brought from all possible places along the coast. In six weeks, he has more than a hundred pieces of ordnance at his disposal.

Now he will give a display of his talents as military commander. What is his plan? He will mount batteries on the tongue of land which divides the bay into twin harbours, and will thus cut off the hostile fleet from access to the sea. The British commander will not stay to be shot at in a mousehole with no outlet. He will set light to the arsenal and withdraw his forces from the town.

"Fantastical nonsense!" say the amateurs, mockingly. But Buonaparte, who has friends in the Convention, has a complaint lodged there against his chief. He also sends to Paris his scheme for the bombardment of Toulon, many pages of manuscript, containing, in addition, counsel of a more general nature: "Our fire must always be concentrated. If we can breach the wall, the balance will incline to our side, resistance will be fruitless, the place will be won. To live, we must divide; to strike, we must unite. Victory is impossible without unity of command. Time is everything!" Thus does a captain of twenty-four write to the central authorities.

He has a powerful ally in Paris, the younger Robespierre, who has the reputation of a man of talent, and is not completely overshadowed by his all-powerful brother. "Should you ever need a man of iron for street fighting," said Joseph Robespierre to Maximilien, "a young man, a new man—then it must be this Buonaparte." Indeed, the Corsican adventurer had already been asked whether he would become military guardian of the terrorists, but considerations of caution had led him to decline. Now his plan was approved, and the painter-general was recalled. Who would replace him?

Buonaparte gnashes his teeth. Another dilettante! The new general is a medical man. He spends his time nosing out conspiracies hatched by the nobility—and meanwhile the enemy occupies the precious tongue of land. From Paris there had come State carriages filled with "men of genius," clad in brilliant uniforms, and resolved to end the siege of Toulon, to take the place out of hand. Buonaparte led them to an unprotected battery. When the enemy opened fire, and they looked round vainly for cover, their guide said gravely: "We do without cover, nowadays; we have patriotism instead." This young man with blue-grey eyes is more interested in actions than in intentions. Further complaints, and a new change in command. This time the chief is a tried warrior, who is prompt to appoint Napoleon battalion commander, and to adopt the young artillerist's plan for driving the enemy from the tongue of land.

When, finally, Toulon is stormed (still in accordance with Buonaparte's designs), his horse is shot under him; and he is wounded in the calf by an English lance—this being his first and almost his last wound. Moreover, it is his first victory, although he is not the official commander; and it is a victory over England. The enemy retreats to the ships, fires the arsenal, and withdraws, all in one night, just as Napoleon had foretold.

Conflagration and death, battle and the terrors of a naval port in which thousands of treasonable burghers are trying to escape the avengers; amid all the fierce passions of this December night, through the reek and the cries, across heaps of corpses, and to the accompaniment of the agonised curses of drowning civilians and the exultant shouts of looting soldiers, a new star rises in the firmament—Napoleon's fame.

XI

The popular festival held in Paris to celebrate the liberation of Toulon and fresh victories on the northern and eastern fronts, spreads Napoleon's name among the masses. He is raised to the rank of brigadier general, and his chief, sending in a report in which the subordinate is given due credit as the originator of the plan of siege, adds (betwixt fear and admiration) the amazing sentence: "Even though the Convention were to slight him, he would still force his way to the front." But five other young officers are likewise mentioned in despatches, and when for the first time Napoleon sees his own name in the "Moniteur" there can be no doubt that he is vexed at being merely one among so many. How hard it is to climb!

Already, however, there are some young fellows who have noted the rising of the new star. Marmont and Junot, unknown officers, want to join their fortunes to his. He appoints them his adjutants; Brother Louis, too, now sixteen years of age. He has a group!

Big guns! The Convention commissions him to fortify the whole stretch of coast from Toulon to Nice. Is not Genoa, Corsica's ancient enemy, farther along the coast? He who takes Genoa, has the island in his hands. Is not Genoa full of diplomats and agents? This is the place for weather-breeding among the neutrals; here, any one with sharp eyes and keen ears can learn a great deal, and keep his information to himself. He gets himself appointed people's commissary, which gives him precedence over the chiefs in Genoa. Ostensibly the appointment is made that he may help in the settlement of frontier questions.

In reality, this is the first step of Buonaparte the diplomatist. He intrigues with agents of various kinds, while taking note whether the representatives of France in that part of the world are genuinely revolutionary or only making a pretence of revolutionary fervour. At the same time, he keeps his eyes open to see where the cannons are. He comes back to Nice to write his report, and, without warning, he is arrested.

For, meanwhile, Robespierre had fallen, and had perished by the guillotine. There is a general movement of repudiation. Every one wishes to make out that only under compulsion did he hold converse with the tyrant. Those who wish to prove themselves guiltless, look round for victims. The best victims will be those who are not in Paris to make a fight for it. Quick, quick, lest we should be suspected of having belonged to Robespierre's faction! General Buonaparte! He has just been on a secret mission to hostile Genoa. Lay the traitor by the heels! He was colloguing with Robespierre to bring about the destruction of our southern army. Hale him to Paris for trial!

Napoleon is in Fort Carrée near Nice. All his papers have been seized. It is his birthday. "To-day I am twenty-five," he thinks, as he glances seaward through the grating. If he could lean out of the window, he would catch a glimpse of Corsica. How many attempts he has made there, only to be defeated! Was the destiny of a young aspiring soul ever before built upon such a series of catastrophes? What has Plutarch to say on this matter? Cashiered, banished, outlawed—as far as Corsica is concerned. Now, after all his plans, he is a prisoner of

France. Next week, perhaps, he will be standing in the barrack yard, with his back against the wall, awaiting a score of bullets. What is to be done?

His faithful followers advise him to flee. He answers in an impassioned tone such as we rarely encounter in the sixty thousand of Napoleon's letters. He thanks them for their friendly counsel, but says: "Men may treat me unjustly; no matter, so long as I am innocent. My conscience is the tribunal before which I judge my own conduct, and my conscience is untroubled. Do nothing, for you would only compromise me." The one genuine phrase in this letter wherein he poses as a martyr, is the last. To Junot, the enthusiastic admirer, he speaks of motives which Junot will understand. In reality, since he knows that there is not a jot of evidence of complicity with Robespierre, he does not wish to compromise himself. Flight would be an admission of guilt.

Writing from prison to an influential diplomat, he says: "I am somewhat affected by the tragical death of the younger Robespierre, for I loved the man and believed him genuine. Nevertheless, had he been my own father I would have stabbed him had he wished to become a tyrant." Is not that spoken like a true Roman? With even more circumspection, he writes to the Convention: "Although innocent of the charge, I shall never make any complaint against the committee, whatever it may decide. . . . But now hear me! Strike off my chains, and restore to me the respect of patriots! An hour afterwards, if the wicked clamour for my corpse, I shall be ready. I hold my life at little account, for I have risked it in the trenches too often. Nothing but the thought that I can serve my country enables me to endure my burdens cheerfully."

A week later, he is free. Saliceti, his fellow-countryman in the Convention, had been his accuser. Now, when the Corsican deputy has got over his first fright and feels that his own neck is safe, he pledges his word that Buonaparte is innocent. But at the close of his statement, he adds a phrase which is an unconscious prediction of the young officer's triumphs: "Besides, we need him in the army."

XII

How he is shunned! Powerful friends, to whom he sends letter after letter, long epistles, make no answer. He writes beseechingly for little things, such as "a good surveying outfit for the army," when he wishes to force an influential comrade to reply. All at once comes a signal from the island. Old Paoli has summoned the English to his aid. Corsica must be saved for France! Back to Paris, in order to fan the flames. The expedition is actually decided on, and he eagerly hopes to secure the command. In a fortnight the fleet is back at Toulon, having sustained a reverse. Fresh disappointment! Why did they not put him in charge? Had he not conquered Toulon, fortified the coast—all with an eye towards the campaign against Corsica?

Reaction is in full swing. Napoleon is suspect. The authorities offer him high command in Vendée, for this will separate him from his adherents. At the same time he is transferred to the infantry, as a "supernumerary." How mortifying to a highly skilled artillerist!

The pale young man grew paler than ever, for he had made up his mind to refuse. He expostulated with the People's Commissary for War, who, in reply, twitted him with his youth. Napoleon looked the commissary, who knew little of active service, straight in the eyes, and said: "A man matures quickly on the battle-field, and it is from the battle-field that I come." Refusal to obey orders; expectation of dire consequences; just as it had been three years before.

What had I better do? Report sick? Apply for leave? The out-of-work general turns the possibilities over in his mind. Better stay where I am. Paris is the world's navel. True, Marmont and Junot, who have joined him without leave, are

(From the "Corpus Imaginum" of the Photographic Society, Charlottenburg.)

General Bonaparte in 1797. After a painting by Jean Guérin. Bibliothèque Nationale, Paris.

also penniless. What's Bourrienne doing? Speculating? Well, I can try that too, but assignats are falling. How badly you staged the last affair. Did you think you could make a coup d'état without cannon? But to Saliceti, who in his turn has had serious charges brought against him, and is being sheltered by a fellow-countrywoman, he writes: "You see, I might have paid you back in your own coin. . . . Who has played the better part, you or I? I might have taken vengeance on you, but have not done so. . . . Go in peace, to seek a refuge where you can, and meditate upon your country to better advantage. My lips will always be sealed about you. Take counsel with yourself, appreciate my motives . . . they are noble and magnanimous."

During these summer weeks, the flood of life is obscurely murmuring, is heavily pulsing against the shores. He is profoundly moved by *Ossian*, the book of melancholy passion; and he is stirred by the tragical end of plays he witnesses, hastening from the theatre that his mood may not be jarred by the subsequent farce. "How preposterous, in this new opera, to give a happy ending to *Paul and Virginie* by having the girl rescued!"—"But what is happiness?" asks the lady to whom he says this.

"Happiness?" answers Buonaparte. "The highest possible development of my talents."

Just now they are lying fallow, that is what troubles him. He is a prey to increasing dejection and dumb rancour. When a comedy is being played (the wife of one of his friends reports this), every one else is laughing, but Buonaparte sits there in frozen silence. Sometimes he vanishes, to reappear with gloomy aspect at the other side of the stalls. Often enough his lips are twisted in an unsuccessful attempt to smile. He is an irresistible raconteur of campaign stories, but his laughter on these occasions is rough. He is often to be seen wandering through the streets, short in the leg, thin, sallow, sickly, irritable of mien, "awkward, hesitant, wearing an old round hat, from beneath which two badly powdered 'dog's ears' project, scurf upon his collar, his ungloved hands are long and lean and dark, ill-fitting boots."

He now plans a book traffic with foreign lands; but his first attempt, with a consignment to Basle, miscarries.

Sometimes he visits drawing-rooms, for, as he writes to his brother, every one here seeks distraction. . . . There are women all over the place, at the theatre, in the Bois, at the Library. The prettiest of girls are to be found in the studies of the learned. Indeed, it is right that women should rule here, for the men are infatuated, living only through and for women.

When Buonaparte is in the salon of Barras, the tribune (who outdoes himself in splendour and extravagance, so that all Paris talks; who can never have enough women round him), when he stands there among women famous for their beauty like Tallien and Récamier, he, who is small and gloomy and angular, can only make an impression by cleverness and caprice. Even then he seems a freak.

Always the solitary, he only "lets himself go" in his long letters to his brothers. He is educating Louis, and writes: "The lad is a good soldier. What especially pleases me is that he combines so many excellent qualities: ardour, spirit, health, talent, trustworthiness, good-nature. . . . He will certainly be the best of us four. Of course, none of us have enjoyed his advantages in the matter of education." He is thinking of having Jerome, the youngest, sent to Paris. He is at odds with Lucien. This talented brother is his rival. Indeed, Lucien vies with Napoleon in his knowledge of men, was the first to understand Napoleon, did so already when he was seventeen while his brother was twenty-three. "In Napoleon," wrote young Lucien to Joseph, "I detect an ambition which is not wholly selfish, but is greater than his love for the public welfare. In a free State he would certainly be a dangerous man. He seems to me inclined to become a despot. I think he would become one, were he king. At any rate, his name would be a terror to posterity and to sensitive patriots." In Lucien's mouth, such grandiose vaticination is no mere playing with words. His own ambition is so intense that in this age and country he regards a development of the kind as quite possible for his brother, and he is mortified at the prospect that Napoleon is likely to outshine him.

For the nonce, Napoleon is in low spirits. He envies Joseph, whom money and happiness have made independent. He offers Joseph support in the way of introductions and papers; advises him to use the depreciated currency for the economical purchase of an estate. Yet we find him already writing to his elder brother, apropos of a letter on political questions: "Your letter was too dry; you must learn to write better than that."

A home! He wants a home of his own, like Joseph. More eagerly in each successive letter he urges Joseph to make sure for him of the wealthy sister-in-law, with whom he has been in affectionate correspondence for more than a year. When she is slow to make up her mind, he presses for a decision. His brother and one of his intimate friends have married well; comrades of his own age occupy prominent positions. Only he, with his surging thoughts and imaginative schemes, remains lonely and does nothing.

"If you are going away for a long time," he writes to Joseph, "send me your portrait. We have lived so long in close companionship that our hearts are intertwined. No one knows better than you how wholly I am yours. As I write these lines, I am more moved than almost ever before, feeling that it will be long before we meet again. I cannot write any more. Farewell, mon ami."

He is in a melting mood, and at times he seems utterly discouraged. "To clamber upwards from step to step, this is rather like an adventurer, like a man who is trying to make happiness." Finally he says: "Life is a trivial dream, which fades away. . . ."

XIII

Suddenly everything is in a flux. A new Minister for War has been appointed, and he is eager to effect changes on the Italian front. Does any one know of a new man to whom the command there can be entrusted? The enquiry passes from one to another, until some one recommends Buonaparte. He is summoned to the War Office. For years he has been making himself familiar with the Italian coast and the Italian frontier, and forthwith he expounds a detailed plan for a campaign in northern Italy, against Sardinia and Austria. It is substantiated by a display of intimate knowledge of the Alpine passes; of the weather and the snows; of seedtime and harvest; of the administration, the temperament, and the characteristics of the territories and the populations concerned. After the conquest of Lombardy, between February and July, the powerful position of Mantua must be wrested from the Austrians. Then the Army of Italy must move northward, and in Tyrol must effect a junction with the sister army, the Army of the Rhine. The joint forces will threaten Vienna and this will compel the emperor to accept a peace which will fulfil all that France has been expecting or imagining for years past.

Overwhelmed by the cataract that issues from this brain, the minister can only say: "Your ideas, General, are equally brilliant and bold. We must examine them closely. Write a report for the committee. You can take your time."

"My plan is ready now. I can write it down in half an hour."

"A notable design," say the members of the Committee of Public Safety when the report has been read to them; "notable, even if impracticable." In any case, such an intelligence as this must be utilised in the Operations Department. A few days afterwards he has a seat in this department, where everything is decided.

The great moment has come, the turning-point of his youth. At length he stands on the threshold of his career. The chance has come suddenly, for everything is sudden in this eruptive era. From now, when he is barely twenty-six, he will for twenty years, with unremitting vigour, move onwards towards his goal, drawing the chain of thought and action after him. Suddenly, twenty years hence, the chain will snap.

Napoleon's work begins. With burning energy, attending carefully to little things because his aim is the greatest of things, he devotes himself to "affairs." The veil is lifted, for here he finds the most secret reports concerning all the armies of the republic. At the same time, his daily association with the leading civilian figures in France gives him authority. The suggestive influence of his personality makes itself felt.

What is the first thing he aspires to gain for himself? Neither the command in Vendée nor the command of the Army of the Rhine. These are attainable, tangible magnitudes. Here, at the centre of all the real fronts, nothing allures him so much as the thought of a command which as yet lives only in his imagination; in a battle-ground which does not exist, but which he wants to create to-day, and which he will again want to create seventeen years hence. Asia! Directly he gets to work at the centre of things, he begins to emphasise the importance of galvanising Turkey into activity, of introducing artillery and the modern art of war on the Bosphorus, for in due time they can from that centre be used against the Russians and the Austrians. In fancy, he already sees himself conversing with the sultan, beyond reach of the eyes of these everlasting republicans, in an obscure and closed country into which the doctrine of liberty has never made its way—a land where a man can still do whatever he pleases. Twelve days after his entry into the ministry, he asks to be transferred to Turkey.

The application is refused. Powerful opponents are already beginning to be afraid of this man. They want to get him out of the War Office; to send him to the front. His protest takes a new tone. As if he were foreseeing all the successes that are still hidden in his own heart, he begins to dictate. "General

Buonaparte, who commands the artillery under the most critical circumstances and has contributed to the greatest successes, expects from the justice of the members of the Committee that they shall reinstate him in his functions, and shall spare him the distress of seeing his position usurped by men who have always kept themselves in the background, . . . but who now press forward to snatch the fruits of victories whose dangers they well knew how to avoid."

In the third person, in the iron style of the historian. Roman.

It avails nothing. Once more the insubordinate officer's name is struck from the lists, and for a second time he has to yield. But he feels that his hour draws nigh; nothing, now, can seriously shake his position. A fresh change of government is at hand. Announcing to his brother the impending transformation, he says that he himself is in the good graces of all the party leaders who will have military posts at their disposal. "The prospect is rosy. Even were it otherwise, a man must live in the present. He who has courage, despises the future."

Because he despises it, it serves him. Henceforward, men will serve him for the same reason.

A fortnight after this letter had been written, a conflict broke out between the government and the moderates, who were backed by the royalists. Once more, there was fighting on the boulevards, as there had been three years earlier. The National Guard is four times as strong as the governmental forces. Either from caution or from cowardice, the general of the Convention parleys with the leaders of the Guard. He is declared a traitor, and placed under arrest. The Convention meets in a panic. It is defenceless, intimidated by the left-wing and right-wing revolutionaries, who, for various reasons, have joined forces.

In the evening, Buonaparte hastens to the Convention, for a successor to the arrested general is needed, and he learns that the name of one of his rivals has been proposed. The heart of the silent onlooker beats furiously. Will his name now be mentioned? If he is asked to take command, shall he accept a task which he had refused in the days when Robespierre was supreme? Does not every one who leads soldiers against the people make himself hated, precisely because of his success? "Appoint Buonaparte!" Yes, his name has come up. "I turned the matter over in my mind for nearly half an hour." Such a mission will not bring renown, but it will bring power. He presents himself before the committee. It is past midnight; the tumult is expected to begin early next morning; everything must be ready within a few hours.

In this situation, he demands that he shall be absolutely free from civilian supervision. This seems a monstrous request to make of the revolution, one of whose new principles it is to lay especial stress upon supervision of the dreaded military arm. "If you appoint me, I shall be responsible, and must have a free hand. To-day, it was the fault of the people's commissaries that the general found himself in so precarious a position. Do you expect that the people will give us permission to open fire upon the people?" The only man he will share the command with is Barras, who is the most powerful among the leaders, but is in his hands. The minutes are passing. There is no choice.—Buonaparte was entrusted with the defence of the government, a fortnight after his name had been erased from the list of general officers.

For seven years the Parisian populace, when roused to action, has had to encounter nothing more than extemporised opposition. That is why the revolution has always made headway. Buonaparte is the first to prepare for the struggle. In one night, he transforms the Convention into a fortress. Even the alarmed deputies are supplied with weapons. They are still more frightened when they hear talk of cannon.

A young cavalry officer, Murat by name, undertakes to bring forty big guns from the suburbs. Murat thus opens a great career on the same day as his chief. Out in the streets he finds the masses, who are likewise on the prowl for artillery. Buonaparte cannot protect the Convention without ordnance. There are hours of tension, during which he must tranquilly devote himself to the disposition of his slender forces. At length, at five in the morning, he hears the rattling wheels of his old friends the big guns. Murat's men were mounted, and they have won the prize. Forward! Within two hours, everything must be ready.

In well-armed companies, the crowd advances threateningly. The lawyers in the Convention are shaking in their shoes. Speech after speech is made from the tribune, urging a parley, advocating the withdrawal of the troops. In the daylight, the situation is so menacing that the civilians utterly lose heart. They weaken; towards noon, some of the troops want to fraternise with the people. Night is falling. Now or never! Is the commander to allow the mob to triumph? In like circumstances, he had laughed at the weakness of King Louis. Shall he himself play the weakling, when he is in command of the guns?

It is probable that Buonaparte ordered the firing of the first shot, or perhaps extorted the order from Barras, although in his report, and subsequently, he declared that his opponents had this "crime against the French people" on their consciences. Anyhow, the firing begins. The big guns win the day; blood besprinkles the pavements; the crowd scatters; in two hours the streets are clear. That night, Napoleon writes to his brother: "At length it is over; my first wish is to send you news . . . We posted our troops, the enemy attacked us in the Tuileries. We killed a lot of them, our own casualties being thirty killed and sixty wounded. We have disarmed the companies of the National Guard, and everything is quiet. As usual, I have escaped without a scratch. Brigadier General Buonaparte. Postscript. Luck is on my side. My compliments to Désirée and Julie."

This is Napoleon's first bulletin of victory. The enemy are

Frenchmen; the battle-field is Paris; the offenders are revolutionists; most of the fatalities are on the opposing side; the signature, which in earlier and subsequent letters consists of nothing but the name, includes, to-day, the writer's military title. Everything is calculated for effect. But his feelings break through, and in the postscript he discloses to his brother the two things he has most at heart: Luck and Woman.

At a later date he said: "I have two men within me, the man of the head and the man of the heart."

XIV

On the tribune of the Convention stands Buonaparte with his officers, hailed by the acclamations of the assembly, to whom the youthful saviour is being presented. He scarcely notices the applause, for such triumphs of the moment seem of little value to him. Coldly surveying the hall, he thinks: "So you are the leaders of the nation. You trembled with fear when you heard the thunder of the guns! You shall not forget how to tremble! I have become your protector. I shall go on protecting you until you have become my humble servants."

As a matter of course, he is appointed to the command of the Army of the Interior. He now has a great following: cashiered officers, who hope to climb in the footsteps of the cashiered general; officials who have dreaded the reaction; all who feel that they have been rescued. But the crowd must be learning to hate him; for, in that darkling hour, hundreds of unarmed citizens, idle spectators, women have perished. What is that to him? It is not his aim to be loved.

Now, when he suddenly has money and servants and carriages at his disposal, he wants nothing for himself, everything for his kin. His younger brothers are given good positions; his mother can once more live a life after her own heart, and gratify her taste for saving; Joseph has the offer of several posts; there are places for the most distant relatives. But the letters become rarer, and the very first of them sounds a new note: "I shall do everything I can to help you, shall spare no effort which can contribute to your happiness." From brother, he has become protector, head of the family.

During these weeks, when he is tasting the joys of fulfilment, he becomes involved in the only passion of his life.

Désirée has missed her chance. Only a few weeks before, writing from the office of the general staff, he had implored Joseph to intervene on his behalf, to demand a prompt answer. "I am burning with desire to have a home of my own." At the same time, in several of his letters, we find more frequent references to charming women, allusions which betray a happy prospect of success. He has come to know la femme de trente ans, in her power and her beauty. He has made advances to two such women, in quick succession: one of them a Corsican of noble birth, a friend of his mother's; the other, a pretty cocotte, Chénier's mistress. Both of them are considerably older than he, and neither of them favours his suit. But the atmosphere surrounding these practitioners of the art of love, the electric atmosphere of the new salon, has exercised its influence on him: "A kiss for the two ladies: for the first, on the lips; for the second, on the cheek." Since he has hitherto known almost nothing of women, his lonely heart is susceptible.

Immediately after his appointment, the new generalissimo issues a decree against bearing arms. A search is made, and all weapons in civilian hands are confiscated. Now a boy of twelve, with engaging manners, turns up at the general's office with a plea for the return of his dead father's sword, which has been taken away from his mother. Napoleon concedes the point, and shortly afterwards the mother comes to thank him. What an elegant woman—wayward, gracious, captivating! Thirty or more; who can say? Not so much beautiful, as enthralling; slender; distinguished, but with a slightly foreign air; the dark skin of the Creole, for she was born in Martinique, though brought up in Paris; and during the days of the Terror she has learned to conquer by her charms.

When the general pays her a visit at the little house in an out-of-the-way suburb, his eyes, sharpened by his own experience of poverty, detect evidence of an endeavour to put a good face upon poor circumstances. This does not trouble him. An army officer, who now, at the age of twenty-seven, can for the first time dispose of means which enable him to live as he pleases, he prizes money, but he does not prize rich people. Just as in the life of affairs, men can only move him by their capacity, by what they can do; so women can only please him by their capacity—by their personal appearance, their nature, and what they can make of these.

Josephine makes a great deal, as she needs to do. From Martinique, her tropical home, she was able to save nothing when she lost her husband, Vicomte de Beauharnais. For years she was separated from him, but was reunited with him after her return to Paris from a prolonged visit to her native island. During the Terror, he was executed as a royalist; and she spent three terrible months in gaol, to be liberated after Robespierre's fall on the very day when Buonaparte was imprisoned. Friends came to her assistance in her difficulties; but her position and that of her two lovely young children, Hortense and Eugene, was precarious.

In this genteel poverty, it is expedient for her to make the best use of her charms. In any case, she is a born coquette, and is urged towards amorous adventures by the spur of her own love of pleasure. At this time, she is Barras' mistress, her handsome friend Tallien having taken up with a wealthy banker, handing over the man of might to Josephine. However, the two women hold Barras in joint control. The Committee of Public Safety supplies them with horses and carriages. But Beauharnais, being of gentle birth, knows how to give attractive dinner parties, and associates with members of both factions, although the counts and marquises who frequent her house leave their wives at home. She has become an adventuress of the revolution.

Well, what about Buonaparte himself? Any change in the political situation may cost him his position. What more is he, as yet, than an adventurer of the revolution? If Murat had failed to shark up those guns the other night, the general would have been shot. Life is insecure, both for him and for Josephine.

What can be easier than to befool this misanthropic and misogynistic man in whose dumb soul the schoolmaster at Brienne had long ago discovered the hidden volcano? For the first time in his life he is in the toils of a woman, an expert in love; he is consumed by his passion for the Creole beauty. To Josephine, it seems a stroke of luck, and in cold blood she decides on marriage.

"You have seen General Buonaparte at my house. He is to become a father to my orphaned children, a husband to my widowed self. . . . I admire the general's courage, and I wonder how much he knows. . . . But, I must confess, I am alarmed at the energy which animates all his doings. In his questing glance there is something inexplicable, which intimidates even our Directors. What ought to please me most, the passionate ardour he displays, is the very thing which makes me hesitate. Now that I am past my first youth, can I hope that I shall be able to keep alive in him an affection so stormy that it borders on madness?"

This lady of refinement does not fully understand what threatens her, and yet in the depths of her soul she shudders at the foreboding that she is to become the play of elemental forces. For, if this man who covets all or nothing and cannot rest until he has all, this man who has never given himself up to any one person or any one thing because it has been his unceasing wish to gain every one and everything, if Napoleon now gives himself for the first and only time in his life, he will stake his whole being, and will fetter it to the personality of the woman whom he clasps in his arms.

"I am waiting for you; I am wholly filled with you; your picture and the intoxicating evening leave my senses no peace. Sweet, incomparable Josephine, what have you done to my heart? Are you angry with me? Do you look sad? Are you ill at ease? . . . But I find calm when I give myself up to my passion, that on your lips, at your heart, I may fan the flames which burn me. How plain it was to me last night that your picture can never replace the real you. At noon you will start; in three hours I shall see you; till then, mio dolce amor, a thousand kisses! But you must not give me kisses, for they burn my blood!"

He does not tell her his plans, and yet he tells her something more. "These Directors fancy that I need their protection. They will consider themselves happy, some day, to secure mine. I shall make my way with the sword."—"What do you think," writes Josephine, "of this faith in success? Can such self-confidence be based on anything else than immeasurable conceit? A brigadier general is to protect the heads of the government! I don't know what to make of it; and yet, often enough, this ludicrous self-assurance makes me believe that anything is possible which the strange man wants to achieve."

We feel as if we were standing in front of the iron door which guards a glowing human heart, and looking through the key-hole into the fiery furnace of a soul.

But this woman, whom he possesses, why does he take her to wife? That he may possess her for himself alone? His egotism is against it, and, besides, he would be deluding himself. To gain advantages? In respect of money, and in respect of influence with the powerful, she can offer him nothing that he does not already enjoy. Of course she might prove useful to him; he is certainly flattered that she is of noble birth; and beyond doubt he has taken into consideration the fact that if she, who had a place in the days of the old regime, becomes his wife, this will put an end to the whispers that he is "only a Corsican." Yet it is as a Corsican, with the family feeling of an Italian (a feeling that has come down to him through the generations, and masters even him), that he desires marriage with a woman of birth. Finally, is it not obvious that this man who is so utterly self-centred must passionately long for a perpetuation of his own ego?

The one thing in the world which Napoleon cannot make without another's aid is an heir, and this heir must be made out of good materials. He is no man of the people. He has come into being amid the struggles of old families, and beneath a coat-of-arms bearing two stars which he now wishes to fuse into one. If he has helped to break down the prejudices against the masses, he has been moved along this course by delight in the elemental energy of action, and never by humanist feelings. Why should he wish to mix his blood with that of the people? When he marries the woman who long ere this has granted him all, he does so because, in both branches of her ancestry, she is the offspring of a long line of noble forebears. It is her birth, in addition to her charms, which makes her a welcome figure in a drawing-room, despite her reputation and her position. Since the Thirteenth Vendémiaire, Barras, the most powerful of the Directors, has regarded Buonaparte as his main prop—and he wishes to bind the general to his service by handing over Josephine. In this realm of erotic freedoms, a man who should wish, of a sudden, to insist on points of honour would simply make himself ridiculous. There are no knights and ladies now, but only citizens and citizenesses, who pair and separate as they please.

Barras has long since decided that Napoleon shall command the Army of Italy; and when Josephine, womanlike, is unable to make up her mind, Barras gives her a definite pledge to this effect. There are good reasons, too, why he should send the dangerous man to the most difficult front. Napoleon's great plan, the one which has procured him his position on the general staff, is now sent to Nice, and comes back with annotations by the commander-in-chief there. The man who has drafted the plan, says that worthy, must have been a lunatic. He had better come and try his own hand at the job. That is exactly what the Directory has been angling for. The writer of the criticism is recalled, and the "lunatic" is sent to take his place.

The position is assured; the prudent Josephine hesitates no longer. A legal friend has to certify that no birth certificate is now obtainable from the blockaded island in the West Indies, and that the authorities must therefore take the lady's word for the statement that she is twenty-eight. Since this knocks five years off her age, the bridegroom is gallant enough to add a year to his own. Thus the marriage begins with a twofold falsification of dates. A marriage settlement arranging for the division of property is signed, although the vicomtesse owns nothing but debts, and the warrior declares that his only possessions are his clothes, his uniform.

In the wedding ring, the words "To Destiny!" are engraved.

Two days later, he leaves Paris. Eleven crazy love letters are sent to her from eleven halting places. In Nice he joins his army, and takes over a command which will lead him beyond the frontiers of Europe.

It is the season of the equinoctial gales. From a turret he looks across at the enemy coast, and thinks: "This is the place I have always coveted as a starting-point. Behind me lies Paris; and her bedchamber, hung with mirrors. That is happiness. It is mine. Over there, across the mountains, in that hostile land, is fame. The goal of my desire."

As he turns away, he catches sight of a familiar line of mountains shimmering in the distant blue. No longer does this hold his attention.

It is his lost homeland. The island.

BOOK TWO

THE TORRENT

So divine an illumination is always linked with youth and productivity; and, in very truth, Napoleon was one of the most productive men that ever lived.—GOETHE.

I

THE towering peaks form a white, serrated ridge that thrusts upward into the blue of morning. Gleaming with perpetual snows, dangerous as the adventure he has undertaken, the Alps look down threateningly upon the bay, and mock the teeming crowds of men. Invincibly does nature, in symbolic fashion, here call a halt to the commander; here she has interposed a barrier between the land of his fathers and his new fatherland.

But he, who never trusts in force alone, who always outbids force with prudence, has to good purpose been pondering the old problem. Hannibal crossed the Alps; he, Napoleon, will go round them. If we come to grips with the enemy at the weakest point, where the Apennines press close to the Alps and a slight depression facilitates an entry, we need not wait for the summer. The earlier in the year, the firmer the snows, and the less danger from avalanches. Forward, into the land of my fathers!

Delay will be fatal. Not that the enemy is a danger to him. His foes are asleep in winter quarters: the Austrians in the east of Lombardy; the Sardinians in the west of the Lombard plain; and the numerous petty republics and duchies, the fragments of Italy, are not expecting an attack until the thaw has come. But the French soldiers are hungry. Paris, on the verge of ruin, through depreciation of the currency, can send them nothing but almost valueless assignats; and all of these disappear into the greedy maw of the army contractors. "France would tremble," said one of the generals in his letters home just before Bonaparte's arrival, "could every one know how many are dying here of famine and disease." What will the new commander do if he brings neither money nor bread with him?

"Soldiers, you are half starved and half naked. The Government owes you much, but can do nothing for you. Your patience, your courage, do you honour, but give you no glory, no advantage. I will lead you into the most fertile plains of the world. There you will find flourishing cities, teeming provinces. There you will reap honour, glory, and wealth. Soldiers of the Army of Italy, will you be wanting in courage and firmness?"

A faint cheer from the ranks answered the new commander when, at the first parade, he addressed his men in the foregoing words. But when they were all back in camp, one said to another: "General doesn't look very weatherproof, with his yellow hide. Fine talk, that, about the fertile plains. He'd better let us have some boots first, so that we can march there!" The people of Israel must have grumbled in much the same fashion when Moses spoke of the Promised Land. The new commander encounters nothing but opposition.

Who knows him among the soldiers of this army, which has now been encamped for three years on the crests of the hills? Those of them who remain, that is to say: for a fourth of the men are in hospital; and an equal number have been killed, or taken prisoner, or have deserted! The officers? Will not they, like those captains in Auxonne seven years ago, be inclined to encounter this wonderful young man's orders with passive resistance rather than ready obedience? Look at him as he sits there writing and calculating; his powdered hair is cut in a fringe over his forehead, but lengthens towards the back of the head to hang down over his shoulders; his coat is simple and scantily embroidered; he walks up and down and issues dictatorial orders, this foreigner whose French is still faulty. Not an officer in his staff is well-disposed towards him, except the three or four faithful followers whom he has brought with him. One of these latter tells us: "They looked upon him as a mathematician or a visionary."

What if he be both at once, and for this very reason a man of genius?

At first, he seems to be nothing but a calculator. Consider one of his early letters to the Directors—for he promptly opens an epistolary campaign, carried on side by side with a campaign of cavalry and by guns, waged with the same ardour and the same success. "You are asking me to perform miracles, and I cannot do that. . . . Only with prudence and foresight can we achieve great ends. It is but a step from victory to defeat. In affairs of magnitude I have learned that, in the last resort, everything invariably turns upon a trifle." But to Carnot, the great army organiser, to whom he can say much that is unsuitable for his official dispatches, he writes, gnashing his teeth: "Would you believe it, that I have not a single engineer officer here, not one who has ever taken part in a siege! . . . You can hardly conceive how furious I am that I have no artillery!" His actual resources totalled 24 mountain guns, 4,000 underfed horses, frs. 300,000 in silver, and enough food to supply his 30,000 men for a month on half rations. With these vestiges of an equipment, he is to conquer Italy!

Nevertheless, having undertaken the venture, he makes the best of the materials at his disposal. Getting to work like a hurricane upon this crowd of pitiful men who have run to seed, upon corps some of which have already begun to sing the royal anthem again, with indefatigable energy he succeeds in transforming them into a republican army.

Here are some of his doings on the third day after his arrival. Sending a hundred and ten workmen to make a road. Suppression of a mutiny in a brigade. Quartering of two artillery divisions. Orders to two generals in case of horse stealing. Answer to the requests of two others concerning their commands. Order to a general in Toulon to bring his men to Nice. Order to another general to call up the National Guard of Antibes. Order to a general to find the most efficient officers in the mutinous brigade. Address to the general staff. Review of troops, with orders of the day.—During the first twenty days, one hundred and twenty-three written orders relate solely to the provisioning of the troops; among them are numerous complaints concerning peculation, short weight, and inferior goods; and these orders are issued on the march, from twelve different headquarters, in the interludes between six skirmishes.

For hardly has he passed through the narrow defiles than, in accordance with his new principle, he has massed his forces to attack first one and then the other of the allied foes, and in two battles he defeats and separates them. In truth, these were mere advance-guard skirmishes, as becomes the nature of the French, and the previous training of these troops, which as yet know nothing of a great movement in open lines. At this stage of his campaign, speed and boldness are more important than elaborate strategy.

When he is on one of these breathless rides, in the deep mountain valleys, through the passes, amid the thunder of his own and the enemy cannon, suddenly the glass covering Josephine's miniature (which he carries in the inner pocket of his tunic, and has kissed hundreds of times) shivers into fragments. Growing paler than ever, he reins in his charger, and says to Bourrienne: "The glass is broken. My wife is ill or unfaithful. Forward!"

Everything depends upon the fulfilment of his first old pledge. He knows that if, this once, he is able to do what he has promised, the army will believe him; and if it believes him, it will soon believe in him. In actual fact, a fortnight after his prophecy had been uttered, the army, which had won its first victories on entering the downward grades, found itself on the last elevation. The soldiers raised a hearty cheer. After the weary days in the narrow valleys, they at length caught sight of the plains of Piedmont lying at their feet, stretching out into the immeasurable distance, blossoming in the spring weather, offering all that they had gone short of for so long. The Po and other rivers were flowing towards the horizon, and at length the world of snows lay behind. "As if by a magician's spell, they had been enabled to cross the gigantic barrier, which had seemed to them like the frontier of another world."

"All this is yours!" Their commander has forced one of the two opponents, the king of Sardinia, to make truce, thus compelling the surrender of everything that grows on Sardinian territory. This first truce of his campaigns was secured by Bonaparte through cunning and bluff, for he threatened the enemy with the use of overwhelming forces, which he did not possess, and, indeed, could not have used, pressed as he was on both sides. The soldiers are amazed; their general is a man of his word! Literally, in a fortnight, he has fulfilled his promise.

Henceforward, the men under his command put their trust in Bonaparte. It is as Bonaparte that he begins to sign himself from the outset of the campaign. Since Italy is the enemy, he will have nothing more to do with an Italian name.

Ere long, he will change his name again.

II

Why was he victorious? How can we explain that during the next few weeks he was able to deliver blow after blow? What is the solution of this riddle?

First of all, he owes his success to youth and health. A body that can endure interminable riding without fatigue; the power to sleep at any moment, and to wake whenever he pleases; a stomach which can digest anything, and makes no complaint at being put on short commons; eyes that see and arrange everything.

But it is to the revolution that he is indebted for the fact that at the age of twenty-seven, when his splendid powers are in their first vigour, he has risen to a leading place, and can wield unrestricted dictatorship. Only, thanks to the new ideas of equality, in a world which prizes a man for what he does and not for his birth, can any one become a leader in the prime of youth and after so rough an apprenticeship.

Look at the men who are in the field against him. Archduke Charles, with his delicately shaped and decadent Habsburg nose, how can he, with his education, vie with the Corsican in indifference to hardships, rival Bonaparte in knowledge of men? How can Beaulieu, the Austrian commander, cope with the French general? The former is seventy-two; the latter, twenty-seven. General Colli suffers from gout, and has to be carried throughout the campaign. Alvintzy is in the middle sixties. The king of Sardinia is an old man. What can the excellent General Wurmser, who is deaf, and a slow, elderly gentleman, cautious in his movements, do against a commander who thinks nothing of changing his headquarters every day, who surrounds himself with young men, and who takes "Time is everything," for his motto?

The oldest man in Napoleon's circle is the faithful Berthier, now forty-two, whom the new commander has taken over from his predecessor because Berthier has a good knowledge of the country. For two decades he is to be Bonaparte's slavishly devoted chief of general staff. Next to be mentioned comes Masséna, a man of ardent temperament, who had been a cabin boy and a vagrant, and had served fourteen years under the Bourbons without rising to the rank of sergeant major; now, within a few weeks, he was to become a general. Augereau, too, a deserter from three armies, boaster, adventurer, and great thief. Such were the men drawn from the dregs of society out of whom their commander, the youngest of them all, was soon to make heroes and generalissimos, and subsequently princes and dukes.

In every dispatch, he recommends for promotion those, and only those, who have displayed courage. Thus, after three battles, a grenadier rises to the rank of colonel, and will climb yet higher. On the other hand, many of the generals whom he has taken over with his command are dismissed with blunt censure: "Good enough for office work, knows nothing of war." His subordinates do not necessarily incur his displeasure because they are beaten: "The fortune of war, dear Masséna, changes from day to day. To-morrow, or later, we shall win back what you have just lost." But a division which has done badly is paraded to hear a rating. He says that he will have a mocking inscription worked upon its colours. Then the soldiers cry to him from the ranks: "To-morrow we will lead the van." Next day, he has a thousand more enthusiasts among the troops. When they are victorious, in the orders of the day he calls them comrades and friends. Thus does he lead the sons of the people.

For it is a people's army that he is leading; that is the second great factor of his success. This, too, he owes to the revolution. Indeed, the people's army is an expression of the revolution. The soldiers on the Austrian side must be used thriftily, for they cost a great deal, and it is not easy to replace them. They are drawn from a larger number of nationalities than the German emperor himself rules. Six different languages are spoken in the army, and there is no community of thought to hold it together. But the French are fighting as a united nation of thirty millions, and their army will be capable of perpetual regeneration for twenty years to come.

What is the French army fighting for? The new freedom of the republic, and to spread throughout the world the few and simple ideas which animate it! The French are fighting for the world revolution, and nothing short of that. But the army is not in pursuit of purely ideal aims. It has to defend liberty against the environing forces of legitimate monarchy, against the legitimists who are more concerned with self-defence than with the cause of the fallen Bourbons. The French cannot achieve their end by simply defending their own frontiers. They are surrounded by kings and emperors who wish to keep their peoples from any attempt to imitate the French revolution, and are therefore trying to destroy the very focus of the new ideas. Thus France is forced to assume the offensive as a means of self-defence. Those who in such a fashion become conquerors in spite of themselves, are surely entitled to declare that their conquests are achieved in the name of liberty.

This brings us to the third factor of Napoleon's success. While the commander is engaged in the attempt to conquer Lombardy, and then Italy, for France, he issues a series of manifestoes to tell the inhabitants of the territories he is invading that he comes to free them from the Habsburgs and the Sardinians, from dukes and patrician senates. Will not all who have been discontented with the old order be roused to action by the torrential force of such appeals? Have not the oppressed masses long had it in mind to rid themselves of their rulers? Have not the ideas of the revolution crossed the frontiers years ago, rousing, in many of the towns, students and burghers to revolt? Here in Italy were young people who longed for freedom; leaders who had been vainly clamouring for "Italia unità." The revolt, though still in chains, was rattling its chains outside the kings' palace doors. The malcontents were ready to welcome the invading army, and to believe in its mission.

The commander, a man of Italian blood, bearing an Italian name, and speaking Italian as his mother tongue, was not for them a French warrior. He was the herald of liberty and equality, and the two great words headed all his letters. How terrible would be the disillusionment, should the invader prove, after all, a foreign oppressor! The commander is well aware how much turns upon this. Will he be able to keep his famished army within bounds? Can he make his soldiers behave as well as if they were fresh from a well-provisioned garrison town?

"Looting is on the wane," he writes home. "The thirst of an army which lacked everything has been quenched. There is an excuse for the poor devils. They have spent three years in the marches of the Alps, and now I have led them into the Promised Land! A famished soldier perpetrates excesses which make one ashamed of being a man. . . . I intend to restore order, for I will not remain in command of a robber band. . . . To-morrow I am going to have several privates and a corporal shot, for having looted the plate from a church. Discipline will be re-established within a day or two. Italy has been amazed at the valour of our soldiers, and shall be amazed at their good behaviour. There have been terrible moments; things have happened which have made me shudder. Thank God, the retreating enemy behaved even worse!"

He puts his men on their honour. "Swear to me"—thus runs one of his early manifestoes—"to spare the peoples you are liberating; otherwise you will be the scourges of the people! Your victories, your courage, the blood of our fallen brothers, will be lost; honour and glory, too! I and my generals would blush at leading an undisciplined army!" Hard to carry out, despite his adjurations. Throughout the campaign, he is hampered by this problem of looting. Again and again he issues orders to his generals telling them they are to shoot any one who fails to hand over his plunder within twenty-four hours, even if the stolen goods be horses and mules.

There are revolts and counter-attacks. Priests and nobles, agents of the princes, incite a town to resist. He is pitiless in his shootings, ruthless in his reprisals, whenever, in the conquered territory, any one raises a hand against the new master. But this becomes increasingly rare, for in the towns he is skilful in enlisting the civic sense on the side of a new order which assumes imposing lineaments. He understands (and this is an additional factor of success) the Italian temperament; knows how to appeal to the sense of historic veneration: "Peoples of Italy, the army of France comes to break your chains. It is a friend to all the peoples. Have confidence! Your property, your customs, your religion, shall be respected." He goes on to speak to them of Athens, Sparta, classical Rome.

History inspires him. While with rapid strokes he is making history, history gives his spirit wings. In boyhood, he had studied Plutarch; as lieutenant, he had read the history of all times; now, from moment to moment, he turns the knowledge to account. Knowing who has ruled in every part of these territories, understanding how the governments he has overthrown came into being, he has appropriate measures for each area. Time-honoured figures are ever present to his imagination; he wants to resemble them, to outdo them. Thus, whatever he does is conceived in a historic setting; and he compels his army, the country with which he is dealing, and, soon, Europe as a whole, to breathe the same atmosphere. These first victories, which in reality are nothing more than big skirmishes, are by the magic of his words transformed into battles, and the battles are magnified into history. In this way, half of what he achieves is achieved by the power of words. To the lands he is freeing, to his soldiers, he invariably suggests that they have done the whole thing themselves. Read his proclamation to the army in Milan.

"Soldiers, like a torrent you have rushed down from the heights of the Apennines. . . . Milan is yours. . . . We are the friends of all the peoples; but, above all, we are the friends of the offspring of Brutus and Scipio and the other great men who are our models. To re-establish the Capitol, to set up there the statues of the heroes, to awaken the Roman people which for centuries has been paralysed by servitude—that is the fruit of your victories, that will amaze posterity. It is your title to immortal fame that you have given a new visage to the most beautiful land in Europe. . . . Then you will return to your homes, and your neighbours will point you out to one another, saying: 'He was with the army in Italy!'"

Did a commander ever before make such alluring appeals to soldiers and peoples, to friends and foes? Who understood so well as Napoleon how to influence people through their imaginations instead of through a sense of obedience? At Arcola he shouts to his men: "Are you cowards, or are you the victors of Lodi?" In a month or two, he will be urging them onward by reminding them that they are the victors of Arcola. "We have crossed the Po, and have opened the second campaign," he writes to the Directors. All his reports to Paris are penned with consummate art. What he writes is the truth, but it is so skilfully adorned that it develops a life of its own as soon as the government communicates it to the press, and when from France it makes its way into foreign lands.

With the pen, Bonaparte rounds off the victories he has won with the sword.

III

"I have received your peace treaty with Sardinia. The army has approved it."

The Directors quake as they read the words. The arrival of this dispatch cancels the joy they had felt at the coming of so many captured colours. When, before, had a general in the field dared to write in such a fashion to his government? "For this letter, the young hero ought to be stood up before a firing squad," cry his opponents. But the fame of his victories, the glory of his conquest of Lombardy, have already secured him so strong a position in the hearts of the people that no one dares attack him. Recently, when the governmental commissary, his fellow-Corsican Saliceti, came to his camp, Bonaparte ignored the official's authority, and himself signed the truce with Sardinia. These negotiations were the first in which he proved his mettle as diplomatist. When the other side wanted to bargain, he took out his watch, named the hour at which he had decided to attack, and said they had better make up their minds quickly. "I may lose battles," he said, "but no one will ever see me lose minutes either by over-confidence or by sloth." With this truce, he for the first time dispossessed a king. Without asking for instructions, he entered into negotiations with the dukes, with Tuscany. Was he not, before long, to do the same thing with the pope? What was the best way of dealing with this dangerous conqueror?

"We will send him a partner," thought the Directors, with a smile. "Let him share the supreme command with Kellermann, while Saliceti decides upon political issues." Orders to this effect reached him at Lodi, on the day of battle.

That was the first real battle he had won. A colossal bluff and a bold movement enabled him to storm the bridge over the Adda and to defeat the alarmed Austrians. There were to be much greater victories in days to come; but, in the history of the man's spiritual development, not one of them was to equal this in importance.

For now, after a battle which decided the first part of his campaign, having taken much booty and sustained only trifling losses, and having made himself master of a territory opened to him by an hour's struggle on the bridge,—this evening, Bonaparte feels for the first time how obscure plans and brilliant exploits of war, dream and reality, are interconnected. The consciousness of his own powers makes him realise that boundless possibilities lie before him. That was the first time on which a word concerning such aims crossed his lips. To his friend Marmont he said: "I feel that deeds await me of which the present generation has no inkling." Long afterwards, in retrospect, he declared: "That evening, after the battle of Lodi, I first became aware that I was an exceptional man; from then I date the awakening of an ambition to do the great things which hitherto had existed for me only as the fantasies of a dream."

Such was his mood when the new orders came from Paris. What? The conquest of two or three continents was looming before his imagination—and he was to go halves with Kellermann? He strode up and down the room, pursing his lips, and then he issued his fiat to the government:

"If you put hindrances in my path, if you make my actions

dependent upon the commissary's decision, . . . you must not expect any more good results from me. . . . Here it is indispensable that you should have absolute confidence in your commander. If I do not enjoy that confidence, I shall without complaint endeavour to win your approval in some other post. Every one has his own way of making war. General Kellermann has more experience, and would doubtless do it better; but, together, we should do it badly. I cannot serve the country unless I have your complete and undivided trust. Much courage, I know, is needed to write you this report, for it would be easy to charge me with ambition and pride! But you are responsible for my having to express my feelings. . . . I cannot serve jointly with a man who regards himself as the best commander in Europe. For the rest, one bad general is better than two good generals. With war, as with governance, it is a question of tact."

The general does not seem inclined to yield up his place to any one. If the authorities in Paris insist on a divided command, is it not likely that he will march ahead on his own initiative, gain further victories with his unaided talents, then turn back to threaten France, and, as a condottiere, overthrow the government? The Directors think it will be better not to insist; with a smile, a wry one this time, they give way. After his first, noiseless victory over the government, Bonaparte feels he is master. Henceforward he behaves, substantially, as a king who is his own commander-in-chief, but who can only secure reinforcements and other requisites by reiterated adjurations. For months and years, therefore, his dispatches are still written in the tone of a subordinate; of one who does not threaten, but advises. Yet in reality he acts all the time as if he were already in the land of the sultan, towards which his masterful character draws him.

The Paris courier has been sent off. Bonaparte's first "No" is on its way. Another restless night in camp, and then to Milan!

In everything, he imitates the Roman general celebrating a triumph. As of old, the prisoners lead the way, the only difference being that nowadays they are not in chains. They are followed by five hundred cavalrymen. The citizens, who are used to seeing brilliant uniforms, are astonished at the tattered tunics, the sorry screws, the jaded appearance of the riders; and they are still more amazed when they see the thin little man on the inconspicuous white nag, at the head of his weary-looking suite. How grey the whole procession looks in the light of this brilliant spring day. At the gate the venerable archbishop, with a train of counts and dukes, bids him welcome. He dismounts, but does not draw near to the reception committee; he merely listens with forced politeness to the words of greeting. The onlookers are wondering what answer he will make. For a few seconds he keeps his lips tightly pressed together, and then contents himself with a single sentence, to the effect that France wishes the Lombards well. Remounting, he salutes, and rides on.

Leaders and crowd are deeply impressed; no enthusiasm, only astonishment. Not a sign of arrogance about this conqueror; nothing but resolution, and a force of will before which all must bend. Was his conduct deliberately planned to produce such an impression, though never before had he experienced anything of the kind? Was he "play-acting"? If so, all the more remarkable his knowledge of men; all the more plain that he was a master of the ruler's art!

Nevertheless, he is absent-minded to-day, for he has not all that he wants.

Now, the streets echo to the shouts of the crowd, who cannot restrain their expressions of astonishment as they watch the men who follow the commander—marching in a slack and almost disorderly fashion, clad in scarecrow uniforms patched with many colours. These Frenchmen seem in almost sorrier case than the prisoners!

The commander is taking his ease in the archbishop's palace.

General Bonaparte in 1796. Engraving from the Kircheisen Collection.

He is having a bath. Hot baths are his one luxury, a luxury that he will continue to indulge in down to the day of his death, taking them hotter and hotter, staying in them longer and longer, as time goes on. Nothing can break him of the habit, for a hot bath is the only thing which really refreshes him, soothes his nerves. In the evening there is a reception. "You will be free, and in a safer position than the French. Milan will be the capital of this new republic, which has a population of five million. You shall have five hundred pieces of ordnance, and the friendship of France. From among you I will choose fifty men, who shall rule the country in the name of France. Adopt our laws, modifying them to suit your own customs. . . . Be sagacious and united, and all will go well. Such is my will. If Habsburg should again seize Lombardy, I swear to you that I will take up your cause, that I will never desert you. If your land perishes, I shall be no more. Athens and Sparta did not last for ever!"

Never since the days of Plutarch's heroes did a commander talk like this. It was the conqueror's first speech from the throne, and was compounded of all the elements with which, in his speeches and letters, he was to work upon the mind of Europe for twenty years to come. Everything is single and definite; there is so much fixity of purpose that every one wishes to comply. You are vassals, but free. I am your master, but I will protect you. Five hundred pieces of ordnance and the friendship of France. "Such is my will." Then it is all over.

Through the May night, the wealthy town blazed with fireworks and resounded with music. The young commander-in-chief has moved on to the Palazzo Serbelloni; the banquet is over, and he stands at the window. The triumphal entry of which he dreamed in youth, towards which his virginal fancy strained, has now been accomplished. Does he look forward or back? With what is his mind busied?

"What do you imagine the Parisians are thinking of us?"

he asks his adjutant. "Do you expect they are satisfied?" When Marmont makes the conventional reply, Napoleon goes on: "But Paris has seen nothing, so far. The future hides much greater victories. The goddess of fortune has not smiled on me that I may scorn her. The more she favours me, the greater shall be my demands. In a few days we shall reach the Adige; then Italy will be at our feet. Perhaps we shall cross the river, and press onward. Our age has produced nothing great. I want to set an example."

IV

A royal couch in the Serbelloni Palace; never has he lain so soft before. But it is far too wide for one! Where is Josephine? What are triumphal entries and victories worth, without her? Fireworks and flags! Why has she not come? Is she really ill? Has she a lover?—He lies awake for hours.

From the very first this man, who inspired respect even in the veterans among the generals, imperilled that respect by his way of showing his wife's picture to all and sundry, and when he was in the middle of a conversation about service matters. "You will come soon, won't you?" So he wrote in one of his almost daily letters. "You must come to me. I want you on my heart, in my arms! Quick! Fly, fly!" He knows her frivolous disposition; that her senses are easily aroused; that she is always ready to give herself up to new impressions, new admirers. But now, now! What can be keeping her? He had expected her to come to Milan. His ambition had been to escape thither from the savagery of the campaign, that in one of the palaces of that city he might give her capricious charms a splendid setting worthy of her and himself.

But there is something which our great calculator has left out of his calculations. By his very feats of arms, he has kept her away from his side. For years in Paris she has been living in the half-world. Now, in this city which she loves, she wishes to shine forth in an assured position, as wife of the great commander whose name is in every newspaper, on every one's lips. Does the little general really think she married him for love? When the first captured colours are exhibited, she drives out among the people, and, while she is loudly cheered, she thinks to herself how much more gratifying this is than to rough it in foreign towns surrounded by unmannerly soldiers. She seldom writes to him. His own words grow ever more urgent. "Have you a lover, have you taken up with some stripling of nineteen? If so, you have reason to dread Othello's fist!" She laughs, and says to Tallien: "A queer fellow, this Bonaparte!"

Another day, in the middle of a letter to Carnot dealing with urgent affairs, he writes: "I am in despair. My wife won't come here. I am sure she must have a lover, and that that is what keeps her in Paris. I loathe women, one and all!" Then comes a letter in which she grasps at an expedient. Since there is no other way of avoiding the dangers and the dirt of camp life, she writes to him that she has hopes. . . .

Thunder and lightning! Have all the spirits of good fortune united to shower blessings on him? Among his successes, that was the only thing he lacked to complete his happiness. For, if destiny is to carry him to the lofty altitudes he foresees, to the heights he has resolved to scale, then his greatest need is to have heirs. But this battle is only planned, not yet won; new dangers are impending. He shudders. Is it true? Is it his child?

"I am sorry!"—the words are penned in his almost illegible handwriting on the commander-in-chief's official stationery. "I have been pestering you with complaints, and you are ill. Love had robbed me of reason. Forgive me, but I think I shall never be reasonable again. My life is an unending dream; gloomy forebodings make it hard for me to breathe; I have lost all hope. Write me ten pages, for nothing else can console me. You are ill, you love me, you are with child, and I never see you. Who takes care of you? Hortense? I love the sweet girl more than ever when I think of her as taking care of you. . . . Soon you are to have in your arms a child as fascinating as yourself. If I could only spend a whole day with you. You know, if I saw a lover with you, I should instantly tear the man to pieces!"

But who is to help her through her time of trouble? There is no friendship in the world, only the ties of blood. "I am in despair," he writes to Joseph under the same date. "My wife is ailing; I do not know whether I am standing on my head or my heels; dreadful forebodings rack my heart. Write to me, I implore you. Since early childhood, we have been bound together by kinship and affection. Do for her what I would so eagerly do for you. . . . You know how much I love her; know her ardent nature; know that I have never loved so passionately, that Josephine is the first woman whom I have adored. Her condition drives me crazy. . . . But as soon as she is well again, well enough to travel, she must come to me. I must have her in my arms; I love her to distraction, and cannot live without her. If she no longer loves me, there is nothing more for me in the world. Oh, mon ami, do not keep the courier more than six hours in Paris; send him back to me with an answer which will give me new life. Be happy! For myself, nature has doomed me to win none but outward victories!"

On the same day, he dictates, inter alia: Order to Berthier to occupy Alessandria; dispatch to the Directors concerning urgently needed reinforcements; ultimatum to the Genoese Senate anent the murder of soldiers; letter introducing Murat to the same Senate; plan to sell some cannon which are still left on the Riviera; order to Masséna to procure ammunition from the arsenal in Venice; order to Lannes to advance no farther; order to send all suspects to Tortona; order to send a division to Toulon; report to Kellermann that money and troops are on the way.

His letter has an effect. Joseph asks Josephine to come with him to Milan. What pretext can she find for refusing? She sighs, packs her trunks, sheds tears at a farewell festival in the Luxembourg, gets into the carriage. After all, to-morrow is the thirtieth of June, the season is at an end, and she has good company for the journey. Of course Joseph, her vis-à-vis, is a homely fellow, but Junot is a dapper young man; Fortuné, her lap-dog, is a darling, as ever. Then there is Charles, another young officer whose acquaintance she has recently made, and who has danced attendance on her ever since. Is he on the lookout for a career, or a conquest? What a choice Christian name, Hippolyte! How fine he looks in his chasseur uniform. He tells such amusing stories, has an expert knowledge of the latest shawls and wigs, and his legs are so well turned!

Milan. Bonaparte is away? More battles near Verona? No matter, this is a lovely place! Such a splendid palace; they all flock to pay their respects. But Hippolyte is hors concours; no one can rival the grace with which, sword clanking, he strides up and down the Corso. What a pity one has to be circumspect in one's behaviour under so many prying eyes. But Hippolyte knows his way about, and has found a discreet staircase. . . .

Suddenly there is a stir of excitement. The commander-in-chief is coming from Verona. For two days and two nights, the lava of this volcano overwhelms her.

V

Thrice do the soldiers of Emperor Francis try to relieve Mantua, which Bonaparte is besieging. Mantua is the key position. Old Wurmser, marching down beside Lake Garda with fresh troops, drives back the opposing forces. If Bonaparte is to make front against him, Mantua must be abandoned for a time. Meanwhile, however, the enemy has blocked the line of retreat upon Milan. A terrible reverse, and the French army is in the utmost danger. Bonaparte, hastening from

Milan, rides under the hot July sun across the plain, busily inspecting one division of the army after the other, gathering all his strength, for the fate of the whole campaign is at stake. A period of the utmost activity, and of extreme tension.

"Since I left you," he writes on one of these evenings, "I have been sad. I can only be happy when I am near you. I spend my whole time thinking of your kisses, your tears, your bewitching jealousy. The charm of the incomparable Josephine is perpetually rekindling the flames of my heart and my senses. When shall I be free, at length, free from cares and duties, free to devote all my time to you, with nothing in the world but to love you. . . . Since I have known you, I have come to respect you more day by day, which shows how wrong La Bruyère was when he said that love comes suddenly. Everything in nature runs its course, and increases by degrees. . . . Be less beautiful, less tender, and above all less jealous. Your tears inflame my blood. . . . Join me quickly, so that, before we die, we may be able to say: 'We have had so many happy days!' A million kisses, even for your horrid Fortuné!"

Neither now nor later could the commander-in-chief rid his home of this lap-dog. He tells us that on his wedding night the dog was in bed with Josephine. "I had to choose between sleeping beside the beast or not sleeping with my wife. A terrible dilemma, but I had to take it or leave it. I resigned myself. The dog was less accommodating. I have the marks on my leg to show what he thought about the matter!"

Amid the hurly-burly, the general's lady arrives at Brescia. Almost immediately she has to be sent back to Milan. She has a narrow escape of being seized by the enemy, together with some recruits and cannon. Now she has an excuse, and, in the future, she will be slower to comply with his invitations.

During these weeks, Bonaparte for the first time loses courage, though it is only for a few hours of one night. Instead of simply issuing orders, he holds a council of war, much to the astonishment of his generals. In this critical situation, he proposes to retreat across the Po, but the mad Augereau thumps the table, shouting: "For the sake of your own fame, I insist that we attack." He flings from the room. The counsels of the others are divided.

See him before the decision, brooding over his maps. He is alone. Moths are fluttering round the candles, and at last burn themselves to death. The midsummer night is sultry. As he listens to the drums and the shouting without, he thinks: "To-morrow will settle whether we can keep Lombardy. Perhaps it will be the turning point in my fame, my destiny. Shall I stake all on one card? What if Wurmser's strength is greater than the reports say? Josephine is sleeping now, in the great bed. Or, who knows, she may be laughing softly in the embrace of some puppy who has bewitched her."

He decides to fight. Next day, he is victorious at Castiglione.

Soon afterwards, he writes: "Three days without a letter from you; I have written daily. This separation is terrible; the nights are long and savourless, the days monotonous." At this time, Josephine writes to Tallien in Paris: "I am bored to death." He is busied in battles and victories; she is fêted and honoured. To both of them life seems wearisome: to him, because she is too far away; to her, because he is too near. Three days later: "The enemy has been beaten, my darling. Eighteen thousand prisoners, the others dead or wounded. Wurmser has only Mantua left. This is the biggest success yet: Italy, Friuli, and Tyrol are saved for the republic. In a few days we shall see one another again, that is the reward for labour and pains. A thousand glowing kisses!"

When the commander can draw breath, the statesman must turn every moment to account. In Modena he assembles deputies from all the States as far south as Bologna, and at a formal sitting he gives them a constitution, that they may unite to form henceforward one State, the new republic. Is he happy, now that he is at work State-building? His wife in Milan must be in love with some one, or she would write to him differently!

"Your letters are cold"—this is from Modena on the same day. "Their tone suggests that we must have been married for half a century at least. Friendship and winter, it is odious and spiteful. What more am I to expect of you? That you have ceased to love me? That is an old story. That you should hate me? Well and good. That is what I wish. Everything degrades, save only hatred. But indifference with a heart of marble, lack-lustre eyes, languid gait? . . . A thousand kisses, tender as my heart."

Fresh crises call him northward once more. He comes, he fights, he is driven back. The gloomy November weeks, in which his fate again trembles in the balance, are not gladdened by any consolation from her. Far from it, for his most intimate friends, alive to all that goes on in Milan, venture cautious hints that my lady Josephine is having a merry time there. This is the day after the defeat at Caldiero. He sends to Paris a despairing appeal for reinforcements.

Complications thicken; courage wanes; every one turns for help to the chief. He seems to be thinking with thirty heads these days, when the battle of Arcola is impending. It is in a crazy mood of despair that he writes to her in the evening, his pen storming over the paper: "I no longer love you, I hate you. You are hateful, stupid, inept. You do not write to me, do not love your husband. What are you doing all day, Madame? What important business makes it impossible for you to write to the man who loves you? . . . Who is the fairy prince that claims all your time, so that you cannot write to your husband? Take care, Josephine: some fine night, the door will burst open, and I shall be there! Quite seriously, I am uneasy, my pretty one. Do write me four pages full of sweet words which will warm my heart with joy and happiness. In a few days I hope to clasp you in my arms, and to cover you with a million kisses, hot as the equator."

How his heart flutters, uncertain whether she is still to be trusted, miserable if she be unworthy of trust. There is a crisis in his own soul as well as out there on the battle-field. Responsibility, uncertainty, storm in the heart of this man, who has perhaps already been dishonoured in his private life, and to-morrow may be dishonoured as a military commander—the man who still hopes to rule the world. During these days, when a suicide occurs among the troops, he issues an order: "The soldier must conquer the pain and the melancholy of the passions."

Two days after the date of the letter last quoted, he is standing near Arcola on a bridge spanning the Adige. The enemy is bombarding this bridge. The French troops shrink back; there seems no way of forcing a passage across the river. At length, after repeated summonses, the soldiers advance once more, but there are calls from the ranks to Napoleon: "Do not go any farther, General. You will be killed, and then we shall be lost!" Marmont is a little in the van. Turning round to see if his men are following, he notices that the commander is in the arms of Muiron, the adjutant, apparently wounded. Around them a group of motionless figures. Now that the movement of the vanguard is arrested, the troops seek the shelter of the embankment. Bonaparte, who has recovered, stumbles and falls into the ditch at the foot of the dyke. His brother Louis and Marmont drag him out. A horse! Confusion, shots; Muiron covers the general with his own body, is hit, and falls. Bonaparte saves himself on horseback.

That evening in camp, he is greatly depressed. Second day's fighting, and a vain attempt to storm the enemy's position. This abominable river. Seems impossible to get across it. For a long time, the fortunes of the third day are no better than those of the first two.

At the eleventh hour, he has recourse to cunning. While the fight on the river rages uncertainly, he sends all the trumpeters and drummers he can get together, with part of the guard, in a wide half-circle to reach a position in the enemy's rear. There the charge is sounded. The wearied Austrians are panic-stricken, and one of their divisions draws back. The French, encouraged by the rout of part of the foe, assume that all the opposing army is retreating, and act accordingly. Courage and ruse have snatched victory out of a morass of despair. The name of another village becomes famous. Arcola medals are struck in Paris. A picture is painted, showing the commander on the bridge of Arcola, waving imaginary colours.

The danger is over for a time. The enemy supports are withdrawn from Mantua, and soon the town must fall. Bonaparte makes a fresh disposition of his troops, and hastens to Milan. At length he will be able to administer the province from the capital, and have Josephine and hold her fast.

But Josephine is harder to catch than Wurmser. "I reach Milan, rush to your house, having thrown aside everything in order to clasp you in my arms. You are not there! You are gadding about somewhere, running away when I come to seek you. You care nothing about your Napoleon. A whim led you to give me your love, and now fickleness has made you indifferent. Inured to dangers, I know how to meet reverses of fortune. . . . Don't put yourself about, amuse yourself, happiness is made for you, all the world is happy to have the chance of pleasing you, your husband alone is most unhappy."

Next morning. "You have no reason to trouble yourself about the happiness or unhappiness of a man whom you do not love. But it is my fate to love you. . . . Take no part in the unhappiness of your husband, who lives only for you. It would be unjust if I were to ask you to love me as I love you. Who can expect delicate lace to weigh as heavy as gold. . . . My fault is that nature has denied me the charms which might bind you to me. What I do deserve is nothing more than this, that Josephine should show me a little consideration, a little respect, for I love her to the verge of madness, her and her alone. Farewell, adorable woman. . . . If I were certain that she could no longer love me, I would hide my pain, and would content myself with being useful to her whenever I could. . . . I open the letter once more, to send you a kiss. Ah, Josephine! Josephine!"

What a confession! With ardour and ambition he pushes forward to the goal, but the enemy has escaped, and what is to be done? Resignation must be the first aim after a failure, not raging and cursing. A man must retain his self-respect, and act prudently. A little mockery, embellished with courtesy, will have its due effect. Next day, he has turned things over in his mind. I must have her. How shall I lure her back? To extol my exploits does not move her in the least. What does influence her? Flattery and service. Such is his calculation. A miscalculation: for he, who is masterful with kings, fails to see that the charming Josephine would fear a master, even though she would not worship him; that nothing makes her more secure in her own position than his confessed passion.

Napoleon's mistake is the outcome of his pride. His pride will lead him to the limits of what is humanly possible, but will in the long run mislead him into the greatest of his blunders. Now, it is pride that prevents his veiling a passion which he does not master because he does not wish to do so. After all his carefully planned phrases to the effect that he wishes to be of use to her, the foolish human heart drives him, with the gesture of a love-sick youth, to tear open his letter that he may "send a kiss."

VI

What is Paris saying?

Paris is radiant, for, after long years, it once more has a hero to worship. Bonaparte's picture is in all the shops; rhymed comparisons of him with the heroes of antiquity are in every one's mouth; the actors speak of him when instructions are sent to announce a new victory; the colours he has taken from the enemy are on show at the Luxembourg; his reports, cut about by the Directors, appear in the "Moniteur."

Songs, medals, caricatures (a recent importation from across the Channel), enliven the boulevards.

He knows all this. He knows, likewise, that the rapid growth of his popularity is alarming the Directors, who feel that he has long ceased to be their creature. "The fellow's perpetual victories will be the death of us," they think, and put their heads together. A people's army is invincible, but it is dangerous unless its officers are genuinely devoted to the government. For the last seven years, it has been the rulers' way to threaten with the guillotine any general who has dared to meddle in politics on his own account. "A commander who does not comply with our orders, who makes light of the commissaries we send to his camp, must be dismissed, even if his name be Napoleon Bonaparte. Saliceti is too much under his thumb, being a fellow-Corsican, and having an uneasy conscience because he betrayed Bonaparte not very long ago. Let us send another commissary, Clarke, who is both prudent and ambitious."

Elegant and high-spirited, himself a general, Clarke, while on the journey to Milan, looks forward to twisting Bonaparte round his fingers. That gawky little fellow in the threadbare uniform whom he had often met at Barras' should be easy enough to deal with. But in the Palazzo Serbelloni, the envoy is abashed before the commander. Napoleon has not grown any taller, certainly; but the manner of his entries and exits, while all wait for his coming or make way for his going, suggests the ruler rather than the simple warrior. The commissary has a courteous reception, but he is far from being able to penetrate Bonaparte's secret plans and report them to his masters. On the contrary, within a couple of days the commander-in-chief has full knowledge of the Directors' private designs, about which Clarke ought to have kept his mouth shut. The commissary has bowed before the higher authority. "Here is the man of the future," says he to himself; and promptly changes sides. Napoleon's suspicions are now confirmed. He knows that the Directors are using his conquests as mere pawns in the game they are playing to secure peace with the Austrians. They have no intention of keeping Italy, and still less do they think of revolutionising it. Now that he is forewarned, he will make all his preparations to thwart the government's plans.

But he still has need of the Directors. "Reinforcements! Reinforcements! Not in name only, not on paper merely, but armed men in the flesh. . . . My best soldiers are wounded; none of my staff officers and generals are fit for active service. The new levies are raw and unsteady. The army is reduced to a handful of exhausted warriors. We are forsaken in the middle of Italy. The few brave fellows left to me, are marked out for death unless you send ample reinforcements. Soon may strike the hour of the valiant Augereau, the indomitable Masséna, Berthier, myself. What will happen then to the lads in the ranks? This thought makes me cautious. I no longer dare to defy death, for if I were to fall it would demoralise those who are the object of all my care."

Could anything be more artfully phrased?

Yes, he has another string to his bow. When he does not threaten imminent destruction, he cajoles with gifts. Month after month, to this government whose only resources have for some time been piles of almost worthless paper currency, he sends a consignment of hard cash, gold extorted from princes and republics by the terms of truce. He is the first commander to send money home, instead of continually demanding money. And in addition he has little presents to spare for the Directors. "I am sending a hundred of the finest horses I can lay my hands on, to replace any you may have that are not really good enough to draw your carriages."

He asks for the troops quartered in the southern provinces of France, and is told that they are needed for home service. "It is better," he rejoins, "that there should be broils in Lyons, while we keep Italy, than conversely." When told to leave all diplomatic negotiations to the commissaries, his answer runs: "For such matters, you do not merely need a one and only general; you must see to it that no one and nothing interfere with him in his work. . . . My advance is no less precise than my thought process. . . . We have to do everything with a weak army: thrust back the German troops; lay siege to fortresses; keep our lines of communication open; threaten Genoa, Venice, Tuscany, Rome, and Naples; show our strength here, there, and everywhere. For this, absolute unity of the military, political, and financial command is indispensable. . . . Unless the general remains the great centre, you will be exposed to incessant danger. I hope this language will not be ascribed to personal ambition. For my own part, I am unfortunately overburdened with honours, and my health has been so seriously undermined that I may soon have to ask you to appoint my successor. I can no longer mount a horse; nothing is left to me but courage. . . . I am continuing the negotiations. Troops! troops!—if you want to keep Italy. Bonaparte."

The more popular he becomes, the more often does he tender his resignation, though his health is in truth excellent, and day after day he rides until his horse stumbles from fatigue. Woe to the Parisian lawyers if they run counter to his wishes! While he strengthens France's power in Italy, he is consolidating his own influence in Paris; this is his new idea. Although he neither champions popular freedom nor believes Italy ripe for it, he insists upon the formation of the "Cisalpine Republic," against the wishes of the Directors—among whom Carnot, at least, is a convinced democrat, though he wants to use Italy as a pawn in the French game.

This is the first occasion on which Bonaparte builds up an organism out of centrifugal forces. In days to come, he will repeat the process again and again, on an ever grander scale of creation, his aim being to establish a United Europe. He now welds together the half dozen petty States of northern Italy, prescribes their constitution, appoints and dismisses their officials. Throughout, he is the dictator, and yet all the time he acts on rational principles and allows for elasticity in matters of detail. He issues brilliant proclamations, announcing that these States are to be free whether they like it or not, and that they are to pay him promptly in hard cash for the privilege.

"The French Republic has sworn hatred of the tyrants, brotherhood with the peoples. This principle of the constitution is the principle of the army as well. The despot who has so long kept Lombardy enslaved, has done great injury to France. . . . The victorious army of an insolent monarch was compelled to spread terror among the conquered. But the republican army, while waging war to the death against its enemies, the kings, gives a pledge of friendship to the peoples it has set free. Respect for property, humanity, and religion—this is our animating principle. But the Lombards owe us, who are their brothers, a fair return. . . . Lombardy must support us with all her resources. We need provisions, for France is so far away that we cannot supply our requirements thence. We are entitled to them by the right of conquest; friendship must hasten to offer them to us. We have to requisition twenty million francs from the provinces. They are so rich that this will not be a serious burden."

Then he takes whatever he wants out of the taxes, the countryside, the camps, the arsenals, and the domains. In the articles of every truce, he demands money, oxen, and pictures. If he sends pictures and statues to Paris, this will not, of course, stabilise the currency; but it will tickle the vanity of the Parisians, and win him popular favour. In a period of intense financial stringency, Bonaparte, with Italy as his source of supply, stocks the Louvre with precious works of art, contributing far more than the most resplendent of kings.

But all the time, while he is ruthlessly extorting money from the Italians, he is not less ruthless with Frenchmen who are trying to feather their own nests. In one of his early despatches, he writes: "The army consumes five times as much as it should, because the commissariat officers are falsifying their accounts. . . . Prodigality, venality, and peculation are rife. There is only one thing to do: a committee of three must be appointed, with power, during from three to five days, to shoot every dishonest administrator." When the deliveries of hay are found to be short weight, he declares: "It is of the utmost importance that not one of these rascals shall escape. Too long have the army and the country been the victims of cupidity." Innumerable are the documents bearing his signature which are directed against these plunderers. When the influx of women camp-followers exceeds all bounds, he issues the following order: "Any woman found among the troops without a permit twenty-four hours after the posting of this notice, will be blackwashed and publicly exposed for two hours."

On the other hand, this strict disciplinarian was humane in his desire to put an end to some of the barbarities which still characterised war in those days: "The infamous practice of flogging men to make them disclose secrets, must come to an end. The only result of torturing people in this way is that the poor wretches say whatever they think will please their captors. I forbid the use of means that are equally repugnant to humanity and reason."

VII

As a diplomat, he strengthens all the instruments of diplomacy: flattery and threats; lying and frankness—or sometimes, even in diplomatic negotiations, he will play the bluff soldier. He is especially shrewd in his dealings with the Vatican.

As thorough-going revolutionists, the Directors wish to put an end to the temporal power of the pope; for the Papal States are the focus of the religion which revolutionary France has rejected. The prospect of this moral success, to be gilded by the wealth of the Vatican, charms them more than all Bonaparte's activities in the formation of border States. They insist upon his advancing against Rome. Now he will be able to see it close at hand, this city with which, from childhood onwards, his imagination has associated power, greatness, and fame. Like Cæsar, he will be able to pluck laurels from the Capitol, for the papal troops cannot stand against him for a moment.

But he holds his hand. For him, the pope is the only ruler who cannot be dethroned by big guns. He sees the idea behind the papacy, with its millennial influence on France and Europe; he knows the moral repercussions of martyrdom, and he has determined not to wage war upon the pope, unless it be a make-believe. "The influence of Rome is incalculable. It was a serious error to break with this power, which will profit by our mistake."

He moves southward, and, literally, crosses the Rubicon, but there he stops. Because he is the stronger, he offers a truce; henceforward this will be his technique. The aged pope accepts the offer, for Bonaparte is wise enough to leave all ecclesiastical questions open. Pius VI promises to pay France several millions; to hand over one hundred pictures, busts, vases, or statues as the French commissioners shall determine. There are only two articles for which the commander-in-chief makes a specific demand: He wants the busts of Junius Brutus and Marcus Brutus from the Capitol. He is a Roman from Corsica; he crosses the Rubicon, spares Rome, and does not enter the city; but he requisitions the busts of the two heroes of antiquity.

When the pope fails to pay up, and makes difficulties, Napoleon sets out towards Rome a second time, but does not go to the city. After a trifling skirmish, he is willing to make peace. He will soon want to use his soldiers in the north. A pope on the run would carry his treasures with him, and what would there be left then for the poor Directors in Paris? On his own initiative, he actually pardons the French priests who have refused to take the oath of allegiance to the constitution and have sought refuge in Rome. He makes friends everywhere among the clergy, compares a "citizen archbishop" to one of the apostles, and writes as follows in several of his letters to high ecclesiastics: "The teaching of the Gospels is based on equality, and is therefore the most suitable for any republic." What will they say to that in Paris, where Christ has been done away with?

Finally, he sends to the pope, who is on the point of taking to flight, an assurance that there is nothing to be afraid of. "Tell the Holy Father that I am not an Attila; and that even if I were, the Holy Father should not forget that he is a successor of Leo." He thus dresses himself in historical trappings when he is dealing with the oldest of the thrones. But when the nuncio is slow to sign the new agreement, the polished man of the world is suddenly metamorphosed into a soldier, who tears up the draft and throws it into the fire. "We are not discussing terms of peace, Monsignore; there is merely a suspension of hostilities." The other side is alarmed. He doubles his demands, and this time he gets what he wants. Thereupon the pope writes his "dear son" a letter, and gives the child of the revolution his blessing.

He never wraps up his doings in mystery, as the diplomats of those days were wont to do. An hour after his first truce has been arranged, he discussed recent happenings with the freedom of a historian in the next generation. Talking to the conquered Piedmontese over the dinner table, he says: "My attack on the castle of Cossaria was needless; but your movement of the 17th was a sound tactical manœuvre."

At the end of the second campaign, he again shows himself a master in respect of both self-confidence and moderation. He has moved forward out of Lombardy in the beginning of March, and by the end of the month he is already in Styria, a few days' march from Vienna. If the Army of the Rhine follows up his blow by similar victories, they will be able to dictate peace to Emperor Francis. Yet he chooses to halt, and to offer peace to the vanquished. True, the Army of the Rhine is still a good way off, whilst Austria and Hungary are arming themselves in frenzied haste. To stay where he is as a menace, this is the conqueror's logic.

Bonaparte, however, is a statesman. The Directors want peace before the elections, and he still has need of the Directors. How would it be if he, he alone, the soldier, were to bring France the peace for which she has been waiting five years? Is he to share the glory of this achievement with his rivals in the Army of the Rhine? The fortune of war is uncertain, and none but the foolhardy will tempt it unless they must. Once more he has broken the troops of the Empire, cut off as they are from the Rhenish armies. For a year, Europe has been afraid of the new commander; it will become him now to make a gesture of peace, so that people may learn to revere the new statesman. Without courtly periphrases, and as an equal, he writes to the defeated Austrian leader, Emperor Francis' brother:

"Commander-in-Chief, Sir! Our valiant soldiers are waging war and want peace. Has not the war lasted six years? Have we not killed enough people; have we not brought enough suffering upon mankind? Everywhere there is a reaction towards humaneness, and almost everywhere the enemies of France have laid down their arms. Your nation is the only exception. The omens of this new campaign are sinister. However it may end, each of us will slay a few thousands of the other's soldiers; and yet, in the end, we shall make peace, for everything comes to an end, even the fiercest hatred. . . . You, who stand so near to the throne, uplifted above the petty emotions of statesmen and governments, are not you disposed to win for yourself the title of benefactor of mankind, saviour of Germany? I regard it as quite possible for you to save your country by force of arms. But, even then, Germany will be laid waste. If these lines could save the life of but one man, I should pride myself more upon my civic crown than upon the melancholy renown of the battle-field."

This letter makes a strong appeal to Archduke Charles. A highly cultured man, declared enemy of all wars, and only acting as commander-in-chief from a sense of duty, with this document in his hand he will be able to make headway against the war party in Vienna and to influence the emperor. For what would happen should they refuse? Bonaparte would certainly publish his letter and their reply. He would have another chance of parading before Europe the humanist ideals of the republic, and contrasting with them the feudal militarism of the empire. He would lay the country waste with fire and sword, while censuring us before the world for our truculence. He is following up his letter by advancing his troops, and he has already occupied Leoben.

The emperor's envoys arrive. The French commander meets them at the foot of the stairs, speaks of the emperor and the archduke with respect. When they beg for a ten days' truce (during which Vienna will be able to continue preparations for war), he answers by inviting them to supper. After the meal, he agrees to a five days' suspension of hostilities.

While comparative calm now reigns in Vienna, the Directors in Paris are much perturbed. Is this general of ours going to make the Great Peace all by himself? If he can do that, he will only have to come to Paris afterwards, and with one hand he will be able to push us from our seats. Most politely, therefore, they instruct him to await the coming of the envoy they are sending. All the more does Bonaparte press the other side for a decision. He knows what reports concerning him are current in Paris, and he cracks his whip over the Directors' heads: "I should like to have a rest. I have justified your confidence in me; in all my undertakings I have hazarded my life; I have covered myself with more glory than the most fortunate man could wish; now I have advanced upon Vienna, leaving Italy's lovely plains behind me, as I advanced once before in search of bread for the army which the republic could no longer feed. Calumny vainly attempts to discredit my intentions. My civic career, like my military career, will be unique and simple."

Ironies, beneath whose mask the writer is moving towards unnamed goals.

Endless negotiations. But why should the matter drag on? Give us Belgium and Lombardy. You can compensate the dispossessed princes with possessions in the Holy Roman Empire! Habsburg accepts this principle, for neither the emperor nor any one of the German princes is concerned any longer about the Holy Roman Empire. It is very old, in poor health, and will soon be laid in the tomb. This plan will give France a finger in the pie across the Rhine. But how Habsburg is to be compensated for the loss of Lombardy, remains uncertain.

Opportune is the arrival of letters from Venice reporting insurrections against the French and the murder of a number of French soldiers. At length the day of vengeance has come! Venice, too, is outworn, and ripe for destruction. "Since the discovery of the Cape route to the Indies and the rise of Triest and Ancona, Venice has been on the decline," he writes to the Directors, to soothe their conscientious scruples—i.e., for use in a justificatory campaign. "It will hardly survive the blow. This wretched and cowardly population, unfitted for freedom, without land or water, must, of course, be handed over to those to whom the hinterland is allotted. First of all, we shall take the ships, empty the arsenal, carry off the big guns, and close the banks; we shall also keep Corfu and Ancona." Thus weakened, the Lagoons were to pass to Habsburg.

Bonaparte dealt in summary fashion with the old lords of the region, with the few patrician families which, as the successors of strong men, had ruled Venice for centuries, and had made of it one of the most reactionary States in the world. "You have stirred up the peasants against us," he wrote to the doge while the negotiations with the Austrians were in progress. "Thanks to you, every one is shouting: 'Death to the French!' Hundreds of our soldiers have already perished through your machinations. Do not lie to me! You incited these disturbances. Do you imagine that because I am in the heart of Germany I shall be unable to enforce respect for the greatest nation in the world? I shall take vengeance for the blood of my companions-in-arms. War or peace! Unless you instantly hand over the ringleaders, I shall declare war."

This is his tone when he wishes to terrify a dozen tottering old patricians. When the envoys from the Senate come to his camp, he pretends to fly into a passion: "I shall have no more constitution and no more Senate. For Venice, I shall be a second Attila. Make me no more proposals. I will be your lawgiver." When the city is being handed over, the doge, a man of ninety, falls dead—the last doge of Venice. Bonaparte never forgot this scene.

Has he done with Italy now? Has not he got all he wants; has not he reached his end?

There is no end, for every step forward opens a new vista. Venice is merely a springboard, whence he can start his swim into the open sea. The islands first; then the Adriatic; and now he contemplates a more distant horizon. When he was in Ancona a while back, forcing his terms of peace upon Rome, he stood on the shore, looking seaward. There were the Ionian Islands, and beyond them lay Turkey. He wrote: "From this point, we could reach Macedonia in twenty-four hours; the place would be invaluable for our influence upon the destinies of the Turkish Empire." As brigadier on the general staff he had thought of engulfing himself in Turkey. From Ancona he sends agents to open up relationships with powerful pashas in Janina, Scutari, and Bosnia.

Now, when he is in Leoben, he makes sure of the island possessions of Venice, arranges for the occupation of Corfu and Zante, "to control simultaneously the Adriatic and the East.

No one will be able to save the Turkish Empire. We shall watch its death agony. The occupation of the Ionian Islands leaves us the choice between supporting Turkey and making sure of our own share of the spoils."

The political reality underlying this is an attack on England. France has long looked forward to the acquisition of strongholds in the Mediterranean, and to thus imposing a barrier between England and India. In Bonaparte, this general aim acquires the impulsive energy of a personal ambition. He does not want the East that he may inflict a mortal wound on England as his arch enemy; he is in search of means to injure England that thereby he may win the East. Since his imagination always runs far ahead of his achievements, Europe, of which but yesterday he first seized a corner, is already beginning to seem too small for him. He says to Bourrienne:

"Only in the East have there been great empires and mighty changes; in the East, where six hundred million people dwell. Europe is a mole-hill!"

VIII

A high-arched room, in the baroque style; the walls are white, picked out with gold. On a long couch upholstered in green silk, a sixteen-year-old lieutenant, a spoiled darling, with the fawning manners of a page, is sitting between two women of ripe beauty. One of them is the youth's mother; but when her smiling glance roves coquettishly over the surrounding group of smartly dressed officers, we gather that she is thinking far less of maternal obligations than of hours in which such boys as hers are engendered. Without words, she seems to add: "Creole women are adepts in the art of love!" Another connoisseur in the same art is the handsome general who stands behind her, craning forward over her shoulder that he may see far down into her corsage—as fashion and the lady's pride in her charms make it easy for him to do. This is Masséna, whose talent as a soldier is to be ever prompt to attack, being too unrestrained and uncultured to count the cost; but his flaming impetuosity often saves his troops in moments of danger. His temperament is so ardent, that he must always have at least two women in his train; and his appetite for money is no less keen. Money and women—he steals both, whenever he has the chance.

All the qualities that Masséna lacks, you will find in the little man with the big head who stands in front of the ladies making conversation. He is ugly, touchingly grotesque in his movements, and at the moment intoxicated by his success in winning—no one knows how—the love of a pretty member of the Visconti family. This is Berthier, chief of general staff, unresting in his activity; a man who will do administrative work one day, and take a fortress by storm the next; a great student of maps, for he is one of the few among these officers who is well grounded in the theory of his profession.

There is Murat, theatrically decked out in green satin, twisting the huge plumed hat he holds in his hands. Of proletarian birth, like most of the men at this remarkable headquarters, he is fond of talking in asides. Now he laughs too loudly because the ribald Augereau, the avaricious and extravagant peasant's son, has been telling him an after-dinner story. Murat, though he fears neither artillery fire nor the frowns of princes, is now painfully embarrassed because Josephine calls to him across the room. She wants to hear the joke!

But Joseph, a man of the world, who dreads what the enfant terrible may blurt out, nods meaningly to Murat, implying to him that for God's sake he must hold his tongue. Elise is sitting in the embrasure of one of the windows. Not so good-looking as the other women, and finding her husband a bore, she is apt to be censorious, and would carry tales to Mother Letizia, who abhors Josephine's loose morals.

Now comes the bright sound of laughter from the garden.

That is Pauline's birdlike voice. She is making the most of the days of freedom left to her before her marriage to General Leclerc, the husband chosen for her by Napoleon. She is playing blind-man's-bluff with Hippolyte, and her pleasure in the game is doubled by the knowledge that she is annoying Josephine.

Here is the chief, coming slowly along the passage. For two long hours he has been walking up and down with the Parisian dramatist Arnault. This companion has been carefully chosen. The newcomer has asked many questions about the army and the battles. Bonaparte has answered them with a detailed report of his own doings, which he knows that Arnault will spread far and wide. Now he has steered the conversation to the topic of the governmental crisis, long drawn out. As the two come into the reception room, he says, ostensibly with indifference, and yet with emphasis enough to fix the words in Arnault's memory: "I can hardly conceive any other way out of their difficulties than that they should bend before the power of one strong man. But where is such a man to be found?"

As Bonaparte enters, the officers rise to their feet, break off all conversation, and look expectantly at this man of twenty-seven, though most of them are older than he and all of them a good deal taller. Only the page continues to loll on the couch, for Eugene knows that his mother is unchallenged mistress of the house.

We are at Montebello, the huge castle near Milan, where Bonaparte is passing the summer. He is almost wholly the statesman now, for the war has been ended by the arrangement entered into at Leoben, and nothing more is needed than a formal ratification. He might be in Paris, receiving the adulation of which he dreamed in youth; but he prefers to stay in Italy. He will not return to Paris until the political consequences of his victories have assumed a concrete form, until the new States are consolidated and the Italian business over and done with. Meanwhile, during the many months he spends at Montebello, the life there is not so much that of a military headquarters, as that of a minor court.

But in no respect does he behave like an upstart. There are no pretences. In everything he will make his influence felt as one who is a child of the revolution that established a regime of equality. He has appointed sons of the people to the leading positions in his army; but he has no fear of what his noble guests, the dukes and princes of Italy, may think of it, should one of his valiant generals commit a solecism. He sees no reason for hiding his origin like a parvenu, although his adoption of French nationality might well incline him to conceal his Corsican birth. In actual fact, he parades it. Before the close of the previous year, he had summoned the whole family to Milan. Now, with lavish oriental hospitality, he has invited them all to Montebello, and those who seek his favour must show his relatives due honour. Half Italy pays court to him, for his name is already acquiring the mythical power of that of a man of destiny. Besides the numerous persons who wish to harness their fortunes to his chariot, not a few come from afar to ask the sage's advice concerning family matters and private affairs.

He has found it hard to persuade his mother, proud and a woman of strict principles, to make friends with Josephine, whose reputation is an offence to her. Josephine reciprocates Madame Letizia's dislike; but Napoleon, though he idolises his wife and can refuse her nothing, compels her to observe the outward forms of respect. Now, the friction between the two women has become even greater than at first. "This Creole says soft nothings to every man, and kisses every woman, instead of attending to her business of bearing children." The Corsican mother has given birth to thirteen. Josephine's barrenness dishonours Napoleon and his family. Letizia fancies that in the eyes of many of his adversaries she can read satisfaction and mockery because the great man cannot procreate a child. But it is not his fault. Josephine has led, and still leads, too loose a life. That is what is amiss.

When Letizia first met Napoleon again, after his battles and victories, she embraced him and said:

"You are thinner than ever! You are wearing yourself out!"

"Not a bit of it. I am really living, now!"

"Yes, for posterity. . . ."

"Well, do you call that dying?"

When he leaves her, he says to her: "Do take good care of yourself, Mother. If you die, there will be no one left with any authority over me." His Corsican clannishness is almost as strong as his cosmopolitan self-confidence.

Three sisters, three brothers, and Uncle Fesch are, in their various ways, enjoying themselves at Montebello. The fascinating Pauline, sixteen years of age, cannot forgive Josephine, who, in deference to Napoleon's wishes, has interfered with her plans for a love marriage. She weds Leclerc in the castle chapel, and at the same time Elise and Bacciochi have to resolemnise their union in church, for the chief is eager to keep in the good graces of the Vatican. After the ceremony Letizia, who has no interest in these intrigues, returns to Corsica.

"This island, this province," as Bonaparte now calls it, as if it were an island or a province like any other, has now been regained from the English, who had occupied it in response to Paoli's call for aid. Bonaparte managed the affair from a distance, while busied in his campaign on the mainland. One foggy night, a couple of dozen Frenchmen, taking with them plenty of money and an abundance of weapons, landed in Corsica "to encourage the patriots," circulate pamphlets, and so on. Napoleon also sent Saliceti, his friend and his opponent of earlier days. Thus, by proxy and from afar, he was able to achieve what he had thrice failed to do in person.

"Can it really be only four years?" thinks Signora Letizia, when those who had driven her and hers into exile receive her with acclamations. Is this the very citadel which was for so long the centre of Napoleon's thoughts and feelings? Now, simply because he orders it, Elise's husband is to be commandant there. For a long while, already, Lucien has been intendant of the forces. To Napoleon, in Italy, his native island now seems an ancient family seat, a romantic and medieval spot where his kindred can dwell when convenient. With a contemptuous smile, not long ago, he had read a letter from the Bourbon pretender, in which Louis offered him the title of duke, or even hereditary viceroy, of Corsica, if he would espouse the royalist cause.

In Montebello, Bonaparte first learns how to separate his private life from his public life—a lesson which those born in the purple learn from childhood upwards.

The guardianship of the castle, strangely enough, is entrusted, not to French soldiers, but to three hundred Polish legionaries. In several of his battles, there had been danger that he would be taken prisoner, so he has formed a bodyguard, forty strong. They are called guides, are chosen from among the tallest and best of his soldiers, and have a dare-devil for their leader.

The castle is thronged with orderlies and couriers. Envoys are flocking from all quarters. The lion of St. Mark and the key of St. Peter gleam on foreign epaulettes; Vienna, Leghorn, and Genoa are also represented at Montebello. Napoleon lives in state. Following the custom of the country, he keeps open house. Interested spectators are admitted to the gallery of the banqueting hall; and he drops a hint, lest they should forget to spread the news when they return home, that like them he drinks the wine of the country.

The reports of those who come to see him on service matters or other official business express astonishment that this young commander-in-chief is never embarrassed. He is dignified and yet perfectly natural; always the most simply dressed man in the company. None the less, he knows quite well how to keep people at a distance. Though nearly every one who comes to see him towers over him in stature, he never tries to appear taller than he is. Instead, those conversing with him are inclined to stoop a little, and thus seem to be paying court to him. Henceforward, throughout life, he is able from his natural defect to derive an advantage whose ultimate psychical consequences are incalculable. One of the visitors to Montebello wrote: "Should this man have the luck to escape death in battle, within four years he will be in exile or seated on a throne." The writer was only three years out in his reckoning.

A student of his epoch, one who knows how fame is manufactured, he has in attendance an able journalist, the first publicity agent in history, whose business it is to blow Napoleon's trumpet in Paris and subtly to discredit the Directors. Being a disciple of Plutarch, Bonaparte knows through whose agency the story of great men's deeds is handed down to posterity; that is why the faces of poets, historians, artists, and men of science are so often seen at his Italian castle. A year before, a few days after the triumphal entry into Milan, and when overwhelmed with urgent business, he had found time to pen the following remarkable lines to a great astronomer:

"The sciences which are the glory of the human mind, the arts which beautify the world and bequeath great deeds to our offspring, must be cherished with especial care in free States. All men of genius, all those who are famous in the world of learning, are Frenchmen, no matter to what country they may belong." Hitherto, such men have had to lead a retired life. Now, freedom of thought prevails; intolerance is a thing of the past, there are no despots left. The talented can foregather under his patronage, and fearlessly tell him all their wishes. Any such person who wants to go to France may be sure of a cordial reception, "for the French people would rather win a great mathematician, painter, or other man of note, than win the wealthiest of provinces. That is why, Citizen, I ask you to make these sentiments widely known among the great men of Milan!"

He commissions an attaché, who, like most of his tribe, has little to think about and nothing to do, to make a register of the art treasures in the possession of the petty States of Italy. In subsequent treaties, he demands the best of these for Paris.

For the Paris Conservatoire, he instructs experts to make copies of the best Italian music. Writing on this topic, he says: "Of all the arts, music has the strongest influence on the passions, and for that reason the legislator must make it one of his chief concerns. An inspired symphony composed by a master cannot fail to stir our feelings, and has far more influence than a treatise on morality, which convinces our reason without affecting our conduct." When he becomes a member of the Institute, he flaunts this title at the head of all the letters he writes as commander-in-chief, and declares: "The true power of the French Republic must henceforward consist in this, that no new idea shall arise anywhere which is not the property of France." In confidential talk he says: "The soldier must, above all, regard his commander as wiser and more cultured than himself; and the soldier will regard this title with respect for the very reason that its meaning is obscure to him.

Such actions disclose, not the statesman alone, but the man born to rule, the prince who regulates every gesture, every word that he says or writes, with an eye to the legend as to his personality which he wishes to inculcate upon his people. But when the door is closed, and he is among intimates, he opens his heart.

Here is a description of Napoleon as he was in those days, penned by an exceptionally shrewd observer: "The power of the man impressed every one with whom he came in contact. . . . His demeanour was still rather ungainly at times; but there was something imperious in his nature, his glance, and his speech. Every one obeyed his orders. In public, he deliberately tried to heighten this impression. In private life, on the other hand, he was unconstrained, genial, and even confidential; with a taste for witticisms, which were never ill-natured, but were merry and discreet. Frequently, he shared in our amusements. He did not take his work too strenuously, not finding it necessary at that time to measure out his hours; and in leisure moments he was always accessible. But when he had withdrawn to his work-room, his door was closed to every unauthorised intruder, without distinction of rank.—He needed a great deal of sleep, like all people of nervous temperament and very active mind. I have often known him to stay in bed for ten or eleven hours at a stretch; but if it was necessary to wake him up, he was unperturbed, and could easily make up for the lost hours afterwards—or could store up reserves of sleep in expectation of a strenuous time. He had the precious faculty of being able to go to sleep wherever and as often as he pleased. Fond of vigorous exercise, he rode very often, and at a great pace, though he had an exceedingly bad seat."

He has a taste for talking, and chooses politics or general questions of life as his theme; if the conversation flags, he suggests the telling of stories; should this be followed by a general silence, he spins a yarn of his own, pregnant and humorous.

The loveliest women set their caps at him in vain; he is wholly devoted to Josephine. Not, indeed, so frenzied in his adoration as he was a year back, when she betrayed or disillusioned him; it is she, and she alone, who has trifled away this passion for self-surrender. Now there is a moving note in his tone towards her; a fervent courtship, a smile, a petition: "You are sad," he wrote to her while still in the field. "You do not write; are you longing to get back to Paris? Have you ceased to care for me? The thought makes me wretched. My life has become unbearable since I have known that you are not happy. Perhaps I shall soon make peace with the pope; then I shall join you at once." Three days later: "The peace with Rome has just been signed. Bologna, Ferrara, and Romagna are ceded to us.—But there is not a word from you! Good God, how have I offended you?—I fear you know only too well how absolute is your power over me! For life, wholly yours."

Now, at Montebello, he is for the first time tasting the joys of uninterrupted connubiality, while he is delighted to watch Josephine's winning charm in social intercourse. Occasionally he steals time for a brief love festival. They drive across to Lake Maggiore; and when, among the rhododendron bushes beneath the baroque stone edifices on Isola Bella, Grassini, the heroine of La Scala, uplifts her thrilling voice and sings an appassionata by Monteverde, Napoleon sits wrapped in thought, his companion's hand clasped in his own.

"In the carriage"—so his adjutant relates—"he would take marital liberties which were apt to be rather embarrassing to Berthier and me. But it was all so simple and natural, that there was no ground for offence."

IX

What is Paris saying?

Since yesterday, there has been a watchman on duty there. Hitherto, the cabinet ministers had all been nothing more than lawyers; now, a statesman was at work in that innermost circle. Sprung from the old nobility of France, a bishop, then as a republican placed under the ban of the Church by the pope, Talleyrand had recently spent years of waiting in the United States. Now he was back in Paris, and had grasped a share of power. The recently elected Chambers were predominantly "right," and had been railing against the Directors; the commander-in-chief in Italy wanted to revolutionise Europe; he wished to perpetuate the war; the rape of Venice was an infamy. Perhaps many of the accusations were only too true, but when the echoes of what was being said in the place of words made their way into the place of deeds, they could not fail to arouse the contempt of the man of might. He sent the Chambers a memorial, or, rather, a memento: "Speaking in the name of eighty thousand men, I warn you that the days when

(Photograph by Braun, Paris and Dornach.)

General Bonaparte. Unfinished portrait by Jacques Louis David. From the collection of the Duke of Bassano.

cowardly lawyers and pitiful chatterers could allow valiant soldiers to be butchered are over and done with!"

At this date, Bonaparte had dispatched Augereau to defend the Directors, as he himself had defended them a year or two before; for the growing power of royalists and priests were becoming an ever greater menace to the new constitution of the Republic. If either of the Bourbon brothers should venture to set foot on French soil, all the malcontents would flock to his standard, and in a hand's turn he would win his way to the throne. But the Bourbons stayed in their safe retreats, and the Directors could risk a little coup d'état. Now, they were five instead of three, and felt more self-confident.

Called to office after this coup, an expert was for the first time in charge of the Ministry for Foreign Affairs. From afar, he measured the strength of his only rival. Though he had never seen Bonaparte face to face, he knew him for the coming man. To begin with, at any rate, he was willing to play second fiddle, and set to work that he might win the confidence of one greater than himself.

In all respects, Talleyrand was Napoleon's counterpart. Not a born negotiator; passionless, except for his avarice; cold and crafty, never natural and frank; always adapting himself to the mood of those he wished to use as his tools. His cynic's head, his long, pointed, prying nose, now surmounted the gold-braided collar of the republic; they would surmount the imperial and the royal uniform; and then, for a fourth time in the service of the ruler of the French, he would don the livery of the bourgeois king. For forty years he served the man who happened to be in power; but never unreservedly, and therefore he was never tied to any ruler's fortunes. Lamed by an accident in childhood, he was unable to enter the army, and became a priest, remembering that, in this guise, the great Richelieu had been master of France. Talleyrand was the only man in the country able to measure his strength against that of Bonaparte. Never would the man of destiny be able to shake off

Talleyrand even when he had come to hate the subtle diplomat; and when the final breach between the two men occurred, it was at the very time when Talleyrand, with a smile, could limp across the body of the master he had cast down and enter the cabinet of the enemy. Talleyrand was the man who overthrew Napoleon; but, if we think of elemental forces, Napoleon was felled by his own hand.

Talleyrand's breadth of view and utter lack of principle make their due impression on the distant Bonaparte. These September days, the commander has gone to Udine, to sign the peace whose preliminaries had been arranged in the spring. In this sprig of the old nobility, in this connoisseur of the rococo, in this cold nihilist, Napoleon sees the tool he will need. Hitherto, he has wanted none but soldiers. Now, when he has become a statesman, he wants and finds a statesman. While he is discussing matters with the Austrians, he sends the new Minister for Foreign Affairs a long letter (a letter of betrothal, we might call it), disclosing his whole political programme:

"The organisation of French power has only just begun—Despite our good opinion of ourselves,—we Frenchmen are still tyros in political matters. As yet we do not even understand the difference between executive, legislature, and judiciary. In such a State as ours, where all authority issues from the nation, where the people is sovereign—governmental power, in the full comprehensiveness I ascribe to it, must be regarded as the true representative of the nation, who rules in accordance with the constitution."

"Does your heart express itself so openly, Bonaparte?" thinks the inscrutable recipient, smiling to himself as he reads.

"It is an immeasurable misfortune that, in the eighteenth century, a nation of thirty million persons should still be compelled to take up arms in order to save the country. These forcible means are a burden upon the legislator, seeing that a constitution for human beings must take human beings into account."

"Is your aim so high?" muses the reader, with astonishment. "He is already sated with martial fame, and aspires, under the new constitution, to become dictator!" Talleyrand reads on:

"Why should we not make sure of Malta?—I had good reason for confiscating the estates of the Knights of Malta.—With Malta and Corfu in our hands, we should be masters of the Mediterranean. If we cannot dislodge England from the Cape, we must take Egypt. With twenty-five thousand men and from eight to ten ships of the line, the expedition could be risked. Egypt does not belong to the sultan. I wish you could find out what impression an Egyptian expedition would make upon the Porte.—The break-up of the huge Turkish Empire, day by day more imminent, must lead us to think of our trade in the East."

As he sits in the Foreign Office, reading this, the diplomat raises his eyebrows yet higher. He feels that the writer is a man of genius, if not the very devil. A week or two later, comes another letter.

"If our doings are guided by a sound policy, which is nothing else than the calculation of combinations and chances, we shall for a long time to come be the Great Nation and the arbiter of Europe. The scales are in our hands, and, should fate be propitious, within a few years there may be great happenings. To-day, these may seem the vague anticipations of a visionary enthusiast; but a cold, pertinacious, and far-sighted man will be able to make them a reality."

X

How slow these German diplomats are to make up their minds. For weeks we have been at it, discussing matters far on into the night, and still the titled negotiators hesitate to sign the document, though any reasonable man would come to a decision in an hour or two! Throughout, the Austrians are looking over their shoulders at the emperor in Vienna. In the room where the conversations take place, there is an empty throne on which the shadowy Francis is supposed to be sitting beneath the canopy. "Better carry that chair away before we begin," says the commander. "I have never been able to see a raised seat without wanting to sit in it."

His letters to the enigmatical Minister for Foreign Affairs, those fervid preludes, had been nothing more than the soliloquies of a man chafing at idleness, to whom weeks spent in thinking about peace seem wasted, even though the peace be one for which Europe has been longing for years. His patience is exhausted, and he assumes a menacing tone: "I have been too lenient with you," he growls to the Austrians. "I might have made the conditions much harsher! You are frittering away my time. I stand before you as the equal in rank of any of your princes. Don't talk to me about congresses. . . . With the means at our disposal, in a couple of years we Frenchmen can conquer the whole of Europe. Not that we want to do so. Our wish is to give our citizens peace, and quickly. . . . You tell me that this, that, and the other are your instructions. If, when the sun is shining, your instructions said that night had fallen, would you insist that it was dark?"

At last, to give them a salutary fright, he bursts into a rage, dashes a vase to the ground, and thus forces them to sign the peace in which every one gets what Napoleon had promised six months before in Leoben.

When Europe learns the news, there will be a sigh of relief. But what is going on in Bonaparte's mind? The day after he has signed at Campo Formio the peace which ends a six years' war, the peace he has fought for and won, he writes to the Directors, in the most matter-of-fact way: "It is absolutely indispensable to our government that we should speedily overthrow the English monarchy. Unless we succeed in doing this, we can be sure that the corruption and the intrigues of these active islanders will ruin us. The moment is favourable. Let us concentrate our energies upon increasing our navy, so that we may crush England. Then Europe will be at our feet." He issues a manifesto to the navy: "Comrades! Now that we have established peace on land, let us conquer the freedom of the seas. Without your aid, the glory of the French name could be carried only through a corner of the Continent. With your help, we shall cross the ocean, and the fame of our nation will reach the most distant lands!"

His mind is full of titanic schemes. As he gallops along the causeway of his great deeds, fame vanishes behind him in the dust raised by his charger's thundering hoofs, but fame ever looms in front of him, beckoning from the mirage of his fresh designs. In this spirit he hastens back to Milan, to Montebello, whence he is to give Italy her final orders; for now, carrying the peace treaty, he will go to Paris. In the tone of a prince speaking to his people, Bonaparte issues a proclamation to the newly formed Cisalpine Republic:

"Yours is the first nation in history to win freedom without partisan struggles, without a revolution, and without a blow. We have given you liberty, and you will know how to keep it! . . . Let your minds be full of the sense of your own strength, and of the self-respect proper to the free man. . . . Had the Romans of old used their powers as the French are using their powers to-day, the Roman eagles would still wave above the Capitol, and the human race would have escaped being dishonoured by eighteen centuries of slavery! To consolidate your liberties, and with the sole end of bringing you happiness, I have completed a task such as hitherto has only been performed by ambition and the will-to-power. . . . In a few days I shall leave you. . . . Your happiness and the glory of your republic will always be matters very dear to my heart."

Is this a warrior blowing a trumpet? Is it a poet, into whose mouth the ecstasy of life puts words that are to arouse popular enthusiasm? During these very days, in the company of a diplomat belonging to this very country, he is strolling to and fro in the park of Montebello. His whole nature is straining towards Paris; his companion is a good listener, and a man of ability. Napoleon, in one of those bursts of frankness which genius sometimes allows itself, delivers himself as follows:

"Do you fancy that I have won my triumphs in Italy that I may help the lawyers of the Directory . . . to achieve greatness? Or can you imagine that I want to stabilise the republic? What a ridiculous notion, a republic with thirty million inhabitants! With our customs! With our failings! France will soon forget these whims. The French need glory and the gratification of their vanity, but they do not understand the elements of freedom. Look at the army! Our victories have restored the French soldier to his true self. I am the idol of the soldiers. If the Directors, for instance, were to try to withdraw my commission, they would soon see who is master of the army.

"The people needs a chief, made resplendent by fame and victory; it does not want theories and governments, the phrases and the oratory of the ideologues. Give the masses a toy! They will play with it, and allow themselves to be led—provided always that the leader is adroit enough to hide his true aims! Here in Italy, it is not necessary for me to be so circumspect. . . . Still, the time is not yet ripe. For the present, it is necessary to yield to the fervour of the moment, so here we shall have two or three republics after the French model. . . . Peace is opposed to my interests. . . . If peace were firmly established, and if I were no longer at the head of the army, I should have to renounce the power and position I have gained, and should have to pay homage to the lawyers in the Luxembourg. If I leave Italy, it is only that I may play the same part in France. But that fruit, likewise, is not yet ripe. Paris is divided. There is a Bourbon party, and I cannot fight on its side. In due time I shall weaken the republicans, but I shall not do so to the advantage of the old dynasty!"

Such are Bonaparte's real plans. What he says is true:

"Everything has happened as I foresaw; and I believe that I am the only person in the world who is not surprised. So will it be in the future; I shall make my way whithersoever I will."

A stream of confessions is forcing a way for itself. The words have come down to us in the memoirs of the man who heard them; of course the speaker would have denied them, had the hearer then ventured to repeat them. But it is true that he is far from being satisfied with what he has hitherto achieved. Seated beside Bourrienne in the carriage in which he is driving away from Italy after a stay of nearly two years, he says: "A few more campaigns like this, and we shall have made a fairly great name for ourselves, a name that will go down to posterity." When his friend interposes that Bonaparte has already secured a notable reputation, the commander laughs him to scorn:

"You flatter me, Bourrienne! If I die to-day, ten centuries hence my record will not occupy more than half a page in universal history!"

XI

The Luxembourg palace has been transformed into an amphitheatre. Weapons and colours, the latest trophies, are displayed, side by side with the gold-blazoned slogans of the revolution, on the venerable walls within which, of old, the satellite peers used to circle round their central luminary, the king of France. Paris has assembled, and all are dressed in gala attire, as if for a May Day festival—though it is chill December. The front seats are filled with pretty women, friends of the men in power, for they want to get a close view of the little commander with the leathery yellow skin, the hero of the occasion.

"He has already been a week in Paris, and not a soul has set eyes on him. Why does he modestly shun the acclamations of his people?"

"There is the signal for the entry! Look, the five Directors are coming on to the platform!"

The chorus sings the anthem of liberty, the crowd joining in the refrain. A pause. The sound of clanking sabres and clinking spurs is heard upon the perron without. People crane from the windows, look down from the roofs. He is coming! He is coming!

Napoleon wears a field uniform, for this looks less pretentious. His mien is grave and unassuming, as with firm step he strides along the gangway to the dais. He carries a roll of paper, and three adjutants follow in his train. But, as well as these, hard upon the heels of the plainly uniformed little figure with the martial gait, comes a man wearing silk stockings, and resplendent in gold lace; he walks with a limp. At this moment, a cannon shot is heard, the first shot of a salute; the sometime lieutenant of artillery is being honoured in appropriate fashion. Thunders of applause shake the building, and are echoed outside by the thousands who are waiting to greet Napoleon on his departure. Quiet once more. Talleyrand is speaking. Brilliantly, smoothly, with undercurrents of meaning which few can understand, he praises the classical simplicity of their great general, the saviour of his country, who scorns pomp, and is a servant of the things of the spirit. The minister closes with the words: "All France will be free; save only him, perhaps—that is his destiny."

Applause, as usual; but is there one among these thousands, even among those in the inner councils, who realises the profound truth of the closing phrase? Does any one of the auditors feel the poignancy of the satire?

Napoleon quietly comes to the front. What is he going to say?

"The French nation had to fight with its kings in order to win freedom. . . . Religion, feudalism, monarchy, have in turn ruled Europe for two thousand years. The era of democratic constitutions has only just begun. It has been your achievement to extend the domain of the Great Nation to its natural frontiers. You have done more. The two loveliest countries of Europe, renowned for science, art, and genius, see the spirit of freedom, buoyed up by hope, rising out of the tombs of their ancestors. These are the pedestals on which two mighty nations are uplifted. I have the honour to present you the treaty of Campo Formio, ratified by Emperor Francis. . . . As soon as the fortunes of the French nation are established upon the best organic laws, Europe, too, will be free."

The soldierly voice is silent. For a moment, not a sound is to be heard. Then come salvos of applause. Are they applauding the speech? It lacks the charm of the popular orations and the speeches from the tribune with which the walls of Paris are often placarded. The hearers are astonished; many of them are positively amazed. Alarm and veneration are the prevailing sentiments. The applause is not for the speech, but for the man. He has spoken on many fronts, has harangued a crowd in Corsica, but has never before addressed society folk, or politicians.

His speech was that of a statesman. At first perhaps not a soul but Talleyrand understood it. All that he had said of their own epoch, seemed false. England and America had been democracies for many, many years. France had been fighting nearly a decade for her recognition as a democracy. Now, at last, recognition had come, in this peace with Germany. There was the tangible proof of it in the parchment which betokened peace on the Continent.

But the story was not finished—such was the implied menace that sounded, with a metallic ring, from the concluding words of the statesman hidden in the soldier. The Directors understood his meaning, knew that the threat was for them. But Barras pulled himself together, delivered a fulsome speech, and then, for the first and last time embraced the little general, whose wife he would infinitely rather have held in his arms.

Josephine, where was Josephine? Why was she absent on

the great occasion? No one knows with certainty how or where she spent these weeks. She did not reach Paris until a month after Napoleon. When she came, she was serene, charming, rather tired. In Paris, she promptly resumed her old life, and took up the threads of some of her old amours.

Meanwhile, another woman had entered Napoleon's orbit. She was handsome, but was too intelligent to please him. This was Necker's daughter, Madame de Staël. An influential woman, as well as an interesting; it was at her suggestion that Talleyrand had been appointed Minister for Foreign Affairs. She besieged Bonaparte with letters; she would fain have harnessed him to her chariot wheels, but he jibbed at the prospect. Now, when she had met him in the flesh, he parried her advances with a few civilities; but he could not prevent this talented woman from seeing further into his mind than most men had succeeded in doing. Here is her pen picture of the commander, an early impression:

"His face is thin and pale, but not unpleasing. Being short of stature, he looks better on horseback than on foot. In social life, he has rather awkward manners, though he is by no means shy. When he is on the alert, he is a little contemptuous in his bearing; whereas his natural demeanour is a trifle common. The contemptuous pose suits him better. . . . When he is speaking, I am enthralled by an impression of his pre-eminence, though he has none of the qualities of the men of the study and of society. If he recounts his personal experiences, he often discloses the lively imagination of an Italian. . . . But I always become aware of a profound irony, which nothing escapes, neither the sublime, nor the beautiful, nor even his own fame. . . . I have known not a few men of note, some of them savage by disposition, but the dread with which this man fills me is a thing apart. He is neither good nor bad, neither gentle nor cruel. He is unique; he can neither inspire nor feel affection; he is more and less than a man. Character, mind, speech—all have a strange stamp. This very strangeness helps him to win over the French.

"He neither hates nor loves; for him, no one exists but himself; all other people are merely 'number so-and-so.' A great chess-player, for whom humanity-at-large is the adversary he hopes to checkmate. His success is quite as much due to the qualities he lacks as to the qualities he possesses. . . . Where his own interest is involved, he pursues it as the just man seeks virtue; if his aim were good, his perseverance would be exemplary. . . . He despises the nation whose applause he seeks; there is not a spark of fervour intermingled with his craving to astound mankind. . . . I have never been able to breathe freely in his presence."

If we discount in these sentences all that may reasonably be regarded as due to the mortified vanity of a notable and much admired woman, enough will still remain to be worthy of careful study. Each moment she tries to pierce his armour, only in the next breath to acknowledge herself his prisoner. She moves in a Rousseauist world of abstract virtue and goodness, with which a dictator can have nothing to do, and she therefore cannot regard Bonaparte with enthusiasm; but nevertheless she foresees his aim, which was not publicly disclosed till near the end of his career, and hers is the credit of having been the first to recognise his genius.

"Picture to yourself a little man," writes a German at this date in one of his letters home. "No taller than Frederick the Great; very regularly and slenderly built; lean, but sturdy; a large head; high forehead; dark-grey eyes; thick, dark-brown hair; Grecian nose, so long that it almost hangs down over the mouth; his mouth is full of humaneness and grace; the firm chin is rather prominent. His movements are brisk, but he has a fine and dignified bearing. You may see him run down a long staircase in five or six strides, and yet, as he finishes the last stride, he stands before you as graceful as ever. Unless he is fixing his gaze upon some object he particularly wishes to examine, he is generally looking upwards. It was always a delight to me to contemplate his beautiful, deep, sensitive eyes, at once severe and kindly, like those of our own Frederick."

XII

On the way to Paris, Napoleon had had to spend a few days in Rastatt, to discuss with the imperial envoys certain details connected with the carrying out of the peace treaty and the evacuation of Mainz. Here, expected with mingled curiosity and scepticism, he had assumed royal airs. He had alternately scolded and made much of the envoys, as best suited his plans at the moment, giving one of these Austrian counts a watch and the other a jewelled hat-buckle. "The two poor envoys were amazed that I had so much money to spend, for they were as poor as church mice."

This oriental lavishness in present-giving, the outcome of kindliness quite as much as of arrogance, will be a persistent characteristic. He will become known as a caliph who loves to shower gifts, displaying a mingled disdain and generosity which throw a searching light upon his own spiritual make-up. But if he has to acknowledge some genuine service, then this same man (who from underlings exposed to danger demands scrupulous exactitude in the fulfilment of duty) will express his thanks in the most courtly fashion, as if he were one of Arthur's knights, and the world a jousting-place. The warrior who has captured so many of the enemy colours is given one of the flags from Arcola, as a keepsake. He passes it on to General Lannes, writing:

"At Arcola, there was a moment when the fortune of the day was so uncertain that nothing but the utmost bravery on the part of the leaders could have saved the situation. Thereupon, bleeding from three terrible wounds, you left the field hospital, resolved to conquer or die. Again and again I saw you in the foremost ranks of the brave. You were the first . . . to cross the Adda. Yours must be the honour of owning and guarding this glorious flag."

He knows exactly how his words will affect the people of Paris. If he makes a public display of such expressions of approval, he is just as sedulous to draw near to the footlights when he has to censure or to condemn. That is one of the tricks of his trade.

Now, he is careful to behave in such a way that all Paris, every one of his opponents, the whole press, shall exclaim: "The modesty of true greatness!" Twice more, during these days, he makes ceremonial appearances, one of them being at a festival held in his honour by Talleyrand. He had hastened to pay his respects to the Minister for Foreign Affairs on the day after his return to Paris. Neither of them had as yet disclosed his ultimate plans, but Bonaparte, in his dealings with this scion of the old nobility, had not forgotten to speak of his own exalted antecedents. "You are the nephew of the archbishop of Rheims," he had said in the first half hour. "One of my uncles, who helped in my education, is an archdeacon—in Corsica, you know, that means much the same as being a bishop in France." In this way Napoleon implied that he was no parvenu whom a man of ancient lineage was, in his heart, entitled to despise. From the first, he looked upon Talleyrand as a possible antagonist.

He has bought the little house in which Josephine used to live. Here he leads a retired life, with his wife, who has at length arrived in Paris. His circle is small, consisting of his brothers and a few friends who come and go. He often wears mufti, drives out alone, avoids parties, is easy of access. When he is cheered at the theatre, he draws back into the recesses of his box. This is the man who, a little while ago at Montebello, was keeping up a princely state. "If I am seen three or four times at the theatre, people will cease to notice me," he says to an intimate. "You expect me to be pleased by such public demonstrations? There would be quite as big a crowd to see me guillotined!"

He invites men of learning to his house; attends most of the sittings of the Institute, and is willing to read a paper there now and again; discusses mathematics after dinner with Laplace, and shows the astronomer new Italian methods of calculating orbits; argues with Chénier about poetry, and even metaphysics (if he can't help himself!).

But he silently follows, all this time, every move made by the Directors, whose power is continually on the wane. Knowing them to be his secret enemies, he keeps out of their path, and has them watched by his brothers. He gathers information as to the relative strength of the various parties, and ponders his own course. "Paris has no memory. A new reputation drives out an old one; and if I linger here inactive, I shall be lost. I must not stay here." Often he walks to and fro in the garden, arms locked behind, thinking.

"Too soon. Better wait until they have made a complete mess of things. Become their colleague, a member of the Directory, just when the pillars are crackling? A good thing that I am not yet forty, as the law demands. Meanwhile, I must capture the fancy of the crowd! How? There is peace throughout the Continent. Hardly a rival left to dread. Hoche, the most dangerous of them, is dead, thanks be! One of Josephine's lovers; a handsome fellow, certainly. His passing troubled her little; she is inconstant by nature. Carnot thrust aside, Moreau defeated. Augereau, in command of the Army of the Rhine, is jealous of me; I must put a spoke in his wheel. The Corsican stalwarts have little influence now; but that woman who came to warn me against the risk of poisoning was stabbed next day; there are conspiracies. Too soon. I must leave Paris once more.

"Get to work against England? That would be the best plan, if only these idiots had not allowed the navy to get into so wretched a condition! I've been worrying them about the matter ever since the siege of Toulon. During the naval war of the last five years, we've lost half a dozen sea-fights. What about invasion? If only that were possible! Any one who could defeat England would be master of the world. Sail along the coast, study the possibilities, and then, if there seems no chance of a successful landing on the other side of the Channel, back to the Mediterranean! Only there, in the East, can I throw off all restraint, and keep France a-quiver with curiosity and excitement. Egypt's the place, in the footsteps of Alexander; and there we can strike England a shrewd blow!"

After long preparations, the general visits Dunkirk and the Flemish coast. He asks questions wherever he goes, not forgetting to cross-examine fishermen and smugglers. Returning unexpectedly, he gives Josephine a fright, but it escapes his notice that she hastens to pen a few lines to the secretary of an old flame. In his campaigns, hundreds of spies have brought him secret missives; what would he say if he could read this one? "Bonaparte has come back this evening. Please tell Barras how sorry I am that I cannot come to supper after all. Say that he is not to forget me. You know better than any one what my position is.—La Pagerie Bonaparte."

Thus undermined is the marriage in which he still puts his trust. Thus equivocal is the position of Barras, the impotent Director, who hates and mistrusts the mighty commander of the forces. Thus nonchalant is Josephine, as with carefree heart she makes her way through society, passing her time in women's boudoirs and men's bedrooms—and, among the men, she has to put up with Bonaparte, although when she signs her married name she prefixes to it her maiden name, as though she were still mistress of her own destinies and free to choose her lover.

No doubt Barras is cursing Bonaparte this evening, but next day the general writes to him and the other Directors a long report, which begins as follows: "Even with our best efforts, it will take us several years to get the upper hand at sea. The invasion of England would be a desperate venture; it will only be possible if we take the islanders by surprise. . . . We shall need long nights, so it must be in winter. Consequently we cannot make the attempt till next year. Before then, it is likely enough that hindrances will have arisen on the Continent. Perhaps the great moment has been lost for ever."

After this amazingly perspicacious renunciation of his scheme for the invasion of England, he goes on to formulate a yet more amazing plan for achieving the same end by other means. Substantially, he proposes eight naval campaigns, ranging from Spain to Holland, all the political conditions and consequences being carefully considered. If, however, ships and money are not forthcoming, the next best expedient will be to attack English commerce, beginning in Egypt, whence Bonaparte could get back to direct further operations against England.

Enough for the Directors to hear the word Egypt, and they are ready to agree to this last plan. He shall have the command there, and all the help they can give. So dangerous a man as this—the farther away he is, the better! Best of all would be, to make an end of him!

The Egyptian plan is not new; it has been mooted at intervals for years. Talleyrand had brought it forward in connection with Bonaparte's letter, though his comment had been: "The leader of this campaign would not need to be a man of exceptional military talent." Was this remark prompted by a wish to keep Bonaparte in France, or was it nothing more than a spiteful innuendo? However that may be, the talented commander, when he read the words at a much later date, wrote in the margin: "Crazy!" But we anticipate. He drafted the terms of his own nomination as chief of the Army in the East: plenipotentiary powers; a commission to take Malta and Egypt, to drive the English from the Red Sea, to cut a canal through the Isthmus of Suez in order that France may be secure in the possession of the Red Sea.

With feverish energy he now devotes himself to preparations

for the new undertaking. He has long been familiar with all the essentials of the problem. The Mediterranean is his home. In childhood, he was wont to contemplate the Moor's head on the scutcheon of Corsica; sailing ships from Africa often visited the island; not long ago, he had deprived Genoa and Venice of their fleets; he was already in touch with Tunisians and Greeks, with Albanians and Bosnians. Over all these machinations brooded the spirit of Alexander, who had chosen Egypt as the centre of his world empire.

For the first time, during these weeks of waiting, do the elements of Bonaparte's nature become formally compacted within him. What has been no more than a scheme of the unbridled imagination, the plan of one who aspires to resemble the most splendid exemplars of the ancient world, is now dissected, pondered, weighed in the calculating brain; it is refashioned, reconsidered; by degrees it is adapted to the actual possibilities of the situation. When preparing his Egyptian campaign, Bonaparte attempts, in the grand style, to unite the calculator with the dreamer, while it escapes his notice that there is an incalculable residue. His imagination, nourished upon dreams of the heroic age, binds him to the fact that we are no longer living in the days of classical antiquity, that caliph and conqueror can no longer command millions of unthinking slaves, that even in distant Africa the peoples are awakening. Bonaparte is making ready for a titanic and insoluble conflict; and the more deeply he becomes involved in it, the more defiantly will he continue his vain attempts to solve it.

This man of genius, born two thousand years too late, is already spinning the threads of his own doom. With the hand of a demigod, he is sketching the outlines of his own fate.

XIII

"I am going to the East," he writes to his brother, "with all the means to ensure success. Should France need me, . . .

should war break out and take an unfavourable turn, I shall come home, and public opinion will be more solidly on my side than it is now. But if the fortune of war should favour the republic, if another commander like myself should appear upon the scene, I shall, perhaps, be staying in the East, do the world more service than he can." When Bourrienne asks how long they are to be away, Bonaparte answers: "Six months or six years."

At the last moment, fate wants to give him another warning. In Rastatt, Austria refuses to cede the left bank of the Rhine; in Vienna, Bernadotte, who is French envoy there, is so provocative that a new war already seems imminent. Would it not be better to stay in Europe? But the Directors speed the departure, saying that matters have now gone too far to withdraw. In May, exactly two years after Napoleon's entry into Milan, four hundred ships set sail from Toulon. Josephine waves farewell to her husband, and (doubtless with more concern) to Eugene. Not until the whole mighty apparatus has been set in motion at the master's nod, does he disclose to his subordinates the goal of the voyage. All are on deck, watching the gradual disappearance of the European coast; but Napoleon, on the "Orient," standing beside the mainmast among the eight-pounders, is not, like the others, looking back at Europe. His gaze is directed towards the south-east.

At the same hour, Nelson and three other British admirals, standing on the decks of their ships, are searching the seas with telescopes for a sign of the hated enemy, who is, it is supposed, about to sail for Sicily. Where is he to be found? Yesterday, Nelson's fleet was scattered by a storm. Days pass before the ships can get together again, and the very storm which had detained Bonaparte for twenty-four hours in Toulon, saves the French. They reach Malta before the English fleet, and seize the important island by a coup de main. By the time the cat arrives, the mouse is gone. Under all sail, Nelson presses on to

Egypt, but finds no one there, for he has outstripped the enemy. He tries the Syrian coast. Nothing! Back to Sicily. No one! "The Devil has the devil's own luck," says Nelson, cursing himself and the foe.

The French fleet is four weeks on the voyage, and Napoleon, who is a bad sailor, spends most of the time in bed. Is not this symbolic? Will the seasick general ever win to the command of the sea? He is restless lying down, and, to pass the weary hours, he makes Bourrienne read aloud to him.

For on board this fleet there are not only two thousand guns. A whole university is sailing to the East. Astronomers, geometricians, mineralogists, chemists, antiquarians, bridge-builders, road engineers, orientalists, political economists, painters, poets —one hundred and seventy-five learned civilians, with hundreds of boxes full of apparatus and books. Everything in this land of ancient story is to be meticulously studied. For France, Bonaparte is to win a colony, and for himself an African reputation. The soldiers have bluntly nicknamed these learned passengers, collectively, "the donkeys." But Bonaparte prizes them, and his wrath breaks loose on any of his officers who grumble at the presence of so many "idlers." He has chosen his experts with the utmost care, and has thought out every detail of what they are to do. He has brought a font of Arabic type, extracted with great difficulty from the State printing house. He has taken especial pains in the choice of books for the library with which the flagship is freighted for the voyage to Egypt. Novels are good for officers; and when he finds them reading novels, he laughs good humouredly. For himself, he has only *Werther* and *Ossian*, works of passion, his inseparable companions. On this journey, however, he seldom reads them.

What does Bourrienne read aloud to the chief? Travels in Egypt, which have been collected from various quarters, from Rome and elsewhere; Plutarch; Homer; Arrian's account of Alexander's campaigns; the Koran, which, logically enough, is housed among the political works, beside the Bible and Montesquieu.

After dinner, he is fond of holding sessions of "the Institute." He uses the name jestingly, and yet in the discussions he takes it seriously enough. He propounds a subject for debate, and nominates the champions. Mathematics and religion are his favourite topics on these occasions, for he has always been both calculator and dreamer. There sits the famous Monge, a man with a crooked nose, a receding forehead, and a massive chin; Napoleon has admired him for years, and thinks more of him than of any of the others. Beside Monge is Desaix, whom Bonaparte has just summoned from the Army of the Rhine; he has a thick nose and thick lips, a somewhat negroid but kindly face, and the strategist rivals the mathematician in the shrewdness of his eyes. Look at Kléber, a man of fearless countenance, full of courage and resolution; beside him, Laplace, who peers earnestly at the company from beneath his eye-shade; next is Berthollet, with a head like a ram. Kléber runs atilt at geometry; but when one of the professors wishes to take up the cudgels on behalf of the things of the spirit, Bonaparte signs to him not to waste breath, and points with a smile to Berthier, who has fallen asleep in the corner over the *Sorrows of Werther.*

The weather is getting much warmer. Napoleon, wishing to breathe the night air, lies on deck till a late hour. His intimates are sitting round him in a circle, and discussion turns on the planets, on the question whether they are inhabited. Pros and cons are voiced by the disputants. This leads to the problem of the creation. The sons of the revolution, disciples of Voltaire, be they generals or be they professors, are agreed upon one point, that the universe and its origin are rationally explicable in terms of natural science, without reference to the idea of God. Napoleon lies there, listening in silence. Then, pointing to the stars, he interjects:

"You may say what you like, but who made all those?"

XIV

Bonaparte rides slowly across the desert sands to look upon the face of the Sphinx. The eyes of stone and the eyes of steel meet. Like the Sphinx, he knows how to be silent, but we can guess his thoughts.

"Alexander stood here. Cæsar stood here. They lived two thousand years after this image was sculptured, as I live two thousand years after them. Immeasurable empires, consecrated to the sun, extended around the Nile. Millions obeyed the will of one. What the ruler dreamed, was fashioned by his slaves with their myriad hands. Everything was possible to him. The king was the son of the gods. All obeyed him as the descendant of the original conqueror. Because that first conqueror named himself king, and son of the gods, all believed him. Here, in the East, it is possible to say to human beings, 'I am your god,' and all believe. Europe is a mole-hill."

Soon, not many miles away, Napoleon makes ready for battle. Eight thousand Mamelukes, the best cavalry in the world, are ready to crush the invader. He rides up and down in front of his troops, points to the pyramids in the distance, and exclaims: "Soldiers, forty centuries are looking down on you." The Mamelukes charge the French, but are driven back by artillery fire; their camp is soon in Bonaparte's hands; they flee to the Nile, crossing the river in boats and by swimming; since it is notorious that they always have gold with them, the fight continues for hours on the bank and in the water until the victors have secured some of the treasure.

In Cairo, he knows how to win the support of the pashas and the sheiks. He gives out that he loves and venerates the Turks and the sultan. He is only attacking the Mamelukes, who are their enemies likewise. Periphrases, bowings and scrapings, elaborate metaphors—these come natural to him, the man of the Mediterranean who is half an oriental. They are devices for lying even more circumstantially than do the diplomats of

Europe with their speedier and directer methods. Here he is following the oriental custom. While still on board the "Orient," he had dictated to his interpreter a letter to the pasha of Egypt. It began as follows:

"Thou who shouldst be supreme over all the beys, but hast, as I know, neither power nor prestige in Cairo, thou wilt welcome my coming. Assuredly thou knowest that I have it not in mind to do anything against the Koran or against the sultan. Come, therefore, to my help, and join with me in cursing the godless race of beys!"

To approximate his own creed to the faith of Allah, he begins, like a conjuror, to juggle with the Trinity. First of all he explains that he has conquered the pope and the Maltese, and that for him the Koran is the word of God just as much as the Bible. But, at a later date, when the forces sent to dislodge his own are being disembarked, he argues as follows: "Allah is Allah, and Mohammed is his prophet. To the divan of Cairo, chosen from among the ablest, most learned, and most enlightened of men! The blessing of the Prophet be upon you!" He goes on to say that he has allowed these men to be landed in order that he may kill them all at one blow, "which will be a glorious sight for Cairo." There were Russians on board the invader's ships. "The Russians hate all who, like you and myself, believe in one God, for, in their own legends, they speak of three gods. They will learn, soon enough, that there is but one God, the father of victory, who graciously fights on the side of the good."

Out of this potpourri of the religious, which ends on a more pagan note than he seems to be aware, he subsequently extracts unchristian France as a political instrument, saying that the religion of France is especially akin to Mohammedanism. He is continually appealing to the Koran as the basis of his thought. The holy book which he has included in the political section of his travelling library, shall be made to do him good service. When he dismisses a dangerous cadi in Cairo, he finds a justification for his action in the Koran: "All that is good comes from God; he gives us victory. . . . Whatever I undertake must succeed. All those whom I call my friends, thrive. But any one who helps my enemies, perishes."

If he had but had the luck to have been born here in Egypt four thousand years ago, he would have gained the victory by the power of suggestion alone. But nowadays even these brown fellows are sceptical! He despises them, while showering them with superlatives; but, at the same time, he threatens to punish with the utmost rigour any of his soldiers who injure a native. The first order of the day to the Army in the East runs: "The peoples with whom we are now in contact do not treat their women as we treat ours. Nevertheless, any one who harms a woman is looked upon as a monster here as in Europe. Looting enriches very few, dishonours all, destroys the sources of aid, and makes us hated by those with whom it is to our interest that we should be friends." No one is to enter a mosque, and groups must not even assemble round the doors. By cajolery and threats, by tolerance and intrigue, by Allah and the sword, by all the methods of the oriental, Bonaparte secures an authoritative position within a few weeks.

At length he can regard himself as master in the East. Is he any the happier for that?

Junot has received a letter about Josephine. If only this letter, like hundreds more, had been intercepted by the English! Then, at least, Napoleon could still have enjoyed the bliss of ignorance! For Junot feels it his duty to tell his commander and old friend all about the matter. It concerns Hippolyte Charles, as well as Josephine. Napoleon had cashiered the young man. Josephine had found him a job with an army contractor, and had lost sight of him for a time. But she has met him again, has come across him at a fashionable dancing school. Her old passion has revived. He has such graceful hips! He makes such elegant sallies! Now he has the added charm of wealth. Meanwhile, Josephine has bought a fine estate near

Paris (though it is not yet paid for); the young dandy is living with her at Malmaison as master of the house. . . .

Bonaparte walks up and down as he talks things over with Junot. He grows paler and paler; his face twitches; twice or thrice he strikes his forehead despairingly with his fist. Suddenly, turning upon Bourrienne, who is sitting in front of the tent, he says: "You are not a true friend! These women! Josephine! You ought to have told me. Junot, he is really my friend. Josephine—and I am more than two thousand miles away! How can she betray me like this? Damn these puppies and coxcombs! I'll make short work of the lot of them. I will divorce her. Yes, a public, sensational divorce! I will write instantly. I know everything. If she is guilty, farewell! I will not be a mock for the flâneurs on the boulevards."

Bourrienne tries to pacify him; tells him that fame is more important than family happiness. "Fame! What is that worth? I would give everything in the world, so much do I love her, if only Junot's news were false."

But the English may intercept and publish anything he writes, so in his letter to his brother Joseph he can do no more than hint at this private calamity. The missive has a peculiar charm, which is perhaps given to it by the writer's enforced restraint, by the need for using veiled expressions. Tædium vitæ of genius at its climax. This private letter is penned the day after a victorious and virile despatch:

"No other country in the world is so rich as Egypt in maize, rice, vegetables, and meat. Barbarism reaches its highest level here. There is no money, not even for paying the troops. In two months I can be back in France. Look after my interests, I beseech you; I have a great deal of trouble at home; the veil has been torn off once for all—I have no one left in the world but you. Your affection is precious to me. Only one thing could increase my bitterness—if I were to lose you, if you also were to play the traitor. How terrible that all my affections should be concentrated upon one personality. You understand me? Make arrangements that as soon as I return home I shall have at my disposal a country house near Paris or in Burgundy, a place where I can spend the winter in absolute seclusion. Mankind has become loathsome to me. I need rest and solitude. Greatness bores me to death. The fount of feeling is dried up. At twenty-nine years of age, I find that fame is vanity. I've got to the end of everything. Only one resource is left to me, to become an absolute egoist. I shall keep my house in Paris, and not hand it over to any one! I have nothing more than what I brought into the world with me. I have never been unjust to you, that you must admit, though I have often wanted to be. You will understand. Kiss your wife for me, and Jerome. Bonaparte."

This cynicism and misanthropy, the desire for vengeance and the demand for satisfaction, have at length, and for the first time, become merged in a symphony of melancholy. The melancholy note had been sounded twelve years before in his diary, but since then it has been silent. A heart that desired to give itself wholly, in which trust had been ever renewed despite many disillusionments, now seems to have been pierced through and through. Victory, glory, to be a second Alexander—all dust and ashes. If a man is deceived where he least deserves it, and where he has trusted with all the ardency of youth, what is greatness to him? He begins his letter with rice and vegetables, and ends with solitude and utter disheartenment. What is left for him in the world besides his brother? "I have got to the end of everything."

XV

A blow quickened him back to life.

Returning from a ride in the desert, he entered Marmont's tent to find that all his associates were greatly perturbed. What had happened? The French fleet had been destroyed.

The day before, there had been a sea-fight in Aboukir Bay, and only four ships had escaped. All the rest had been sunk or captured by Nelson.

The officers stood in gloomy silence. The grenadier on sentry duty in front of the tent understood, every one understood, the meaning of this reverse. Napoleon's face paled, but he recovered his composure instantly, realising that it was his business to restore the morale of the others. After a brief pause, he was ready with encouraging words: "So we are cut off in Egypt. Good. We must keep our heads above the stormy waters; the sea will soon be smooth once more.—Perhaps we are predestined to change the face of the East. Here we must remain, or achieve a grandeur like that of the ancients!"

A terrible reverse! What will Paris say? He is not admiral of the fleet, and was not present at the battle of the Nile, but the disaster will certainly affect his prestige. How are we to get home again? On Turkish ships? But will the sultan remain neutral any longer? He has been wavering between Russia and France, and will be likely, now, to turn against the French. England, too. The fleet annihilated; thirteen battleships gone. How many years will it be before we can again face England on the high seas? A decade, perhaps. Allah is Allah, but behind what cloud was my star hidden?

No, not my star! For, when he reports the defeat, he conceals nothing, but is careful to explain in his official despatches that fortune had delayed Nelson's return until the French had been able to secure their footing in Egypt.

Weeks of uncertainty. This is a new phase in Bonaparte's life. He must remain inactive, while he waits for news that will throw light upon the state of affairs in Europe. If England keeps good watch, perhaps no letter will be able to cross the seas. For the first time in his career, he begins to wonder how he can kill time. The administration of a whole army, the suppression of disturbances, the rehabilitation of crumbling fortresses—these are no more than variants of idleness. The hours hang heavily, and he becomes more nervous, more fanciful than of yore. Bourrienne tries to tranquillise the commander's mind, saying: "Let us wait till we hear what the Directory proposes to do!"

"The Directory? A dung-heap! The Directors hate me, and will leave me here to rot!"

If he could only ride! But it is too hot, at any rate to ride in uniform, and an attempt to wear Arab clothing has been abandoned. Sometimes he goes for a ride, in spite of the heat. When, on his return, he finds that no despatches have come, he grows meditative:

"Do you know what I have been thinking, Bourrienne?—If I ever see France again, my greatest ambition will be to conduct a campaign on the Bavarian lowland. There I could win a great battle, and take vengeance for Blenheim. Then I should retire to my country seat, and lead a quiet life, perfectly contented." The fire still glows; the kettle goes on simmering! In the plain of the Po, his restless spirit was yearning for the East; having made his way to Egypt, he craves for Bavaria; and always he thinks in terms of battles.

Now, when his future is so uncertain, when he is perhaps cut off from all chance of returning home, and when there is no longer a strong tie of personal affection to bind him to distant Europe, he opens negotiations with the shah of Persia and Tippoo Sahib, England's enemies: asking the former for a right of way to India; and offering the latter an alliance, and deliverance from "The iron yoke of England." The prospect of following in Alexander's footsteps looms nearer. But when he comes to practical calculations he begins to doubt the possibility: "Only if fifteen thousand men can be left here, and I have another thirty thousand at my disposal, shall I be able to venture a march on India."

Although all remains in the realm of fancy, such imaginative excursions fill Bonaparte's happiest hours; he luxuriates in these vast plans. Four years later, he declares: "In Egypt alone did I feel free from the trammels of civilisation; and there I seemed to have the means of realising all my dreams. I pictured myself on the road to Asia, the founder of a new religion, mounted on an elephant, wearing a turban, and holding a new Koran which contained my own message. My plan was to weld the experiences of two worlds, to force history into my service, to attack the English power in India, and, through my conquests there, to reopen communications with Europe."

Are these the visions of a poet? Or is it that the conqueror and the poet are close kin? In Egypt, he has a romantic name for himself, "Sultan El Kebir"—he is, in truth, always the sultan, more or less. El Kebir is his third name, as visionary as the whole campaign.

His lively imagination, his spleen on account of his wife's infidelity—these combine with the influences of climate and lack of occupation to drive him into an amourette. A pretty young woman, the wife of a lieutenant, had sailed with the army from Toulon, in male attire. She was the illegitimate daughter of a cook, had herself been a dressmaker before marriage, was piquant, blonde, violet-eyed. He takes her to himself, and sends her husband back to France on official service. She soon learns to play Cleopatra's part boldly and charmingly; graces the head of his table; drives out with him. But Eugene, her rival's son, is adjutant, and his duty is to follow the carriage on horseback. This conjuncture is disagreeable to all parties, and so the young man is given furlough.

Eugene knows more than he cares to know about the scandal attaching to his mother's name; Bonaparte has himself enlightened the youth. What a painful situation! His mother, not far on in the thirties, is a coquette, and makes his stepfather (the hero of the nation!) ridiculous in all men's eyes by her open and shameless intrigue with a young coxcomb who is but little older than her son. Eugene himself has to look on while Napoleon, commander-in-chief of the army and pasha of the new French colony, flaunts his mistress before the public gaze. The little dressmaker, who would probably find the handsome adjutant more to her taste than his stepfather, laughs gaily, showing her white teeth. Anyhow, she has cut out the Creole countess, and she glories in the new spirit of equality. Napoleon Bonaparte is the central figure of the composition. All he asks of the young woman is that she shall give him a child.

An heir, that is what he has been wanting for years! If she will but provide one, he will marry her, for divorces can be arranged. One of his ruling passions is the desire to found a family. The mother would be of working-class origin? So are most of his generals! What matter, so long as the child is legitimate, and of the blood of Bonaparte? He believes in the equality of all who play an active part in the world; but he believes no less strongly in legitimacy. The hereditary succession of kingship is over and done with. The hereditary succession of efficiency is the new doctrine. Such is the fallacy by which his mind is enslaved.

After a while, he says savagely to one of his confidants: "The silly fool of a woman does not even know how to make children!" The gibe is retailed to her, and she exclaims mockingly: "It's not my fault, you know!" Bonaparte hears of the rejoinder, and his face is shadowed. He has no proof to the contrary, nothing but the inner consciousness of a productivity such as no mortal has ever had before.

His spirit embraces the whole world in its grasp. But if nature has denied him the capacity for reproduction, the foundation of all activity has been shattered. His self-confidence would collapse.

XVI

In the Institute, the commander-in-chief sits as an equal among equals. He never tries, in argument there, to gain a victory by rank instead of reason. Yet many of the questions that are discussed relate to army matters of immediate practical importance, such as the filtering of Nile water, the erection of windmills, the search for ingredients needed to make gunpowder. On one occasion, Napoleon grew heated. Berthollet said quietly: "You are wrong, my friend, for you have lost your temper." A naval surgeon supported Berthollet. "You men of science are as thick as thieves," exclaimed Bonaparte. "Chemistry plays the cook for medicine, and plays the assassin for science!" The surgeon's answer came pat: "But how, Citizen-General, would you define the conqueror's art?" Within the republic of learning, this equality pleased the dictator, whom elsewhere hardly any one now ventured to contradict.

For weeks in succession, the orders of the day ended with the words: "No news from France." Everything was at a standstill; widespread uncertainty prevailed. Amid the general inertia, the travelling university was an exception; the savants were hard at work, studying, advising, ever ready to help in the second line. As far as they were concerned, this time of waiting was a great opportunity for research. A thorough investigation of the country and its resources was in progress: the fishes of the Nile and the minerals of the Red Sea, the flora of the Delta and the constituents of the desert sand—all were now for the first time being elaborately scrutinised. The exploitation of the natron lakes and the Nile mud was under consideration. The physicians of the expedition were enquiring into the causes of oriental plague; and of trachoma, the terrible form of ophthalmia which is so frequent a cause of blindness in Egypt. A dictionary and a grammar were printed; some of the buried temples of Upper Egypt were disinterred; the Wells of Moses were discovered. One day, an engineer officer came back from Rosetta bringing with him a granite slab on which there was a polyglot inscription, chiselled in Greek and in two variants of the ancient Egyptian picture-writing. The riddle of the hieroglyphs had been unriddled.

What especially interested the commander, however, was the possibility of cutting a canal through the Isthmus of Suez. He made long journeys in the desert, always exposed to the danger of Bedouin raids; traced the line of the ancient canal; planned the course of a new channel. All his speculations were confirmed half a century later by Lesseps. Not like an adventurer whose schemes have miscarried, but in the spirit of a conqueror, he designed to separate the continents and link the seas.

Now at length! Some merchants on small vessels have managed to slip through the English lines. From them, Napoleon learns that the destruction of the French fleet off Aboukir has brought about a general transformation. The sultan has entered into an alliance with Russia, and the two powers have declared war on France. Achmed, the Turkish commander, is marching on Egypt through Syria. The malcontents in Cairo, encouraged by these tidings, rise in revolt. The insurrection is quelled by artillery fire, and the heads of the rebels are exposed on pikes as a warning. "This will have a salutary effect. Clemency is no good here."

On the whole, the commander is more relieved than alarmed. If the Turks are marching southwards, so much the better; at length he will have a chance of beating them in open fight.

From most of his close associates he conceals his deeper cause for anxiety. When he left France to occupy Egypt, his aim was to secure a position that would help him in his scheme for the conquest of India. "With ships, we can cross the seas; with camels we can cross the desert." He had allowed fifteen months for the conquest of Egypt and the consolidation of his power there, and for the preparation and equipment of his forces for the Indian campaign. That would need forty thousand men, as many camels, and one hundred and twenty field-guns. He had asked for extensive reinforcements; ships, guns, and men. These were to support his land army by sea.

The battle of the Nile had frustrated his fine schemes. The English were blockading the coast; the sultan had become his enemy; Egyptian sentiment was now hostile. But it was Napoleon's way to adapt his plans to changing circumstances, and it seemed to him that he could derive advantage from the turn of events. The Turks and the English are going to make a joint landing? That threatens our very existence here? Well, then, let us attack to escape destruction! Seize all the magazines and ports from the Turks, arm the Syrian Christians, stir up the Druses! If we were to take the fortress of Acre, opinion in Cairo would veer round to our side. By June, we shall be in Damascus; shall thrust outposts forward into the Taurus; march eastward with 26,000 Frenchmen, 6,000 Mamelukes, and 18,000 Druses. Desaix will come direct from Egypt. The sultan will find it expedient to keep quiet. The shah of Persia has already agreed to our marching by way of Bassora and Shiraz. By March, if Allah favours us, we shall reach the Indus.

Once more, Bonaparte fashions a splendid dream out of pressing embarrassments. He sets out for Syria.

There are practically no roads. Sometimes he rides as many as forty-five miles in fifteen hours, invariably by night, without water, and almost always with the vanguard. When Jaffa falls, three thousand Turkish soldiers surrender. What on earth is he to do with them? Keep them prisoner? His own men are on short commons; and, besides, he would then have to spare thousands of Frenchmen to guard the Turks. Send them home? He has no ships. Exchange them? The Turks have no prisoners. Set them free? Then they will reinforce Acre, the next stronghold. What on earth is he to do? Council of war!

All are in favour of killing the prisoners. Only a few days before, the Turks killed one of our envoys! Our own troops would be infuriated if they were to go hungrier still because of these fellows. Bonaparte wavers, thinks matters over for three days, and finally agrees. The prisoners are marched down to the sea and slaughtered. Subsequent military critics, especially the Germans, have agreed that there was no choice.

Acre lies before us. There we shall find stores of new weapons. Then onwards towards the north! The great dream renews itself during these weeks. Now that Turkey has declared war, he is completely isolated, and forced into a life-and-death struggle. Everything is possible, for needs must when the devil drives. But he is not quite easy in his mind about the Indian scheme, for he mentions an alternative plan to one of his officers: "After I have seized Acre, I shall march upon Damascus and Aleppo, augmenting my army as I go, for I shall announce to the people the overthrow of the tyrannous pashas. Then, with overwhelming forces, I shall take Constantinople, make an end of Turkey, and found a new and great empire. This will bring me immortal fame. Perhaps I shall then make my way home through Adrianople or Vienna, after annihilating the house of Habsburg."

Always the same visions, magnified now, when the situation grows desperate.

He reaches Acre. Not a big fortress, but well supplied with modern weapons, and defended by English officers and artillerists. Three successive attempts to storm the place are fruitless. English battleships arrive to support the besieged, and threaten the besiegers.

At last, after eight months, he has direct news from Paris! It is little to his taste. Talleyrand has not gone to Constantinople to treat with the sultan. Is the rogue hedging? The French Republic is at war with Naples and Sardinia. Moreau and Augereau, Bonaparte's rivals, have high command. Why, in God's name, do we squat here on the burning sands, inactive? Storm the place! Are our schemes to be wrecked against these miserable walls?

Who is in charge of the defence! Phélippeaux is there, a skilled engineer, one of Napoleon's old comrades at the Cadets' School in Paris, afterwards an émigré who had entered the English service!

Why can they not take the place by storm? Bonaparte has

no patience for a slow siege, for starving his enemy into surrender. The whole idea is foreign to his impetuous temperament. A fortress, like a woman, must be taken by storm, or not at all. He cannot beg, serve, or woo; and he cannot wait. Now time presses, and to wait is out of the question. Storm!

The soldiers begin to murmur. Even among the officers there are mutterings which are the heralds of mutiny. "Let us have Kléber for our leader; he is humane and gentle."

Bonaparte sits in his tent, thinking matters over. A terrible hour! Is England to be ever invincible, even on land, even here in the East? Is the siege to drag on for months? Impossible! Europe is full of the clash of arms. Turn back, without having won a victory? An unprecedented experience, an entirely new feeling; but there is no choice. The enterprise must be abandoned. Back to Egypt! It is only half the truth to say that Acre barred his march upon India. Who can tell whether, if the fortress had been taken, he would have pressed on towards the Indus notwithstanding the ominous news from Paris. We should have to reckon with incalculable feelings here. Every coincidence is symbolical. Before Acre and on the Po, France is at war with the same monarchical coalition. None but the son of the revolution can save the situation. Contrary to his usual custom, he does not ride in the van, but for hours after the columns have started southward, till nightfall indeed, he stays behind on an elevation to contemplate the stubborn fortress, his mind filled with a sort of ferocious melancholy.

A ghastly retreat. No roads, no water, the plague as rearguard. Is Bonaparte's career to be ruined by the desert and the black death? Calm of aspect, he visits the sick in hospital, and encourages them wherever possible. The doctor points to fifty cases as hopeless. They must be put out of their misery, thinks Bonaparte; their path to death must be smoothed. With a royal assumption of responsibility, he orders a lethal dose of opium. The doctor demurs. It remains uncertain whether some one else carried out the order. "In such circumstances," he says later, "I would have had my own son poisoned."

Two thousand sick men and six thousand who are still in health make their way slowly through the desert. Every four of the healthy has to carry a comrade who is too ill to walk, for there are not enough horses to bear the sick and the maimed. The staff officers are all marching with the rest. This is by Napoleon's command. An equerry asks him which horse he will ride. "Did you not hear the order?" retorts the commander, striking the man with his whip. "Every one on foot!"

At length the retreating army reaches Cairo. By entering with a triumphal display of captured colours, and by proclamations and marches, he makes a vain attempt to delude the people of Egypt.

What is Paris saying? What shall he tell Paris? We did not occupy Acre, because the plague was raging there! That was why we withdrew from the siege! In the Institute, a committee is appointed to substantiate this tale. A doctor stands up, and, in the presence of a hundred savants, refuses to attach his name to this fiction. The commander yields with a wry face, but bears no grudge against the stalwart, whom he promotes more than once in years to come.

The Turks now arrive by sea, intending to make an end of the French. Once more, the whole existence of the expeditionary force is at stake. The enemy is to land in Aboukir Bay, just a year after the battle of the Nile. He lets them land, and then inflicts a crushing defeat on them, though their army outnumbers his by two to one. After the battle, Murat meets him, and embracing him, says: "General, you are as great as the world, but the world is too small for you!" Bonaparte writes to Cairo: "You will have heard of the battle on the shores of Aboukir Bay, one of the finest I have ever seen! Of the army the enemy had landed, not a man escaped."

At this time he notices among the Mamelukes who have

entered his service a tall, handsome fellow with blue eyes, a Georgian named Rustam, who has five times been sold as a slave. Fidelity is written on his countenance. Napoleon gives him a sword with an enchased hilt and scabbard, and makes him his body-servant. For fifteen years, Rustam sleeps outside his master's door.

After the victory at Aboukir, Napoleon enters into a parley with the admiral of the blockading fleet. Ostensibly he wishes to discuss an exchange of prisoners with the English. Really he is hungering for news; newspapers are worth more than king's crowns. Some one manages to get hold of what he covets, and an adjutant brings them into his tent. The commander is asleep. "Here are newspapers, General. Bad news." He sits up. "What's happened?"

"Scherer has been beaten. We have lost nearly the whole of Italy." Napoleon jumps out of bed, seizes the papers, and goes on reading them all through the night, with an occasional pause for an outburst of wrath. At dawn, he sends for his admiral-in-chief, is closeted with the seaman for a couple of hours, and then sets out for Cairo.

"I have made up my mind to return to France," he says behind shut doors to the faithful Marmont. "You will come with me. Our armies in Europe have been defeated. God knows where the enemy will have got to by now. Italy is lost. What are they about, these incompetent idiots at the head of affairs? Stupidity and corruption! I have borne the whole burden single-handed, and by my victories have propped up a government which could never have maintained itself but for me. As soon as I leave, everything collapses. If I start at once, I shall get to Paris almost as soon as the news of my latest victory. My presence will restore confidence to the troops, and will reanimate the citizens with hopes for a happier future."

"My future," he thinks, as soon as Marmont has gone. "People will say I have abandoned the army in Egypt. It will get along all right under Kléber. I came here to found a colony. It is founded, and the Turks have been beaten. Help can only come from France, and no one but myself can send it. I have nothing more to gain here, but everything to win on the battle-fields of Europe. Thirty years! How many days before I can get away? The admiral says it is a bad wind for Toulon, and that English warships swarm in the Mediterranean. I'm afraid I can't get to Paris in an air-balloon! But Paris is the heart of the world. I must risk the sea passage."

XVII

They show no lights, the two small frigates which had once flown Venetian colours. The vessel freighted with the commander is the "Muiron," thus rechristened in memory of the lieutenant who had died to save him at Arcola. Fifteen years later he is to do still more honour to this name. Here, off Cape Bon, is the most dangerous point. Literally, they sail through the English fleet, for they know the ships by their lights. An August night, but cold, for the mistral is blowing. They sit on deck in the starlight, feeling dull and rather depressed. Let's liven things up with a game of cards; there's just light enough to play! Bonaparte cheats, and is delighted that no one notices. Next morning, with mischievous glee, he owns up, and restores his ill-gotten gains.

What a different voyage from that of fifteen months ago! Only two ships now, and then there were four hundred. Half of the army is dead bones. True, France still holds the land of ancient story—but for how long? The hopes of striking an effective blow against England have been dashed. What has become of the plan for a landing at Dover? Gone to join the scheme for the invasion of India! He has had to steal away furtively from Egypt, for there might have been a mutiny had his impending departure become generally known among the soldiers of the army of occupation. Kléber was not appointed commander-in-chief until Napoleon had gone. The last order of the day had been dry and brief. The civilians had been sent to Upper Egypt, for Monge and Bérthollet, who were in the know, and were now on board, might have blabbed the news to their colleagues. But poets were a nuisance! One of the fellows, keen-witted, had guessed what was in the wind, and had stolen aboard the frigate, whose destination was still undisclosed. Oh, well, let the beggar come along. He and his tribe are the brokers of fame, so we can't do without them. After the last victory, Paris will be on our side.

For weeks, the two frigates are in continual danger. "What would you do, if the English fleet were to heave in sight? Fight? Impossible! Surrender? You would none of you like that any better than I should. The only other alternative is to blow up the ship." A general silence. Monge, who is sitting beside the commander, grows pale. "That shall be your charge," adds Napoleon, turning to him with a mischievous smile. A few days later, a ship is sighted, and is wrongly supposed to be an English man-of-war. The mathematician vanishes, and is found afterwards at the door of the powder magazine.

This incident gives us the measure of Bonaparte's authority.

After a six weeks' cruise in the Mediterranean, an island is sighted on a fine October morning, a familiar ridge of mountains is seen on the horizon. The captain of the frigate consults his chart. "That is Corsica," says Bonaparte unhesitatingly. Does he order the seamen to clap on all sail and make for the island? No, they must find out, first, whether the place is still French. But a strong wind is blowing shoreward, and, even under light canvas, progress is rapid. His thoughts run swiftly, too.

" 'Still French?' My question used to be, 'French yet?' Only six years ago. I was twenty-four then, and to be master of this island seemed to me the greatest thing in the world. Since then, I have had Italy at my feet; Egypt has been conquered; Paris smiles. All has happened as if by natural sequence. The wind is freshening. What will be the answer from the shore?" The signals show that the harbour is open to a French ship. The native island of the man without a country is home to him once more.

They land, and all Ajaccio crowds to the harbour; thousands who once cursed the name of Bonaparte are now eager to welcome him. He regards the throng cynically. Many address him with the familiar "thou"; and hundreds wish to shake hands with him. He accepts these demonstrations unmoved. But suddenly he hears a voice: "Figlio! Caro figlio!" Camilla is speaking, his old nurse, a vigorous peasantwoman, hardly fifty years of age. The sight of her is the only thing that stirs his emotions.

Napoleon makes for his ancestral home, which his mother has had set in order once more, though she is away just now. He summons those best fitted to give him the news he craves. There, beside the family hearth, he learns what has, during the last three months, happened to his creations. Mantua and Milan have gone, and with them most of Italy, won by his feats of arms three short years ago. Genoa is still French, though hard to keep. Masséna has been forced back through Switzerland! The English have landed in Holland! What is the first thing to do? Make for Nice! Instantly take the lead! Win back all in a storm of victories. "What's that you say?" Two of the Directors forcibly removed! Only by such tricks can the shaky government still keep in power? General Moulin is one of the Directors? Moulin, who the devil is he? The other substitute? Sieyès, you say? Another coup must be impending—perhaps a forcible change of government. We must make all speed for Paris. On board! On board! Take a big rowing boat in tow!

Two days' sail towards Toulon. Twilight when the coast is sighted. The look-out man reports English ships. "Put about!" orders the admiral. "Forward!" thunders Bonaparte.

In case of need, we can make the shore in the big rowing boat! Once more his star blinds the enemy; once more he escapes capture by the English. Night falls. Impossible to land at Toulon? Let us make for Fréjus, then. Uncharted rocks there? Rocks everywhere! In sight of the French coast after a seven weeks' voyage, we must run all risks to land!

Does this Italian love the country on which he now sets his foot? To him it is nothing more than the fiddle on which he can play a better tune than on any other instrument.

Next day, in the little town of Fréjus, Bonaparte's name is on every one's lips. Why is the harbour full of rowing boats, laden with sightseers? Why this popular rejoicing? What has the man done in Africa, that the inhabitants of the provincial town should greet him as if he were a Roman imperator celebrating a triumph? An official says something about quarantine. "We prefer the plague to the Austrians, and the Austrians are almost at our gates!" shouts the crowd, escorting him through the streets as a deliverer.

"France seems to be in a bad way," thinks the man in the carriage, as he acknowledges the vociferations. "It looks as if every one had been waiting for me. A while back would have been too soon. To-morrow would have been too late. I have come at the right moment."

He drives westward from Fréjus, and stays for a time in Aix, questioning every one he meets. At Aix, a copy of a letter comes into his hands, an old letter that had miscarried: "The Directory is waiting for you, General; for you and your brave companions!" This was written in the panic of rulers who are at their wits' end for a saviour! What had he better do? Stay where he is for a time, and write before going to Paris. "Egypt is wholly ours, and safe from invasion.—I was cut off from newspapers till the end of July, but when I heard of your troubles I instantly set out for home. I had to take all risks, for my place was the spot where I could be of most use. Had there been no frigate, I should have wrapped myself in my

General Bonaparte in 1797. Drawing by Wocher in Basle.
Town Library, Basle.

cloak and should have sailed in the first cockle-shell I could find. With Kléber in command, Egypt is in good hands. When I left, the whole country was under water—the best Nile for fifty years."

This carefully worded epistle goes as a herald to Paris. The people there must be told who is on the way. His northward journey is a via triumphalis; salutes are fired everywhere. Passing through Valence, he recognises among the onlookers the good woman who keeps the café where he used to lodge, the place with the billiard room; he gives her a keepsake from the East. In Lyons, he waits two or three hours to see the performance of a hastily extemporised drama, "The Hero's Return." Everything shows the powerful spell already exercised by his name. Perhaps the most signal instance is the sensational end of Baudin, one of the best of the deputies, who utters a shout of joy on hearing the news of Napoleon's return, and drops dead from surcharge of emotion. The light that radiates from the commander is so strong that it kills.

Paris draws near. He is still gathering news. But about private affairs, about Josephine, he can ask no questions. Is he already a divorcé? Where are his brothers? The news of his coming has been noised abroad; why has no one come to meet him? She, where is she? Will she, after all, be waiting for him in the mirrored room, ready to welcome him with a smile? In the grey dawn he passes the octroi, drives along the outer boulevards, turns into his own little street. There is the house. A woman stands alone at the door. Who is it?

His mother.

XVIII

"Bonaparte's landing is one of those events which at first we hesitate to believe. The news spread over night at theatres and in social gatherings. In the most obscure pot-houses, people were drinking to celebrate his return. . . ." "Every one hails him with delight, for he brings us new hope. . . ." "Glory, peace, and happiness follow in his train."

These and similar items catch Bonaparte's eye as he flutters the newspapers. Day by day he can read an abundance of details, mingled truth and falsehood, concerning his aspect, demeanour, and dress. Even the opposition press pins its hopes on him: "His Egyptian campaign has miscarried; but what matter? He is satisfied with having undertaken it, and it is difficult to say whither his rashness may lead. All the same, his bold ventures restore our courage."—He is received with acclamation, and his plans are consolidated.

But his wife is away. When the news that he had landed reached Paris, she was dining with Gohier, the first of the five Directors. She and her host were equally alarmed. Both had uneasy consciences, and now the volcano was rumbling beneath them. Some time ago, Barras (who during this period seems still to have been an occasional recipient of her favours) had advised her to procure a divorce from the absent and almost vanished adventurer, and to marry handsome Hippolyte. She had received no letters from Napoleon. If he had written any, they must have miscarried. But her brother-in-law's hostile attitude showed her what was in the wind. Barras was right. She would do well to act first.—Then Paris was electrified by the news of Napoleon's great victory over the Turks. Perhaps it would be wiser, after all, to stay in her present safe harbourage. Unstable and frivolous, she had of late been coquetting with the thought of reconciliation. A glance at her own image in the mirror, a knowledge of the way she could turn men's heads, sufficed to convince her of the possibility.

Now, at Gohier's table, she pulls herself together, and her host tries to outdo her in self-command. They drink to the general's return. She hurries home, packs up all that can set off her beauty to the best advantage, and in a trice is driving southward. As her carriage rattles past the barrier, she thinks: "Act promptly, and take the enemy by surprise—is not that the secret of his military success? On the return journey, I shall be with him day and night, and shall win him over before the tale-bearers can get at him!"

But she misses him, learns that he has passed her, and hastens back to Paris. She has lost three precious days, during which his relatives have told him all the scandal. True, some of his intimates warn him against applying for a divorce. In Paris, a cuckold is always a figure of fun. He is resolute, however: "I have done with her. What do I care about the chatter? It will only last for a day or two." He has her trunks packed, and carried down to the porter's lodge, so that she shall not enter the house. Could he give plainer proof that he dreads his own weakness?

She comes, breaks through the first line of defence, enters the fortress. He has locked himself in. She calls to him and pleads with him through the door. During her journey, the more she has come to realise that his name is in every one's mouth, the more fervent have been her hopes for a reconciliation, and the more has her pride been humbled. But the citadel holds out. At length she decides to call up reinforcements for a final assault. Hortense and Eugene must come to her aid. They clamour, beseech, shed tears. Thus a night passes.

No dispassionate observer can fail to understand Josephine's motives in making this ridiculous scene. What of Bonaparte himself, the man with so profound a knowledge of the human soul? Was he duped by a woman?

There he lies, returned after a long absence, with his head full of schemes for the conquest of a nation. Let us try to follow his thoughts. "They have deceived me one and all. The government, the political parties, my own companions-in-arms, were all endeavouring, during my absence, to exclude me from power, for they regarded me as a danger to themselves. As long as I was out of range, no one wanted me back; my brothers no more than the rest. This capricious woman, whose pretty whims I have never tried to restrain—would it be reasonable for me to expect that she should have spent a year and more thinking of no one but her absent husband, whose return seemed ever more unlikely as the days went by? When I am there, she is fascinating. If I make truce with her now, when the game is in my hands, she will agree to all my conditions, and I can exact guarantees for the future. What a lovely voice she has. There cannot have been any falling off in her charms, or she would not have so many admirers. What a fool, compared with her, was that little woman in Egypt, and even she could not give me an heir. Where shall I find a woman who will make a more perfect lover and a better wife than Josephine? Besides, she has had two children, and may yet have more."

He opens the door and, heroic in his silence, suppresses, once and for all, the accusations with which his heart is filled. In this matter, as in others, he holds fast to his resolves. Next day she confesses that she is in debt to the tune of two million francs. He pays without a word.

It is hard for his brothers, and still harder for his sisters, to accept the situation; but they do not venture a remonstrance.

Nor is there time for the further discussion of family matters. Events are on the wing. His brothers have not been idle while he has been away. Joseph, after being envoy in Rome, is now on guard as one of the Parisian deputies. Lucien is leader of the opposition, although, being only twenty-four, he is under the legal age. A brilliant orator, dreaded in debate, a Hotspur with a taste for theatrical displays, burning with ambition, too headstrong for constructive work. He and Sieyès have been working at plans for a coup d'état on their own, but they lack the support of a great soldier whom the troops would follow. Now the soldier has come, and Lucien will keep his private wishes to himself. He, too, is a Bonaparte.

Dangerous, inscrutable, and cunning is Joseph's new brother-in-law, Bernadotte. He is slow in coming to greet Bonaparte. When he does come, and Bonaparte speaks of the desperate situation of the republic, Bernadotte rejoins: "It will be able to make headway against its enemies both abroad and at home!" He looked searchingly at his interlocutor, and for a moment the masterful eyes of the two men clash. But Bonaparte, controlling his emotions as usual, attempts a diversion to political issues, speaks again of the dangers, and then passes severe strictures on the Jacobin Club. Thereupon Bernadotte breaks in: "Your brothers founded it!"

Bonaparte is still loathe to take offence, and replies: "Well, well, General, I would rather live in the woods than in a State where there is no security!"

Bernadotte, mockingly: "Good God! What security is lacking to you?"

Now, Bonaparte is about to make an angry rejoinder, but Josephine intervenes to keep the peace. And yet the hidden fact is that Josephine is, in a sense, the cause of the dissension. For Bernadotte has married Désirée Clary, to whom Napoleon had once paid court, with whom he had not found favour when he was still obscure, and to whom he had preferred Josephine when his fortunes were on the mend. Now he can forgive neither himself nor Bernadotte. Throughout his career, Bonaparte will try, by showering benefits on her, to atone to Désirée for what she has lost by not marrying him, though it was mainly her doing that they did not become man and wife. For her sake, he continually advances Bernadotte, who no less persistently betrays him.

All that his brothers and other intimates have told him about affairs in Paris during his absence, their picture of anarchical corruption and violent impotence, fills him with forebodings and urges him to speedy action. The number of the holders of power must be reduced, and their term of office must be lengthened. The government is a plateau; it must become a towering peak. A ten years' triumvirate—that will be the best plan.

At the Luxembourg they are all uneasy, now that he is back. Every one of the Directors mistrusts him, and each of them is suspicious of his four co-Directors likewise. Which of them is intriguing with Bonaparte? Sieyès is on friendly terms with Lucien, Barras with Josephine, Gohier with both. What about Ducos? Is General Moulin to be relied on?—Immediately after reaching Paris Bonaparte had sent Moulin a Damascus blade with a diamond-studded hilt, and Moulin could not in decency refuse the gift.

Such are the secret thoughts of the Directors. Look at Bonaparte's get-up when he first came to pay us his respects! Did any one ever see a general in such a rig? Much more like an adventurer! Mufti; green coat; round hat; Mameluke sword. The man wants to dazzle Paris into believing him a pasha. Did you notice that he has had his hair cut short? Wants to win people by an affectation of simplicity! Yet today he comes to call in great style. General on horseback, with all his aides. Brilliant uniforms. Paris agog. Very sinister, this change of aspect. Look at the way he sits and questions the five of us, as if he were a monarch holding audience.

"Why do you let the man impose on you?" say his enemies angrily to the Directors. "He made a frightful mess of the Egyptian campaign. Your proper course is plain enough. Have him arrested for deserting the army under his command! He's got something up his sleeve, you may be sure!"

Bonaparte, meanwhile, receives visits from Jacobin leaders and Bourbon agents; gives advice to all and sundry, but tells no one what he really thinks; behaves like a man of family who has just returned from a long journey, and, with an air of good-natured boredom, allows his relatives to tell him all about their squabbles while he has been away. He has been home for two weeks now. The tension is increasing. Affairs of State are at a standstill, or nearly so; for the Five, who should be carrying on the work of government, are busied in intrigue. Amid the general confusion, the Councils have utterly lost prestige. The new constitution is rocking in the blast, but no one seems to know from which quarter the wind is blowing.

Who is the real holder of power in the State? Who controls the army? General Moulin? General Bonaparte?

While no one can tell from day to day how the relationships between Napoleon and the government are likely to shape themselves, he goes to the Institute to deliver a lecture on the vestiges of the ancient Suez canal, and describes the Rosetta stone. On November 1st, there is a State banquet in honour of a victory won by Masséna. Where is Bonaparte? No doubt it is not to his taste to celebrate the triumphs of a brother-in-arms!

That evening he is closeted with Lucien and Abbé Sieyès. Talleyrand has at length brought him in touch with the ablest of the Directors. Sieyès and Bonaparte, the man who has rediscovered the constitution and the man who has rediscovered the secret of power, sit face to face; they vie with one another in ambition and in intellectual ability. "I have made the Great Nation," says the general. "You could not have done so, had we not first made the Nation," counters the abbé.

They discuss the details of the proposed coup d'état. On the critical day, they will spread the report that a Jacobin conspiracy is afoot. The Councils, in alarm, will transfer their sessions from Central Paris to Saint-Cloud. "As a measure of precaution," Bonaparte will be entrusted with the command of the Paris garrison. Sieyès has come to an understanding with Ducos. Persuasion, threats, or money, will induce the other three Directors to resign. Barras will take money. But what about Gohier? "Make short work of it," says Lucien. "Dissolve the Councils by force." But at night Napoleon, when he is alone, turns matters over in his mind:

"Force! How silly it was to use force four years ago! We see where it has led! The supreme art is to maintain the appearance of legality. Without cannon or bloodshed, without arrests and parties, that is the secret of the ideal coup d'état. Otherwise you set up something that may last a year before it wears out. After ten years of revolution, the republic is heartily sick of it all. She is an amazon who has borne arms till she is tired, and now asks nothing better than to be led by a strong man. She is ready for me.

"Can I depend upon Sieyès? Behind that receding forehead of his, he thinks too much. For ten years he has been building constitutions, but he is nothing more than the ideologue whom a vigorous general can use before casting aside. Had I not arrived in the nick of time, he would have joined forces with Moreau. I shall turn the pair of them to account. I know I can trust Berthier, Bourrienne, Murat, Marmont, and Leclerc. Is Lucien faithful? For the time being. Bernadotte? His spiteful look betrayed his true feelings. Still, he will not come into the field against me. What about Talleyrand? A dangerous man, and for that very reason I must have him on my side. Moulin? No time to waste; there are too many generals in Paris. Watch out!"

Next evening he went to Talleyrand's, for a private talk with that intriguer. They sat late, discussing plans. Suddenly there was a noise in the street. Trotting horses, which stop in front of the door. The patrol? "Bonaparte turned pale, and I fancy I must have done the same," wrote Talleyrand in his Memoirs. Both men believe that they are about to be arrested. Lights out, and on tiptoe to the balcony. False alarm! An ordinary street scene, nocturnal revellers and police, nothing more. The conspirators breathe again. But why do not the Directors have them arrested on suspicion? The answer is simple. Bonaparte is already too commanding a figure to be touched!

On the 6th, there is a banquet at the Luxembourg. Bonaparte and Moreau are the guests, but the latter has the place of honour, and the hosts eye Bonaparte askance. He reciprocates his entertainers' suspicions, and eats nothing but bread and eggs, handed him by a trusty servant. After half an hour, he makes his excuses, and goes back to his confederates, to talk over the plan for bringing about the downfall of the men with whom he has just been dining. Next evening, Talleyrand, Roederer, and Sieyès, dine with Bonaparte; Jourdan and Bernadotte, who are to be won over, have also been invited. After dinner, he asks Jourdan what is to happen. This simple question is evidence enough of the prevailing crisis. Two generals who have never before exchanged a word except about commonplaces, meet, and look one another in the face. "What is going to happen?" enquires one. The other significantly grips his sword-hilt. The plotters agree to take action in forty-eight hours. The parts to be played by members of the inner ring are assigned. Murat, Lannes, and Marmont are to inform the officers of the three branches of the service; Berthier will acquaint the general staff.

Lucien undertakes to manage affairs in the Council of Five Hundred. He is president for the month, having been elected in honour of his brother's return. The president of the Council of Ancients is also a party to the conspiracy. The bedells will be told to overlook certain names when notices of the sitting are sent out. As soon as Bonaparte has been appointed commander of the Paris garrison, he will hand over the Tuileries to Lannes and the Palais Bourbon to Murat. Gohier and his wife will be invited to breakfast by Josephine—eight o'clock. Bonaparte will offer himself to Barras for luncheon, in order to put Barras off his guard. Joseph will persuade his brother-in-law Bernadotte to keep quiet, if Bernadotte will not actively participate. Roederer writes the proclamation. His son knows a friendly printer who will set it up and machine it—on the quiet.

"Was Brutus' mood so paltry?" thinks Bonaparte. "But, in truth, we too wish to slay some one—Anarchy! A new era, a new century, to be ushered in by such petty and distasteful means! Camp life is cleaner!"

XIX

November 9th, a foggy autumn morning; the Eighteenth Brumaire is dawning. A bustle in the street opposite Bonaparte's house; officers arriving on horseback and in carriages. Is the blow to be struck at last? Most of those present were with him in Italy. The house is too small for such a concourse. They stroll up and down in the garden, discussing their chances; lively and cheerful as if they were on the Rhine. Appearances must be kept up. No one must be able to say that uniformed officers were about so early. All goes well. Messengers come to confirm the carrying out of the programme; both Councils were summoned at seven o'clock, but undesirable members have not received notice. The initiates were the first comers, and, as soon as there was a quorum, Lucien in the Council of Five Hundred and his colleague in the Council of Ancients had proposed Bonaparte's appointment to the command of the Paris garrison.

Here is the messenger with the commission, duly sealed! The formalities are being strictly observed. The general joins his faithful followers. Everything goes on as if they were in camp. With a great suite, he rides through the town, to the amazement of a huge crowd, which does not, however, show any political interest. A dragoon regiment which had been through the Italian campaign with Napoleon turns up on the Boulevard Madeleine without awaiting the orders of its colonel. Other officers follow with Ducos and Marmont. The latter summoned them at an early hour. When they said they could not come for lack of horses, he borrowed some from a riding-school.

The Tuileries garden is crowded. Many remain on horseback; but Bonaparte dismounts and enters the Council of Ancients. Is he going to make a speech to people whom he despises, in this dark and unfamiliar hall? Why does he not take the oath to the constitution, the constitution he is about to destroy? The law directs that a general appointed to a new command should take this oath. Evading the formality, he speaks from the rostrum:

"The republic is in danger. . . . Recognising this, you have passed a law that will save it. Do not search history for examples that may give reason for restraining your activities. No epoch in history is like the end of the eighteenth century, and in that end there is nothing like this moment. . . . We want a republic based on liberty and equality. We shall have it. With the aid of all the friends of liberty, I shall save the republic. In my own name and in that of my companions-in-arms, I swear it to you!"

"We swear it!" comes like an echo through the open doors of the hall. The Ancients move uneasily in their seats. "Companions-in-arms?" But Bonaparte has left the hall, drawing a breath of relief. These lawyers'-eyes; bespectacled eyes! Effete pygmies! Has he noticed that he spoke to them as if he were on the parade ground, and that they did not like his tone?

His words and his voice have a very different ring outside, when, having remounted his charger, he summons his troops to save the republic. Then comes a report from Lucien, who has meanwhile adjourned to the following day the sitting of the Council of Five Hundred. What is that you say? The Directors' guard is on the way hither? Do they come as friends or foes? "Is Sieyès sending them?" Their colonel says no. The two men laugh.

In fact, Sieyès, pale of countenance, is still at the gate of the Luxembourg. For the last fortnight, our clever abbé has been taking riding lessons. It had been his design to ride at the head of his guard to join his new comrades. Before all the world, he would show his equality with these comrades by leaning from his saddle and embracing them. But the guard has started without his orders; their colonel has brought them to the Tuileries, riding hell-for-leather, too hot a pace for the abbé. Almost unnoticed, and much crestfallen, Sieyès drives after them in a carriage, with Ducos, who is pliable, by his side. Every one in the know is aware by this time what will happen to the other three Directors.

Moulin looks at the matter from a soldier's standpoint. He estimates the opposing force at the Tuileries to be eight thousand strong, and his adjutants report to him that all the important points of the town are in Bonaparte's hands. He writes, therefore, saying: "At your service."

Honest Gohier is at home, blustering ineffectually. He had not thought it advisable to accept the strange invitation to an eight o'clock breakfast, and had been content to send his wife. Now, a sort of hostage, she is drinking tea with Josephine, while Bonaparte is betraying her husband—not, indeed, stealing his mistress, but stealing France. When the first news comes, Gohier sends to his colleagues, summoning them to a meeting of the Directory. No one turns up. Moulin has joined Sieyès and Ducos. Barras says he is in his bath.

When Talleyrand, the messenger of fate, visits Barras, the Director is shaving; he seems to be devoting the day to the arts of the toilet! But, at a glance or two from the other augur, he throws up the game, being content to ask for a safe-conduct. When his secretary brings this demand to Bonaparte, the general harangues the man publicly in the Tuileries garden: "What have you done with France, that I should let you off so easily? I gave you peace, and I find war. . . . What have you done with the hundred thousand Frenchmen who were the companions of my glory? They are dead! We can go no farther along that road, for in three years it leads to despotism! We want a republic based on equality and liberty, toleration and morality!"

Thus berated, the little secretary shakes in his shoes. In reality, Bonaparte is perfectly calm, but it suits him to simulate wrath in the presence of so many witnesses. In a couple of hours, all Paris will hear of it.

Here comes Gohier. He does not lack courage, anyhow.

Bearding the man of power surrounded by his troops, Gohier reminds him of his duty to the Directory.

"The Directory no longer exists!" storms Bonaparte. "The republic is in danger, and I intend to save it. Sieyès, Ducos, and Barras have resigned." As he speaks, a letter from Moulin is brought to him. "Are not you in league with Moulin? No? Well, here is his resignation too. You are the last. Do you intend to hold out all by yourself?"

Gohier is a stickler for the law, and refuses to give way. He goes back to the Luxembourg, and there he and his friends are kept under guard by five hundred men until all is over. Barras is waiting at home, uneasy till he has the answer to his message. What if Bonaparte were now to take vengeance? Who can depend on Josephine's moods? Here is Talleyrand back again, with the safe-conduct and a bag of gold. As to this last, no one knows whether Barras had the fingering of the money, or whether Talleyrand kept it as messenger's fee.

Thus the five heads of the republic were rendered powerless by General Bonaparte. But this was only the first day. To-morrow, at Saint-Cloud, greater difficulties may have to be faced. Lucien, who has been all over the place, and is fully informed, exclaims with well-grounded anger: "The whole job ought to have been finished in one day! You have left them too much time! The Five Hundred are already crying out that they have been tricked! To-morrow all will be in the melting-pot once more! The only thing to do is to send soldiers to clear out the Chambers, and to put the most dangerous members of the Councils under arrest."

Certainly there may be complications to-morrow. Bernadotte had wanted the Jacobin Club to appoint him general of the opposing forces. "But the fellows were in too great a funk!" The generals unsympathetic to the coup d'état must be put under lock and key. Bonaparte's associates urge this again and again, but in vain. He is resolute to maintain the semblance of legality.

"People would say I was afraid of the generals. No one shall have a right to accuse us of illegality. No parties; no force! The whole people must be associated with the decision through the votes of its deputies! No civil war! What begins with the shedding of civilian blood, will come to a shameful end!"

But at night, prepared for all eventualities, he has loaded pistols handy to his bedside.

XX

Next morning, an endless string of carriages and carts, an endless succession of riders and pedestrians, makes its way to Saint-Cloud, as if to see a great military review. Bonaparte, too, drives instead of going on horseback attended by a bevy of mounted officers. That might be provocative. He has made up his mind to observe constitutional formalities to the very last moment. Could any one say that there had been a breach of law the day before? Are not the Councils entitled to remove their sittings to a spot beyond the precincts of the town, if they think that this would be safer? Is it not within their competence to appoint a new commander for the Paris garrison? Had not the Directors the right to resign? Will any one pretend that the Jacobin peril, which is the occasion for these happenings, is imaginary? To-day, at public sittings, the Councils will alter the constitution. Three rulers will be provisionally appointed. Borrowing a title from ancient Rome, they can be called Triumvirs, or, perhaps better, Consuls. Then the Councils will be prorogued, everything being done in due form of law.

But the deputies hold other views. Like cloud-drifts hanging low, they flit through the valleys of this forsaken palace, discussing the situation, and giving vent to their protests. Since the hall that is being furbished up for the sitting will not be ready before one o'clock, they have plenty of time to foment their wrath.

In a small room fronting on the park, sit the three men who will be Consuls to-morrow. At least Sieyès and Ducos remain seated most of the time, but the third walks up and down impatiently, as his adherents come and go to report. He thinks: "How infernally slow civilians are! They have needed a whole morning to arrange a few benches. Then they must take an oath one by one, a thing which our recruits do in chorus, and get through it all in a couple of minutes! Why should I have to wait in a back room while these lawyers are deliberating in the council chamber?"

The Ancients meet upstairs in the Salle Apollo; the Five Hundred, downstairs in the Orangerie. Spectators, safe people, throng the hall of the Five Hundred. When, after the swearing-in, the discussions at length begin (Lucien is in the chair), the protests of the opposition gain weight from the circumstances. Speakers point to the threatening force of soldiery outside. When some of the orators exclaim: "No dictatorship! This Cromwell wants to bind us in chains!" almost all the delegates applaud. The reports that come to the back room are more and more unfavourable. The officers grow restive: "Chase the beggars out! What else have we got our men here for?"

Bonaparte's only answer is a cold glance. Buckling on his sword, he silently mounts the stairs to the hall of the Ancients. Two or three of the stalwarts follow him, shaking their heads. Is he going to talk once more, as he did yesterday, instead of shooting? Amazed but curious, the president allows him to speak. Will he put up a better case than yesterday, speaking to the point, and not simply haranguing them about himself?

"Yesterday, I was sitting quietly at home when you summoned me. . . . To-day, I am overwhelmed with calumnies. . . . Since my return, all parties have been busied with my name. . . . The Council of Ancients must decide quickly. I am no intriguer. You know me. Have I not given proof and to spare of my devotion to the country? . . . Am I, a man whom even the great coalition could not conquer, to tremble before a few rioters? If I am a crafty schemer, you may well be all Brutuses!"

Uneasy stirrings; smiles. Why does he speak, instead of acting? He is not sure of his ground, for he goes on to say: "All France shall know what we have lived through.—Every one of the parties wishes to turn this crisis to its own account, and every one of them would like me to side with it. But I have come to the Councils. If you hesitate, and if liberty is overthrown, you will be answerable to the world and to posterity!" His periods grow ever more confused. The Ancients surround the rostrum, interrupting him, demanding names. Suddenly he turns, and waves his hand towards the doors, as if pointing to the soldiers, who are out of sight. He seems to be looking for an exit. He apostrophises the invisible soldiers:

"You, comrades, whom I see united in this circle, raise your bayonets with which we fought our way to victory together, raise them against my breast! But if an orator in foreign pay dares to call your general an outlaw, smite the wretch with the thunderbolts of battle! The god of battles and the goddess of good fortune are on my side. . . ."

Will not a burst of laughter sweep the speaker away, and his coup d'état along with him? At length Bourrienne comes up to him from behind, takes him by the arm, and whispers in his ear: "Do stop, General. You really don't know what you're saying!" He turns, and follows Bourrienne from the hall. A deputy devoted to his interest takes the floor promptly, and does his best to put a good face upon the matter.

Outside, he draws a breath of relief. What could have been the matter with him? Why had his brain been clouded? Amid all the turmoil of battle, he is calm, fully master of himself; his decisions are well-rounded, brilliant, and cool, like polished

General Bonaparte in 1798, during the voyage to Egypt.
Sketch by André Dutertre.

marble spheres. Why is he unequal to the occasion on this day of days, when his whole future is at stake?

Because he is a man who knows how to command, but does not know how to beg. He can cajole, threaten, feign hesitation, lie; outdoing in these arts all the diplomatists with whom he negotiates treaties. He meets them as equals, but is always sustained by the feeling that, if he does not get his way by diplomacy, he can enforce his wishes by artillery fire. He can endure everything, except having to ask favours, and except having to submit to a law which is not of his own making. He wants order and legality, but not such as existed before he established them!

With titanic energy, as he already foresees, he will lead this country towards order, will found an orderly State after a decade of chaos. No one will be the worse for humble birth or for poverty, since all will have equal opportunities. But in these halls to-day sit lawyers, ridden by the spirit of faction, corrupt, outworn, besoiled by the grime of party politics. He is to implore them to be good enough to give him (and others) a power which has long been his, and which stands outside there, impatient to get to work!

He, who in the Institute could sit quietly among the savants, learning and questioning, is so little able to understand the mood of these legislative assemblies that he actually fancies the day already won. He sends a message to Josephine to tell her that all is going well; says a few encouraging words to his followers, and goes quickly downstairs to play a similar part before the Council of Five Hundred. It is just as well that his friends take the precaution to send into the hall with him four stalwart grenadiers, whose strength and loyalty can be thoroughly depended on.

No matter that this escort is quite out of keeping with his determination to be strict in the observance of parliamentary forms! Followed by his grenadiers, carrying hat and riding whip in his hand, he enters the hall of the Five Hundred.

"Bonaparte!" All turn towards the door. The Jacobins shout: "Down with the tyrant! Down with the dictator! Outlaw him!" A few of the more hefty among the Five Hundred hurl themselves upon him; the grenadiers rally to his protection, encircling him, and sheltering him with their big bodies from the angry Jacobins' blows. The combat sways to and fro for a while, a knot of struggling and shouting people. Then, step by step, the five force their way backwards towards the door. Outside, surrounded by his own supporters, he is for a moment too much discomposed to speak; but, rallying quickly, he makes for the back room.

During the Italian campaign, Bonaparte was under fire in the front ranks on several occasions. At Lodi, and again at Arcola, he had been in imminent peril. But here, he was for the first time involved in a rough-and-tumble affray where firearms and cold steel are against the rules. Towards the close of his career, he was to have a similar experience. In such a chance medley, he could not draw his sword. He must assume his antagonists to be unarmed, though some of them were in truth armed. To use his sword seemed to be in hopeless conflict with the fundamental principles of the coup d'état—as he envisaged it.

But at length he has to abandon these principles of his. In person, he has been rescued from the blows of his adversaries, but their fists have shattered his doctrine. Force has been used against him. He strides furiously up and down the room; his pride is touched to the quick; in his anger, he scratches his cheek till his finger-nails are bloody. Blood? In an instant he has recovered his composure. This blood will be most useful! Attempted assassination in the council chamber! He will show his soldiers how these villains have manhandled the commander of Paris! The pretence that the other side had been the first to break the law, frees him from the tyranny of his principles.

In the assembly hall, meanwhile, Lucien is fighting for him. "Hors la loi! Outlaw him!" cry most of the deputies. Lucien tries to still the clamour with voice and bell. The attempt is vain. A formal demand is made for a vote on Bonaparte's outlawry, and every one knows what that means in revolutionary Paris. Since there is no other way out of the difficulty, Lucien, whose pose to-day is that of the defender of law and order, with an imposing gesture throws off his toga and storms out of the hall. None too soon!

He finds his brother with the troops. Napoleon had turned pale when the news had been brought of the vote of outlawry. Then, running to the window, he called to the troops: "To arms!" Going out, he mounted, and was quick to notice that the soldiers were not sufficiently moved, were not yet ripe for action. Night was falling, and all were waiting on events. Lucien came out, leapt into the saddle, and the two brothers rode up and down the front. Outside the railings were Sieyès and Ducos in a carriage, ready for flight to-day, or to become rulers to-morrow, as events might decide. The movement seemed to be without a head.

Then Lucien grasped the opportunity. He could make a better job of speaking to the soldiers than Napoleon had made of speaking to the deputies:

"Soldiers, as president of the Five Hundred I tell you that in the hall there the majority is being terrorised by a handful of armed Jacobins. These rascals are in English pay. They have dared to outlaw your general, who was appointed by the Councils. They actually tried to assassinate him. Look at the wounds! Use your bayonets to guard him against their daggers, so that the deliberations concerning the welfare of the country can be conducted in peace! Recognise as deputies none but those who come with me into the midst of your ranks. Drive out the rest, all who would stay in the hall!"

Napoleon listens with pinched lips. When Lucien has finished, he speaks in his turn, shouting: "Kill any one who resists. Follow me! I am the god of battles!" Lucien, who is afraid of another speech, hisses: "For God's sake, hold your tongue!"

"Long live Bonaparte!" shout the soldiers, who regard the brothers as military and civil authority conjoined. But not a man moves. All is lost, if they will not march now. Lucien grasps at the last expedient. With a theatrical flourish, he snatches an officer's sword and points it at Napoleon's breast: "I swear that I will run my brother through, should he ever dare to threaten the liberties of France!"

The phrase has the desired effect. Murat orders the sounding of a general advance, summons a troop of soldiers to follow him, and shouts: "Lads, chuck the whole rabble of them out of the hall!" At length he has raised a laugh. With bayonets at the charge, but good-humouredly and without hurting any one, they thrust from the hall any of the deputies that are valiant enough to offer resistance. In the failing light, there is a confused scene in which red togas, birettas, and the caps of the guardsmen are intermingled. The last of the fleeing deputies escape through the windows.

The priceless Lucien now hastened upstairs to the Council of Ancients. Grossly exaggerating the injuries sustained by his brother at the hands of the Jacobin deputies, he induced the Ancients, in a panic, to appoint the three Consuls, and to adjourn their sitting until a late hour that night. Then the leaders foregathered in a small café for a meal, being all much in need of food.

That night, the most trustworthy among the deputies reassembled in the deserted hall at Saint-Cloud. By the light of a pair of candles, the thirty who were left to represent the people of France voted whatever they were told. While a hundred or so people of fashion, pretty women and their gallants, mockingly watched the midnight ceremony—while all went smoothly, society-at-large being quite undisturbed and the proletariat unruffled—the indefatigable Lucien insisted that the political mass should be worthily celebrated. At two in the morning, to the sound of drums, the three Consuls took the oath. "Long live the republic!" called a few weary voices.

At three o'clock, Consul Bonaparte drives back to Paris with Bourrienne. He looks straight in front of them, saying never a word. Not until he is at home, and Josephine is present, does he open his mouth:

"I say, Bourrienne, did I talk a frightful lot of nonsense to-day?"

"A fair amount, General."

"Those idiots drove me crazy. I'm no good at speaking in public assemblies."

Then, instead of going on to talk about the coup d'état, or to congratulate himself upon its amazing success (for from tomorrow onwards he will rule France) he alludes to personal enmities. Bernadotte's conduct is what rankles!

"That fellow Bernadotte! He wanted to betray me! His wife—his wife has a great deal of influence over him. I should have thought I had done enough to placate him! You were there, and you know. I regret having gone so far to please him. He will have to clear out of Paris. There is no other way in which I can pay my score. . . . Good-night, Bourrienne. Tomorrow night we shall sleep in the Luxembourg."

BOOK THREE

THE RIVER

One who thoughtfully ponders the centuries,
Surveys the whole in the clear light of the spirit;
All that is petty has vanished from sight;
Oceans and continents alone are of account.

—GOETHE.

I

About twenty men are seated round a large oval table. Some are quite young, some middle-aged, some elderly. They are plainly dressed, in accordance with the fashion of 1800, when wigs were no longer worn, and lace was out of date; those of them that are in uniform are not resplendent with gold braid, and they wear no orders. Some have the bold, self-confident look of the man of action; others, the thoughtful mien of the savant. From town and from countryside, from office and from laboratory, they come, but are unified by a common experience and a common aim. For ten years, they have been living through a revolutionary epoch; they meet to bring that epoch to a close. Around them is the chill splendour of the Tuileries, the palace of the last Bourbon kings. The golds and the reds of the rich carpets and the silken hangings are out of keeping with their bourgeois circumstantiality; the silvery sheen of the candles, reflected in rainbow tints from the myriad facets of the candelabras, recalls an era that scintillated with light and glowed with colour.

The Directors before them had been wont to entertain their lady friends in royal halls, but that was in the Luxembourg, the former meeting-place of the peers of France. The Tuileries seemed full of Ghosts. Did not a curse lie upon the place? The dictator had broken the spell. Two months after the coup d'état, he had come with his fellow Consuls to take possession of the palace, which exerted a magical lure upon his imagination. Yet when, seven years after the arrest of the last scion of the royal line, the first of the bourgeois rulers made his formal entry, the affair had a strong flavour of burlesque. The Parisians could not but laugh to see the numbers of the hackney carriages peeping out from beneath the slips of paper which had been carelessly pasted over them. This seemed to symbolise the ludicrous aspect of time's revenges.

The Consul's own mood was no less haphazard as he looked round with childlike curiosity. "Well, here we are in the Tuileries," he said to one of his friends; "let's see to it that we stay here!"

Several of those now seated at the oval table, had waited here of old—wearing powdered wigs, lace jabots, and pumps—tremulous with eagerness to learn whether His Majesty would receive them, and when. Some of them had sat at a similar table in the Luxembourg. There had been no stability about those deliberations. Laws had come and gone, urgency orders and exceptional provisions; transitional decrees had pushed foregoing decrees out of the way; three constitutions had risen and set, had shot up into the air swiftly and brilliantly like rockets, to vanish like these and to fall like rocket-sticks. The whole decade during which the new ideas had been trying to realise themselves in the concrete, had passed swiftly over Paris like a single night, amid a confusion of flashing lights and rumbling drums. The city had been like an armed camp with no fighting fronts and no battles, but perturbed by the to-and-fro march of armed political parties, deafened by the noisy wrangling between the old order and the new wishes, dazzled by the glare of venturesome ideas, confused by the clamour of disappointed hopes and the clash of warring ambitions—a titanic bacchanal of liberty, equality, and cozenage. Surveying the medley, looking down from the skies, were the shades of the two men whose books had set the whole in motion: Rousseau, with eyes of disgust; Voltaire, with a mocking smile.

But suddenly the tumult had been stilled. That little man at the head of the table had stilled it, the little general in the well-worn green uniform. Not that he, presiding over the Council of State, is in fact presiding over the State; the parties have withdrawn into their caves, satisfied or rancorous, but at any rate silenced. France, weakened by clubs and corruption, by the Terror and the demagogues, is turning back (like an adventuress weary of errant amours) to the arms of a strong man who can master her.

Enough, now, for Bonaparte that he should aspire to fulfil this masterful lover's role. No longer did he need to fight for the position. The man for whom France was longing, must be a man of order; must be one who had never before held power, who belonged to no party, and who none the less enjoyed popular favour. He must, therefore, be a soldier and a conqueror. Moreau lacked the self-confidence and adroitness needed to make him a successful rival; the other great generals were dead or overshadowed; there were no civilian competitors. After Bonaparte's outstanding military successes, it was easy for him to win supreme power in the State. He would have won it without a struggle had he not been so stubborn in his desire to observe constitutional formalities.

The attempt to be strictly constitutional had been a ludicrous failure, and had imposed artificial obstacles in his path. Yet this very fact was a token and a guarantee of his political talents. He was a man with a firm grip on the sword-hilt, but he was also a man who clearly understood the limits of the power of the sword. "Do you know," he said in those days, "what amazes me more than all else? The impotence of force to organise anything. There are only two powers in the world: the spirit and the sword. In the long run, the sword will always be conquered by the spirit." Napoleon was the greatest military commander of his day, but neither now nor later was it his habit to strike the table with mailed fist, neither in Paris at this juncture nor elsewhere when negotiating a truce or a peace or an alliance. He was a political genius, who prized the sword, indeed, but prized it only as one of the two powers. His ear was never deafened by the clash of arms. As now, so for fifteen years to come, he is ever on the watch for indications of public opinion; always listening to the voice of the people, a voice which defies calculation; a voice which Napoleon, a man of figures, vainly tries to calculate. Precisely because of his failure to do this, the attempt to reckon with public opinion is always alluring to the imaginative side of his nature.

Because Bonaparte believes in the power of the spirit more than in the power of the sword, he strives for order and peace more resolutely than for war and conquest. The history of the next ten years will prove it.

For him, order denotes equality, but not liberty. He adopts into his dictatorship the former of these two gods of the revolution. Except for a few vacillations, he will cherish equality to the end, despite appearances to the contrary. But liberty? What is liberty? "Both the savage and the civilised man need a lord and master, a magician, who will hold the imagination in check, impose strict discipline, bind man in chains, so that he may not bite out of season; one who will thrash him, and lead him to the chase. Obedience is man's destiny; he deserves nothing better, and he has no rights!" These threatening words of the misanthropist disclose no more than half of his secret thoughts. Through all the phases of his rule, he is ever in search of the efficient man, and to such a man he grants power over thousands; just as he himself, through energy and diligence, through natural and acquired superiority, has won to power over millions. In spite of all, he is the son of the revolution; and in this sense he will remain the son of the revolution, whatever forms his power may assume.

In part, that is the explanation of the mysterious influence he wields. The wider his domain extends, the more plainly do all realise that they are living in a system which promises to every efficient man the gratification of his wishes, and guarantees to every efficient man place and power and wealth; which does these things because the Master has himself risen out of the crowd. He shows this, now, in his very first step. Sieyès has drafted a constitution. There is to be a grand elector, a president who can only represent and sign his name. With soldierly curtness, Bonaparte puts his pen through the item.

"Away with this fat hog!" Instead, there is to be a First Consul, with plenary powers, and plenty of work. He is to be war lord and also director of foreign policy; he is to appoint all ministers and envoys, councillors of State and prefects, officers and judges. Thirty nominated senators are to elect their colleagues; but neither the Senate nor the Legislative Assembly nor the Tribunate is to have any power to initiate legislation. These bodies are merely brought into existence to give politicians a platform for their orations, and to provide senators with high salaries and opportunities for a resplendent life.

Although everything was dependent upon the will of one man, that one man insisted that those dependent on him should themselves be men, and not mere names. Neither birth nor pretentiousness nor prominence in a political party could lead to the front in the army or in civil life. Nothing but energy and capacity could ensure promotion. Such was the principle upon which Napoleon chose the members of the Council of State.

This last was a round table of experts, selected by the dictator on his own initiative. Among them was Laplace, whom, to honour the Institute, Napoleon had also appointed Minister for Home Affairs—an appointment the great mathematician held for a time, until he turned back from the mechanics of the State to the mechanics of the heavens. There, too, was Roederer, official and journalist, the most independent man to be encountered by Napoleon during twenty years, and the most valuable recorder of conversations. Tronchet, also, one of the finest jurists of the age, was there. In the council chamber, all alike were citizens, and addressed one another by that plain title. Royalists and Jacobins sat there side by side, under a regime of equality, since reason was enthroned.

When the minutes of the sittings are shown to the citizen-consul, he says: "It is essential to give a full and accurate report of the opinions expressed by legal luminaries, for their words are weighty; but what we soldiers and moneyed men think is of little account. In the heat of the moment I have often said things which an instant afterwards I saw to have been unjust. I do not wish to seem better than I am." When he noticed that the councillors were simply echoing whatever he said, he was quick to call them to order: "You are not here, gentlemen, to agree with me, but to express your own views. If you do that, I can compare them with mine, and decide which is better."

The sittings, often enough, do not begin before nine in the evening, for up till then the Consul has been dealing with the urgent affairs of the day. They may last till five o'clock in the morning. The councillors get very tired during the small hours. Perhaps the Minister for War goes to sleep. Napoleon shakes them up, exclaiming: "Do let's keep awake, citizens. It's only two o'clock. We must earn our salaries." He, who presides, is indeed one of the youngest of the company, being now thirty. But in three campaigns he has learned how to watch over the interests of hundreds of thousands. Was not the management of an army which set out from the Alps, crossed the sea, and marched far into the desert—was not this the best school for the study of State administration? There, too, he had to think of money and bread, of rights and laws, of rewards and punishments, of rest and obedience and order.

During the very first night after the coup d'état, he had appointed two committees to draft a legal code; this was the first act of his dictatorship! The prevailing chaos had been the outcome of a lack of law. Down to the outbreak of the revolution, there had been no unified legal system in France. The revolution brought the promise of such a system; but even now, after eleven years, the promise was unfulfilled. That first summer, three great lawyers were set to work; four months later a draft of the Civil Code, subsequently rechristened the Code Napoléon, was ready; then the draft was discussed in the Council of State. In eighteen months the laws were voted. They passed into effect in 1804.

After more than a century, this Code is still the law of France; it was adopted in many of the lands conquered by Napoleon, having great influence on the legislation of Central and Southern Germany, Prussia, Switzerland, and Spain; and its influence spread still farther afield, to Central America and South America. All that is new and morally decisive in the Code Napoléon is revolutionary law. The law-book which the Dictator discussed in all its details for many months, the law-book, many of whose most contentious points were the direct outcome of his decisions, borrowed the fixed principles of reason that had been sketched in the first days of the revolution. Experienced and dispassionate minds, under Napoleon's guidance, worked them up, purified them, and made them into a new system of the rights of man. In this system, there was no longer a hereditary nobility; all children had an equal share in inheritance; all parents became legally responsible for the maintenance of their children; Jews became equal with Christians before the law; civil marriage was open to all, and was dissoluble.

Concerning this matter, as concerning all matters of family law, his Corsican family feeling persistently influenced his judgments: "We know that adultery is not a rare occurrence, but an ordinary one; that it can happen on any convenient sofa. . . . Some sort of restraint must be imposed upon these women who commit adultery for trinkets or verses, for Apollo and the nine Muses."

His sense of order leads him to be a thoroughgoing supporter of marriage. He even sees to it that women shall follow their husbands into transportation, "for how can we forbid a woman to do so when she is convinced of her husband's innocence? Or is this conviction of hers to deprive her of her rights as married woman; is she to lose the title of wife, and to become the man's concubine? Many men have only become criminals owing to their wives. Are we to forbid those who have been the cause of the misfortune from sharing that misfortune?"

He also thinks highly of the custom of old Roman days, when, at marriage, the woman was formally described as passing from her father's guardianship into that of her husband. "That would be excellent in Paris, where women do as they please. It would influence some of them, though not all."

Therefore, though he favours divorce, it must not be too easy: "What would happen to the most intimate of natural ties if people were suddenly to become estranged? Unless we make divorce difficult, a young woman will be ready to marry a quite unsuitable man, for fashion, convenience, simply to get a roof over her head. The law must warn her against this. . . . In truth, there are only three valid grounds for divorce: attempted murder, adultery, and impotence."

Such are the plastic thoughts of this expert in human nature, whose mathematical talents still leave him free to subsume facts under ideas; one who has an intelligence well fitted for the consideration of laws, seeing that it is equally swayed by theory and practice, by energetic activity and sceptical suspense. The conflict of trends within the legislator's mind is obvious, and it was intensified by his thoughts concerning Josephine's former infidelity and present faithfulness. (We know that she manifested a lively interest in the drafting of those sections of the Code that related to divorce! Napoleon at this time was already wondering whether, if his wife remained childless, he would not have to divorce her for reasons of State. Her own dread of this possibility led her to use her influence in favour of strengthening the marriage tie, whereas he was driven by self-interest to insist that marriage must not be indissoluble.)

It is a personal feeling, too, which drives him to avoid scandal, to save the honour of marriage. He opposes the interference of the law-courts in conjugal questions; prefers that such matters should be settled by mutual understanding, so that the veil shall not be stripped off. "The desire of both parties for divorce is an indication that divorce is necessary. It is not the business of the court to establish the fact that this mutual desire exists; the court has simply to pronounce the divorce when the desire exists." His strong family feeling leads him to add that maltreatment, perversion, and adultery should be concealed beneath the formula of mutual desire; the need for divorce is to be settled at a family council, and the judge has merely to confirm this decision.

For the same reason, he introduces a semi-divorce, a judicial separation from bed and board. This is always to be arranged after a mutual private understanding, for it will be a barrier to the possibility of reconciliation if the grounds for the separation have been made public. His aim in all these matters is to maintain family life; he is a champion of order, an anti-revolutionist. His social sense is so strong that he maintains it would be necessary to punish an adulterous woman by criminal procedure unless she were punished by being divorced. Similar considerations regarding the sanctity of marriage lead him to raise the age at which marriage becomes permissible. At the revolution it had been lowered to thirteen for women and fifteen for men; he insists upon fifteen and twenty-one respectively.

For children, the Code promises all the things which the ensuing century is slowly to build up. Under the fatherhood of the man to whom they are born in lawful marriage, they have a secure position even before they enter the world. True, "the father cannot recognise the child as his own if he has been absent for fifteen months"—the figure is specified by Napoleon—"and has fought at Marengo." But, a man of position as well as a man of the world, he concludes by saying: "I will sacrifice honour to truth, but why should I sacrifice the wife's honour when no one will gain thereby? If the husband is not sure of his dates, he had better hold his tongue; the child's interest is paramount."

When some one proposes to restrict the elder children's right to maintenance, he rejoins: "Is a father to have the right to drive his fifteen-year-old daughter out of the house? Let us suppose him to have an income of sixty thousand francs, can we allow him to say to his son: 'You are old enough to tend for yourself; be off with you to work!' If we limit this duty, we shall tend to make children entertain thoughts of putting their father out of the way." The suggestion is made that adoption shall be feasible by simple declaration before a notary, with revolutionary speed. He opposes the plan:

"We are not concerned here with a trivial formality. Human beings are controlled through their imaginations; that is what distinguishes them from animals. The main defect of the newer legislation is that it makes no appeal to men's imaginations. A soldier does not face death in order to earn a few pence a day, or to win some paltry order of merit. None but the man who touches his heart, can stir his enthusiasm! A notary cannot touch our hearts merely because we pay him a fee of twelve francs; that is why we need a legislative act. What is adoption? An imitation of nature, a sort of sacrament. By the will of society, the offspring of one human being's flesh and blood is supposed to become the offspring of another's flesh and blood. Could any action be more sublime? Thanks to it, two creatures between whom there is no tie of blood, become inspired by a natural mutual affection Whence must this action come? Like the lightning, from on high!"

"In these sittings," says Roederer, "the First Consul manifested those remarkable powers of attention and precise analysis which enabled him for ten hours at a stretch to devote himself to one object, or to several, without ever allowing himself to be distracted by memory or by errant thoughts."

Bonaparte is filled with respect for the logicality and mental energy of the octogenarian Tronchet; and the old lawyer responds with admiration for the analytical faculty and the sense of justice of the young Consul, who, in the case of every ordinance, asks: "Is it just?" and "Is it useful?" He is never tired of enquiring how predecessors have solved the problems under consideration, paying special attention to Roman law and to the legal institutions of Frederick the Great.

Not only are thirty-seven laws discussed at this table; furthermore, the Consul propounds question after question concerning other matters. How is bread made? How shall we make new money? How shall we establish security? He makes all his ministers send detailed reports, and this is a great tax upon their energies. But he affects not to notice that they are overworked, and when they get home they often find letters from him requiring an immediate answer. One of his collaborators writes: "Ruling, administering, negotiating—with that orderly intelligence of his, he gets through eighteen hours' work every day. In three years he has ruled more than the kings ruled in a century." He spoke to every expert in the phraseology of the craft, so that none of them could ever plead in excuse that his questions had not been understood. Even the most hidebound royalists were amazed at the technical accuracy of his enquiries.

His unfailing memory was the artillery wherewith he defended the fortress of his brain. Ségur, returning from an official inspection of the fortifications on the north coast, sends in a report. "I have read your report," says the First Consul. "It is accurate, but you have forgotten two of the four guns in Ostend. They are on the high road behind the town." Ségur is astonished to find that Napoleon is right. His report deals with thousands of guns, scattered all over the place, but the chief pounces on the omission of two.

By slow degrees, the huge machine (which for ten years has been standing still or moving backwards) is set in regular motion once more. Throughout the last decade, all the reports from the provinces have been full of complaints regarding the lack of public safety, sanitation, and order; the louis-d'or used to exchange for twenty-four francs, but now the ratio is one to eight thousand; the Directory's attempt to stabilise the franc has been an utter failure; the newly enriched have bought up the State domains, the Church lands, and the seignorial estates. No one is paying taxes. What is the new dictator going to do about it all?

Within a fortnight after the coup d'état, he had arranged for the establishment of tax-collecting offices in all the departments, for, as he put it: "Security and property are only to be found in a country which is not subject to yearly changes in the rate of taxation." Two months later, the Bank of France came into being; next year, there were new boards to supervise taxation, the registration of landed property, and forestry. Whereas his predecessors had simply squandered the State domains, he used what was left of them to defray repayment of national debt. The funds rose from 7 to 17; he continued the process of debt cancellation, renovated the Chambers of Commerce, regulated the Stock Exchange, put an end to speculation in the depreciated currency, stopped the frauds of the army contractors and other war profiteers, and by these and similar measures restored manufacturing industry whose productivity had sunk to a quarter or half of its former level.

What was his magical spell?

At the head of affairs was himself, a man of indomitable energy, and incorruptible. Men of the same stamp, energetic, diligent, and bold, were put in charge of the ministries, the departments, and the prefectures. Favouritism was done away with; sinecures were abolished. Preferment was obtainable only by the efficient, and to them it came regardless of birth or party. All officials, down to the mayors, were appointed from above, and paid from above—"a hierarchy, all First Consuls in miniature," to quote his own words.

There was no political opposition. "No reaction is possible," he prophesied. "I have not relied upon the credit or upon the strength of a party, and am therefore indebted to no one.—The men of intelligence who, a little while ago, were perpetrating crimes, are now being used by me to upbuild a new social edifice. There are excellent workmen among them, but the trouble is that they would all like to be master builders. Typically French, that trait; every one thinks himself competent to rule the country!" Being careful to satisfy all parties, he gives the two most coveted portfolios to two rogues, mutually hostile, but both men of remarkable ability. Having done this, he is able to say: "What revolutionist can fail to have confidence in the social system when Fouché, the Jacobin, is Minister of Police. What nobleman would be unwilling to live under Talleyrand as Minister for Foreign Affairs? I have one of them on my right, and the other on my left. I open a wide road, in which all can find room."

To all the prefects and all the generals the order went forth: "No more clubs; no more parties. Tell the National Guardsmen and the citizens whenever you can, if a few ambitious fellows still feel the need to hate, that the rudder of State is now in strong hands, accustomed to overcome obstacles." A few weeks after the coup d'état, he issued a great proclamation, commending the new constitution to the people. It closed with the simple and lofty words: "Citizens, the revolution has returned to the principles with which it began. It is at an end."

II

It is not war.

"Returning to Europe after eighteen months' absence, I find that war has broken out once more between the French Republic and Your Majesty. The French people summons me to the first position in the State." In these terms, shortly after the coup d'état, he addresses the German emperor, just before marching against him. Napoleon writes as proudly as any monarch, as if before the journey he had already been the first man in the State; and he writes with the natural dignity to which, in large measure, he owes his success. That is his way. In this manner he puts his adversary in the wrong. But the emperor is unmoved. Well, Bonaparte's plans were made long since; he has only to carry them out.

First of all he surrounds himself with a guard, every member of which must have been through four campaigns—as many as the commander, but no more. Then, while he sends Moreau to fight on the Rhine, he makes his own preparations for an adventure in Italy. If he were to come along the coast, as he did four years ago, they would be ready for him. He must find a new plan! At Dijon, in full view of the Austrian spies, he collects from the rawest levies a pitiful reserve corps, and smiles as he reads the mocking comments in the Viennese papers. Meanwhile, he prepares a force of 32,000 men, no more, but the finest soldiers under his command. They are for a bold venture of which no one dreams, any more than they dreamed of his Egyptian campaign. Did not Hannibal cross the Alps, bidding the mountains make way for him? But nowadays a general must get cannon through the passes! Cut down trees, then, and make huge sleighs on which to drag the ordnance over the snows!

Thus in the spring after the coup d'état an army climbs the Great St. Bernard, for the first time in two thousand years. The old monks in the hospice can hardly believe their eyes. The herdsman who guides the commander's mule, prattling the while about his wishes and his troubles, will soon afterwards learn that he has been talking to a fairy godmother, will be enriched by the gift of a house and a farm. Even the common soldiers seem to realise the epic character of this campaign, and vie with one another in their zeal to drag the guns. They are following their tried and trusted leader; they are returning to that Lombardy whither, four years ago, he had led them as to the Promised Land; these reflections, and the urgency of the occasion, increase the mysterious suggestiveness of the expedition. So little do the Austrians realise what is impending, that their chief, writing to a lady friend in Pavia, tells her she is quite safe there; no need to leave. Twelve hours later, Bonaparte enters the town.

Nevertheless, the great blow seems to him a questionable success. When, in the middle of June, he attacks the Austrians in the plain, the enemy, whose forces greatly outnumber his, drives him back. Where is Desaix with the promised reserves? The affair begins to have the look of a general rout. The commander, by the roadside, flicks the dust nervously with his riding-whip, as he watches the beaten army pass by. "Stand firm! Wait a little! Reinforcements are coming! Only an hour! But the flight continues. Has fortune, too, been routed? At length Desaix arrives, and hurls himself on the dismayed Austrians; the dragoons charge; the enemy's lines are broken. The battle of Marengo, which Bonaparte had lost at five o'clock, was won by Desaix at seven—but Desaix fell in the hour of triumph.

Sad at heart, Napoleon remained on the field of battle. The best of his generals was dead; but an even more painful thought was that Desaix, not himself, had won the victory. He himself had been defeated. Maybe he was consoled by the knowledge that he alone had designed the whole campaign, and that he alone was responsible for the plan of battle in accordance with which Desaix had arrived in time to snatch success out of the jaws of failure. Perhaps he realised that this great battle, which opened and closed the campaign, had been won by him no otherwise than the Eighteenth Brumaire. Then, also, he had lost the day, and the crown of victory had been gained for him by another!

Yet in neither case can this judgment be maintained when all the circumstances are reviewed. Only three or four miles from the spot where this evening he dictates to Bourrienne the report of the battle, is the point on the map into which, four months earlier, he had thrust a pin, saying (to this same Bourrienne): "Crossing the Alps at the Great St. Bernard, I shall fall upon Melas, cut off his communications with Austria, and meet him here in the plains of the River Scrivia at San Giuliano."

This was no time for reminiscences! Statesman as well as commander, he was already parleying with Vienna, acting on the principle: "We must fight and negotiate at the same time." Now, on the battle-field, he writes again to Emperor Francis:

"The cunning of the English has neutralised the effect which my simple and frank advances must otherwise have had on Your Majesty's heart. War has become actual. Thousands of Frenchmen and Austrians are no more.—The prospect of the continuance of such horrors is so great a distress to me, that I have decided to make another personal appeal to you.—On the battle-field of Marengo, amid grief and pain, surrounded by fifteen thousand corpses, I implore Your Majesty, it behooves me to give you an urgent warning. You are far from the scene, and your heart cannot be so deeply moved as mine is on the spot. You rule over many States.—Let us give our generation peace and tranquillity. If the men of later days are such fools as to come to blows, they will learn wisdom after a few years' fighting, and will then live at peace one with another."

This long letter, of which only a few of the most weighty sentences have been quoted here, is as brilliant as had been his plan for the battle of Marengo, and it was as fruitful as his victory. For the first time it gave plain expression to his longing for peace. In days to come, he will write half a dozen such letters after as many decisive victories. Is Bonaparte, the great military commander, a pacifist after all?

By no means, but he is not a swashbuckler either. His nerves always remain sensitive to the impressions of the battle-field; and he has an unfailing reserve of scepticism as regards successes won merely by the sword. He is fond of camp life, and he has a chessplayer's love for the great game of war; but, before all, he is a statesman. It was in this very plain of Lombardy that the sense of statecraft first awakened in him. It was there that, with kings and countries as pieces, he began to play that other great game of chess, the diplomatic game. Delight in the use of spiritual force has taken possession of his soul. He will never renounce the sword, will never allow its edge to become blunted. It is as the wielder of the sword that he is acclaimed as the hero of Europe. But he also has the Golden Goblet, and does not wish to risk it anew every year.

He knows, too, that, while France is always eager for glory, an even greater need at the moment is tranquillity. Above all, the country has need of him, personally; but he has enemies in his rear. Before, it mattered little that he should be away for a year or two at a time; but now, when he is dictator, so long an absence would be fatal. These multiple considerations explain his letter to Emperor Francis—surely an unparalleled despatch from a conqueror on the battle-field. As soon as he has written it, he hastens to Milan.

What is Paris saying?

Is the capital satisfied at length? Is it not like Josephine, before whom one can pour out all the treasures of the world—to find only that she takes them as a matter of course, and holds out her hand for more? Paris is by no means enthusiastic about the new master. "For eleven years," writes Roederer in his diary, "the Parisian's first thought on waking in the morning had been: 'When shall we be able to rid ourselves of tyrants?' Now, the Parisians were saying: 'Everything seems to be going on well. But these enterprises that are being started, this capital that is being invested, these houses that they are building, these trees that they are planting—what will happen to the lot of them, if the Man should perish?'—His supreme calling was not the general's, but the statesman's. His victories, indeed, had made him the cynosure of all eyes; but it was his talent for statecraft that had raised men's hopes." Thus the Parisians are uneasy, but wellwishing. One among them, however, foresees the future, and writes to Napoleon at the theatre of war:

"General, I have just returned from the Tuileries, and shall not attempt to describe either the enthusiasm of the French or the amazement of foreigners. . . . Will posterity believe the miracle of this campaign? Favourable, indeed, are the auspices that preside over your homecoming! Never has there been an empire that was not founded upon miracle. In this instance, miracle has become reality."

Napoleon smiles, thinking: "In truth, Talleyrand is more than a flatterer; he is a soothsayer! But why does he give a name to my secret thoughts? Would he play the part of the Roman of old, who tempted Cæsar with a crown?"

Here is another missive from Paris. A police report from Fouché, who tells how Talleyrand had recently summoned a few intimates to discuss what had better be done should the Consul have a misadventure, or perchance be defeated. The news of Marengo had come while they were at supper! "So he was alarmed!" thinks Bonaparte. "There were stirrings of what remained of a conscience. Good friends! Fine confidants! Their alleged concern for my safety, is but the mask for their secret longing to rid themselves of their master!"

Is it a mocking smile or is it an expression of pensive anxiety that purses Napoleon's lips? Certainly, he must be back in Paris as soon as possible! But this evening he goes to the Scala, where the heroine is the lovely Grassini—whose advances he had scorned a year or two back. Now she sings for his ear, has eyes for him alone; and though she may be piqued that his beckoning nod comes so late, the handsome Italian prima donna gives herself to the conqueror of Italy for the asking. She shall go to the Paris opera. As star, or as his mistress? Time will show!

Since in Germany, too, the enemy has been defeated, the subsequent peace of Lunéville is extremely favourable to France, the Rhine frontier being conceded, and the re-establishment of the Cisalpine Republic agreed to. Could more have possibly been achieved by a few weeks' campaign? His colleagues and other false friends make ready to receive him as hero of the hour; they write to him about plans for a triumph. "I shall make an unlooked-for entry into Paris," he rejoins, with malicious double meaning; "and I have no desire for triumphal arches or any kind of ceremonial. I have a sufficiently good conceit of myself to scorn such plummery. The only genuine triumph is public content."

A little later, he writes in a vein that is equally modest, or equally proud: "I accept the offer to erect a monument in my honour and should like a site to be chosen. But I would rather leave the actual building of the monument to future centuries, should these confirm your good opinion of me." It is as if he could sense the coming storm of iconoclasm, could foresee that in less than twenty years his idolators of to-day will be rolling his eagles in the dust!

After his return, the dictator devotes all his energies to the consolidation of peace. He outsoars himself: for whereas formerly, by forced marches and crashing blows, he has imposed his will on one country after another, now, by shrewd negotiation, he cements peace with his sometime foes. Within two years of his seizure of power, France is at peace with Austria, Prussia, Bavaria, Russia, Naples, Spain, Portugal and even with England.

Nine legitimate and therefore ardently legitimist rulers now recognise the republic which they had been fighting for a decade. France, which two years before had been threatened by disruption from within and by dangerous impacts from without, had become the leading power on the Continent.

It is as First Consul, not as general and not as emperor, that Bonaparte leads the revolution to victory. In a Europe all the rest of which (except for Switzerland) is ruled by kings and princes, he not only establishes peace between the new ideas and the old forces, but also, unchallenged, compels his border States, Holland and northern Italy, to adopt the consular constitution. Neither Austria nor England attempts to interfere when, with a turn of the hand, he extends his grip over Piedmont, Genoa, Lucca and Elba. At the same time, when the compensation of the princes on the left bank of the Rhine is in question, the members of the oldest reigning houses of Germany throng around the great huckster, the man who has robbed them of their lands—thus teaching him to despise birth and heritage, nobles and crowns.

Only one chasm gapes in the structure he is building, but he will be able to close it.

At the opening of the revolution, Reason took the place of Christ. Indeed, this anti-Christian notion became extremely popular. Bonaparte stood almost alone in his rejection of it. Four years earlier, in Italy, he had granted the pope all kinds of things which Paris wished to refuse; and, for reasons of his own, he had always been chivalrous in his attitude towards the clergy. Now he wished to heal the breach that had existed for ten years between France and the Church. He did not do this because he was a believer. "Among the Turks, I was a Mohammedan; now I shall become a Catholic." He knew that this oldest of the powers could not be conquered either by the sword or by the spirit. He must come to terms with it in order to make use of it. "Catholicism kept the pope in being for me," he said later: "and, in view of my grip upon Italy, I continued to hope that sooner or later I should be able to bend him to my will. What immense influence I should then wield! What a means to have at my disposal in my dealings with Europe!"

It will be difficult to make Paris accept the rehabilitation of the Church! As a preliminary step, he is actually willing to present himself before the bishops in the guise of a philosopher: "I am aware that in no State can a man be truly virtuous and upright unless he knows whence he comes and whither he is going. Unaided reason cannot tell us these things. Without religion, we grope in the dark. But the Catholic faith throws a clear light upon the origin and the destiny of human beings." Rome is dumbfounded for a time, when this and similar speeches are reported; but the shrewdest of worldly sages can find his master in the Vatican. When Cardinal Consalvi comes to Paris in order to discuss matters with Napoleon, and, at the first official audience, the consul wishes to browbeat him, the prince of the Church smilingly stands his ground. What a spectacle for Talleyrand, who looks on in silence! Still, agreement is reached on various important points, such as the celibacy of priests, the choice of bishops by Rome, and the re-establishment of the old canon law. But though these concessions are made to the Church, the payment of stipends by the State, which gives the latter decisive influence, is to remain.

A great ceremony in Notre Dame seals the agreement. The Consul, with the other State dignitaries, had wanted only to come for the Te Deum; but he found it expedient, after all, to attend Mass, stipulating that he was not to be expected to take the sacrament, "or to participate in all the rest of the hocus-pocus that makes a man ridiculous." To his brother, he said on this occasion: "We're going to Mass to-day. What will Paris say about it?"

"The audience will look on at the play, and will hiss if it does not please."

"Then I shall have the church cleared by the guards!"

"But what if the grenadiers join in the hissing?"

"They won't. My old war-dogs will be just as respectful in Notre Dame as they were in the Cairo mosques. They will keep their eyes on me, and when they see that their general is serious and well behaved, they will follow his example, saying to themselves, 'Those are the orders of the day!' "

III

The ground is still unsteady beneath his feet. His consulship is for ten years only, and there are but eight years more to run. Then a rival may take his place. He is dependent on popular favour, which he must court, and which he despises.

What sort of a position is that for the head of a State in his dealings with foreign potentates? They will not take him seriously, any more than if he were an American president. Turning these thoughts over in his mind, he makes a sign to the Senate.

Always compliant (being dependent on his good graces), the Senate now proposes to ensure that the First Consul shall hold office for an additional term of ten years after the expiry of the present term. Put out of humour by this suggestion, he jogs the senators' thoughts and induces them to propose a lifelong tenure of the consulship. But, prudent as Cæsar, he says that the matter must be referred to the "people," the source of all power. A plebiscite is taken, and there are nearly four million ayes against a handful of courageous noes. His powers are enlarged. He now has sole authority to sign treaties with foreign States; he alone appoints the senators, who are themselves entitled to dissolve the Chambers; and he is granted the right to appoint his successor. When he compares his position with that of other European rulers, and notices that they all wear crowns, he consoles himself with the naïve sophism: "Henceforward, I am as good as the other sovereigns, for they, likewise, rule for life only!"

By no means all among the millions who have voted for him are his whole-hearted adherents. Even in Paris, when he makes a triumphal entry into the Luxembourg, there is so little public applause that he says afterwards to his Minister of Police: "Why did you not work up opinion beforehand?"

Said Fouché: "We are still the children of the ancient Gauls, of whom it was said that they could neither endure liberty nor tolerate oppression."

"What do you mean?"

"I mean, Citizen Consul, that, in your last steps, the Parisians fancy they see the loss of liberty, and a tendency towards absolutism."

"I should not care to rule for six weeks, if I had but the shadow of power, and could not be master!"

"You have only to be humane, strong, and just, at one and the same time," rejoins the fox (who never showed any of these qualities himself), "and soon you will win all hearts once again."

"Public opinion is capricious. I shall know how to mend it," said Bonaparte, turning his back on his interlocutor.

A two-minutes' talk like this, and Napoleon has made up his mind. He dismisses Fouché, but not because he is afraid of the ex-cleric (whom he despises, rather). He abolishes the Ministry of Police, and transfers its functions to the Ministry of Justice, "for I wish to show Europe that my policy is peaceful, and that the French love me sincerely." We must get used to such phrase-mongering, in which he cloaks his policy. To keep Fouché quiet, he makes the ex-minister a senator. When, on leaving office, Fouché discloses to the Consul a reserve fund of two and a half million francs, Bonaparte is amazed, and tells him to keep half the sum "as a token of personal regard." In the anteroom, the departing Fouché grins over his mental arithmetic, adding the undisclosed residue of the reserve to the amount of the First Consul's gift.

Such are Bonaparte's methods with a dangerous man who knows too much. As for public opinion, he can take his measures to get that on his side. It is because he is determined not to be indebted to any party or any individual, that he demands a popular ratification of his appointment as Consul for life, just as he had asked for popular approval after the coup d'état. The result gives him assurance that the revolution is over. "This consultation of the people has a twofold advantage. Besides confirming the prolongation of the consular term, it throws light on the sources of my power, which otherwise might have seemed ambiguous." The phrasing shows that he is aware of his dangerous position betwixt revolution and legitimacy. To the very last, he will be worried by this problem.

Like a Roman imperator, Bonaparte wishes to concentrate all the powers of State in his own hands; but whereas the Roman's title to power was the commandership of the armies, Napoleon is supreme because of his supreme efficiency. That is why he bases his power, not upon the army, which loves him, but upon the people, to which he is hostile. He wants to be "tyrant," in the classical sense of the term; but he wishes to be tyrant on a democratic footing, as the outcome of a free popular decision. The people, the source of power, is to transfer power to Napoleon. None knows better than he the weakness of any such fiction, but it is imposed on him by the spirit of the age. After all, Bonaparte can fearlessly quote in his own favour the revolutionary principle that power must go to talent instead of to birth, for where can a more talented man than himself be found? But instead of contenting himself with talent as the source of his power (the talent that has brought him victory in war and in peace, the talent that has enabled him to grasp the reins), he muddies this splendid source by a popular vote, feels morally compelled to do so, and even fancies that he is clarifying the waters by his action. If Bonaparte saves the revolution, he certainly kills the republic.

These ideas are not the outcome of calculating policy, but of the mood which seeks its stimulus in classical life. It is the same mood as that which draws him towards the East; the same mood as that which, on the day of the coup d'état, led him to make a fool of himself before the Councils. "Your place is among the men of Plutarch," said the first who really understood Bonaparte in early youth. The Consul was not a democrat in the sense that he believed in popular sovereignty. What he lacked was such days as those of classical antiquity, when genius did not need to entrench itself behind representative assemblies, but held sway on its own initiative; or Asia, where, even in modern times, there are monarchs in the literal sense.

In his work-room at Saint-Cloud there are two busts, Scipio's and that of Hannibal's. No other position than that of Roman emperor or that of caliph was suited to his temperament.

Immediately after the coup d'état, the Bourbons, with a childlike frankness, had made advances to him. The brother of the executed king, now Count of Provence, and in future days to reign as Louis XVIII, asked the son of the revolution to help him to the throne. The demand was thrice repeated, and a handsome reward was offered. The Consul made no answer to the first two applications. To the third he replied as follows:

"Sir, I have received your letter, and thank you for what you are so kind as to say about myself. You cannot seriously wish to come back, for your return would cost a hundred thousand lives. You must sacrifice your personal interests to the peace and happiness of France, and history will thank you for the sacrifice. I am not insensitive to the misfortunes of your family . . . I shall be happy to do all in my power to contribute to the welfare and tranquillity of your retirement. Bonaparte."

Very different is Napoleon's reception of the Vendée royalists, for he hopes to win them over to his side. At first they fail to understand him when, after a long time of waiting, the man of destiny, wearing his old green coat, and with untidy hair, makes advances to them.

"Come over to my side. Mine will be the government of youth and enthusiasm! . . . You struck shrewd blows for your princes. . . . But your princes have by no means covered themselves with glory. Why were they not in Vendée to lead the fight? Was not that their place?"

"They were kept in London by political considerations," answered the nobles.

"They should have crossed the Channel in the first fishing smack they could get hold of," he answered passionately, and, so the report runs, "in a voice that seemed to come from the depths of his stomach." Yes, my fine noblemen, from the depths of his stomach! The phrase carries with it the implications of an incident in universal history which was still recent, still vivid in Napoleon's memory. That was the tone proper to the bold adventurer who, in a tiny frigate, had made his way across the storm-tost Mediterranean, through the enemy fleet, to reach the coast where power was his for the seizing. Hear how he mingles flattery and threats, the young wizard who has turned the whole continent upside down!

"What would you like to be? General or prefect? You and yours can have whatever you please, if you will come over to my side. Nothing? Would you think it a disgrace to wear the coat that Bonaparte wears? . . . Unless you will make peace, I will march against you with a hundred thousand men, and burn your towns to ashes!"

"If you do," answers the count firmly, "we shall annihilate your columns."

"You dare to threaten me?" he exclaims—this time "with a terrible voice." But upon receiving a matter-of-fact answer, he is calm once more. The noble emissaries retire in disgust, having achieved nothing, having been perplexed by his foreign accent, and by the impetuous imagination, which leads him to complicate the issues to such an extent that it is often hard to follow his meaning.

None the less, the Consul induces a great many of the émigrés to return, disarming their hostility by making suitable provision for them. Forty thousand families promptly come back. At the same time, he negotiates with the Jacobins, although these, "with their metaphysics, are enough to ruin twenty governments." He feels sure of the support of those who follow the middle courses of democracy, for the democratic masses feel safe under his rule, now that Paris is no longer a sort of civilian camp, and now that (a benevolent despot) he is doing all in his power to bring better times.

Consider these instructions issued to various authorities:

"If the cold should be sharp, as it was in 1789, you must

have fires kept alight in the churches and market-places, so that as many people as possible can warm themselves."—"The winter is very severe, meat is dear, we must provide work in Paris. Get on with the cutting of the Ourcq canal, with the construction of the Quai Desaix, with the paving of the back streets."—"The law directs that all beggars shall be laid by the heels. Were we to do nothing more than this, our conduct would be barbarous and absurd. Arrest them, certainly, that you may give them work and food. We must have several homes of refuge in every department."—"There are a great many out-of-work shoemakers, hatters, tailors, and saddlers. See to it that five hundred pairs of shoes are made every day." He writes to the Minister for War saying that special orders for supplies for the artillery are to be issued. To the Minister for Home Affairs: "We must provide work, especially this month before the holidays. Issue an order that in May and June two thousand of the Saint Antoine workmen are to supply chairs, chests of drawers, armchairs, etc. . . . Send me your proposals to-morrow, so that a beginning may be made promptly."

He reads a by-law that no one wearing a workman's blouse is to walk through the Tuileries garden. Instantly he has the regulation cancelled, and gives express permission for such people to go through. He learns of a proposal to close the public reading-rooms: "I won't allow anything of the kind. I have not forgotten my own experience, how useful it was to know of a well-warmed room where I could read the newspapers and recent pamphlets. I will not allow others who are as poor as I was then to be robbed of these comforts." In the Théâtre Français, the stalls are to be very cheap on Sundays, "so that the people may enjoy the performance." There are to be no gambling hells in France: "They bring families to ruin, and I should set a bad example were I to tolerate them."

By his new education law, he establishes public elementary schools, middle schools, lycées, and technical colleges, throughout the country. There are to be six thousand free scholarships, and a third of these are to be reserved for the sons of specially deserving persons. Within three years, there are 4,500 elementary schools, 750 middle schools, and 45 lycées. He honours the Institute by choosing a third of his first senators from among its members. The Ministry for Home Affairs is instructed to draw up lists "of the ten best painters, sculptors, composers, musicians, architects, and other artists whose talents make them worthy of support." He orders great frescoes to be painted, which shall depict striking incidents in his battles. He gives his reasons for this State regulation of art, saying: "People complain that we have no literature. That is the fault of the Minister for Home Affairs!"

But if he tranquillises persons of all occupations by bringing them prosperity, what opening will be left, in this nation of the ambitious, for the pursuit of fame? If there is to be no war and no court life, where will the French find an outlet for their vanity? He answers this question by founding the Legion of Honour.

The Legion will form a group of stalwart supporters, for those who have taken a solemn oath to resist any attempt at the restoration of the feudalist regime will not be so likely to side against Bonaparte. Besides, it is not to be merely an officers' club, inasmuch as the aim is to provide distinctions for all who do good service. He therefore appoints a natural philosopher to the office of arch-chancellor; and when, in the Council of State, a warning reference is made to the kinship between these orders of distinction and the abuses which have been swept away, he answers with perfect seriousness:

"I doubt if there has ever been a republic without such distinctions. You declare that they are toys for children. Well, grown men are led by toys. I would not say that from a rostrum, but in a council of sages and statesmen I can speak my mind. I do not think that the French love liberty and equality; they have not been changed by ten years of revolution; they are what the Gauls were, fierce and fickle. They are accessible to only one sentiment, the love of honour. That is why we must have distinctions. . . . Soldiers must be allured by fame and pay. . . . Here is a new kind of money assessed at a different valuation from current coin. Its source is inexhaustible. With no other kind of money, is it possible to reward actions which are so sublime that they cannot be valued in current coin." In these notable words, we hear the rippling of the three fountains of his soul: contempt for mankind, understanding of the masses, and the critical aloofness of the foreigner who has chosen a new fatherland.

IV

On Christmas Eve, 1800, the Consul was driving to the opera. Josephine and her daughter were following in another carriage. In a narrow street an empty cart partially blocked the way, and caused a halt. The cart was pushed aside, and the coachman whipped up his horses. The instant after the carriage had passed, an infernal machine hidden in the cart exploded. About twenty persons were killed, but no one in either Napoleon's or Josephine's carriage was hurt. On reaching the opera, Napoleon went straight to his box. When his wife arrived, he said calmly: "Josephine, those rascals wanted to blow me up; send for a copy of the music." Outwardly unmoved, he listened to the performance of Haydn's recent work, *Creation.*

Ordinarily, good music made him forget all his schemes; but this evening his brain was busily at work, pondering the causes and foreseeing the consequences of the attempt on his life. It mattered little who "the rascals" were, revolutionaries of the left or revolutionaries of the right. He knew well enough that he had plenty of enemies on both sides. The question was, whether it would suit him best to assume that his would-be assassins belonged to the right or to the left. His mind was soon made up on this point. Had the attempt been successful, the consequences for France would have been immeasurably great. Well, the consequences of the unsuccessful attempt should be no less momentous. It was a lucky chance, and he would make it solve the problem of personal power.

Next morning, when people came to offer congratulations on his escape, and when all were agreed in the opinion that the outrage must have been planned by the royalists, with assumed heat Napoleon declared they were absolutely mistaken. "This was the work of Septembrists, intellectuals, the non-commissioned officers of the revolution—persons with a bolder imagination and more culture than the masses, but in close touch with them, and always ready to spur on the workers!" When, in the Council of State, a proposal was made to institute special proceedings, Bonaparte objected on the ground that the method would be too slow. His speech was impassioned:

"Either we must do nothing at all, and, like Augustus, forgive the sinners; or else we must act promptly, take far-reaching steps which will guarantee social order once for all. . . . No ordinary criminal procedure will suffice; this is a matter for statesmanship. . . . Blood must flow. As many of the guilty must be shot as there perished innocent persons in the streets. Two hundred of these raging wolves must be seized and transported. They are always watching and waiting for their prey. All our troubles are due to these metaphysicians!"

Old Tronchet shakes his head. The attempt had been the work of émigrés and Englishmen.

"Are you proposing that I should transport noblemen or priests?" asked Napoleon angrily. "Vendée is quiet, and I do not want to banish the servants of the most widely spread religion in the world. I shall have to dismiss all the members of the Council of State, for, with two or three exceptions, every one of you believes in this fable of a royalist plot. . . . Do you think me a child? Am I to say that the country is in danger? Has France ever been in better case since the revolution, the army more victorious, the country more peaceful? A pretty thing that men who have never been among the true friends of liberty, should now display so much concern for liberty! Do not think to excuse yourselves by saying: 'I defended the patriots in the Council of State.' That might go down in a drawing-room, but it will not go down here, among the most enlightened men in France!" He abruptly closes the sitting. Do the councillors understand his drift?

These alarums and excursions are not the outcome of any sense of personal danger, for if that were his motive, if his own alarmed will-to-live were at work, he would seek out the real offenders as object for vengeance. The whole scene was statecraft. Whom can we frighten here at home? Whom can we pacify across the frontier? That is what the Consul is asking himself. Those are the considerations that guide his actions. Of course, there is a personal motive as well. He thinks that his own safety can best be guarded by draconian measures. "I did not sleep well o' nights," he said at a later date, "until I had had these leaders of the great towns sent across the seas. I was not afraid of the sort of conspirator who gets up at nine o'clock in the morning and puts on a clean shirt!"

At the same time, he is infuriated by an anonymous pamphlet, "Cæsar, Cromwell, and Bonaparte," in which the writer advocates the establishment of a hereditary monarchy. Who is daring to disclose his own secret thoughts, even though the indiscreet pamphleteer is a sympathiser? When one of his confidants says that the only thing wrong with the pamphlet is that the disclosure is premature, Bonaparte lets the observation pass. But these two attempts, the attack on his body and the attack on his mind, have terrible consequences as far as freedom is concerned. The Tribunate and the Chambers are purged of a fifth of their numbers, Constant, Chénier, and other noted democrats being excluded; sixty-one out of seventy-three newspapers are suppressed; pamphlets and plays are subjected to a censorship. When the Council of State reminds him of the freedom of the press, he answers: "Do you think that, in such a situation, we can allow public meetings? . . . And is not every journalist an orator? Do not the subscribers to his newspaper really form a club? Calumny is like an oil spot, which always leaves traces. . . . In England it is different; there the Government is old-established; here it is new. People would write worse things about me day by day; saying, for instance, that I am so afraid of being poisoned that I dare not eat! . . . The only way of keeping the political parties in check is to deprive them of their battle-ground."

Sound reasoning, appropriate measures. But the spirit of free thought stands weeping at the door; her fascinated gaze is fixed upon power enthroned.

V

The man who was certainly in part responsible for the before-mentioned pamphlet, perhaps its author, the man who had thus inflicted a grave injury upon the First Consul, was the very man who had been his main buttress on the Eighteenth Brumaire, and who had saved the situation that day—Brother Lucien. The most gifted of Napoleon's four brothers, six years younger than the Consul, scaling the heights of ambition at an even earlier age than his great brother, though helped in his upward progress by that brother's prestige, Lucien coveted the highest for himself. To stand in the shadow of Napoleon's great name, to be under his protection, and even to be the object of his love—these were more galling to Lucien than Napoleon's disfavour in later days. He never forgot the incidents of the coup d'état. He had been the king-maker. How, then, could he obey the man whom he had raised to the throne?

Needs must, however. Shortly after Brumaire, he becomes Minister for Home Affairs, a mere instrument of the master brain. Is it not natural that he should critically examine all

(Photograph in the Kircheisen Collection.)

Bonaparte as First Consul. Painting by Girodet. Musée Nationale, Versailles.

that comes to him from the chief, wondering whether he can make a better job? Hostile to Josephine, he is hostile to her confidants. This brings him into conflict with Fouché, who is always ready to blame the Minister for Home Affairs for anything untoward, like the publication of the pamphlet.

By temperament, Lucien was as unscrupulous and amoral as his brother. Though very like his brother, he lacked the boldly calculating brain, and may even be said to have had semi-criminal traits beneath his smiling exterior. A Napoleon, like the other, but one degree more adventurer and several degrees less statesman. At twenty-five years of age, Lucien was powerful and yet embittered, his audacious spirit urging him to more and yet more hazardous adventures. His first wife was an innkeeper's daughter; he sold monopolies; speculated in grain; lived beyond his means, instead of setting to work; bought the finest house in Paris, furnished it sumptuously, rebuilt it, and refurnished it; gave splendid banquets, indulged in amateur theatricals, wrote verses. All these extravagances were undertaken in the half-conscious desire to eclipse his brother.

Between two such men, in such a relationship, how can a breach be avoided! Lucien taunts the Consul, saying that he, Lucien, had won the victory on the Nineteenth Brumaire. In the first flush of his wrath, Napoleon has it in mind to banish Lucien; but, in the end, he is content to deprive the young man of ministerial office. This will put a term to the monetary scandals attaching to Lucien's abuse of his position. Lucien goes to Madrid as envoy. His ability in this new post enables him to work successfully against England, and also to divert the flow of a good many millions into his own pockets. Being now a widower, he soon returns, and marries his lady love, a beauty whose reputation is of the same sort as Josephine's in earlier days. The First Consul is furious, for he has been working to promote a marriage that would have brought political advantages.

Joseph, too, man of the world and good fellow, is inclining to join the ranks of the sceptics, now that, with his brother's aid, he has risen to wealth and power; he frequents Madame de Staël's circle, and speaks critically of the Consul. He is no longer content with the position of envoy in Rome, refuses the presidency of the Italian Republic and the chancellorship of the Senate; cannot forget that he is the eldest; looks upon himself as head of the family.

Louis still vacillates, the poet in his temperament taking charge from time to time. For years he is in love with one of Josephine's relatives, and has no affection for Hortense, whom he is forced to marry. Years afterwards he will sing the love of his heart.

Jerome, the youngest, good-natured and frivolous, is brought up by his brother with paternal strictness. "I send you Citizen Jerome Bonaparte, who is to serve as a midshipman. As you know, he must be kept under strict discipline. See to it that he fulfils all his duties."

His sisters, again; he has loaded them with money and honours, but they give him little thanks, and are incessant in their demands for more. There is Elise! She and Lucien, her favourite brother, vie with one another in escapades that are the talk of Paris. At amateur theatricals, they disport themselves in pink tights, and the Consul thunders: "Disgraceful behaviour! While I am wearing myself out trying to make people moral and respectable once more, my brother and my sister appear before the footlights almost naked!" But as soon as his back is turned, they laugh merrily, and follow their own bent.

Caroline, who has married General Murat, is already involving her husband and Bernadotte in intrigues against the Consul. The public learns nothing of these matters, but they come to Napoleon's ears, and he says angrily that Murat deserves to be shot.

Pauline loses her husband in a colonial campaign. She does

not regret the loss. By her second marriage, she becomes Princess Borghese in Rome. Her innocence is no more than a cynical pose, but her brother remains fonder of her than of any of the others. Even when the looseness of her life imperils his reputation, and he thinks it necessary to remonstrate, he words his remonstrances cautiously.

Uncle Fesch, at first a priest, and then an army contractor, now enters political life and resumes the clerical habit. Napoleon secures his appointment as archbishop and then as cardinal. All the Bonapartes exploit the man of power, that they may win money and position, lead a splendid life, and enjoy themselves, whereas in his life of superhuman toil there is little scope for pleasure.

Only his mother continues to hold aloof. Although she is not better pleased with Josephine now than formerly, although she is still the woman of Corsica and continues to talk an island dialect, he invites her, immediately after the coup d'état, to come and live with him in the Tuileries. She refuses, prefers to stay with Joseph. At the first great parade he holds in the courtyard of the palace, when she appears on the balcony among the highest State officials, she is very simply dressed, all in black, and yet looks prouder than Josephine, hard by, decked out in peacock array. Letizia mistrusts all this splendour, being now inured to the vicissitudes of life. When any one tries to flatter her by speaking of her son's greatness and power, she sagely answers, in her Italian French: "Pourvou que cela doure."

What is the source of these family dramas, some of which will end in farce, others in tragedy?

In Napoleon's heart, had he been nothing more than a parvenu of the familiar type, he would, when pressed by his nearest and dearest for a share in his good fortune, graciously or ungraciously, but infallibly, have kept this dozen or so of men and women far from his circle of influence, for he would have been fain to conceal an origin which conflicted with his affectation of French nationalism. He is dictator of France, and yet every time his mother opens her mouth she reminds all the nationalists of his foreign birth. Here is the sister of a man who ranks with kings, and she plays the maddest pranks before the eyes of the monarchs of Europe, who naturally delight in pointing the finger of scorn at the ill-breeding of the upstart's relatives. His brothers wallow in the practice of corrupt methods which it was a primary aim of the revolution to abolish. All this occurs in Paris, where irony has ever been the fundamental tone of criticism!

Yet he does not merely tolerate these embarrassing kinsfolk; he is continually showering honours on them, promoting them to high office, making them his representatives abroad.

Herein we see the working of his Italian blood, and, above all, of his island upbringing. Every Corsican family, patriarchal by tradition, is clannish to the core, while filled with sentiments of hatred and vengefulness towards the rival houses of the puny isle. Such traditions are older than those of many of the royal families, and as a result of them the urge towards the gratification of pride and towards the vindication of honour is more powerful than the desire for wealth. With this inborn clannishness is associated and intertwined the intense longing of a conqueror to preserve for the heirs of his body all that he has snatched for himself by the strength of his genius and through the favour of fortune. Nevertheless, destiny (tragical in its working, being conditioned by his innermost sentiments, and therefore inexorable) has made this man childless. The wife, into whose arms he has been driven by all the passion of love, the wife who has borne two healthy children in previous marriage, remains barren in her second union; and the infirmity of barrenness, but for which the history of Europe would have taken a different turn, is obviously a consequence of her devotion to the art of love, of the facile amorousness with which she won Bonaparte's affection and held him for a time in thrall. For, when she first met him, she was little over thirty; and, as for him, in subsequent relationships with other women, he was able to procreate three sons. He urgently needs a legitimate heir. Even an heiress would serve his turn. There can be no doubt that Josephine's failure to satisfy him in this crucial instance had a decisive effect on his plans.

In view of the plenitude of his powers, how could it be otherwise? During the first years of his rise, Roederer propounds the great theme: "The royalists are saying: 'Who will be Bonaparte's successor!' If you die to-morrow, what will happen to us? You must nominate your successor."

"What you suggest would not be a strong policy."

"France would be more at ease if she knew who was to succeed you."

"I have no children."

"You could adopt one."

"That would not meet the difficulties of the moment. I can see no other way out than that the Senate should appoint my successor. Only three of the senators and myself should know his name. But who is it to be?"

"They had better choose a lad of twelve."

"Why do you want him to be a child?"

"A boy who can grow up in your school; one whom you can train and love."

At length the Consul, driven into a corner, exclaims: "My natural heir is the French people."

The man who speaks is not old. He is little more than thirty. Though he is appointed dictator for ten years only, he plainly foresees that he will be monarch. But he is already alarmed by the dangers of the position. When he looks round in search of an heir, his only hope is in his brothers. The best return they can make for the gifts he showers on them is that they should raise up heirs to his name, heirs who will at least have the advantage of Bonapartist blood. That is why Napoleon is so furious with Lucien, not because he has taken a wife with a bad name, but because he has taken a wife with no name.

Lucien must get a divorce, and thus win freedom to marry a woman of royal blood.

Lucien refuses, quite as much owing to spite for his all-powerful brother as owing to affection for his wife. He is, indeed, fond of her; but he is so ambitious that he would sacrifice anything in the world for the sake of supreme power. After a stormy scene between the pair, Bonaparte comes into Josephine's room, and his voice is shaken with emotion as he says: "It is all over! I have given Lucien his dismissal."

Similar considerations explain the long-lasting quarrel with Louis, to whom Josephine looks for the salvation of her own line. He cannot endure Josephine's daughter Hortense, who reciprocates the dislike and loves another man. Josephine, however, forces her to marry Louis, and the son of this ill-assorted union becomes Napoleon's darling, and is looked upon as likely to be the heir. Thereupon, his sisters begin to intrigue, spreading abroad the report that Napoleon is really the father. Through these disputes, the unity of the family is shattered, at the very time when Europe envies it for its good fortune. Letizia sides with the young people who have been forced into a marriage; and also espouses the cause of the ostracised Lucien, whom she follows to Rome. There she can live happily, far from the glowing star that has sprung from her womb. There she can live as an Italian, a wealthy and respected associate of Rome's leading families, and treated by the pope with all the honours due to a woman of royal blood.

What if Bonaparte were to divorce Josephine? His sisters, who hate "the old woman," do what they can, and trot attractive beauties up and down in full view. As Josephine grows older, Napoleon's relations with her become more tranquil, but he needs her friendship. He has ceased to be fastidious and has transient love affairs with one pretty actress after another, or makes this or that companion of his sisters the mistress of a few evenings or a night or two.

Georges, who, like all the rest, is afraid of him, describes him as "an amiable and considerate man," who plays hide and seek with her, helps her to undress, and bends to her "childish caprices." Since her Christian name is Josephine, he refuses to call her by it, and invents for her an Italian name. She is Giorgina. He asks her to tell him her own story, listens attentively, and nods approvingly—for he has taken care to learn all about her, and is pleased that she tells him the truth.

Sometimes the Consul's servants catch sight of him in the evening, as, in his stockinged feet, he steals up a secret winding staircase to visit the lovely Duchatel. She is gentle, slender, and blonde—the type he prefers. Duchatel is one of Josephine's ladies-in-waiting. He likes to play cards with her sometimes, talking to her in an undertone about matters of love, while the uneasy Josephine, at another card table, strains her ears to catch what he is saying. The lady-in-waiting retires. Napoleon follows, to find her in the place of assignation. His wife, beside herself, pursues them, rattles the door-handle. Napoleon comes to the door in a rage. Next day he threatens her with divorce, but he is softened by her tears.

These amours are but occasional. He is always up to the eyes in work. Besides, he has made up his mind to avoid what has proved disastrous to so many kings. He will not squander his resources on inamoratas, and he will not allow them to interfere in matters of State. As regards affairs of love, he is prematurely old. It is with a sense of shock that we find this man of thirty writing in a letter to a friend: "My old heart, which now knows human beings for what they are . . ."

Josephine is racked with anxiety about his conduct, just as formerly he was racked with anxiety about hers. She relies on dresses, hats, the arts of the toilet; spends more than the late queen of France; and has still so little reticence that, though she is the first lady in the land, she cannot refrain from telling her maid when the Consul has spent the night with her. He forgives her much. Sometimes she sits at the weary man's bedside, reading to him in her lovely alto voice. He thanks her with his eyes. He is conservatively inclined, this man of the revolution. Rarely does he part with a general, dismiss an official. How, then, shall he divorce this woman whom he loves, despite her faults?

In the pleasant gardens at Malmaison, where during his year's absence in Egypt she lived with her light-of-love, Hippolyte, he runs races with Bourrienne, Rapp, and a few men of letters, while Eugene and Hortense look on. When he trips and falls, he joins merrily in the others' laughter. Then he gets into his carriage for the drive to Paris, saying:

"Now I can put my head in the collar once more."

VI

"Bonaparte very seldom writes with his own hand. He dictates everything, while walking up and down his study; dictates to a young man of twenty named Méneval, the only one who has the entry to this study and the three other rooms of the private suite. No use approaching Méneval; nothing to hope in that quarter; indeed, no one would dare to try. But the First Consul himself jots down the memoranda that relate to his most important plans. This . . . very special map, he locks up with his own hand, and always carries the key about with him. If he leaves his study, Méneval has to put the map away in a cupboard screwed to the floor. Of course the map might be stolen, but it would instantly be missed. Suspicion would at once fall upon Méneval and the underling, who cleans the study and lights the fire, so the underling would have to make a bolt for it. . . . All the secret memoranda concerning his military operations must be in it, and since the only way of overthrowing his power would be to destroy his plans, the theft of this map would bring everything to naught."

Who writes the foregoing? A Bourbon spy? Or is it a traitor among the Consul's intimates?

Neither the one nor the other. The young man of twenty

named Méneval writes it; and it is dictated to him by his chief, the First Consul, who is walking up and down the study. Acting on Bonaparte's orders, the Minister for Justice is sending a provocative agent to Munich, where the man is to get in touch with English agents of the Bourbons. The letter is to be part of the outfit. Many other details are given. We are told more about the royalist menial who cleans the study and lights the fire; what this fellow will get if he brings off the coup successfully; where he will spend the night during his escape. The commander is drafting the plan of a little campaign directed against himself.

He has good reason to be on his guard. Uneasy winter weeks are these, during which he collates the data sent in by a hundred spies in London, Vendée, and Paris itself. "Has the time come to strike?" his agents are continually asking. "Wait," he replies, and quietly goes on gathering information. At length he has all the proofs in his hands. His deadly enemies of the extreme right and the extreme left, the royalists and the Jacobins, have joined forces for the destruction of their great enemy. Pichegru, the friend of the Bourbons, and Moreau, the champion of the republicans who are opposed to the dictatorship, are working together. Both the generals are his rivals. Now is the time to strike.

When the plot became public property, alarm spread across Europe. The legitimate rulers were amazed at Napoleon's perspicacity, but put their trust in his enemies, whose number must be greater than the "Moniteur" was willing to admit. The English ambassador compromised! The great Moreau in jail! —Bonaparte hesitates a long time before arresting Moreau, having high esteem for the man who had shared his laurels. On the day of the arrest, the Consul sends repeatedly for news. Is his memory at work? Less than four years ago, he himself had a scare that night in Talleyrand's house when he believed his own arrest to be imminent! The trial is distressing; Moreau's complicity is clearly proved; but Napoleon thinks it better to pardon the victor of Hohenlinden on condition of withdrawal to the United States. Pichegru is found strangled in prison. Thirteen of the conspirators are executed. A man named Querelle, personally involved in the conspiracy, reveals that one of the Bourbon princes has been privy to the plot.

The Consul lends an eager ear. A Bourbon prince! Talleyrand draws attention to the fact that for a long time the duke of Enghien has been living close to the Rhine frontier—presumably in order to watch through a telescope what is going on in France. Would a man spend his time thus inertly in Baden, simply in order to make love to a cardinal's niece? The duke of Enghien is a scion of the house of Condé; he is a Bourbon, and is in English pay. Most likely he is the Bourbon prince incriminated in the affair. At any rate, he is in touch with the agents who swarm in South Germany. An example must be made of this suspect of the blood royal. That will put an end to the reiterated attempts on the part of the exiled Bourbons to disturb the peace of France and to trouble the sleep of its master!

In a lengthy despatch, the Consul orders an attack on the little Badenese town of Ettenheim, just across the Rhine. The number of boats and the soldiers' rations are prescribed with as much care as if the expedition were the siege of Mantua. Three hundred dragoons make a raid into Baden and carry off the duke. Four days later, he is brought in secret to the fortress of Vincennes.

Two of Napoleon's confidants warn the dictator that no compromising documents have been found among the duke of Enghien's belongings. But Talleyrand, who has ever an eye to his own future, advises court martial and the severest measures, knowing that the moral reprobation thus aroused will, in the end, prove disastrous to Napoleon. Brother Joseph is alarmed at the same thought. He reminds Napoleon of the veneration they had shared for the great Condé during their cadet days; of the verses they had recited about the hero of the seventeenth century. Was the only remaining descendant of that famous man to be slaughtered?

"I have made up my mind to pardon him," answers the Consul. "But that is not sufficient. I feel that I am strong enough to have him fighting on my side."

Joseph returns home, able to reassure Madame de Staël and his other quests.

The duke, who was two years younger than Napoleon, and who would probably have won renown but for the peculiar political circumstances which had brought Napoleon fame and power, was tried by court martial the same evening. With a brave and knightly bearing, he faced the twelve staff officers who formed the court, while a member of the Council of State, acting as prosecutor, asked the questions that had been drafted by Napoleon.

"Did you never have any dealings with English agents?"—"No."—"Was it not your intention, if Pichegru's conspiracy had been successful, to cross the Rhine and invade Alsace?"—"No."—"Have you been in receipt of an English pension?"—"Yes."—"Did you wish to enter the English service?"—"Yes, in order to free my country."—"This means that you placed yourself at England's disposal in order to take up arms against France?"—"How can a Condé return to his homeland except under arms?"

A death sentence follows, and next day at dawn the duke of Enghien is shot.

In one respect the treatment of the duke of Enghien was definitely illegal. The French had no right to kidnap him in foreign territory and to bring him across the frontier. Once he was on French soil, there was legal warrant for condemning him to death as a person who (according to his own admission) desired by force of arms to overthrow the extant form of State. With the primary reservation regarding the French raid into Baden, of course absolutely indefensible, the condemnation was technically just.

Nevertheless, as Talleyrand subsequently said of the affair, it was worse than a crime—it was a blunder. In time of revolution, hundreds are put to death who are more innocent than was this prince. Even though he may not have been privy to the plot, he would have hailed with delight the assassination of the usurper, and would, sword in hand (to quote his own words), have joined in the march on Paris to take vengeance on any of the regicides who remained alive. There would have been very little said about the court martialling and shooting of this young officer, had he not been a Bourbon, had he not been a symbol of that prince-ridden Europe whose system had been ended on French soil by the revolution. The shooting of the duke of Enghien was a challenge to a dozen thrones, and to the many millions of Europeans who believed in rule by divine right. It gave the signal for a rallying of forces against the dictator who had had neither part nor lot in the reign of terror, and who during his seven years as military commander and as statesman had never committed an outrage.

The day after the execution, a few tongue-tied and crestfallen guests were seated at his board. Josephine was doing her best to hide her fears, and Napoleon had been taciturn despite his tumultuous thoughts. Then, suddenly, he broke out: "At any rate, they will know now what we can do. Henceforward, I hope, they will leave us in peace." After dinner, he walked up and down the room, explaining to the silent listeners his reasons and what he thought of it all. Continuing to pace the room, he went on to speak movingly of genius, of statesmanship, and above all of Frederick the Great, for whom he had so profound an admiration:

"Ought a statesman to indulge in feelings? Is he not an isolated individual, always alone though always in company? Policy is his telescope, which must neither reduce things in size nor magnify them. Even while he is attentively watching the course of events, he must be pulling the strings which move them. Often enough, ill-matched horses are harnessed to his chariot. Do you think he can allow himself to heed some of those feelings which may in other respects be of great importance to the welfare of society? . . . How often he will have to do things which seem quite out of keeping with the whole! . . . Try to get outside the limitations of your own epoch, enlarge your imagination instead of being content merely to blame, and you will see that those great personalities you had regarded as violent and cruel, are nothing but statesmen! They know themselves better than others know them; they are the best judges of their own conduct; if they have true ability, they will even know how to control their passions, for they will be competent to calculate the precise effect of these."

Suddenly breaking off this monologue, which discloses some of the deepest recesses of his soul, he sends for the documents bearing on the conspiracy and has them read over to him.

"You see," he says, "we have incontrovertible proof that the conspirators wanted to spread disorder in France, and hoped, through killing me, to slay the revolution! It was my business to defend the revolution, to avenge it! The duke was a conspirator just like another, and had to be treated in the same way as the others. . . . The madmen seek to kill me, though they would gain nothing by it, for a gang of fanatical Jacobins would take my place. . . . These Bourbons! If they ever do regain power, I will wager that their first concern will be with etiquette. If they were prepared to share in the rough and tumble of the battle-field, with its blood and its grime! . . . But how can they expect to win back a kingdom with a letter dated from London and signed Louis? All the same, letters like that will incriminate incautious recipients . . . I have shed blood; I had to. Perhaps I shall shed more in the future. But always without passion, quite simply, because blood-letting is indicated. I am a statesman: I am the French revolution, and shall know how to protect it!" Abruptly he dismisses his guests.

Such is his mood; such are his motives, his views, the

undercurrents of his feelings. But his notable inferences are not yet disclosed.

VII

A week after the court-martialling of the duke of Enghien a committee of the Senate comes to see the Consul, with a very remarkable twofold request: for the establishment of a State tribunal and the foundation of a monarchy. This is a cautious improvisation, to test the current of popular opinion. Can anything be more logical, or simpler? To scare the terrorists, to safeguard the head of the State, two things are requisite, a State tribunal and an heir!

As with all the decisions of his life, so also this premature resolve to become an emperor is an outgrowth of circumstances. In none of the decisive moments of his career, do we find evidence that he had a definite scheme of life, which he systematically endeavoured to realise. When he first invaded Italy, it was not in search of the crown of Milan, and still less in search of the crown of France. But, as he winged his soaring flight, the natural sequence was that wider and ever wider vistas of land and sea should unfold themselves before his eyes. What happened, was a fulfilment of his own guiding principle: "He will not go far who knows from the first whither he is going." Improvisation, which, in amazing fashion, characterises so much of his activity, merely deprives him of the nebular glory of the mystical hero. As far as details are concerned, it leaves him free to make exact preparations, while restoring to him, as a whole, a liberty and a guilelessness which strengthen his genius.

Was the desire to become emperor a mistake? What urged him towards the adoption of such a role?

First of all, the imaginative side of his nature, which for the second time is blinding the cold reason of the calculator. Thus was it in Egypt, and thus was it to be for a third time in

Russia. His ideal drives him to take this step. He had grown to manhood amid dreams of the antique world; classical imagery had filled his mind; his dictatorial nature necessarily craved for the forms of Roman imperialism. A poetical temperament which makes him look upon the successive occurrences in his life as phases in the unrolling of a saga, and makes him feel, on the very evening after a battle has been won, that the battle has already passed into the realm of history; this engine, driven by the power of fantasy; this eye that looks upward and beyond to see how posterity will crown his deeds with fame—they need a symbol which no one has to-day, but which shone over Europe two thousand years ago.

Yet the mathematician in him also needs this symbol; the statesman needs it, that he may safeguard his country without perpetual wars. Lastly, and perhaps most passionately of all, the man with strong family attachments needs it; the man who feels he has won nothing, if what he has won be no more than an adventurer's prize that will perish with the winner.

"The name of king is outworn. It carries with it a trail of obsolete ideas, and would make me nothing more than the heir of dead men's glories. I do not wish to be dependent upon any predecessor. The title of emperor is greater than that of king. Its significance is not wholly explicable, and therefore it stimulates the imagination." Here, in two or three sentences, are compendiously disclosed the impetuous and the hot, the cunning and the cold, motives of his soul.

Does he see the dangers, or does he overlook them? What are his antitoxins? "What is a throne? A piece of wood covered with satin!" When he has become emperor he will ask the question and answer it thus, more than once. But with this satin-covered piece of wood, as he knows, he can influence grown men, just as he could influence them with the toys of the Legion of Honour. Indeed, the glamour of the throne is stronger, and therefore he will take the establishment of his throne more seriously than he took the foundation of the Legion of Honour. It is an instrument of policy, a means for the management of men. In the real world, where no one can call familiar spirits to his aid, the private person, the poet or the philosopher, can raise his head heavenward without bearing the burden of a crown; but the statesman needs the insignia of power, for the dull populace cannot believe in the reality of power unless he who wields power wears the insignia.

Are we to suppose that he, who can calculate all eventualities, does not see the danger that lurks in the symbol of the crown? Does he not know that for thousands of years people have regarded the monarch as akin to God? If he is aware of this, how without disaster will he be able to harmonise the illusion with his political cynicism? If the crown is the gift of his genius, how can he bequeath it without bequeathing the genius?

Nevertheless, all his endeavours, like those of the emperors of ancient Rome, are now concentrated upon the bequest of power. He, whose own genius has taught him that genius is always aboriginal and primary; he who with his own eyes has seen hereditary power perish amid blood and grime, and whose inmost heart said aye to the act of regicide; he, who to-day reproaches the Bourbons, not with their origin, but with the cowardice that keeps them trembling in their mouseholes; he, Napoleon Bonaparte, who feels himself to be the one man of a millennium; he, a principle of whose rule it is to grant honour and wealth only to merit and courage and talent; he, who is the symbol of revolt incorporated in human flesh—believes that in the place he has fought and won for himself through the storms of eight years, he will be able to perpetuate his blood for the sole reason that it is his own!

He knows Plutarch and the story of the Cæsars. He has studied the history of the great kings of France and England and Prussia, and has learned to look with contempt upon their decadence. And yet he is ready and eager to restore the hereditary principle for the succession to this, the highest office in the State! Here, and here only, he wishes to combine the newest of the new with the old, so that, as he says later in a phrase both profound and tragical: "I might achieve that harmony which I regarded as essential for the tranquillity of the world, a solitary man, driven forward by the impetus of my own personality. That is why I dropped sheet-anchors everywhere."

But side by side with these heroic words, which sufficed to class him with the heroes of Plutarch, were housed the simplest feelings of domestic life. For, when his confidant Roederer urged him to seek a new wife, who would bear him a son, Napoleon answered in great excitement:

"Hitherto I have always ruled justly. It might be to my interest to seek a divorce. But what right have I to put away a good wife merely because I have become a greater man than I was when we married? She would have followed me into exile or imprisonment. Now I am to divorce her? I am not strong enough to do that. A human heart beats in my bosom; my mother was not a tigress." After Josephine's death, he would be free to choose a new partner. But, as things are, what will be the best way of solving this problem of the succession? "My brothers, like myself, were born in petty circumstances, but they did not force themselves upwards unaided as I did. The man who is to rule France must either be born to greatness, or he must be one of those whose inborn strength enables them to distinguish themselves from the herd."

In this last idea is implicit the disastrous error which in due time is to lead him to inevitable destruction.

For the nonce, however, all is done quietly and soberly, just as on two previous occasions. Wishing to be independent of the parties and to stand above them, he again demands a popular vote; and the very Frenchmen who twelve years earlier had destroyed, not only the king, but kingship, now re-establish both, doing this with even more enthusiasm than when, two years before, they had made Napoleon Consul for life. In a few days, everything is settled. First of all there are votes in the

Chambers. In the Senate, only three adverse votes, those of personal enemies. In the Tribunate, Carnot is alone in recording his dissent, Carnot who admires Napoleon, but is a far-sighted devotee of the principle of freedom. The result of a plebiscite is overwhelmingly in favour of the adoption of the imperial title with hereditary succession. In May 1804, the new constitution is promulgated. It is short and businesslike, as if it were a mere paragraph modifying an old constitution.

He never affects to believe that his power has a mystical origin, or even that it really springs from the people. See him, a few days after he has been proclaimed Emperor, seated in a bow window one evening after dinner. He is astraddle on a chair, with his chin resting on the back. For a long time he is silent while Josephine and Madame de Rémusat are talking (the latter records the incident). Then he stands up, turns to Madame de Rémusat, and, after posing for a while as an easy-going and cheerful man of the world, of a sudden, with that free gesture which always amazed his associates and still amazes posterity, he tore off the veil, disclosed his motives, expounded his thoughts as if he had been writing a predecessor's history:

"You were all very angry with me about the execution of the duke of Enghien. You seem still to be fond of traditional memories. My own memory goes back only to the time when I began to be something. What is a duke of Enghien to me? An émigré, more important than the others, and therefore one whom it is all the better to destroy. . . . Two years ago, power dropped into my hands in the most natural way in the world. . . . It is true that the duke compelled me to cut the crisis short. I had expected to carry on the Consulate for another two years, although its forms conflicted with the reality of things. France and I could have walked along arm-in-arm for a while longer, for France had confidence in me, and wanted everything that I wanted. But after this conspiracy, which was to set the Continent in motion, it was necessary to show Europe the error of her ways. . . .

"The political parties I wished to conciliate, the royalists and the Jacobins, will not lose heart as long as they have somebody to dread. I realised, therefore, that no pact between them could be concluded, but that it would be possible to conclude one with them to my own advantage. . . . Now, they have been reduced to silence. Still opposed to me are the republicans, the cranks who believe that Europe will look on quietly while a republic is being established upon the ruins of a monarchy. . . . That is why I preferred the imperial dignity to a dictatorship, for in an empire people no longer feel that they are travelling in unmapped country. . . .

"You will soon see what a lure court etiquette will exercise on the émigrés. The old familiar forms of address will win over the nobility. . . . You French love monarchy. It is the only form of government which really suits you. I will wager, Monsieur de Rémusat, that you feel a hundred times more at ease now that you call me 'Sire' and I address you as 'Monsieur' . . . Your vanity was always being bridled; the strictness of the republic would have bored you to death. . . . Liberty is no more than a pretext; equality is your hobby horse; the people are content to be ruled by a prince who comes from the army. . . . To-day, soldiers and people are on my side. A man who could not rule under such conditions would be an idiot."

He broke off, resumed a formal demeanour, and gave Monsieur de Rémusat an order of no importance whatever in the dry tone of the absolute master.

These moments of confession; these quarters of an hour in which we stand opposite him, silently listening and watching, while he lounges on his chair, this newly made emperor of thirty-four in his well-worn green coat, looking askance up and down the room, rising to walk restlessly to and fro, pouring out his most intimate thoughts and then with a brusque transition cutting off all the springs of familiarity; when we see him in such movingly close proximity, in scenes full of nature and purpose, full of surrender to destiny and animus against the present—we can see and hear for ourselves even more than he frankly discloses in simulated self-forgetfulness. We become aware of his easy contempt for persons of noble birth, which is none the less conjoined with a secret wish to make a good impression on them; we discern programmes which he is always willing to adapt to changing circumstances; we observe the robust cynicism aroused in him by the folly of mankind, and see that it exists side by side with the foreign character traits of this Corsican, the very traits which enable him to rule the lovely Marianne with such gallant rigour.

Of course he discloses no more than half his motives, for he is here confining himself to political issues. Still, at the outset of the imperial epoch these political issues exert a predominant influence. It seems as if, to begin with, he regards the change of title with the utmost sobriety: "My brother will not hear a word of his new title," writes Napoleon to Madame de Staël. "He says he is just the same man he was before, and at the same time he puts on great airs. The truly great man is the one who fully realises that such empty names, which only the system of society compels us to assume, make no difference to friendship, to family life, or to social relationships. I am certain that since I have been 'Your Majesty,' not one of those who live with me will have been able to detect any difference in me."

Yet it is an event that now for the third time he takes leave of his name. It may be nothing that the leading persons in the country who appear at the first court reception address him and Josephine as "Sire" and "Madame," and that the members of the noblesse, who on this same polished floor fifteen or twenty years earlier had said "Sire" and "Madame," should feel their hearts revive as they bandy courtiers' compliments. That may be nothing. Certainly, as regards essential nature, clothing, and deportment, the Emperor of to-day is no different from the Consul of yesterday.

But the proclamation, the thousand and one letters, memoranda, and decrees, will henceforward be signed with a new name. For eight years they have been signed with the rudiments of a "Bonaparte." Now he signs with a name which he himself has never written since he was a child, and which his nervous hand will speedily compress into an initial N. and a flourish. Josephine has always addressed him as "General." His brothers and his sisters have for a long time past spoken to him with the ceremonial "you" instead of the familiar "thou" (the change was initiated, not by the Consul himself, but by Joseph). Only his mother in rare moments of expansion has occasionally used her son's Christian name; and she utters it in her own dialect as "Napolione."

There is a profound significance in the newness of this name when, adding to it a brand-new title, he writes for the first time in his life:

Napoleon I., Emperor of the French.

VIII

With the first steps, the dilemma begins. The new coins he issues bear the legend: "Emperor according to the Constitution of the Republic"—this paradox will dog him for another four years. When the anniversary of the taking of the Bastille and the outbreak of the revolution comes round once more, he celebrates it with imperial pomp. The gesture may look sublime, but it is nothing more than a measure of political expediency. Even on this very first occasion, the anniversary of the day of liberation is postponed to a Sunday. A year or two later, the commemoration is completely ignored. With it vanishes the revolutionary calendar, for the old one is restored by degrees.

All flock to his standard. Ere long, one hundred and thirty of those who twelve years earlier had voted for the king's execution, hold office under the Emperor. This is the revolutionary picture caricatured in France, while Europe looks on, watching how first the forms, and then by slow stages the content, for whose sake so much blood has been shed, are laid aside in the museum of history. What can Europe do but smile?

Still more broadly smiles the old noblesse. In the Faubourg Saint-Germain, which the emperor watches as closely as he watched the working-class quarter of Saint Antoine, anecdotes are rife concerning the new master in the old Tuileries. Now that he is called "Sire," just like the last of the Bourbons, all the lorgnettes are turned on him, and he has become the focus of criticism. As far as his own personality is concerned, so great is his native dignity that he is practically above criticism; in Milan, already, when no more than a general of the French Republic, he ruled simply because he was there. But his relatives, with their childish curiosity and jealousy, and with their gossip about everything that goes on in the palace, soon become the targets of mockery. Magnified by rumour, and carried across the frontiers, this ridicule besmirches the master.

Henceforward England keeps in Paris, in addition to ordinary spies, a horde of quilldrivers, whose tales find credence whenever they are enlivened with wit. Caricatures pass from hand to hand, showing the little lieutenant being taught by the great Talma how to walk like an emperor—Napoleon, who has often taught Talma the best way of playing the royal roles in Corneille! How otherwise could old Europe defend herself against this saga which had become reality? The only resource was to degrade to farce what was being staged with all the crude seriousness of tragi-comedy.

For the Emperor needs a court! It is his way to do everything with due attention to detail; but the details of court life are beyond the range of his studies, and he has to call in the experts of the old regime. The sometime chamberlain at the court of the late king must lay aside his pen (literature had been the resource of his retirement), to resume his staff of office. Josephine, who at first is attended by no more than a few of the ladies of the former court, is at a loss as to the management of an empress' train. What has become of Marie Antoinette's lady-in-waiting? She is still alive, and keeps a school in Paris. Bring her forth from her obscurity! She comes, and in the same rooms, before the same mirrors, arranges the folds of the train round these Creole feet which know very different dances from those of the poor dead queen.

The Emperor organises his court with the same seriousness and the same precision as if he were organising the general staff of a new army. No one knows better than Napoleon the vanity of these things: "I am well aware that plenty of people are writing unfavourably about them. Even you, Monsieur Roederer, are not complaisant enough to suppose that I have a little common sense! You ought to understand without my telling you why I have given my new marshals, plain republicans though they be, the title of 'Monseigneur'; it is only to safeguard my own imperial title of 'Majesty'? The marshals, having grand titles of their own, cannot make fun of mine." His very first undertakings as Emperor involve him in the toils of such contradictions.

The two ex-consuls (these are the only offices suppressed by the Emperor) become respectively arch-chancellor and arch-treasurer of the Empire. Talleyrand, as grand chamberlain, brings back the old arts and graces into the old house. How easy it would be for the Emperor to appoint none but gentlemen and ladies of the old regime to the leading offices at court! Instead, he chooses the scions of the proletariat and the bourgeoisie, the men who have risen with him: Berthier, Murat, Lannes, Ney, and Davoust. Fourteen generals, who in youth had been bakehouse lads, stable boys, waiters, cabin boys, or vagrants, must now exchange their campaigners' uniforms for the gold-braided coats of the marshals of France, must double their military duties with offices at court, must wear lace ruffs and buckled shoes; their wives must learn how to curtsey in the grand manner, how to stand and sit properly, how to scratch at the door instead of knocking—all that Europe may see how the Emperor, who was himself a lieutenant, promotes his lieutenants according to merit. Marmont is there, still wearing his arm in a sling; he is decked out in silk and satin and gold; but the slit sleeve, with its reminiscence of martial glory, seems to mock the splendour of his breeches. The Emperor tactfully drops out of the ceremonial two details that were degrading to the dignity of the courtiers: the presentation of the shirt at the king's levee, and the kissing of the ruler's hand.

But how is the charm of the rococo court to be revived, now that a soldier sits upon the throne? True, that, after hours of deliberation, it is possible to decide what colours the empress and the highnesses (Napoleon's relatives) must wear when they go out hunting. When, however, the time has come to bring down the stag, and the Emperor's thoughts are wandering in other fields, no one else ventures to shoot, with the result that the stag escapes because the chief sportsman has so much else on his mind. The ceremonial "was conducted as if to the sound of drums; everything seemed to happen at the storming pace; and the dread which he inspired in all, drove away grace and ease. . . . Court life was cold and dull, was gloomy rather than dignified. Since we were following a prescribed ritual, our inner feeling was that we were only machines which some one had placed upon the new gilded couches."

The Emperor is bored by ladies' society. With blunt circumstantiality, he asks how many children they have had, and whether they suckle their own babies. He tries to make himself agreeable, but often fails, when his thoughts range to other matters. At Saint-Cloud, in a room full of ladies, he can find nothing to say but, again and again: "How hot it is here!"

All the same, every one attached to the court grows rich. He gives princely salaries to the court officials, and only shows thrift in his payments to some of the members of the old noblesse, maliciously implying that such work is nothing more than their duty. In general, he pays munificently, for "ambition is the mainspring of action. People work so long as they are aspiring upwards. . . . I have made senators and princes in order to promote ambition, and to make them dependent on me." He thus uses both honours and money to attach people to his cause, making, not friends, but dependents.

He knows the value of money; and though at all the critical moments of his career he surprises us by improvisation, we are, in general, just as much astonished by the way in which he continually displays a bourgeois rationality and foresight. His own demands are moderate. The Emperor's personal salary is fixed at twenty-five millions, the amount paid to the late king; but where as Louis had spent forty-five millions, Napoleon saves twelve. The whole court, resplendent though it is, does not cost a fourth as much as the Bourbon court. France, which has to foot the bill, owes this economy to the care and knowledge of the master, who once had to live on ninety francs a month, and even now declares that he could get along well enough with twelve hundred francs a year and a horse.

There was no change in his routine of life. The Emperor was called at seven, and held his first reception at nine. Most of the day, his secretaries were engaged in taking down from dictation. This dictation was at the speed of ordinary conversation, and must be transcribed with perfect accuracy. At night, when he had some difficulty in sleeping, Méneval must come to record his master's night thoughts. His dinner took twenty minutes, and he hardly noticed what he was eating. He was much more plainly clad than his gaily bedecked courtiers; and when, on State occasions, he had to dress ceremoniously, he was always in a bad temper while being arrayed, and greatly relieved when he could doff his finery. When he entered Saint-Cloud after the place had been done up, he regarded it with disfavour, saying: "Rooms like this are suitable for a kept woman; they lack seriousness."

He does not allow himself to be enslaved by anything, and never insists that his bed or his meals or the lighting shall be just so and no otherwise. Even the snuff-box that he always carries is no more than a toy. The only things which the Emperor finds indispensable are open fires, hot baths, eau-de-cologne, Chambertin, and clean linen twice a day.

Josephine is extravagant. Her seven hundred dresses and two hundred and fifty hats, her jewels, her shawls, and her hair-dressing, cost millions; and although the Emperor wants her to shine in all the splendours which he scorns for himself, he often grumbles at the preposterous totals of the bills.

His brothers and sisters squander money too. He gives them everything, and they are never satisfied. There is an absurd rivalry between the five couples (Lucien is still banished) and Josephine, whom all the others detest. Of the six grand dignitaries who draw fabulous salaries, four are his near relatives, by blood or by marriage. Joseph is grand elector; Louis, constable; Eugene, arch-chancellor of State; and Murat, high admiral. Since the brothers are to be styled Imperial Highnesses, the sisters have their noses put out of joint, and make a collective demand, complaining that Hortense, as the wife of Louis, has become Imperial Highness, while they are "nothing." He eyes them for a moment, and replies with a witticism which deserves a place in universal history: "When I listen to you, I can almost believe that His Majesty our father of blessed memory must have bequeathed us crown and realm!"

Indeed, one could almost believe it. For when he complies with their demand, with a good nature he is not apt to show towards others, and when for ten years to come he showers honours and wealth, crowns and territories, upon these brothers and sisters who show no gratitude, who never obey him, and never cease to trouble him—we cannot but ask ourselves once more what can be the prejudice which blinds his eyes where they are concerned. His pride is great; he is lonely in his self-confidence; his path is that of a pioneer; in this instance as in others, his motives must be mixed; in part obscurely felt, in part coldly calculated.

He is half an oriental, and it tickles his fancy to bestow diadems as he used to bestow swords and snuff-boxes; but all the same, he warily contrives that power shall be given to those only on whom he can rely. Well, what is thicker than blood? Even his companions-in-arms seem to him less trustworthy than his relatives; but for his trust in them, his relatives will repay him with ingratitude, and in the end his sister will betray him. Because in this one respect he infringes his own principle of equality and departs from his determination to choose only the efficient, because he appoints brothers and nephews to high office and looks upon them as his heirs, he cannot give them the free hand which it is his way to give all his generals within the limits of their commissions. By treating his relatives as an all-powerful minister treats princes who are still under tutelage, he enrages them, and lays up a store of bitterness for himself.

Joseph is already animated by a mocking spirit. He tells his daughter to address His Majesty as "Consul"; holds disputations in democratic circles; refuses to become a minister of State; but accepts an allowance of two millions as an imperial prince, and lives at the Luxembourg, which his brother hands over to him. At length Napoleon loses patience. The ostensible cause of his anger is a trifle, but all the rage of his heart is now vented in this complaint:

"What on earth is Joseph thinking about? Does he imagine that he has been made prince in order to hobnob with my enemies and walk up and down the streets of Paris in brown surtout and round hat? I have sacrificed my own personal pleasures in order to become what I am. I am as well fitted as another to shine in society! . . . But things of that sort do not help a man to rule. Does he dream of disputing with me for the supreme power? My strength is builded on a rock! . . .

"Do you know what he ventured to say to me recently in the presence of two others? I ought not to have my wife crowned; the step would be opposed to his interest; it would give Louis' children a better position than his, because they would be the grandsons of an empress! He had the impudence to talk to me about his rights and his interests! He wanted to touch me on the raw! He might almost as well have boasted he had slept with my mistress, or hoped to do so soon. My mistress! Power is my mistress! The conquest of that mistress has cost me so much that I will allow no one to rob me of her, or to share her with me!"

Thus does the volcano suddenly spout forth great rocks, in the midst of a conversation about trifles. But the rest of the conversation does not turn wholly on trifles. He speaks bitterly of his brothers and sisters, comparing them with Eugene and Hortense. "My stepchildren always side with me. If their mother is put out because I take a fancy for a pretty girl, they say to her: 'Oh, well, he's still quite young, you know. You mustn't make a fuss. No doubt he has faults, but you must not forget how much he has done for us all.' "

But nothing will keep him from pushing his brothers' advancement. When Joseph refuses all other occupations, Napoleon forces him into the army. "He must have military rank, get a nice wound, and win a good reputation for himself. I shall only give him easy jobs. Then he can win a battle, and I shall be able to promote him to a higher rank than all the other commanders." It sounds like the education of a degenerate son by a great father.

Louis has an enthusiasm for poetry; he becomes chief of the imperial guard, so that he may have a dignified position; but he can stay at home when the guns begin to shoot.

Murat and Caroline are frightfully extravagant; their table service is of gold. "As for Caroline, my own sister, if I have to discuss anything with her, I must make longer speeches than at the Council of State. . . .

"The whole lot of them are always thinking about my death. It's rather nasty of them to be continually bringing that into my mind. . . . Were it not that I find some happiness in my home life, I should be miserable! Why are they always so suspicious of my wife? What has she more than they? Diamonds and debts! . . . She's a good wife to me, and does them no harm! She's rather fond of playing the empress, with her jewels, her dresses, and the whimsies natural to her age. I have never been blinded by love. But I am just. She shall be crowned, even if it costs me two hundred thousand men!"

Thus he is continually bickering with a family which he could reduce to nonentity in a moment, but from which he is unable to cut adrift.

Only one of them is incorruptible, asks for nothing, and holds aloof. Lucien writes from Rome:

"Mother thinks that the First Consul is wrong to take the Bourbons' crown. She has uneasy presentiments which she will not confide to me. Her dread is that a gang of fanatics will assassinate the Emperor."—While this dignified mother of the family, still a beautiful woman though well over fifty, is led by her knowledge of the world and her gloomy forebodings to keep herself to herself, while she holds her tongue and only mentions her anxieties to a few intimates, in the Tuileries her children are quarrelling about titles and precedence, disputing who is to sit at the Emperor's right, debating whether they are entitled to walk out of the room in front of a sovereign prince!

Then Napoleon summons Madame Mère to Paris. But here is one who will not obey him. At first she makes excuses. When more urgent commands are sent, she sets out on the journey, but takes her time, and does not reach Paris for the most splendid festival that a mortal mother can ever have witnessed. She hears and reads all that a gaping world says and writes about the affair. Her only comment is: "Pourvou que cela doure!"

IX

Meanwhile, Letizia's protector the pope has become more compliant, and is already on the way to Paris. What else could the Holy Father do? The man of might had summoned him, and the Emperor must be kept in a good humour. Besides, he who is to be crowned is an Italian. As one of the cardinals had put it, in the decisive conclave: "After all, we have this satisfaction, that we are taking vengeance on the Gauls by setting an Italian family to rule over these barbarians." Napoleon is still regarded as a foreigner in France! But why does he not go to Rome for his coronation? Why is he not content to be anointed in Rome, as Charlemagne had been, and all the emperors of the west since Charlemagne's day? What does he want a pope for at all?

In this matter, once more, he is trying to harmonise the new with the old. At first he is silent about details, and merely asks the pope "to give the highest religious consecration to the anointing and crowning of the first Emperor of the French." For weeks, letters have been exchanged between Rome and Paris, but the exact nature of the ceremony still remains obscure. Pius VII. is in an uneasy frame of mind as he draws near to Paris, and his spirit is by no means one of benediction. Never before has a pope been summoned in this way, much as a great physician is summoned. When the Emperor meets the pope at the gate of the city, the Holy Father does not fail to note that Napoleon neither kneels to receive a blessing nor kisses hands in token of fealty. Paris is a town where people's faith is unstable and where popes are held in little honour. The visitor is chilled.

But Josephine is different. All devotion, she confides to him that she and her husband were not married in church, and that therefore from the pope's point of view they are not married at all. She is eager to grasp the opportunity of consolidating her union, which seems to her frail in view of her barrenness. Taking the hint, Pius insists upon a religious celebration of the marriage before he will crown her as empress. In the palace chapel, two days before the festival, Uncle Fesch, clad in purple, solemnises the union of the pair who eight years before had needed the intervention neither of priests nor civilian officials before coming together. There are no witnesses, not one who could laugh over this comedy in which cheating is still the order of the day—for even the Corsican uncle is not aware what is about to happen.

On December 2, 1804, in Notre Dame, an abundance of precious stones reflects the light of a myriad candles, so that the place looks more like a banqueting hall than a church. Everything has been prepared for weeks beforehand. A skilful museum director has even produced a colourable imitation of Charlemagne's sceptre. Ancient parchments from the days of the Roi Soleil had been consulted, to ensure that the crowning of this revolutionist should vie in every respect with that of the legitimate monarchs of France. Ségur had studied the etiquette of the occasion with the utmost care; Isabey had rehearsed the whole affair with an array of dolls; the old palace, Paris, France, were in a fever.

The Emperor is in a pleasant humour. Early in the morning he makes sure that Josephine's crown is a good fit. The great procession drives to the cathedral. Napoleon, robed in an antique imperial mantle, strides to the high altar leading the empress by the hand. Josephine's charm helps to divest the great moment of a certain sense of embarrassment. Surrounded by attendant cardinals, the pope is seated, waiting. The organ peals forth.

Then, when the appointed instant has come, and all are expecting this man who has never bowed the knee to any one, to kneel before the Holy Father, Napoleon, to the amazement of the congregation, seizes the crown, turns his back on the pope and the altar, and, standing upright as always, crowns himself in the sight of France. Then he crowns his kneeling wife.

None but the pope had known his intentions. Informed at the eleventh hour, Pius had lacked courage to threaten immediate departure. Now, all he could do was to anoint and bless the two sinners. Moreover, the crown on the Emperor's head is not a Christian crown at all, but a small pagan circlet of golden laurel leaves. All who describe the occasion agree in saying that the Emperor was pale but handsome. He resembled Emperor Augustus; and from now onwards, as if by some mystical power, his features grew more and more like those of the first emperor of Rome.

Thus, in this symbolical hour, Napoleon reduces to mockery the legitimate formalities he is affecting to copy. Furthermore, he makes a laughing-stock of the pope, who will not forget the slight. In an instant the cloud of Bourbon reminiscence has been scattered; the flavour of imitation and parody has vanished; and on the steps of a temple there stands a soldier, a Roman imperator, whom a dozen years before this day no one had ever heard of, who since then has performed no miracles but only done deeds, and has now crowned himself with the golden laurels of these deeds. But his mantle is broidered with golden bees, the emblem of activity.

Several incidents show that he has not, throughout this day of his coronation, wholly surrendered to the mood of a man who has made his own destiny.

When he was seated on the throne, crown on head, with the pope in front of him, he said in a low aside to his brother: "Joseph, if only Father could see this!" The remark, poignant at such an hour in the mouth of a man who was never wont to speak of his father, is fundamentally natural. The perfect simplicity, the unsophisticated innocence, of his course of action, lead his mind back to his origin. Memories of family feuds on the island, of the pride and ambition of the Corsican clans, direct his thoughts towards the stock from which he has sprung.

Semblance never holds his attention, which always reaches out to the core of reality. Thus he is not bewildered even in this amazing hour. When he wants to whisper something to his uncle, who stands just in front of him during Mass, he gives the cardinal a gentle dig in the back with his sceptre. As soon as all is over, and, alone with Josephine, he goes in to dinner, he

(Photograph in the Kircheisen Collection.)

Bonaparte as First Consul. Pencil sketch by J. D. A. Ingres.
Germain Bapst Collection.

says with a sigh of relief: "Thank God we're through with it! A day on the battle-field would have pleased me better!" At their little dinner he tells her to keep on her crown, as if he and she were poet and actress, for, he says, she is charming, his little Creole woman as empress. Thus, in the most natural way in the world, he unmasks the whole masquerade, and we are at ease once more as we see the son of the revolution laughing his own empire to scorn.

The freedom of spirit shown by the foregoing petty details is splendidly illuminated by an admission he made the same evening, when, to a confidant, he summed up the whole matter with sceptical emotion: "No, Decrès, I have come into the world too late. There is nothing great left for me to do. I do not deny that I have had a fine career, but what a difference between me and the heroes of antiquity. Look at Alexander, for instance. After he has conquered Asia, he declares himself to be the son of Jupiter, and the whole East believes him, save only his mother and Aristotle and a handful of Athenian pedants. But if I, nowadays, were to declare myself the son of the Father Eternal, every fishwife would laugh in my face. There is nothing great left for me to do."

This was said a few hours after he had crowned himself emperor; said quite simply and quite truthfully. Is it not plain why the East has always allured him, and will continue to allure him? By nature he is endowed with immense powers, and is overburdened by their incredible weight. Nothing can be adequate to his aspirations, now that he has learned how readily people obey the man who can command obedience by his skill and by his deeds. He is strong in his own strength; what does Voltaire's enlightenment, what does Rousseau, matter to him? How can he wish to establish democracy, to install popular government, when he knows the weakness of the popular instincts, and all the corruptness of the leaders of the people? To expand his sway, to spread his name widely and ever more widely, to leave more record of himself in the book of universal history than that half page of which he spoke a few years ago, to sacrifice life itself to the little golden circlet on his head, to do these things without enjoyment and without leisure and without pause—this is all that life now offers.

When, during these days, the sketch for an imperial seal is laid before him, and he sees a lion couchant, he draws his pen across the picture, and writes in the margin: "An eagle volant."

X

But with a sinister energy the dangerous fluid of divine right radiates from the golden circlet, and slowly spreads its waves through the brain of the wearer, the chosen man. Vainly he endeavours to master and transform the millennial force that has been stored up in this crown, or to make light of it; it masters him, and from time to time forces him to quit the realm of his self-control. When, a year after his coronation as emperor, he crowns himself in Milan with the iron crown of the Lombards (for the border States, like France itself, are to become monarchies), his voice reverberates through the cathedral as he thunders the traditional formula of the Carlovingian kings: "God gave it to me, woe to him who touches it!" Of course, it is only the statesman who speaks, for sound political reasons saying something he does not believe. But, though he is well aware of the contradiction, he will not always be able to solve it with the same vigour as in Notre Dame.

In the first place, the new position makes it necessary to impose new fetters on the mind. The Ministry of Police is revived; and France is parcelled out into four great sectors, in which the most trusty members of the Council of State, each with an army of spies, keep watch upon the mood of the country, for he wants to collect "moral statistics." Fouché is reappointed Minister of Police, and, since Napoleon's ties with Talleyrand become increasingly close, the Emperor is by degrees enmeshed in the nets of the two great intriguers—though he is aware that they are playing a double game between himself and the Bourbons, and, by a second relay of spies, fruitlessly endeavours to keep watch and ward over his watchers.

Sinister figures, these two ex-clerics, whom he hates, who hate him, but whom he will never be able to shake off.

Fouché is a man of humble origin, pale, with a cold manner, taciturn, parchmenty. Though orders flash on his breast and a lace ruffle waves there, were it not for his piercing eyes he would look like a mummy in court dress.

Talleyrand is in all respects the man of noble birth. Lame though he be, the prettiest women pay court to him. His charm is that of a rolling sphere, whose living summit is everywhere and nowhere. The assertion that he betrayed his master only for the sake of France, is belied by his immeasurable avarice and venality. For the nonce, he continues to serve the Emperor; but, from the first, the two men have mistrusted one another. Once, indeed, Talleyrand made a sacrifice for Napoleon. Late in the evening, when the two were on a journey together, the Emperor summoned the minister to his bedside for a talk about public affairs. Suddenly Napoleon fell asleep, and Talleyrand sat on guard till morning, not stirring, lest he should wake his master. That is his version of the affair. But the man's whole nature is so remote from any idea of sacrifice or sympathy, that we may suppose rather that his motive was the hope that Napoleon might reveal some important secret by talking in his sleep.

A dozen times every year, the name of Madame de Staël crops up. Afraid of her and her works, he keeps her away from Paris with an obstinacy which arouses wonder. Yet she says of him: "His look grows infinitely tender when he speaks to women." Throughout Europe, the champions of the freedom of the spirit fall away from him; Byron, who had greatly admired him; Beethoven, who cancels the original dedication of the *Eroica* to Napoleon. With painfully mixed feelings the Emperor must have read the tribute of the mad tsar Paul, who had already acclaimed the First Consul as the suppressor of the revolution.

Since Marengo, he has been doing his utmost to maintain peace on the Continent, and for four years he has been successful. His hope is that the re-establishment of monarchy will appease the united princes, will assuage the anger they still cherish against France. The death of two men comes to thwart his plans. Tsar Paul is murdered, and this enemy of England is succeeded by a youthful son, an idealist, trained by French apostles of the enlightenment, a man with democratic leanings, gentle, muddle-headed, animated by the wish to be a better sovereign. Alexander, therefore, quickly comes to an understanding with England, where, after Fox's brief predominance and death, a transient attempt at peace with France has been followed by a revival of the old jealous enmity. England fails to evacuate Malta as had been arranged, imposes new conditions, and is the first to break the peace. Once more there arises the menace of a European coalition under English leadership, a coalition that will aim at a Bourbon restoration, for talent enthroned in France sets so dangerous an example to all other countries.

Thus, a year after the coronation, the war with England is resumed, and will not end until Napoleon's star sets. There is no campaigning, at first; simply a state of war, in which this great military commander cannot force a decision, and which, therefore, he cannot bring to a close. England has two notable advantages over her continental rivals, and over France in particular. It is an island realm; and it spreads athwart the world. Napoleon's historical sense, growing ever more alert, shows England to him as a new empire of Alexander, extending like Alexander's from homeland isles and peninsulas to Asia and to Africa, invincible so long as it remains a united whole. The dream of our new oriental splits upon this rock.

On this rock, too, are wrecked the mathematician's calculations. The day after Aboukir, he had said that a decade would be needed for the rebuilding of France's fleet. Half that time has elapsed, and England's naval predominance has steadily grown. During the brief peace, the soldiers of the unsuccessful Egyptian campaign are brought back to France in English bottoms; England is confirmed in the possession of the Cape and other overseas colonies; and France has more urgent claims on her energies than the building of the new fleet.

Fundamentally, what was a ship to the Emperor? He was competent to design a big gun, to cast it, to place every screw; and to repair every wheel and every shaft of an ammunition wagon. He knew when every horse in a cavalry squadron would have to be re-shod, and how much it would cost; and he knew exactly how many loaves a field bakery could turn out a day. This far-reaching knowledge was one of the secrets of his predominance; made his subordinates zealous in their terror of his incessant control, whether in peace time or in war time; aroused respect for the all-embracing intelligence of the chief; and ensured the exact carrying-out of his military ideas.

But one who would know a ship, must grow up in a ship, just as one who would know ordnance must have passed his youth among big guns. Even though his admirals were astonished to find how quickly he made himself at home in naval matters, how shrewd were his questions, and how sensible were his orders, still their commendation of Napoleon was no more than the praise of a kindly expert who, tacitly, is criticising a talented amateur. Napoleon knew this well enough. Since he lacked a great admiral quite as much as a great fleet, and had never been willing to entrust the conduct of a campaign to any subordinate, he invented a new kind of war which was to enable him, after all, to get the better of England. The European ports from Hamburg to Taranto were to be closed to English ships, and thus the nation of traders was to be vanquished in a trade war. At the same time, he revived his plans of invasion; for, could he but set foot on the island, he would be the military commander, and in his own element.

Just as he had done before the Egyptian campaign, so now in Boulogne, he studies the possibilities of embarkation and disembarkation. On land, his fantasy has found satisfaction and his mathematical powers have gained conquests in ardent imaginings; and yet, all the time, his battles have been realities, have realised these imaginings. But here, at sea, he is an amateur, not an expert; is, for the first time, the onlooker instead of the man of action. In none other of his private letters do we find sentences akin to those which he writes from the coast to Josephine after a stormy night in which a gunboat has broken away from her moorings: "A wonderful sight! The minute-guns were firing; watch-fires were lighted along the coast. A raging, foaming sea; uncertainty and anxiety throughout the night. But a kindly spirit brooded over the ocean and the night. No lives were lost, and I lay down to sleep with the feeling that I had been witnessing a romantic and epic vision—so that I could almost believe that I had been looking on quite alone."

A wonderful sight; but, alas, only a sight! The Ossianic note is sounded again, for the first time after fifteen years. Napoleon waxes romantic. How moving and how significant are the closing words of this artist, who suddenly feels that he has been robbed of the human material with which he works, and who is even a little alarmed (we cannot help but read this through the lines) at the unwonted sensation of being quite alone.

The unfamiliar element leads him astray. When a storm is threatening, he orders a naval review. Admiral Bruix does not carry out the order. The Emperor finds that no preparations are being made, and sends for the admiral. A terrible scene.

"Why did you not obey my orders?"

"Your Majesty can see that for yourself. You would not needlessly risk brave men's lives in such weather!"

The Emperor, surrounded by his rigid officers, turns pale with wrath, and says: "Sir, I have given you an order. The consequences are no concern of yours. Do what you are told!"

"Sire, I cannot obey."

An ominous pause. Napoleon strides towards Bruix, riding-switch in hand, threateningly, though the switch is not raised. The admiral draws back a step, and lays his hand on his sword-hilt. A petrified group.

"You will leave Boulogne within twenty-four hours, and betake yourself to Holland. Rear-Admiral Magon, carry out my orders."

A naval review is held in a raging storm. A number of chaloupes are capsized, and their crews struggle in the water. The Emperor, to save himself, jumps into the first boat; all who can, follow his example. Two hundred bodies are washed ashore next day.

This incident, unique in Napoleon's career, a blunder, an act of cruelty, a direct disobedience on the part of a subordinate, is a warning symptom. But there is a third indication.

A year before, an American inventor had come to Paris, and had offered the French admiralty two new inventions: one of them a ship to be propelled by steam power instead of by the wind; the other, a submarine boat which was to sink ships by the discharge of a kind of torpedo. "The man is a charlatan," was Napoleon's comment on Fulton, after an experiment in which the inventor's "plunging boat" had secured a partial success; and he brushed the whole matter aside. If the American had brought him models of a machine gun and a field telegraph, he would have opened his purse.

Napoleon failed to conquer England because this was the one matter in which he was not confident of victory. Failure was inevitable because here, and here only, his self-confidence was at fault; because his belief in his own powers was weakened by his want of expert knowledge and by the inaccessibility of the foe. By land! Yes, if he could only get at this island by land! The thought brings back to his mind the scheme of five years ago, when he had planned an attack on India by way of Herat. But for such a scheme, quiet and time are needed.

His first aim is to keep the peace, to bring about which he has worked with his best powers for years. Immediately after the coronation, he writes in this sense to six monarchs, addressing each in a style appropriate to his correspondent's character, thinking out the effect of every detail, and considering even the exact working of his signature. Note, for instance, how he writes to the shah:

"My reputation reaches so far, that you cannot fail to know who I am and what I have done; how I have made France supreme among the nations of the West; and how great an interest I take in the rulers of the East. . . . Orientals are full of courage and spirit, but their ignorance of certain arts and their neglect of military discipline put them at a disadvantage in war when they are faced by soldiers from the North. . . . Write me your wishes, and we will renew friendly and commercial relationships. . . . Written in my Imperial Palace of the Tuileries . . . in the first year of my reign. Napoleon." But, in the heading, the document sets forth a title which never existed, a title which Napoleon obviously uses to show the ruler of Persia that the writer is the general who made himself famous in the Egyptian campaign. The document purports to come from "Bonaparte, Emperor of the French."

On his table, as he signs the letter to the shah, lies a letter to George III., though England and France are at war. It is penned with wonderful art, and is both moving and politic: "Does not all the blood that is being shed without apparent advantage to any one, touch the consciences of the governments? I am not ashamed to take the first step. It seems to me I have shown the world that I have no dread of war and its caprices. My heart, indeed, longs for peace; but war has never dimmed my fame. I implore Your Majesty not to deprive yourself of the good fortune of restoring peace to the world! Do not leave this precious task to your children.

Never was there a more favourable opportunity of stilling angry passions. If this chance be missed, what will be the outcome of the war? During the last ten years, Your Majesty has won more territory and more treasure than all Europe possesses. What further could you expect from the war?"

How could the writer fail to smile at the realisation that the last argument could with equal force be turned against himself? The appeal is fruitless, for neither England nor the rulers on the mainland will tolerate the new power of France or its upstart emperor. A fourth coalition of the princes against the republic is imminent.

During the years of peace, he has been tolerably well content. His intimates at Malmaison have often described him as cheerful. Now he must take up arms once more, and resign himself to the knowledge that "it lies in the nature of things to continue this struggle between the past and the future, for the enduring coalition of our enemies makes it essential to attack them if we are to escape annihilation." There is the simple truth, spoken without exaggeration and without bitterness. If he did not create this nature of things, at any rate he stabilised it. Even though the first wars of France in the revolutionary epoch were purely defensive, the subsequent campaigns became offensive, and were transformed into wars of conquest by the impetus of the people's army and the outstanding genius of its commander.

Nevertheless, when he is thus challenged by opponents whom he has twice defeated, can we wonder that concrete plans which have hitherto followed his soaring imagination at a respectful distance, should now, likewise, begin to outsoar the boundaries of reason? In the opening years of the nineteenth century and here in the West, the Emperor might have kept the peace for another decade, that in the end he might measure his strength against England's in Asia. But when Europe's persistent desire for revenge upon revolutionary France spurs him into action, he conceives the great plan of a unified European realm.

Now for the second time (and for the last time down to our own days) a great and saving work will be attempted, and the attempt will fail.

Thus it is that Napoleon's crowning political thought issues out of a personal defensive. Now, when a new coalition is being formed, and formed against him, his ideal takes a fresh shape. For years his inward gaze has been concentrated on Alexander; now, instead, he sees the figure of Charlemagne. He goes to Aix-la-Chapelle, for a ceremonial visit to the tomb of the great Frankish emperor. "There will be no peace in Europe," he says at this time to his trusted companions, "until the whole continent is under one suzerain, an emperor whose chief officers are kings, whose generals have become monarchs. . . . Would you tell me that this plan is but an imitation of the old imperial constitution? Well, there is nothing new under the sun!"

This gradual transformation of his ideal, and the sustenance of the new ideal by the historical imagination, has immeasurable consequences. Precisely because the adoption of the Carlovingian scheme involves for him a renunciation, he storms forward in pursuit of it as if he were fighting for a province. The haste with which he tries to reconstruct the empire of Charlemagne is new, is symptomatic of a fever which will drive him towards new goals before he has reached the old ones.

XI

Since the spring, his army has been assembled in Boulogne in readiness for the repeatedly postponed landing in England. But in the autumn, when the menace of a fresh Austrian attack becomes a certainty, with a change of plans which is decided on in a couple of days and is carried out in a fortnight, he directs all his forces eastward, and is across the Rhine in advance of the news of his first movement. Just before leaving the coast, he dictates to Daru the whole scheme of the attack on Austria, "the order and length of the marches, the meeting places of the columns, the attacks by storm, the movements and the blunders of the enemy—all this two months before the events, and at a distance of six or seven hundred miles from the scene of action."

Austria had good reason for taking up arms once more. On the knob of the new king of Italy's sceptre, the lion of Venice was graven. This, and the seizure of Genoa, were urgent warnings to the Habsburg ruler not to venture across the Alps a third time. Francis must be content to fight the matter out on German soil. England was liberal with proffers of money; and the inexhaustible forces of Russia were again available for the coalition, as they had been when it was victorious during Bonaparte's absence in Egypt. The new tsar was determined to overcome Europe's old prejudice against Russia, and, with an exchange of roles, to draw his sword against the tyrant of the West. The secret of Napoleon's fighting technique had been learned, and this time the engineer should be hoist with his own petard.

But the soldier of genius can evolve new methods of victory. By forced marches he encircles the Austrians before they realise what is afoot, encloses them in an iron ring at Ulm, and compels the capitulation of an army which has not even a chance to fire a shot. "I have attained my end, and have annihilated the Austrian army by simple marches. Now I shall turn against the Russians. They are lost."

The habit of success is making him thrifty of his words. "I had a rough time of it, rougher than necessary," he writes to Josephine; "wet through day after day for a week, and my feet very cold." Among the gold-bedizened marshals, who are for the first time parading their splendours on foreign soil, stands Napoleon to receive the capitulation of Ulm. He wears the uniform of a private soldier, a mantle weather-worn at elbows and skirt, a hat without a cockade. His arms are locked behind. Of the imperial purple there is no sign.

Once more, as on the evening after Marengo, he offers peace, sends an admonitory letter to the defeated Austrian emperor, writing as usual with the frankness which is so annoying to the diplomats of Europe: "You will understand that it is only right and proper if I take advantage of my good luck to impose, as condition of peace, that you should give me guarantees against a fourth coalition with England. . . . Nothing would make me happier than to combine the tranquillity of my people with your friendship, upon which I venture to make a claim, despite the number and strength of my enemies in your entourage." At the same time, he marches on Vienna.

Then, while he is advancing at topmost speed, comes a blow. He learns that two days after his victory on land had come the sea-fight of Trafalgar, when England had almost annihilated the French fleet. Eighteen ships have been lost; Nelson is dead; the French admiral is a prisoner. Is this another disastrous hour, like the one when the news of Aboukir reached him in the desert? Courage! Then the situation was a hundredfold more difficult. We are not now cut off from Paris by the sea; we need no ships. With redoubled speed he marches on Vienna, which the enemy surrenders without a blow.

But the tidings of Trafalgar have renewed Francis' fixity of purpose, and have made Alexander firmer than ever. Both try to win over Prussia, which hesitates, and protracts negotiations. Napoleon vainly tempts the tsar with the promise of Turkey. In Brünn there is a great game of hide-and-seek, in which each power tries to keep the others in suspense and is disavowed by its own plenipotentiaries. The Emperor is the only ruler who improvises a political idea. Two days before the decisive battle, for which preparations are already being made, he writes to Talleyrand, who is negotiating in Brünn:

"I should have no serious objection to handing over Venice to the elector of Salzburg, and Salzburg to the house of Austria. I shall take Verona . . . for the kingdom of Italy. . . .

The elector can call himself king of Venice if he has a fancy that way.

"The electorate of Bavaria would become a monarchy. . . . I will give back the artillery, the magazines, and the fortresses, and they must pay me five millions. . . . To-morrow, I think, we shall have a pretty big battle with the Russians. I have done my utmost to avoid it, for it is only useless bloodshed. I have exchanged a few letters with the tsar, and learn from what he writes that he is a good fellow, with bad counsellors. . . . Write to Paris, but don't say anything about the battle, for that would make my wife anxious. You don't need to worry. I am in a very strong position here, and my only regret is for the almost needless bloodshed which the battle will cost. . . . You write home for me; I have been in camp among my grenadiers for the last four days, and have to write on my knees, so I can't manage many letters."

Such is the Emperor's mood just before the most famous of his victories. While he is studying his maps, noting the name of every Moravian village, the width of every stream, and the condition of every road, and while he does his best to keep himself warm by the camp-fire, he is thinking of the ministers in Paris who are awaiting his commands, and of his wife who may be anxious. In the same half hour, he drafts a new programme for the partition of four or five States, talks of new crowns, of war indemnities, and of handing over fortresses. Twice his laments for the useless bloodshed light up the written page like the rising sun of one of these December days. Need we be surprised that such a man conquers the legitimate princes, who at this moment are dining in their palaces?

In the evening, when he learned the enemy's movements, he clapped his hands, and, "trembling with joy" (the words are his adjutant's), said: "They are walking into the trap! They are delivering themselves into my hands! By to-morrow evening, their army will be annihilated!"

Then he sits down with his staff to supper in a peasant's hut, and, an unusual thing with him, remains at table for some time after his meal, emotioned and musing. He goes on to speak at considerable length concerning the nature of tragedy. From this, he passes to Egypt: "If I had taken Acre, I should have donned a turban, have clad my soldiers in wide Turkish trousers. But only in the utmost need should I have exposed my Frenchmen to serious danger; I should have made of them a corps of immortals, the Holy Battalion. I should have fought the war with the Turks to a finish by the use of Arab, Greek, and Armenian levies. I should have won a great battle at Issus, instead of in Moravia, should have become Emperor of the East, and should have made my way back to Paris through Constantinople." The concluding words, so one who heard the soliloquy tells us, were accompanied with a smile, as if to show his awareness that he was being carried away by a rapturous dream.

But is not the scene we are describing a dream? Must we really and truly believe that, little more than a century ago, a mortal man, the understudy of a demigod, stormed across modern Europe and remoulded it in accordance with his will? Did it not all happen in the Homeric age, when two princes in single combat would settle the fate of generations? Or, perhaps, he is a character in a fairy-tale, this man in the middle thirties, a little fellow, seated in a wattle-and-dab hut, on an unknown plain. He wears a greasy coat, a clammy shirt; stuffs potatoes and onions into his hungry mouth. Next day, by this one battle, he will renew the glories of Charlemagne, dead a thousand years since. Now, over night, his unbridled imagination wanders across Asiatic deserts, where a stone-heap successfully resisted him; dwells on that old frustrated plan; while his errant thoughts follow the wraith of the Macedonian to the Ganges.

Day dawns. A year ago, on the altar steps in Notre Dame, he had crowned himself with the circlet of golden laurels. In a fervent proclamation, he reminds his soldiers of that day, and concludes with the promise that for this once he will keep out of the firing line.

Never before has history recorded such words uttered by a commander. They have always been eager to declare their determination to defy death in the forefront of the battle. Napoleon, whose grenadiers have seen him in twenty fights and regard him as a heavenborn leader, can venture to tell his men that he will reward their valour by being careful of his own safety.

Then the Emperor defeats both his enemies, and makes famous for a thousand years an out-of-the-way spot of which no one had ever heard before—the plain of Austerlitz.

"Soldiers," he says next day to the victors, "I am pleased with you. . . . Name your children after me, and if one of them should prove worthy of us, I will make him my own son and appoint him my successor!" That is the emotional note he keeps for the army. To his wife, he writes as simply as possible: "I have beaten the Russian and Austrian armies. Rather tired, after a week in the open, when the nights have been chilly. To-night I shall sleep in a bed, in Prince Kaunitz' fine castle. I'm wearing a clean shirt, the first time for a week. . . . I hope to get two or three hours' sleep."

Quite a simple matter, these momentous happenings! It is but a new song in the rhapsody when, a day later, Emperor Francis comes to Count Kaunitz' castle, to beg for an interview with the little Corsican lieutenant. But the bird has flown. When the two men meet at length, it is in a windmill. Napoleon greets his brother emperor courteously, saying: "I regret, Sire, that I must receive you here, in the only palace I have entered for two months." What self-confidence in the soldier interviewing the man born in the purple; what subtle mockery in the mouth of one who knows that in his distant capital, at news of his splendid victory, flags will soon wave and songs resound.

But the distinguished guest, a man of sound sense and good breeding, knows how to parry the thrust: "Your present quarters are so profitable to you, Sire, that I think they cannot fail to please you." Both smile; and unobtrusively they eye one another up and down, for, though they have fought for a decade, they have never met. Of the same age, they had both reached power at twenty-six or thereabouts, though in such different ways; and neither of them can foresee how close Napoleon's will-to-peace is one day to bring them, or how widely Francis' will-to-revenge will ultimately sever them.

"Yesterday I had the German emperor in camp with me and we had two hours' talk. . . . He threw himself on my generosity. But I took good care of myself, as I am used to doing. . . . We have agreed to make peace promptly. . . . The battle of Austerlitz is the finest of all I have fought. We have taken forty-five regimental colours, more than one hundred and fifty guns, the flag of the Russian guard, twenty generals, and thirty thousand prisoners in all. More than twenty thousand killed—a ghastly sight!" Did the jubilant outburst of a conqueror ever come to a stranger close? He luxuriates in the figures of his gains, and then, suddenly, the corpses of the dead rise before his eyes! Henceforward, such references become frequent; he writes in simple and heartfelt words about bloodshed.

In the peace negotiations, the minister has a contest with his master. The day after Austerlitz, Talleyrand writes to the Emperor: "How easy would it be, now, to destroy the Habsburgs once for all. But it would suit our book better to strengthen them, to give them a fixed place in France's system!" Napoleon, however, enforces the peace of Pressburg, in which the old German empire is shattered into fragments, while Austria vanishes from Germany and Italy. What is in the conqueror's mind?

Europe! A league of States under French hegemony. Russia is Asia; England is detached, an island. The Continent must be unified, must consist of middle-sized and small powers overshadowed by the eagles of France, and democratically ranged side by side. Now, after Austerlitz, the new thought takes shape. The victory has put it within his power to realise the greatest aim of a European, the unification of Europe.

He did not set out towards this goal. It was a gradual growth, the fruit of circumstances. He did not deliberately provoke the wars that were fought when the new idea was in its inception. Since Marengo, his chief wish has been for peace. At that time, Austria had been loath to make peace. The Austrian renewal of the attack was a logical outcome of legitimist theory, for Habsburg and the revolution could not jointly rule Europe. Austerlitz had settled the dispute once more. Now it had become possible to reunite Charlemagne's resurrected Europe. But neither the kings and emperors (who were only beaten, not convinced), nor he himself (who had gained all by the sword and not by persuasion), could march along the way of the spirit towards the unification of Europe. The determinisms of his own past left Napoleon no option but to create his United States of Europe by force. Not till ten years later did he come to see that he had been seeking to achieve a great end by false means.

When he came to understand this, it was too late; he was impotent, in the great epilogue of his exile.

XII

"Tell the pope that I am keeping my eyes open; tell him that I am Charlemagne, the Sword of the Church, his Emperor, and as such I expect to be treated."

Thus threateningly he writes to Rome. If he must bow before this mole-hill, at least he will enforce obedience. His demeanour is infused with a new tone since Austerlitz and Pressburg. From conquered Austria, he writes in a dictatorial style which neither he nor Europe has hitherto known.

The queen of Naples, despite his yearlong warnings, has permitted English ships to anchor in the bay. An army order is issued: "The Bourbon dynasty has ceased to reign in Naples." Simultaneously, he writes to Brother Joseph: "I think I have already told you that I intend the kingdom of Naples to accrue to my family, so that, like Switzerland, Holland, Italy, and the three German kingdoms, it may belong to my federated States or, rather, to the French Empire."

Henceforward he endeavours to make the plan a reality, the plan whereby Europe shall be governed by one emperor with kings as vassals. Paris, which now acclaims the conqueror, shall be the capital city of the Continent. The Emperor has, in the best sense of the term, "come home again." He exclaims: "This campaign has made me fat! I believe that if all the princes of Europe were to ally themselves against me, I should develop an absurdly wide paunch!" In such a mood does he hurl himself from recent events into new adventures and allow them to run their course.

During the next few months he organises, from Paris, the following realms: Joseph becomes king of Naples; the princes of Bavaria and Württemberg are turned into kings; Baden is changed into a grand duchy; Eugene weds a daughter of the House of Wittelsbach; a Badenese hereditary prince marries a niece of Josephine's; a Württemberg princess is reserved for his youngest brother; sixteen States of southern and western Germany are joined together to form the Confederation of the Rhine, vassals of the Emperor, liable for the payment of tribute and the provision of troops, and the sixteen German princes hasten to Paris to vow allegiance, hoping to get a share for themselves in the great mart; a dozen small principalities are wiped out; imperial fiefs are established for Talleyrand, Berthier, and Bernadotte.

Meanwhile Napoleon announces, curtly and conclusively: "Holland has no executive. She must have one. I will give her Prince Louis. We will frame a treaty. . . . For me the whole matter is settled: either thus, or annexation to France. . . . Not a minute must be lost." Why "not a minute"? Holland has been dependent for years; she only needs a crowned vassal; her dependence is to be made clearer by the phrasing, "Napoleon bestows his brother on Holland." The Dutch object? Then they shall be gobbled up; the choice is quickly made. Louis does not care for the honour; climate bad; health weak? "It is better to die sitting on a throne, than to live a mere prince in France." Hortense must become a queen, Josephine is aglow for the consummation; the Dutch must present a solemn petition, and must be graciously received by the Emperor in the Tuileries. But Napoleon is so overcome by the irony of the situation, he is so contemptuous, that after the audience he cannot resist telling his little nephew (son of the new king of Holland), in front of the ladies of the court, the fable of the frogs who wanted a king.

What next? His sisters are complaining and intriguing. Are there no more kingdoms available? The pity of it. Oh well, a few grand duchies must be vacated! Through Murat's promotion, Caroline becomes grand duchess of Cleves; Elise is made grand duchess of Tuscany; and the lovely Pauline Borghese weeps because she is nothing more than princess of Guastalla. "Why, it's no more than a village! And I'm to be princess of that?" Still, she soon finds consolation in an ocean of diamonds and lovers.

None of the clan are equal to the occasion. King Joseph, in his first proclamation, compares the love of his subjects (who have never clapped eyes on him till yesterday) towards himself with the love of the French towards their emperor. He covers himself with ridicule, and makes the Emperor furious. King Louis utters piteous sighs because the war with England forces him to interfere with "his country's" trade; and he sends, instead of troops, long letters to the Emperor filled with complaints. "Really, you are throwing unnecessary burdens upon me," replies Napoleon, in a hectoring tone. "It is all due to your narrow-mindedness and your lack of interest. . . . I wish you were not always whining! . . . Leave wailing and complaining to women; a man must be determined. . . . You are governing far too gently. You allow me to bear the full brunt of the war expenses. . . . See to it that you raise an army of thirty thousand men. You only think of yourself; that is neither good nor magnanimous. . . . More energy!"

Elise, who dominates her husband, gives a constitution to Tuscany, holds reviews of the troops, changes her favourites every quarter, and amuses Napoleon by an assumption of the imperial style: "My people is content; the opposition is crushed; your commands, Sire, have been carried out. I am much pleased with the Senate; it is showing deference to my authority."

Murat, for excess of zeal, draws upon himself a reprimand phrased with Napoleon's customary bluntness: "I have seen decrees issued by yourself which are quite senseless. You seem to have lost your reason! . . . All you appear to have in mind is to reign and nothing more!"

Pauline, however, is immortalised by Canova, in a work which outlasts all the realms Napoleon has set up.

Young Jerome, who has gone to America in his capacity of midshipman, has meanwhile married a lady of the middle class without consulting his family. The Emperor, who has more crowns to dispose of than siblings to give them to, and cannot spare any of his brothers, is outraged by this marriage. He pursuades his mother to utter a prohibition. When the young man's ship puts in to Lisbon, the vessel is surrounded; Jerome alone is permitted to land. Bidding the lady farewell, the youthful husband swears everlasting troth; he travels alone to Paris; is received by the Emperor with threats and lures; at length he gives up his spouse for the sake of princely honours and a post as admiral; maybe, even, he will become a king. The wife fruitlessly endeavours to land on the Continent; she journeys to England, where she brings a child into the world.

There she meets Lucien, her companion in misfortune. He has been well received by the English, and settles in the island realm with his wife and children. He writes poetry. An epic. What is it called?

Charlemagne.

The only member of the family who is active, loyal, and, for the most part, judicious in his undertakings is Napoleon's step-son Eugene. The Emperor loves him, publicly praises his work whenever possible, and now, when Eugene becomes viceroy of Italy and spouse of the Bavarian Princess, Napoleon writes: "You are working too hard, dear son. That is all very well for yourself, but you have a young wife who has hopes. . . . Why do you not go once a week to the theatre and occupy the royal box? . . . One can accomplish much business in a short time. I am leading the same kind of life as yourself, but my wife is getting on in years—also I have more business to deal with!" To his step-daughter-in-law, from whom he categorically demands a male heir (seeing that Hortense's son has but one life, and the dynasty needs additional safeguards!), he writes: "Do not give us a daughter, please! Here is a recipe for you: drink some undiluted wine, daily—only you'll never believe me!" When, in his despite, she gives birth to a daughter, he says: "If one begins with a daughter, one is destined to have a dozen children!"

How marvellously Napoleon, the great stylist, can accommodate his tone to every circumstance—to inspire dread or to flatter, to praise, to spur on, to punish, or to persuade. He pours this out upon a family which is ever acting in opposition to him, and expends himself thus in the interludes of all his other business.

The Emperor's mother lives in Paris, as retired a life as her son will allow. She is watchful and conciliatory. He has installed her in the Trianon; gives her one million a year. No one understands why she is so thrifty. Some use the word "miserly." But she maintains that "we Corsicans have experienced many revolutions; all this may come to an end; what will then happen to my children? It is better that they should come to their mother, than go to strangers who might leave them in the lurch." From time to time she holds a reception, where she carries herself with natural dignity, and far more regally than many of her children who wear the royal crown. If any one haggles as to the price of the beads with which she works, she smiles and says: "No, you can't impose upon me. I do not play the princess as my daughters do." Though she is the mother of the Emperor, and of kings and princes, she laments that not a single trustworthy person is in her immediate entourage. She only unbends over a game of reversi with old friends of hers; or when she chats of an evening with her faithful servant, discussing "the happy days gone by. . . . They all say that I am the happiest of mothers. In truth I am always full of worry. Every news item makes me tremble lest the Emperor lie dead upon the battle-field."

On Sundays, following the tradition of her patrician ancestors, she dines with her children at the Tuileries. She does not invariably obey the Emperor; and when he constrains her, she is resentful. No doubt he is aware that she is too proud to accept the relationship which circumstances have established between them; and whenever he looks in the mirror, he cannot fail to see his increasing personal resemblance to his mother, in forehead, mouth, eyes, and hands. Sometimes he teases her:

"Do you find life at court tedious? Look at your daughters! Why do you hoard your money? You ought to spend freely!"

"You'd better allow me two millions instead of one, if that is what you want. But it's my nature to be thrifty."

She has as keen an eye for the detection of flatterers as Napoleon himself, and gently warns him against them from time to time. Though she never asks anything for herself, she will often enough beg him to help the numerous Corsicans who come to visit her, and thus does her best for whilom family friends. Once, indeed, and late in the day, she puts in a plea for something she has much at heart. She would like Ajaccio to become the capital of Corsica, instead of Corte. A stirring of family pride! The Emperor issues a decree to this effect, understanding perfectly well what moves her, and says: "My mother was born to reign over a kingdom."

But she cannot get him to do anything for Lucien. "I love him more than all the others," she says, "because he's not been so lucky." The Emperor is adamant: "No feelings of affection can weigh against reasons of State. I will only accept as relatives, those who serve me. He who does not soar with me, ceases to belong to my family."

XIII

At Paris, in his study, Napoleon has a silent witness of his activities; a bronze bust of Frederick the Great.

He had grown up in the days when the renown of the last of the famous commanders was still fresh; and, indeed, he had become lieutenant before the king died. Like all the generals of the day, in the art of war he was a disciple of Frederick. He had not yet come into personal contact with the Prussian army, but he still had considerable respect for it, although Frederick's immediate successor had won no laurels against the soldiers of France. He knew Frederick William III. to be foolish and weak; and if, none the less, he tried to induce the Prussian ruler to enter into an alliance, and hoped to turn Prussia's antagonism towards Austria and Russia to his own uses, it was because he continued to entertain an unavowed respect for the only foreign army in Europe which had covered itself with glory during the eighteenth century. But when Prussia showed him, not her strongest side, the military, but her weakest, the political, his respect waned.

In the previous year, before Austerlitz, he had offered

Frederick William an alliance. After Trafalgar, when Francis and Alexander were courting Prussia, and after Austerlitz, when the indications were in favour of France, the weakling monarch continued to vacillate, always hoping to better his position by neutrality. Then, when the Emperor was stronger than ever before, the Prussian ruler seized the first pretext for making warlike preparations against France. Had not Napoleon violated Prussian neutrality last year by marching through Ansbach?

What has really decided the king's attitude is the mood of the democrats, in conjunction with his dread of mortified national pride, and, in especial, with his uncertainty as to the loyalty of some of his bellicose generals. In Nuremberg, a bookseller had been tried by court martial and shot for publishing a lampoon against the French army and circulating it in places which, in accordance with the terms of the treaty, were legitimately occupied by French troops. The decision of the court was formally just; but the indignation it aroused, being moral, was juster. The Emperor realised this, and wanted to avoid war. He proposed a mutual withdrawal of troops. Through the mouth of his envoy, he explained that Frederick William had only to say whether the presence of French soldiers in Westphalia annoyed him. Then he wrote personally to the king: "I hold unalterably to our alliance. . . . But if your answer shows me that on your side you repudiate this alliance, and put your trust solely in the power of arms, then indeed I shall be compelled to make war. Nevertheless, battles and victories notwithstanding, my feelings will remain unchanged. Since I regard this war as a wicked one, I shall, even then, propose peace."

In private, however, with mingled feelings of anger and contempt, he says hard things about Prussia. He cannot believe that country to be so mad as it seems. "Its cabinet is despicable; its sovereign a weakling; its court ruled by young officers who will risk anything."

A fortnight before the outbreak of war, he still finds it impossible to believe in its coming.

He is mistaken. The men of noble birth who officer the Prussian army, the men who, under Frederick the Great, defeated France, and were subsequently defeated by France, want to rehabilitate themselves. The middle classes are inspired with ardent nationalist sentiments. The Prussians are ready to "risk anything"; their eyes are fixed on a protectress in whom they trust. The queen of Prussia is a passionate advocate of war, for the tsar is now allied with Prussia, and during his stay in Berlin she has recognised in him the manliness that is lacking in her husband. After Austerlitz, Alexander had promptly withdrawn into his own realm, to await a more favourable opportunity. Now the opportunity had come.

We learn from Talleyrand that Napoleon was full of secret disquietude at having to draw the sword once more. He had been dazzled by the feats of the great Frederick's soldiers. Never before had he fought against an army famous in story. "I fancy we shall find them tougher metal than the Austrians." All the more reason for getting quickly across the Rhine! A week after the beginning of the advance, he gains his first victory. At Saalfeld, the best of the Prussians fell, Prince Louis Ferdinand, the first and finest blossom shattered in the first storm.

Confusion prevails among the Prussians, and the king contributes to its spread. General Scharnhorst had advised him to attack two weeks earlier, but the irresolute ruler had waited for the French offensive. The duke of Brunswick is commander-in-chief; but instead of leaving the management of the campaign to this officer, at the last moment the king comes to the fighting front. "We don't know whether the headquarters should be called royal or ducal." The duke obeys the king when he ought to command. Questions of precedence necessitate the division of the forces into three army corps, for Prince Hohenlohe, who is a reigning prince, cannot possibly fight under a duke. Once more the enemy holds out the hand of friendship. Two days before the main battle, and while confident of victory, Napoleon writes:

"I do not wish to derive any advantage from the folly of your advisers, whose blunders in statesmanship amaze Europe. . . . Well, we are at war. . . . But why should we lead our subjects to slaughter one another? I care nothing for a victory that is bought with the lives of many of my children. If I were at the beginning of my career, and had reason to dread misadventure in battle, I should have no right to use such language. But, Sire, you will be defeated. You will sacrifice the quiet of your days and the lives of your subjects without the smallest justification. . . . I have nothing to gain from Your Majesty; I do not want and never have wanted anything from you. This war is unwise! I know that my letter may wound your royal sensibilities, but the circumstances make bluntness essential. I am telling you what I really think. . . . Restore peace to yourself and your territories. Even if I could never be your ally, you will always find in me a man, . . . whose greatest wish it is never to shed blood by making war with princes who are not the adversaries of his industry, his commerce, and his policy."

Louise, who has followed her husband to the front, is a woman with more peaceful instincts than is pleasing to the ambition of the generals on the headquarters staff. When the letter is read, however, she agrees with their scornful view that Napoleon writes as he does because he is afraid of a catastrophe to himself. Is she, then, unable to realise that destiny has placed her among these men to-day, that she may influence her weak-willed husband in the direction of a humane settlement of the dispute? She cannot see it! Napoleon is nothing but "an infernal monster risen out of the mire," and tomorrow he must fall!

"My affairs march very well," writes this monster, meanwhile, to his wife. "Everything is going just as I should like.

The king and the queen are in Erfurt. If they want to see a battle, they will have this gruesome delight. I feel splendid. Although I am travelling from eighty to a hundred miles a day, I have put on weight. I go to bed at eight in the evening, get up at midnight, and remember when I do so that you have not yet retired to rest." The last night before the battle he refuses to go to bed. At three in the morning, one of his officers urges him to take a nap, but he exclaims: "Impossible! I have my plans here" (he touches his forehead), "but nothing yet in my maps!" Then he quickly explains the whole plan. "Do you understand? . . . To horse with you and find me a place from which I can get a commanding view of the battlefield. I shall be there at six." Then he throws himself on the camp-bed, and instantly falls asleep.

In the course of that night, the Prussian headquarters staff is informed by its scouts that remarkable movements are going on among the French troops. Oh, well, to-morrow will be time enough to discuss the matter! But before the day dawns, the Emperor has ridden along the front, has fired his guard with enthusiasm, has recalled the day of Austerlitz.

He defeats the Prussians near Jena, while simultaneously Davoust is routing a superior force of the enemy at Auerstädt.

When the valiant duke of Brunswick is fatally wounded, no one ventures to take over the command. They all lose their heads, and what is left of the army of the great Frederick flees in disorder through Saxony eastward.

"Chère amie, I did some fine manœuvring against the Prussians, and won a great victory yesterday. Twenty thousand prisoners, and we took about a hundred cannon and colours. . . . Have been camping here for a couple of days. I'm feeling splendid. Farewell. Take good care of yourself, and love me."

In Weimar, he meets the reigning duchess. Charles Augustus, the duke, has been in a warlike frame of mind for the last twenty years. He is Prussophil, and, in defiance of advice, has joined issue with the Emperor. Now, as Prussian general, he is in full flight after the disaster at Jena. No one knows his whereabouts. The court has also fled from Weimar. Only the duchess and her minister, Goethe, remain behind. When the Emperor sees the lady for the first time, he says: "I am sorry for you! How could the duke. . . !" But to his amazement (for he is always against women's rule—in especial, when the woman happens to be a German) the duchess answers him with so much clarity, simplicity, and dignity, explains the duke's friendship with Prussia in so steadfast a manner, that he is shaken, behaves courteously, returns in the evening in order to have a long talk with her, and, after having vowed the annihilation of her dynasty, promises her that nothing shall be done to injure the duchy. Why?

Because this woman has never interfered in politics, has not now affected a knowledge she does not possess, but in simple camaraderie has spoken on behalf of her absent husband, and with princely demeanour has pleaded for her country. She has made use neither of cajolery nor anger, but has kept the golden mean between pride and deference becoming to a conquered monarch. Years afterwards, the Emperor remembered this woman who by her noble bearing had saved her country and her dynasty.

In Berlin, he meets another woman. Count Hatzfeld, who has been negotiating with the conqueror on behalf of Berlin, writes indiscreetly to one of the discredited generals, and gives him details concerning the strength of the French troops. His letter is intercepted. The Emperor, in a rage, declares he is to be shot as a spy. Berthier is depressed by the command; Rapp endeavours to soften Napoleon. Countess Hatzfeld is brought to see him; she falls at his feet. He invites her to Potsdam: "When I showed her the count's letter she answered me guilelessly, with a sob, and with deep emotion: 'Yes, that is certainly his handwriting.' As she read the document the tone of her voice moved me to my innermost being. I pitied her.

You see," he concludes his report to Josephine, "I love good, simple, and gentle women."

Love? There stands the man of might; the countess is naught to him as far as her womanhood goes; hardly has he noticed her figure or her dress. But these natural passions, womanly pleadings, tears, and silences, move him deeply. He throws the letter into the fire: "The proof I had has been burned. Your husband is safe."

Thus does Napoleon the Conqueror deal with two German women whose husbands have fought against him. He deals leniently with them because their conduct appeals to his heart.

He dislikes Queen Louise. A politician, that woman, who has driven her country and her consort into a disastrous enterprise, who has egged this quiet-loving man into war when he could have had peace with honour. Napoleon execrates such a woman. Since she seizes every opportunity to spit fire at him, he determines to strip her of all her womanly dignity. He jeers at her in official bulletins: "She is a woman with beautiful features but little brain. . . . She must be terribly tortured by pangs of conscience for all the suffering she has brought upon her country. Her husband is a man of honour who desired happiness and peace for his people."

He has made a triumphal entry into Berlin. His suite is brilliantly dressed, but he is as simply clad as ever, and his hat is adorned with a cockade worth about a penny. Nothing interests him so keenly as Sans Souci. He holds the sword of the great Frederick in his hands, and takes it away as a trophy more priceless than any other he could ever find in his whole life. He would not exchange it for the throne of Prussia. But he heartily despises Frederick's descendants, and publicly attacks the queen:

"In the queen's rooms was found the tsar's picture, which he himself had given her. Also there was her correspondence with the king. . . . These documents go to prove how unhappy those princes can be who permit their wives to interfere in affairs of State. Notes and State papers reeked of musk, and lay beneath ribbons and laces and other fal-lals of the toilet."

An unworthy tone! He seems to have forgotten the patriotic impulse of the queen. If, however, we compare these taunts with what the best and greatest of contemporary Prussian statesmen, the non-Prussian Baron vom Stein, wrote about Queen Louise, we can understand the Emperor's humour, though hardly excuse it.

Serious considerations restrain him from destroying the house of Hohenzollern, though he had already drafted a decree to dethrone the king. Napoleon has to bear the tsar in mind. In Berlin he thinks in terms of Europe as a whole: "On the Elbe and on the Oder we have won our India, our Spanish colonies, and our Cape of Good Hope." The grandiose words as yet only announce the start of the voyage; but with mighty strokes of the oar he is now to round the cape of his hopes. In the castle at Charlottenburg he dictates the greatest, most unbloody, and most dangerous of all his declarations of war: Charlemagne closes all the harbours of Europe against English ships. If the island cannot be reached by his sword? Well, henceforward, Europe shall be placed out of her reach! All merchandise, parcels, postal communications, etc., from and to England and her colonies are to be held up; every Englishman at large on the Continent is now a prisoner of war.

How is the carrying-out of the scheme to be supervised? Hitherto, action has always followed close upon the heels of thought. Now, he has to make treaties with various States, and, first of all, with Russia and Austria. Austria has fragments of the sometime realm of Poland within her frontiers; but Russia wants them for herself; Poland, tossed between the two, pays allegiance to neither. As to a god, the Poles turn to the Emperor. He, the champion of the freedom of the peoples, must come to their aid and free them. What is to be done? How does Napoleon solve the Polish problem?

"Shall I set up the throne of Poland anew, and thus restore a great nation to life? God alone, who has the fashioning of all things in his hands, can solve this riddle." Words of Delphic cunning, which he sends forth throughout Poland. God alone sees the smile with which he signs the proclamation! In addition he takes three measures. He demands that the Poles shall provide troops, for "not until you have an army of forty thousand men will you be worthy of the name of Nation." Next he proposes to the Austrians an exchange of Galicia for Prussian Silesia. But the real key to the Polish problem he fishes out of the Bosphorus, for he tells the sultan to drive the Russians out of Moldavia, and to meet him, the Emperor, on the Dniester; thereby he hopes to bind, not only Russia, but also the trembling Austria, to the lower Danube.

There he sits in Sans Souci, the ancient candelabra in Frederick's study scintillate over his head, Voltaire's picture smiles sideways, through the wraith, at his great fellow-countryman. He sits alone at his game of chess, calculates the moves of his unseen opponent, his glance takes in wider and wider circles; suddenly the traits of his new ancestor suffer a change, the big blond beard vanishes, the nose is flatter, the eyes lose some of their confident glance, then become bolder again: instead of the great Charles, he is facing the great Alexander. Yes, now, indeed, he will conquer England in India! World dominion hovers before his eyes.

A new opponent leaps on to the board. Couriers bring the news of a revolt in Spain. He pales. The whole game is imperilled. Once more Napoleon sees clearly that he who would vanquish England must gain Russia's friendship. But in order to conquer Russia or to win her over to his side, he needs a fulcrum. He has one ready to hand: Poland in revolt. Napoleon journeys to Warsaw.

While in imagination he had, during these weeks, been weighing the fate of continents, his heart had felt lonely. Yet he did not trouble himself about women. Only to his wife did he write gallant things: "I love you, and long for you. . . . These Polish women [in Posen] are all Frenchwomen in their hearts. But for me there is only one woman. Do you know who she is? I would tell you what she is like, only I should have to flatter her too much, so that you could recognise yourself in the description. Seriously, my heart can say naught but good of her. Oh, these long nights, all alone!"

Josephine, with the keenness of a foxhound, senses a rival under these cajoleries. But she has no reason, as yet, to be jealous, or to make so long a journey. He answers her that "the agitation of your letter tells me that you beautiful women know of no limits to your powers. What you wish must come to pass. I, on the other hand, recognise that I am the most enslaved of men. My master has no mercy on me, for my master is the nature of things."

Hardly has he finished touching upon these airy trifles in weighty words, when a courier brings him tidings of the great consequences of a trifling affair: the beauty to whom Caroline had introduced him in the previous winter, and who was expecting a child before he went away, has been confined. At last! It is then proved that he does not lack the power which Dame Nature grants to other men! A great gift from above. A boy. He turns to his intimate and exclaims with the ingenuous delight of a youth: "Duroc! I've got a son!"

XIV

The brilliantly lighted ballroom forms a background where Poland displays her greatest beauty and her most precious jewels. This is the evening of evenings. In the old palace of Poland's kings at Warsaw, the Emperor of the French is to be shown the calibre of the nation that has been suffering so long. Will he admire the national dance, its music and its figures? Will the eyes of the ladies ravish him, those eyes which are pools of Slavic melancholy? Will the flattery of the speeches

Bonaparte in 1802, as First Consul. Engraving by Alexandre Tardieu. After a drawing by Jean Baptiste Isabey.

or the idolising comparisons appearing in the newspapers make his heart as wax? Such, according to the sanguine, are the questions upon which hang the fate of the nation. The procession has passed by; he has spoken to many in cheerful vein; now he is standing in a recess, dividing his attention between his interlocutor and the dancers. He is thinking of Paris, where, for seven years, he has never failed to be in January.

Suddenly his gaze is focused on a special point, and he forgets to carry on the conversation. A hundred watchful eyes follow the glance of the huntsman. Who is the quarry? A little later he approaches a group, asks for the names of those composing it, and smilingly, with a courtliness of manner rarely shown by him on public occasions, he draws the lady of his choice out of the circle of her companions. She is a gentle, fair-haired beauty, dainty and small, has blue eyes, appears to be of a yielding disposition, and is eighteen years of age. She is simpler in her dress than any of the others, and her behaviour is correspondingly quiet and without display or the lures of coquetry. The Emperor chooses her as partner in a contradance, delights in her grace and her lovely voice, finds her broken French bewitching. While she smiles and is covered with confusion, her name is whispered from room to room throughout the palace: Countess Walewska.

"Who is she?" asks Napoleon later of his friend Duroc. She is the daughter of an ancient line, the family so impoverished that the lady has been married off to a wealthy old count whose youngest grandchild is ten years older than the new wife.

"I had eyes only for you," he writes to the countess next day. "I admired only you, and longed to be with you alone. Send me an answer quickly, in order that the fire which is consuming me may be appeased. N." But the messenger, Duroc, returns with neither answer nor tidings of any sort. The Emperor is nonplussed. Something quite new. Twelve years ago the brigadier general had had such a rebuff. But Napoleon, never. Have not all women, whether princesses or actresses, have not all the beauties, invariably come to him at his slightest nod of invitation? The more enchanting, therefore, is this lady who shrinks back so virginally from the unveiled desire of a man.

"Have I displeased you? I hoped the opposite. Or has your first feeling vanished? My passion grows. You rob me of my rest. Vouchsafe a little joy, a little happiness, to the poor heart that would fain worship you! Is it so hard to give me an answer? You now owe me two." This second letter is unsigned. Suppose an amateur of such matters to come across it in a collection of love letters, would he dream of ascribing its authorship to Napoleon? Neither heavy nor dictatorial, neither emotional nor stilted, but romantic rather is the tone. Nevertheless, since worldly convention demands that she should pay no heed to his suit, again his missive remains unanswered. Terrible the position of the adjutant who for the second time has failed in the carrying out a movement ordered by his chief. The Emperor, controlling his passion, thinks:

"If neither my pleading nor my rank has any effect on this tender creature, I must try to gain my end by a half-promise, which I need not regard as binding." He writes: "There are moments in life when high position is a heavy burden. That is borne in on me at this moment. . . . If only you would! None but you can overcome the obstacles which separate us. My friend Duroc will do what he can to make it easy for you. Oh, come, come! All your wishes shall be fulfilled! Your country will be even dearer to me, if you have compassion on my heart. N."

Now we should recognise his wonted style, even without the capital N. Nevertheless, how amazingly the loneliness of the man of might breathes from these lines. The third love-letter is intelligently composed, and therefore achieves its purpose—but it discloses to us the tragical mask of destiny, the destiny of one who wishes to walk along the course he has planned for himself, and who is sacrificing his human happiness to this heroical monomania. He roams through the splendid palace, arms locked behind. For weeks his mood has been one of yearning, but always he has been alone. For months he has hardly been near a woman. Now, having fallen passionately in love, storm-tost, he dismisses his secretaries, will not discuss matters with his generals, refuses to admit deputations, will not go out riding. The whole mechanism he has constructed is stationary. The palace, the army, Paris, Europe—let them wait. He, more a slave than any other, refuses to-day to obey the nature of things; a man of thirty-seven whose wife, well past forty, no longer stirs his passion. Profoundly moved by a girl, twice rebuffed, he must devise lures from his other realms, must tempt her with the freedom of her country, in order that, after nearly a decade of quiescent feeling, he may spread upon the shoulders of a young woman the mantle of his yearning for tranquillity.

She, alarmed at the assault of this virile will, sits the same afternoon among her friends and relatives who are urging the sacrifice upon her, for Poland's sake. In this mood, she at length goes to see him. The three evening hours she spends with him are spent in tears. By gentle arts he restores her to calm, and to her astonishment she finds that this dreaded man of iron is a tender wooer.

"Marie, sweet Marie, my first thought is yours!" she reads next morning. "I shall see you at dinner. I pledge you my word. Please wear the nosegay that I send; it will be a secret messenger of our feelings amid the crowd; thus we shall understand one another. If I lay my hand on my heart, you will know that it is wholly yours; for answer, press your flowers to your bosom. Love me, my charming Marie; do not take your hand away from the flowers."

Not until three days later does she become his. Then she comes to see him every evening. But, as well as this, she must be present at every reception, for otherwise he stays away. What is she to him? The second creature in the world who asks nothing from him; his mother was the first. Never has he known another woman who did not expect his magician's hand to shower on her the treasures of the universe: jewels, palaces, crowns, money. This woman wants nothing from him, and gives him everything. Countess Walewska is the quiet and loving companion whom Napoleon's stormy soul has sought. It will be long before he will be willing to part from her. "She is an angel. It may justly be said that her spirit is as lovely as her features."

Josephine wants to come? Now? He smiles. Since the Cairo days, Bonaparte has never had a mistress while campaigning, whereas his generals have had plenty of love-affairs. There can be no doubt that the story of this intrigue, distorted of course, will quickly be carried to Paris, and in a veiled form will find a way to Josephine's ears. She is waiting there, waiting to be summoned to his side. Now, in the most graceful way in the world, he deceived the wife who had deceived him for years. The weather, the roads, the public insecurity, made it impossible. "How gladly should I be spending the long winter nights at your side. . . . If you are always weeping, then you lack courage and character. I cannot endure cowardly people. An empress must have courage!"

Now he betrays her. "I laughed when you wrote to me that you had taken a husband in order to be with him. In my simplicity, I had believed that woman was made for man; man for country, family, fame. Forgive my ignorance. One can always learn something from lovely women. . . . Besides, I could not think of any lady with whom I was exchanging letters. If there really were one, I can assure you she would have to be as beautiful as a newly opened rose. Does that apply to the lady of whom you speak?"

See how this ambiguous trifling amuses him. His heart is so light sometimes. He can play the gallant as if there had never been a revolution in the world. When, after a few weeks, he resumes a campaigner's life, his farewell to his Polish inamorata is an au revoir.

Now Russia is open to him for the first time, a land like the desert. Endless steppes, covered with snow or mud; no bread, and hardly any roads. After a few skirmishes, the tsar slowly retreats. Can we follow him? Whither is he enticing us? Who will feed the army? There is nothing in this land to be seized, nothing such as there is in prosperous Germany, no storehouses. Had not a few hundred Polish Jews, shrewd speculators, seen the chance of striking good bargains, the regiments would have perished, at this early date, in the year 1807. When the Emperor, whose carriage has perforce been left behind, is riding towards Pultusk, he hears murmurs from the ranks. This is a sound he has almost forgotten; he heard it for the first and last time eight years ago at Acre. His generals report suicides among the men. Thousands of starving soldiers desert, to become marauders. The Emperor is dumbfounded at the news, but what can he do? "I know my Frenchmen," he says. "It is difficult to march them on distant expeditions. France is too beautiful."

It is not surprising, therefore, that when he compels the Russians to fight, for the first time he should fail to conquer in the open field. He is not actually beaten at Eylau, but both the contending armies sustain terrible losses, and the issue is indecisive. A first warning not to campaign against Russia! Report after the battle: the soldiers are rifling the potato clamps for food, and the horses are tearing straw from the roofs. The whole countryside is filled with invalided soldiers, and none of the colonels know how many men are left in their commands. The Emperor speaks:

"We shall stay here a couple of days more, and then withdraw a few miles. Post guards on all the bridges over the Vistula; no one must be allowed to cross, except the amputated. Don't bother about stragglers; no punishments." But these signs of the disintegration of his army trouble him more than in former days. A cramp of the stomach, from which he has already suffered at times, becomes more frequent, and he says: "I bear within me the germs of an early death, and shall die of the same trouble as my father." Cancer is the family heritage: his grandfather, his father, his uncle, Lucien, and Caroline, all perished of this disease.

He writes to his brother: "We are living here amid snow and mud, without wine, bread, or brandy." But this is a private missive. From Osterode, where he is housed in a barn among the soldiers, and eats whatever they can shark up for him (a comrade among his men, as he had been years before in Italy), his bulletins to Paris speak of a great victory, and of a Russian rout. The casualties are stated at a third of the true figures. The French army is in fine case, and can stay where it is for a year if thought best.

For the second time he must learn that his nerves are not made for waiting. Here, as in Egypt, this commander finds that there is something uncanny about standing still. Only once more in the whole course of his fifteen years as a conqueror will there be another such pause of two or three months in a place far from Paris. Both these epochs of tedious consideration, cautious negotiation, are filled out in the interludes of work by giving free rein to his pent-up emotions. They are filled out with idylls.

Finckenstein, a fortified Prussian castle, is now the scene of his activities, while he is awaiting the thaw on the roads and in the hearts of his adversaries. There are huge fireplaces, which are a delight to him, "for I love to look into the fire at night when I can't sleep." The place is roomy enough to house the envoys and couriers. For ten weeks, the world is ruled from here. In the great bedroom upstairs, he has had his iron camp-bed set up beside the huge four-poster.

No one knows that the Polish countess occupies the next room—or hardly any one except Constant, his valet, and Rustam, the Mameluke. She rarely goes out, and then only after dark. The time is passed in embroidery, reading, and waiting, until the door opens, and he enters, to devote himself to her for a time. He has his meals with her alone. In these two rooms are the commander's headquarters, and here the Emperor has enshrined his idyll. There are no dynastic wishes to trouble him as in Paris, no jealousies, and no bargainings for jewels; there is no wish to shine; nothing but the desire to remain hidden from the world, a wordless wish in the eyes of this sweet girl of eighteen who has learned to love him.

"I know," he says to her, "you would rather live without me. Yes, yes, don't protest; I know it! But you are good and gentle; your heart is pure. You don't want to rob me of the few hours of happiness which you can give me every day? To think that people regard me as the happiest of men!"

A dispatch comes to tell him that his nephew and heir, the son of King Louis, is dead. How the news affects him is shown by his moving words to Josephine; but he cannot tell his wife all the thoughts that now enter his mind at Finckenstein. That little cocotte in Cairo, what he had really hoped from her was a son. How if this beautiful woman, this noblewoman whom he loves, were to give him an heir? Would he then make her his empress? Why not? He looks at Walewska, but keeps his own counsel.

What is Paris saying?

With ear attent, he listens to the rumours that reach him across the Polish steppe. The funds are falling. Malicious jests are current on the boulevards. "Where are our brave lads?" ask the Parisians. Caution is needed! What begins as a gentle shower, may turn into a raging storm; and the man who knows how to control the thunder is far away. He offers the beaten Prussians a separate peace, and even proposes a conference, but Queen Louise holds firmly to the alliance with the tsar. Austria, too, is deaf to his voice.

Despite all, here and now, with enemies to right and to left of him, and without any firm standing-ground, he begins to dream once more of the conquests of Alexander. Messengers bearing heavily sealed letters ride forth from the courtyard of Finckenstein; strangers bringing dispatches arrive from remote lands and make their way to him across distant mountains. To this northern headquarters comes a Persian envoy, and the messenger of the King of Kings reverently bows his head to greet the sublime Emperor of the West. Next day, Napoleon and the Persian emissary come to an understanding. The Emperor will force the tsar to give back Georgia to the shah. In return, the shah will spur on the Afghans and the tribes of Kandahar to attack the English in India; he will equip an army for the invasion of Hindustan. If the Emperor wishes to send an army against India, his men shall have free passage across Persia.

Hardly has the Persian departed, when a gorgeously attired Turk rides in past the astonished sentries, bringing golden gifts and a dispatch. A bespectacled oriental expert translates it. Standing in front of the fire, the Emperor, having reduced the eastern bombast to sober proportions, dictates a letter to the sultan: "I regret very much that you ask for no more than five hundred men instead of several thousand. . . . State your demands clearly, and whatever you want shall be instantly done. Get into communication with the shah of Persia, for he, too, is an enemy of the Russians. . . . I offered your envoy the artillerymen and other soldiers you need, but he would not accept them, being afraid of hurting Mohammedan susceptibilities. I am so powerful, and I am so desirous for your victory (I wish this because of my friendship for you, and not on political grounds alone), that I can deny you nothing."

The same day, he writes to Brother Louis, who has been sending urgent appeals from his new kingdom, a letter which may be regarded as a sort of general instruction for kings, and which occupies five pages of print. He also sends orders to Joseph, as to the latter's conduct in Naples. To Jerome, who in Breslau is commanding a corps of pretty actresses instead of his soldiers, Napoleon writes to ask why his brother never sends complete reports, and why he has left six hundred men in Schweidnitz, four hundred in Brieg. "Let me know your exact plans, down to the smallest details, so that I can form an accurate picture of your situation." He likewise sends a missive to all the bishops in France. They are to institute a public thanksgiving for the Emperor's victories; but he aims, also, at exercising personal influence on each of his episcopal correspondents, for he has learned that the dispute between himself and the pope is making the ecclesiastics more and more uneasy in their consciences. Meanwhile he sends a dozen orders to Fouché: concerning Madame de Staël, and the extent of her influence; concerning the salons of the aristocratic quarter; and so on. He enquires about the two leading Parisian theatres; their condition, their finances, and their repertoire. "What has become of my librarian?" he asks in another letter. "Is he dead, or enjoying himself in the country? That would be a fine way of fulfilling his duties! I ordered him to send me all newly published books, and to let me have the publishers' announcement lists, but I have not had a word from him." Draft for a new historical university, where young people may learn about modern happenings as well as the story of ancient days. To the Minister for Home Affairs: "Literature needs encouragement. Let me hear your proposals for livening up the various forms of belles lettres." Enquiries as to the building of a new Stock Exchange and of the Madeleine. How can six millions be best applied for the encouragement of manufactures, and what will be the best way of raising the money? Two millions are to be spent in renovating his palaces. Arrangements must be made for the Paris newspapers to publish articles ostensibly based on information from Bucharest and Tiflis, and describing Russia's desperate situation.

He smiles, glancing at his demure little friend. "You marvel at my manifold activities? I have to keep watch on all my posts. Before, I was only an acorn. Now I am an oak, the ruler of nations. All eyes are fixed on me because I am in so outstanding a position. A man must play his part, and cannot always be natural. But, for you, I will become the acorn once more." Simple words, tranquilly uttered. One more evening with her, and then he must take the field again, for May has come, and the idyll ends with the leaving of winter quarters and the extinction of the fires at Finckenstein. He will see her again. They are both sure of this. But were he to forget her, he could read the posy in the ring she gives him:

"If you cease to love me, forget not that I love you."

XV

On the Memel, where it flows past Tilsit, a huge raft is anchored in mid-stream. The tree trunks and the planks are covered with carpets, and in the centre a tent gleams in the June sunlight, with the colours of France and of Russia flying above it. On the western and the eastern banks are ranged the guards of the two emperors. Boats set out from either shore. Napoleon and the tsar enter the peace-tent simultaneously. The soldiers, who were shooting one another only ten days back, cheer lustily, and those in front, who can see, pass the word to the thousands in the rear. The foes of yesterday have embraced, their masters have made friends.

Immediately after the great victory of Friedland, Napoleon, as was his way, had offered his hand to the vanquished. At the opening parleys, since the appropriate response had not been made by the sultan, he had given a hint that the tsar might well hope, some day, to establish the cross once more on the dome of St. Sophia. The words were carefully chosen, for he knew that the man to whom they would be reported next day, a romanticist and a mystic, would be amenable to their influence. Alexander had been prompt to take the proffered hand of friendship. Now the enemies of Austerlitz and Friedland stood face to face in amicable converse. Napoleon coldly scrutinised his only serious rival on the Continent, a young man with feminine lineaments, compact, delicately moulded, rosy; hearing and eyesight rather weak. In an instant he felt assured that the tsar was a man whom he could win over.

By the end of a fortnight, the sometime adversaries have not merely entered into an alliance, but have made friends. How has this come about?

"He is an amiable and pleasant fellow, a hero of romance," says Napoleon of him at this time. Inasmuch as the Emperor is bored by novels, and has no use for heroes of romance in the practical world of his calculations, there is an undercurrent of criticism in these pretty phrases. But he adds: "A handsome young man, more intelligent than is usually supposed." At a later date, Napoleon utters profound truths regarding Alexander: "The tsar is an attractive figure, well formed to exercise a victorious charm on those with whom he comes in contact. Had I been inclined to surrender to superficial impressions, I should have become devoted to him instantly. But there is something peculiar about him, which I can best express by saying that in all he is and does there seems to be something lacking. The strangest point about the matter is that it is impossible to foresee precisely what will be lacking in any given instance, for the defect is infinitely variable." Thus, the man whose friendship is all-important to him seems to him utterly feminine. His final judgment takes the form of an overwhelming compliment: "Were Alexander a woman, I think I should fall passionately in love with him."

It is not surprising that such a man should in a trice be mastered by the seductions of the man of power; nor is it remarkable that subsequently the tsar should forsake the Emperor, for the surrender and the abandonment are both feminine. No one has ever given a better description of Alexander than Metternich: "A mingling of masculine merits with feminine defects; favourite ideas, imperfectly thought out, initiate sudden impulses. As a result, sudden embarrassments. He gives his word too quickly, and then finds it very difficult to keep; not strong enough for ambition in the grand style, and not weak enough for mere vanity; the man of the world rather than ruler. There is a sort of periodicity in his enthusiasms and disenchantments, a periodicity of five-year terms during which an idea waxes and wanes. At the close of each cycle, a new one opens. To begin with, he is a liberal. Then he is filled with hatred for the Frenchman; then he passes under the Frenchman's influence."

Five years hence, the new period will come to an end, and the friends of to-day will be at war again.

Maybe Napoleon already foresees this in the splendid tent, where for two hours the emperors discuss the affairs of the world; certainly he foresees it during the long dinners and during the rides and drives together. Napoleon's handling of Alexander is masterly. At first, the Emperor assumes the role of the cavalier, who cannot sufficiently extol the heroism of the Russians; then he conveys the implication that ere long he must surround himself with a bodyguard of his ministers, lest he should be carried away by the tsar's charm. At table, in order to dazzle Alexander, he talks of his good luck—a thing to which the man of destiny rarely alludes. He tells an anecdote, for which this is the only warrant, of an incident that had happened in Egypt. He had fallen asleep beneath an ancient wall, which had suddenly crumbled to pieces without injuring him. Awaking, he found in his hand something which at first he believed to be a stone, but which, on examination, he saw to be a wonderfully beautiful cameo of Augustus. Could any playwright invent a more marvellous scene than this one invented by the Emperor, in an after-dinner hour, to stir the imagination of the mystical idealist, his companion?

Enthralled, the tsar listens to the man of wonders. If he could only know all that Napoleon knows! "I feel that I am not really emperor as you are, for I am dependent on my generals." He asks a hundred questions about the art of war.

Naïvely, when the two men are out walking together, the tsar asks: "What sort of position is this? How would you defend it, and how would you attack it?"—"I explained matters to him; and I told him that, if I were ever again at war with Austria, he should lead an army corps of thirty thousand men under my orders, so that he could learn the art of war."

Was ever woman in such humour wooed? Soon an offensive and defensive alliance is concluded.

"The lands between the Elbe and the Memel" (this is a secret note to the treaty), "are to form the barrier between the two great empires, a barrier to render harmless all the pin-pricks which, in disputes between nations, are apt to precede the firing of the guns." In this treaty, each party to the alliance gives only in order to take; and in a couple of words the tsar sacrifices Prussia, the Emperor Poland, although each of the two rulers has pledged a woman to maintain the integrity of her country. Almost grotesque is the calm with which, seated in a small room in an out-of-the-way and little known town hard by the shores of the Baltic, the two men pore over the map and cut pieces out of countries like Hotspur and Owen Glendower in the play. The Emperor gives Coburg, Mecklenburg, and Oldenburg, whose rulers have ties with the tsar, receiving the Ionian islands and Cattaro in return. Only when the tsar asks for the Bosphorus, does the Emperor demur. "Constantinople? That carries world dominion with it!" In the thorny thicket of these negotiations, we have stumbled upon the decisive word that slumbers beneath the treaties and notes. It is plain that when two men are dividing the world between them, they will in the long run come to blows.

The king of Prussia joins their company; and, since he lacks dignity and intelligence, he is ignored by both the emperors. Napoleon privately considers him a dullard, possessing neither talent nor character, and adversely criticises everything connected with him; even his dress, which is the uniform of a hussar, headgear and all complete. Since the king is anxious about the very existence of Prussia, he leaves no stone unturned to secure the safety of his State, and summons the queen to Tilsit. The Emperor, curious to see his beautiful foe, intimates that he would be pleased to receive the lady there. He uses the neutral zone as a pretext for not setting out to meet her; but he has a charming residence prepared for her reception. Then, with a brilliant suite, though himself dressed in the simplest attire, he rides forth to visit her, and is received by the queen, who stands at the head of the flight of steps to welcome him.

She is clad in white silk, adorned with ancient jewels, beautiful and bitter. With seemingly innocent words, Louise breaks down the unbearable constraint:

"Sire, I hope you will excuse these narrow steps."

"What would one not excuse to reach such a goal," he answers. But when he continues to speak in this complimentary tone, she says with dignity:

"Sire, have we come here to speak of trifles?"

Then she pleads as spouse and mother, and appeals to his "magnanimous heart."

"You will be glad to be back in Berlin?"

"Not in all circumstances. It depends upon you whether we return home without sorrow in our hearts."

"Madame, I should be only too pleased. . . ."

When she moved to speak, he interjected:

"Madame, how came Prussia to venture upon this war?"

"The fame of Frederick the Great deceived us as to our strength."

"How many times have I offered peace? Austria showed more wisdom after Austerlitz."

"To-day, I beg you to establish a claim upon our gratitude."

"Have you not, yourself, destroyed my friendship for Prussia?"

"Your heart is noble; it unites with other fine qualities, the possession of a great character."

"Unfortunately, general considerations often stand in the way of special wishes."

"I do not understand questions of high politics; yet I do not feel that I am foregoing any of my dignity as a woman if I assure you . . ."

He listens to her with growing interest. She notices "a kindly smile trembling at the corners of his mouth, which seemed to guarantee success,—when, at that moment, the king entered the room."

The conversation has no political consequences, but the human appeal has been very great. "It was just as well that the king put in an appearance when he did," the Emperor says to the tsar with a spice of coquetry. "I might have made her promises. . . . An exquisite woman. Instead of depriving her of a crown, one is tempted to lay one at her feet." After another talk with Queen Louise, Napoleon writes to Josephine: "She is a bewitching woman, and is most amiable in her behaviour towards me. But you have no cause for jealousy. . . . I should have to pay dearly for it were I to play the gallant here. . . . She has been punished for her love of domination; but she has displayed much character in the midst of her misfortunes. . . . One has to concede that she said many sensible things."

Even more amazing is his effect upon her, who had once called him an infernal monster. She writes: "His head is shapely, his lineaments are those of a thinker, his whole appearance reminds one of a Roman emperor. When he smiles, his mouth assumes a kindly expression. . . ."

This is Napoleon's greatest victory. What other woman has, after a few weeks' acquaintance, been able to portray him more charmingly? And yet she has reasons enough to detest him, for, in spite of the humility of her attitude, he is as unyielding as iron. Soon, however, she arouses his irritability. When, at last, everything has been signed, and the Emperor, "in consideration of his friendship for the tsar," has secured the kingdom of Prussia against dissolution (though monstrous cantles have been sliced off!), she cannot refrain from making renewed attempts to soften him. Finally, he sees her into her carriage, and she seizes this opportunity to ask him, for the last time, why so mighty a man should have foregone the chance of earning her eternal gratitude. He throws courtesy to the winds, and answers with ironical bitterness:

"What will you, Madame? I am to be pitied, for this is obviously the work of my evil star!"

XVI

What is Paris saying?

"Even were I ten thousand miles away from my homeland, I could not leave the field free for bad citizens to stir up my capital to strife!" He has now been ten months absent—longer away than ever before or afterwards.

He tightens up the home government all the more rigorously since he fears that his censorious Parisians are slipping out of his hands. This city, renowned for its biting wit, is not only venting its feelings in songs and jokes that are the delight of the boulevards; it is now assuming a sceptical tone, and is more amused than impressed by his expeditions. Yes, he is right, these Parisians need to be ruled by "an iron hand in a velvet glove." Now they are to experience both again, only the velvet seems to have worn rather thin. Indeed, the whole tone of the capital has become lax and disorderly. Do they want to return to Directory days, when every one said and printed exactly what he pleased?

A new and more rigid censorship of newspapers and plays is introduced. Historical drama must deal only with matters of the remote past; and even Corneille, his ideal, is pruned of certain passages. Before every opera he must be consulted, not merely as to the general question of acceptance after it is written, but earlier, as to the choice of topic; religious subjects are forbidden, and mythology is recommended. With lavish means, on the imperial scale, a university is founded, modelled after the Jesuit schools he detests; the professors are exempt from military service, but to some extent celibacy is insisted on. Chateaubriand is attacked, and his "Mercure de France" is suppressed, because in opposition salons he has criticised the Emperor, and has quoted Tacitus the historian as having taken vengeance on Nero the tyrant.

Madame de Staël's new requests for permission to return to Paris are rejected, "for she is able to make people think, people who had never learned or had forgotten how to think." To the arch-chancellor he writes: "Summon Count R., and let him know that his wife's boudoir is the talk of Paris." To Fouché: "You are not policing Paris properly. Malicious gossip is ripe. Keep watch on the speeches that are being made at Citerni's restaurant and in the Café Foy." That young people may learn who pleases God, every child in France patters the following catechism: "We owe our Emperor Napoleon I. love, respect, obedience, loyalty, military service, . . . ardent prayers for his welfare, . . . because God has showered gifts on him in peace and war, and has made him God's image on earth."

He has moved a long way. When the heir of countless generations believes such things of himself, others (or some of them) can believe them of him. But it is only three years since the Emperor, on the day of his coronation, had said that every fishwife would laugh in his face were he to declare himself the son of God. . . .

Is he no longer the same man? As of old, in personal matters he renounces display. He will not have money lavished on his study. Here, apart from the great writing table, there are only a small settee (on which he lounges when he is dictating, unless he wanders about the room), two tall bookcases, a couple of chandeliers, and the bust of Frederick the Great; in another simply furnished study, he has a bust of Cæsar. Looking through some bills, he says: "I was charged much less when

I was lieutenant. Why should I pay more than any one else?" When the private theatre of the palace is to be done up, he remarks: "There must still be a lot of upholstered benches and candelabras that were supplied at great expense for my coronation. No doubt they are stored away somewhere."

When Rémusat exceeds the Emperor's wardrobe allowance of twenty thousand francs, he is dismissed, and his successor is handed a long inventory of requirements, a list personally drafted by the Emperor: "I think we can make a few more savings even than this. See to it that the tailor does his work properly. Lay the new clothes out for my inspection and approval on the day of delivery, and then put them away at once in my drawers." In the case of uniform coats which are to be delivered every quarter, he remarks: "This coat must last three years. . . . In addition, forty-eight pairs of white breeches and waistcoats, at eighty francs a suit=frs. 3840. One pair of breeches and one waistcoat must be delivered every week, and they must last three years. . . . Also twenty-four pairs of shoes, to be delivered a pair every fortnight, must last two years=frs. 312." Shirts are the only things he orders in large quantities, to be delivered a dozen every week, must last six years.

Here, in his intimate life, he is the same man as before; just as, when he is campaigning, he is the old Bonaparte—a man of few enjoyments. But upon the formalities of majesty, upon court ceremonial, upon all the outworn display of the world whose power he has broken, he will squander, not money alone, but, more precious, time, and, more precious still, human dignity and his own freedom.

He no longer laughs sarcastically when those who dwell in the aristocratic quarter frequent his court; he is genuinely pleased. His mood is difficult to understand. The men of birth who had mortified him in his cadet days by making fun of his poverty, now throng the court of this same Corsican, and their shadows on the shining parquet floor seem to mock the humility of their gestures. They are all back in the Tuileries now, the Montmorencys, the Montesquieus, the Radziwills, the Noailles, the Narbonnes, the Turennes, who for years had sworn the death of the upstart. The princes of the Confederation of the Rhine clank through the halls in their German uniforms; the Mecklenburger pays his court to the empress; the heirs apparent of Baden and Bavaria are privileged to hear the discussions at the Council of State. To the old nobility this was a pastime; to the Emperor it was policy, for he wished to make sure of the allegiance of their class.

But now there happens something which should never have happened. Napoleon, the man who counts his coats as he counts his soldiers; the man who in the army gives promotion only for good service, and will never make an inefficient soldier a lieutenant merely because he is some one's son or nephew; the man who sits contentedly in a barn among his officers, or by the camp-fire among his grenadiers; the man who has expunged the privileges of birth from his legal code; the man who has contraposed the new idea of individual ability to the old idea of hereditary dignity, and has thus turned a whole continent upside down—this same Bonaparte, in the autumn of the year 1807, founds a new nobility, "because it is a part of human nature that a man should wish to hand down to his children, not property alone, but also tokens of esteem." Counts and princes, dukes and majorats, were created, not, as before, in order to bestow a supreme dignity upon the bravest marshals, the ablest senators and ministers, but that the sons and grandsons of these new nobles, ne'er-do-wells, wealthy Parisian idlers, and degenerates, might enjoy the privileges which the men of a whole decade had fought and bled to abolish!

Even the Legion of Honour was now desecrated by its own creator, for these appointed knights, every one of whom had done good service to his country, were to be entitled to bequeath the semblance of this service as well as their property; and the great dignitaries were to bequeath their princely rank and appellation. Certainly, the bequest did not carry with it any special civic privileges, but none the less the new institution conflicted with the spirit of the Code Napoléon. "Liberty," he wrote with too much truth in a private letter at the time of the issue of this decree, "liberty is only the need of the few whom nature has endowed with exceptional talent; and there is no danger in restricting it. The crowd loves equality. I do not injure the many when I distribute titles without raising the old question of birth; they are bourgeois crowns, which any one can win. Clever men impart their own movement to those whom they rule. My movement is an upward one, and therefore the nation must move upwards. . . . I know that these dukes whom I am endowing so richly that I make them independent of me, will endeavour to elude me, and that they are relying on what they call the caste spirit. But I can run quicker than they, and shall soon overtake them."

Rarely has a great error had so grand a foundation. Not many months before, in his letters, he had positively cudgelled his brother for having founded a nobility in Holland; and, speaking of his own intention to do the same thing, had excused himself by saying that the Dutch were a trading people, and that in the militarist French Empire matters were on an altogether different footing. But in the very fact that he himself had transformed France into a militarist State, lay the first danger; and the second danger was the imperial crown, which, with inexorable logic, was now diffusing its ancient symbolical power athwart his realm.

Before, when he had been Consul, he could with impunity bestow civic crowns, gather honour and glory into a Legion, and transmit the stupendous momentum of his flywheel to the strongest of the lesser wheels in his country. But when he granted estates to the best among his followers, he had to supply titles to go with their estates, titles which were necessarily inheritable; and when to the second and third best he now gave titles without lands, the recipients naturally begged that the titles, too, should be hereditary. Thus in a generation, several thousand, and in three generations, as many as twenty thousand, would bear these new titles, not for services rendered, not for deeds splendidly performed, but with the semblance of superiority, and, if not with the political privileges attaching of old to birth and title, still with the social privileges which in former days had aroused revolt in the masses.

The treason and ingratitude which he is here laying up in store will in due time open his eyes to his mistake. In truth, the death sentence he passes on equality will prove to have been a more grievous blunder than the execution of the duke of Enghien. Then he was destroying a scion of the past; now he is creating forebears who will resuscitate that past.

The resolve issues from a moody mind; for this is a dark year in Napoleon's soul, although nothing seems to be going awry. "You do not understand the nature of human motives," he said at this period to an honest democrat. "You democrats are unable to draw distinctions between one another, whereas personal interest plays its part in what every one does. Look at Masséna. He has won an abundance of fame; but what he wants now is to become a prince, like Murat and Bernadotte. Soon he will get himself killed in the forefront of the battle, thanks to his eagerness to win this distinction. Ambition is what spurs the French!"

He grows colder in his manner, forbids his brothers to speak to him uninvited, is less regular in the arrangement of his work, needlessly extends sittings far into the night. Even at Fontainebleau, in the interludes between hunting and festivities, he will have nothing but tragedies staged; rises from his bed at midnight, and dictates to his secretaries till morning; can only soothe the increasing irritability of his nerves by spending hours in a hot bath. The cramps in his stomach trouble him more frequently and grow more severe.

He has periods of gloom like those from which he suffered in youth, speaks of the roaring of the sea and the moaning of the wind, has the candles shaded when he is listening to the mournful songs of Italian singers. None of his associates understand these moods; they can only wonder, and they guess at political motives. They do not realise that now, when the dream of his fancy is being fulfilled, he cannot but be disillusioned by the fulfilment, which comes otherwise than he had dreamed, and far too slowly. "You are just like all the rest of them," he says roughly to one of his ministers who congratulates him on the treaty of Tilsit. "I shall not be master until I have signed the peace of Constantinople!"

Worldwide power! Asia! These are the thoughts that continue to pulse in his brain. If he, who is always studying the tragical figures of the heroes of antiquity in search of his own image, could find the true reflexion of his own soul, it would be in the verses at this time being written by a German poet to describe the inner aspect of the Faustian unrest which he, the Emperor, with ever more violent blows, is now producing in the countries of Europe.

But these dark hours are followed by others in which his mind recovers the wonted clarity of its calculations. Thus, to the tsar, the other ruler of vast territories, he writes this imaginative programme:

"An army of fifty thousand Frenchmen and Russians, with perhaps a few Austrians, could march to Constantinople, and thence hurl itself upon Asia. Once it had reached the Euphrates, England would lie at the feet of the Continent. . . . Within a month of our coming to an understanding, our armies can be at the Bosphorus: the influence will make itself felt as far as India. . . . Of course the arrangements could only be concluded in a personal interview with Your Majesty. Everything can be signed and sealed before the middle of March. By May 1st, our troops will be in Asia, yours in Stockholm. England will collapse beneath the weight of the events with which the atmosphere will be charged. It is true that Your Majesty and I have proposed to enjoy peace within our far-flung empires.

. . . But it is always wise and politic to do what destiny commands. . . . That will make this crowd of pygmies bow their heads, the pygmies who cannot see that the prototype of the present age must be sought in the remote periods of history, and not in the newspaper articles of the century that has just closed. . . . In these few lines I am pouring out all my soul before Your Majesty."

All his soul? Part of it, since the jewels are cut for the delectation of a muddle-headed idealist whose own dreams will be reflected with rainbow tints from their sparkling facets. But the undertaking has its elements of well-considered realism. At about this time he has an interview with a general who has been in India. This expert declares the scheme practicable, and the Emperor's hesitations superfluous. Thereupon, the latter repeatedly strokes his visitor's face with both hands, and "bubbles over with an almost childlike joy."

Thus imaginative was Napoleon.

The present leads him once more to the shade of Charlemagne. The previous year he had thought of visiting Rome to have himself crowned Emperor of the West. The pope was to lose all temporal authority, and to content himself with a few millions as revenue; but the cardinals had vetoed the scheme. Thereupon he had rancorously exclaimed: "The whole of Italy will be subject to my laws. I will not disturb the independence of the Holy See, if Your Holiness will pay me the like consideration in temporal matters. No doubt Your Holiness is sovereign in Rome, but I am Emperor of Rome!" This threatening demeanour, this Carlovingian defiance, is in sharp conflict with the constitutional law on which his power is assumedly based. In Rome, as in India, he aims at the forcible realisation of things which only the vision of his great forerunners created.

More and more frequent become the signs which show that Napoleon's historical fantasies are tending to outsoar the limits which, were he still an accurate calculator, he would regard as attainable—and terrible will be the ultimate result.

In Rome, for the time being, he is still the stronger; but so much has the habit of command grown upon him, so overweening has his belief in his unconquerable sword become, that he has lost sight of the moral canons which, ten years earlier, he (then a mere military commander with no experience in political matters) had with clear insight defended against the hectoring Directors, and had subsequently, though at considerable risk to his popularity, incoporated in the Concordat. Now he writes to Eugene that one of the cardinals has died leaving a history of the popes. "If it represents an attempt to set forth all the harm the popes have done to the Church and to Christendom, let it be published forthwith."

Because the pope refused to exclude English ships from his ports, the Emperor occupied Ancona, relying "upon the protection of God, who crowns all my enterprises with his glory— If Your Holiness would like to give my envoy his papers, you are at liberty to do so. I should even prefer that you should receive the English, or the caliph of Constantinople.—In conclusion I pray to God that he may keep you for many years more at the head of our Holy Mother the Church. Your pious son, the Emperor of the French and the king of Italy, Napoleon."

The year before, simultaneously with these burlesque menaces, he had sent warnings through Uncle Fesch that his own role resembled that of Constantine, and had touched upon the old struggle of the Middle Ages about investiture: "For the pope, I am Charlemagne, seeing that I have joined the crowns of France and Lombardy, and that my dominions border on the East. . . . On condition of good behaviour, I shall make no change in the outward semblance of things, but if the pope thwarts me I shall degrade him to the status of a Roman bishop, . . . and shall introduce the Concordat into Italy: for whatever can make people happy in France, can make them happy in Italy as well; and what does not contribute to the happiness of life in one land, cannot do so in the other."

This is truly Lutheran terminology! The man who lets his imagination riot when his temporal affairs are merged in historical mysticism, becomes circumstantially clear when religious mysticism is a cloak for worldly concerns. Napoleon's reasoning inclined him towards Protestantism throughout life, and it was only on grounds of policy that he resisted the inclination to impose Lutheranism on France. Having determined to make short work of it with the Head Shepherd (since the pope hesitated to give England the go-by), he proposes to sweep away the hindrance that severs the North Italian and the South Italian kingdoms, that he may at length have all Italy for his own—the Italy of which he wrongfully calls himself king.

Now he writes to Eugene, the viceroy, in the style of his military decrees: "The present pope has too much power. Priests are not made to rule. Why will he not render unto Cæsar the things that are Cæsar's, and refrain from troubling my States? Perhaps the time is not far distant when I . . . shall summon the Churches of France, Germany, Italy, and Poland to a council, and settle matters without the pope." He wants to secure a majority among the cardinals by the appointment of French cardinals, but the pope will not allow their number to be increased, and proposes to make up for this refusal by agreeing to crown Napoleon Emperor of the West. Now, however, what he had vainly asked for a year earlier has ceased to charm his imagination. Since it has become possible, he regards it as already achieved; and when the pope shows himself pliable in money matters, Napoleon makes this an occasion for further exactions. He threatens "to reunite this group of my crown lands with the Empire at once, and to revoke the gift of Charlemagne."

In a word, having a large appetite, he will make one mouthful of all the Papal States. Thereupon the enraged pope breaks off the negotiations, the Emperor has Rome occupied, and in April the Papal States become a province.

Napoleon, who has ranged from Cairo to Vienna, and will range from Madrid to Moscow, Napoleon, who has often been in Italy, hesitates to set foot in Rome; caution or circumstance always keeps him away. He never confirms by actual inspection the image he has carried in his mind from boyhood upwards. Now for the second time his generals take possession of what he had been wont to regard as the Eternal City. No member of his entourage protests against the occupation. But his mother feels it to be a mistake, and her distress affects her health. Whereas formerly she had been content to say sceptically of her son's great fortune: "if only it lasts!" now, with a presage of destruction, she confides her misgivings to her intimates:

"I foresee that he will bring disaster on himself and all his family. He should be content with what he has. He tries to grasp too much, and will lose all!"

XVII

"What the German peoples ardently desire is that persons who are not of noble birth but are talented shall have equal rights to your consideration and to office, so that there may be an end, once and for all, to any kind of subordination, and to all intermediaries between the ruler and the lowest classes of the population. The advantages brought by the Code Napoléon, publicity of legal procedure, and trial by jury, will be characteristics of your monarchy. To lay my whole thought before you: for the consolidation of this monarchy, I look more to the effects just named than to the results of the greatest victories. Your people must have a liberty, an equality, and a prosperity hitherto unknown in Germany. This way of ruling will be a stronger barrier between you and Prussia than the Elbe, than fortresses, than the protection of France. What nation would ever wish to go back to Prussian rule when it had once experienced the advantages of a liberal government?"

In these sentences (which are written as a private lesson, and are not penned with an eye to public effect), the Emperor expounds to his youngest brother the great mission that is being entrusted to the latter when he takes charge of the new kingdom of Westphalia. Jerome's task was to plant the fundamental ideas of the revolution on German soil, a pioneer work, this introduction of the first glimmer of self-government in a part of western Europe where hitherto the inhabitants had known only how to obey. In Holland and Italy, ideas of self-government were by no means new. But as far as concerned the princes of the Confederation of the Rhine, although, acting under orders, they could introduce the new legal codes, they lacked the traditions and the talents that might have made it possible to initiate such changes from within. We can now understand the historic mission of the youngest of the Bonapartes. He was to make a great experiment in democracy; he was to transform four million Germans from subjects into citizens. Had this impetus been successful, the whole nation might have been spared resubjugation to princely arrogance after the War of Liberation.

But the young man of twenty-three who, coming at the end of this long family, had been reared as a prince, regarded his kingship as a gallant adventure, in which money and vital energy could be squandered. Youth was like champagne, which bubbles when the cork is drawn. He forsook the arms of his Württemberg consort for those of innumerable mistresses; ran into debt, became involved in manifold scandals, and procreated children all over the place; amused himself more than his subjects; and, by this traditional deportment of one born in the purple, succeeded for decades to come in discrediting the fine notion of the choice of the fittest. There was something to be said for the German view that, if they must have a prince to ride across fields and men, they would like him to be one who had inherited the position. Jerome, however, laughed at the world's mockery, and even laughed at his great brother's exhortations.

Napoleon had a predilection for his youngest brother, the sort of weakness that fathers are apt to have for the latest born of their sons. The brio of the young man's life was in keeping with his own tempo. Besides, Jerome was always amiable, took nothing amiss. For instance, on one occasion he asked Napoleon to make him commander-in-chief, and showed no offence at a refusal couched in the following terms: "Are you serious? After you have been through six campaigns, and after you have had a half a dozen horses shot under you, you can ask me again!"

When Jerome went to war, he took his whole court with him —not the queen, indeed, but all the prettiest of her ladies. He issued proclamations in the style of the Roi Soleil. But he was not mortified to receive the following imperial admonition:

"I have read an order of the day issued by you, in which you make yourself ridiculous. You are king, and the Emperor's brother! Fine qualities in war! In war, a man must be a soldier before everything. When I am in camp, I need neither ministers nor luxury. You must camp with the advance guard, be in the saddle day and night, march with the advance guard, so that you may get all the news without delay. If you don't like that, you had better stay at home in your palace! You make war like a satrap! God in heaven, you never learned that from me! I ride in front of the skirmishers, and do not allow even my minister for foreign affairs to follow me. . . . You make vast claims; you have a certain amount of talent and a few good qualities, but these are put quite in the shade by your follies. Furthermore, you are insufferably conceited, and know absolutely nothing of public affairs."

The king sticks the letter into his jabot with a laugh. But the Emperor? Cannot he realise, while he talks to his brother like a father, that every one to whom he gives unmerited power endangers the very essence of power? That these golden crowns and the extemporised coats-of-arms he provides for them create very unstable kings and princes? That homunculus escapes from the phial and makes fun of his master? This perennial weakness where his relatives are concerned leads him, at times, to assume what is a very unusual role for him, that of the good-natured man; for, though he begins by issuing orders to his brothers, he very often gives way to them in the end. "My brother, inclosed you will find the constitution of your kingdom"—thus he begins a missive of instruction in matters of high politics, with a sentence that might have been taken out of a comic opera. When he is in a friendly humour, he will end a letter full of reproaches with a paternal smile: "Mon ami, I love you, but you are so frightfully young!"

Napoleon is no longer young. Inevitably, as his plans grow, there must be an increase in that harshness which, in him, is mainly the outcome of overwork. When, twelve years earlier, he had come down from the Alps as a conqueror and his fame had spread before him across the plain of Lombardy, his youth had endowed the novelty of this campaign with a sort of romantic innocence which carried his contemporaries off their feet. Now, when the mountain torrent has long since widened into a river, bearing on its broad bosom ships freighted with the treasures of the world, and when the river is drawing near to the ocean in which its waters will soon mingle with all the waters of the earth; now, the gravity of this labour of Atlas has stamped its imprint upon his features, has written its message in his heart. Rare have become the hours of tranquillity, few the moments of merriment and sportive humour; and the heroical cynicism of his mission moulds him before the eyes of the world into a statue of bronze.

True, he had sent for his Polish countess. She was installed in the very street where Josephine had first charmed him, and where, again and again, a quaint superstition led him to house his lady friends. Walewska is munificently provided for, and Napoleon's physician visits her every day. But, though there is no secret about the matter, she leads a retired life, does not use the box at the opera he has reserved for her, and seldom sees him now that she has come to Paris. This is an interlude between one idyll and the next. He has made up his mind that the child she is to bear him will be a son; and the event may have still greater consequences to-day than it would have had yesterday.

For the first of his illegitimate children, the one of whose birth he had received tidings in Berlin (when he had been reassured to learn that there was no justification for the common belief that he was sterile), has been put out of court by the mother's unwise importunity. Shortly after his return to Paris, she had called. He would not see her, sending a message to say that he received no one whom he had not summoned. He provided her with a house and an income, and would have nothing more to do with her. But he had the boy brought to him, and playfully teased the little chap. For a moment, he even thought of adopting him. All had to be done secretly. The invisible master, whom he called the "nature of things" and on rare occasions "fate," forbade him the unconcealed enjoyment of this most natural of scenes in our human life, one in which Napoleon could not play his part until he was nearly forty. At length he had a son of his body, who might become his heir. Yet he, Emperor of the West, could not step forward and say: "This is my son!" Wishing to give the boy at least half his own name, he called him Léon.

But the mother had become completely estranged from him, and Napoleon soon ceased to have any serious thought of making the child his successor. Perhaps he thought that the boy came of a bad stock; maybe he had a foreboding that this half Napoleon would become a half criminal and an outright ne'er-do-well.

All the more vigorously does his advance in years urge him towards a new marriage. There are long conversations between Napoleon and Josephine, between reason and sorrow; and after them it is not Josephine alone in whom the servants note the traces of tears. "How terrible to die childless!" he says on one occasion. Nevertheless his fondness for his helpmate increases. We know how difficult he found it to break with any of his collaborators; and his temperamental conservatism makes him cling to this first companion of his rise. "If I were to divorce her," he says to Talleyrand who advises him to take this step, "the witchery of my home would be gone. I should have to go to school again in order to understand the ways and fancies of a young wife. The empress adapts herself to me perfectly, and understands me so well. Besides, it would be very ungrateful to divorce a woman who has done so much for me." Such are the motives, tender and reasonable, respectable and convenient—in a word, thoroughly middle class—which make the man cleave to his wife.

But the difficulties grow in number, and the need for a decisive step becomes more urgent. While he ponders the moral impression which his divorcing Josephine will make in France (where she inspires far more personal affection than he does), he, as his manner is, lays his plans deliberately, that, at last, he may make an advance which no one anticipates, and will enable him to fulfil two wishes at once. He arranges for an interview with a man whom he has long needed, and whom he may now need more than ever. His mother is always interceding with him on Lucien's behalf; now, Napoleon, who is travelling in Italy, sends for Lucien.

The conversation between the brothers is the most interesting of all Napoleon's recorded conversations, and has been reported by Lucien with fidelity and picturesqueness. Napoleon is there portrayed to the life.

XVIII

Lucien was now just thirty-two. It was on a December evening when he had reached the castle of Mantua, after a journey during which the dread of imprisonment, aroused by his brother's summons, had been continually present to his mind. On entering a room extravagantly lighted by numerous candelabra, he was blinded for a moment by the glare. Then he heard Rustam's voice announcing him: "Sire, your brother Lucien!"

The man to whom the announcement is made does not stir. He is seated at a large round table, which is covered by a huge map of Europe, the biggest Lucien has ever seen. Supporting his head on his left hand, with the other hand he is thrusting coloured pins into the map, pins which presumably represent army corps or whole armies. It is so many years since Lucien has seen his brother, and Napoleon has changed so much, that the visitor is not quite sure whether he is looking at the Emperor, and he remains motionless for several minutes. At length the man sits up, yawns, rubs his back against the chair, takes up a small bell from the table, and rings it with one strong movement. The visitor advances a step or two:

"Sire, I am Lucien."

The Emperor jumps up from his chair, dismisses the servant, and takes his brother by the hand affectionately, though with a certain amount of reserve. Lucien feels called upon to embrace Napoleon, who does not repel the advance, but accepts it with a passive coldness, as if no longer used to such intimacies. Then, taking the visitor by the hand once more, he pushes Lucien gently away to scrutinise him the better:

"So it's you, is it? How are you? How is your family? When did you leave Rome? Have you had a pleasant journey? What about the pope? How is he? Does he like you?"

Lucien notes the nervousness masked by this flood of questions, turns them off lightly, and says he is glad to find his brother in good health.

"Yes, I'm very well." He pats his waistcoat, and adds: "I'm getting fat, and I'm afraid I shall get fatter still." He looks keenly at Lucien, takes a pinch of snuff, and says: "As for you! Do you know that you are looking uncommonly well?

(Photograph by Braun, Paris and Dornach.)

Bonaparte as First Consul. Painting by J. D. A. Ingres.
Musée de Liége.

You used to be rather too thin. Now, you are almost handsome."

"Your Majesty is good enough to make fun of me."

"No, no, it's quite true. But let's sit down and have a talk." They seat themselves opposite the huge map, the Emperor fidgets with the pins, and Lucien waits for him to begin. But, since Napoleon does not open the ball, the younger man says, hesitatingly: "Sire . . ." At this moment, the Emperor sweeps all the pins flat, and says abruptly: "Well, what have you to say to me?"

Lucien replies that he hopes his brother has forgiven him.

"You can have my pardon soon enough. It depends entirely on yourself."

Lucien expresses his willingness to do anything compatible with his honour.

"Well and good, but what sort of things will square with your honour?"

Lucien speaks of nature and religion.

"But politics, Sire; do politics mean nothing to you?"

Lucien demurs, saying that he has retired into private life.

"It rested entirely with yourself. You could have been a king just as well as your brothers."

"Sire, my wife's honour, my children's position. . . ."

"You keep on speaking of your wife, when you know perfectly well that she has never been your wife. Is not, and never will be, for I shall never recognise her."

"Ah, Sire!"

"No, never, though the heavens should fall! Since you are my brother, I can forgive the wrong you have done me. But upon her my curse will rest!" There is a long tirade, until at length Lucien intervenes, laughing nervously, and saying:

"Moderate your words, Sire. There is a proverb: 'La processione torna, dove esce,'" and Lucien thinks it expedient to add a French translation. When Napoleon continues to talk of his brother's wife as a woman of bad reputation, and Lucien shows signs of taking offence, the Emperor tries to mollify him by admitting that these reports may be calumnious, but adds that nothing will induce him to recognise her. Besides, it is now a fundamental law, as firmly fixed as the Salic law, that no marriage in the Emperor's family is valid without the Emperor's consent. Lucien reminds him of the date of the marriage, and Napoleon answers: "Yes, but the law was passed because of what you had done!" This Napoleonic logic makes Lucien smile.

"What are you laughing at? I don't see anything laughable in it! I know what you and your wife and my enemies say about the matter. You choose your friends from among my enemies. But no good Frenchman approves of what you have done. The only way in which you can regain popular esteem is by espousing my cause, like Jerome."

Lucien, who is in the Emperor's hands, has absolutely determined to let nothing affront him. But he is spurred into opposition, springs to his feet, and does not sit down again:

"Your Majesty is mistaken! When your courtiers approve your attitude towards me as thanks for the services I was so happy to render you, they are only acting after their kind. On my side, too, my servants tell me that I am right!"—At these words, Napoleon's brow is furrowed, his eyes flash, and his nostrils work, "an unmistakable sign of rage in members of our family." But Lucien has taken the bit between his teeth, and goes on: "What ought the nation to do for me? What gratitude does it owe me? It ought to look upon me as the saviour of the man who has saved it. . . . I am proud to think that it will rather be inclined to compare me with you than with Jerome. No, Sire, public opinion, which is mightier by far than all the kings in the world, assigns every one to his true place, whatever courtiers may say."

Napoleon grows calmer. Instead of flying into a passion, as Lucien dreaded for a moment, he controls himself, and says quietly:

"Talleyrand is right. You speak of the affair with an ardour worthy of a political club. Such eloquence, Citoyen, is, believe me, long since out of fashion. I am well aware that you did me good service on the Nineteenth Brumaire; but as for having been my 'saviour,' of that proof is lacking. This much I remember clearly, that you disputed with me the unity of power which I needed for the saving of France, and that I and Joseph spent half a night before we could get you to pledge yourself to silence when these questions should be touched upon. . . . Finally, after the victory, you were inclined to oppose my personal elevation, and this conduct on your part releases me from all obligation to show gratitude.

"But you, do you owe me no gratitude? When you 'saved' me at Saint-Cloud, were not you yourself in mortal peril? I sent my grenadiers to save you from the hands of assassins. And if you, a bad brother, an unnatural brother, had really allowed that vote of my outlawry to be taken, do you imagine that I should have been such a fool as to accept the decree unresistingly? Had I not adherents enough, with God's aid, to defend this head that was destined to wear so many crowns?" He goes on to speak for a whole hour of those days, and of Corsican compatriots who had helped him; suddenly gives the conversation an intimate turn; speaks of his generals and the extent of their devotion; refers to political conflicts in which the brothers had held divergent views, and shows how his view had been right. Then he changes the subject, saying abruptly:

"Enough. That is all ancient history, like your great day of the Nineteenth Brumaire. I did not summon you that we might deliver lectures to one another." A long pause.

"Listen to me, Lucien, and weigh my words carefully, for, above all, let us avoid getting heated. . . . I am too powerful to have any desire to lose my temper. You have come to me trustfully. Corsican hospitality shall never be violated by the Emperor of the French. This virtue of our forefathers and fellow-countrymen is a guarantee for your absolute safety."

The Emperor strides up and down the hall for a long time, pulling himself together, and then turns to Lucien, whose hand he takes and presses:

"We are alone here. You see? We are alone. No one can overhear us. I am wrong about your marriage. . . . Knowing your wilfulness as I did, knowing your self-love—for everything, you know, depends on self-love, which regards itself as a virtue, just as we princes dignify by the name of policy everything which turns on our passions—I ought not to have interfered with your union. People slandered your wife to me, though some ventured to speak well of her, especially Mamma, who loves her, saying she makes you happy and is a good mother. . . . Lebrun, indeed, has sung her praises so often that Josephine once told the good fellow he must be in love with her himself. I was very much amused at my wife, who has more of a temper than people fancy. Still, I must say that Josephine never shows her claws to me! Well, I have no disrespect for your wife, but I detest her because this passion of yours for her has robbed me of the most capable of my brothers. However, her beauty will pass; you will be disillusioned; then, returning to political life, you will oppose my policy, and I shall have to take measures against you whether I like it or not; for—let me say this to you—unless you are on my side, Europe is too small for the pair of us!"

"You are making fun of me."

"No, I'm in earnest; friend or foe! It is easier for you today than ever before. You need not be surprised: there has been a change in my family policy. You will see soon enough. Your children, which hitherto I have wanted to exclude, can now be of great use to me, but they must be dynastically recognised. The offspring of a marriage I do not recognise can have no right to the throne. Tell me, then, what would you do in my place?"

Lucien advises him to make the Senate pass a simple resolution to the effect that the children come within the right of succession.

"Of course I know that I can do that, but I must not. As you said just now, public opinion has to be conciliated. What would the family, the court, France, which all watch my slightest movements, say about such a step? A recantation of that kind would do me more harm than the loss of a battle."

Lucien points out that he cannot possibly ask pardon for a marriage which had been entered into long before Napoleon's accession to the throne. "Grant my request, Sire. You will have no more faithful servant than I. All the rest of my life will be an expression of my gratitude."

The younger man goes on talking for a long time, and throughout his speech Napoleon is incessantly taking snuff, but spilling most of the tobacco, so nervous is he, growing more and more anxious; in his perplexity exclaiming at length: "Good God, you press me hard, and I am weak. But I shall not be so weak as to move the Senate to pass the resolution you ask for. I cannot recognise your wife!"

Thereupon Lucien, who is now almost beside himself, says: "Well, then, Sire, what do you really want of me?"

"What do I want? Simply that you should divorce your wife."

"But you have always maintained that we are not married, so how can we get a divorce?"

"I expected you to say that. What do you think I can mean by asking you to procure a divorce? Obviously, thereby I recognise your marriage, but not your wife. The divorce will be the best thing for your children, just like all that you have hitherto refused to do, all that I have so much wanted you to do: to annul the marriage and divorce her."

"That would be a dishonour for me and my children, and I will never do it!"

"Why is it, that with all your mother wit, you cannot see

the difference between my earlier proposals and my present ones. In the former case, if your marriage had been declared null, your children would have become bastards!"

Lucien points out the difference between his children's dynastic rights and their civic rights. "You can bestow your thrones upon whom you will, Sire, for you won them at the point of the sword. But no one shall cheat my children out of their share in the modest heritage of Carlo Bonaparte, for they are as legitimate as any one else's both by canon law and by State law. The pope has even given one of my daughters the name of his mother!"

"Calm yourself! . . . Of course the divorce I ask for implies the recognition of your marriage. Nor do I wish to force an actual separation from your wife. She shall be honoured in accordance with her merits if she will make this sacrifice to my policy and to the future interests of France. I would even pay her a visit. But if she refuses, you and she will both be blamed for having sacrificed the true greatness of your children to your own egoism, and your children will curse your memory!"

Lucien answers mournfully.

"You are really incorrigible," rejoins Napoleon. "You take everything so tragically. I am not asking for any tragedies! Think it over."

After Lucien has again and again insisted upon his point of honour, and has several times wished to take leave, the Emperor once more brings up the distribution of the thrones. Eugene's position in Italy is merely provisional, and he would much rather see Lucien installed there. Napoleon complains about Hortense, too. None of them are satisfied. "Pauline is naturally the most reasonable in the matter of ambition, for she is the queen of fashion. Besides, she grows more lovely day by day. Josephine is ageing, and is greatly distressed about a divorce."

Lucien pricks up his ears. Napoleon goes on as if he were talking at random:

"Can you believe it? She always bursts into tears when her digestion is a little upset, for she fancies she is being poisoned by those who would like me to marry some one else. That is despicable. Still, in the end, I shall have to get a divorce. I ought to have taken the step long ago, and I should have had quite big children by now; for, I may as well tell you"—he speaks earnestly—"people are wrong in thinking it is my fault we have no children. I have several. Two I know of for certain." He mentions, without naming her, Léon's mother; and then, wonder of wonders, the Polish countess. "She is an exquisite woman, an angel. . . . You laugh to see that I am in love. Yes, I really am; but I never forget considerations of policy. She wants me to marry a princess. Of course, as far as feelings go, I would much rather raise my beloved to the throne. You, in your dealings with your wife, ought in like manner to be guided by considerations of policy!"

"Sire, I should act as you are doing if my wife were only my mistress."

The Emperor grows more and more animated; speaks of a fixed intention to get a divorce; deplores having given the Bavarian princess to Eugene, who does not care for her and did not choose her for himself; remarks that he might long since have had Lucien's daughter betrothed to the prince of Asturia "or some other great prince, perhaps even a great emperor. . . . Your divorce would have to precede mine, or be simultaneous. Then there would be less chatter about my divorce; for yours, in view of your obstinate refusal for so long previously, will certainly arouse more interest. Will you do me this service? I think you really ought to."

Lucien looks at him so quizzically that the Emperor is amazed, eyes his brother up and down, and says: "Why not?"

Lucien smiles at the unreasonableness of the demand. Napoleon is embarrassed, but returns to the charge. Suddenly he addresses his brother as "my dear President" (Lucien having long ago been president of the Council of Five Hundred), and adds with emphasis: "Service for service, of course—and this time you will not find me ungrateful!"

Lucien sank "into a sort of reverie, which was by no means unpleasant," so that for a few moments he hardly noticed what Napoleon was talking about. Before long he realised that the Emperor was saying, confidentially, that his only reason for wanting Lucien's divorce was that this would probably minimise the effect of his own on public opinion. Lucien, as tactfully as he could, alluded to his own advantages, pointing out that his wife was a young woman and was not barren. Napoleon took no offence. "Your wife, oh, yes, your wife, didn't I tell you? She will become the duchess of Parma, your eldest boy will be her heir, without having any claim of succession to your rights as a French prince. For this is only the first stage to which I shall raise you, until something better can be found: an independent crown."

At the word "independent," Lucien cannot restrain a smile, for he is thinking of the part his brothers have to play. Napoleon notices the expression on his face.

"Yes, independent. You will know how to reign. . . . You need only take your choice!" His eyes flash fire, and he bangs the enormous map with the flat of his hand. "I'm not talking at random. All this belongs to me or soon will. Even to-day, I can do what I please. Would you like to have Naples? I will take it away from Joseph. . . . Italy, the loveliest jewel in my imperial crown? Eugene is no more than viceroy. He hopes to become king, expects to outlive me, but he will be disappointed in this matter. I shall live to be ninety, for I cannot do with less than that for the complete consolidation of my empire. Besides, Eugene will not suit me in Italy, after I have divorced his mother. Would you care for Spain? Do you not see that it is ripe to fall into my hands, thanks to the blunders of the Bourbons you are so fond of? Would you not like to be king in the country to which you went as envoy? What would you prefer to have? It is for you to say. Anything and everything is at your disposal, if only you will divorce your wife before I divorce mine!"

Lucien is spell-bound for a time by the feverish haste with which Napoleon speaks. At last he says: "Not even your lovely France, Sire, would bribe me to this divorce; and besides . . ." He hesitates; but the Emperor guesses his thoughts, and says dryly, with an imperious air such as Lucien has never before seen him assume:

"Do you think that you, as a private individual, are in a more secure position than I upon my throne? . . . Do you believe that your friend the pope is strong enough to protect you against me if I should seriously propose to take measures against you?" After reiterating arguments and enticements, he says in a formal tone: "You may be quite sure of this: everything for the divorced Lucien; nothing for the undivorced!"

Lucien glances at the door, as a hint to the Emperor that he would be glad to be given his dismissal; but Napoleon takes him by the hand, and says "in a vague tone, and with a demeanour which might mean anything":

"If I get a divorce, you will not be the only other one. Joseph is merely waiting for my divorce to arrange for his own. Madame Julie has been good for nothing but to bring girls into the world, whereas I urgently need boys. The only use of girls is to marry them off in advantageous alliances. Besides, your eldest girl is nearly fourteen, so you tell me; just the right age. Won't you send her to Mamma? If you do what I want, I will get Mamma to arrange something good for her. . . . You are not afraid that we shall do any harm to your spoiled darling? Tell her we shall be good friends, and that I will not pull her ears as if she were a child. . . . I need more nephews and nieces! The divorced Josephine, the grandmother of Hortense's children, will always be the enemy of my legitimate and my adopted sons." Then, murmuring as if to himself, "It must be done. I have no other way of undermining the power of Louis' and Hortense's children."

He comes back to the subject of his own illegitimate children, says he intends to adopt them, enters into details, and suddenly exclaims: "You cannot suppose that I have not the power to legitimise my natural children, just as Louis XIV. declared his bastards, the fruit of a twofold adultery, to be within the right of succession to the throne." Again he speaks of Joseph's intention to procure a divorce, and, when Lucien is sceptical, he rubs his hands delightedly, saying:

"Yes, yes! Joseph and you will both divorce your wives! We will all three get divorces, and then marry again, all of us, on the very same day!" He adds a number of quips in the like merry vein. Then, suddenly: "But why have you become so serious? One might think you a sage of classical antiquity! You must stay with me for three days. I'll have a bed made ready for you in the next room to mine!"

He presses this invitation. Lucien, who dreads his brother's blandishments, has to invent an excuse, and says that one of his children is ill.

His wife, he goes on to say, has suffered because of the Emperor's dislike; so much so, that he had been afraid at one time her anxiety and distress about the matter would be too much for her.

"Is that really so? I'm sorry. You must take care of her! Whatever happens, she must not die before you get your divorce, for if she did I should not be able to legitimise her children!"

Lucien pretends that he will think the matter over.

"That's all right. Well, well, go if you must! But be sure to keep your word!" Napoleon takes Lucien by the hand, and at the same time presents his cheek for a kiss, which is not as brotherly as it might be. Lucien departs, and when he is in the anteroom he hears the Emperor calling: "Méneval!"

Lucien quickens his steps, for again the dread of imprisonment has seized him.

No one, no historian and no imaginative writer, has ever

given a more brilliant description of Napoleon than the foregoing, penned by his brother with obvious fidelity. This evening, the Emperor is in a quandary. He wants the help of a man whom he cannot coerce, and one who in certain respects is his equal. In the light thrown by Lucien, Napoleon's character becomes positively transparent. He develops himself under our very eyes, showing us all the interplay of his motives.

He lavishes temptations in the endeavour to overpersuade his adversary. Every move is carefully thought out, that it may exercise its appropriate influence upon the ambition of his interlocutor, whom he tries to win by the studied gradations of the dialogue. The visitor finds him brooding over the map of Europe, and is greeted in a way which is to alarm and to inspire confidence by turns. The wife, the bone of contention, is first vilified and then extolled. Napoleon goes back to the phraseology of the Jacobin Club, calls his brother "citizen," pulls out one emotional stop after another. He reminds Lucien that they are both Corsicans; says with a challenging irony that Europe is too small for the pair of them; talks of Mamma and Pauline, of Joseph and Louis, using names that carry with them reminiscences of the nursery in which the Bonaparte children had played together. Thus he spins his web round Lucien.

And yet—this is the marvel—we are shown the bubbling up of his nature, the beating of his heart, the quivering of his brain. Again and ever again, imagination and passion seem to carry him beyond the limits of self-restraint. Though his brother is a declared opponent, he makes all kinds of confessions: about Josephine and the countess; about his stepchildren and his generals; about his own blunders and his new, far-reaching plans. There is a flood of confidential admissions. Why?

Because this Lucien, though an adversary, though no less gifted than Talleyrand, is a brother, and therefore, to the clannish Napoleon, is, in spite of everything, worthy of confidence. It moves us to see the way in which Napoleon detains him in private talk for hours, till midnight is long past; how he presses Lucien to stay for a few days, that they may thrash matters out; and how Lucien insists on going, not because he really needs to, but because he does not wish to bow before the force of his brother's genius. For there is a secret contest between the pair, not about love or divorce, not about honour or crowns. To-day, just as seven years before, when the younger man could not bring himself to obey the elder, the contest is between the innermost self-esteem of one rival and of the other. After all these years, in the privacy of his own thoughts Lucien is still convinced that he could have managed everything much better than Napoleon.

And yet, all the time, he loves him after his own fashion. Every word of his report betrays the obscure enmity between the brothers, the enmity that lives side by side with love. That is why he concedes nothing. The memory of the Nineteenth Brumaire has to be revived, and once more each of them is confident he was right. While these expert realists are talking, with the old phrases on their lips, the old verbiage about the greatness and the safety of France, they are really moved by nothing but their own passions. We seem to see them posturing before the crowd (a doubt seizes them—"We are alone here. You see. We are alone. No one can overhear us"); but in truth they are alone, in a strange and foreign castle, beneath huge candelabra, on which the candles are burning low.

Nevertheless, despite Napoleon's wealth and all his crowns, despite his stupendous powers of intellect and imagination, how poor a man he is, entangled in the threads of destiny, the threads which he has spun, but which are now spinning themselves in defiance of his wishes! For all his omnipotence, he is the slave of an incalculable, much-courted power, public opinion, which will not allow him to effect a reconciliation with his brother, to recognise his own children, or to marry the woman he loves. The impotence of the man of might is displayed in his own exclamations. He asseverates his power to do anything and everything—and yet he dare not do what he wants. How pleased he is with his brother, whose affairs he could manage so beautifully now that they have met after many years of separation. If Lucien would only stay with him, were it but for three days, they would certainly be able to come to an understanding. "Good God, you press me hard, and I am weak."

During this night when an emperor was offering his brother a choice among the thrones of Europe, was there not talk of the heritage of Carlo Bonaparte, a poor nobleman, on a small, out-of-the-way island? Did the Emperor of the French, who will never hear a word of his being a foreigner in France, conjure up the shade of the Corsican; was it he who evoked the penates of his birthplace for the protection of Brother Lucien, a negotiator in a hostile camp? Surely what we are recounting is a saga, told at midnight beside the fireplace in Mantua? Yes, it is the saga which the little Corsican lieutenant has woven out of the threads of his life: first a narrow band; but as he trails it after him, twists it and loops it, mixes colours and patterns, by degrees a carpet is formed; greater and more varied become the pictures produced out of the one thread, pictures of lands and thrones, of seas and men.

The whole has been woven in the most natural way in the world. Not by a miracle, but only through the working of his talents, has the man become master of men. To-night he wants to add yet another to the long list of his subjects. He has not enough time, even though he hopes to live till he is ninety. He cannot allow his brothers to have girl children, or to live with the women of their choice. But if these undesired nieces throng his stage, he must set up new nephews against them. If a wife is in danger of dying of grief, she must at least be good enough to wait until she is divorced. When the men of the family have at length forsaken the wives who are barren or can only bear daughters, then, on the same day, they will take new wives unto themselves—and all will go happily ever after. Look at him, when the conversation is drawing to a close, rubbing his hands in his satisfaction, the little magician who stands in front of his immense map. By the time he has impaled all the countries with his coloured pins, impaled them like butterflies to put away in his collection—well, by that time the candles have burned out and a large slice of to-morrow has already been devoured.

XIX

The Spanish dynasty seemed about to fall. Immediately after the conversation recorded above, war was declared. Had not the Emperor already predicted it? A king who had degenerated into being his wife's souteneur; a queen who only lacked courage to be a Messalina; a faithless minister; hatred between father and son; rascality, bribery, and corruption—to such a pass had sunk the house of Bourbon! He who wished to dethrone those who represented it, must use the same means as were used by the Spanish royal house itself. Never before had Napoleon's actions been more fiercely unscrupulous; never before had the degeneracy of his opponent been a more useful weapon to his hand. He had always adapted his methods to his adversary; and, in the case of this decayed dynasty, he had recourse to the wiles and trickery similar to those which the Spanish house availed itself of in a last effort to preserve its integrity. Absorbed in his schemes, he forgot the Spanish people, which was in no way responsible for such princes, and which in no way resembled the royal rulers: in days to come the Emperor was bitterly to rue his forgetfulness.

He who is for England, is against me! In support of this principle, Napoleon had already chased the Portuguese royal family from the throne. Now, since Spain, too, is on the side of England, in a prolonged intrigue he turns to his own advantage the struggle between the king and the crown prince; brings the latter to the front; then orders him to withdraw in favour of the father; and, finally, at a meeting of all parties in Bayonne, is able, by threats and cunning, to ensure that the

Spanish crown shall be his own. The Mediterranean must belong to him; the coasts at any rate, from Gibraltar to Cattaro. This is an essential part of the war on England.

At first his generals have an easy task in their work of conquest. "Do you know why I am invading Spain?" says Napoleon to Metternich. "I must feel safe at my back." Alas for him when he is no longer safe in that quarter!

On the critical day when he has settled matters with the Spanish princes, and has arranged that they shall be kept in a mild imprisonment, he is in a condition of moderate intoxication. The new crown gives him fresh impetus. He no longer sees Spain; his eyes are turned to contemplate the worldwide empire of Spain in the days of her vanished glory. On this occasion, a witness tells us, "the Emperor spoke, or rather dictated, at great length, in the Ossianic vein, . . . like one whose heart was uplifted. . . . In his picturesque, metaphorical style, he referred to the powerful kingdoms of Mexico and Peru, describing the might of their rule and their influence. Never have I heard him display such a wealth of imagery as on this day. He was sublime."

The one thing he lacks is an occupant for the vacant throne, since Lucien has not accepted the bribe. The only way out of the difficulty will be a general post, like that which occurs when a vacancy is filled in the upper ranks of the officialdom and every one is promoted a step. Let us do away with the kingdom of Holland, make it into a province, and discrown Louis. The victim protests: "It does not suit me to be governor of a province. A king must rule by divine right. . . . How could I demand loyalty from my people if I myself were false to the oath I swore when I ascended the throne?" Napoleon is troubled once more by the consequences of having founded a dynasty. This modern Roman should have put his provinces in charge of generals and regents, whom he could recall whenever he pleased. But the ermine in which he dresses his puppets, all the apparatus of coronation and Mass and anointing, awaken ideas which were being laid to rest, and fully justify little King Louis in his refusal. Joseph is more accommodating. Till yesterday, he was king in Naples: why should he not be king in Madrid to-morrow? Shortly after the Bayonne intrigue, King Joseph I. enters his new capital, acclaimed, not indeed by the hearts of the people, but by the proper number of salute guns and all the ceremonial suitable to the occasion. Murat, whose wife has long been pestering her brother for a crown, Murat the son of the proletariat, becomes king of Naples, and thus the imposing couple gain a statelier field for their intrigues, and in due time for their treason.

But this Spanish affair is a great adventure, and has serious consequences. There is muttering "at the Emperor's back," for the Spaniards are proud, and will not endure the conquest without a struggle. In front, across the Rhine, all the Prussians and all the Austrians who hate the Emperor have now reason to dread that Prussia and Austria may share the fate of Spain, and have good grounds for yet another renewal of their offensive. In Berlin, Napoleon had declared that on the Elbe he had conquered the Ganges. Now he fails to see that in his dealings on the Tagus he is raising up new enemies on the Danube. But he knows that he cannot do as he pleases in Spain unless the tsar holds Austria in check for him. The tsar is a man of unstable character. The only way to win over Alexander is by suggestion, as two years before, in Tilsit, and for this a personal interview will be necessary. The Emperor thereupon proposes to meet the tsar in central Germany, half way between their respective empires, thus initiating a form of policy new to him, a conference. Always before, when he has left France, it has been sword in hand, and he has invariably paved the way for negotiations by fighting. Now, to avoid a fight, a conference table is established in Erfurt.

Napoleon prepares for this new sort of campaign with as much care as if he had been preparing for a military expedition. Day after day he summons court officials and other dignitaries. "My journey must be extremely imposing. I want great names for the headquarters, . . . and I wish to amaze Germany by the splendour of the occasion." For others are coming besides the tsar. The great double stars are attracting all the lesser stars. How can he best influence this assembly? The play's the thing wherein he'll catch the conscience of the kings! He stage-manages his theatre elaborately, devotes much thought to the cast, amends passages, and gives Talma (for whom he feels something akin to friendship) hints as to what requires to be emphasised—all with an eye to the royal audience. "You are going to play your parts in a theatre where the stalls will be filled with kings."

In actual fact, the evenings at the theatre form the climax of the Erfurt weeks. Among the audience are four kings and thirty-four princes, rivalling one another in the splendour of their retinues. The Emperor of the West and the Emperor of the East occupy the royal box. Almost every evening, this distinguished audience sees and hears what the kings of saga or the kings of history proclaim, what they struggle for, what they suffer. Talma, as Orestes, thunders forth:

The gods are the rulers of our times,
And yet fame is created by our own deeds.
Why should the heart allow the heavens to threaten?
Resolve to become immortal
And you will be as gods upon the earth!

The next evening they see Voltaire's *Mahomet*, of which the Emperor is especially fond, were it only because the hero so seldom quits the stage. The prophet's disciple exclaims:

All men are equal; it is not birth,
But virtue alone which makes them different.
There are certain mortals favoured by the gods,
Who achieve everything by their own merits,

Who owe nothing to their forefathers.
Such a one is he whom I have chosen as master;
He alone, in all the world, has deserved his position.

Is there any one among the audience whose heart does not beat faster as he glances at the man up there in the royal box—though the passion may be a passionate antagonism? The princes by right of birth may dread to look at the Emperor, but at least their eyes will seek one another as if to secure a common understanding. They do not dare to smile. They tremble before the man who sits there in a plain green coat, the man who is revolt incorporated in human form. He knows what the German princes in the stalls do not yet know, that a new and stronger utterance will soon be made by Mahomet:

See, the Roman Empire falling into ruins,
That great torn body, whose scattered limbs
Lie spread about the earth dishonoured and lifeless:
On these fragments of a world we shall upbuild the far-flung East,
A new god reveals himself to the blind world!

Finally, the Emperor's policy of to-day and to-morrow is voiced in the words:

Who was it made the master a king?
Victory alone has crowned him! But now
To the name of Conqueror he will add
The name of Peacemaker.

At this instant, when all glance at him questioningly, Napoleon makes a slight movement as a sign that such is actually his intention, and for a political instant the illusion of the theatre is dispelled. But when, next evening, Œdipus proclaims: "A strong man's friendship is a gift of the gods!" the two emperors rise and clasp hands.

Napoleon knows well enough that Alexander is not a strong man, that his friendship is not a gift of the gods. He tries, therefore, by suggestion, to win over this vacillating personality. If the tsar is to be influenced to move along the lines laid down in the letter previously quoted, if he is to agree to divide with Napoleon the empire of the world, he will require a course of psychomagnetism, renewed from day to day. Napoleon rarely leaves the tsar to his own thoughts, but treats him like a woman who is to be wooed and won. The only person who is allowed to help the Emperor in this matter is Talleyrand.

The diplomat still limps after Napoleon as the Emperor strides forward, though recently the differences between the two men had found vent.

Talleyrand's shrewdness had led him—sooner than Napoleon, sooner than any one—to detect the first cracks in his master's system. A year before, after the drawn game of Eylau, he had foreseen the possibility of his master's failure in Russia. This had come to him as the vision of a great statesman, and he had promptly deduced therefrom the mission of a great and statesmanlike traitor. Matters had been privately arranged between Napoleon and Alexander; the Emperor was relying on the tsar (to the exclusion of Talleyrand); Napoleon was cherishing a Carlovingian dream, interpenetrated with thoughts of Cæsarism: the fantastical elements in Napoleon's schemes for world conquest had estranged Talleyrand from his master's policy. But instead of cutting adrift from Napoleon, he had been content, on specious pretexts, to resign his ministerial post, receiving instead a lucrative position among the dignitaries of the empire. Both men hoped to gain by the change; Napoleon thinking that he would be able to keep better watch on Talleyrand, and Talleyrand fancying that he would be able to keep better watch on the Emperor's secret thoughts. He was still grand chamberlain; and Champagny, his successor as minister, was a butt for Napoleon's shafts of ridicule. Thus, even after the divorce from his master, Talleyrand remained the sultan's favourite, and his power was redoubled by his shifts as a trickster no longer hampered by official responsibility.

His doubts as to the stability of Napoleon's position were confirmed by the progress of events in Spain. Directly he saw that the Emperor's mind was set on this act of plunder, he realised that its upshot would be disastrous, and for that very reason encouraged his master to the venture. Since the days of Louis XIV., said Talleyrand, the Spanish crown had always been an apanage of the rulers of France. Napoleon, when his mind had been rendered effervescent by this and similar pseudo-arguments, decided upon the occupation of Catalonia "for the duration of the war with England." Now the intriguer promptly returned to a critical attitude, and laughed to himself when the Emperor gave him the ignominious task of entertaining the infantes of Spain in their durance at his mansion near Valençay.

He wants privacy, that he may keep watch on the kidnapped princes, and, through their instrumentality, not only spy upon England, but also keep England informed. Thence it is but a step to open betrayal, and that step Talleyrand now takes. This is in keeping with his whole career as a statesman. Henceforward he sends Tolstoy and Metternich (the envoys of Tsar Alexander and Emperor Francis in Paris) private information. How can he make his duplicity square with his duties to the master, to whose service he is pledged as imperial official, court official, and confidential adviser?

There is a scene about the matter.

"Well, you see," says the Emperor on his return from Spain, "they all walked into the net I spread for them!"

"I think, Sire, you have lost more than you have won by what has happened at Bayonne."

"What do you mean?"

"Something quite simple. Let me explain my meaning by an example. If a man of standing commits follies, keeps mistresses, treats his wife and his friends badly, he will be blamed;

but his wealth and his power will enable him to regain the good opinion of society. But if the same man cheats at cards, he is expelled from good society, which will never forgive him."

The Emperor turns pale—so Talleyrand reports and will not speak to him for the rest of the day. Why does he not drive the plain speaker out of his circle? Why does he not banish Talleyrand to the West Indies? Napoleon receives a moral castigation from a scion of the old nobility, and still keeps the man in his entourage! Or was Talleyrand lying? We may have all the more confidence in the diplomat's memoirs, seeing that they were written twenty years later, after the Restoration; were written to show how he had always played double, and (of course, owing to his respect for the claims of the legitimate rulers!) had served his imperial master only by halves. We can assume that the words were actually spoken, and to a man to whom hardly any one now spoke the truth, to a man whom even fewer now ventured to affront. Why does Napoleon keep Talleyrand in his service?

"He is the only one who understands me," said the Emperor of Talleyrand again and again. That accounts for much. Talleyrand's unscrupulous way of thinking, his freedom from all qualms of conscience, furnished a tilting-ground on which the Emperor could joust freely when running a political course. The others had principles or considerations which must first be leapt over. Because Talleyrand was exempt from all prejudices of class and time, and also lacked the ordering ideas with which Napoleon fashioned his realm out of the chaos of chances, the wily opportunist, whose only passion was for money, was the best adviser of the other realist, who could only assuage his stormy imagination in a perpetual succession of new plans.

That is why they understood one another, though only in the superficial regions of their respective characters. Napoleon never plumbed the depths of the treason that Talleyrand was preparing.

Here, in Erfurt, the great day for the double-dealer has at

last dawned. When the German princes gather round him and listen as he talks of the Emperor, he gives little heed to these pygmies, for there is some one else who will pay a far higher price for information, will pay both in political advantages and in ready cash.

Alexander is prompt to seize the opportunity! The Russian has been well informed by his representative in Paris, and is almost as inquisitive concerning this Frenchman as he is concerning the Emperor. Talleyrand soon meets the tsar in the reception room of the Princess of Thurn and Taxis, who keeps open house every evening after the play. Talleyrand's report of the encounter, written several decades later, reads like the utterance of a Mephistopheles: "The arts which I had prepared for the capture of the tsar were quite unneeded. At my first word he understood me, just as I had wished him to understand."

The play of their eyes conveyed a meaning which was not manifest in the words, for on the first day Talleyrand had said to the tsar: "Sire, what are you thinking of doing here? It lies with you to save Europe. But you will not succeed in your task unless you become a match for the Emperor. The French people is civilised: their ruler is not. The ruler of Russia is civilised: his people is not. Thus, the ruler of Russia should be the ally of the French people. . . . Your Majesty should not allow yourself to be inveigled into any disciplinary measures against Austria, but should consent to undertake the same duties towards that country as those my master has undertaken."

During the long evenings, over a glass of punch or a dish of tea, Talleyrand (who, like Napoleon, knows the manifold arts of the seducer) instils into the tsar's brain all the truths and the hopes he wishes to bring to life within this suggestible spirit. The tsar shows his appreciation of the diplomat's indiscretions at France's expense by bestowing his favour upon the Emperor's confidential adviser. He promises the hand of a Russian princess to one of Talleyrand's nephews; she is the richest heiress in the eastern realm.

Alexander, who in any case had come to Erfurt in a cautious frame of mind (for his relatives had succeeded in arousing suspicions before he started), is now for the first time able to resist Napoleon. In their private interviews, each is always trying to humbug the other; the honeymoon atmosphere of Tilsit has vanished, and the tsar's enthusiasm for the Emperor is a thing of the past.

Napoleon is taken aback. He makes Talleyrand draft the new treaty of alliance. Then, with great labour, he transcribes it, inserting his own emendations, and takes it to Alexander, who has to promise that no one shall hear a word of what is written in this secret document. The tsar gives the required pledge; but the very same evening he hands Talleyrand the amended treaty, so that the author of the draft learns what alterations his master has made. In the end, this treaty is not signed.

At night, the Emperor summons Talleyrand, who plays the part of Iago admirably. The Emperor says: "I can make no headway with him; he takes such short views."

"But he is completely under your spell, Sire."

"He makes you think so, and you are taken in by him. If he is really fond of me, why won't he sign?"

"He is a man of knightly faith," answers Talleyrand. "His simple word and his inclinations will bind him more strongly than a treaty."

"I shall not talk to him about this matter any more; for if I do, he will think I have it very much at heart. Our private interviews will be enough to make Austria believe that there is a secret treaty. . . . I cannot understand your fondness for Austria, a country whose whole policy recalls that of our old regime!"

When fundamental principles are under discussion, Talleyrand is apt to become more communicative: "It seems to me that Austrian policy is also that of the new regime, and I venture to say it ought to be your own policy. People count on you, Sire, to safeguard civilisation."

"Civilisation! . . ." Napoleon halts in front of the fireplace, and, with a sudden change of tone, says softly: "Do you know why no one will negotiate with me plainly and straightforwardly? Because I have no children. . . . That is the secret. People are afraid of me, and every one wants to snatch what advantages he can. This is an unfortunate state of affairs for the world, and it must be altered."

A few days pass. Intercourse between the two rulers seems more cordial; etiquette has been forgotten; they come and go freely, like ordinary friends in private life. Napoleon spreads his nets cunningly. He says to the tsar: "Yes, I need rest; I need a home. How can one get these when one has no children? My wife is ten years older than I," he goes on, falsely adding four years to Josephine's tale. "Please excuse me. What I have just said may sound rather absurd, but I do not wish, where you are concerned, to hide the stirrings of my heart." A pause. "Hullo, I see it's almost dinner time, and Baron Vincent is still waiting my leave to depart."

The kings of the drawing-room are fond of describing Napoleon as a man of camps; but how prettily he can introduce a delicate topic just before dinner, so that he can slip away without having it discussed at this state. Late that evening he summons Talleyrand to his bedside; orates, questions, suggests combinations, and issues orders by turns. At length he speaks of divorce. "Fate constrains me to it, and it is essential to the tranquillity of France. I have no successor. Joseph is a man of no account, and his children are all girls. I must found a dynasty, and my consort must be the daughter of a great line. Alexander has sisters, and one of them is of suitable age. Have a talk with Romanzeff. When the Spanish affair is settled, I shall discuss the partition of

Turkey. Tell him this, and use other arguments as well. I know you have long been in favour of the divorce."

Next day, Talleyrand broaches the topic with the tsar, who has been influenced by the suggestion the Emperor has instilled with his assumption of melancholy overnight. "No one fully understands the man's character," says Alexander, much moved. "All the commotion he spreads abroad is an inevitable outcome of his position. No one realises how good he is. You know him so well. What is your opinion?"

Talleyrand has no intention of saying what he really thinks, but deems it expedient, at this juncture, to let Alexander know what Napoleon had let fall about the Russian princess. "I should have no objection," rejoins the tsar promptly, "but I cannot dispose of my sister's hand without my mother's consent."

Thereafter, a long conversation between the emperors, and a renewal of intimacy; Alexander spends some more evenings with Talleyrand, talking over the teacups—but no conclusion is reached. The expanded treaty of alliance between the emperors is not signed at Erfurt, nor is the marriage to Alexander's sister arranged. Although Napoleon receives more adulation than ever before, he is disappointed at having to leave without his treaty and without his Russian bride. The only one who brings home substantial advantages is Talleyrand, for he has secured the new niece's millions.

Meanwhile the thirty-eight princes have been cajoled or threatened, rewarded or ignored, by the Emperor and his train. "In Erfurt," writes Talleyrand, "not a man among them was bold enough to face the lion. . . . On the last day he was surrounded by princes whose armies he had seized or destroyed, whose States and existence he had curtailed, but not one of them ventured even to proffer a request. The only wish of them all was to be seen; and to be seen last if possible, in order to remain in his memory."

In any case, Napoleon thinks Vienna will believe that to have been settled which unfortunately has not been settled. Fear will achieve what he has failed to secure through a treaty. He does not know that Talleyrand has betrayed him to Metternich, saying: "It rests with you to restore your relationships with Russia to the intimate footing that existed before Austerlitz. Nothing but an alliance between Austria and Russia can save the vestiges of Europe's independence." The Austrian diplomat writes exultantly in his report: "At length we have entered a new epoch, in which allies offer themselves to us from within the French Empire."

Farewells are taken. The Emperor, watched by the princes, exchanges a brotherly kiss with Alexander. All the onlookers are profoundly impressed by this token of friendship in the pair who rule the world. But Talleyrand, hat in hand, smiles inwardly, for over the teacups at the German princess' he has been able to undermine the foundations of this friendship.

In four years his labours will bear fruit, and the fruit will poison Napoleon.

XX

Brightly, against this dull background of German princelets, shines the torch of the German spirit. "I have gained only one thing here to take back with me to Paris: that you will have a pleasant memory of me." To the Weimar circle, the Emperor says these words on the evening of his departure, for here and in Erfurt he has spent several evenings among those who are the true princes of Germany—princes who have no ancestors, but only genius. Himself a genius without ancestors, it is solely among them that he feels at home; though, during this fortnight, he experiences so much that increases his misanthropic contempt for his fellow-men, a contempt which has its counterpart in the respect he feels for the German spirit. The works of the masters of German literature are, indeed, unknown to him; but he knows their reputation, he knows the position they occupy in the invisible German and the imperial French Republic. That is why he seeks them out.

Two years before, in Potsdam, he had summoned Johannes von Müller to his presence, and nothing throws a stronger light upon the significance of their conversation than the reserve with which the Prussianised Swiss historian treats the incident. With all the precision of a mind that knew so well how to classify its materials, the Emperor was able, without periphrases, to come direct to the topics which must interest every historian, and were especially interesting to this one. Within three minutes, the pair were deep in the profoundest problems of history.

The Emperor spoke of Tacitus. Then he sketched the main epochs of intellectual life, and waxed enthusiastic concerning the wonderful manner in which Greek culture was renovated by Christianity when Roman culture was decaying. How adroit had been the Greek tactic, when Greece, conquered by the Roman sword, had found a way to reassert her dominance over the things of the spirit. These words, addressed by Napoleon so soon after the battle of Jena to a man of learning in Prussian service, convey both recognition and a challenge. The Emperor showed himself even more affable by going on to advise Müller to write a history of the Napoleonic exploits—advice he had never given to any Frenchman. Then he spoke of the basis of all religions, and of the need for religion. "The conversation was a long one," writes Müller. "It embraced nearly all lands and nations in its scope. . . . The more interesting he became, the more did he drop his voice, so that at length I had to come very close to him, and no one else in the room can have heard what he was saying. Much of it, indeed, I shall never disclose."

From this remarkable conclusion to a bald report, we may infer, not only the discretion of the grave historian, but also the splendid frankness which the Emperor could show when holding forth in monologue to a man of mark.

Now, in Weimar, he pays especial attention to old Wieland, compares him to Voltaire, but asks him rather critically when he mixes up romance and history. "A man of outstanding intelligence, like you, should know how to keep them apart. Running them together is apt to lead to confusion."

Something more serious than literary criticism is involved, for when Wieland ably defends his misuse of history, and goes on to speak of virtue as an example, the Emperor pulls him up with customary bluntness, saying: "But don't you know what happens to people who are always expounding virtue in the realm of fable and nowhere else? In the end they come to believe that virtue itself is nothing more than a fable."

Napoleon turns back to Tacitus, for he always keeps a sharp eye on this Roman historian, as if the man, like Madame de Staël to-day, might still work mischief in Parisian drawing-rooms. As a development of this criticism, speaking in a modern ball-room, Napoleon utters great things concerning the activities of men: "Tacitus has not sufficiently studied the causes and the inner motives of events. His enquiries into the mystery of actions and states of mind have not been sufficiently profound to enable him to hand down an unprejudiced judgment to posterity. A historian should take men and nations as they are, should appraise them as their time and their circumstances have made them. . . . I have heard him extolled because he would fain make tyrants dread the people, but that would be very unfortunate for the people! Perhaps I am boring you? We did not come here to talk about Tacitus. Look how beautifully Emperor Alexander dances!"

Wieland has been waiting for this moment. In a carefully prepared speech, he defends the old Roman against the new, so that, at the end, the Weimarian dignitaries and any others who are listening cannot restrain their jubilation.

The Emperor has listened attentively. All now look at him, wondering what he will say. Will he politely withdraw from the discussion? Napoleon, as if on the battle-field, has been wondering upon what private information his adversary's unexpected attack can have been based, and how the onslaught can best be parried. Unquestionably, the speech was not improvised. But how on earth had it entered Wieland's mind to get up that particular topic? Suddenly the Emperor, who in the interim has talked to hundreds upon hundreds of persons, recalls his conversation with Johannes von Müller two years back.

"I certainly have a strong opponent," he says, when the old gentleman his finished the harangue. "You make full use of your advantages. Do you happen to be in correspondence with Herr Müller, whom I met in Potsdam?"

Every one in the audience smiles, including Wieland, who is fonder of wit than of himself, and frankly rejoins:

"Yes, Sire, it was he who told me that you do not like Tacitus."

"Well, I do not admit defeat," says the Emperor. He returns to his Greek and Christian ideas, develops them further and more boldly, for he sees that the clever old Wieland is a sceptic: "Furthermore," he says in low tones, shading his mouth with his hand, and coming close to his interlocutor, "it remains an open question whether Christ ever lived."

Conqueror and poet. One of them is still in his prime, a ruler who has re-established the Christian faith upon the ruins of the revolutionary cult of reason, but is now more or less at odds with the Church. The other is a venerable poet, a pagan whom Napoleon has just coupled with Voltaire, a man who has maintained the cause of reason against the cause of Christ, a member of a conquered nation, and physically so frail that again and again he has to lean on the back of a chair. The former whispers to the latter that it is probable Christ never lived. But the old man has for half a century been justly regarded as the wittiest among the Germans. He will show the Emperor that, in the intellectual world at any rate, a German can courteously exchange thrusts with a Frenchman, and he hastens to reply: "I know that there are foolish people who doubt that Christ lived. But it would be just as absurd to doubt that Julius Cæsar lived; or that you, Sire, are alive to-day!"

Thus with a sally in the French manner Wieland upholds both German courtesy and wit, and the historicity of Christ. The Emperor, without committing himself, is content to drop the subject, and to clap the poet on the shoulder, saying: "Excellent, excellent, Herr Wieland!" Then raising his voice, he talks to his ball-room audience about the value of Christianity as one of the buttresses of the State. But although he was obviously eager to continue his talk with Wieland, the latter showed plainly that he was too tired to stand any longer, and thus the old man's fatigue put a premature end to a scene which the aid of a couple of chairs might have made even more valuable.

One of the silent witnesses of this conversation was Goethe.

A few days earlier, in Erfurt, the Emperor had had an hour's talk with Goethe. They were together in a room where, as was Napoleon's custom when on a journey, he breakfasted, received, commanded, philosophised, and signed documents. Their conversation was a union of two minds, the balancing of counterpoised electrical forces. It was a process of mutual accommodation in which the two greatest men of their day contemplated the world together; a duologue in which most of their thoughts were never uttered, and in which the best elements were an expression of the homage the two paid one another. Goethe, who learned everything from nature, though in the reality of the world of men he could only find the confirmation of his previous imaginings, felt that this conversation was one of the greatest events in his life, and he described it as such. To the Emperor it was less significant.

For Goethe had followed the Emperor's course for a decade, marvelling all the while; and in his old age he said such profound things about Napoleon that a century after their utterance they have not been excelled. Napoleon, on the other hand, knew almost nothing about Goethe; in especial, he never surmised the poet's personal admiration for himself, since the German had hitherto confided his feelings only to his intimates, and even now kept his own counsel. Though the Emperor had read *Werther* several times, the mood that work had aroused was as completely a thing of the past as those youthful feelings which are merely compensatory derivatives for an unoccupied imagination. What this grey-headed poet now signified, was at that time not realised by more than a hundred Germans, and hardly one Frenchman; and, since his name in his own country was little known (and, where known, was unpopular and evoked no enthusiasm), it was natural that the Emperor should know nothing of him save that he had written some wonderful things which were unknown to any except the poet's immediate circle, and that Goethe, at the time of the battle of Jena, was minister to that Saxon prince who had incurred the Emperor's displeasure. When Napoleon summoned Goethe to an audience, he had less to expect from the poet than he had expected from Müller and from Wieland.

But such as Napoleon and Goethe need but look in a man's eyes to know all about him. Napoleon sits breakfasting at a large, round table; on his right is Talleyrand; on his left, Daru. Now he looks up, and, seeing the poet framed in the doorway, invites Goethe to approach. The Emperor is silent, amazed. There stands the sexagenarian, the most beautiful, the halest of old men, Goethe in the calm of his age, at the pinnacle of a strenuously wrought harmony of spirit, a harmony he had never possessed before and was so soon to lose. Napoleon is too full of admiration to speak. Then, more to himself than to his companions, he says:

"Voilà un homme!"

That is the golden shaft which pierces the heart and illuminates the scene: the word of a seer, deeply felt, an impression rather than a judgment—and it is meet that such it should be. For, precisely because the world ruler does not know that a world ruler is now before him, this utterance, the like of which he had never made to or of any one in the past and which he is never to make in the future, shows the godlike kinship of a genius with his brother genius. It is as if two elemental forces hovering on high had recognised each other through a rift in the clouds, and had, despite themselves, stretched out arms to one another until the tips of their forefingers had met; then the mists of time once more rose between them. A fleeting moment in the course of a thousand years; there has been nothing to compare with it since the meeting between Diogenes and Alexander.

Goethe's discretion prevented him from recording the conversation for many a year, and even then the record was incomplete. Other memoirs provide us with fragments only.

Napoleon praises *Werther*, and adds: "I do not like the end of your romance."

"I can well believe that, Sire. You would rather that a romance had no end."

The Emperor calmly accepts this wellnigh threatening epigram. He then continues to criticise the story, saying that Werther's love was not the only factor of the catastrophe, for ambition was likewise at work. The poet laughs (in two letters Goethe mentions this—a freedom rarely indulged in when the Emperor was present), and admits that the criticism is sound; but he adds that surely an artist may be forgiven for using an artifice which few readers will detect.

The Emperor is well content with his little victory in the other man's domain. Turning now to drama, he makes "very remarkable observations, like one who had studied tragedy with the closest attention, in the spirit of a judge presiding over a criminal trial, and of one who keenly regretted the departure of the French theatre from nature and truth." He spoke unfavourably of the drama of destiny, saying that it was a relic of less enlightened days:

(Photograph in the Kircheisen Collection.)

The Coronation. Detail from the picture by Jacques Louis David. Louvre, Paris.

"What have we to do with destiny now! Politics are destiny!"

As he utters these words, he gives an object lesson in his own fashion, turning to Daru to discuss requisitions, and then speaking to Soult who has just entered. Turning back to Goethe, he manœuvres to get the poet to himself, and asks personal questions. Then he assumes the offensive:

"Does it please you here, Herr Goethe?"

But Goethe, too, knows how to seize political opportunities, and rejoins: "Very much; and I hope these days will also prove advantageous to our little country."

"Is your people happy?" asks the Emperor, not noticing that he has phrased the question as if he were talking to a sovereign prince—for he must often have used such words in conversation with rulers. Really, he has no interest now in Saxony, and is thinking: "How can this man of genius be useful to me? What a pity he does not write history. But as a novelist he might describe this congress, or he might write a play.—He would certainly do either much better than our folk; and, besides, this would have redoubled value coming from a foreigner." He therefore says:

"You would do well to stay here for the whole period of the conference, that you may write your impressions of this great drama. What does Herr Goethe think of the suggestion?"

Napoleon ends with this question (so unconsonant with his customary dictatorial manner) almost all his advances to the poet who is so hard to lure out of his reticence. Goethe says cautiously:

"I have not the pen of a classical author."

"That's in the political vein," thinks the Emperor. But what he says is:

"Your duke has invited me to Weimar. For a time he was sulky, but now he is in a better humour."

"If he was sulky, Sire, the punishment was certainly rather

sharp; but perhaps I ought not to express an opinion on these matters. At any rate, we all owe him reverence."

"Splendid!" thinks Napoleon. "He stands in front of his master, but lets me see he knows that the duke is a donkey. I must get this man to write my 'Cæsar' for me! The effect in France would be bigger than that of winning a battle!" His spoken words are:

"Tragedy should be the school of kings and peoples; there is no other field in which the poet can win such laurels. Why do you not write 'Cæsar's Death,' more worthily, more splendidly than in Voltaire's attempt? This might be the greatest work of your life. The aim of the tragedy would be to show how much happiness Cæsar would have conferred on the human race had he been given time to carry out his far-reaching plans. Come to Paris! I urge you to do so! Thence you will get a wider prospect of the world, and there you will find the most abundant materials for new imaginative creations."

The poet expresses his thanks for the proposal, and says he would deem himself happy were it possible to accept.

"That is as far as I had better go," thinks the Emperor, as he had thought recently in his dealings with the tsar; "if I am too insistent, he will fancy I have a strong interest in the matter. It is very strange! He wants nothing from me, not even to shine in my presence. What can charm him out of himself, this incorruptible man? He must come and see the plays we are presenting here; that will stimulate his ambition to write better ones."

Out loud: "I hope you will come to the theatre this evening. You will find a lot of princes there. Do you know the prince-primate? You'll see him in his box, fast asleep, with his head pillowed on the king of Württemberg's shoulder. Do you know the tsar? You ought to dedicate something to him in honour of Erfurt!"

Thus the Emperor gives a third hint. Will Goethe take it? But the poet only smiles civilly, and candidly declares:

"I have never done anything of that sort, Sire, and therefore I have never had occasion to repent it."

A touch! A touch! The Emperor of the French cannot but feel it! Marvellous to relate, the son of the revolution tries to strengthen his position by referring to the Roi Soleil:

"In the reign of Louis XIV., our great authors held other views!"

"No doubt they did, Sire; but we do not know whether they may not have repented."

"How true!" is the Emperor's thought when he hears this sceptical answer, which is really a skirmisher's attack on the part of the German. Consequently, he makes no attempt to detain the poet when the latter, with a deprecatory gesture, himself closes the interview and bids the Emperor farewell—another breach of court traditions, with which Goethe is perfectly familiar.

Thus the amazing upshot of this uncanny conversation between the two men of genius is that the Emperor, to whom the duologue was merely interesting, had vainly solicited a favour of the poet to whom it was the greatest encounter in his life. The explanation is simple: The Emperor wanted to make use of the poet, whereas the poet did not need the Emperor. Napoleon wanted Goethe to write for him. But to Goethe, Napoleon's actions were merely the precious material which enabled him to penetrate to the heart of the other's genius; and he could do this without a journey to Paris.

Although the poet did not respond to the Emperor's invitation by so much as a poetically worded compliment, years afterwards, in a tragical moment, Napoleon remembered the man whom, by three great words, he had set apart from all contemporaries.

XXI

Two months after this conversation, Napoleon is in Madrid, standing in front of the picture of Philip II. He has been over the palace, and has made a quick transit through the galleries; but here, in front of this conqueror's image, he stands so long that the members of his suite watch in dumb amazement while the Emperor seems to be holding converse with the king. The man contemplating the picture is unable to say: "Upon my realm the sun never sets." Perhaps this worldwide empire cannot be achieved without the aid of the Inquisition—which Napoleon has just suppressed, when invading Spain. Has he always been too lenient? Too democratic? Still, he has, in a dozen countries, put liberty in harness, that she may be broken in to dragging the dictator's chariot. Perhaps the trouble is that he talks and writes too much? Philip, with the unfathomable eyes, was always silent. He does not look happy. But who is happy?

A gloomy and joyless war had led the Emperor to this southern capital, for the intrigues with which the Spanish affair had been begun had wrought their own revenges. The kings and princes with whom he had dealt so high-handedly in the previous spring, had deserved no better fate; but the Emperor had failed to understand the temper of the Spanish people. When these had taken up arms in defence of their injured pride, the Emperor had regarded the insurgents as mere windbags. "They were worthy countrymen of Don Quixote. Ignorance, arrogance, cruelty, cowardice—these made up the spectacle before our eyes. Monks and inquisitors had stolen away Spanish brains. . . . Their soldiers were like the Arabs, and would only fight from behind the protection of walls; their peasants were no better than fellaheen; their monks were ignorant and dissolute; their grandees were degenerate, and had neither energy nor influence."

Entangled in this error, he failed to realise that, though he might conquer them to-day, his conquest would be for the day only. To-morrow the Spaniards, supported by England (which here finds its greatest rallying point), will begin to shoot once more from the houses, and who shall hinder them? The Emperor was already willing to admit it to his confidants. To Vincent, who had been a comrade in his earliest campaigns, he said:

"This is the stupidest thing I have ever done in my life! Can you think of any possible way in which I can free myself from the embarrassment?"

"You have simply to withdraw, Sire, and leave the country to itself."

"Fine words! Remember my position. I am a usurper. To gain this position, I needed to have the best head and the best sword in Europe. If I am to keep what I have won, all must be convinced of this. There must be no falling off in the prestige of my head and my sword. In face of a watchful universe, it is impossible for me to say that I have made a serious mistake, and to withdraw with a defeated army. You must see for yourself that the thing can't be done. I am still asking for your advice!"

Conviction that he has made a blunder, and that it is impossible for him to retrieve it; crude admissions made to an old companion-in-arms, whose advice he asks; is this young Bonaparte, or Napoleon growing old? In a week, he had beaten Frederick's famous army. But in Spain, he effects very little in eight months. When he has to deal with armies in a country which can feed his soldiers, a country with roads and towns, he is always victorious; but when he must campaign in trackless regions, such as the desert, the plains of Poland, or the mountains of Andalusia, the tempo is too tedious for his impetuous nature, and the circumstances are too incalculable for his mathematics.

His royal brother, instead of supporting him in this perplexing situation, makes difficulties. King Joseph wants to be a Spaniard, and to win his subjects by kindness. There are scenes between the brothers. With good reason the new king feels that he has made himself ridiculous by having to run away, and because he can only return under shield of the advancing

Emperor. But with even better reason does the man of iron complain to Roederer about the king:

"Joseph wants to be loved by the Spaniards, and to make them believe in his affection. Kings cannot inspire affection through tenderness. They must make themselves feared. . . . He writes that he wants to retire to Morfontaine; at this busiest of moments, he proposes to leave me in the lurch. . . . He says that he would rather pass the time at his country-seat than in a land bought with blood unjustly shed. . . . The blood is that of the foes of France! If he is king of Spain to-day, it is because he wanted to be; he could have stayed in Naples had he wished. Support me? I need no family. . . . My brothers are not Frenchmen, as I am. . . . The king of Holland, too, talks about going into private life. It seems to me that I, if any one of us three, have the best right to retire to Morfontaine!"

Why does he not break with Joseph? Here is Marshal Soult, commander in Spain, and perhaps the most highly prized among all his generals. Why does he not give Soult a crown, just as he has given one to Murat? "Joseph writes to say that if I value any one more highly than himself, that is the man I had better make king. I certainly did not make Joseph a king because I thought such a lot of him! If I distributed thrones according to merit, I should have made a very different choice! I need my family to stabilise my dynasty, for that is the system on which I am working."

Now, in Madrid, he issues decrees to establish the new order of things; which is welcomed by few, loved by no one, threatened by England, and detested by the Spanish people. Nothing can restrain him. Only last October he had written to his wife from Weimar, saying that the tsar had been dancing, but he himself would not dance, for "forty years are forty years." Moreover, he often makes fun of the way in which he is putting on fat. Yet on Christmas Eve, afoot, he crosses the Sierra de Guadarrama in a snowstorm, as if he had still been the general at Lodi. He defeats the English; but on these miry roads, deep in snow, he is no more able to follow them in retreat than he could follow the Russians after Friedland; and he gnashes his teeth when the enemy escapes to the ships. Shall he follow up the other portion of the English forces, away there in the mountains? That would be to withdraw the nucleus of his power still farther from France. Here he is, waiting in the centre of Castille; but what is Paris saying?

He is in camp at Astorga when the courier arrives. Now he will learn what is going on at home. As he is reading one of the letters, he begins to tremble with a dumb wrath. Silently he paces up and down for an hour, without saying a word even to those who are deepest in his confidence. Then he suddenly issues order that the headquarters staff is to return. For his own part, leaving army and generals, he hastens to Valladolid, and thence to the frontier.

"King Philip was right with his unfathomable gaze!" thinks the Emperor as he drives northward in his travelling carriage. "Instead of abolishing the Inquisition in Spain, I should have set it up in France. A conspiracy in Paris, and not one organised by the enemy! Fouché and Talleyrand, whom I could only use because they hated one another, and because each watched the other and told tales, have become reconciled and have entered into an alliance. Murat in it, too!"

The warning letters, which had decided him to return, were from Eugene and from his mother. Letizia is active in spite of her years; active in playing her part when danger threatens, though she withdraws when festivals are the order of the day. She is the Corsican mother, and safeguards her children. The scope of Talleyrand's treason, and how long he has been playing a double game, can at present only be guessed. That he has advised the Austrian envoy to take the offensive against France immediately, now when the Emperor is busy elsewhere, is not known, for there are no incriminatory documents. Even if such documents were in the Emperor's possession, how could so great a master have such great servitors arrested? Slowly and invisibly has the power proceeding from himself grown in their hands, ultimately to be turned against him whom they hate. During the fortnight's journey to Paris the waters of his wrath are rising against these creatures of his making.

Arrived in the capital, the Emperor calls a Council of State composed of many senators and all his ministers, that they may be witnesses to his vengeance. The two delinquents are present. Napoleon loses no time before he begins his attack on Talleyrand: "You are a thief and a scoundrel, for whom nothing is sacred. You would sell your own father! I have showered benefactions upon you, and yet there is nothing that you would refuse to do against me. You it was who advised me to undertake the mad venture in Spain, and now you criticise it to all and sundry. It was you who informed me of the duke of Enghien's whereabouts and incited me to take ruthless measures against him. . . . You have intrigued with the dethroned Spaniards who were placed in your charge. To-day, because you consider the Spanish affair a mistake, you have the effrontery to declare that you had always warned me against it. . . . You shall restore to me the keys of your office as grand chamberlain. . . . I could break you like glass if I chose; I have the power! But I despise you too much to give myself the trouble! . . ."

For half an hour, Napoleon holds forth in this fashion. His hearers sit petrified. Silently, Talleyrand bows, and withdraws: "What a pity," he says smilingly to a friend he meets outside, "that so great a man should be so ill-mannered!" Within the council chamber, the Emperor now proceeds to his attack on Fouché, whom he charges with having failed to work up public opinion, with having supported the enemies of the Emperor. . . .

His hearers sit petrified. Silently, Fouché bows—and remains! The Emperor commands that the higher officials shall renounce all right of criticism; they are to become mere tools of his thoughts. He declares menacingly that doubt is the first step on the road to betrayal, which, in its turn, becomes actual as soon as it takes the form of opposition.

Meanwhile, all Paris is convinced that both the unfaithful servants are to be banished or placed in confinement. But neither is dismissed! Fouché remains, for who could replace the man with a hundred eyes? Talleyrand, smiling as ever, continues to come to court; he has retained his official position; at the Sunday receptions, he always places himself so that his master cannot fail to see him; answers in the stead of his neighbour when the Emperor has put a question to the latter; and, in general, demonstrates the truth of Lannes' soldierly judgment: when Talleyrand is kicked from behind and one is conversing with him at the moment, not a sign of his feelings can be detected in his face! Ere long he is to be seen once more, limping away from the chill festivities in the brightly lit Tuileries, following in his master's wake to resume his labours in the Emperor's study, for "he is the only man with whom I can really talk!"

Weighty matters have to be talked over. Germany has awakened; slowly she is beginning to stir; all eyes are fixed on Austria. The Prussian king hesitates as usual; and an order, dated from Madrid, has banished Baron vom Stein from Prussia. Tyrol is seething with mutiny, like Spain; Austria, now allied not only with England but also with Turkey, is arming for the fifth time. What matters it, then, that Saragossa, after a heroic struggle, should have fallen? Troops cannot be withdrawn from Spain so long as insurrection is rife. How can a war be undertaken, seeing that a vast army of a quarter million men is tied up in Spain? It is precisely on account of this situation that Austria has found courage to take up arms against the Emperor.

The Russian menace is Napoleon's last hope. When the Russian envoy, Romantzoff, is leaving for St. Petersburg, the Emperor overwhelms him with gifts and with promises. Thinking to make himself agreeable to the tsar, he pledges himself to the evacuation of Prussia; and urges Alexander, for his part, to proclaim the alliance of the two emperors to a trembling central Europe.

But Alexander vacillates; he allows himself to be reassured by Vienna, Berlin, and London; timid and hesitant as he is, he yields to the threats of his grand dukes (who to a man detest Napoleon), and yet cannot make up his mind to go wholeheartedly over to their side; Vienna's hopes of securing one of the tsar's sisters as bride for an Austrian archduke are frustrated: the tsar elects to remain neutral!

The Emperor is cut to the quick by his friend's breach of faith; indeed, it is the unkindest cut of all. He has given too much personal confidence, his pride is wounded, his labour lost. Literally, there remains nothing for him to do but to raise an army out of the very earth: the levies for the following year are now being called up, a year in advance; money must be procured by every possible and impossible means; the funds have fallen to 78, in consequence of the Spanish affair. Still, Austria is ready far earlier than he had expected. When, in April, the semaphore announces that the enemy is on the march, and Napoleon is informed of the news in his bed at ten o'clock that night, he orders the mobilisation of his troops for midnight, and is furious when the unwieldy machine is not ready until four hours later.

When he arrives in Bavaria, he sees the mistakes committed by the Austrians in their advance. He can hardly believe his good luck; it was as if "he grew; his eyes gleamed, and with a delight which his glance, his mood, and his movements all betrayed, he exclaimed: 'I've got them! Their army is lost! A month hence, and I'll be in Vienna!'" He underestimates the time: he will be there in three weeks! He incites his soldiers to marches of over sixty-five miles in forty hours, and beats his foe in a series of five battles. Later he was to call these five days his finest achievement from the point of view of manœuvring.

The last day he is wounded on the foot; and, since fate wills that the legend of his invulnerability (in which the army whole-heartedly believes and to which even he is inclined to lend an ear) shall be exploded, the bullet hits his Achilles' tendon.

But he speeds away again, and crosses Germany. Napoleon's carriage is outwardly plain, but within it is comfortably built. The Emperor can sleep in it; by day he can govern from it, just as well as from the Tuileries or from a tent. He is the first to overcome the friction which brings movement to a standstill; and, though he does not travel as fast as we do nowadays, he travels faster than any man ever travelled before. Five days take him from Dresden to Paris. In a number of lock-up drawers within the carriage, he collects reports, dispatches, memoranda; a lantern hanging from the roof lights up the interior; in front of him hangs a list of the different places he must pass through, including where relays of horses are awaiting him. Should a courier reach him, Berthier, or another official who happens to be at hand, must take down the more pressing orders, while the carriage goes jolting on its way. Before long, orderlies are to be seen flying off in every direction.

On the box seat, the Mameluke is enthroned in solitary grandeur. Two postilions whip up the six horses. The carriage is surrounded by a crowd of equerries, pages, and light cavalrymen; when the procession sets forward, the road is all too narrow to accommodate it, eddies of dust and heat envelop it, night and fog encompass it. The peasants stand aside to let the tornado pass; they are agape with wonderment and firmly believe that the devil is hiding inside the great Napoleon. He leaves behind him a trail like that of a paper-chase: for he throws out of the windows of the carriage, not only all the envelopes and other useless paper, but all the reports he does not wish to file (torn into tiny fragments); all the newspapers he has read; and, finally, books, which he glances at when he has a moment to spare, and then consigns to their fate in the mud of the highway.

Wherever he gets out of his carriage, a hot bath is ready for him. Then, at two in the morning, he will dictate till four, snatch three hours' sleep, and start off again at seven. At his halts, four light cavalrymen surround him in a square, and follow him in all his movements, if, for instance, in the daytime he studies the country through his small telescope. Should he need the large telescope, he uses the shoulder of the page in waiting as a rest. Whether his halt be short or long, in wartime the map is always ready to his hand, in carriage or tent, in camp and by the watch-fire. Any member of his escort who fails to show him in the map the precise point where the halt has been made, the area he now wishes to study, receives a volley of abuse—be it Berthier himself, Prince of Neuchâtel. Through all countries, for the whole duration of his life, the map follows him, pierced with coloured pins, illuminated at night by twenty or thirty candles, and with a pair of compasses lying on it. This is his altar, before which he offers up his prayers. It is the real home of the man who has no home.

Now, without a blow, he takes Vienna for the second time, and occupies the same room as of old in the palace of Schönbrunn; but the war is not over.

For what has meanwhile been happening in his wide realms is unfavourable to him, and encourages the enemy. There is bad news from Spain; in northern Italy, Eugene has been fighting unsuccessfully; and since, at this instant, Murat has to advance from Naples, the Roman Emperor makes as short work of it with Rome as the Hohenstaufen had done many centuries before. Four years ago, at the same writing table, he had penned a decree annihilating the royal house of Naples. Now he repeats the manœuvre with the pope. Since Napoleon, at this juncture, has to strike with his sword in all directions, he no longer troubles himself about moral and political consequences, and ventures this dangerous edict for little better reason than that a junction must be effected between his armies in Italy.

But anger is a contributory cause. When he had been in Spain at the beginning of the year, he had let fall expressions showing how out of humour he was with Rome: "Last year, the pope was impudent enough to neglect sending us the consecrated candles he sent the heads of other States. Write to Rome saying that we don't want any, not even for the three kings of our house. Say that at Candlemas I always get consecrated candles from my own clerics, and that the value of these things does not depend upon purple or the other insignia of power. In the realm of the shades, there will be priests just as good as the popes! Thus a candle blest by one of my own clergy will be just as holy as one sent by the pope. I won't have his candles, and none of the princes of my house may accept them."

In this way he trumped the pope's trick, like a Protestant, like a revolutionary. Such was Napoleon's mood, in the slough of the Spanish roads and battles. Now, in Schönbrunn, he bluntly deprives the Holy Father of power as sovereign prince. The pope is relegated to the Vatican, and assigned a revenue of two millions.

Many members of the Emperor's retinue are shocked, for some of them are good Catholics, and it is only five days from the feast of Pentecost. Is he not challenging God? Those in whom faith becomes intensified into superstition are likely enough, ere long, to find confirmation of their presentiments. In five days, at Pentecost, Napoleon will be defeated for the first time in his life.

Some regard the battle of Aspern-Essling as indecisive; at any rate, no one can consider it a success for Napoleon. When the bridge across the Danube was swept away, this was just as much and just as little due to chance as were all the great happenings whereby at Lodi, Rivoli, Marengo, and on many other occasions, he had, by precisely such improvisations, wrested victory from God. A friend of his youth, Marshal Lannes, is mortally wounded. Napoleon hastens to the dying man's side, and, so the story runs, his old comrade shows hostility both in word and glance. That evening Napoleon sits long before his untasted supper, silent, and refusing to see any one.

"Conquered? Conquerable?" he muses, staring forth gloomily into the future. "Has Achilles' heel indeed been hit? That marksman aimed better than Talleyrand. No, it was my own fault. Too hazardous to cross the river in full view of the enemy! Lannes was right; he was already half way over. What is Paris saying? What will be the best way of reporting this in Paris?" In uneasy mood, he goes back to Schönbrunn, a huge, lonely palace in the midst of a hostile land. His Polish mistress! If only he had had the lovely Walewska with him. She is sitting now in a Polish castle, far away, but her thoughts fly towards him. His hopes of a child by her last year had been dashed.

He sends for her.

Strange news from Rome! To Napoleon's edict of deposition, the pope has promptly replied by a bull of excommunication. Does this alarm the Emperor? He laughs. He laughs at Catholic mediævalism, and the soldier, the self-made man, thinks:

"Is this vengeance for my having, in Notre Dame, snatched from him the crown which the holy man wanted to place on my head with his own hands? And what is holy? It is doubtful if Christ ever lived; the only certain thing is that we can make use of him. But in these enlightened days, none but children and nursemaids are afraid of curses. I have been outlawed twice ere this, on the Nineteenth Brumaire, and in Corsica. Such farces bring good luck!" Much refreshed by these thoughts, he prepares for the counterstroke on the Marchfeld, and at Wagram is again victorious, as in thirty battles, his excommunicated weapons being too much for the pious archduke Charles. Towards the end of his two days' battle, when all was going well, and the commander was overpowered by fatigue, he made Rustam spread a bearskin for him on the battle-field, told the Mameluke to call him in twenty minutes, lay down, and fell fast asleep for the prescribed period, to awaken fully reinvigourated. The war was finished, and a truce was agreed on. Next day, reporting the new victory to his wife, he adds: "I've been burned as brown as a berry." He has been thoroughly toned up, and his mood is rejuvenated.

Returning to Schönbrunn, he finds Walewska awaiting him. How many lovely women have glided through the secret portals and discreet chambers of this vast palace, to revivify the Habsburgs? Now the adventurer from the Mediterranean sends evening after evening to fetch the countess, who is housed near by; and again and again he warns the groom of the chambers to be careful lest the carriage should be overturned on the rough road. For the second time, the pair live three months together. He had looked forward to this in Finckenstein, and had promised her that it should happen; but the where and the when depended on the course of universal history, and not wholly on himself.

In a few weeks, she knows that she is with child. Will she this time give him the gift that he has been asking from women for twelve years, and has only once received? Thus, the idyll gains a new content; and when, at midnight on August 15th, lying in her arms, waiting for his fortieth birthday to dawn, and thinking how early next morning salutes and bell peals will hail the coming of this day, throughout France, and indeed in all the countries over which he rules,—the day to which the pope had complacently transferred the feast of St. Napoleon—may it not seem strange to him that the first to congratulate him should be this beauty of twenty summers, who can speak but haltingly the two languages in which he is at home, and whose glances convey more meaning than her words? His thoughts may well fly back to that time ten years ago when he sailed homeward from Egypt, hazarding all to the luck of the seas, out of which the great English net could so readily have fished him. Now he is a different man, but not a happier one, for he is the slave of "the nature of things."

He is different, also, from the man he was two years ago in Finckenstein. Then he was the builder of a world empire, the potentate to whom the kings of the East and the kings of the West paid homage; now, that empire is on the defensive, and even a great victory like that he has just won, can only be turned cautiously to account.

On the day of Wagram, his people in Rome had committed a blunder of which he has only just heard:

"I am very much annoyed at the arrest of the pope. That was an idiotic thing to do! You should have arrested Cardinal ———, while leaving the pope at his ease in Rome." He had laughed at the symbolic power of the bull of excommunication. "Excommunication" is an empty word, an airy nothing, which the French bishops can blow away; but as statesman he realises instantly that the imprisonment and deportation of the Holy Father are very serious matters. This rash action has put him in the wrong, for a banished pope is morally stronger than a pope fulminating bulls.

Other letters are coming to hand, from Spain this time, telling how England has made good her losses there; and how, in the forest wilds, the visible-invisible Spanish people, allied with England, is standing more stoutly to arms. The news from Paris is that Fouché has overstepped his orders, and has called up the National Guard everywhere; his obvious intention has been to intensify the dread of England throughout the country, and to fan the flames of discontent among the newly levied conscripts.

A difficult and dangerous situation, and one whose difficulties and dangers thicken as the radius widens. The despatches from Rome and Paris are a week old, and those from Spain date from more than a fortnight back. By the time fresh orders from Schönbrunn can reach Valladolid, the whole position will have changed. If only he had the power to issue his commands with the velocity of light, then he would be able to rule the world from this office on the Danube. As things are, he must cut short the negotiations, which Austria, encouraged by England and Hungary, has been protracting for weeks. When, recently, the victor demanded a third of the monarchy, with nine million souls, he was met with a refusal. Now he pursues a different plan. With the splendid frankness which is so baffling to diplomats of the old school, in one of his endless conversations (this particular talk with Count Bubna lasted seven hours), he explains his own difficulties to his opponent:

"I was to blame for Aspern-Essling, and suffered for my mistake: but the confidence of my soldiers remain unshaken." In broad outline, he sketches his own tactics on the battle-field. "But I will tell you the mistake you are always making. . . . You draw up your plans the day before the battle, when you do not yet know your adversary's movements, or what positions you will have to occupy. But for my part, I never issue orders long in advance, and am especially cautious over-night. At peep of day, I send out my scouts, survey the field for myself, and keep my troops in mass formation as long as I am still in doubt. . . . Then I hurl myself on the enemy, attacking him wherever the ground makes attack most favourable. . . . You are right when you remind me that my free use of artillery fire causes much bloodshed. But what am I to do? My troops are weary; my men want peace. That is why I have to be sparing with the bayonet, and to use cannon more than formerly."

Later he comes to the condition of the alliances: "To-day I am sure of the tsar, but what guarantee have I that he will stand by me? As regards Prussia, I have known for a long time that that country is oscillating between you and me." Suddenly he demands only half of what he had asked before, disavows his minister, and offers an alliance. Needs must, for he has to get back to Paris. A new basis for negotiation! Austria is to lose a fragment to the Confederation of the Rhine, and another to Russia; a pathway to the Balkans has to be left open for Napoleon. Several more weeks pass in negotiation. His impatience is soothed by the bright glances of Walewska.

In October, Napoleon is holding a great review in Schönbrunn. A young man forces his way into the palace. He is arrested. When searched, he is found to be carrying a long knife and the picture of a girl. Examined in the guard room, he refuses to give any information, and says he will only explain himself to the Emperor in person. Soon the lad of eighteen, a fair-haired youth, serious of aspect, frank and courageous but courteous, is confronted with Napoleon. His name is Friedrich Staps, and he is the son of a Tyrolese pastor. Napoleon questions him in French, Rapp acting as interpreter.

"Yes, I intended to kill you."

"You must be mad, young man, or ill."

"I am neither mad nor ill, but in the full possession of my faculties."

"Then why do you want to kill me?"

"Because you are ruining my country."

"Your country?"

"It is mine, as it is that of all good Germans."

"Who was the instigator?"

"No one. My heart told me that by killing you, I should do good service to Germany and to Europe."

"Have you ever seen me before?"

"In Erfurt. Then I believed you would make no more wars, and I was your greatest admirer."

The Emperor sends for his physician, in the hope that the young fellow will be declared a lunatic; but the doctor, having made his examination, says that Staps is of sound mind.

"I told you so," says Friedrich.

The Emperor is uneasy. He is loath to make an end of so frank and bold a youth. He has not to do here with a partisan, with a conspiracy, with one who is out to destroy a principle; he has not to do with an ideologue, but with an idealist. Germany has sent forth against him a Brutus with a long knife.

"You are distraught. You are bringing affliction on your family. Ask my forgiveness, and say you are sorry. Then I will grant you your life!"

Never before has Napoleon spoken thus, at any rate to an assassin. The young man remains steadfast. Has Napoleon lost the power of suggestion? "Well?"

"I do not want your forgiveness, and I am not sorry. My only regret is that I have failed."

The Emperor grows angry.

"The devil! A crime means nothing to you, then?"

"To kill you would not be a crime, but a public service," says Staps, still perfectly respectful, indeed, thoroughly well bred.

"Hm. Whose portrait is this?"

"The girl I love."

"Will she approve this attempt of yours?"

"She will be sorry it has miscarried, for she hates you as much as I do."

"What a pretty girl," thinks the Emperor looking at the miniature in his hand. "Am I really to be baffled by this young fellow? No, I will save him, will pardon him. What does it matter to me if he hates me?" Still holding the miniature, he looks Staps squarely in the face: "If I pardon you, I suppose it will gladden the heart of this girl?"

Friedrich's blue eyes flashed, and he says firmly:

"Then I shall be able to kill you after all!"

The Emperor turns away, and leaves the prisoner to his doom. To Champagny, who is present, he talks for a long time about the Illuminates. Then, with a sudden transition he says:

"We must make peace. Drive back into the town. Summon the Austrians. We are practically agreed on the main points, and the only trouble relates to the war indemnity. The difference amounts to fifty millions. Reduce the demand by half. Get the matter settled. I was satisfied with the last draft.

Add whatever clauses you think necessary. I leave everything in your hands. Make peace."

So great is the impression wrought by the youth. We cannot call it alarm. Caution is too mild a word. The trouble is that a shadow has fallen across his soul. After negotiating for three months, the Emperor, simply that he may save one day, leaves the conclusion of the peace to his minister. He has Staps examined once more, but the enthusiast prefers death to recantation. Next morning at six, the minister brings the treaty which has been arranged during the night. The Emperor, well content, praises his minister:

The same morning, the assassin is shot, and the Emperor returns to the topic: "The thing is unprecedented! So young a man, a German, a Protestant, well brought up; and such a crime! How did he meet his end?" The answer is that Staps, in face of the firing squad, had cried in loud tones: "Liberty for ever! Death to the tyrant!" The Emperor holds his peace.

Napoleon commands that the long German knife shall be brought back with him to Paris.

XXII

The Empress Josephine is lying in a swoon on the floor. Napoleon summons the palace prefect, and orders him to bear her to her chamber. The Emperor goes in front, carrying a lighted candle. Since the staircase is narrow, he passes the candlestick to a servant, and helps Bausset to carry Josephine. He carefully lays her on her bed, and, in a state of great excitement, leaves the room. Hardly is he out of sight, when the empress opens her eyes: cries and fainting fit were all a pretence! Bausset betrayed her secret later, stating that, as he carried her up the stairs, she had whispered that he was holding her too tightly, and was hurting her.

All the same, fear and sorrow are in very truth her portion; for she has been informed that she must leave the Tuileries, where, for more than a decade, she has ruled as queen. The Emperor himself has broken the news to her. Matters cannot continue as in the past: every one is counting on his death: across the frontier are the Germans with their long knives; here at home is Fouché, colloguing with the English. Napoleon needs a son; and his son must be the child of a princess of royal blood. The scene with Josephine took place shortly after his return from Schönbrunn. Probably he was feeling sore because he could not place his Polish love, who bore his child in her womb, straightway upon the throne. For a certainty, he did not as yet know the name of his future bride.

Mother, sisters, brothers, are sitting in silence, with stony faces, round the table, in family conclave: Josephine is likewise present. She can detect the smothered joy in the minds of these witnesses who at last have gained their end. The "old woman" must go! With uncontrolled emotion in his voice, the Emperor declares that all hope of an heir from the empress is quenched, and that it is solely on this account that he must part from her. "God alone knows how hard a step this is for me to take. . . . But no sacrifice is too great for the sake of France. . . . For fifteen years, the empress has made my life beautiful by her presence. She was crowned by my own hands. . . . I have determined that she shall preserve the rank and the title of empress; and, above all, that she shall look upon me as her lifelong friend." Josephine exercises admirable self-control, but asks the arch-chancellor to read her words of acquiescence.

The memorandum concerning the divorce is then signed by all. Napoleon's signature is more legible than usual. It is vigorous, and a long, firm flourish underlines his full name: he thus brings a very serious matter to a close, in manly fashion. Nervously, Josephine adds her signature to the right of his, quite near, as though pleading for his support. Madame Mère writes her M. as her son has written his N., and follows him, likewise, in the concluding flourish.

That night, Josephine makes an amazing entry into his room,

and approaches his bed, tears streaming down her face, and her hair falling round her shoulders. Next day, supported by Napoleon, a veritable Niobe, she quits the palace and drives to Malmaison. Before leaving, however, she has (foolishly perhaps) besought Méneval to speak of her as often as possible to the Emperor.

Napoleon went alone to Trianon, which was at this time unoccupied. There he held a death watch such as no lover had ever held before over the love from whom he was to be eternally severed: he remained there for three days, absolutely inactive—this being as great an achievement as if a Buddhist holy man had for three days done Napoleon's work! He received no one, he dictated never a word, read nothing, noted down nothing; for three days the mighty wheel stood still, the wheel which for fifteen years had rotated by the strength of its own impetus. Soon afterwards he visited his divorced lady at her house in Malmaison. Then he wrote to her:

"I found you to-day in a worse condition of mind than I had hoped, mon amie. . . . You should not give yourself up to so profound a melancholy. Take good care of your health, which is so dear to me. If you love me, then show me how strong and happy you can be. You cannot doubt my fondness, or all the tenderness I feel for you. You cannot believe that I shall ever be happy if you are unhappy. . . . I was very sad when I got back to the Tuileries; the great palace seemed so empty; I felt so lonely. . . . Farewell, chère amie; sleep soundly, and remember that I wish it thus. . . ." After fifteen years of intimate association, the man of forty writes in so natural and so grateful a fashion—though at the same time we may detect a gentle hint of a determined will that commands.

Then come endless calculations: he will allow her three millions per annum; the set of rubies he will pay extra for: "this will cost me quite four hundred thousand francs and I will have it valued, for I do not wish to be cheated by the jeweller. . . . In the wardrobe at Malmaison you should find five to six hundred thousand francs. You can take this money in order to increase your silver plate and your underclothing. I have ordered a beautiful china service for you, but I have told the makers to await your commands, for I wish it to be really lovely. . . . The page who saw you this morning, tells me you were weeping. . . . I shall take my meals all by myself. . . . Have you really lost courage since going to Malmaison? And yet that house has been the witness of our happiness, and our feelings for one another. These feelings must never change; nor can they, at least as far as I am concerned. . . . I should so much like to pay you a visit; but first I must know if you are a valiant woman or a weakling. I am rather weak myself, and am suffering greatly. Farewell, Josephine. Good-night."

A melting mood has once more taken possession of him. The tone resembles that of the passionate letters sent from Milan by the young general to his faithless wife in Paris. It is set in a minor key; and the same melody that surged up and soared above the whole orchestra of his senses in those days, is now played by the 'cello as a solo echoing through the desolate halls of the Tuileries.

Shortly after this, a masked ball was given by the archchancellor. Among the guests was Princess Metternich, whose husband had formerly been envoy at the court of Paris. A man clad in a green domino took her by the arm and led her aside. Every one knew who he was, for although no one fully knew Napoleon unmasked, the masked Napoleon was impossible to mistake: the tragi-comedy of genius in this world. After a few quips, he asked her whether she thought that an archduchess would accept the offer of his hand.

"I do not know, Sire."

"Were you in the archduchess' place, would you accept the offer?"

"I should certainly refuse it," says the Viennese lady with a smile.

"How unkind! Will you write to your husband, to ask his views on the matter?"

"I think you had better say that to Prince Schwarzenberg, Sire; he is the envoy now."

Thus with one of his improvisations does Napoleon begin his new wooing after the divorce. It is a splendid return to the straightforwardness of the revolution. The same evening, he instructs Eugene, who next morning approaches the Austrian ambassador. None of the Habsburg clan understand promptness and simplicity in such campaigns; but to the Emperor these qualities come naturally. The tsar makes no sign. Vienna, beaten in four wars, must at length be pacified. What could be more obvious than this solution? Why get a divorce if you do not forthwith do your utmost to attain the unattainable?

The Corsican family feeling is at work once more. He, who so rarely holds a council of war, summons a family council before the divorce and before the marriage. There they sit, just as six weeks earlier, round the oval table; all the great dignitaries are there; according to the report of one of those present, general embarrassment prevails. The Emperor announces his desire for an heir, and then speaks with an assumption of dubiety:

"Were it possible for me to be guided by personal feelings alone, I should choose my bride out of the circle of the Legion of Honour, from among the daughters of the heroes of France, and should make the worthiest of Frenchwomen empress of the French. But a man must adapt his actions to the customs of his own century, to the usage of other States, to political considerations. Many sovereigns have sought my alliance, and I do not think there is any reigning house to which I cannot propose this personal tie. Three of them have now to be considered: the Austrian, the Russian, and the Saxon. I should like to hear your views."

Thus does the curse of legitimacy break once more into the mighty dictator's private preserve. Legitimacy is the rock on which he will be shipwrecked. Why should he not choose Countess Walewska whom he loves? Or, if the empress is to be a Frenchwoman, why not a daughter of one of those heroes to whom he has given kingdoms? He has shaken the old world to its foundations; has with his own hands placed two crowns on his head; has kept kings of ancient lineage waiting in his anterooms; has dethroned one such, and placed an innkeeper's son upon the vacant throne. Has he done all these things that today, debarred from the choice of the woman of his heart, on the prowl for an heir, he must "adapt his actions to the customs of his own century"—customs which hitherto he has defied like a demigod?

But no such unconventional possibilities are discussed in these cold, imperial halls, for one and all are against a Frenchwoman. Eugene and Talleyrand are for Austria. Murat demurs, saying that Marie Antoinette had brought bad luck to France. Some voice the advantages of a Russian alliance. Others favour Saxony. The Emperor listens to their views, closes the sitting, and does what he has already made up his mind to do. That same evening he sends a message to Vienna. The only one present at the council who saw clearly was the minister who had strongly urged the claims of Russia, but who did not venture to utter his real reasons except in private; "Within two years, we shall certainly be at war with both the monarchies with whose ruling house the Emperor does not ally himself by marriage—and Austria is the only one of the three a war with which would not be dangerous!"

By the Emperor's instructions, the court of St. Petersburg is informed that he has been kept waiting too long. Furthermore, it would be inconvenient to have a priest of the Russian Orthodox Church in the Tuileries. Finally, he has been informed "that Grand Duchess Anna, who is fifteen years old, is not yet ripened to womanhood. Inasmuch as, in young girls, two years elapse between the appearance of the first signs of womanhood and complete maturity, this will not suit the aims of the Emperor, who does not wish to be married for three years before he can have a child." This gynecological excursus is the last we hear of the Russian wooing which had begun so inauspiciously in Erfurt.

But the Habsburgs are a prolific family, so that he may regard an Austrian princess as practically guaranteed against barrenness. When he learns that the mother of his chosen bride has given birth to thirteen children, that one of her ancestresses has had seventeen, and another actually twenty-six, the Emperor exclaims: "That's the kind of womb I want to marry!" There could be no doubt about the answer to his proposal; Francis would accept it, and his eighteen-year-old daughter would comply. . . . Acceptance is taken for granted in the first letter of his courtship, which the Emperor writes with his own hand, legibly in places, for it is penned with Méneval's aid, and with more pains than might be gathered from an inspection of the schoolboy script:

"Chère Cousine, The brilliant qualities which distinguish your person have aroused in us the desire to serve you and to honour you. Inasmuch as we are approaching the emperor, your father, with the request that he will entrust us with Your Imperial Highness' happiness, may we venture to hope that you will graciously accept the sentiments which move us to this step. Dare we flatter ourselves that you are not deciding on this step solely from a sense of duty and filial obedience? . . . If Your Imperial Highness has no more than a trace of inclination towards us, we shall carefully cherish this sentiment, and make it our supreme task to be agreeable to you always and in all things, so that we may look forward to the happiness of winning your whole heart. . . ."

Did ever a great genius write a more preposterous letter? He knows perfectly well that her acceptance will be dictated by filial obedience and nothing more; that she cannot possibly have a trace of liking for the devil who, during the years of her childhood, has been despoiling her father of one province after another, so that she has learned to cross herself at the sound of his name. He knows that he has better things to do, that he has other supreme tasks, than to make himself agreeable to a little goose, who is not distinguished by any other quality than by the luck of being born a Habsburg; who is neither beautiful nor wise, neither brave nor passionate. Yet the equivocal nature of his position constrains Napoleon, who has never asked a favour, to write such a letter as the foregoing!

With the gesture of a sultan, he gives to his friend Berthier (who is to woo for him by proxy in Vienna) tokens of affection for his bride: his miniature set in diamonds, and jewellery worth one-and-a-half-millions. But at the proxy wedding in the Hofburg, Napoleon is represented by the bride's uncle, Archduke Charles, whom he has worsted in a dozen battles.

The Emperor, meanwhile, gives more attention to clothing and furniture than to affairs of State; orders for Marie Louise a trousseau to the tune of five millions, for what she is bringing with her has cost only half a million; studies all the details of Marie Antoinette's journey, lest the Habsburgs should be able to plume themselves on breaches of etiquette; orders fashionable coats from his tailor, and buckled shoes from his shoemaker; goes out hunting, rides vigorously, in the hope of sweating off his fat; even finds that his dancing days are not yet over.

While on her way to Paris, Marie Louise receives a love letter, quite illegible, for all she can make out is the capital N. of the signature; flowers greet her wherever she halts for the night; in Compiègne she is expecting to be received by the terrible man whom she is to wed; he is waiting there for her with all his family.

But suddenly, with a surge of vigorous youth, the firm will and the fierce impatience of the revolutionist break through this hedge of antiquated formalities. Laying aside his new embroidered coat, and donning his old uniform, he jumps into a calash undecorated with armorial bearings, and drives to meet the bridal procession. There it is; the horses are being changed in a downpour of rain. He wants to take Marie Louise by surprise, but her master-of-the-horse, recognising him, exclaims, "His Majesty"; so the little coup fails to come off. In a moment he is in the carriage beside her, dismisses the lady-in-waiting, kisses his bride, laughing the while, for he is wet through. In her embarrassment, she finds a pretty phrase: "Your portrait does not flatter you, Sire!"

"She is by no means beautiful," he meditates, as he takes stock of her. "Marked with smallpox, though not badly, thick lips; watery blue eyes; full-bosomed for her years; but fresh and young."

With disgust, that evening, the masters of the ceremonies see their whole programme, which has been rehearsed for weeks in advance, torn to tatters. The meeting with the imperial family has been effected with scant formality; all come and go as they please; the girls who present bouquets must cut their compliments short, for every one is wet and cold; supper is improvised, with Caroline as third at table. At one in the morning the whole company retires to rest. But the Emperor has taken his uncle the cardinal aside, and has asked Fesch, as an authority upon these matters, whether Marie Louise is not already his wife, thanks to the proxy marriage in Vienna. "Yes, Sire, according to civil law," answers the priest, foreseeing what is about to happen.

Next morning the Emperor has breakfast for two brought to the empress' bedside. Within an hour all Compiègne knows.

By this night attack, made on the spur of the moment, Napoleon conquers the world of legitimacy after the same fashion as he has conquered it in the field, taking the Habsburg fortress by storm, as beseems his reputation.

With a mischievous double meaning, he writes next day to his unsuspecting father-in-law: "She fulfils all my hopes, and we do not cease to give one another proofs of the tender feelings that unite us. We suit one another exceedingly well.

. . . Allow me, therefore, to thank you for this lovely gift." Uncle Fesch does not give their union the blessing of the Church until after they have made their imposing entry into Paris. In Josephine's case, he was eight years too late; this time the sanctification has been delayed no more than a fortnight.

The Emperor finds his bride charming. "You should all marry Germans," he tells his intimates; "they are gentle, good, unspoiled, and as fresh as roses." He is delighted that she gets on well with his family. Domestic peace is new to him. He graces the intimacies of the toilet with his presence; pinches her cheeks caressingly; calls her his "bonne petite animale."

Two or three weeks later, there is news from Poland. The child conceived during the weeks at Schönbrunn has been born —a boy. There is a strange medley of feelings in Napoleon's soul. From that same Austrian palace, where he has stayed only in the absence of its rightful owner, has come the new wife, who as yet gives no signs of capacity for doing her duty. He vacillates; sends for the Polish countess. But, soon after this, Marie Louise finds that she is with child. "The Emperor's jubilation almost passes description," writes Metternich to Vienna. At this early stage, the empress' condition is solemnly announced to the Senate and the nation; prayers for the successor to the throne are to be said; there is to be a festival of rejoicing as sumptuous as those of pagan times.

When the lovely Walewska arrives, he gives her everything she can ask for; sees the baby and fondles it; makes it a count of the Empire, with the chancellor for guardian. But nothing beyond this unites the sometime lovers. Napoleon has become a respectable married man.

In all respects, now, this man's career seems to be transcending familiar limitations, outstepping traditional horizons. Thus among the women who have crossed his path new relationships begin. The Polish countess, whose eyes Josephine would at one time have been glad to scratch out, is invited to Malmaison. Walewska brings Josephine Napoleon's son, that son whose absence from her own womb decided Josephine's fate. See the group on the terrace. One of them is a grey-headed woman, who was born in the West Indies, had a taste of prison, and then became empress of the French. The other, young and blooming, was brought up in an impoverished Polish noble family, was married off to a wealthy old man, and was then switched into a new career through Napoleon's chance glimpse of her at a ball. Between them is the child of the man who had loved both and forsaken both, that he might compel a stupid little Habsburg girl to immortalise a name which had long ere this immortalised itself.

When the empress' hour comes, he has to make a choice great as destiny itself. Paris knows, France knows, that the young wife is in labour. All are waiting for the heir; enemies are dreading him before he is born; the common people, who at such moments are always dynastically inclined, are praying for mother and child. Throughout the night Napoleon has been watching by his wife's bedside, but has withdrawn for a time. The accoucheur brings him dread tidings: "The child is in a bad position; there is danger to the life of both mother and infant!"

The whole structure of his dynastic schemes is tottering. What will he say, this man of iron, when the doctor asks whether the first thought is to be for the mother or for the child? Will he not answer that, before all, it is necessary to save the child, for whose first cry millions besides Napoleon are waiting? What does Marie Louise matter? When she has borne him a healthy boy, she will have fulfilled her earthly mission. Surely the Emperor can have no choice?

"Do exactly what you would do if an ordinary citizen's wife were in labour. The mother's life comes first!"

Two hours later, however, the baby has been born, and the mother is in good case. With rapt attention, Paris counts the cannon shots. Nineteen, twenty, twenty-one—so far, it may only be a girl. But when the twenty-second gun booms out, the whole city is in a frenzy of delight. The crowd surrounding the old Bourbon palace cheers madly. The salute is still thundering. The little lieutenant of artillery stands by the window, mechanically noting the calibre of the guns from the pitch of the gun-fire, glancing down upon the mutable many without —while his thoughts reach far back into the past, and roam yet farther forward into the future.

The groom-of-the-chambers sees that there are tears in the cold, grey-blue eyes.

(From the "Corpus Imaginum" of the Photographic Society, Charlottenburg.)

Napoleon as Emperor. Painting by Vigneux. Count Primoli Collection.

BOOK FOUR

THE SEA

It is essential that this man shall be ruined! . . . But since, here below everything takes place by natural causes, the daimons trip him: thus, in the end, even Napoleon is overthrown.—GOETHE.

I

The old struggle in Napoleon's mind between mathematics and fantasy had ripened. The issue of the struggle was now to decide the history of his world dominion.

For now, at the climax of his career; fortified by his ties with the Habsburgs, ties for whose sake he had broken the familiar associations of years of married life; fortified by having a legitimate heir, whose birth gave firm anchorage to his adventurer's dynasty; having gained the mastery over conspiracies, and having learned to dominate all the political parties—he was once more free as he had been eleven years earlier, when the victory of Marengo had safeguarded the tranquillity he needed for the internal development of France. True, England was unconquered; but Russia seemed still friendly. True, Spain was uncoerced; but Europe from Reggio to Hammerfest was allied to France, this being a euphemism for dependence on France. For the last time in his life, he was free to make a great decision.

Had he been nothing more than a mathematician, he would have been content with his calculations within the resuscitated realm of Charlemagne, and dreams of world dominion would have yielded place before the reality of the United States of Europe under France's leadership. Had he been nothing but a visionary, he would have aimed, like a new Alexander, to march towards the Ganges; and England would have been merely a pretext for his onslaught on India. But he was both mathematician and visionary, and was therefore in danger of disavowing himself. For, as calculator, he failed to grasp an eminently real factor which could not be expressed in figures. The moods of un-uniformed men in Spain and in Germany could play no part in the cipherings of a military commander who thought in terms of army corps and big guns. Nevertheless such moods should have come within the scope of his visions as a seer!

Thus during these decisive years, after the birth of his heir, and before his next warlike designs have become active, his mind is alternately dominated by his two fundamental impulses, and the whole future depends upon which of the two will be supreme when the moment for action comes. Will his awakened fantasy warn him that it is dangerous to brave the anger of exasperated peoples, or will his calculating faculty disclose to him the danger that will await him on the distant road to the East? What will happen should he err in both respects? Then, indeed, his whole world will go up in flames.

He feels that his powers are ripening. In addition to the two energies we have been considering, a third is growing to maturity, the sense of destiny. Words unheard before, or rarely expressed, now find voice: "I feel that I am being driven towards an unknown goal. But as soon as I have reached it, as soon as I no longer have an inexorable mission, an atom will suffice to overthrow me. Till then, no human powers can effect anything against me. The days are numbered."

Truly they are numbered; and through these prophetic words there already breathes the foreboding of an exit, although he does not know the way thither. Now, on the path towards the tragical catastrophe, the clarity of his inner vision is dimmed. Yet he himself speaks of the campaign against Russia as the "fifth act," though the full significance of the term is not apparent to him. Tones like those of his youthful days resound in the new harmony. "I have got to the end of everything," he had said when he was thirty, on the Nile. Now, at forty-three, he declares in the Council of State: "All this will last as long as I do, and no longer. Perhaps when I am dead, my son will think himself well off if he can be sure of an income of forty thousand francs a year."

But at the same time his ardour increases. Since those days

when it seemed to him that (thanks to the acceleration of genius) he had got to the end of everything, since the days of the Egyptian campaign, he had been guided by a religious faith that it was his destiny to become a second Alexander. Now, when for the first time he is equipped with means for the carrying out of his design, is he to annihilate his dream by figures, which are not more potent in the world than dreams? When the arch-chancellor wishes him a happy new year, he answers, as if suddenly rejuvenated: "I must grow wise if you are to be able to repeat this greeting thirty years hence."

Napoleon never grew wise, but he was always clever. When he finds that his commercial warfare is reacting to the detriment of his own country, he disregards his own prohibitions, and grants licenses for the import of certain raw materials and dyes from England, in part because they are urgently needed for French industry, and in part because the articles in question are among the requirements of Parisian luxury. Soon, in all continental countries, huge sums are made by smugglers who import the very colonial produce which the Emperor wishes to prevent his chief enemy from marketing. These goods are then retailed at a great profit. Is the smartest dealer in Europe to be robbed of his gains by smugglers? He would rather have the business under his own control, so he imposes a fifty per cent. duty on all the colonial produce his agents can find on the Continent, and pouches these receipts for France. Since at the same time he has all English woollen textiles that he can lay hands on burned, he opens opportunities for illicit gains which are so large that for their sake people will ignore the risks of draconian punishments. He has to carry on a guerilla warfare, just as in Spain, though this time he is fighting the nation of shopkeepers with trade weapons.

It is likewise a war of decrees. Since Paris has prohibited all trading in English wares, London reciprocates by demanding from all neutral countries enhanced dues for permission to call at the blockaded ports. Paris counters this move by declaring that the vessels of neutrals which shall call at the ports of London or of Malta, run the risk of capture as prizes. London responds by sending her ships out under false colours, and Paris thereupon has all merchantmen trading in Mediterranean waters overhauled and searched. The American government forbids its citizens to have business dealings with Europe, or even to have any private intercourse with the Continent; but the Emperor promises all kinds of privileges to the Americans if they will cease to call at English ports. So paradoxical is the situation resulting from the endeavour to strangle overseas trade, by which Napoleon had hoped to extort the freedom of the seas!

The Emperor's hopes are rising. The English pound sterling is still quoted at seventeen francs, the English banks are failing, and in parliament the opposition is against the continuance of the war. In spite of this, his peace proposals are rejected. The disturbances in Spain are at once the cause and the consequence of England's defiant attitude.

There is still an army numbering a quarter million men stationed in Spain; and, despite all endeavours, Wellington's thirty thousand are not driven out, for the bands of native insurrectionaries led by officers and monks carry on unceasing guerilla warfare against the French invaders. The Emperor's quarrel with the pope stiffens the antagonism of the monks. While French children on the northern slopes of the Pyrenees are being taught that Napoleon is God's vicegerent, Spanish children on the southern slopes are learning that the Emperor is the devil incarnate and that the murder of a Frenchman is a deed pleasing to the Almighty.

In so fanatical a land, where hardly any regular troops are left for the French to fight against, Napoleon's generals feel out of their element. Disunion prevails. Masséna is sent against Portugal. At the same time, Napoleon deprives Joseph of four provinces. When the king journeys to Paris to demand the cancelling of the decree, the Emperor declares that his brother has ceded these lands. Napoleon places a general to administer each province, and appoints a marshal in supreme command. He carries out this Roman system of ruling through military governors thus ruthlessly and persistently because of his intense disappointment in the rule of the members of his family to whom he has allotted crowns, and, above all, in the behaviour of his brothers. Terrible battles, made more ghastly by famine and disease, are meanwhile forcing Masséna to retreat. The Emperor, in a fury, recalls him.

Will Napoleon at length realise that his presence is essential? Marshals, officers, and, above all, the rank and file of the army, eagerly await his coming. Full well does he know this; and yet he does not go. Does he fear assassination at the hands of some fanatical Spaniard? Or is it treachery at home that deters him; such conspiracies as those which called him back to Paris so suddenly when he was encamped near Astorga? Is he to get enmeshed in this southern corner of his empire at the moment when the whole is at stake? What is Spain to him? He chooses the oldest of his companions-in-arms: Marmont is sent to clear up the mess and bring the campaign to an end.

The second kingly brother had, with good reason, thrown up his job. Napoleon had deprived him of all the Dutch territory on the left bank of the Rhine; had insisted upon the removal of the rest of the protective duties against France; and (this was the worst of all) had angered the Dutch, who are traders and seamen, by the measures he had compelled them to take against England. The Emperor had expected both his brothers to run counter to the currents of national feeling in their respective kingdoms, underestimating alike the strength of popular sentiment and the sense of honour of the two men he had forced to become monarchs. It would have been easier for military governors to cope with the rising tide of nationalism and to dispense with a feeling obligation towards the people they ruled, than it was for kings burdened with historic crowns.

When Louis found it impossible to put up any longer with

the Emperor's tutelage, he abdicated in favour of his younger son, and fled by night from his kingdom for an unrevealed destination. Napoleon's catchpolls sought him far and wide in Europe, to discover him at length in Austria. The Emperor was greatly enraged, yet he could not but see that he was himself more to blame than Louis. He therefore made no attempt to punish, but sent his own body physician to care for the fugitive, who had excused the flight on the ground of illness. To his mother, the Emperor wrote saying that there were tidings of Louis' whereabouts. "You need not be anxious; but his conduct has been of a kind which can only be explained by his illness. Your very affectionate son, Napoleon."

The wording of this subscription stands out among the numberless letters in which the dictator of Europe was accustomed to express his will to those who usually received these missives with trembling. The fugitive king, meanwhile, drawing a breath of relief, settled down to a literary life in Graz, writing in three volumes under the title *Marie, ou les peines d'amour* (1808), the story of the love affair which the Emperor had so ruthlessly frustrated. But when Joseph wished to follow Louis' example, feeling that he would rather retire into private life than continue to play the part of king in a pack of cards, he was restrained from abdication by the iron hand of the Emperor. Napoleon considered that his democratically inclined brother would do more mischief as an intriguer in Paris than in his position as nominal chief and military commander; so Joseph had once more to put his hand to the task of war, for which, to the Emperor's great annoyance, he was utterly unfitted.

The most frivolous members of the family, Jerome and Pauline, were amusing themselves with love affairs. Murat and Caroline were immersed over head and ears in old and new intrigues. As for Elise, she had so much printed in the Tuscan newspapers anent her reviews and hunting parties that the Emperor was even more annoyed by her craze for notoriety than by the things she actually did, and wrote to her, saying: "Europe pays very little heed to what the grand duchess of Tuscany is doing."

The most dangerous man in his family circle has not yet become an object of his menaces. Since the old king of Sweden was on friendly terms with England, the Emperor had made him abdicate in favour of an uncle; and the new ruler, who is devoted to the cause of Napoleon, has declared war against England. Being old and childless, he thinks he cannot please the Emperor better than by appointing as successor one who is closely connected with Napoleon by marriage. Thus it is that Bernadotte, Joseph's brother-in-law, who during the wars has made friends in Swedish Pomerania, is unexpectedly nominated crown prince of Sweden—as a result of a complicated intrigue, in which Fouché has played a considerable part. The Emperor would have found it difficult, in any case, to object to this selection of a French general as heir to a foreign throne; and it was practically impossible for him to interfere with the promotion of his sometime rival, the man who had nearly prevented the coup d'état of the Eighteenth Brumaire, and had subsequently become the husband of the woman whom Napoleon had once thought of marrying. "A good soldier," growled the Emperor; "but with no talent for ruling; one of the old Jacobins, with a bee in his bonnet like the rest of them, and therefore he will never be able to keep his position on a throne. . . . Still, I could not interfere, were it only because it would be impossible to do anything more effective against the English than to set a French marshal upon the throne of Gustavus Adolphus. . . . I am glad to be quit of him."

Is he really so carefree? Hitherto these folk whom he cannot trust have always been kept under his own eyes in Paris.

Bernadotte triumphans! Soon, at last, he too will wear a crown, and will not even have to thank this detested Bonaparte for the gift. To Napoleon, therefore, who till yesterday was Bernadotte's supreme war lord, the crown prince of

Sweden now writes a bitter-sweet letter, offering soldiers and iron, but asking for money. The Emperor smiles. He knows what is written between the lines, and makes no direct answer. He has Bernadotte informed that he does not correspond with royal princes. His old opponent will not forget the gibe. In less than two years, Bernadotte will take vengeance for it, and for all that has gone before!

Ruefully, the Emperor watches the flames that are springing up everywhere, the flames his family mania has lighted. He does not conceal from his intimates that he is disappointed with his kin and his nobles. Writing to one of them at this time, Napoleon says: "I ought never to have had Murat and my brothers crowned. Live and learn! . . . It was a mistake, too, to give back the confiscated estates to the émigrés. I should have kept the lands as State domains, and have been content to allow the former owners a modest income. I can't stomach them, these people of the old regime; their light and airy graces are out of keeping with my serious temperament. I myself did not succeed to a heritage, but was content to take what belonged to no one. I ought to have been satisfied with the appointment of governors and viceroys. Some of my marshals, even, are beginning to dream of greatness and independence."

At length he has realised that it is dangerous to play the emperor! His troubles are the fruit of his wish to safeguard a dynasty (this meaning that the spirits of revolt and of genius, from whose union Napoleon has sprung, are to be taught to walk in the paths of legitimate mediocrity). They are the outcome of the weak moments of a man who in his hours of strength believed in the immortality of deed and of fame, of a man who in these hours of strength felt no need of the perpetuation that is achieved by means of a family line. The brothers, and brothers-in-law, and marshals, who all shine by reflected light, will take vengeance ere long. When his star pales, and the skies of Europe are overcast, they will still try to shine across the Continent in the afterglow of his splendour!

Deeply ingrained in him was the illusion that his good fortune would be transmitted to his son. When, after the boy's birth, a great reception was held, and all the notables came to offer congratulations, the Schwarzenbergs were among the guests. Schwarzenberg, as Austrian envoy in Paris, had done much to promote the marriage. The Emperor, full of gratitude, went up to Princess Schwarzenberg and, taking from his coat a scarab pin, presented it to her, saying:

"I found this scarab in the tomb of an Egyptian king, and have worn it ever since as a talisman. Please accept it; I no longer need such a mascot."

He feels that the birth of his son has placed him above all possibility of danger, and that everything will go well with him in future. He can have no further need for an amulet!

These kings, these brothers, have been but a substitute for the sons that were lacking. Now, when he can feast his eyes on a son of his body, he recognises his mistake, and the disastrous consequences of Josephine's barrenness are plainer than ever. Too many battles have been fought, too many years have passed, there has been too much self-restraint and self-denial, for it to be possible now to give this heir a great place in his system. The boy has been born too late. The tempo of Napoleon's life has been so rapid. The man who at two-and-twenty was still a lieutenant, had become an emperor at thirty-four. Such a man should have had his first-born son long before the age of forty-one. He has recklessly expended his vital energies, and cannot look forward confidently to many years of power. How can he reasonably expect to establish the child securely as his successor?

It is, indeed, a poignant sight. Watch this man who is now growing old with fearful speed, as he dandles the long-desired infant on his knees, tries his own hat on the baby's head, watches the child crawling on the floor while he sits at breakfast, and even (when the youngster grows a little older) allows him to run about the study. Napoleon is playing the war game, with little wooden rods representing soldiers dispersed over the floor, and is planning how to make an end of Wellington in Spain. The boy is brought to the door. According to the rule of the house, the governess may not cross this threshold, so Napoleon himself goes to the door for the child, sets him down among the mimic armies, and, with the tolerance of a grandfather, lets the child play riot with the battle. Laughing, he pulls faces at his infant son in front of the looking-glass; buckles round the body of the two-year-old the sword with which he has conquered Europe; and, with his actor's instincts, feels that the boundaries between jest and earnest are being broken down. Imaginings are ripening into reality, while all that has seemed to him real is not more than an image and a parable.

He says that the child is "spirited and sensitive. Just what I want him to be. . . . My son is sturdy, and in splendid health. He has my lungs, my mouth, and my eyes. . . . I do hope he will turn out well." In such simple fashion he writes to Josephine, and to her only. He insists upon her keeping up the old tone of comradeship, and scolds her when, after the divorce, she writes to him as "Your Majesty." "You have written me an unkind letter. I am always the same; my feelings do not change. . . . I shall say no more until you have compared this letter with yours. Then you can judge for yourself which of us two is more friendly, you or I." To no one else can he speak so simply, unless it be to Berthier, whom he often calls his "wife." The only thing that annoys him with Josephine is that she is always running into debt. He thinks that she ought to be able to save half of her allowance of three millions. "Then in ten years you would have put by fifteen millions for your grandsons. . . . Let me know that you are quite well again. I am told that you are getting as stout as one of our good Norman peasant women." But when Josephine continues to be spendthrift, he tells the steward of her property not to make her any further payments till evidence is forthcoming that she is no longer squandering money.

He sees very little more of her, however; and he will have nothing to do with the lady friends of earlier years. His attitude towards marriage is that of a respectable citizen, and that of an Italian. Besides, as a sovereign prince he wishes to set a good example to his subjects. Since Marie Louise makes no nationalist pretensions (for, being of a dull, easy-going, and fickle temperament, she has promptly come to regard herself as a Frenchwoman), the two get on very well together. He has always time to spare for her. When she is learning to ride, he walks patiently at her bridle. He, who has never waited before, will even wait when she is late for dinner. She is not afraid of him, and is saucy enough to tell the Austrian envoy that she thinks her husband is a little afraid of her. It is important to the Emperor that he should make a good impression upon the Hofburg. Regarding it as politically expedient that a report of his wife's happiness shall be sent to Vienna, he brings Metternich to see the empress, and tells the envoy to stay until some one fetches him. Napoleon goes away, locking the door of the room after him. He does not release the prisoners for an hour, and then, with a sly laugh, asks Metternich whether he is satisfied, now, that the empress is happy.

These are nothing more than jests, but that he can find it possible to make them in a period of grave decisions indicates that there is a certain release of tension in his heavily laden heart. In truth, Marie Louise's only service to him was that, during the years with which we are now dealing, her freshness did actually bring him such a solace.

But the marriage did not effect the desired release of political tension. Felix Austria, accustomed to gain advantages by these royal marriages, had hoped for a couple of provinces as dower, but had received nothing. All the more, therefore, must Emperor Francis feel rancorous on account of the humiliation inflicted upon him by the little Corsican; for, as soon as the gates of the Hofburg had closed behind Marie Louise, he could not but regard the marriage as detrimental to his dignity. To appease his legitimist misgivings, the Habsburg ruler had a search for Buonaparte ancestors made in musty old Tuscan documents, and when next he met his son-in-law was able to assure the latter that the Buonaparte lineage had been traced as far back as the eleventh century. At that time, said Francis, there had been members of the family in Treviso. Thereupon the first and last of the Buonaparti made the delicious answer:

"Thank you, Sire. I prefer to be the Rudolf of my race!"

Witty, but unwise, for such words from an upstart sovereign could not but rankle in the mind of this descendant of an ancient line! When, as would soon come to pass, the question whether the emperor of Austria was to take sides for or against his son-in-law was to be decided by Francis' mood, the memory of this and similar slights may have played a considerable part. Napoleon recognised this when it was too late. "Had I but made myself agreeable to that simpleton, who knows but that in the plains of Leipzig there might have been a hundred thousand fewer men in the opposing army!"

All the same, the revolutionist admired many of the ways of the legitimate ruler. One day he caught sight of a letter his wife had addressed to her father as follows: "His Sacred Majesty, the Apostolical Emperor." Napoleon considered this an excellent idea; and in private, no doubt, his thoughts turned to Alexander of Macedon who had declared himself to be the son of Jupiter.

The apostolical emperor was especially out of humour with his son-in-law on the pope's account. Napoleon was continually tightening the bonds round the Holy Father. Pius VII. was kept at Savona. A man by no means learned in canon law, he was cut off from his advisers, and subsequently deprived of his papers, in order to make him pliable. A schism was threatening. Thirteen of the cardinals had failed to put in an appearance at the Emperor's wedding, for the pope would not recognise the divorce which Fesch had pronounced. Now Napoleon has cases filled with the Vatican State papers brought to Paris, thus arousing the belief that he really intends to make this city the capital of Christendom; he summons a council at which the prelates of his European realm appear; he extorts a decree depriving the pope of the investiture in case of dissent, and ultimately compels Pius to agree to this—at any rate for France.

Europe is troubled by these matters, and split into factions. On the whole, the Russians and the Poles are glad that things are going ill with the Roman pontiff; the Prussians and the English are, of course, delighted; but what arouses general surprise is that the inhabitants of the Papal States are also on the side of the Emperor. This little country, now doubly robbed of its master, is glad to accept the Code Napoléon, modern education, a rational system of administration, vigorous road construction, and the draining of the Pontine marshes. Whereas the son of the revolution has long since brought back the old spirit of Rome to Paris, he now transplants young revolutionary practice from Paris to Rome. Thus does Napoleon build bridges.

The excommunicated Emperor cunningly tries to turn the curse against the pope. When, in newly annexed Holland, he receives the clergy in the presence of the Protestants, he rebukes the bishops as follows: "Are you of the religion of Gregory VII.? I am not. My religion is that of Jesus Christ, who said: 'Render unto Cæsar the things which are Cæsar's.' In accordance with the same text, I render unto God the things which are God's. I have received my sceptre from God. But I wear a worldly sword, and know how to use it! God erects thrones. I did not raise myself to my throne: God set me upon it! You poor mortals wish to resist? You will not pray for your monarch, because the priest of Rome has excommunicated him? Do you think I am the sort of man to kiss the pope's toe? . . . Prove to me, imbeciles, that Jesus has appointed the pope his vicegerent, and that the pope has power to excommunicate a monarch! . . . Be good citizens, and sign the Concordat. You, Mr. Prefect, must take such measures as will prevent my hearing any more of these matters."

To so preposterous a travesty of his own innermost thoughts has Napoleon come. He does not believe a word of what he is here thundering out; and in private mocks at this official doctrine, as he has always done. Nonetheless, to the circlet of golden laurels with which he had crowned himself before the eyes of the priest of Rome, there now attaches a vestige of divine right which makes the crown a heavy one to wear.

II

"Kindly inform me why the price of salt in the neighbourhood of Strasburg has risen one sou."

Closely following upon the heels of this enquiry to the Ministry for War, comes a command to the Admiralty: two entire fleets are to be constructed in the course of the next three years, one Atlantic fleet and one Mediterranean fleet; the latter against Sicily and Egypt, the former against Ireland. As soon as the Spanish affair is in better case, preparations are to be made for an expedition to the Cape in 1812. An army of from sixty to eighty thousand men is to be got ready for an attack on Surinam and Martinique. "Having eluded the enemy cruisers," the expeditionary forces are to share out the two hemispheres.

We see how closely at this date, when imaginative fantasies threaten to develop into adventures, the exact observations of the father of his country are allied to the rhapsodical plans of the world conqueror. For that is what Napoleon now attempts: he is actually trying to realise his old dream of world conquest.

"You want to know whither we are going? We shall have

done with Europe; then, as robbers of robbers less bold than ourselves, we shall march to the attack, seize India, over which they have made themselves masters. . . . I must take India . . . in the rear, if I am to strike successfully at England. . . . Just imagine Moscow occupied, the tsar conciliated or killed by his people, perhaps a new, dependent throne,—and tell me whether an army of Frenchmen, reinforced by auxiliary troops from Tiflis, cannot press forward to the Ganges, and thence, at a touch, destroy the whole structure of English commerce! . . . At one blow, France would have established the independence of the West and the freedom of the seas!" A witness reports that while he was voicing these ideas "his eyes shone with a wonderful light, and he went on to point out the reasons for the adventure, all the difficulties it entailed, the means of achievement, and the prospects of success."

Shall the tsar be conciliated or killed? That is the question which troubles the Emperor the whole year round. Calculations and presentiments make him desire to have Alexander as his friend rather than his enemy. Napoleon has nothing to gain by a defeat of Russia. On the contrary! He dreads being forced into this war, and endeavours, as on former occasions, to avoid it; though only if the tsar, as previously agreed, shall participate in the great final struggle as an ally. Napoleon keeps the tsar under observation, and perceives that suggestions are having less and less effect upon Alexander. He therefore writes to a prince of the Confederation of the Rhine in these amazing terms: "This war will break out in spite of the tsar, in spite of me, and in spite of the interests of the two empires."

Never before had the Emperor or the Consul declared, in such words, that war was unavoidable. Precisely because all rational need for the campaign was lacking this time, he found it necessary to proclaim the war with the tsar to be the work of fate. At the very first handclasp, in the peace tent on the Memel, the seed of this war was sown. During the days of intimacy which followed, when the encounter blossomed into friendship, that seed invisibly took root and grew. In later days, Talleyrand's treacherous diplomacy cherished its growth; and when, at Erfurt, the emperors embraced, they could already feel between them the coils of the snake. That they did not become related by marriage was neither an accident nor the outcome of a conscious desire: it was consequent upon the mistrust which had invaded the tsar's mind, a mistrust of which he could not rid himself and which was to prove well founded. Two men wishing to divide Europe between them, could not see with complacency the half in a rival's hands. Their intentions were honourable at the outset; but they were impossible of fulfilment. The day of contest must inevitably come at last. "He alone is still weighing upon the pinnacle of my edifice. My rival is young; daily his strength is waxing; daily mine is waning." This gloomy recognition spurs him ever onward.

It is useless to try to interpret such decrees of destiny as the outcome of political causes.

Somewhat earlier, the Emperor has asked the tsar to lay an embargo on all neutral ships, as he himself has done, and thus give England the death-blow. The tsar cannot agree to this, for it would fatally injure his own sea-borne trade; he will only continue, as before, to confiscate all the prohibited goods he discovers, but he needs colonial wares from the neutrals. Being unable to stop this leak in the East, the Emperor has to exercise redoubled care on the German coast, and he therefore annexes the mouths of the Weser and the Elbe with the Hansa towns and part of Hanover. "Circumstances demand these new guarantees against England." Oldenburg is swallowed up with the rest, though the heir to this duchy has married Alexander's sister.

The Emperor's high-handed proceedings were a logical outcome of his policy, but they were necessarily an offence to the tsar. Alexander regarded them as a breach of the treaty of

Tilsit, in which the integrity of Oldenburg had been guaranteed. He issued a circular to the powers protesting against this insult to his house, a remonstrance almost equivalent to a declaration of war. In this document he enquired what could be the use of alliances unless the treaties in which they were incorporated were strictly observed, so that the cabinets of Europe could not but smile at the concluding words of the circular, in which he described the alliance between Russia and France as permanent. His next step was a ukase in which he threw Russia open to colonial goods, while imposing prohibitive import duties on wine and silk, the products of French industry.

The maps lie spread on the tables in St. Petersburg and Paris. Where can either power best harass the other? The tsar proposes to make peace with Turkey. The Emperor incites Austria to seize Serbia, to advance towards Moldavia and Wallachia, promising not to interfere; this will keep Alexander busy. Metternich nods assent, but does not move. "What about Poland?" thinks Alexander. "Has not Napoleon already enlarged the duchy of Warsaw by the addition of Galicia? Is there any guarantee that he will not re-establish the kingdom of Poland?" Caulaincourt, French ambassador in Russia, who admires the tsar and wants peace, gives the desired guarantees. But the Emperor would only agree to a secret ratification. If the differences between France and Russia should culminate in war, he will need Poland for his operations against the tsar; Polish hopes must, therefore, be fostered. Penetrating this design, Alexander demands an open treaty, which shall put an end to Polish expectations.

When Masséna is defeated in Spain, the Emperor entertains fresh doubts. Caulaincourt, who is back in Paris, does his utmost to intensify these misgivings, dilates on the tsar's will-to-peace, and ventures far in his defence of Alexander. The Emperor leads him on; hears all he has to say; asks a thousand questions concerning the tsar and the court, Alexander's piety, the nobles, and the peasants; takes Caulaincourt by the ear, a sign of affability.

"You must be in love with him!"

"I am in love with peace."

"So am I. But I will not allow any one to dictate to me. Evacuate Danzig, forsooth! Next I shall have to ask Alexander's permission before I can hold a review in Mainz. You are a fool. I am an old fox, and know the people with whom I am dealing. . . . We must deprive this Russian colossus and his hordes of the power to inundate the south once more. . . . I shall advance northwards, and reestablish there the old boundaries of Europe."

Quite unsubstantial reasons, masks, mere pretexts. Warningly Caulaincourt quotes Alexander's words: "I shall learn from his own teachings, which are those of a master. Our climate will make war for us. The French are not inured to it as we are. Miracles only happen when the Emperor is present, and he cannot be everywhere." Napoleon is greatly moved by these words; he tramps restlessly up and down the room; the conversation lasts for hours. Since he cannot refute Caulaincourt's arguments, he makes vague answers behind which his titanic wishes loom.

"A well-fought battle will put an end to the fine resolves of your friend Alexander. . . . He is false, ambitious, and weak; he has the character of a Greek. Believe me, it is he, not I, who wants this war, for he cherishes a hidden design. . . . He is out of humour because I did not take his sister." When Caulaincourt gives proofs to the contrary, Napoleon says: "I have forgotten the details."—Forgotten! This is a new word in the Emperor's mouth. He knows his position to be weak; himself a man of facts, he now brushes away those which he finds inconvenient.

He sends a more resolute envoy to the tsar. When a proposal comes from St. Petersburg that Warsaw shall be exchanged for Oldenburg, the Emperor says threateningly to the Russian ambassador, raising his voice so that every one in the room may hear: "Not one Polish village!"

But these political incidents and discussions are merely the forms of destiny. Schemes flash like lightning through his brain; his soul is devoured by wishes: and he will rather reveal these things to a dangerous enemy like Fouché than to a shrewd adherent like Caulaincourt. He cannot rid himself of the ex-Jacobin and ex-cleric. Last year, he had cashiered the Minister of Police, for Fouché was obviously intriguing with England. But Napoleon was as lenient as he had been at the time of the conspiracy which had brought him back hot foot from Astorga. Instead of banishing the man, the Emperor had appointed him senator—at the same time writing to him words which give a glimpse into the inferno of these struggles between the monarch and the spy: "Although I do not doubt your devotion, I find it necessary to have you watched all the time. This is a fatiguing necessity, and I should not be called upon to do anything of the kind."

But though he dismisses Fouché from his ministerial post, and has the watcher watched, Napoleon cannot get on without him, and talks to him about the most private matters.

"Since my marriage, people fancy that the lion is asleep. They will soon learn whether I am asleep. I need eight hundred thousand men, and have them; I shall tow all Europe in my wake. Europe is nothing more than an old woman, and with my eight hundred thousand men I can make her do whatever I please. . . . Did not you yourself say to me: 'You let your genius have its way, because it does not know the word impossible.' How can I help it if a great power drives me on to become dictator of the world? You and the others, who criticise me to-day and would like me to become a good-natured ruler—have not you all been accessories? I have not yet fulfilled my mission, and I mean to end what I have begun. *We need a European legal code, a European court of appeal, a unified coinage, a common system of weights and measures. The same law must run throughout Europe. I shall fuse all the nations into one.* . . . This, my lord duke, is the only solution that pleases me. . . ." Having said this, he suddenly sends Fouché from the room.

Here we have it plainly disclosed, Napoleon's vision of the United States of Europe. The plan is recorded by one who, in his memoirs, would fain have discredited the Emperor—this plan with its extremely rational deductions and its daimonic inspiration. Europe is no longer a "mole-hill" as it was in the days of Milan and Rivoli, when he was nothing more than General Bonaparte, and when to the young man of genius all possible adversaries seemed too petty. Fifteen years later, Europe has become a plastic material; and Bonaparte is the emperor, the legislator, the great orderer, the enemy of the anarchy out of which he sprang, the modeller who would mould the clay into a splendid whole. Throughout the intervening years he has been marching along a predestined path; now he displays before us, in this statement of his aims, the productive consequences towards which he has been moving along that road of force through ever new hecatombs of slaughter. Behind him lie Charlemagne's visions of a united Europe; in front of him glide new forms; and Cæsar, half way towards the realisation of his dream, is well aware that the spirit will ultimately overpower the sword. He has himself said this; and what he is now striving to establish by force with the aid of eight hundred thousand men, will some day come into existence as a voluntary amalgamation based upon reason and necessity. All the nations will fuse into one.

This, my lord duke, is the only solution that pleases me.

III

While Napoleon is pouring his thoughts into Fouché's ears, Alexander is pouring gold into Talleyrand's pockets, and no doubt Talleyrand is going shares with Fouché. The bank could have informed Napoleon to whom Count Nesselrode, the new secretary to the Russian embassy, was paying out such large sums of money. From month to month Talleyrand lets Russia know how the French preparations for war are advancing, and when they will be completed. The limping Mephistopheles must have smiled to himself, sometimes, when Russia paid him for his information with licenses for the import of English goods into Russian harbours—documents which he could sell for hard cash in Paris!

Is the tsar richer than the Emperor? Russia is still allied to France, but the Russian market has been closed to French goods, and the famous 1811 vintage has one purchaser the less. Since England and Spain have long ceased to be customers, French industry is in a bad way. But when the Minister for Finance urges peace because tranquillity is essential to the restoration of French finances, the Emperor cuts him short by saying: "Not at all! It is true that our finances are disordered, but that is why we need war!"

This argument was valid in the past, when the general had sent from Italy the money which the indebted Directory needed, and when, as Consul and Emperor he had made money by his wars. The French State, suffering more than any other from the effects of the blockade it had itself established, showed a deficit for the first time, though the deficit amounted to hardly more than fifty millions. Yet, even now, the Emperor refused to sanction any kind of State loan; "that would be immoral, for it would lay a burden upon later generations." Nevertheless, he introduced indirect taxes and monopolies; nor did he act unwisely in doing so, since he expected to acquire fresh markets, and thereby more stable finances, from the Russian war. But victory was essential!

He enthusiastically lays his plans before the Chambers of Commerce. "England has harmed herself far more by her blockade than she has harmed any other country; she has taught us how to dispense with her products. In a couple of years' time, Europe will have adapted herself to the new ways of feeding her populations. Soon, we shall have more than enough beet sugar and shall be able to do without cane sugar. . . . Every year I draw only nine hundred millions revenue from my own country; three hundred millions I put away, and store in the cellars of the Tuileries. The Bank of France is full of silver; the Bank of England has none. Since the peace of Tilsit, I have received more than a milliard francs in indemnities. Austria is bankrupt. England and Russia will soon follow suit. I alone have money!"

All the same, no one has much faith in his fine words. The more the Emperor's plans for world conquest force the pace of recruiting, the more keenly does he keep watch upon the internal tranquillity of France. As the ruthlessness of his dictatorship increases, the mood of the citizens of France becomes gloomier and gloomier. Any criticism, even in the remotest corner of the realm, is immediately pounced upon and prosecuted. There are more than three thousand persons locked up in gaol without trial, because this one "hates the Emperor," or this other has certain "religious outlooks," or another has written, "in private letters, unfriendly expressions in regard to the government." A new press bureau, with the absurd name of "Bureau of Public Opinion," is established to manufacture political trends. When a Dutch newspaper publishes the statement that it is within the competence of the pope to excommunicate kings, not only is the journal suppressed, but the author of the offending article is arrested. In a certain book, an appreciation of the English constitution has to be deleted; another work has to be rechristened "Campaigns of Napoleon the Great," whereas the author's original title had been "History of Bonaparte."

While oppression of thought is rampant, it is not inconsonant with the imperialistic spirit to find that such men as Monge and Laplace, Guérin and Gérard, are willing to accept baronial honours. And when the French version of *The Robbers* is prohibited in Hamburg, the last of the republicans recall with ironical bitterness the day twenty years earlier when the revolution had conferred the right of French citizenship upon its German author.

What cares the Emperor for the mood of these ideologues? Under the spell of the evolution of his own powers, his eyes fixed upon the goal of his life's aspiration, he misjudges now, as earlier in his struggle with the pope, the moral impression he is making upon his contemporaries. Yet in the past he had never failed to take this into account; at each step, he had questioned public opinion. Now, he allows the newfangled Bureau to manipulate public opinion: "What do I care for the opinion of the drawing-rooms and the babblers! I recognise only one opinion, that of the peasants!" Certain it is that the peasants are his most faithful supporters, mainly because he rescued their lands from the dangers threatened by the revolution. Now that the Spanish war has swallowed up larger and larger armies, the peasants have to pay eight thousand francs for a substitute, simply to save the few remaining sons to carry on the work of agriculture on the lands of their fathers. Many thousands of these young men are trying to evade service; and those who in the early days of the war would have joyfully rallied to the colours, have now to be rounded up by mobile columns or forced into the ranks by threats against their families and the communes to which they belong.

Why should the Emperor be surprised at such a change of mood? Had not General Bonaparte set out to carry the ideas of the revolution to the peoples groaning under the yoke of emperors and kings? Did not the First Consul go forth to repel in his one campaign, did not the Emperor likewise go forth to repel in his three wars, the ever-renewed onslaughts of the allied monarchs? That by wars thus forced upon him he won more than freedom for the land of his adoption, that by the battles of Austerlitz, Jena, and Wagram he obtained new provinces from the enemy, was the outcome of his genius, and encouraged the people's army to fresh deeds of valour. Even the rivalry with England was comprehensible to the French people; had it not been ever thus in the days of their fathers and grandfathers before them? But what could the peasant of Provence make of these purely political struggles in Spain and in Russia? The Emperor could not explain to him the plan for setting up a United States of Europe. Men had disappeared in the rivers of Andalusia, the names of which fell haltingly from a Frenchman's lips. The peasant needed the support of his son's young arm, now that the years were creeping onward. So it was that he purchased his son's freedom from military service, and growled as he paid.

What had the German peasants to say when, addressed as "contingents," they answered the call of their kings and accompanied the foreign Emperor into distant lands? Thousands of peasants from the valley of the Main were dispatched to Spain; Jerome sent thirty thousand Westphalians to the Oder; Saxons guarded the Vistula; Württembergers and Bavarians flowed in a steady stream eastward, for "if the princes of the Confederation of the Rhine" (thus writes the Emperor to one of these same princes) "give me the least cause to doubt their willingness to undertake a joint defence, then, I tell them frankly, they are lost. I prefer open enemies to untrustworthy friends." Such is the crack of the master's whip. He deals more politely with the Habsburg. All being well, Austria may even be rewarded for her aid by receiving Silesia.

Germany, composed as she is of many small and disintegrated fragments, serves Napoleon admirably in his jig-saw game with the nations. The three southern States have had their inhabitants and their lands bartered and exchanged at will; and, since Eugene has lost his throne to the Emperor's son (the baby was made "King of Rome") he is immediately installed as ruler in the hastily concocted "grand duchy of Frankfort."

What of Prussia? Why should Prussia continue to exist? Had he not, in Tilsit days, merely preserved this kingdom to please the tsar? But he is about to destroy the tsar! By notices and decrees, the Emperor announces that now, just before the war with Russia begins, Prussia is to be parcelled up. Does he not know that for the last year Prussia has been the ally of Russia, and that in a secret treaty the tsar has promised Frederick William his assistance? The Emperor hears much of defiant songs, of volunteer corps, of discontent in the universities, of the Tugendbund. Beware! Remember Spain! Do not trust to the proverbial "tolerance and coldness of these north Germans"! Surely it would be wiser to utilise the Prussian army before destroying it. . . .

The great-hearted Scharnhorst assures Frederick William that now is the time to strike. But Metternich, in Vienna, tricks the Prussian general when he proposes an alliance, and advises him to seek alliance with Russia rather than with the Habsburg emperor. For only if the man with whom he exchanges these words of false friendship, becomes an opponent, only if Prussia enters the war as Austria's enemy, can Austria hope to enclose Silesia once more within her borders. At the same time Hardenberg bends before the Vienna wind, to-day as always. The king, who will take no risks, and who considers Napoleon absolutely unconquerable, at last makes up his mind to enter into alliance with the Emperor; his resolution comes too late to secure favourable terms. Silesia and Poland are already alive with troops, and Prussia is surrounded. In such circumstances it is natural that she should be treated as a vassal, should have to tolerate the passage of armies, should have to put up with requisitionings, should have to look on patiently while her eastern fortresses are manned by French soldiers and her auxiliary corps commanded by foreign marshals. Metternich writes to his master in gleeful mood: "Prussia need no longer be reckoned among the powers."

And yet! And yet! Although Europe, from Capua to Tilsit, at the outset of 1812, is rallying to Napoleon's standard, although his arm reaches from Finisterre to Bukovina, he feels how uncertain is the outcome of his campaign, and, as Count Ségur tells us, starts up from the conning of his interminable lists and calculations to exclaim in terror: "I am not ready to undertake a war in such far-off lands! I need three years more!"

But the machine rolls on; no master hand can stay it. An inner impulse urges him forward; the whole history of his rise to power impels him; all the shades of vanished years drive him on. He, who has built so many harbours wherein to seek refuge in times of storm and stress, is in the end tossed out upon the open sea, more roughly, more speedily than he had wished, and, with the wild determination of the adventurer, he now recklessly seizes the steering-wheel which for so long he has manipulated with statesmanlike care. "Do you not see," he exclaims to his brother, "that I can only keep my seat upon this throne by means of the fame which brought me to it? That a private individual such as I, who has merely risen to become a ruler, dare not call a halt? That such a one is constrained to mount higher and ever higher, and is doomed to perish the moment he stops climbing?"

His soul is a-flicker with excitement, so that at one moment he is eager for the final struggle, and at the next dreads it. His letter to the tsar, with which, as heretofore, he begins the campaign, still preserves a friendly tone. At the same time he says to a Russian colonel who is on spy duty in Paris: "Since the tsar is young and I have yet many years to live, I had thought to preserve the peace of Europe by means of our good feelings towards one another. My feelings have not changed. Tell him this; and say, in addition, that if the fates decree that the two greatest powers of the world are to come to blows over girlish peccadilloes, I shall enter the lists as a gallant knight, without hatred and without enmity. I suggest to him the possibility of our meeting for breakfast together between our respective outposts. . . . I still hope that we shall not spill the blood of hundreds of thousands of brave men, simply because we cannot agree as to the colour of a ribbon!"

How his own unrest vibrates through these brilliant subterfuges, which he specially adapts to cajole Alexander's feminine disposition! A grey gauntlet of steel is hurled from one world power to the other; the great fight between birth and genius is now to take place in all its grandeur. And he who, after two decades of dreaming, sees his dream descending out of the clouds earthwards, talks as if nothing more were at stake than a girl's quarrel or the colour of a piece of ribbon—when in reality the fate of the world hangs in the balance!

IV

What is passing in Alexander's mind? Estranged from the Russian nobility, railed at by his mother, cheated out of his hopes of setting up the cross once more on St. Sophia, deeply concerned about Poland (which his adversary threatens to liberate)—there are reasons enough, both in political and court life, why he should no longer regard Napoleon as his friend. After Tilsit, Metternich had said that it would take five years for the tsar's feelings to swing to the opposite pole. That period had now elapsed, and although the tsar's was one of those nervous temperaments in which moods decide actions, on his side, too, the struggle could assume allegorical greatness. But he lacked a grand aim and a lofty thought. He was not even fighting to win warlike renown against the master craftsman in the art of war. The impulses that drove him to the fight were merely the outcome of a confused mysticism, in whose waters he had drowned his old veneration for the magician of Tilsit.

Politically, he makes two successful moves in the game, one of these being intimately adapted to the peculiarities of human character, and therefore weighty with consequence. To cope with Napoleon, he needs tranquillity on his southern and his northern borders. He finds means to keep the sultan neutral; but in the case of Sweden he manages even better, for he is able to secure an alliance. He and Bernadotte meet on the frontier; and here, for the second time, the tsar of all the Russias succumbs to the charm of a French revolutionary. Sweden is in danger of English vengeance. Norway belongs to the Francophil Danes. The community of interests between Sweden and Russia secures expression when Russia, in return for a promise of help in the coming war, guarantees that Sweden shall have Norway.

But this prospect of territorial enlargement is not the thing that spurs Bernadotte to action. He, who is king in Napoleon's despite, cares no more about his new subjects than those who had become kings by Napoleon's favour cared about theirs. But the tsar, too, has an imagination. Looking forward to the winning of this game, he sees in broad outline what lies beyond. He sees, not only the Emperor's defeat, but the Emperor's destruction; and while Napoleon, at the head of the greatest army known to history, is slowly advancing to swallow up the tsar, Alexander is promising Bernadotte, the friend of Bonaparte's youth, no less a prize than the throne of France.

To such heights, this summer, do the opposing eagles soar.

In Dresden, the Emperor treats all the princes to the spectacle of a review, just as he had done four years earlier in Erfurt. The only sovereign from among that company who is absent, is the one he is now to fight. But Alexander's place has been taken by the Habsburg ruler. Only once before have Napoleon and Francis met, on the day after Austerlitz. Twice, since then, has the victorious Emperor of the French occupied the Austrian's abandoned capital. When peace had been made between them, and the victor had wedded the daughter of the vanquished, the girl had been sent alone from Vienna to distant Paris.

Now Marie Louise sits between husband and father at the

sparkling board, and to outward seeming all is well. The father-in-law is pledged in alliance, and the Emperor has appointed his wife regent of France. But vainly has he forbidden her to be so foolish as to attempt the outshining of her stepmother on these festal occasions. The empress from Paris sheds tears at the prohibition, while the empress from Vienna weeps because her pearls are smaller than those worn by Marie Louise. The old jealousies between the principalities and powers now find vent in family quarrels which the courtiers try to gloss over. When a health is drunk to the boy who should be a tie between all four of them, both the men and both the women drown their thoughts in their champagne, though each knows perfectly well what the others are thinking.

The December meeting in the windmill near Austerlitz, and the May meeting in the palace of the Saxon kings! Son-in-law and father-in-law will never set eyes on one another again.

Meanwhile, half a million men are being ranged between Königsberg and Lemberg. The master of these legions journeys to Posen, and announces the "Second Polish War," for his ostensible aim is merely to wrest Poland from the tsar—most of the old kingdom, at any rate, as far as Smolensk. "There or in Minsk," he tells a confidant, "the campaign will end. I shall winter in Vilna, organise Lithuania, and live at Russia's expense. If, then, peace cannot be secured, I shall, next year, advance into the centre of the enemy's land, and stay there until the tsar becomes pliable." The whole disposition of Napoleon's troops is made in accordance with this scheme. At Russia's expense? What supplies can he get from Russia? Has he accurate information regarding the resources of this foreign land?

In Gumbinnen, he sends for a Prussian president. Speaking of the stores of grain he has collected in the German ports, and proposes to have sent to Kovno, he says:

"I presume there are plenty of mills in Kovno?"

"No, Sire; very few mills are to be found there."

The Emperor looks at Berthier "dubiously." This glance of the supreme war lord at his chief of general staff is a foreshadowing of the disillusionments he is to experience in the unknown land beyond the Memel. It is not the mere lack of mills which disturbs him, but the fact that he is taken by surprise. For a whole year, the Emperor has been preparing the great campaign. Troops, parks of ammunition, reserve corps, fourteen hundred pieces of ordnance, siege trains, bridge-building materials, pontoons, have been assembled from seven realms, counting the Confederation of the Rhine as one. Eight Baltic fortresses are used as storehouses, to which hundreds of ships and thousands of wagons bring wheat and rice. Some of the wagons are drawn by oxen which are destined for the slaughter house at the end of their journey—a symbol of compulsory military service, in which a man serves only that he may die. Now Napoleon learns that he is about to enter a country without mills. He can build them, no doubt; but at what cost in time and men! Are other surprises awaiting him across the Russian border? It will be impossible to carry fodder for one hundred and fifty thousand horses. That is why he has waited till June, when the grass will be green. But what if the steppe should disappoint him here?

And what if his men's spirit should disappoint him?

On the frontier, warning voices make themselves heard. He is told that these young recruits are hardly able to endure the long marches, and that the heat will be too much for them. In Dresden, Murat had vainly asked for furlough. Now, in Danzig, he and Berthier and Rapp are dining with the Emperor in gloomy silence. Napoleon, emerging from his thoughts of world conquest, suddenly asks Rapp: "How far is it from Danzig to Cadiz?" Rapp is bold enough to answer: "Too far, Sire!" Thereupon the master rejoins:

"I can see, gentlemen, that you no longer have any taste for fighting. The king of Naples would rather be back in his pretty kingdom; Berthier would like to be playing the sports-

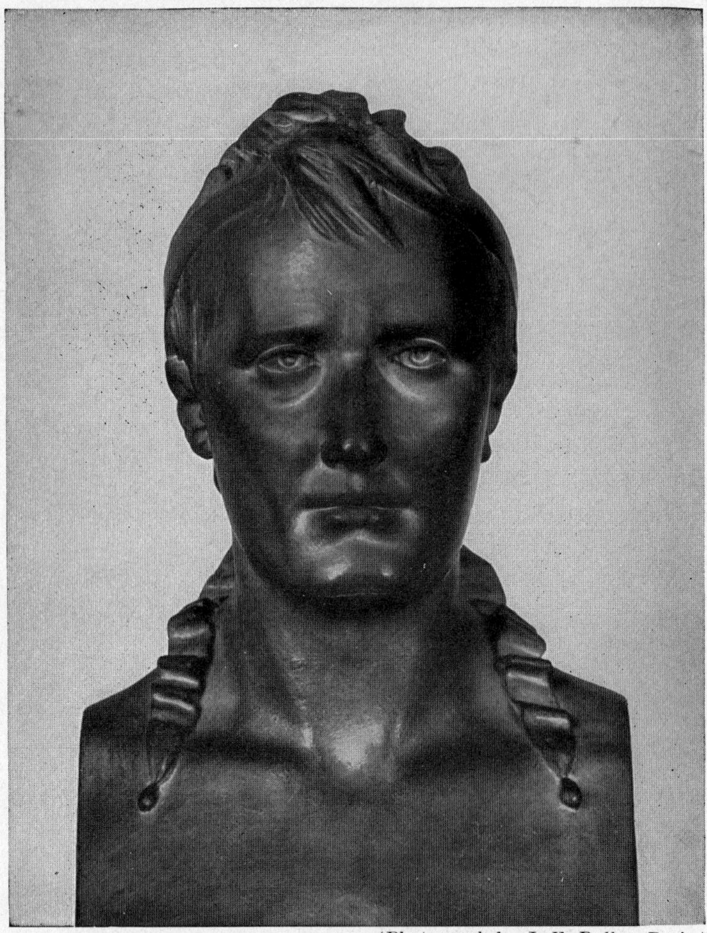

(Photograph by J. E. Bulloz, Paris.)

Napoleon as Emperor. Bust by Houdon, Musée de Dijon.

man in Grosbois; Rapp would fain be enjoying the sweets of Parisian life!"

The marshals answer never a word, for they will not deny that it is so. But that it should be so, is a new experience for Emperor Napoleon.

When he reaches the Memel, the symbolic significance of the Russian frontier captivates his imagination to such an extent that he is the first to cross the river, and he gallops several miles eastward before returning slowly to the bridge. Well, he is over now, and this time, in very truth, he has crossed the Rubicon. At his nod, three armies advance into the interior of Poland. The main army is under his immediate command, the second being commanded by Eugene, and the third by Jerome. Why does he venture to entrust a whole army to the leadership of this amateur (who made such a fool of himself in the last war), even with the safeguard of veteran generals as advisers? Napoleon thinks he can risk it. The enemy has at most three hundred thousand men.

Where is the enemy? In two armies, led by Barclay de Tolly and Bagration. They are somewhere in Lithuania, far away, and the total force is only one hundred and seventy thousand. Napoleon's overestimate of the strength of his opponents was a disastrous error, for if he had himself had fewer mouths to feed, he would have had a much better chance of getting adequate supplies for his soldiers. Why is he so keen on superiority of numbers? General Bonaparte was used, with forty thousand men, to defeat an enemy that greatly outnumbered him, his method being to crush one wing of the foe after another. The cumbrous multitude he has collected for the present campaign is symptomatic of his own increasing age, and of the lust for power which makes him pile up weight, instead of equipping the spirit with wings. Is he no longer the commander of the days of Rivoli?

In a sense, he is still that commander, for, even with this gigantic array of troops, he will be a victorious invader. His first army will march from Tilsit upon Vilna, to take up a position between the Russian detachments, so that his second and third armies can separately defeat the enemy. But the Russian distances weaken his influence. Upon a front of such vast extent, he cannot show himself everywhere. Those who command under him are too independent of one another (Davoust and Murat nearly fight a duel), and yet they are too dependent upon him. Never did he suffer more than in this campaign from the lack of speedy means of communication. His was the central brain in all his undertakings, so that a telegraph would have been far more useful to him than to his opponents.

The Russians are aware of their own weakness. Neither of the two commanders ventures to stand firm. Both of them withdraw before the invaders, at first without any mutual understanding, to get into touch later, far in the rear. These are not the tactics of inspired leaders. Though the Russians do the right thing, it is merely because they are afraid of the forces that outnumber theirs, and because they dread the great name of Napoleon. They are but instruments in the hands of fate.

For a time, the Emperor pauses in his advance. In Vilna, he says: "If Monsieur Barclay imagines that I am going to run after him to the Volga, he is making a great mistake. We will follow him to Smolensk and the Dvina, where a good battle will provide us with quarters. . . . It would certainly be destruction were we to cross the Dvina this year. I shall go back to Vilna, spend the winter there, send for a troupe from the Théâtre Français, and another to play opera. We shall finish off the affair next May, unless peace is made during the winter."

News from the outer world is satisfactory. At length the United States has declared war on England, and has gained some victories at sea. In England the opposition, which wants peace, is gathering strength. Even in Spain things are not going so badly. Forward! A good battle!

But where is the enemy? The Emperor goes scouting, accompanied by only one officer; there is no trace of the Russians. Uneasiness grows. Since the invaders are marching light, and therefore too quickly, part of the army, on bad roads and amid heat and rainstorms, gets separated from its commissariat, upon which everything depends. In Vilna he fails to find the tsar, though Alexander has been there just before. At this moment, news is brought that the supplies are delayed, for the commissariat wagons have stuck fast in a morass, and the vessels that are bringing other supplies have run aground in the river; moreover, ten thousand horses have perished, through gorging themselves upon rank grass. The shortage cannot be hidden from the troops, who scatter through the town, and plunder so recklessly that there will be no supplies left for the next comers.

The Emperor can get nothing from the inhabitants of this land either by threats or cajoleries; and yet he detests rapine, which leads to chaos. The Lithuanians note that even now he has not granted the Poles the promised kingdom. They do not hail him as a liberator, as the people of Lombardy had done long years before. They give no help; they give nothing; they are hardly willing to accept in payment the forged rouble notes, millions of which he has had printed in Paris. They pray.

What is to be done? Now is the time to win over the tsar. He writes: "All that has taken place is out of keeping with Your Majesty's character, and with the personal consideration you have sometimes shown me in the past. . . . When I crossed the Memel, I had it in mind to send you an adjutant, as I have always done in previous campaigns." But, since the tsar had refused to receive his last envoy, "I realised that the invisible providence whose power and dominion I recognise would decide this matter, as he had decided so many others. . . . Nothing, therefore, is left but to conclude with the request that you will remain convinced of the steadfastness of my kindly feelings towards you."

Before writing this long and unctuous letter, in which nothing is genuine except the perplexity and the faith in destiny, he has had a conversation with a captured general who is to convey the missive. The way in which the Emperor hectors the prisoner, smacks of comic opera: "What does the tsar expect from this war? I have seized one of his best provinces without firing a shot, and neither of us knows what we are quarrelling about!" Then, as his way was, he spent an hour or more pointing out the Russians' mistakes, asking why they had not defended Vilna, and talking to this captive just as if he had been berating one of his own generals in Spain. "Are you not ashamed of yourselves?" is the burden of his song. He waxes enthusiastic about the Poles, whom as a rule he frankly despises; but now it suits him to make much of their contempt for death. He says that he has thrice as many soldiers as the tsar, and much more money, so that he will be able to carry on the war for three years. These falsehoods are uttered in simulated anger, which he allows to flash out by fits and starts. The Russian meets bluff with bluff, saying that in Muscovy they have made preparations for a five years' campaign. But now the turn has come for one of the Emperor's bursts of frankness, in words suited to the ears of this officer blown him by a chance wind, but of course designed to impress the tsar, to whom they will be reported.

"I am the man of calculations. When I was in Erfurt, my reckonings convinced me that it would suit my book better to walk hand in hand with you Russians, instead of quarrelling with you. We might still have been good friends. . . . Then the tsar made peace with me, when his country wanted war; now he makes war on me, when his country wants peace. It puzzles me that so distinguished a man can have anything to do with such persons as some of his present advisers. . . . How can any one make war through a council of war? If at two in the morning a good idea enters my mind, in a quarter of an hour I have issued my orders, and half an hour later my outposts are executing it. But what happens among you?" Napoleon shows the prisoner a letter from the Russian general staff which his men have intercepted. "You can take it with you, for it will while away the tedium of your journey. . . . Tell the tsar I pledge him my word that five hundred and fifty thousand men have already crossed the Vistula. But I am a man of calculations, not a man of passion. I am still willing to enter into negotiations. What a glorious reign he might have had, if he had not broken with me!"

The general is alarmed by this flood of confessions. But in the evening, when he dines with the Emperor and three of the marshals, he is placed on an entirely different footing, for the Emperor proceeds to cross-question him like an explorer eager for information.

"Have you any Kirghiz regiments?"

"No, but we are making experiments with Bashkirs and Tartars, who are very like the Kirghiz."

"Is it true that when the tsar was in Vilna, he went to tea every day with a pretty lady there? Let me see, what was her name?"

"The tsar is courtly to every lady."

"Is it true that Baron vom Stein dined with the tsar?"

"All persons of note were invited to dinner."

"How can the tsar tolerate such a man as Stein at his table! Does he think the fellow can be fond of him? Angels and devils cannot be good companions. . . . What is the population of Moscow? How many houses? How many churches? . . . Why are there such a lot of churches?"

"Because our people are very pious."

"Nobody is pious nowadays. Which is the shortest way to Moscow?"

"All roads lead to Rome, Sire. You can choose your own route to Moscow. Charles XII. marched by way of Pultava."

At this mischievous answer, the Emperor thought fit to turn the conversation. As for the general, he had wit enough to report in St. Petersburg that Napoleon was extremely nervous.

This nervousness increases mile after mile. The Emperor tries to join battle, but the Russians evade the issue. Barclay, who is waiting for a junction with Bagration, retreats aimlessly; Bagration does not come, for he believes that he is facing, not Jerome, but the main body of the invaders. Still, Bagration retreats. Jerome, who ought to follow him up, is too slow in his movements, so that Davoust, who is waiting for a junction with Jerome, has to let the enemy slip. The Emperor, in a rage, cashiers Jerome (who retires in dudgeon to Cassel), and gives the command to Davoust. Too late! His fondness for Jerome, the braggart, has cost him the chance of a decisive battle. As difficulties increase, the Emperor redoubles the pace of his advance; but as the tempo is quickened, the difficulties are redoubled. There is no means, now, of providing for the army. The retreating Russians burn their storehouses. No bread, no vegetables, nothing but meat. Dysentery breaks out. The horses eat the thatch from the roofs, and collapse in great numbers, so that their corpses line the road. During this advance in which there are no battles, the Bavarian leader estimates the losses of his corps at nine hundred men a day.

What is Paris saying?

Very little news comes to hand; hardly a word even from the empress. It seems as if the couriers were already being cut off. But here is a report from the Tuileries, written by the governess, to let him know how the child is getting on. He rejoins: "I hope to hear from you soon that the last four teeth have been cut. I have seen to it that the nurse shall get everything she needs. You can assure her of this."

See the Emperor in the sun-parched steppe; before him rises the smoke of the burning villages he has yet to reach, behind him the stench of decomposing bodies. The strange food and the unaccustomed heat lead to a recurrence of his attacks of gastric spasm; he can no longer bear to ride, and, since wheeled traffic is constantly coming to grief, he covers great distances on foot, accompanied by the whole of his staff, pursued by the thought: Where is the fight to take place? Couriers arrive less frequently, and, when they do come, bring no news calculated to interest him in his present state of nervous tension. Yet here he is, pacing up and down within his tent; and the pen of his secretary, instead of, as usual, ordering masses of men to move from one place to another, hastens over the paper to record the master's concern about the four teeth which are still lacking to an infant in a forlorn palace twelve hundred miles away. Soon the Emperor will be in Vitebsk. How far is it thence to Paris?

"Too far, Sire," is re-echoed from unseen lips.

At last! We've got him! There stands Barclay, held in check for the moment by Murat! He thinks to escape to Smolensk on the morrow; such are the tidings! The hour has struck. But the Emperor is ill, irresolute. With unwonted consideration, he does not wish his exhausted army to go straight from the heat of the march into the heat of battle; with unwonted caution, he wishes to collect more troops than he really needs before beginning the attack, in order that the battle may be "another Austerlitz." He waits till morning.

The Russian laughs. Under cover of the morning mists, he makes good his retreat; and when the air clears not a trace of the foe is to be seen, nor can a guess be made as to the direction he has taken. At midday the Emperor returns from the search, flings his sword on the table, and exclaims:

"Here I remain. Let us rally our forces. The campaign of the year '12 is at an end." When Murat urges him to continue the forward march, Napoleon answers: "In '13 I shall be at Moscow; in '14 at St. Petersburg. This war will last three years!"

It is time that the scattered army should be reorganised. Nearly a third of the forces has been struck off the lists, although no battle has taken place; the country has devoured them. Where are the auxiliaries—the Prussians under Macdonald, the Austrians under Schwarzenberg? Trustworthy news is lacking. Too far! What a country! How is one to pass the weary hours when there is no fighting? Wait? In Cairo there were a hundred men of science in his train, and the country was full of unsolved riddles.—The following letter bears witness to a sense of boredom the Emperor has not known since the days of his lieutenancy:

"Send us some entertaining books," the secretary writes to the librarian in Paris. "If there are some good novels, new or old, which the Emperor has not read, or memoirs pleasantly written, we should be most grateful; for time hangs so heavily on our hands in this place."

Can we not see him standing in front of his tent in his old green coat? He takes one pinch of snuff after another, and from time to time looks through his telescope across the plain. Then a grenadier approaches with a paper in his hand; the Emperor reads it, puts it away; the two secretaries gaze dumbly from the gloom of the tent, like two tamed animals awaiting the nod of their tamer. Rustam sits apart Turk fashion; for him alone is the weather never too hot. All movement is paralysed, activity is stopped, one can go neither forward nor backward. Napoleon calls towards the tent: "Méneval! Order some novels!"

News comes at last: England has secured a treaty with the tsar and with the Spanish regent. This arouses the Emperor: he sees in it the birth of a fresh coalition; perhaps, even, encirclement. Must he really lie up here till Europe rises against him or goes to sleep? Over there is Smolensk. The two Russian armies have doubtless by now met in the town. That is where the real Russia begins: surely they will not evacuate and burn the old town of the Blessed Virgin, as they have been doing in the Polish and Lithuanian wilderness! Should victory be achieved at Smolensk, then the march on Moscow or St. Petersburg can be undertaken at will.

He questions his generals. Many of them utter words of warning. But the Emperor replies: "Russia cannot continue this sacrifice of her towns. Alexander can only begin negotiations after there has been a big battle. No blood has yet been spilled. Even if I have to march as far as the holy city of Moscow, I am determined to force a fight and win!"

At last the two Russian armies have effected a junction; they plan a systematic retreat, preceded by a stubborn resistance; wave after wave of the weary French army breaks against the walls of Smolensk. The veterans think of Acre, thirteen years gone by. . . . In the end, the town falls, but it falls amid the flames; a heap of ruins is all that is left in the victor's hands. Is the Emperor beginning to understand the moral strength of this people? Can he not see that day by day its mood becomes more fanatical, that it would rather burn its ancient holy things than leave them to the enemy? There remains nothing for a starving army to plunder.

The Emperor, indeed, is in sorry plight. King Lear upon the heath. Power crumbles in fragments from his body; every gesture melts in the air; from afar the laughter of the rational world comes echoing, to be lost in the void. An end must be made. A second message is sent to the tsar. No use writing, for that last letter from Vilna has remained unanswered. Once more a captured general is ushered into his presence, and once more the Emperor's secret meditations are unveiled. In conclusion he says:

"Can you write to the tsar? No? Still, you can write to your brother at headquarters and tell him what I am saying to you. You will greatly oblige me if you tell him that you have seen me and that I have charged you to write to him. He would do me a real service if he himself would let the tsar know, or get the grand duke to do it for him, that my greatest wish is to conclude peace. . . . What are we fighting for? Of course, if you were the English, that would be a different matter! But the Russians have done nothing to me. You want to buy coffee and sugar cheaply? Very well. That can be arranged. But do you fancy it will be easy to beat me? Then get your council of war to consider the situation; if it thinks the Russians can achieve a victory, choose your battle-ground. . . . Otherwise I shall be compelled to take Moscow, and, in spite of every precaution, I shall perhaps not be able to save it from destruction. A capital which has been in the possession of the enemy, is like a woman who has lost her honour. . . . What do you think? If the tsar wishes to conclude peace, surely none will oppose him?"

As a young lieutenant, as a young general, he had never asked a favour; he could not; he knew only how to command. Even to kings he wrote in the tone of a commander, and the word "please" had only twice passed his lips during the course of this last decade: the first time, when he asked the pope to anoint him emperor; the second time, when he besought Francis of Habsburg for his daughter's hand. Yet to-day, what a tone! What thoughts must be passing through the captive's mind at the moment when his sword is given back to him!—Can this be the master of the world? Has he not begged me, a poor man, begged me and my brother, to do him a service? How came these things to be? Has he no other messenger? Coffee and sugar are to blame, it seems, for the fact that an army of hundreds of thousands of men is perishing in my land! And, as though the whole thing were some brilliant game of chess, the master player sends his challenge, while Little Mother Russia is suffering and weeping, and sees one of her cities after the other go up in flames, and the images of her saints reduced to ashes!

The letter to the captive general's brother is duly written, passes Berthier's censorship, is delivered—but is never answered. The Emperor is beside himself with rage: he passes through a period in which he makes impulsive and vacillating decisions. When Rapp asks whether the army is to go forward or to retreat, Napoleon answers: "The wine is poured out; it must be drunk to the last drop. I am for Moscow. . . . Too long have I played the emperor; it is time I became the general once more." The eyes of the officer light up as he recognises the old ring in the voice!—We are at the beginning of September.

On the sacred soil of the heath near Borodino, Kutusoff, Barclay's successor, must at length put up a fight. The armies now are of equal strength: this is the game the Emperor proposed. No one sleeps, for to-morrow, to-morrow at last, the battle will be joined! Then will golden Moscow lie at our feet, and all our troubles will be at an end. In the middle of the night, a courier arrives from Paris. The Emperor, bending over his maps, asks if there is anything urgent to attend to. Silently his secretary hands him a dispatch from Spain: Wellington has gained a decisive victory over Marmont in the fight near Salamanca. The Emperor reads the report, makes no comment, and resumes his interrupted work. At the eastern extremity of Europe, at the point where it loses itself in the Asiatic wastes, in a few hours he is to vanquish the Russians. This is no time to trouble his mind as to the significance of the victory of the detested Briton at the southern extremity of Europe. Day has dawned. To-day, as every day, the guards call the salute: "Vive l'Empereur!"

He shows them his son's picture, which the courier that night had brought him from Paris. There they stand, the old wardogs, never dreaming that France has been beaten in Spain, but admiring the portrait of the beautiful boy who is their leader's very own son. When the picture is brought back to the tent, the Emperor says, speaking like a poet: "Hide it away. He is too young to look upon a battle-field."

In fierce fighting, on this day of Borodino, salient points are taken, lost, and retaken. The guards shout. They want to decide the issue, here, on the Moskva, as they have so often done before. His generals beseech him to order the advance, and his intimates urge him to action, but he will not give the word. For the first time, when the fight is on, he will not stir from his place. He is feverish, panting for breath, racked with a cough, and his legs are swelled. He sits motionless on his horse, and cannot make up his mind to order the advance of the guards, although the fate of the day seems to hang on it. "Suppose there should be another battle to-morrow? What men shall I have left to fight it with?" At night the Russians withdraw. Next day, when the fallen are counted on the field, they number seventy thousand dead or half-dead—more than in any of his previous battles. The Emperor exclaims:

"Fortune is a strumpet. I have often said so. Now the truth is coming home to me."

But the way to Moscow is open. Half a million men had been chosen for the invasion. One hundred thousand of them are still following him, when, from an elevation, with his back towards the setting sun, he first sees the city of a thousand cupolas, and upon the hill in its centre that fragment of the East, the Kremlin. Napoleon, as he gazes at the sight, is filled with weariness rather than with exultation, and he says in a low tone:

"Moscow! It is time!"

V

"Where are the keys of the city? Why are not the mayor and corporation here to hand them over?"

For the greater part of the afternoon he waits while the army marches past him, waits for the keys of the town. At Vienna and Milan, at Madrid and Berlin, he had ridden through the gates as a conqueror. Are these Tartars ignorant of the fine old Roman custom? From afar can be heard the noise made by Kutusoff's soldiers, as the half-beaten army evacuates the Eastern side of the town, while Napoleon's men are streaming in from the west. The advance guard of the French and the rear guard of the Russians are almost in touch.

It is a silent entry, for the town is like a city of the dead; the houses are empty. "Still, there are plenty of houses," think the weary campaigners; "we shall find food, and be able to sleep at our ease."

The Emperor and his staff ride slowly through the streets whose silence is so ominous. The Kremlin is their destination. Here is the ancient fortress. The newcomers look with astonishment at its walls. All the gates are open, but there is no one there to act as guide. The golden and red halls are forsaken, as in the vision of a dream. The invaders make their way into a huge room where the windows are boarded up. The grenadiers knock the boards away with the butt ends of their muskets, and the Emperor recognises by the canopy that he is in the coronation room of the tsars of Muscovy; but the throne is veiled.

Peace is the only thing lacking to him in this moment of fulfilment. Where is the peace? He has nothing but a victory. Who has cheated him of its fruits? Only the vast, strange land; the steppe has cheated him to-day, as the desert cheated him thirteen years ago. Why did he not free the serfs in Lithuania, and thus win guides and new soldiers, as he had planned to do aforetime with the liberated Arabs? What if he were to adopt this policy now? The town is deserted, but there are peasants in the surrounding countryside. Why not summon them, make terms with them? We are masters here; this enigmatic realm can still offer much of what we desire!

Night comes, but sleep is coy. "Let us do some work, then, to distract our minds," he says to Caulaincourt. He opens the map of Poland; satisfies himself that it was impossible to stay there; in six weeks he can be in St. Petersburg. The muster rolls (they are his Bible, which he always takes with him on a journey, and perpetually cons even in peace time) show him what forces are still at his disposal. His spirits rise as he looks at the columns of figures. "In a few weeks I could get together a quarter of a million men here. There are plenty of roofs to cover them, but what about food? The city seems to be in the middle of a desert!"

A red glare shows through the windows. Fire! Oh, well, we're used to that. There were several fires here and there yesterday evening. But orderlies rush in, and generals arrive. A hundred messengers have reported the outbreak of fires all over the city. Not accidental fires, but prearranged, for the fire-engines have been broken or removed. Do these lunatics mean that Holy Moscow should go up in flames? What will the Emperor do? Ségur, who was with him in these dark hours, tells us what happened:

"It seems as if the encircling flames have spread to the Emperor's mind. By turns, he leaps to his feet, sits down again, or tramps hastily through the rooms of the palace. His abrupt movements betray his terrible agitation. He abandons an urgent task, resumes it, abandons it once more, that he may fling the window wide. He exclaims:

"'What a dreadful sight! Their own work! So many palaces! How stupendous a decision! Who could have expected anything of the kind? What men they are! They are Scythians!'

"Suddenly we are informed that the Kremlin has been mined. Some of the servants are panic-stricken; the guard quietly awaits orders. The Emperor smiles incredulously, but he continues to pace convulsively to and fro, halting at every window to watch the raging element as it seizes the bridges and the gates, simultaneously imprisoning him and besieging him. The air is full of smoke and flying sparks; the equinoctial gale increases the fury of the conflagration.

"Murat and Eugene arrive hotfoot, force their way to the Emperor, and urge him to flee. In vain! Napoleon, master in the palace of the tsars, is steadfast. He will not yield even to devouring flame. But suddenly comes the cry: 'Fire in the Kremlin!' The Emperor is to see the danger close at hand.

"A Russian military policeman has been seized in a turret

of the arsenal. Brought before the Emperor, the man admits that he has fired the Kremlin, acting under orders. The Emperor makes a sign of rage and contempt. The prisoner is led out into the courtyard and is cut down by the grenadiers. This incident decides the Emperor's action.

"We hasten down the northern staircase, and the Emperor orders us to guide him out of the town. But all the gates of the citadel are blocked by the flames. At length an alley-way leading to the Moskva is discovered between two rocks. Through this narrow passage we are able to escape from the Kremlin. But what has been gained? How can we cross the river? The soldiers, blinded by the sparks and deafened by the storm, do not know where they are, and the streets are hidden amid the smoke. The only way out of the inferno is through a winding street where the houses are on fire.

"Heedlessly the Emperor strides along this dreadful exit, undismayed by the crackle of the flaming beams and by the crash of the falling roofs. . . . We can hardly breathe, so intense is the heat. Our guide loses his way, and we should all have ended our lives in the flames had not some marauders belonging to the first army corps recognised the Emperor and found a way for him and the rest of us out of the smoking ruins.

"We meet Davoust. He has been injured on the Moskva, but has had himself carried back among the blazing houses, hoping to find the Emperor or perish with him. The general embraces Napoleon in a fever of delight. The Emperor responds in friendly fashion, but with that calm which never leaves him in the hour of danger."

He awaits the end of the conflagration in the Petroffsky palace, a suburban retreat. On the fourth day, he returns to the Kremlin, where very little damage has been done. On the fifth day, his patience gives out. For the third time, he writes to the tsar. Even now, when he is in possession of the capital, he feels he is grasping at the air. He is so cut off from the enemy that once more he has to make use of a Russian prisoner (this time only a captain), in order to find a contact with the tsar. Napoleon receives the man in the throne room. Does he sense the heroic grotesqueness of the scene? An officer of no account, powerless, unknown, is the representative of Holy Russia; before him, in the storied hall of the tsars, stands the mighty Emperor of the French, the conqueror at whose slightest nod all Europe trembles. The Emperor speaks, chaffers, poses conditions with this man, as though the occasion were another Tilsit and the captain the tsar.

"I am conducting a purely political war," Napoleon reiterates. "All I need is the fulfilment of our treaties. Had I taken London, I would not have offered to leave it so speedily. From here, however, I intend very soon to withdraw. If the tsar wants peace, he must let me know of his desire. . . . I am setting you free, but on condition that you make your way to St. Petersburg. The tsar will be glad to see an eyewitness of recent happenings in Moscow. You must tell him everything."

"I shall not be permitted to enter his presence, Sire."

"Appeal to Court Chamberlain Tolstoy. He is an upright man. If he fails you, get the tsar's body servant to introduce you to his presence, or you must approach His Majesty during one of his daily walks. . . ." The captain gets cold all over; it seems to him that he is being urged to commit a crime, an attempt on the tsar's life. He can promise nothing; stammers.

The Emperor says: "Very well. I shall write a letter to your emperor and you must see that he gets it." This last missive, which finds its way from one emperor's hands into those of the other, is the strangest of the trio.

"My Lord Brother. . . . Beautiful, magical Moscow exists no more. . . . This deed is loathsome, and to no purpose. Did you wish to rob me of my means of support? They were in the cellars, to which the flames never penetrated. How could you consign to destruction the loveliest city in the world, a city it has taken hundreds of years to build; how could you lay it waste for so little gain! . . . Out of kindness, and in the interests of Your Majesty, I have now taken charge of the town which the Russian army had sacrificed. At least the municipal authorities and the militia should have been left in the city, as was the case in Vienna, on two occasions, and in Berlin and Madrid; Milan, likewise, acted thus when Suvaroff entered at the head of his army. . . . It is surely impossible that you, with your high principles and your good heart, can have consented to such abominations, for they are unworthy of a great ruler and a great nation. Your people were so busy getting the fire-engines away, that they abandoned one hundred and fifty pieces of ordnance. . . . I have warred against Your Majesty without bitterness. A sign from you, before or after the last battle, would have stayed my forward march; nay, for Your Majesty's sake, I should have wished to forego my entry into Moscow. . . . If you have preserved any of your former friendship towards me, you will receive this letter favourably. In any case, you will be grateful to me for informing you of the recent occurrences."

The letter of a tutor to his pupil, angry and threatening, written from the depths of his isolation, with intent to rouse the recipient. Thus might an impeccable moralist write to a ne'er-do-well! The whole epistle turns upon the two words "receive favourably"; this is the aim; on these words are built up the writer's hopes. Will the letter fulfil its mission?

The advance of the invader, the threatening proximity of the foe, the burning of Moscow, have filled all hearts in St. Petersburg with despair. The court is for peace. Can a more favourable opportunity present itself? The enemy is becoming more embarrassed day by day. Emperor Napoleon is eager for negotiations. The madcap grand duke Constantine is in favour of a parley; the tsarina-mother, she who hates the upstart, who refused her daughter to him as bride, who railed at

Alexander for weeks after the Tilsit meeting, even she advises the tsar to clasp hands once more in friendship with the Emperor. Now is the time!

But Alexander held firm. Two men were responsible for his unwonted steadfastness. One was a Frenchman, Bernadotte. He and the tsar had recently met in Finland, and Bernadotte had strengthened Alexander in his determination to persevere, had even handed back the Russian auxiliary corps which the tsar had lent for the conquest of Norway. Bernadotte's hatred was so fierce, he had so inflexibly made up his mind to destroy Napoleon, and he so greedily coveted the crown of France which the tsar had promised him, that he would stick at nothing.

The other was a German, the best the nation had nurtured in its downfall and in its fight for freedom. Four years had passed since Napoleon pronounced a verdict of outlawry on Baron vom Stein. The baron spent them far from his homeland; and had become the tsar's trusted adviser. In every respect he was Napoleon's exact contrary. He was now to fight the Emperor to a decisive issue.

This time Stein would conquer.

VI

In many lands, among the many wise and energetic men, who for seventeen years had pitted themselves against the General, the Consul, and the Emperor, none proved equal to the task except Talleyrand and Stein: The former did so, because he succeeded in paralysing Napoleon's productive will by the genius of his malicious cunning; the latter, because, to Napoleon's amoral energy, he contraposed a moral energy which was wedded to fervour. Just as Stein embodied the virtues of the Germans, so Napoleon gathered into himself the talents of the Italian character; and yet, since neither Teutonic virtues nor Italian talents are mutually exclusive, but, rather, cut athwart one another, each man could understand the opponent so far, that Stein, had he been a Frenchman (Carnot's blood brother), might have proved the mainstay of the Emperor. Pride and practical good sense would have brought the two men together.

But this mutual respect could never have bridged the abyss of alienation which must have continued, in spite of everything to hold them asunder. For, just as Napoleon lived entirely without feeling for a fatherland; just as he would gladly have made his career anywhere, and merely placed the French before other peoples because he chanced to be their emperor, so, on the other hand, Stein lived and wrought entirely for the sake of his fatherland; and his Teutonic solidity (firmly rooted in the native soil), the whole weight of his rich soul, remained estranged from the agility, the swiftness, which was so essential a part of Napoleon's make-up, and which the Emperor utilised so adroitly. Here was a statesman whose one thought was Germany and the Germans, who wanted unity among the stocks speaking the same speech, even if such unity had to be achieved against the wishes of the weakling princes. Over the way stood the man who could only think in terms of Europe and Europeans, people whom he wished to weld together for a fight against the selfsame princes.

A baron of the empire, and therefore an independent though petty prince, Stein was a worthy son of ancestors who for seven centuries had tilled and ruled the same fragment of German soil. Having left the home of his fathers for one reason only, that he might serve the nation, he regarded with mistrust, and soon with growing contempt, the other German princes, who were so eager to barter lands and liberties—their own and their subjects—for the favour of the world conqueror. Napoleon, sprung from an impoverished noble stock, a man who had in early youth been driven forth from the ancestral vineyard, despised these lickspittle princes as heartily as did Stein, and in secret he honoured none but the few irreconcilables.

But whereas the contempt with which he regarded the decadence of the European princes was mingled with amusement, Stein's attitude towards them was purely one of rancour. Their innate impotence, which encouraged the self-confidence of the brilliant upstart, was a challenge to the self-respect of Stein, the man who would fain believe in the knightly order to which he belonged; and just as the Corsican used his own career as an argument to strengthen his conviction that a new and splendid epoch was in the making, the German could not fail to consider the behaviour of his fellow-princes as melancholy evidence of the collapse of the old order, and must perforce regard the king of Prussia with a contempt no less hearty than the hatred he cherished for the Emperor of the French.

Thus Napoleon's pronouncement of outlawry against Stein was symbolic of the differences between the two men in respect of nationality, class, and epoch. Had the imperial baron been a king, he would, far more worthily than any Habsburg, or Hohenzollern, or other among the defeated monarchs, have embodied, in opposition to the son of the revolution, that idea of legitimacy for which the German nation was willing to battle with no less ardour than it would display in the fight against the foreigner. Apart from the duke of Brunswick and one or two of the younger princes, Stein stood alone in those days as saviour of the pride and dignity of the German rulers.

Now his great moment has come. From Madrid, the Emperor had sent forth his decree of banishment against the Prussian minister. Twice, for this, time was to exact vengeance. Now was the first occasion. Nothing but the sentence of outlawry had brought Stein into contact with the tsar, for whose soul he was wrestling with his old enemy. In all Alexander's vacillations, no influence did more to strengthen him than the indomitable spirit of the German exile. When the Emperor, not long before, holding forth to the Russian general, had spoken with so much acerbity about Stein, it was because, from afar, he had sensed this influence, and because he was afraid of the imperial baron. He knew Stein to be a vigorous idealist, an undismayed monarchist; and he knew that in the decisive hour such a man was likely to exercise a potent suggestive influence upon the tsar, also an idealist, though irresolute and timid. Stein, knowing human character as he did, and knowing that the tsar, in a hazy fashion, was eager to live in accordance with the moral law, would dilate upon Napoleon's contempt for morality and itch for dictatorship. Stein would not tempt Alexander with countries to be annexed, but with principles to be obeyed; and would rouse to action a modern monarch who would know better than the German princes how to defend rule by right divine.

This German was the only person at the tsarist court who had no axe to grind. Driven from his own home by the homeless Napoleon, he was ready betwixt night and morning to change his present hospitable asylum for any other. The tsar knew that Stein was not a place-hunter, but an independent foreigner whose counsel was not tainted by any thought of personal advantage; for this reason, he had more trust in the German baron than in his own Francophil minister. Perhaps he had heard of the splendid words uttered by the German when the news of the burning of Moscow had arrived. Stein, sitting at table, had raised his glass, and had exclaimed: "Three or four times, ere this, I have lost my baggage. We must get used to throwing away such things. Since we must die, let us be valiant."

His enemy in Moscow will soon make up his mind to the same thing. He throws away the baggage of the past, and marches on; he makes up his mind to retreat. Not a word has come from St. Petersburg. Five weeks have been wasted, and the winter draws near! He has been waiting on events, waiting and listening; this is ill suited to his temperament, out of keeping with his energetic nature. The novels he has ordered from Paris have not yet come to hand, so he hunts up whatever can be found in the Kremlin. But he reads very little. After meals, which, contrary to his usual custom he protracts to the uttermost, he sometimes lies for hours, book in hand, but meditating with fixed gaze.

What is there to do in a burned city where nothing is left to organise! On one or two evenings, the Emperor has some French plays performed by a troupe of actors which had remained behind at the time of the evacuation. This reminds the holiday-making ruler of the charter of the Comédie Française, and he sends instructions for its amendment. Half the day is whiled away in issuing army orders which by no means appear to emanate from a wearied brain, and are far from being commonplace; on the contrary, they are as crystal clear as in earlier days. But since nothing remains to be hoped for, since provisions are dwindling and the cold season is imminent, he calls a council of war in mid-October, although he knows that only one way lies open to him.

Daru counsels: make the winter quarters here; await reinforcements from liberated Lithuania; in the spring, march upon St. Petersburg. The Emperor remains for long in a brown study. Then he says:

"That is the advice of a lion. But what will Paris say? Who can calculate the effect of six months' separation? France may grow accustomed to my absence; Germany and Austria might turn it to account." The only possible order is for the whole army to turn back. What trophies shall we bring back with us to Paris? The giant cross of gold from the church of St. John within the Kremlin walls is taken down from the cupola that it may be set up on the dome of the Invalides. But can we not devise some better revenge against the false friend? The Emperor orders the Kremlin to be blown up.

Eight miles away from Moscow he reins in, and waits for news of the explosion. The unending stream of the grand army flows steadily by the Emperor; it is flanked by the sick and the wounded; it is laden with booty, rested but undisciplined. At last come tidings: the explosion has missed fire. He is silent.

But when Rapp expresses anxiety about the approach of winter, Napoleon rebukes him, saying: "Can't you see how lovely the weather is, even to-day, on October 19th? Do you not recognise my star?"

Such words hardly ever fall from his lips, and this day he is full of cares. He realises that the baggage train is going to cause delay, and yet he has not the heart to order his men to leave their booty behind; they must have something to take home. Russian troops have encircled the French army, and recently they pressed so hard on Murat's squadrons as to drive these back upon the town. On the eastward march, the Emperor had longed for nothing so much as a good action to take place; but now, on the westward march, there is nothing he dreads more than to have to put up a fight. Get to Smolensk as quickly as possible; we will find winter quarters there!

Is the beginning of his career falling into step with the end? Again, as in Egypt, the army marches with the baggage in the middle; again the troops have to defend themselves from the swarming enemy. Once the Emperor is saved from being made prisoner only by the presence of mind of one of his men. "Cossacks! Turn about!" cries Rapp, pointing to a thicket. The Emperor will not follow this advice. The adjutant, thereupon, seizes the bridle-rein and turns Napoleon's horse round. "You must!" Never, in his whole life has he heard such an order addressed to him. What is he to do? Reason tells him to flee.

But the Emperor remains where he is, and draws his sword. Rapp, Berthier, Caulaincourt, do the same. They place themselves to the left of the road and await the riders, who are barely forty paces away. Then the officers of the suite cover Napoleon until the guard cavalry comes to the rescue and puts the Cossacks to flight.

New thoughts flit through his brain after this adventure. Shall Alexander harness him to a triumphal car? He procures a dose of poison from his physician, and wears it always in a black silk bag around his neck, in case he should be made a prisoner. Since the day when he was so nearly captured, the ambition of every Russian flying column is to procure the head of the "wicked infidel." Russian headquarters issues a warrant against the Emperor; it is embellished with his picture, and orders the corps leaders to have "every man of small stature" among the prisoners brought before them for examination: any one of them may be Emperor Napoleon!

As in Egypt the heat of the march had killed hundreds of men, so now does the Russian cold devour them by thousands. Snow and ice bring down the horses, guns get stuck, munition wagons are blown up, cavalry soldiers must pad the hoof, frozen men line the roads.

Not more than fifty thousand reach Smolensk, one-tenth of all the invading host. They have no more supplies, and cannot winter here. The freezing army pushes forward. Thousands have thrown their weapons away; now, even the guard weakens. The Emperor comes among his grenadiers:

"You see the disorder of my army. These poor deluded men are throwing their muskets away. Are you going to follow this shameful example? If so, then there is no hope left to us! On you the whole future of the army depends!" He marches among them. A silent procession (thus described by one who met it): first come the generals, few of whom are mounted. Ghosts in rags, in scorched cloaks, lean, grey, with matted beards, bent and silent: prisoners of fate. These are followed by the Holy Legion, a legion composed of officers, most of them leaning upon sticks, their feet swathed in remnants of sheepskin. Then come the survivors of the cavalry guard.

Last of all three men on foot: to the right, the king of Naples, no longer concerned about his peacock splendours; to the left, the viceroy of Italy. In the middle walks a little man, wearing a Polish fur coat and a cap of red fox, and helping himself along with a birchen staff. Thus in silence he wends his way through Russia.

VII

What is Paris saying?

He does not know. For the first time since he was in Egypt, his calculations concerning Paris have no solid foundation in fact. Not to know what is going on in his capital: a dreadful position this, like that of a traveller who fancies that during his absence his wife may be betraying him! Writing to Maret in Vilna, he says: "For more than a fortnight I have had no courier, so that I am in the dark as to all that is going on . . . in France and Spain. . . . The army is terribly disorganised. It would take at least a fortnight to set things straight, but we cannot possibly spare the time. Shall we be able to maintain our position in Vilna? Only if we are not attacked during the first week. Food! Food! . . . Make sure that there shall be no foreign envoys in Vilna, for the army is not in a fit condition to be seen. Send them all away."

Here is the courier at last. Why does the Emperor turn pale? What terrible news can have come from Paris? Can anything have happened there worse than what he has just been living through? The fact is that, through English newspapers, through letters, and through rumour, France has long since learned the whole truth, which had been glossed over in the Emperor's bulletins. Many of the Parisians are fickle, and many of them are easily reduced to despair. A good part of Paris has already given up the Emperor for lost. Alarmist reports and spiteful quips are rife on the boulevards. But what is this item?

A coup d'état had been planned, and had been frustrated. But what a background of discontent is revealed! Malet, who had been a general in the days of the republic, had years before been concerned in a conspiracy, imprisoned, and then committed to a lunatic asylum. Having received distorted news about the Emperor's disasters and the burning of Moscow, he had escaped. With a number of accomplices, he had published a forged dispatch announcing Napoleon's death. The conspirators had seized the Minister of Police; had declared a provisional government; had bamboozled the National Guard, the militia, the prefects, and even veteran generals. At length, however, two undismayed officers had seen through the cheat, had seized the conspirators, and from the balcony of the governor's residence had shouted, "Vive l'Empereur." Therewith the spectre had been laid.

In his tent, on which the snow is falling, the Emperor contemplates this document with dismay. More serious news even than that which recently arrived from Salamanca! The offenders had been shot; the whole affair had fizzled out. But for a time the conspirators had been masters of the Paris police, and one who controls the Paris police is master of France! No carriages would venture into the streets! When an elderly nobleman had asked what was afoot, a workman had laughed, saying: "Citizen, the Emperor is dead. At noon the republic will be proclaimed!" Greatly shaken by the tidings, the Emperor drops the newspaper containing these details, and says to his intimates:

"What about the dynasty? Did no one think of my wife, my son, all the institutions of the Empire? I must get back to Paris instantly!"

The dangerous possibilities revealed by this interlude, flash like lightning through his mind. "The workman who laughs—he is the people! I toil day and night for years at my great building; I break with the woman I love, and take an emperor's daughter to wife, that our heir, the pledge of earthly immortality, may grow up in our palace. Then some foolhardly officer, a man no one has ever heard of, has merely to call out that the Emperor is dead, and instantly a clamour about 'citizens' and 'republic' rises once more from the people! The regent, the heir, the Council of State—all these count for nothing? The bottomless cask of the Danaids! But I will make a bottom for it. Like the Capets, I will have my son crowned in my own lifetime, and muster my faithful supporters in Paris!"

Fortified by the approach of danger, the Emperor grips the reins firmly once more. "He is pale, but his face is calm; nothing in his features gives any sign of trouble." His health is better, too. Now the army nears the Beresina. Having received false intelligence to the effect that the auxiliary armies are close at hand, he draws his own forces more compactly together, and has the rest of the baggage train burned, that the horses may be freed to draw the remaining guns. If only the bridge is still standing! He writes: "Should the enemy have seized the bridge-head and burned the bridge in order to prevent our crossing, it would be very serious."

Next day they come to the river. No bridge, no boats; two armies outnumbering the French are waiting on the other shore; between runs the broad river with marshy banks. Is there any way out of the difficulty?

He makes a shrewd plan, like those of his early days as general. He will decoy the Russians away. Out of eighteen hundred horseless cavalrymen of the guard, of whom only eleven hundred still have their weapons, he forms two battalions. Then he has all the regimental eagles burned, for even in this dread hour Napoleon thinks of honour and glory, and he will not risk the loss of colours to the enemy. After midnight, he at length lies down in his tent, where he overhears Duroc and Daru, who believed him to be asleep, discussing in an undertone the possibility of a catastrophe. The phrase "State prisoner" has caught his ear. He fingers the black bag he is wearing round his neck, and sits up in bed:

"You think they would dare?"

"I would not trust the enemy's magnanimity," says Daru, composedly.

"But France! What would France do?"

Daru's answer is evasive; but when pressed, he says: "I

think, Sire, the sooner you are in Paris, the better. When you are there, you will have a better chance of saving us all."

"Then you feel I am a burden on you here?"

"Yes, Sire."

"And you don't want to be State prisoners?"

There is a long silence. Then the Emperor resumes:

"Have my ministers' reports been destroyed?"

"Hitherto you have always refrained from giving us the order."

"It must be done. Destroy the lot of them. We are in a very difficult position."

This is the only admission of the kind made by the Emperor during all the weeks of the Russian campaign. It is the voice of a man who regards himself as a moriturus. But nature is more sensible than fate, and in a few moments he is fast asleep.

Next morning, while the enemy has been lured down stream and is being kept at a distance by artillery fire, the sappers, neck-deep in the freezing water and amid the drifting ice, hastily build two bridges. The crossing of the river takes two days more. With the cavalry, which swims the stream, the army still numbers about twenty-five thousand men. The Emperor, though the risk of his being taken prisoner is imminent, remains until all have crossed; and then, on the third day, surrounded by the old guard, he too makes his way over the river. But there are still stragglers to come, and these perish during the next few days betwixt ice and fire.

In the ensuing week the Emperor's life is twice in danger. The first peril is from a Cossack attack. On the next occasion the trouble is an assassination plot in which one of his own Frenchmen is engaged. It is early on the morning of December 5th when Major Lapie meets the officers of the Prussian guard of honour in front of the Emperor's tent. "Now then, gentlemen, the hour has come!" The senior captain is to cut down the Mameluke, and then to make an end of Napoleon. Presumably the conspirators have seen Schiller's

Wallenstein on the German stage! The Prussian wants the Frenchman to do the deed, but Lapie says he is not sure of his men. Then Caulaincourt, to whom the conspirators' behaviour seems suspicious, comes forward, claps his hands, and says: "Now, gentlemen, it is time to start!"

That evening the Emperor, who has not heard a word of the affair, summons his marshals. "I shall be stronger when I can speak from my throne in the Tuileries than I am at the head of an army which has been destroyed by the cold. . . . Had I been a Bourbon, born to rule, it would have been easy for me to avoid making mistakes." He takes the marshals aside by turns, asking each for his advice; he flatters, praises, and encourages; he smiles and charms. Obviously his design is to counteract the possibility of revolt.

Next, he tells Eugene to read them his latest bulletin, the first in which he admits disaster. "Men who had not been sufficiently steeled by nature to rise superior to all vicissitudes of fate and fortune, lost courage and equanimity, and could dream of nothing but misfortune and defeat. But those who were equal to the occasion were able to keep up their spirits, and regarded every fresh difficulty as a fresh opportunity for glory."

The only reason why the army had wasted away was the rigour of the climate. "His Majesty has never been in better health."

The unfeeling, metallic tone! Again we are listening to General Bonaparte who, having recovered confidence in his destiny, and having regained health, is able to use the old language. The incisive sentence at the close is, of course, added for the special benefit of Paris, which for several weeks has had no news as to his state of health. But, on the whole, the mood in which he ends the Russian campaign, exactly six months after it had begun, is one of heroic cynicism. The command of the army is handed over to Murat, who is to lead the survivors home. There are still nine thousand men under arms.

Now there is something new. The Emperor embraces every one of the generals present. Is this the last coup of a trickster who wants to strengthen their waning loyalty? Is he really overcome by his feelings? Every one of these soldiers, that evening, could feel the beating of the Emperor's heart.

He gets into the sleigh with Daru and Caulaincourt, and the three drive away. To be on the safe side, he travels under an assumed name, that of his secretary, Rayneval. This is his fifth name. The fourth had been Napoleon.

When they are driving through the snows across the Polish plain, he suddenly has the sleigh stopped at a cross road. This must be near Countess Walewska's mansion; he wants to go there. Napoleon is on the flight from Russia, his head full of world-shaking plans; he is forsaking his army because Paris needs him and he needs Paris—and now comes this lyrical thought, the painful recollection of a frustrated idyl. But the urgent warnings of his companions, who remind him that they are alone in a couple of sledges and that Cossacks are scouring the countryside, induce him to abandon his plan. He wraps his furs around him once more and goes to sleep.

Five days afterwards he leaves the sleighs waiting on the bridge near Warsaw, and at noon goes on foot with Caulaincourt into the town. Should any one recognise him, they will face it out, and declare that the interlocutor is seeing ghosts, or must be mad. Napoleon sends Caulaincourt to the embassy; but, in order to keep his own identity secret, he himself goes to an inn, which, of all names in the world, still calls itself the Hôtel de l'Angleterre. The low-ceilinged white-washed room is cold; there is only green wood, and the maidservant cannot get the stove to light; he must keep on his furs, his cap, and his big boots, while he tramps up and down the room, thrashing his arms like a coachman to keep himself warm. It is thus he is found by two Polish noblemen for whom he has sent through the embassy. They can hardly believe their eyes, but the ghost laughs at their astonishment.

"How long have I been in Warsaw? A week? No, only a couple of hours. It is but one step from the sublime to the ridiculous. How are you, Monsieur Stanislas? . . . Dangers? Not a bit of it. I thrive on excitement. The more I am tossed to and fro, the better I feel. The shadow kings grow fat in their palaces, but I put on flesh when riding my nag in the field. . . . So you've been anxious here? The army is in splendid condition. I have still one hundred and twenty thousand men! Gave the Russians a good hiding everywhere. They never ventured to stand up against me. The army will winter in Vilna. I am returning to Paris, and there I shall raise three hundred thousand soldiers! In six months I shall be back on the Memel.

"I have been through other fights! At Marengo I was beaten until six in the evening, but next day I was lord of Italy. At Aspern-Essling I made myself master of Austria, though the archduke believed he had held me in check there. It was not my fault that the Danube rose sixteen feet in one night. But for that, I should have finished off with the Habsburgs once for all. However, it was written in the stars that I was to marry an archduchess. . . .

"The same thing in Russia. I can't prevent its freezing there. Morning after morning, the report was that ten thousand horses had perished during the night. Bon voyage! Our Normandy horses cannot endure the cold like the Russians; the same with our soldiers. . . . Perhaps people will say that I stayed too long in Moscow; but the weather was beautiful, and I was waiting for peace. A great political drama! Nothing venture, nothing have. One step from the sublime to the ridiculous! . . . Who could have foreseen the burning of Moscow? . . . I never felt better in my life!" . . .

Such is the spate of words that for two hours flows from the mouth of a man who, after unspeakable losses, wishes to give the impression of desperate courage.

Napoleon becomes an adventurer. To impress these Poles, who will pass on what he says, he invents an army which has vanished long since; cold which really did nothing more than complete the destruction that other forces had begun; battles he never fought. He intersperses these figments with historical parallels of worldwide significance; treats what has just been happening as if it were ancient history; appeals to providence; and repeats no less than four times the cynically imposing aphorism about the sublime and the ridiculous, which blunts the edge of criticism. Great realist though he is, the world and what he is doing with it are becoming drama to him; and thus Napoleon, when his own fortunes are declining, is slowly mounting the ascent towards supreme irony.

The two Poles see nothing of all this. Their thoughts are concentrated upon their country's debts, and they would fain get money from this man who is still numbered among the great ones of the earth. They seize their opportunity when at length there is a pause in the torrent of speech. He gives them an order on the treasury for six millions, which he thinks will buy support for him in Poland. Then his visitors wish him a happy journey, and, with secret scorn, watch the incognito drive away hastily in his sleigh.

Day and night, night and day, they glide swiftly westward; for Germany, too, is under snow. Day and night, night and day, questions, commands, and plans are churning in his brain. "Is England really invincible? Now, the English can trade freely in the Baltic; English goods can enter Cadiz, and can make their way into the Levant." He must put off his scheme for the conquest of India, but will abate no jot of his other designs! Will the Confederation of the Rhine still answer to his nod? How will it be possible to explain this crash in Russia? The disaster cannot be hushed up indefinitely. Is there any chance of raising another hundred and twenty thousand men in France? Next year's levies must be called up in advance. Make peace with the pope at once, and with Spain likewise, for he must feel safe at his back. A National Guard, that was the best thought of the revolution; in that way he will be

(Photograph in the Kircheisen Collection.)

The Emperor's profile. Sketched during Mass in the Tuileries. Germain Bapst Collection.

able to raise a million armed citizens within three months."

Night. Change of horses. He thrusts out his head. "Where are we?"

"In Weimar, Sire."

"Weimar? How is the duchess? And how is Herr Goethe?"

VIII

Forty bowed backs receive the beaten war lord on his return home. The sight of the court dresses which he has embroidered with his contempt revives his belief in the folly and the weakness of these men whose only wish is to be ruled. But his glance strays to the bars of the golden cage in which the son of liberty has locked himself up. He does not realise that the people of his capital are weary and disaffected; and instead of following the example of his own youth, instead of with disarming frankness acknowledging the faults he hopes to better, he postures as Cæsar before his servile officials, and rails at the weather god, though but yesterday he had boasted his power to make what weather he pleased throughout Europe.

During the nine days' drive from Warsaw to Paris, the uncertain mood of the adventurer had given place once more to the steadily aspiring flame of the imperator. Although the Russian winter had set in later than usual, he carries off the reverse by saying: "The army sustained heavy losses, but that was because the winter began so early. . . . The king of Naples is not fitted for high command, and he lost his head after my departure. . . . All the same, I have three hundred battalions left, without bringing a single man back from Spain."

Has his contempt for his fellows risen to such a pitch that he can serve up these fables to experienced men who have known the truth for months? But their consciences are uneasy. They feel responsible for the October putsch, or at any rate guilty for not having made an end of the whole business within the first quarter of an hour. On the other hand the Emperor, whose own heart accuses him, is glad to play the accuser, for it galls him that in the decisive hour they should have forgotten the empress and the heir to the throne. In memorable words, at the first reception in the Tuileries, he tries to hammer his point into the heads of his councillors.

"The apostles of the rights of man are really to blame for all that has happened. They declared rebellion to be a duty. They flattered the people, imputing to it a sovereignty it is incapable of exercising. They destroyed respect for law by establishing the supremacy of an assembly which knew nothing of administration and law, instead of holding fast to the nature of things! Any one who wishes to build up a State once more, must be guided by the very opposite principles. History depicts the human heart, and we must study history if we would learn the merits and defects of legislation. . . . When I undertook the reconstruction of France, my prayer was that I might be spared for a considerable number of years, seeing that what has been destroyed in a moment will take a long time to refashion. The State needs courageous officials. 'The king is dead; long live the king!' That was the watchword of our fathers. The phrase makes us realise the advantages of monarchy."

Were it not for the prettily turned expression about history and the human heart, Emperor Francis might have subscribed to this speech, and it might have been an ornament to the pages of any of the familiar expositions of monarchical doctrine. Why should people go on quarrelling about such matters? The ancient dispute between tradition and revolution has been settled, now that the son of the revolution has acknowledged the supremacy of tradition. No matter whether an heir be named Bourbon or Bonaparte! When we compare the two fathers we see that they are very much alike! His marriage with the daughter of one who rules by right divine has complicated the problem, and has sophisticated his own genius.

Or does he believe no more than half of what he is saying?

Before setting out on the Russian campaign, he had frankly explained his plans to Metternich: "The legislature belongs to me; all I need is to put the key of the deliberative chamber in my pocket. France is less suited for democracy than a good many countries. . . . When I get back, therefore, I shall transform the Senate and the Council of State into an Upper House and a Lower House, most of whose members I shall myself nominate. These will constitute a real popular representation, consisting only of experienced business men, without an ideologue among them. Then France will be satisfactorily ruled, even under a prince who is a mere figure head (and such will come), for whom the ordinary education of hereditary princes will suffice."

These Cæsarist ideas betray the monarchist, but also the sceptic. Although, when he shows people his son's portrait, they tell him that the little boy is the loveliest child in France, the flattered father knows perfectly well that dynasties last a long time whereas genius is fleeting. Foreseeing the decadence of his own blood, having studied that decadence in the annals of all princely houses, he wants to rid himself of waverers that he may fortify the position of his heir. For the very reason that he understands the contradiction inherent in monarchy, he wishes to build his own monarchy on a rock.

For the time being, his business is to buttress it anew with the power of the sword. What has been the fruit of the war games in which he moved his myriads over Europe? Those leather-bound muster rolls of his contained the death sentences of numberless youths, even though there were marshals' batons to be won by a few among the best of them! Of the old guard, four hundred men, and of the cavalry guard, eight hundred men, made their way back to Königsberg; a few thousand officers and sergeants, broken men most of them, have survived the storms of war. Except for the auxiliaries, who are not under France's orders, that is all that remains of the Emperor's hosts. Marshal Ney, on his flight from Russia, seems like a hero out of a Greek tragedy when he reaches Prussia, and makes his way into the first Prussian government office on his route. When old acquaintances look at him incredulously, as if questioning who this man can be, he rejoins with a superb gesture: "I am the rear guard of the Grand Army."

A new army must be made, and it must be made in a few weeks. The year 1813 will supply one hundred and forty thousand recruits, but where are the rest to come from? The Emperor has a magic wand, and can conjure up men whenever he needs them. The passing of a new law is all that is requisite for the levying of the National Guard and for the drafting of eighty thousand soldiers from the dependencies of France. Add one hundred thousand belonging to the oldest conscript levies; and call up the youngsters who should not, properly speaking, be enrolled until 1814. Soon he will have half a million under arms once more. "The French people," he says to the Prussian envoy, "will follow me whatever I do, and, if needs must, I shall arm the women!".

With unbroken will, he charms into existence the innumerable machines without which he cannot ply his trade. But how shall he explain these unexpected measures to the people? The enemy is far from the frontier.

A stroke of luck! At the close of the year, Yorck, a Prussian general, acting on his own initiative, enters into an agreement with his Russian neighbours, declares the force under his command neutral, and thus opens the door to a change in the military situation for which the German nation has long been eager. The Emperor can use the incident in order to whip up the enthusiasm of the French. For the moment, the treason of his ally costs him no more than twenty thousand men; but it serves as the text for a manifesto in Paris, and for hectoring letters to the princes of the Confederation of the Rhine. He would not, says Napoleon, need their help at all, had not Yorck's secession compelled his army to withdraw.

The summons of France is actually obeyed. The German

princes, including the Habsburg ruler, once more collect money and levy troops. One of them is servile enough to send an assurance that he is "delighted to be able to give the Emperor opportunity for winning fresh laurels." The king of Prussia cashiers Yorck, and assures the Emperor of his fidelity to the alliance. But Frederick William conveys a hint to the tsar, goes to Breslau, wobbles between the parties, what time a wave of enthusiasm is spreading far beyond Prussia's borders, and threatening to sweep away the debile monarch. Youths, politicians, and poets are voicing the call of national sentiment. Stein is the man to treat with the tsar on behalf of his country, and in Königsberg the baron takes matters into his own hands.

The Emperor is ever on the watch. In a circular, he warns the princes against the intrigues of those "who by rebellion and revolution are trying to give Germany a new form. Should they succeed in infecting the Confederation of the Rhine with their doctrines, intolerable sufferings may await these territories."

He feels the stirring of the new spirit. Now, for the first time, does the Emperor seem to become aware of the growth of a national sentiment among the Germans, as among the Spaniards. Shortly before the Russian campaign, he had said that hardly so much as a night watchman was needed to keep the Germans quiet. "Since Germany has no America, nor yet a sea, nor yet a great number of strongholds, nor even Englishmen as there are in Spain, there is nothing to be afraid of, and would not be though the Germans were as lazy, dirty, superstitious, and monk-ridden as the Spaniards. How could there be anything to fear from such honest, reasonable, coolheaded, and patient people, who have so little inclination to violence that throughout the war not one of our soldiers has been murdered in Germany?"

A wonderfully true picture of the Germans, and yet there is a slight miscalculation. He has overlooked the romanticism by which these people can be stirred, and without a knowledge of which they cannot be understood. Of course the Italian, with his fiery imagination, cannot grasp the nature of an imagination that works slowly and lacks ardour. Napoleon, who knows how monarchical the Germans are in their sentiments, believes that when he holds the princes in his hands he must be master of the German people.

Besides, were the Germans a people? Was this realm, which ten years earlier had been formally liquidated by the abdication of the last of its emperors, really anything more than a "metaphysical concept"? Only for a moment, only for two years, will the German peoples be united. Then, as soon as the enemy's power has been broken, they will fall asunder once more. Not for half a century, and not until another Napoleon threatens them, will they at length become a nation—though even then, only a fragment. So atrophied was Napoleon's own sense of nationality, that the quarrels and jealousies of the German princes made him believe that the Germans were disintegrated for all time; whereas, had he been able to understand the forces that were at work, he would have realised that the jealousies of the rival sovereign houses were the only obstacle to the reunion of these kindred stocks.

But the sublime breathing of history sometimes determines the rhythm of an epoch even in despite of the will of the genius that animates it. In sweeping curves, during these years, the spirit of liberty returns to her primal home in the hearts of the people. For, just as Bonaparte, in the name of liberty, had defeated the princes and stirred the peoples to revolt; so now, in the name of liberty, the peoples arose to defeat him, the prince of princes. Doubtless this great movement of destiny was complicated by numerous petty wishes, and blurred by minor circles. It is not the force of legitimism which now, after twenty years, is at last gathering strength to slay the spirit of revolt. Pallid, disunited, decadent, and with never a great figure among them, are the princes in the league they form against the one man who rules in virtue of his self-made power.

But the fact that the peoples of Spain and Germany are eager to force their princes into the fight, gives to the tragical collapse of the usurper a semblance of poetical justice, and that is why we who look on find it easier to bear the sight of the slaying of the lion by the spears cast by such a legion of hunters.

IX

Letizia looks anxiously at her son. His face is clouded, though he keeps his thoughts to himself. What can she do to help him? Intimates? Many of them, she sees plainly enough, are betraying him. He needs his brothers, that he may have the support of steadfast hearts, even though he thinks them lacking in intelligence. She therefore puts her trust in her other sons, writes to London and to Graz, smooths the path for reconciliation. One day, after a decade of estrangement, comes a letter from the ambitious Lucien, who says he is always at Napoleon's service.

But the Emperor cannot believe that he, the mightiest of his family, needs any assistance from the others. Though he has always regarded Lucien as the most capable of his brothers, he proposes merely a formal promotion. In imperial fashion, he answers through his mother: "Please write to let him know in my name that his letter has awakened an echo in my heart. I think of raising him to the throne of Tuscany. He loves the fine arts. It will suit him to reign in Florence, and to revive the glories of the Medicis." There is no place for Lucien at the centre of things! As for Louis, who also offers to devote his powers to the cause of France (in so far as he can honourably do this), and who sends a copy of his last volume of verse —the ex-king of Holland is met with a rebuff: "The idea you seem to have formed about my position is quite erroneous. I have more than a million men under arms, and two hundred million francs in my war chest. Holland remains French. . . . Still, I am ready to greet you in the spirit of one who brought you up as if he had been your father."

The Emperor reads this answer to his mother before sending it. She tries to mitigate its harshness in a long covering letter; tells Louis how pretty his children have grown; urges him to come to Paris in any case. "The Emperor has forgotten to give me your poems. I will ask him for them, and will let you know what I think of them when next I write."

Next day, the old lady finds a savage article in the "Moniteur," in which she learns that the king of Naples will have to recall his envoys from Vienna. When she asks what this signifies, her friends reluctantly explain that Murat has been persuaded by Caroline to intrigue with the Habsburgs, so that the pair are now playing double. Letizia writes to upbraid her daughter. Joseph is out of humour, for he thinks that Napoleon is not supporting him properly in the Spanish war. She does her best to appease him through the instrumentality of his wife. Furthermore, she tries to mollify Jerome, whom the Emperor had sent home in disgrace. Finally, she gets to work on Hortense, who is doing all she can to hinder Louis' coming to Paris.

Now a woman well over sixty, she does her utmost to keep the peace between her sons, daughters, sons-in-law, and daughters-in-law. But it seems to her that the greatness for which the world envies her family has brought in its train nothing but discord, jealousy, arrogance, ostracism, and betrayal. Her thoughts fly back to her native island, where her kindred always formed a united front against other clans. Moreover, her eyes, though old, are clear-sighted; and she sees that the star of the Buonaparti is paling.

The Emperor has little personal feeling about these matters. In his present situation, he regards them from a purely political outlook. No doubt he says to himself that Murat and Caroline are traitors; but his main concern is, how he can make sure of the support of Murat's soldiers. He therefore writes in a conciliatory strain to Caroline; keeps her husband informed about the impending campaign; and asks for troops, which Murat ultimately agrees to send, for both he and Caroline think that Napoleon may prove victorious after all, and are afraid of being dethroned unless they keep in his good graces. At the same time, they wish to have a secure footing in the other camp, and therefore conclude secret treaties with England and with the ex-king of Sicily (whose dominions they themselves have filched).

Napoleon even seeks to conciliate Bernadotte, though he cannot but regard the crown prince of Sweden as a treacherous kinsman and an enemy of his house. He offers Pomerania as the reward of alliance and the prize of victory. But for Bernadotte, the bid is not high enough; this Frenchman prefers to join the coalition against France. His ambition is to reign there; France is worth more than Pomerania. Bernadotte enters into especially close relationships with Prussia. In Berlin he meets Madame de Staël, and these fellow-countrymen of the Emperor, united in their detestation of him, foregather among the oppressed Prussians.

A third enemy, whom the Emperor approaches with blandishments during these feverish weeks, is the captive pope. Pius VII. has been brought to Fontainebleau, and Napoleon gets to work on him through the instrumentality of prelates devoted to the imperial cause, adding personal suggestion until the old man gives way. How great will be the power of the Church (this is the Emperor's theme) when Catholicism has been re-established throughout Germany! By trifling concessions upon matters of form, and by cunning devices, Napoleon is able to secure a new Concordat. Thanks to this reconciliation with the Church, he is able to recruit new Catholic soldiers in all the lands under his sway. When the pope, a week after signing the Concordat, wants to revoke it, the Emperor says with a smile: "Your Holiness, being infallible, cannot have made a mistake in entering into this arrangement!"

During these weeks, a desire for peace suddenly spreads throughout Europe. The pope wants peace on the Vistula, and Metternich wants it in London. Count Bubna, with whom Napoleon had negotiated years before in Schönbrunn, comes to Paris to advise peace, for Vienna can neither send nor refuse the troops which the Emperor has demanded. In February, peace can be had for the asking. Why does the man who needs peace most of all, make impossible stipulations?

For ten years, one war after another has been practically forced upon the Emperor as a consequence of his first victories. Now, when he is in grievous peril, and when his isolation is increasing, the will-to-war grows in him as in the early days of his career. When unconquered, he would gladly have laid aside the sword; now, after his defeat, he craves for new victories. But though his shield has been tarnished in Russia, though he would fain win fresh glories for himself and for France, these are but the pretexts of destiny. In very truth, he is stiff-necked, and will prove himself to be so at three congresses during this year 1813. The reason is that all the elements of his character are now rolling inexorably forwards; the reason is that, "in accordance with the nature of things," he is advancing along a road on which he must march to the bitter end.

Forward! Since the war must be, the allies are arming everywhere. England makes treaties with Sweden and Prussia; to conciliate the latter, the tsar renounces his claims to East Prussia; Prussia calls Germany to arms; Austria makes a truce with Russia, tries to enter into an agreement with Saxony and Bavaria and even King Jerome. Emperor Francis withdraws his troops to Cracow, ostensibly to save them for the coming campaign.

"The first step towards desertion!" exclaims Napoleon, when

this news comes to hand. He must now withdraw his own forces from the Vistula to the Oder. In Vienna, he once more offers Silesia. The offer is declined with thanks, for the Austrian role is to be one of armed mediation. While the whole world is thus preparing for the struggle, and when in the middle of March the first signal is given in Paris by the Prussian declaration of war, Talleyrand, in his open ambush, says with a smile: "The hour has struck; the Emperor Napoleon must become king of France."

A remarkable flash of insight, on the part of one who cannot but hope that no step so sensible as this shall be taken—and who must, none the less, at bottom, wish for it. Nevertheless matters have gone too far; not the levying of troops alone, but the preparations in the minds of men. Every one knows that the last great combat is imminent, that nothing can avert it. The only one who could have called a halt, and will not do so, is driven onward in his own despite, and he is weary. There are new signs of this growing weariness.

First of all, there is the simplicity upon which he insists in his environment. "I want my journeys to be very differently arranged. I shall not take so many people with me; fewer cooks and less table furniture; no meal to consist of more than three courses. . . . I shall not take any pages with me; they are of no use whatever; only two bedmakers instead of four; two tents instead of four; and so on." At the same time, he orders plans for a small palace, "a comfortable place rather than an imposing one (the two things are incompatible); . . . my room must open on the garden; . . . or, preferably, I must have a north room and a south room, according to the season; all arranged as in a well-to-do country gentleman's mansion. . . . It is to be a holiday seat, or a dwelling for a man in his declining years."

In 1805, when he was in the plenitude of his powers, he had said: "The war need not take long. I am still good for six years, but then it will be time to call a halt." Now, when he takes the field once more, four months after his return from Russia, his mien is quiet and careworn as he steps into his travelling carriage in the courtyard at Saint-Cloud. He leans back among the cushions, with his hand pressed to his forehead. To Caulaincourt, his travelling companion, he acknowledges his distress "at having so soon to leave my good Louise and my lovely boy. I envy the poorest peasant in my dominions. By the time he grows old, he has already paid his debt to his country, and can stay at home with his wife and children. I am the only person whom an inexplicable fate leads back ever and again into the field."

No more pages, he is in his declining years, wants to stay at home with wife and child—and this is only seven years after the programme just quoted! Are these fourth-act moods, these shadows that fall across his soul, merely the consequences of the Russian catastrophe? Are they not, rather, the essential causes of new defeats? The moods of a man growing prematurely old, one whose work is often interfered with by illness, one who is being increasingly mastered by the natural inclinations of a family man well on in the forties. He wants to spend at the domestic fireside the evening of a life which is not equipped for seven or eight decades like that of his mother or his brothers.

He is himself in the frame of mind with which he had reproached his marshals at Danzig less than a year ago, when he had declared they would rather have an easy life of it in their country seats than go campaigning with him. Is not such a longing natural in a man who has been working himself to death for twenty years, and who has chosen the bee for his escutcheon?

But those on whom the Parcæ bestow the ecstasies of youth, must pay for it by the oncoming of age. He has had such wonderful successes that he must not expect to garner also the joys of content in achievement. He has conjured up the gods; now they have come!

X

At the first review in Mainz, there are only one hundred and eighty thousand men instead of the three hundred thousand he had hoped to assemble there. The army is very short of cavalry; the equipment is inadequate, for it has been far too hastily got together; the best guns have been lost in Russia, or are tied up in Spain; the general staff has been decimated; the ambulance service is defective. He sees all that is amiss, but even this imperfect army reminds him of old times and old happiness. He recalls the April days in Cannes and Nice, seventeen years before, when he had taken over the command of half-starved and ragged soldiers, that he might lead them through the mountains to victory. With these memories surging up in his mind, he gathers his energies, and utters the darkly challenging words: "I shall conduct this war as General Bonaparte."

Such is the signal, a mingling of impetus and self-restraint, with which he launches himself into the first battle. At Lützen, he exposes himself more than he has done for years. During the first day's fighting, he does not sleep at all; on the second day, when everything is going well, he has his bearskin spread on the ground in the middle of Marmont's corps; and when, an hour later, they wake him to let him know that all is going on well, he leaps to his feet with the ironical remark: "You see, the best things come to one while one is asleep."

But hardly has the general won this victory than the emperor-politician resumes the ascendant. He sends letters in all directions; forces the vacillating king of Saxony to a decision, talks to the princes of the Confederation of the Rhine about providence and the fortune of war, that he may keep them up to the scratch; sends his ministers to the Russian outposts; abruptly and informally offers the tsar Poland in exchange for Prussia, and suggests other territorial rearrangements, until Alexander weakens; and he writes to Emperor

Francis in terms of unusual self-commendation: "Although I personally led all the movements of my army, and was several times within range of grape-shot, I have not had even a graze." The words and the actions are those of one who feels weak, and would fain appear strong. Henceforth the warnings of fate thicken.

True, he gains another victory at Bautzen, but does not take any prisoners. On the second day of the battle, he is riding under fire, accompanied by Caulaincourt and his friend Duroc—the latter having for a decade been his inseparable companion in the field. Men are being shot down in his immediate neighbourhood. He gallops to an adjoining elevation; adjutants follow him. Dust and smoke; a tree close at hand is smashed to splinters. He thunders past. On the hillock, a young officer comes up to him and stammers: "Marshal Duroc has been killed."

"Impossible! He was at my side a moment ago!"

"The cannon ball which struck the tree, brought down the marshal as well."

The Emperor slowly rides back into camp. He says:

"When will fate have a little discrimination? What will be the end of it all? Caulaincourt, my eagles are again victorious, but my star is setting."

Duroc has not been killed outright, but he is dying. Terrible is the aspect of this shattered comrade. Greeting and farewell, both men in tears. Duroc murmurs: "I told thee at Dresden what would happen; the inner voice . . . Give me some opium."

This tone, the sudden use of "thee," the last request of a man who has no fear of death. The Emperor walks unsteadily as he leaves the cottage.

From a farmyard, he contemplates for a while the spot where his friend had fallen, and then makes his way to the place where the guard is encamped, with his own tent in the middle. That evening, wearing his grey field-coat, he sits gloomily on a campstool, apart from his suite; he listens to the sounds of the camp, where the guardsmen are cooking supper and calling to one another; in the distance, the men of a yager corps are singing a song. Bivouac fires are glowing in the half-darkness of the May night; two burning villages flame like torches in the sky. An officer draws near, and hesitates to give his report. Before the words are spoken, the Emperor understands that Duroc is dead.

Next day, he orders the purchase of land where a memorial is to be erected, and he pens the inscription: "Here died, gloriously, in the arms of his friend the Emperor, struck down on the field of battle by a cannon ball, General Duroc, Grand Marshal of the Emperor Napoleon."

General Bonaparte used to have no time for such feelings. He concealed his heart-ache, and stormed onward, even when he lost his wife's love. Now it behoved him to push forward into Silesia, to follow up the Russians into Poland, to take advantage of the misgivings of the allies; and, by delivering blows in rapid succession, to fetter the vacillating Austrian to his side. In later years, he said frankly that his failure to do these things had been the greatest mistake in his life. Once more, the deliberations of the emperor are impeding the activities of the general. His private letters from France are full of reports concerning the clamour for peace. "What especially determined my course of action was Austria's preparation for war, and the desire to gain time. This led me to interrupt the course of my victories." In Silesia, at the beginning of June, he agrees to a six weeks' truce, thus giving his adversaries time to attain complete unity at the congresses of Reichenbach and Prague.

Is he deceived as to the frame of mind of the wavering German princes? He knows them all. "The Saxons are just as German as the others, and would gladly follow Prussia's example. The king is faithful to me, but I do not trust his troops. . . . Austria's impudence is indescribable. While uttering honeyed words, she tries to snatch from me Dalmatia and Istria. . . . There never was anything so false as the court of Vienna. If, to-day, I were to grant Austria's demands, she would ask to-morrow for Italy and Germany." Now, when he sees that the Habsburg ruler is about to go over to the enemy, he realises too late that his marriage has been a mistake, for he has gained nothing by it, and has lost much. His own patrician family feeling had made him believe that there must be an imperial family feeling. The old tone of contempt for hereditary monarchs is at length heard once more. To his intimates, he again and again says frankly what he thinks of the kings who are kings by birth:

"Among those who are born to sit on the throne, the ties of nature count for nothing. The interests of his daughter and his grandson will not move Emperor Francis an inch from the calculations of his cabinet. These men have no blood in their veins, nothing but frozen politics! What pygmies they are, the kings by the grace of God—and the grace of Napoleon! My leniency has been my blunder. In Tilsit I could have crushed them, but I was too generous. History should have taught me that houses so degenerate deserve neither loyalty nor faith! Now, England is filling their coffers with gold. But I shall prove myself a better statesman than these born kings who never leave their golden cages!"

In this atmosphere of intrigue, when he has to rub shoulders with princes who dare not fight either for him or against him, traitors are his best confidants.

The Emperor therefore summons Fouché, to whom he says: "Your friends Bernadotte and Metternich are my worst enemies. Your Bernadotte can do us an immense amount of harm, for he is able to give my enemies the key to our policy, and he can explain to them the tactics of our armies. . . . His head has been turned because legitimate princes flatter him!" There we have it once more, the word whose mystical power explains half of Napoleon's perpetual unrest. He can never refrain from a tremor when he speaks of the legitimate rulers, whom he regards with mingled contempt and envy. Whether he is mimicking them, or whether he is railing at them, he, who is an upstart, is always pondering this problem of birth.

Instead of listening to the call of the nations, which soon rises clear above the babble of the princes, he can only look on with malicious delight at the manœuvres of the chessplayers in the cabinets. He watches how England doles out subsidies to Prussia; how Alexander and Francis hold converse about the weakness of their ally, the king of Prussia; how Frederick William, in his dread of revolution, disbands the enthusiastic Landsturm, refuses to give high office to Scharnhorst the boldest and to Stein the ablest of his advisers, dismisses and banishes Schleiermacher for a speech voicing the popular sentiment. The Emperor sends Fouché on a secret mission (in plain words, as a spy) to the congress of Prague.

In Spain, meanwhile, though Napoleon in the north has been strengthening his position by two victories, Joseph has been utterly crushed by Wellington at Vittoria. The king of Spain has run away. When the princes learn in Prague that the south of France now lies open to an English invasion, their inclination to defiance is promptly strengthened. The Emperor, who had left the best of his generals to fight for Joseph in Spain, is beside himself with wrath. "He alone is to blame!" writes Napoleon to Paris. "The English reports show how utterly stupid was his command. Never was anything so absurd! Of course he is no soldier, but he is responsible. . . . Make the king understand that he is not to see any one till I come back. . . . Otherwise his house in Paris will become a centre of intrigue, and I shall have to put him under arrest, for my patience is at an end. I will no longer have my affairs imperilled out of consideration for idiots who are neither soldiers nor statesmen!"

His eldest brother is his closest intimate in the family,—and now the Emperor thinks that Joseph in a private house in

Paris is more to be dreaded even than as king in Madrid! Will Napoleon at length learn his lesson, and, after this outburst, leave Joseph at peace? Hardly! For even little Jerome has an army once more, and is again making a mess of things; he gives one of the generals new marching orders, with the remark that he is acting on instructions from the Emperor. The latter hears of it too late. "I will not tell you in plain terms what I think of your conduct; enough that I will not tolerate it any longer! If you again make false representations of the kind, I shall publish an order of the day to the effect that in future no attention is to be paid to anything you say. . . . By such behaviour you may disturb the march of my whole army. It is sheer cheating!"

Soon afterwards Junot, one of the oldest of his comrades, becomes affected with megalomania; he loses a battle in Illyria, and then, in a fit of frenzy, throws himself out of a window. Bourrienne, who had for a time been cashiered on account of peculation, and had then been appointed chargé d'affaires in Hamburg, had, after all, to be dismissed once more for the old offence. "If he dares to interfere in public business, I will have him arrested, and make him disgorge his ill-gotten gains!" Bernadotte, the most faithless, has actually landed in Pomerania with his Swedes, has advised the allies to stand firm, and will deceive them as he has deceived others. To crown all, a sworn enemy of the Emperor is now to join the opposing combination. General Moreau, who had been exiled to America for his share in Cadoudal's conspiracy, is on his way to join the foes of France, and will share with Bernadotte the distinction of fighting against his native land.

In this situation, on the horns of a dilemma, too cautious to turn his victories to account, and too powerful to accept the terms on which alone he would be able to make peace, the Emperor has recourse to his whilom methods. He invites Metternich to Dresden, and tries to win over the Austrian diplomat by suggestion. The interview is typically Napoleonic, lasting nine hours without a break. The Emperor gains nothing by it, but posterity gains a great deal.

Standing in the middle of the room, his sword buckled on and his hat under his arm, the Emperor receives the minister. After making formal enquiries about his father-in-law's health, he forthwith assumes the offensive: "So you, too, want war. Well, you shall have it. I have crushed the Prussians at Lützen, and have beaten the Russians at Bautzen. You are waiting for your turn? Be it so, we shall meet again in Vienna. Men are incorrigible! Three times I have replaced Emperor Francis on his throne; I have promised always to live at peace with him; I have married his daughter. Even at that time I thought: 'You are making a fool of yourself.' Still, I did it; and now I regret it!"

We see that he is not disposed to be civil; that to his father-in-law's envoy, on whom he wishes to make a good impression, he is blunter than he had been to Francis on the day after Austerlitz. Metternich speaks of world peace, which will only be possible if the Emperor is willing to accept a reasonable curtailment of his dominions. It will be necessary to give back Warsaw to the tsar and Illyria to the emperor of Austria, to set the Hansa towns free, to enlarge Prussia.

"What you are asking is that I shall dishonour myself. I will die rather than cede a hand's breadth of soil. Your born kings can accept defeat twenty times over, and still go back to their palaces. I am the child of fortune, and I cannot do this! My power will not outlast the day on which I cease to be strong, on which I cease to be feared. . . . Through the cold of Russia I lost everything except honour. . . . Now I have a new army; you shall see it; I will hold a review for your benefit!" Here we have once more the pride of the born soldier facing those who are born kings; here we have General Bonaparte. When the minister ventures to declare that this army of which Napoleon speaks would be glad if peace were made, the Emperor cuts Metternich short with one of his amazing outbursts of frankness:

"It is not the army that wants peace! My generals want it! Really, I have no generals left. The cold of Moscow has demoralised them all. There, the bravest among them cried like children. A fortnight ago, I could still make peace; now, after two victories, I can no longer do so."

"Europe and you, Sire, will never come to terms. When you have made peace, it has been nothing more than a truce. To you, success and failure are equally strong motives for war. This time the whole of Europe will fight against you."

The Emperor laughs savagely:

"Do you think to destroy me by a coalition? How many of you are there, then, Messieurs les Alliés? Four, five, six, twenty? The more, the merrier!" He goes on to warn Metternich against counting on Germany, whose peoples he is holding together by the presence of his soldiers and whose princes are held together by their dread of Austria. He advises armed neutrality, so long as the negotiations are going on in Prague, whereas Metternich talks of armed mediation. These finesses of the old diplomacy are to mask the gulf between them. Then, for a whole hour, they dispute about the relative strength of the opposing armies, each claiming the possession of exact information about the other side.

"I have detailed and accurate lists of your forces," says the Emperor. "I have had so many spies at work, that I know to a unit even how many drummers you have. But no one knows better than myself how much or how little value to attach to these secret service reports. My calculations are based on more exact data, upon mathematical inferences. In the last resort, no one has more than he can have." The Emperor shows the Austrian envoy the muster rolls of the Austrian army, which till yesterday had been part of the French alliance. Metternich can see for himself whether the figures are accurate. The Emperor then spends hours upon a description of the

Russian campaign. When the minister remarks that the imperial troops are composed of striplings, and asks what Napoleon will do when these children, like those who have gone before them, have been swallowed up by the war, the Emperor is overcome with wrath. He turns pale, his features are distorted, and he shouts at Metternich:

"You are not a soldier. You do not know what passes in a soldier's mind. I grew to manhood on the battle-field. Such a man as I does not care a snap of the fingers for the lives of a million men!" He flings his hat into a corner of the room. Now, there is nothing assumed about his anger, and what he has just said is the revelation of an innermost truth. The man who turns pale at the sight of a dying horse, who cannot bear to see a human being pass away, remains and must remain impassive when, in his army lists, he adds up the figures, shifts the hundreds of thousands from column to column, and erases the myriads of slain. Is not war made with human lives, and does it not end with corpses? What is the use of reproaching a craftsman for using the tools of his trade? But as far as morals are concerned, the minister has the best of the argument, and he would have been glad if all France could have heard Napoleon's words.

"France has no reason to complain," says the Emperor more calmly. "To spare France, I have sacrificed Germans and Poles. In Russia I lost three hundred thousand men, but only a tenth of them were Frenchmen!" Meanwhile, he has picked up his hat for himself, a thing he has certainly not done for the last ten years; he has acted sensibly, as if he had still been General Bonaparte. Then he plants himself in front of the Austrian and says:

"It was exceedingly stupid of me to marry an archduchess. I was trying to weld the new with the old, to make Gothic prejudices square with the institutions of my own century. Now I can see the whole extent of my error! The blunder may cost me my throne, but I will bury the world beneath its ruins!"

This tragical admission is the climax of the interview, and the turning-point of the problem of war or peace. The rancour engendered in him by his own mistake spurs him on, regardless of prudential considerations, into the fight with a coalition whose forces outnumber his by three to one. Like a great gambler who realises that he has made an irretrievable blunder, he is impelled by the stubbornness characteristic of such natures as his to stake all upon a single throw. He will show that, blunder notwithstanding, he can still win.

By the time he dismisses Metternich, he has fully recovered composure. His hand on the door-handle, he says: "We shall see one another again before you leave?"

"I am at Your Majesty's service. But I have no longer any hope of succeeding in my mission."

The Emperor looks at him quizzically, and taps him gently on the shoulder: "Do you know what will happen? You will not make war on me!"

After three days' negotiation, Metternich wishes to depart, but the Emperor is afraid of the final rupture. Napoleon summons the Austrian envoy several times, and then invites him to an early interview in the garden. The two men walk up and down.

"Now then, you must not assume this injured air!" In ten minutes they arrange for a prolongation of the truce, and talk about further conversations in Prague. Everything is left hanging in the wind; and in the memorandum he signs with Metternich, the Emperor recognises his father-in-law's position of armed neutrality, which can only be a stage on the way to war. Then he drives off to Mainz, that he may see once more the wife who is daughter of that same Austrian ruler. He has appointed her regent in Paris again, but has expressly forbidden his ministers to submit certain kinds of documents for her consideration. "There are details with which a young woman's mind must not be besmirched."

Had the Habsburg archduchess been a staunch wife and an

affectionate daughter, she would have journeyed on to Vienna, and would have brought about a reconciliation which there was really nothing to prevent except the two men's wounded pride. She had a passably good understanding. Only a few weeks before, the Emperor, writing to Francis, had said: "She fills the post of prime minister to my great satisfaction." We cannot for a moment suppose that now, at the height of the crisis, he can have failed to let her know all the hazards of the hour, were it only to ensure that in the event of a breach her feelings would be on his side. But the little goose made no move. Her only concern was to send costly gifts which would make an impression on her relatives.

In Prague, each party keeps the other in suspense; Fouché does his master harm by gossiping with all and sundry; Bernadotte cements his alliance with his new friends. When, at the last moment, it seems possible that the Emperor may give way, Alexander and Frederick William are so much alarmed at the prospect that they compel Metternich to make the terms more exacting, for they realise that so favourable an opportunity is not likely to recur. The Emperor now angrily draws back, and on the day after the expiry of the truce he receives his father-in-law's declaration of war. No doubt, in the interval, he has secured reinforcements; but he can no longer trust the Confederation of the Rhine, and has to keep watch upon his German auxiliaries. He stands to arms in Saxony and Silesia, faced by Schwarzenberg in command of three armies, two of them, respectively led by Blücher and Bernadotte, holding Silesia and the north. With Schwarzenberg is Moreau, who has just arrived, and who, on his last visit to Germany, had been the conqueror of that country.

Thus paradoxical is the marshalling forces in the game of chess. Under the Emperor of the French, are fighting three German kings against a German general, who a little while back had been the Emperor's subordinate in the war against Russia. Against Napoleon, are fighting two French generals.

One of them is leading Prussian troops against the man who had for years pushed him to the front; nor is this general really a royalist, for he, too, is a son of the revolution. Blücher is the only true-hearted foe, for Blücher, whom Napoleon defeated seven years earlier, has never fought on the Emperor's side, and has never espoused his cause. The one element in Napoleon's favour is that three monarchs have their fingers in Schwarzenberg's pie, three commanders who know as little about the trade of war as Brother Joseph did in Spain.

At the end of August, the Emperor opens the second Saxon campaign with a great victory near Dresden. But on the third day, when he might have followed up the allies and scattered them, he is seized by a violent attack of gastric spasm. For a whole hour he fancies he has been poisoned; his will is paralysed, and he withdraws instead of pursuing. Thereby he loses an army corps, and thus (according to the report of Daru, his daily companion) "causes the disaster of 1813." In this first battle against the hated Bonaparte, Moreau falls. Is it an omen? When the Emperor hears the news, the rivalry of his youth flames up anew, and from his very soul he cries: "Moreau is dead! My star!"

His other army has been defeated by Blücher on the Katzbach. Once more, considerations of statesmanship outweigh those of generalship. How can I divide my adversaries? It will be better to spare Bohemia for the sake of Austria, for the defeat has aroused alarm there. He will make a surprise march on Berlin, and will thus lure the Prussians out of Silesia.

But what the tsar had said years ago is still true. . . . Miracles only happen when the Emperor is present, and he cannot be everywhere. He is thus hampered in his great enterprise. Lack of fighting spirit, difficulties of food-supply, and the frequency of desertion, are continually making it necessary for him to visit his flanking armies: so that in popular parlance, in consequence of his rushings to and fro, he is nicknamed the

"Bautzen Messenger." His armies suffer more and more from lack of food. They are so thickly set upon the ground that they have long since eaten the country bare.

Nevertheless, he has not nearly enough soldiers. Since the 1814 levies are already with the colours, he orders the Senate to call up also those of 1815, and even the men whose liability to service has nearly expired on account of advancing years—the very peasants whom, when setting forth on this campaign in a mood of self-pity, he had envied for their fortunate position. But when will the reinforcements arrive? Who will train them, and how long will it take? Vainly now, at the end of September, he sends an envoy to his father-in-law, to talk of peace; he is prepared to make great sacrifices, "if only you will listen." But Francis remains firm, and is at length able to detach an important member of the Confederation of the Rhine: the king of Bavaria falls away. Thereupon the anxious chessplayer, round whom the clouds are gathering, says to his old comrade something which he has never before been willing to admit:

"Marmont, my game is going awry."

With this admission, the Emperor's genius spreads its wings and flies away.

XI

On Düben Heath is a Saxon fortress, Düben Castle. There, one morning, the Emperor is at work, planning the march on Berlin, the defeat of Bernadotte and Blücher, smashing blows which will finish off the enemy.

Then a number of generals are announced. He comes out of his study to meet them, knowing what they want, for his intimates have kept him informed of the growing discontent among the leaders, who wish to winter quietly on the Rhine. Marshal Ney has recently reported: "I am no longer master of my army." One of the visitors begins to speak hesitatingly;

a second puts forward dubious reasons; then, nodding to encourage one another, they all obsequiously beg him not to march on Berlin. Leipzig will be a better point of attack.

The Emperor listens to them in silence as he wonders: "Is my power vanishing?" At length he replies: "The secession of Bavaria is imminent. A movement on Leipzig, a backward movement, will arouse despair among the soldiers. But I will think over what you have said." He spends the rest of the day alone, refusing himself to all visitors, brooding over his maps. Caulaincourt, on duty outside, listens for sounds from within, but can only hear the windows rattling in the October gale which is howling round the castle. At length he is allowed to enter. The Emperor walks up and down, and, speaking rather to himself than to Caulaincourt, he says: "The French cannot endure reverses." Then he sinks into a reverie.

Next day he announces that they will go to Leipzig. It is October 15th: general animation; orders are issued; every one is delighted. Discussing with Marmont the latest steps of the Habsburg ruler, Napoleon says in conclusion: "I prefer a man of honour who simply keeps his word, to a conscientious man who does what he thinks right. . . . Emperor Francis has done what he believes to be the best for his subjects; he is conscientious, but he is not a man of honour."

Next day begins the great "Battle of the Nations." The Emperor has only one hundred and eighty thousand men against three hundred thousand of the allies; by the evening he has won only part of the battle-field. On the second morning Bernadotte arrives with reinforcements. The Emperor sees that things are going badly, and would like to withdraw, but he cannot make up his mind to a step that would give the impression of defeat. Once more he tries negotiation. General Merveldt has been taken prisoner; his sword is restored on parole; he is to go to Emperor Francis with proposals for an armistice.

"I will retire behind the Saale, while the Russians and the

Prussians withdraw beyond the Elbe, and you Austrians go back into Bohemia; Saxony must remain neutral." Then, livening up, he develops to this enemy general nothing less than a new plan for Europe. Hanover is to be returned to England; the Baltic coast is to be freed; any of the princes of the Confederation of the Rhine who wish to do so can leave the Confederation; Poland, Spain, and Holland are to be independent; the only reservation is as regards Italy, which must not become Austrian. "Be off with you! You have a splendid peace mission. Should fortune favour it, you will earn the love of a great nation. But if your side refuse peace, we shall know how to defend ourselves."

General Merveldt departs in amazement, and his report seems incredible to his master. What! The Emperor Napoleon, in the course of war, between battles, is willing to renounce half Europe and chooses a prisoner to bring this offer? We did not know he was so weak.

The Emperor is anxiously awaiting his emissary's return. Till far on into the night, therefore, he refrains from issuing orders for the morrow; he speaks of the ties of kinship, and of his wife and child. Suddenly he is attacked by his gastric trouble, and staggers against the wall of the tent, his face pale. They wish to send for his physician. "No! my tent is transparent. If I am up and about, every one is at his post."

"At least lie down, Sire!"

"No, I will die standing."

"Do let me fetch the doctor, Sire."

"No, I tell you! I can send a sick soldier to hospital. But who can send me?" Terrible moments pass. "I'm getting better now. See to it that no one comes into the tent!"

Half an hour later, he issues orders, but not for a retreat. Instead, the army moves a little nearer to Leipzig. The enemy now outnumbers him by two to one.

When day comes, he takes up his headquarters in a windmill. The attack upon the French starts from three sides. It appears that, at the last moment, Bernadotte has persuaded the Saxons to turn their guns against France. "Infamous!" exclaims the Emperor, and all around echo the word. Saxon officers who remain faithful to him, break their swords. A dragoon belonging to the escort wheels his horse, and shouts: "We'll do for them yet, the scoundrels! We Frenchmen, too, are here! Vive l'Empereur!" The whole escort follows him at the charge. Soon a young officer, who has seized one of the Saxon eagles, gallops back with it to the Emperor, and collapses from his wounds as he arrives. "These sons of France!" says Napoleon softly.

On the second day of battle, he loses sixty thousand men. He is beaten, but even the German critics say of the affair: "The allies did not secure an overwhelming victory, such as might have been expected from the enormous preponderance of their forces."

During the hasty retreat of the defeated army through the town of Leipzig, the Emperor dictates orders for the withdrawal. "They had brought him a wooden stool," writes an eyewitness. "On this, he now fell into a slumber of exhaustion, his hands loosely folded in his lap. In gloomy silence the generals were standing round the fire, while the soldiers were marching past a little way off."

Next morning the pursuing enemy spread disorder in the streets; a bridge was blown up prematurely, so that the rear guard was forced to surrender; one of the marshals escaped by swimming across the river, another was drowned, several were wounded and taken prisoner. When, subsequently Macdonald came across Augereau, for whose corps he had been waiting, Augereau laughed him to scorn: "Do you think me such a fool as to let myself be slaughtered in a Leipzig suburb? I won't do that for a madman's sake!"

Here we have it for the first time, a sign that one of Napoleon's oldest companions-in-arms has become completely indifferent to the Emperor's fame; is animated by the mere will-to-live, reasonable enough in a private soldier, but unworthy of a marshal of France. On the very same day, another friend of Bonaparte's youth writes to the Emperor, complaining that in the report of the previous day's fighting his services have been overlooked, although for ten hours he had held a part of the plain for whose defence another man is now given the credit. "Never in my life have I served you more faithfully than I did on this occasion. . . . Sire, I could not suffer anything worse than to be forgotten at such a time." The letter is signed, "Marmont."

These two utterances on the day after Leipzig are the shadows of coming events. Marmont and Augereau will both desert the Emperor in the decisive hour.

Fifty miles away, Goethe is sitting in his room at Weimar. Napoleon's picture has fallen from its nail. The poet has heard the sound of the Leipzig guns. The first news of the French defeat has arrived. Though none of the allied generals can say, yet, whether the Emperor may not be able to collect his forces once more, and to resume his career of victory, Goethe, who only a few months earlier had declared Napoleon to be invincible, already realises the full extent of the disaster. On the day of the retreat, as if everything had happened a hundred years before, and the whole matter had become legendary, he writes the following verses:

He who feels courage in his royal breast
knows no shudderings, treads gladly
the undermined road leading to the steps of the throne,
knows the danger and nevertheless mounts confidently.
The golden circlet's tremendous burden,
he does not try its weight; resolute and calm,
he presses it gladly on his bold brow,
and bears it lightly, as if it were a laurel crown.
Thus didst thou. What seemed so far away,
thou hast tranquilly learned to make thine own;

and whatever fierce obstacles might block the path,
thou sawest them, contemplated them, and understood them.
A joyful day dawned, it summoned thee,
thou wast summoned, and thus it came to pass. . . .
And thou still standest despite all that has happened to thee,
despite the foe, who, with war and death
threatens thee from without and from within. . . .
The peoples are agape, they chatter, they are full of vain imagin-
What do they care for, but games? . . . [ings—
The false world, it wooes us for our treasure,
for our favour, for our position,
and, even if one makes one's lover one's equal,
love does not suffice him, he wants the whole kingdom.
So was it with this man!—And now, declare it abroad,
even if it cost you your life:
To every man, be he whom he may,
there comes a last happiness and a last day.

At the same date, Schelling writes: "I do not believe that Napoleon's end is yet very near. If I am right, he will still be spared; and, even if all his helpers fall away from him, he will still live to drink the cup of humiliation to the dregs." When, almost immediately afterwards, the Bavarians definitively changed sides, Hegel wrote: "In Nuremberg, the mob has welcomed the incoming Austrians with the most hateful jubilation. . . . Nothing more contemptible can be imagined than the mood and the conduct of the burghers."

Three outstanding Germans, immediately after Leipzig!

Certainly, it is far from being a final defeat. Fighting, and fighting victoriously, the Emperor withdraws. In Erfurt, Murat presents himself, wishing to go back to his kingdom. The master allows him to do so, saying: "By next May, I shall have an army of a quarter of a million on the Rhine!" Thus does his intelligence work; such is the quality of his imagination; he can still think only in hundreds of thousands. In Mainz, his troops are attacked by typhus, and he hastens to move what is left of them across the Rhine. During the retreat, he works from three in the morning till eleven at night.

Meanwhile, the advancing allied headquarters are thronged

by the princes who are deserting the cause of Napoleon. All is promptly forgotten and forgiven. But there is one honest man left who finds strong words to describe what is happening: "What do you think of these wretches' behaviour? . . . They have had better treatment than they deserve. . . . All these princelets are weaklings, to whom a far more honourable existence has been conceded than their pitiful conduct would seem to justify. . . . The retention of their sovereignty, which consists in pretentiousness, pleasure seeking, and the lust for dominion, has cost them nothing more than the blood of their subjects."

Such is Baron vom Stein's judgment concerning his peers, the German princes.

XII

Letizia is sitting by the fire. In her hand is a letter from Mainz, in which her son answers her intercession for Louis by imposing certain conditions. But this is not what troubles her; she is thinking of the Emperor's parenthetical allusion to the turn in his fortunes. He writes: "In this situation, when all Europe is rising against me, and my heart is so full of care. . . ." She has never warned him of the impending dangers; they are both of them too proud for that. But she has often uttered her foreboding to intimates, with her phrase "Pourvou que cela doure!" She has never been disturbed by the thought of any disaster to herself. She thinks only of her dear ones. Who will help them when everything falls to pieces? To whom, she is now asking herself, can the Emperor look for support?

When he returns, she has to endure the recognition that the treachery begins among her own children. Murat, who is always led by a keener intelligence than his own (that of Caroline), signs a truce with England and enters into an alliance with Austria. Elise has an adviser, Fouché, who keeps away from Paris until the Emperor's fall. "The only thing that could save us all would be the Emperor's death." Such are the ex-minister's words to the Emperor's sister. But Elise writes to her mother asking what dances are to be given that winter in Paris. Louis defies orders, and, being unable to stay in Austria any longer, comes to Paris without leave. Napoleon proposes to banish him to a distance of two hundred miles from Paris. The mother intercedes between the pair; there is a further interview, as a result of which Napoleon and Louis are once more estranged. Jerome has left his subjects in the lurch, and has fled incognito from Cassel. Joseph, despite the Emperor's reiterated requests, persists in his refusal to undertake the defence of Paris. Lucien keeps his distance, still in a bad humour.

Such is the gallery of brothers and sisters, the relatives upon whom for a decade the Emperor has been trying to build up his dynasty. What can be the feelings of a mother who has always cherished the most tender affection for that one of her children who happened to be suffering most keenly?

But in Morfontaine a cheerful mood prevails. The company there consists of Joseph, the Spanish king without a country; Jerome's wife, a queen in like situation, whose father has gone over to the allies; the sometime grand inquisitor of Spain says Mass in the chapel; there are two colonial bishops; German, Spanish, and Italian courtiers without a court—a brilliant company, like the audience at private theatricals, watching actors who will soon come down from the stage to take their place on the floor of the drawing-room. Only one of them hopes to draw a big fish out of the troubled waters, Bernadotte's wife, Joseph's sister-in-law, the woman to whom twenty years before the Emperor had given the go-by. She knows that her husband, commander of one of the allied armies, is already on the Rhine; she hopes that ere long, in Notre Dame, he will place Josephine's crown on her pretty brown head.

At this country-seat, more intrigues are carried on against

Napoleon as Emperor in 1809. Woodcut from a medal by J. P. Droz.

Napoleon than Joseph is aware of; for Joseph is not himself an intriguer; he is merely easygoing and vain. The Emperor recognises this, now that it is too late, and says to Roederer:

"That has been one of my mistakes. I fancied I needed my brothers for the dynasty, but it is safe without them. It has been brought into being in the heart of the storm by the nature of things. The empress suffices. . . . Everything has been quiet for a year past. There is only disquiet when Joseph lives in Paris. . . . He cannot forget that he is the first-born. Was there ever anything more absurd? If he were talking of our father's vineyard, that would be another story! . . . His interests are in women, houses, furniture. He likes to go out rabbit shooting, and to play blind man's buff with the girls. I am tied to nothing; care not a jot for houses or for women; though I do feel a little concern about my son."

Thus does his monomania make headway in these weeks of increasing peril. We see that all the rest, court included, has been nothing more than a game. He cares not a jot for anything outside the one passion of his soul—except that he is a little concerned about his son.

He now quickly makes up his mind to restore the Spanish crown to King Ferdinand, who is set at liberty; but the Cortes must approve the treaty. This is Talleyrand's advice, for Talleyrand has now been recalled to the Tuileries. Insistence on ratification by the Cortes will delay matters. The traitor's aim is to keep a French army in the south, so that France may be weakened for the benefit of the allies, for whose cause Talleyrand is now working. Joseph protests.

"My present situation makes it impossible for me to think of any sort of foreign dominion," writes the Emperor to his brother. "I shall deem myself lucky if the peace treaty will allow me to keep the old boundaries of France. Everything is crashing round me. My armies have been destroyed, and it will hardly be possible to make the losses good. Holland is gone, and Italy is uncertain. . . . Belgium and the Rhine province are discontented; the Spanish frontier is held by the enemy. . . . How is it possible, at this crisis, to think of a foreign throne?" When the prefect of police advises him to leave a larger body of National Guards in Paris, during the campaign that is now imminent, he rejoins: "Who can guarantee that they will be faithful to me? Am I to leave so large a force in my rear?"

He is in despair. Surely there is no other word for the description of these thoughts? His family, his allies, his own capital, all seem untrustworthy to him. Thus completely has his mood changed since the battle of Leipzig. Count Lavalette, Postmaster General, one of the most honest men in Paris, who often came to see him at this time, found him one evening in a condition of great depression. Napoleon received Lavalette in his bedroom, standing in front of the fire, his hands stretched out towards the blaze. The visitor, though a stout-hearted fellow, advises peace, saying that the French are mutable. But when he ventures to mention the name of the Bourbons, on whom perhaps the Emperor's mantle may fall, Napoleon turns away from the fire and silently throws himself on the bed. When, a few minutes later, the count draws near, he finds that Napoleon is sleeping.

These healthy reactions are a sign of returning courage. Napoleon's overthrow is close at hand; he foresees the catastrophe; but when people talk to him about the Bourbons, to whose throne he has mounted and who may dispossess him in turn, he cannot be bothered with the topic. It bores him, and he goes to sleep.

Awakening reinvigorated, he recognises that the Bourbon sympathies of the northern provinces are a danger; he notes that the funds have fallen to fifty, and that the shares of the Bank of France have declined to half their former value; and he finds that the new National Guard, which after all he is obliged to call up, fails to materialise. He therefore gladly accedes to a proposal that issues from the allies in Frankfort.

They are as disunited as he can possibly wish. Metternich, being a statesman, thinks it will be better not to occupy Paris. The tsar, being a romanticist, wants to take vengeance for Moscow by blowing up the Tuileries. In the end, Austria gets her way. The offer to France is that the country is to retain her natural frontiers; the Rhine, the Alps, the Pyrenees. The Emperor feels that he is saved. Without a moment's delay he will accept the Frankfort proposal. Maret has actually drafted the dispatch.

Suddenly he changes his mind. Why? Perhaps he has been put out of temper by the opposition voiced in the Chambers. There, at length, the members are showing themselves refractory. "We will not vote further armaments unless the government agrees that they are to be used only for defence. The Emperor must pledge himself to carry out all the laws that protect liberty." Thunders of applause greet these words. For the first time in fifteen years, an assembly has ventured to criticise Napoleon. In his hatred for all Chambers, the Emperor flies into a passion, forbids the printing of the speech, closes the House, receives a few of the deputies, scolds them:

"The throne is nothing more than a piece of wood covered with satin. I, and I alone, represent the people. I am the State. If France wants a different constitution, let her find another monarch for herself. Do you think my words proud? I utter them because I have the courage, and because France owes her greatness to me." After this language in the vein of the Roi Soleil, on New Year's Day he openly threatens the deputies, and says he will have them closely watched.

That very day, Blücher crosses the Rhine.

Thus, after twenty years of effort, and after six great wars, the more or less united powers of Europe and the old monarchical idea, incorporated in a Prussian field marshal, have made their way back across the boundary river of the revolution—and in the same hour, the heir of these modern ideas scatters their representatives and threatens imprisonment.

With a similar logic, the manifestoes of the conflicting worlds have changed places. In Notre Dame, where for twenty years nothing has been heard but thanksgiving services, prayers are now offered up on behalf of the success of French arms. From the allies, on the other hand, who have so long heard talk of success of the French arms as heralding the liberation of conquered peoples, come assurances to conquered France that the invaders are "liberators."

The legitimists have at length learned from their great foe the technique of his battles and his proclamations. But if they are able to turn the lesson to good account, it is only because of their preponderance of power, and because of the weariness of a nation, which, after twenty years of glory, now seeks nothing but repose.

To begin with, they weaken their position by asking too much; for when they offer nothing better than the old frontiers of 1792, the Emperor breaks off negotiations, and makes ready to repel their onslaught. In spite of all difficulties, he is able to strengthen his fighting front. His spirits are now steadily rising. When a pious count advises him to send the empress and her ladies to kiss the relics of Ste. Geneviève, Napoleon bursts out laughing, and says: "You're a pretty bigot! I am going to fight it out!"

But to whom, in this stern moment, does he entrust the capital? Who merits all his confidence?

Joseph! Joseph, who understands nothing about war and has been keeping open house for the Emperor's enemies, becomes lieutenant general of France and governor of Paris! This domestic peace treaty throws a glaring light upon the Emperor's isolation, upon his lack of confidence in his supporters, and upon his family feeling. Shortly before leaving for the front, Napoleon has coldly ordered his brother to choose between openly declaring himself to be the friend of the empress-regent or continuing to be banished from Paris. "You can live in retirement at your country-seat, so long as I am alive. If I die, you will be killed or imprisoned. At Morfontaine, you will certainly be of no use either to your own people or to France, but at any rate you will not do me any harm. Make your choice. Feelings, whether friendly or hostile, are useless and out of place."

The tone is that of a man fighting to save his crown. He reckons with the likelihood of death; burns a great many State papers; and provides for his natural sons. Little Léon is to receive a fixed income, Walewska's boy is to have a big majorat. As for his legitimate heir, who is now nearly three years old, Napoleon has the child in his arms when he takes leave of the officers of the National Guard. "I entrust to you the dearest of my possessions. You are answerable!" Once more he urges tenacity on his brother; once more he leaves his wife regent of their son's realm. Next morning he quits Paris.

He will not re-enter the city for more than a year, after devious wanderings.

XIII

In a few weeks he is beaten.

His first strokes are successful. Near Brienne, where he forces Blücher to retreat, and where he himself takes so active a part in the fight that he is obliged to draw his sword in self-defence, he recognises the tree under which "as a twelve-year-old youngster I used to sit and read Tasso." A romantic encounter which links his later life with those early days when his dreams were first dreamed! His historical feeling concerning himself grows in such circumstances to legendary proportions.

Immediately thereafter, Blücher gains a victory over him near La Rothière. Paris is threatened. The Emperor's strength seems broken. Caulaincourt, in a letter, begs him to yield; Maret does the same by word of mouth. Napoleon pays little heed to what Maret is saying; absently, he flutters the pages of a book by Montesquieu. Then, pointing to a passage, he bids Maret read aloud. "I know of nothing nobler than the determination of a monarch of our day to prefer to bury himself beneath the ruins of a throne rather than accept proposals to which no king should ever hearken."

"I know of something nobler still!" exclaims Maret. "That you should sacrifice your glory and thereby fill the abyss wherein, otherwise, France will find her grave!"

"Very well," answers the Emperor. "Make peace. Caulaincourt can conclude it, and sign the documents. I shall bear the shame. But do not claim from me that I myself should dictate my own abasement!" Maret writes to Caulaincourt in Châtillon, where he is negotiating anew with the enemy. Caulaincourt demands confirmation. Meanwhile the Emperor has veered about. He writes to Joseph: "Hold the gates bravely. Have two guns mounted and see that the National Guard takes up its position there. . . . Place fifty men at each gate armed with service muskets, one hundred with fowling pieces, and one hundred with pikes. Thus, each gate will be guarded by two hundred and fifty men."

Crœsus has become a beggar! Only six months ago, nay, even three months back, Napoleon would have added three noughts to the figures! But now, encircled by the conglomerated forces of so many princes, two cannon and a hundred fowling pieces must suffice to save Paris! He sees the absurdity, for the same evening Maret finds him depressed. The minister, however, tries to persuade the Emperor to dictate the conditions of peace: Belgium and the left bank of the Rhine are to be free, Italy must be yielded up, everything which Bonaparte and Napoleon conquered must be given back in order that he may keep Paris and the piece of wood covered with satin. He will sign to-morrow, he says. Those who love him, tremble at thought of the moment when with one stroke of the pen he will lose all that his warlike deeds have won.

But fate guards him from this. News comes during the night. The enemy's position is worse than it seemed the previous day. Once more the war lord's imagination gets to work. When, next morning, Maret arrives with the papers for the Emperor's signature, he finds his master brooding over the map. Napoleon hardly notices his entrance. All the minister can catch is a few hurried words:

"Other matters are to the fore! I am determined to smash Blücher!" When, at the self-same hour, Joseph's letter arrives wherein he states that Paris is in peril, Napoleon, in the interludes of issuing army orders, dictates, from the depths of his heart, this rock-like answer:

"Should Paris be taken, I shall no longer continue to live. . . . I have commanded you to do all that is needful to safeguard the empress, the king of Rome, and our family. . . . I have the right to claim the assistance of my kin, for I have helped them so often in the past. . . .

"If Talleyrand considers that the empress should in any case remain in Paris, this advice is secret treachery. Do not trust him! For sixteen years I have associated with him, and have often given him favours. But nothing is more certain than that he is the greatest enemy of our house, now that luck has forsaken us. Take my advice to heart. I understand events better than the young folk. If I lose the fight and die, you will be the first to hear of it. . . . I fancy that Madame Mère could find asylum with the queen of Westphalia. For God's sake, do not allow the empress and the king to fall into the hands of the enemy! Austria would then lose interest in the war, and would take the empress to Vienna. England and Russia would make the French see things from their outlook, and our cause would be lost. . . .

"Perhaps I shall conclude peace in a day or two. . . . Never since the world began has a sovereign allowed himself to be taken alive in an open city. . . . So long as I live, I must be obeyed. If I die, my reigning son and the regent his mother must not allow themselves to be taken, were it only for France's honour. On the contrary, they must withdraw with the last of their soldiers and entrench themselves in the remotest village. Otherwise it might be said that I had sacrificed my son's throne. . . .

"I would rather know that my son had been killed than that he was being brought up in Vienna as an Austrian prince. I have never seen *Andromache* played without lamenting the fate of Astyanax, and I have always regarded it as a stroke of good fortune that his father did not live to see it. You do not know the French people. The consequences of these vast events are incalculable!"

This hunted man is panting for breath. For the first time since his youth, death or collapse seems close at hand; perhaps both. When he writes commanding Joseph to prepare for either eventuality, the two main elements of his soul are mingling, and both are scattering sparks. His calculating temperament is reckoning up the disastrous consequences that would ensue, should Austria's ambition cease to be operative; but at the same time his idea of the destiny of his nearest and dearest takes a soaring flight. Were he to fall next day, this letter would remain to show that honour and glory had been the last flames of his heroic imagination. But to-day, as always, everything discloses a meditation upon the historical parallels which have throughout life been his spur to greatness.

Thus the letter is the burning-cold document of a statesman and poet, and only in this frame of mind is it becoming for a Napoleon to perish.

At the same time, he is a great military commander to the last. When he divides the remnants of his army into two halves, and begins by defeating Blücher with one of them in a brilliant advance, the six battles he fights in nine days, from Champaubert to Montereau, are still in the avalanche tempo of General Bonaparte. But that the names of these battle-fields are French, tells us the whole story; hitherto his victories have always borne foreign names. At Montereau he is an artillerist once more, training the guns with his own hand as at Toulon.

He cries: "Forward, comrades! The cannon ball that will hit me has not been cast!"

He has settled accounts with Blücher. Now to deal with Schwarzenberg! But the Austrian is afraid of having his renown as commander dimmed, and is sedulous to avoid a decisive conflict; he actually writes direct to Berthier, suggesting that a truce be arranged in Châtillon. Enough for the Emperor to read this, and his lust for battle is redoubled. Another letter to Joseph, written with his own hand this time, breathing defiance, shrewd, bold:

"You have been talking to my wife about the Bourbons, but you should avoid such topics. I have no wish to take shelter behind my wife. . . . That would only sow dissension between us. . . . I have never tried to win the applause of the Parisians, for I am no stage puppet. . . . Besides, the real Paris is something very different from the passions of the three thousand persons who are raising all the clamour. Of course it would be easier to explain that one cannot levy any soldiers, than it is to make the attempt. . . . Je vous embrasse!"

It is many, many years since he has penned these words at the close of a letter. Not since the Marengo days has he written thus to any of his brothers or to any of his commanders—and Joseph is both. His heart is beating more vigorously. Next day, writing to Savary, who has informed him about a petition to the monarchs, and about the regency and fears and intrigues, his phrasing is more incisive, and bears witness to the excitement of a campaign:

"They shall learn that I am still the man of Wagram and Austerlitz! I will have no intrigues in the State. . . . Let me tell you that if a petition against the public authority is being circulated, I will arrest King Joseph and all the others who sign it! . . . I want no tribunes of the people! I myself am the great tribune!"

Meanwhile the allies are quarrelling. The tsar wants Paris to be placed under a Russian governor until the nation chooses

Bernadotte or another; Austria will hear of nothing but a Bourbon restoration; Schwarzenberg wants peace to be made at once, and instead of joining battle is content to assume "a military attitude." But Blücher, who has remarshalled his forces, simply cries "Forward!" and is on the march. When the allies once more send a proposal for the re-establishment of the old frontiers of France, the Emperor is enraged, saying: "I am so angry, that I feel dishonoured by the mere suggestion." Being reminded that the enemy outnumbers him by three to one, he answers heroically: "I have fifty thousand men. Add myself, and you get a hundred and fifty thousand!"

Now, at the beginning of March, when he is to attack Blücher once more, for the command of his other army he puts his trust in Marmont, his earliest companion-in-arms.

But the spirit of revolt is rising. It had shown itself to Napoleon at Düben Castle in the previous autumn; during the winter it had been fomented in his brother's circle; now it was to eventuate in treason under fire. Marmont, the first among men still above ground who had served under Napoleon, is also the first to betray him. Oudinot and Macdonald have lost the battle of Bar-sur-Aube. Now, at Laon, Marmont makes no more than a pretence of fighting, leaves his artillery in the town square, thus snatches victory from his master, and even allows himself to be surprised in his camp. "The Emperor would have been justified in cutting him down," says Berthier, "but is so fond of him that, after making a scene, he has left him in command of his corps."

What is more natural than that, during these days, his heart should go out to the friends of his youth? But Marmont is not the only traitor to whom he is lenient! Augereau, who had fought beside him at Rivoli, begins to make signals to the Austrians, fails to be at his post. The reprimand he receives is an affectionate one. Napoleon writes to him almost as if they were still brothers in the field, as of old.

"Six hours' rest were not enough for you? . . . What pitiful excuses you are making, Augereau! No money! No horses! I command you to take the field within twelve hours of receiving this. If you are still the old Augereau of Castiglione, you can keep your command. But if you find the burden of your sixty years so heavy, hand over the command to the oldest of your generals. The country is in danger! . . . You should be the first in the firing line. We must all put on our seven-leagued boots, and must find the reckless courage of '93. If the French soldiers see your plumes at the outposts, you will be able to lead your men whithersoever you please."

Here we have General Bonaparte once more. The red of sunset reminds us of the glories of sunrise.

Owing to Marmont's retreat, the Emperor is left unsupported at Arcis-sur-Aube, and has no more than a few thousand men with which to face a great army. Defeat is inevitable. During the height of the battle, a dust eddy sweeps across the field. A thousand dragoons are panic-stricken, and take to flight, shouting: "The Cossacks!" The Emperor gallops forward into the press. "Dragoons! Turn and fight! You are running away, but I stand firm!" He draws his sword and charges the enemy, followed only by his staff and the bodyguard. Six thousand Cossacks take to flight. It is years upon years since he has led a cavalry attack. His horse is shot under him, and he mounts another. Berthier reports that the Emperor was obviously hoping to find death on the field.

But death does not come for the asking. No more than Cæsar, Cromwell, or Frederick, is Napoleon destined for this swift, heroic end. Such men are something more than military commanders, and must live out their lives as leaders of nations, —even though they have to fight against their own nation. Henceforward the blows thicken, and each blow is symbolical.

But who can wonder if, at last, men forsake the despiser of men? He has made princes of his soldiers; should it surprise us that they prefer their princedoms to a soldier's death? Need we wonder that a wife sprung from an ancient ruling house, married off to an upstart, should be quick to repudiate him and to become a Habsburg once more? That his brothers, in whom he has shown too much trust, should, when disaster comes, think of themselves rather than of the man to whom they owe everything?

When, in his last letters to Marie Louise, he asks her to write to her father, she complies with a bad grace, and, instead of following the example of Maria Theresa, she pens cold letters which can serve as hints to her father and his ministers. News reaches the allied headquarters that the English have landed in Bordeaux, and that the Bourbon flag has been hoisted there; a letter from the Emperor to his wife is intercepted, a letter in which he announces his intention to withdraw behind the Marne. It is enough; at length all are agreed for the march on Paris.

In this utmost danger, Napoleon has still a last bold shift. He will arm the peasants as a national reserve; they will be ready to his hand, for they hate the invading foreigners. But now tidings come that Marmont has allowed himself to be beaten once more, and is withdrawing to Paris with Mortier. Like one who hears that his house is on fire, the Emperor storms back towards Paris, entrusts the command of his troops to Berthier, and rides citywards with his body-guard. Then, leaving everything behind, he jumps with Caulaincourt into a post-chaise, hoping it will not be too late to seize the reins of power. After how many victories has he not driven in such a carriage through the gates of his capital? Always his thoughts have circled round the problem, "What is Paris saying? How shall I find things there?" But now there is only one idea pulsing in his brain: Will three persons stand firm till I come; three to whom I can entrust the safety of the realm? The empress as regent, Joseph as governor of Paris, Marmont as leader of the strongest corps!

Night. Change of horses. A squad of soldiers led by an officer. The officer reports: "I am under Marshal Mortier's orders, and am seeking quarters for the troops that are being withdrawn."

"Troops being withdrawn? Where is the empress? Where is King Joseph?"

"Her Majesty, with the king of Rome, fled yesterday to Blois. King Joseph left Paris to-day."

"Where is Marmont?"

"I don't know, Sire."

Beads of sweat form on the Emperor's forehead; his lips twitch nervously; he is horrified at the news. He breaks out: "Forward! To-morrow the guards will be here. The National Guard is on my side. Once within the walls of Paris, I shall only leave the town as a conqueror or as a dead man!"

With difficulty, Caulaincourt persuades him to renounce this foolhardy design. The Emperor orders that Marmont's corps is to take up its position behind the Essonne. Then he says to his minister: "Hasten to Paris! Go on negotiating for a treaty. I have been betrayed and sold. You have full powers. I will wait for you here. It is not far. Forward!"

He drives a hundred paces nearer, and can see the waters of the Seine. But what is mirrored therein? The enemy's watch-fires! At the outposts, the invaders are cooking supper and singing songs; while the Emperor, on the left bank with two post-chaises and a few servants, watches them under cover of the darkness.

Then he has the carriage turned, and drives to Fontainebleau.

XIV

Next morning, Talleyrand is sitting in his bedchamber, submitting to the ministrations of his valet. This statesman of the revolution still has his wig dressed in the rococo style. The door is thrown open, and almost before the servant has time to announce him, Count Nesselrode hurries in to greet the friend of many years' standing. He gets covered with powder from head to foot, Talleyrand informs us. Two hours later, the tsar himself comes to stay with his intimate friend as guest; he will not put up at the Elysée for fear of bombs. The moment for which Napoleon's minister has worked indefatigably for six years has come at last, and the smiling victors shake hands with a sense of moral righteousness: virtue has triumphed! After knocking at the gates of Paris for two and twenty years, the legitimist monarchs have at length been admitted. This is their great moment. They have ridden into the city. A small party of Bourbon supporters has hailed them as liberators; the Faubourg Saint-Germain has rallied. Elsewhere in Paris, silence reigns. Every one is calmly waiting to see whether, on the morrow, Napoleon or Louis is to be called master.

The Emperor's fate is sealed, for Joseph, in his cowardly flight and in spite of Napoleon's warnings, has not taken Talleyrand along with him, but has left that cleverest and most dangerous of enemies in Paris. It is not fixity of purpose on the part of the nation that brings the Emperor to his doom; nor are the four allied foes unanimous as to his fate. He is ruined by the co-operation of faithless servants and treacherous friends, under the guidance of a man who is both—for Talleyrand, with the good graces of the tsar, takes upon himself the spiritual leadership of the next ten days. Now the intriguer is in his true element.

Yesterday he received another guest. Talleyrand by no means hates the Emperor, but has from the first sign of Napoleon's decline, forsaken his master in order that he himself may climb. He has no wish to wreak vengeance on a prisoner, and, indeed, has no reason for revenge. Still, it would be convenient were the disturber of the peace quietly to disappear; and therefore he promises a goodly reward to a certain Maubreuil (a monarchist officer with an adventurous past) if this man "will carry out an important commission on the road to Fontainebleau." But the adventurer's heart fails him at the last moment, and he is content to attack Jerome's brave young wife and carry off her jewels, instead of making an attempt on Napoleon's life. Blücher, too, on his own initiative, has sent a detachment with definite orders to make an end of the Emperor.

"Well, what does France want?" asks the tsar of the abbé, as a man of wide experience. Talleyrand has long had in mind the restoration of the former king, but he thinks it best to ask whom Alexander would recommend. Somewhat diffidently, the tsar mentions the name of Bernadotte. Talleyrand smiles: "France does not want any more soldiers. If we wanted one we should keep the one we have already, the finest soldier in the world. No other, in his place, would find a hundred men to follow him." Talleyrand says this to the conqueror, says it in plain words to the tsar; the defeated Emperor at Fontainebleau could have wished no greater tribute of admiration than such words from such lips in such a situation.

A day later, Talleyrand summons the Senate, and the legislature confirms the decision that the Emperor must abdicate. There is a general swing of opinion in this direction. Caulaincourt is the only one who puts up a fight for Napoleon, and tries to win over the tsar. For a moment, Alexander's impressionable heart is touched; the image of his whilom friend rises before his mind; he wavers, and says that he will do his best with his allies to save the crown for the king of Rome.

But while the impotent Caulaincourt is trying to persuade the vacillating tsar, and is doing what he can to save the house of Bonaparte, at this same hour on the third of April, Talleyrand has summoned Marshal Marmont who, with his twelve thousand men across the Seine, is still a power, since the main body of the allies has not yet reached Paris.

See them sitting there, Napoleon's companion-in-arms and senior officer, hobnobbing with the doyen of the Emperor's ministers. The diplomat reasons coldly with the soldier, who hardly needs to listen to the arguments. He is hopelessly disillusioned, tired out. His faith had been shaken three years ago in Spain. His thoughts run this wise: "What is the use of trying to march with a dead man? The king is dead; long live the king! At the military academy, we were all monarchists. His defeat is a proof that the Bourbons have the right of it. The only choice is between being stood up in front of an old wall or taking one's stand behind an old throne. The oath of allegiance? That has been abrogated. The ties of friendship? Only the other day, he was scolding me after the Laon affair." Acting on the suggestion of his old acquaintance, Marmont writes to Schwarzenberg, the allies' commander-in-chief:

"By the decree of the Senate, the army and the people have been released from their obligation of fealty to Napoleon. I am ready to promote an understanding between people and army, in order to avoid civil war." Upon this pretext, which he subsequently endeavoured to fortify with the excuse of patriotism (the paltry argument of every turncoat), the Emperor's senior marshal destroys the Emperor. Augereau, in a shameful proclamation, is quick to follow Marmont's lead.

At the time when Talleyrand is winning over the marshals, the Emperor in Fontainebleau is reviewing his guards. To them he exclaims: "Never shall we allow any one to wear in Paris the white cockade of the émigrés. . . . In a few days we will attack the enemy in Paris!" The officers brandish their swords enthusiastically, shouting: "À Paris! Vive l'Empereur!" He waves his hand to them, and, smiling joyfully, he briskly mounts the steps, surrounded by his last ministers in their embroidered coats.

Soon afterwards, a carriage draws up in the courtyard. Caulaincourt steps out; he is pale, having passed the night in a vigil. He approaches the Emperor. Berthier enquires: "Well, my lad, how goes it?" The minister hesitates to answer, for he does not like Berthier's tone. Are the very nearest going to fall away too? He finds the Emperor at work.

"What do they want of me?" asks Napoleon eagerly.

"Great sacrifices, that you may retain the crown for your son."

"You mean that they refuse to treat with me! They want to make a helot of me, to hold me up as a warning to all those whose genius enables them to rule men and to make the born kings tremble on their ancient thrones!"

Bonaparte's metallic tone! Such is the mood produced in the Emperor by the sight of his guards, by the perusal of his latest muster rolls, by the study of his maps. Now the minister mentions the most moderate of the tsar's demands. Napoleon is to abdicate in favour of the king of Rome, and then the terms of a regency will be discussed. But there is talk of a Bourbon restoration. The Emperor leaps to his feet:

"They are mad! The Bourbons in France; they would not be able to hold their position for a year! Nine-tenths of the nation cannot endure them; my soldiers will never serve under them. They have lived for twenty years upon the alms of a foreigner, at war all the time with the fundamental principles of their homeland! The Senate consists entirely of regicides, or the sons of regicides. I was a newcomer, with nothing to take vengeance for; a man whose only business it was to upbuild. . . . No doubt they can draw profit out of the crash, can exile me and my family; but the Bourbons—never!"

Thus does his work roll before his mind as in a rhapsody, lighted up by his contempt for those whom he succeeded and who are now to succeed him. He becomes the soldier once more. "They demand my abdication. Will the crown then be secure for my son? I have still fifty thousand men. They will march with me to Paris. After the victory, the people shall decide. If, then, the French want to chase me away, I will go." See the conflict in his soul. As statesman, he is willing to abdicate, that his son may reign; as soldier, he is still eager to fight, that he may retain all.

But while enthusiasm grows in the rank and file of his army, while the common soldiers are willing to give their lives for the

Emperor, the marshals are malcontent. Although they have not yet heard of Marmont's defection, they cherish like wishes, and would gladly shake off their allegiance to Napoleon if they could do so decently. This marked difference between the mood of the men and that of their leaders is once more a vengeance for the system of titles and monetary rewards with whose aid the military commander, when he had become an emperor, had transformed generals into marshals. Next day, the seniors among them are of one mind. Ney, Macdonald, Oudinot, and Lefèvre, in the most subservient way possible, speak to him of the advantages of abdication.

The Emperor shows them his maps, which are again beset with coloured pins; he points out to them that the enemy is in an unfavourable position, and enumerates his own resources. All is vain! The frame of mind they had shown in Düben Castle, intensified a hundredfold, blocks his way. Silently he dismisses them, for he wants to think over a plan. Mentally, he has mustered his forces, and the total of his additions does not seem to him a bad one. A conditional renunciation, therefore, will not betoken anything more than an armistice, a postponement.

A few hours after the audience of the marshals, he sends for Caulaincourt, and points to a holograph document on the table:

"There is my abdication. You can take it to Paris."

The minister reads:

"Since the allied powers have declared that Emperor Napoleon is the only obstacle to the peace of Europe, Emperor Napoleon, faithful to his oath, declares himself ready, for the welfare of his country, which is inseparable from the rights of his son, from those of the regency of the empress, and from the maintenance of the laws of the Empire, to descend from the throne, to give up France and even life itself."

What a style! A diplomatic document, involved in its phraseology, cautiously worded, ambiguous, penned for the inspection of diplomats of the old school. Nothing of Napoleon in it. The minister begs for the companionship of two of the marshals for so important a mission.

"Take Marmont and Ney," says the Emperor, adding, "Marmont is my oldest comrade."

"Marmont is not here."

"Macdonald, then."

Late that evening, three hours after the interview with Napoleon, the plenipotentiaries are at the Elysée confronting the allied princes and ministers. Most of the negotiations are carried on between the tsar and Caulaincourt. The latter's contention that the French are heartily against the Bourbons has its effect; the parleys continue far into the night. Suddenly an announcement is made in Russian; the Frenchmen do not understand. Thereupon the tsar speaks: "You are relying, gentlemen, upon the unshakable loyalty of the troops towards the imperial regime. Well, I have just been informed that the advance guard, the sixth army corps, has deserted the Emperor. It has come over to our lines."

The allies' task has become easier; they now demand instant and unconditional abdication. Meanwhile the Emperor sends one courier after another from Fontainebleau to his minister. He writes:

"If they refuse to negotiate with me, what kind of a treaty will it be? . . . Bring back my act of abdication, I command you. . . . I will sign no treaty!"

Next day at six o'clock in the morning the Emperor is at work with Berthier. A captain is introduced, an adjutant of Mortier's.

"Well, what news?"

"The sixth army corps has gone over to the enemy. It is marching to Paris."

The Emperor seizes him by the arm and shakes it.

"Marmont? Are you sure? Did the troops know where they were being led?"

"During the night they were led into the Austrian camp.

They were told that they were marching against the enemy."

"My men have to be duped before they can be torn away from me! Did you see Marmont at the time he set out?"

"No, Sire."

"The cavalry, too?"

"In close columns."

"Where is Mortier?"

"He sent me to tell you that his corps will be loyal to you in life and in death. He awaits Your Majesty's orders. The young guard is ready to die for you. All young France is ready!"

The emperor steps close up to the young officer, looks him straight in the eyes, and with a friendly gesture allows his hand to slip under the fringe of the epaulette so that it may rest on the captain's shoulder. Thus does the ageing Napoleon find support once more in the young men of France.

When Caulaincourt brings the demands, he is accompanied only by Macdonald.

"Where is Ney?"

Silence. A pause. Then he is told the conditions. They probe him to the quick. To disavow the dynasty! For a decade the dynasty has been his goal.

"My personal withdrawal did not suffice? Must I, with my signature, disinherit my wife and my son? I cannot do this! I won their throne for them by my deeds!" The paradox has taken such deep root in his thoughts that he has ceased to be aware of his existence. Then he counts his troops again.

"I have twenty-five thousand men here; I can speedily bring up another eighteen thousand from Italy; Souchet has eighteen thousand, Soult forty. I shall fight! . . ."

The remaining troops are loyal, but the leaders are weary of the struggle. Why does he not place himself at the head of his guards? Because he can only think in terms of marshals, because the feudalist atmosphere is cutting him off from his stalwarts.

Here they all come again! They warn him, even Berthier joins with the others now, that Fontainebleau can easily be surrounded. He listens to them with dignified composure. Then he abruptly asks them whether they are prepared to march with him to the Loire; or to Italy, where they can join Eugene's forces. Behind the proposal, we sense new plans of our adventurer. But the men who stand before him are marshals and Frenchmen; they breathe the words "civil war"; they advise him to abdicate. The island of Elba has been chosen for his dwelling place; he had better take what he can get! He dismisses them.

"None of them has either heart or reins! I am not so much beaten by fortune, as by the ingratitude of my brothers-in-arms. It is infamous. All is over!"

Without, in the drawing-room, groups of courtiers and dignitaries have assembled. Voices are hushed as though a king lay dead. All are awaiting the signature. The Emperor is well aware of this, he allows no one to enter his room, he will keep them waiting till morning. After a feverish, sleepless night, his negotiators find him sitting in his dressing-gown before the fire, a broken man and pitiable.

They bring him the deed which they have signed in Paris that night. He is to receive Elba, and two million francs as annual subsidy; he is to retain the title of Emperor; he is to have a guard of four hundred men. Talleyrand had warned the allies that this proximity of the lion to France was a menace; he suggested Corfu, and even mentioned St. Helena. Fouché endeavours to shield the Emperor from a slow descent from the heights; in elegantly phrased letters he suggests that Napoleon should go straight to America, where, as a free citizen, life could be started anew.—The farther away from the coasts of Europe, the better!

All this leaves the Emperor cold. He is visioning something different. He sees how Macdonald is standing the test; in his secret heart he is comparing this marshal with those others who have shown so much ingratitude; he feels now that he has not honoured the man enough. In this hour when he has to sign his abdication, Napoleon says:

"I have not sufficiently rewarded you. Now I can do no more. Take the sword which Sultan Selim gave me and keep it in remembrance." While all are waiting for the signature, the Emperor sends for the gilded scimitar, and embraces the general as he presents it. Then Napoleon signs the act of abdication.

"The allied powers having declared that Emperor Napoleon is the sole obstacle to the re-establishment of peace in Europe, the Emperor, faithful to his oath, declares that he renounces, for himself and his heirs, the thrones of France and Italy, and that there is no sacrifice, not even that of life, which he is not ready to make for the interests of France."

The deed is done! All breathe freely again. The generals and the courtiers leave Fontainebleau; Maret alone remains. They hasten to Paris; even Berthier throws himself into the arms of the provisional government. Talleyrand and Fouché are at the head of things.

But the Emperor remains another nine days in his palace, and he is not alone. Around him, unshaken, his guards are encamped; they still muster twenty-five thousand men. Who else is with him? His brothers have taken to their heels. What is Josephine doing, at Malmaison? After she has wept, and sworn that she will follow the forsaken Emperor, she receives Napoleon's conqueror with sparkling eyes and adorned with all the pitiful appeal of a Niobe. The tsar wishes to play the part of a knightly cavalier, and succumbs to the renowned charms of the first empress. But Hortense, her daughter, receives the tsar's visit coldly and off-handedly. As soon as he is gone, she hastens to Fontainebleau and remains with the Emperor till his departure.

At first, his mother is with him. But, wishing to see her in safety, he persuades her to go away with Jerome. They will meet again later. When the empress says good-bye to Letizia, she utters polite commonplaces and wishes her mother-in-law well. The old lady, who sees through Marie Louise, and knows that all she cares for is security and enjoyment, answers this daughter of the Habsburgs: "That will depend upon you, and upon your future conduct."

The Emperor has no word from wife or son in reply to his numerous letters and messengers. While for himself he asks neither land nor money, for her he demands that, in addition to Parma, she should have Tuscany, or at least a strip of it which would bring her lands nearer to Elba and thus set up a link between man and wife. He writes to her advising as to the best halting-places on the route; Corvisart is to decide which waters will do her health most good; she is to take her personal treasure with her. Then he writes to the palace prefect that all the diamonds which are not her or his personal property must be given back to the treasury, for they belong to France.

Meanwhile the government has sent a confidential agent to the Tuileries with orders to seize the imperial treasure. All the gold and securities, valued at one hundred and fifty millions, were taken away; in plain words, stolen. These sums had been saved by Napoleon from his civil list during the fourteen years of his rule. His silver plate, all personal articles of value, his golden snuff-boxes, and even his handkerchiefs embroidered with the initial N., were taken at the same time. The order for this bears, among others, Talleyrand's signature. The Emperor, who until yesterday was the wealthiest man in Europe, journeys to Elba with three million francs as his fortune!

He is profoundly disheartened. Can anything disillusion him further? Lucien writes to the pope the day after the abdication, and becomes a Roman prince. Murat, acting on the advice of Fouché (who holds the net of intrigues during these last weeks), has entered Rome, has advanced his troops towards Tuscany, invading Elise's realm—always spurred on by Caroline, and always in alliance with England, which has occupied Tuscany. Elise, who at the last moment has staked on the wrong hazard, and has through a false calculation remained faithful to her brother, flees before her sister's troops, brings a child into the world while lying up at a mountain tavern, and in Bologna is taken prisoner by the Austrians. The only two of the pack who have behaved decently are Jerome and his wife.

The last days pass in sinister silence. "If a carriage drives into the palace yard, all prick up their ears. Is any one coming to bid Napoleon farewell? No one comes while affairs are being wound up. But a day or two before the departure, a veiled lady arrives, late in the evening. No one knows her, and she is not admitted. Countess Walewska waits a whole night, and when she goes away in the morning she leaves a letter for him. He sends after her, but she has gone. He writes:

"Marie! . . . The feelings which animate you touch me profoundly. They are worthy of your lovely soul and the goodness of your heart. . . . Think affectionately of me! Never doubt me! N."

As soon as he has recovered his old tranquillity of mind, the Emperor is promptly animated with new energy. Has he not an island as base of operations? Who knows what may come of it? Corsica, too, is an island in the Mediterranean! He orders a monograph and studies the geography and statistics of Elba. "The air is wholesome, the inhabitants are honest folk, and I hope that my good Louise will like the place well enough. He chooses his four hundred men; but the whole guard wants to go with him, though this will involve leaving wife and children. Among them are men whose hearts he had won two-and-twenty years earlier when he had been captain in Toulon, men who had followed his fortunes from Cairo to Moscow, through sixty battles.

He cheers up. Discussing predetermination with the palace prefect, and how death has passed him by during the last battles, he adds:

"A violent death is cowardice. I can see no greatness in shirking responsibility in that manner, like one who has gambled away his fortune. . . . Suicide is incompatible with my principles and with the position I have occupied in the world." They walk up and down the terrace in silence for a time, and then he says with a smile: "Between ourselves, a living drummer is better than a dead emperor!"

All the formalities have been accomplished; the allied commissioners who are to accompany him to Elba, four in number, have arrived; the start is fixed for noon. He writes in simple terms to tell his wife, and concludes: "Farewell, my good Louise. You can rest assured of the courage, the tranquillity, and the affection of your husband. N." He adds as a postscript: "A kiss for the little king!"

The start will be an easy matter, for no one has come to take leave.

But there are to be leave-takings after all. The old guard is waiting for him in the palace yard, drawn up in a square. As he comes down the steps, thousands of eyes are fixed on him. He must say something. What can he say? For twenty years he has only spoken to these men just before a battle and just after a victory, to inspire them or to thank them. Well, he will thank them now, though there has been no victory; he will thank them for the hundred victories of the past. He steps forward. "Vive l'Empereur!" He enters the square, and says:

"Soldiers of my old guard, I take leave of you. For twenty years I have seen you always upon the path of honour and glory. During the last few weeks, you have been models of bravery and fidelity, just as in the years of good fortune. . . . But there would have been civil war. That is why I sacrificed all other interests to those of the country. I am going away. . . . You, friends, continue to serve France. Her happiness has been my only thought. My good wishes go with you. Do not mourn my fate. If I have determined to go on living, it is that I may increase your fame. I shall write the story of the great deeds we wrought together. Farewell, my children. I would gladly press you all to my heart. At least let me kiss your colours!"

The general holds out the colours. Napoleon embraces him, and kisses the flag. "Good-bye, comrades!" He gets into the carriage. "Vive l'Empereur!" He drives away.

The war-hardened veterans stand there, blubbering like children. Their father has gone away. Never had he spoken to them more movingly. The dignified pathos of ancient Rome, the ardent imagery of his manifestoes, the similes and the exaltations, have vanished with the fever of battle. This Emperor spoke like a commander, this commander spoke like a company leader. His words were manly, blunt, and restrained. When he kissed the colours, it was an unparalleled gesture; never before had he done anything of the kind. They will tell their grandchildren what the great Emperor, their "petit caporal," has said to them this day. The grandchildren will tell their grandchildren in turn, and so the story will go down the generations.

But hardly has he left this soldierly atmosphere, in which he grew to manhood and then to greatness, when he has to face the mob. After the sobs of his old soldiers, come clamour, cries, and curses! As the train of carriages drives swiftly through Provence, the threatening shouts of the people deafen him: "Down with the tyrant! Kill the wretch!" In the villages where the horses are changed, women rage round his carriage, screaming at him, flinging stones, trying to force the coachman to shout "Vive le Roi!" At one of these villages, the crowd has prepared an effigy, a uniform coat stuffed with straw and smeared with mire and blood. Here they hail him with the cry: "Kill the murderer!" The carriages press on at top speed and the journey becomes a flight. Napoleon's first flight.

With rigid face, the Emperor looks at the mob and listens to the cries of execration. Are these the same people who ran beside his carriage, eager to catch a glance from his eyes? They are indeed the same! What he is now experiencing, he had foreseen, with the seer's vision of the misanthrope, at his first entry into Paris when the crowd had jubilantly welcomed him as conqueror. He sits huddled in a corner of the carriage, pale and silent; at each halt, the foreign commissioners jump out to guard the windows of his coach. Will he bear all this without making a sign? Will he draw his sword? He does not wear one now. In mufti, he can get away from his country, but not in his green uniform. Only once before has he had such an experience. It was on the Nineteenth Brumaire, when the radicals were shaking their fists at him. Then he did not draw his sword. Then, as now, he was powerless against the mob, for it was not his trade to beat the mutable many, nor was it his talent to persuade them. He is not a tribune; he is an emperor. One who can command as well as he, can do nothing but command. If he fights, it must be in a battle.

Movement! Air! In a lonely road, he has the carriage stopped, and one of the post-horses taken out of the traces. He fixes a white cockade on his plain round hat, and rides in front of the carriages, outstripping them, his servant following. Thus he makes his way to Aix, but halts short of the town, enters a wayside inn, and gives his name there as Campbell, a British colonel. This is his sixth name.

The little Provençal maid who waits at table prattles: "They'll finish him off before he reaches the sea!" "Colonel Campbell" nods, saying "Of course, of course!" to all her utterances. Then, when he is left alone with his servant, his head droops on the man's shoulder, he has a nap to make up for two sleepless nights. Kindly nature, this is your gift to the greatest of your warriors! When he wakes, the recent sounds and sights recur to his mind. With a shudder, he says in low tones:

"Never again! I shall be happier in Elba than ever before.

The sciences now, nothing more. I do not want to wear another European crown. You have seen what the people really is. Was I not right to despise man?"

When the carriages reach the inn, he thinks it wise, warned by his previous experiences, to change his clothes once more. Since time presses, he puts on the uniform of an Austrian general which belongs to Commissioner Koller; surmounts it with the cap of Truchsess, the Prussian colonel; and has a Russian cloak hung round his shoulders by Shuvaloff. Thus bedecked in a carnival costume, pieced together from garments belonging to the three allied powers, a fool on the heath, does Emperor Napoleon escape from his country.

Fréjus at last! This is the port where he landed on his return from Egypt, a beaten commander, who had lost all the battleships of France, and ought to have been tried by court-martial! But how enthusiastic, then, had been his reception by this leaderless people, for the memory of his successful Italian campaign was still fresh. Then, he had driven through triumphal arches on the journey to Paris; the journey he had now been making in the reverse direction, in danger of being stoned, and escaping murder only by a mummer's disguise! Fifteen years lie between, the rebirth of a State, the glory of a nation. Europe lies between, the clash of arms, dead soldiers rotting in their graves, the returning hero received with frenzied acclamations, a marshal rising from pothouse to palace, men of genius taking sides for and against the conquering nation—and a circlet of little golden leaves which the foreigner from the Mediterranean island had, with the simplicity of the self-made man, placed on his own brow.

XV

How big Corsica is! How high her mountains! Bastia is an admirable harbour; its fortifications can be seen through a spyglass. If taken from the eastern side. . . .

When the ruler of Elba rides among the hills of his new home, the silhouette of his old home lies spread before him; everything looms larger across the water. Forty times bigger, ten times as many inhabitants; he has all the figures, to a unit, in his head. Elba is nothing more than a mole-hill.

On the clear May morning when he landed, he was welcomed by a deputation of peasants and petty burghers in Porto Ferrajo. Timidly they had paid their compliments to the man who was to reign over them. But their astonishment was great when, instead of inviting them to a banquet, he leapt into the saddle and rode off to inspect the fortifications. On the morrow, orders began to fly about the sleepy little isle: Pianosa was to have two more batteries; the mole must be lengthened; the roads improved. When first the four hundred grenadiers appeared in the land, the natives looked at them askance as men of a foreign race. Soon, however, the forces were increased by the creation of a foreign battalion, and a National Guard. Napoleon once more has an army of over a thousand men; soon he has a small flotilla likewise. What for? Just for him to see after and take care of. He has a Council of State; Bertrand and Drouot (the generals who have accompanied him into exile) and a dozen inhabitants of the island, are members; and, together with Napoleon who presides over the assembly, they discuss improvements in the iron mines and the salt pits. Have you no mulberry culture here? The silkworms bring in good money over there, in Lyons; and if the French government imposes a tariff upon our produce, we can easily sell to Italy.

Save! We are so poor, and France makes no move to pay the promised allowance. The white house is smaller than the one in Ajaccio, and very much simpler; but there is no money for building additional accommodation; and when the "grand marshal" Bertrand draws up a list of mattresses and other bedgear, his master underlines the mistakes,—for he has every detail of his establishment by heart.

Is this indefatigable man never to realise what a parody is his administration over the tiny island, the diminutive army, the small household? Never! Here in Elba, where in the best of spirits and health he throws himself whole-heartedly into his undertakings, he comes to realise that it was not the masses that had allured him. To order, to build, to press his finger into the wax of humanity, these things he must do, urged onward by the impulse of his artist's soul. But, since humanity is not as wax, and since his constructions can never be finished and are always vibrant with life; since the opposition of material forces also takes a hand in the game, even when matter seems to have been conquered—he can only fulfil his mission by coercing and conquering the human spirit, by issuing orders and bringing suggestions to bear, by constant vigilance and constant upbuilding; in a word, by ruling. He has never been a dilettante or a parvenu; and, this being so, he drives the little wheel to-day with just as much precision and earnestness as he had driven the earth's sphere in former days.

But soon, when most of his enterprises are in good going order, he feels he is becoming lazy, even when he is studying mathematics. This causes him to reconsider his position.

"It is by no means difficult to accustom oneself to a life of meditation," he writes, "if one possesses within oneself the necessary reserves. I work hard in my study; when I emerge I have the delightful spectacle of my old grenadiers in front of me. . . . Born kings must suffer terribly when they are dethroned, for pomp and etiquette are the very marrow of their lives. For my part, I have always been a soldier, and became a king only by chance, so that these things have been nothing but a burden to me, whereas wars and camps come naturally. Out of my great past, I regret naught but my soldiers. After all my treasures and my crowns, my most cherished possessions are the couple of French uniforms they have allowed me to keep."

These are the words of an unpretentious king. Do people

not believe him? And does Europe laugh when, in his kingdom of Lilliput, he preserves the forms of kingship? Does Europe begin to suspect a secret in the island? The innate dignity, whereby long ago the young general had wrung respect from the bearers of inherited rank, to-day is still able to hold satirical visitors in check. Every one admires the natural simplicity of the lonely man who, despite the exiguity of his dwelling, still holds to the title of "Majesty." He lives in his island sans palace or fittings, sans court or ministers, only surrounded with the aureole of his deeds.

This return home brings solace to his heart—for Elba is Italy. The peasant speaks to him in the language Napolione had learned at Letizia's knee. The Mediterranean amid whose waters he was born and reared, the islands with their quiet shores, do they not all of them bring back memories of youthful days? Stone-pines, fig trees, and crags; the white houses among the vineyards; the sails, and the fishermen's nets; pride of clan, and the headkerchief worn at church; all these things seem to take him gently by the hand and lead him back to the dreams of childhood. Now the storm-racked nerves relax, and at length know a spell of repose. In these wholesome months, the Emperor comes to look upon his career as a visionary flight into the land of childish imagination; and it is only when he contemplates the men of his old guard that he realises something did happen during the years that separate Corsica from Elba.

"The Emperor lives very contentedly on his island," writes one who accompanied him there. "He seems to have forgotten the past. The management of his small household gives him occupation; he is now looking out for a suitable site to build his country-seat; we ride, and drive, and sail round the coasts as much as we please."

Since he has plenty of time on his hands, and since thrift is essential, he examines everything, to the minutest details. Just as, in the Tuileries, he himself drew up the list of his clothing, so now, in Elba, he says to Bertrand: "My underlinen is in a lamentable state. Part of it has never been unpacked, and it has not been marked. Give orders that everything must be laid out in drawers and presses, and that no one is to be given anything belonging to our court without furnishing a receipt. . . . There are not enough ordinary chairs. Have a sample sent from Pisa; they must not cost more than five francs apiece."

Europe laughs when it hears of this. Posterity stands bewildered before such energetic renunciation.

Once only do we hear a gentle sigh. He has climbed to the top of a hill whence he can look over the whole of his realm. Surveying the prospect, he says: "One must acknowledge that the island is very small." Like distant thunder, the fate of a man seems to rumble in these words; for an all too great imagination, confined within the narrow limits of Europe and cribbed within the circle of the folk intelligence of the nineteenth century, is doomed at the outset to be crushed.

With the summer, comes his mother. She, alone, is happy. Her son is no longer threatened with assassination or with battles. Here, all is peaceful and warm; Elba is almost as lovely as Corsica. Daily intercourse with him renews for her the good old times. It is as well that she has come; for, from the millions which she alone has put by, she now brings her son what he needs; and when he receives her banknotes, may we not picture mother and son smiling at one another? On his name-day, she invites him to a little rustic feast.

A dozen and more St. Napoleon days she has spent in Paris; the guns would fire the salute from the Invalides, Masses would be said; Senate and ministers, the court and foreign diplomats, would throng the halls of the Tuileries. When, in the evening, the rooms were filled with guests, and, amid the strains of music, there came and went all that France possessed of great names, of beauty, and of precious jewels; when the fireworks filled the August night-sky with brightness, and thousands of

(From the "Corpus Imaginum" of the Photographic Society, Charlottenburg.)

Napoleon as Emperor. Engraving by Bourgeois, after a painting by Jacques Louis David.

tiny lamps formed the initial N.—Letizia, surrounded by the kings who were the fruit of her womb, would stand silent and proud, thinking the old words so full of ominous warning. But to-day she is blithe; to-day she compares this jocund festivity with the little town of Ajaccio; to-day, for the first time, she thinks: "All the same, we achieved something fine!"

Letizia had been able, while in Rome, to heal many wounds dealt in the heat of the fray. The pope, on his return, had pardoned the mother of his sometime foe. She was not surprised when the whole court, when even her secretary (a Corsican), speedily went over to the Bourbon king. Has she not always foretold it? Caroline, alone, is not permitted to appear before her.

Pauline, Princess Borghese, merry and brilliant, does not hang long in the wind. She has always been the most affectionate, and has been clever enough to prefer real diamonds and nights of love to uncertain thrones and crowns. She comes to the island, so that, with her mother, she may bring cheer to the Emperor. She shakes out a basketful of gossip and news for his delectation.

Hardly a word from his brothers. One letter comes from Lucien. What propositions can he be laying before his banished brother? Will he, who lives in princely fashion in Rome, with magnanimous generosity offer Napoleon money or bring his influence to bear in his imperial brother's behalf? What does the "Prince of Canino" by the pope's grace write in his letter? He owns smelting furnaces, and Elba has iron ore wherewith to feed them: he asks his brother to provide him with the minerals. Crowns and gold, he has refused; but iron, which his brother still possesses, he can make good use of. Maybe he, who is a poet, is enjoying the farce of these blast-furnaces! Is it not a kindness that one still thinks of the exile? Who else writes?

Josephine is dead. A few weeks after Napoleon's departure, she died at Malmaison. No one knows if she ever wrote to him; what is certain is that she left debts amounting to three millions, which he had to pay. Hortense has been separated from her husband. She has become a duchess, and has made her most graceful curtsey before the Bourbon king, in the very room where she and her mother had held sway for so long. Little Léon, whom Letizia had for a time with her in Rome, resembles his father; he is reported to be courageous and full of pranks. These are all the members of Napoleon's family about whom he has news.

An English vessel brings the unknown lady who visited Fontainebleau to the island. In a marquee, beneath the chestnut trees, the Emperor receives Countess Walewska. For two days and two nights they are inseparable. The Emperor only issues forth to give the necessary orders, and the four-year-old boy, dressed in the Polish national costume, plays in the meadow with the tall grenadiers. The Emperor would like to keep Walewska by his side, but he does not wish to provide the empress with an excuse for not coming to live with him. Thus, for the second time, he sacrifices on the altar of the Habsburg princess the phantom of his happiness. Walewska sails away. Her ship encounters bad weather, and the Emperor is filled with restless anxiety until he receives tidings that she has arrived safely at Leghorn.

How marvellously are the threads weaving themselves into the tissue of a legend! With wizard spells this man of forty-five links up epochs and customs. Here he is, a petty prince on a Mediterranean isle: he receives his beloved, the lady with whom he had lived in the imperial palace at Schönbrunn when he himself was an enemy and unknown to the proprietor; to-day he is once again this man's foe, and another woman whom he had invited to his arms from the self-same palace has long since forsaken him; yet his natural son, born in a lonely castle in Poland, is playing beneath the trees of the southern land and wears the dress of a foreign folk which the Emperor had once promised to free. Who could believe that all this had come to pass within five years? A hundred years seemed likelier for the accomplishment of so many events. With such nets, what other fish could one expect to catch but the golden ones of the fairy tale? A thousand years ago a great emperor was banished and left forsaken on an island; but from a distant realm a beautiful, tragical woman found the way to him across the sea, and brought him his son.

In truth Napoleon is forsaken by wife and child. This loss cuts him no less, maybe even more cruelly, than the loss of power, for his conception of marriage is conservative and bourgeois. Constantly, even during the via dolorosa of his last journey through France, he has written to Marie Louise; he has planned a new house for her. But his letters remain unanswered. Believing that his correspondence has been intercepted, he at last writes to the grand duke of Tuscany, her uncle, begging for news; for "I trust that Your Royal Highness has preserved a little friendliness towards me, in spite of the events which have changed the sentiments of so many men. . . . If so, I beg that you will look favourably upon the tiny commune which feels the same towards you as does Tuscany. . . ." Ay, thus writes the prince of this diminutive isle, a prince with no more than twenty thousand subjects, to the mighty grand duke! But the grand duke keeps silence.

When Napoleon realises the sluggishness of the human heart, his old defiance regains the ascendant. It is with a sense of relief that we hear his well-known voice ring out again, after the anguish of this grovelling letter—a letter that would never have been written but for his wife's sake. He exclaims: "These sovereigns, who were wont to send me, in all solemnity, their delegations of ambassadors, who gave a daughter of their blood to share my bed, and who called me 'Brother,' are now cursing me as a usurper, and spit upon my picture since they cannot spit upon the original. They have bespattered the majesty of kings with mud! What is the title of emperor? Had I no other name to bequeath, posterity would laugh. . . . In classical days, the vanquished were robbed of their children, that these might be paraded before the people when the conqueror was celebrating his triumph. . . ."

What must be the tenor of Napoleon's thoughts when he learns how, on that shameful day of cowardice and confusion, the lad of four had refused to leave the palace of his father; of how, when the little king of Rome had met his grandfather for the first time, he had uttered the innocent words: "I have seen the emperor of Austria. He is not handsome." This was precisely what Napoleon had wished to avoid. The fate of Astyanax has been prepared for the boy; and even though he is made much of, the child is well aware that he must no longer mention his father's name. Though he has received the symbolical names of Napoleon Francis and thus embodies the unhappy union of two antagonistic worlds, the name of Napoleon is soon destined to be heard no more. For, when the young cuckoo is introduced into the Habsburg nest, he is called Francis, and nothing else. Later, when the empress' secretary is leaving Vienna and presents himself to take farewell, the boy draws him into a window recess and says in a hurried whisper: "Tell my father I love him tremendously!"

What must be the tenor of Napoleon's thoughts when he hears gossip about a certain Neipperg, an Austrian officer, a man of no account, and one whose only way into history is through the bedroom of a Habsburg princess—who would herself never have been heard of had it not been for her marriage to Napoleon. Thus terrible are the blows of fate, and his intimates think it natural enough when they see their master weeping over his boy's portrait.

But now Pauline arrives, fascinating as ever, in the best of spirits. To amuse him, she mimics the grimaces that are made by the worthies of the island and their wives when, at the weekly receptions, the Emperor asks them how many children they have, and whether they think he ought to build a hospital. As the year draws on, Italians from the mainland come in increasing numbers. Persons with satisfactory recommendations—historians, poets, men of birth, and even Englishmen—secure a good reception; and he will talk to them for hours, though only of the past, with never a word about the future. He is delighted to hear such visitors rail at the Austrian regime which has now been set up once more, but he will pay no heed to conspirators who wish him to come to Italy as leader of a revolt. His thoughts range towards the other coast, and by slow degrees mature into plans.

What is Paris saying?

To him this is still the question of questions. The news brought to him in the journals twice a week, and the information he gleans from his visitors, lead him to turn new possibilities over in his mind. But it must not be supposed that Napoleon began the new epoch with a definite plan. When he landed in Elba, it was an open question in his mind whether he would ever quit the island. Still, the thought of future possibilities was intensified in him by the usual forebodings of an adventurer—the adventurer he had become since the failure at Moscow. "A living drummer is better than a dead emperor." Slowly, as the conditions change, he makes plans and rejects them, renews and modifies his designs. They turn upon what is happening in Paris and in Vienna.

What is Paris saying about the Bourbons? Hardly is Napoleon away, when they make their "entry" after the usual manner of exiled kings who return; and though the newspapers, under duress of the censorship the Emperor had established, lie like troopers, in his remote island he can learn the ridiculous truth. Four persons are sitting in a small carriage. The Parisians, whose risibilities are easily touched, certainly have something to laugh at. The king is there, in an amazing rig-out, in plain clothes, but decked with gigantic epaulettes; a man so fat that he has three chins; and he smiles at the gaping crowd. Beside him is the duchess of Angoulême, her face tearful with reminiscence. On the opposite seat are the prince of

Condé, a very old man, and the duke of Bourbon; they wear the uniforms of the good old days, which none of the younger onlookers have ever seen before. This carriage, freighted with the resurrected ghosts of those who had been laid to rest twenty-two years ago, was attended by Emperor Napoleon's sulky-looking guard, men whose uniforms, shot and slashed, bore witness to the titanic struggles that had been waged in the interim.

The Emperor makes eager enquiries concerning the habits of his successor on the throne, and is gratified to learn that Louis has taken over his room without making any changes. The king's demeanour is said to be far from regal. According to a German description of this date, Louis was "extremely obese, so fat that he can hardly walk. Wearing black satin boots, he is supported on each side, and would stumble over a straw. He is clad in a sort of blue soutane with a turn-over red collar and hanging golden epaulettes of an antique pattern." This sort of thing keeps the Emperor amused for a whole hour. For a dozen years, England has been publishing caricatures depicting Napoleon's camp manners in the palace of the Bourbons, and now this legitimate ruler, set up by England, is a veritable caricature of a monarch. What is Louis doing to show his good will towards the people?

He has granted a constitution? But soon comes news that this gracious gift exists only on paper. The old inequalities, the privileges of caste, which had cost the present king's brother his head, are quietly stealing in through the back door. The nobles are not liable to military service, and men of humble birth have no chance of rising to high office. The new nobility is made a mock of. King Louis, a good old man, reasonable enough, is led by his brother, the gloomy count of Artois. Around the latter are concentrated the vengeful émigrés, who are demanding the return of their property; but the law guarantees the rights of the actual holders. The king, therefore, gives peerages and large pensions to the émigrés.

What is this? So the clergy is rising to power once more! The priests are on the side of the old nobility, and by threats of hell-fire induce the dying to execute wills in favour of the sometime owners of confiscated property. On Sundays, though the new constitution guarantees religious freedom, all business is suspended under threat of punishment. Religious processions again make their way through the streets. But there is a reaction against ecclesiasticism. When Christian burial is refused to an actress who has lived a gay life and is the darling of the Parisians, there is a riot, the first under the restored regime.

People are beginning to see how much they owed to their foreign liberator. With intense delight, the exile contemplates a caricature showing Louis riding pillion behind a Cossack, making his way into France over French corpses. When Wellington, the conqueror of Spain, comes to Paris as British ambassador, he meets angry glances when he walks the streets. What is the new regime doing for the thousands who may no longer remain soldiers? The officers are put on half-pay, and those who are not practising Catholics are cashiered. A new royal guard, consisting of gentlemen of noble birth, is richly endowed; the nobles' military academy is reopened; but the schools for the orphans of members of the Legion of Honour are done away with. Disillusionment spreads through France more quickly than the Emperor had expected.

But the tone in Elba is not Jacobin. Napoleon does not abandon his system, although he recognises his mistakes: "France needs an aristocracy. For its foundation, however, time and memories are requisite. I made princes and dukes, and gave them land and wealth; but they were men of low birth, so it was impossible to make noblemen of them. I tried, therefore, to unite them by marriage with old families. Had I been granted the twenty years I wanted for the establishment of France's greatness, I could have done much. Fate willed otherwise."

On the whole, like a chessplayer when the game is finished, he frankly acknowledges the wrong moves that have led to his defeat. Nor is he cautious in the choice of persons to whom he pours out such confessions. He tells English visitors that he ought to have made peace after Dresden. But when they ask why he did not make peace in Châtillon, he answers proudly:

"I could not make a peace dishonourable to France. Belgium was part of France when I rose to power. Could I cede the lands I had conquered, and go back to the Bourbon frontiers? Never! . . . I am a born soldier. Suddenly, I found myself in the midst of the revolution. The throne was vacant. I took it, and kept it as long as I could. Now I am once more what I was to begin with, a soldier. . . ."

Those who know the man will recognise from such thoughts that he is still unbroken. But what amazes us is the freedom with which he speaks of the past. Never, in Elba, does he show any desire to falsify his history. And yet, during the first months, he believes his career finished, and has no thought of trying a new coup de main. He even fancies that he would like to become a justice of the peace in England. "What would happen to me if I went to England? Would people throw stones at me? The London mob is a dangerous factor." The Englishmen to whom he thus talks assure him that their country is hospitable. He makes a mental note of this assurance.

The Vienna congress is the first thing to set him in motion. Four monarchs, allied against one republic, were at length able, after a decade, to annihilate it; five monarchs, now all united, had assembled to reorganise Europe, and there was no longer an enemy worth considering to hold them in check; but four and a half conquerors (if the Bourbon ruler can be accounted as half) were soon to be disunited, thanks to the inborn jealousy with which each one of them regarded his fellows. Does the tsar want to take the whole of Poland as his share of the spoil; and does Prussia want Saxony? What will happen, then, to Galicia; and what about the worthy king of Saxony, Bourbon's ally? A split is inevitable. By New Year, three months after the opening of the congress, the coalition has been broken up. Ministers and potentates who had so recently been celebrating their victory in a series of festivities, have begun to cheat one another. The Habsburg ruler is now allied with England and France against the Russians and the Prussians, by whose side the Austrians had a few months earlier been fighting against Napoleon.

Metternich's levity, laziness, vanity, intriguing disposition (this is Stein's description), dominated the situation: "he twists our excellent and victorious monarchs round his fingers." A Saxon nobleman writes from Vienna: "The king of Prussia is the embodiment of wrath. . . . The king of Denmark is . . . well-meaning and sometimes intelligent. The king of Bavaria looks like an uncouth and morose wagoner. The grand duke of Baden is huge, gloomy, vain, and robust. . . . The old duke of Weimar lives as jovially as ever he did." The hopes of the man of Elba rise as he reads and hears all this. "My time will come," he thinks, "when the congress goes up in the air!" Henceforward, he is in receipt of secret information concerning the currents of opinion in Vienna. The faithful Maret is able to arrange an intelligence service. But while the congress, a brightly lit pleasure ship, rolling for lack of ballast, is intriguing and enjoying itself, in the crow's nest sits Napoleon's old enemy, keeping anxious watch. He has his spies in Leghorn, who report every ship that sails to Elba, and tell him the names of the passengers.

Thus do the old adversaries eye one another across mountains and seas and across the documents of the diplomats, until it seems as if all these people of importance had come together in Vienna to furnish a lively setting for the game of chess the two experts are playing. Does either of them recall that night just before the Eighteenth Brumaire, when they had been scared by the clatter of hoofs from the mounted patrol, and had turned pale in their dread of arrest?

This much is certain, that at Vienna Talleyrand remains a shrewd judge of men. Regarding Murat as a dangerous personality, he would like to have the king of Naples shipped off to the Azores, nearly a thousand miles from the nearest continent. But his ruling passion, avarice, comes in the way. At the congress, Murat, driven into a corner in the defence of his kingdom, promises Talleyrand a large sum of money in return for the minister's princedom of Benevento. Talleyrand therefore drops the plan against Murat, and concocts a new scheme. The Emperor is to be kidnapped. But the spies in Leghorn report that this will only be possible if one of the four captains who command his ships can be suborned.

When Napoleon gets wind of these intrigues, the adventurer's blood of his Corsican home runs swiftly through his veins. He has the defences of Elba strengthened, and his artillerymen are trained in the use of hand-grenades. "I am a soldier, and am ready to face a firing squad. But I will not be deported! Before they can do that they will have to take my citadel by storm." No attempt is made. In Vienna there is now a better understanding, and the likelihood of the rupture of negotiations diminishes. In France, however, disaffection to the Bourbons is growing. The general upshot is to stimulate the Emperor's determination. His thoughts run as follows:

"If the congress closes with a peace festival after all the documents have been signed, the phalanx will have been reconstituted. But now, when it is still imperfectly consolidated, a touch will break it to pieces. France is murmuring against the Bourbons; Paris makes fun of them; every one detests the allies. There are a hundred signs to show that the old army is devoted to me—the Emperor. The Bourbons are fainthearts, and will run away. As soon as I regain my position, my son and heir will be sent back to me."

Calculations, only calculations; and never has he reckoned more soberly. None the less, though he considers his figures with the utmost care, in the last resort he relies upon psychological reactions. "I count upon taking them by surprise. A bold deed upsets people's equanimity, and they are dumbfounded by a great novelty." He adds: "I am the cause of France's unhappiness. I must effect a cure." In the end of February, he sends for his treasurer. "Have you plenty of money? How much does a million in gold weigh? What is the weight of a hundred francs? How much does a box filled with books weigh? . . . Take a couple of packing cases, put all the gold coin you have at the bottom, and fill up the case with my books; my valet will give them to you. Discharge the present staff of servants; pack their trunks and pay them off. Everything must be kept strictly secret."

In alarm, the man hastens to General Drouot. They exchange glances, but keep their own counsel. Next day, Napoleon orders that no ships are to leave the harbour. Everything has been quietly prepared; an expedition like that to Egypt, but on a small scale.

On the eve of his departure, he plays a game of écarté with the ladies; but he soon leaves the table and goes into the garden, whence he does not return. His mother, according to her own story, finds him sitting under a fig tree. After brief hesitation, he lays his hand on her forehead, and says, much moved:

"I will tell you all about it. No one else must know, not even Pauline."

Then he goes back to his old tone, as if he were talking to Berthier:

"I must tell you that I am leaving next evening."

"Where are you going?"

"To Paris." A pause. "I should like your advice."

The mother's heart stops beating for a moment. How she has enjoyed the last six months; the period of quiet intercourse with her son. An end to the tranquillity and the security!

But Letizia is a proud woman and a clever one. She knows that nobody can hold him back when he has made up his mind, and that the only effect of anxious dissuasion will be to disturb his composure. She says:

"Follow your destiny. It cannot be God's will that you are to die from poison, or after an inactive old age; though it may well be his will that you are to die sword in hand. Let us put our trust in Mother Mary."

On the last evening, the authorities are summoned by their sovereign. He announces his imminent departure. "I have been extraordinarily well pleased here. As a sign of confidence, I am leaving my mother and my sister. To your care, too, I entrust this country, to which I attach great importance." The governor and the mayor express their lively regret. The tone befits the departure of a distinguished guest, who has been spending a few months in a lovely island for the benefit of his health, and is sorry that the time has come for his return home.

He goes on board, and at dawn seven little frigates, carrying a thousand men and a few guns, set sail for the French coast. He stands on the deck. The outlines of Elba, where he has lived so peacefully, and of Corsica, where many years before he had made stormy attempts to force his way upwards, fade into the distance. Slowly the coast of the French Riviera begins to show clearly through the mists of the first day of March. Let us look into the Emperor's mind:

"What is the minimum? Defeat and death. What is the maximum? Europe? No use thinking any more about Europe! The dream of the United States of Europe is finished. I cannot get another million Frenchmen, and the foreign nations are not ready for my scheme. I must give France a constitution, and must accommodate myself to governing through Chambers. The time for dictatorships is over. Besides, we are not in Paris yet. What will the army do?"

His thoughts are coloured with the spirit of the time. He is a man of forty-five, with more past than future; no longer young enough to take the world by storm, but not too old for a desperate venture. Thus does Napoleon again draw near to French shores, in a mood betwixt courage and renunciation.

XVI

The mountains are calling, the valleys are echoing, as the procession of a thousand men who landed at Cannes wends its way through one Alpine village after another. An enthusiastic crowd encircles the old guard which has pursued its way along the road of history without jubilation and without sorrow, imperturbable as a rock. The peasants, these sons of the hills, in the selfsame hamlets, had once before seen him, a lean, small, unknown general; in those days he had relieved them from the burden of maintaining an undisciplined soldiery, and had led the troops over the Alps to victory. These mountain folk were the first to see the miracle he wrought; they plumed themselves on the thought that from their villages the Emperor had gone forth. And now, of a sudden, he is among them again! Surely the procession of the thousand will work a spell, and seem to be the march of prophets and saviours?

They come from their mountain fastnesses; women and children bring up the rear; songs against the king are composed and sung; in the lesser towns, the bolder spirits force the city fathers to go forth to meet the new comer; for more than a hundred miles he encounters none but peasants.

Napoleon had reckoned upon this. He would not face a march through Aix and Avignon, through the monarchical provinces. He preferred to leave his few cannon behind in the snow-covered mountain paths, in order the quicker to reach Dauphiné. Here the peasants had received the most generous distribution of the nobles' lands. They are full of anger now against king, priest, and émigré, who, after the lapse of twenty-five years, are contesting the peasants' right to hold these lands. Was not the great revolution made to protect the poor?

Was it not made by peasants in the country and workmen in the town? The Consul had not taken back anything from them; even the Emperor had only called up their sons; they have never ceased to look upon him as one of themselves, for their minds moved slowly and their hearts were constant. Now, the king had come back again, and forthwith the nobles had begun to squabble over the fields the peasant had tilled.

The souls of the countryfolk were heavy at the change of fortune. Fifteen years ago the mood had been similar when Napoleon, returning from Egypt in his little ship, had landed, and the whole of southern France had hailed him as saviour. What can have happened in the last ten months, to make these people receive with every token of joy the man whom they had so recently execrated? True, he had passed through another part of the country at that time; and the national misfortune had needed a scapegoat. His disfavour among the folk had been as brief as his defeat. But belief in him lasted as long as the years of his glory.

What will the first troops we meet do? He himself, when he took leave, had urged them to serve the fatherland. And the fatherland was the king! They wear the Bourbon's white cockade, they eat the king's bread, from the lips of patrician officers they have received a new and ugly picture of the erstwhile leader. Everything will depend on his power of suggestion. Uncertain feelings govern his heart as he strides inland from Cannes. To his left, lies the fort of Antibes. Does he recognise the tower wherein he was thrown when Robespierre fell? In just such a tower, the Bourbon will fling him, against just such a wall Europe will stand him, if he should fail on the morrow to accomplish what his glance and his word have so often succeeded in doing before.

Outside Grenoble, near La Mure, he has his first encounter with the royal troops. They have orders to exterminate him and his "band of brigands"; the officers have taken the oath to the king just as in former days they had taken the oath to the

Emperor. The order to attack is given. Is the blood of brethren to be shed? That is what Napoleon has spent a lifetime in avoiding. Is this highway to be turned into a battlefield? He alights from his horse, takes ten strides towards them, and shouts:

"Soldiers of the fifth army corps! Don't you know me? If there is one among you who wishes to kill his Emperor, let him come forward and do so. Here I am!" Saying which, he throws open his grey cloak.

A terrible pause. What will happen?

Those are our brethren! This is our general! We have seen him in so many battles, standing on a hillock, or sitting over the bivouac fire, or facing the musket shots and cannon balls! Must not nature and remembrance overpower the influence of recent vows? The soldiers cry: "Vive l'Empereur!" A general running to and fro ensues, guards and soldiers mingling; caps are stuck upon bayonet points—what does one more hole in the blue cloth matter? An hour later, two thousand instead of one thousand fall in behind their leader.

This encounter on the high road to Grenoble, this moment of time, his call, his aspect, were decisive. The man of action had won back to leadership through his own deed; the middle-aged warrior had regained life, power, and realm, by a look and a word. Thus he reaches Grenoble. By a manifesto he communicates his thoughts to the people:

"Frenchmen! . . . After the fall of Paris my heart was torn, but my spirit remained unshaken. . . . My life belongs to you, and must once more be made useful to you. In my exile, I heard your plaints and your cries. . . . You accused me of too long a slumber, saying I was sacrificing the interests of the country to my own repose. Encompassed by dangers, I have sailed over the sea. Now I am in your midst, to demand my rights, which are also your rights.

"Soldiers! We are not conquered! . . . Marmont's treachery delivered the capital into the hands of the enemy, and disorganised our army. . . . Now I have come! Your general, who was elected to the throne by the suffrage of the people, and raised aloft on your shields, has returned to you. Rally to him! . . . Wear the tricolour cockade again, the cockade of our days of victory! Let the eagles which you bore at Ulm and Austerlitz, at Jena, Eylau, and Friedland, at Eckmühl and Wagram, at Smolensk and on the Moskva, at Lützen and Montmirail, once more wave on high! . . . Possessions, rank, and glory, for yourselves and for your children, have no worse foes than those princes who have been forced upon you by foreign powers. . . . Victory will guide us forward through the storms, and the eagles shall fly from one church steeple to the other until at last they alight on Notre Dame!"

Vive l'Empereur! The troops in Grenoble, together with the imperial nobles, come over. Seven thousand men follow him to Lyons. Lyons comes over. Masséna, who had been serving the king, journeys from Marseilles and pays homage to the Emperor.

"Where is Ney?" Embarrassed silence. "With the king?"

They tell him about the council of war in Paris. Since the terrible news was brought, the fat king and his lean court have sat there trembling. The "Moniteur," which had lied in Napoleon's favour for fifteen years, now lies on behalf of the king: the Emperor, it announces, is dead. Just as they are deliberating what to do, old Count Condé enters the room and asks his royal cousin whether on Maundy Thursday the king himself should not officiate at the washing of feet. The king is writing a manifesto to the army. But who is sitting by him, his mainstay, the true leader of the Bourbon army? What is the man's name?

It is Marshal Ney. When, on the retreat from Moscow he had been cut off from the main body and appeared to be lost, his master had cried: "Ney is lost! I would give the two hundred millions from my cellars in the Tuileries, if I had him again!" Now he rises from among the royal plenipotentiaries gathered round the conference table; he swears to annihilate his sometime master. But when the breeze of general enthusiasm sweeps by him, he veers; his corps dons the tricolour cockade, and in Besançon he sends word to the Emperor that he would like to write a vindication of his conduct. But the Emperor waves the proposal aside, saying: "Tell him I love him the same as ever, and that to-morrow I shall embrace him."

What a master-stroke! True, he forgives; but he leaves Ney on tenterhooks till the morrow. Next day, the marshal stammers: "I love you, Sire; but as a son of the fatherland. . . . I was forced to kneel down before that fat hog to receive the cross of St. Louis! Had you not come, we should have chased him away ourselves."

"Marvellous! How vacillating he is, how pale!" These thoughts flit through the Emperor's mind as he asks his questions.

The count of Artois has fled. The very morning of the flight, the guards had sworn to die with him; by midday, they had rallied to the Emperor. Such behaviour does not please Napoleon, and he keeps this portion of the guard at arm's length. But there is one man who had remained loyal to Louis until the Bourbon was in safety; not till then does he change sides. This recruit, Napoleon welcomes, and with his own hand decorates him with the emblem of the Legion of Honour!

But what a change! The more this avalanche of soldiers grows as he marches forward towards Paris, the more peaceful do his speeches become. In one town after another, he addresses the municipal councillors and the citizens in the following words: "War is at an end. Peace and liberty! The principles of the revolution must be protected from the onslaughts of the émigrés. The treaties with Europe must be adhered to. France will win back her glory without war. We must be content to be the most esteemed nation, without trying to dominate other countries."

Does the people grasp the significance of the new tone? If the nation understands, is there belief in its genuineness? Must one be content? Glory without war? To a high official, an old acquaintance whom he meets on the march and in whom at length he finds an intelligent listener after addressing dull-witted citizens and partisan officers, he gives this political explanation:

"The spirit of the people is changed. In earlier days, the nation thought only of glory; now it thinks only of liberty. In the past, I brought the nation glory; I will not withhold liberty now. Freedom can be enjoyed in full, when power rests upon a good constitution. . . . Only—no anarchy! That would bring us back to the days of the despotic republicans, when every one had a finger in the pie. I shall retain only so much power as is essential for governing properly."

In the naïve closing sentence lies the new problem. He has broached the question; he is determined to stabilise the basic ideas of democracy. One thing is the same as on the Eighteenth Brumaire: no party politics! "I don't want to write to them," he says, when advised to forgive the turncoats. "They would believe that I was pledged to them. How are things in the Tuileries?"

"Nothing has been changed; not even the eagles have been removed." He is gay, bubbling over with good humour. He laughs.

"I suppose King Louis found the eagles decorative! What are they playing at the theatre? How is Talma? Were you at court? I've been told that the Bourbons looked like parvenus, did not know what to talk about, nor how to behave."

How inquisitive he is! How full of malicious joy! How he yearns for the air of Paris! He seeks his revenge in mockery, he whom the others had so long held up to ridicule. He is told of the parsimony of the court. He is shown the king's effigy on a twenty-franc piece.

"Do you see? They've got it again: 'God protect the king'!

My device is: 'God protect France'! They've left out those words. They were always like that: everything for themselves; nothing for France!" In the course of three minutes he enquires after twenty persons. When he is told that Hortense has been made a duchess, he answers simply:

"She should have called herself Madame Bonaparte. That name is worth more than all the rest."

His words are symbolic of the new epoch. If he calls himself Bonaparte once more, grants a constitution, allows liberty, and does not grasp at more power than he actually needs, he can make himself king of France. Then, after the failure of his attempt at the unification of Europe, he will still be able to become the happy exemplar of a modern prince by God's grace. He has always ruled as circumstances might dictate. Now, called to power for the second time, and after his imaginative flight towards far horizons, he will still prove himself a master. The road lies open.

The road to Paris is likewise open. The Bourbon king has run away, and the majority of the inhabitants are on the Emperor's side. Any one who might still have dreaded a fight with the last royal troops, must have overestimated them. When the Emperor is yet a hundred miles from the capital, the remnants of the royal guard flee from the city. The Emperor's army overtakes the king, but allows him to escape to a seaport, being content to take the silver he is carrying off with him in sixty carts, and to seize his cannon. France has a hearty laugh at this fat old gentleman, who had been escorted from England to Paris by enemy soldiers, and now makes all speed back to England with the soldiers of France chasing him.

Paris is calm. The town has long since forgotten how to take the initiative. During the twenty days between the Emperor's landing in the south and his arrival at the capital, the thermometer of the press registers the following degrees: "The monster has escaped from his place of exile."—"The Corsican werewolf has landed at Cannes."—"The tiger appeared at Gap, troops were sent against him, the wretched adventurer ended his career in the mountains."—"The fiend has actually, thanks to treachery, been able to get as far as Grenoble."—"The tyrant has reached Lyons, where horror paralysed all attempts at resistance."—"The usurper has dared to advance within a hundred and fifty miles of the capital."—"Bonaparte moves northward with rapid strides, but he will never reach Paris."——"To-morrow Napoleon will be at our gates."—"His Majesty is at Fontainebleau."

When, at length, without having had to fire a shot, the Emperor mounts the steps of the palace he had been compelled to leave thirteen months before, Paris is overawed by his soldiers, and the émigrés have fled with the king. All is quiet. He notes the fact, listens attentively, and says: "They have let me come, just as they let the others go."

Now he has his first disappointment! The march on Paris had been glorious, and in after days he spoke of it as the most splendid experience in his life. But here, in the city which will ultimately decide his fate, the city whose favour he has wooed more assiduously than he ever fought for any realm, the city he has never wholly conquered, he encounters moral resistance. Those whose favour he courts are no longer in the arms of their new friend; but they are listless, as if, after excess of passion, their vital energy had run down. Still, here he is, and he must bestir himself.

He looks to Vienna for a sign.

A week after Napoleon's landing in France, Metternich goes to bed at three o'clock, and is awakened at six by a messenger who hands him a despatch. He reads the inscription on the envelope, "General Consulate, Genoa," angrily turns over and goes to sleep again. He does not open the missive till several hours later, to read: "Campbell, the English commissioner, has just called to enquire whether Napoleon has been seen in Genoa. He has vanished from the island of Elba."

The bomb! Those who were yesterday still intriguing

against one another, now become thick as thieves once more. The vows which have so often been broken are renewed. The first to think of declaring the man an outlaw is Baron vom Stein, whom Napoleon had outlawed five years earlier. The possibility is discussed, but father-in-law Francis of Habsburg cannot make up his mind to the step; he would like to ask Marie Louise first. Four years ago she was devoted to her husband. She has never breathed a word of complaint to her father or to any of her women friends. Why should she? Napoleon had done whatever she wanted; she had been courted and wealthy; he had been the most equable of husbands; the parents had shared in the games of the little boy. Will she now become the Emperor's advocate?

The wife of Napoleon and the mistress of the Austrian officer prefers to take up her pen and write a formal declaration to the congress. She will have nothing to do with the Emperor, and she will put herself under the protection of the allies. Such is her answer to that hour when Napoleon had had to choose between the mother's life and the child's, and had decided in favour of the mother. Not until his wife has cast her vote against him, is the Emperor made an outlaw: "The powers declare that Napoleon Bonaparte has placed himself outside the bounds of civil and social relationships, and that as an enemy and disturber of the peace of the world he is consigned to public prosecution."

The tidings leave him unmoved. He is used to being outlawed. When he left Corsica, he and all his relatives were under sentence of outlawry. The word "outlaw" had been shouted at him in the Orangerie at Saint-Cloud. The pope had pronounced the major excommunication against him. All three anathemas had glanced harmless from his coat of mail, so that he deemed himself impregnable. But this fourth ban will lay him low.

He still continues to hope in the Habsburg. Announcing his intention to summon the Electoral Colleges of the Empire to a great assembly, he speaks of the gathering, in Carlovingian terminology, as a Champ de Mai, for he intends to have the empress and his son crowned there. He thinks that this will ensure Austrian support, and writes to his wife:

"I am master of France. The people and the army are wild with enthusiasm! No one but the so-called king has run away to England. . . . I expect you here in April with my son." The thought of his dynasty is ineradicable.

But even this most natural of feelings assumes a distorted form, for his feelings are in pawn to the old world. Writing to the man who has just outlawed him, he says: "At the moment when providence has recalled me to the capital of my States, it is my chief desire, the object of my tenderest inclination, to see my wife and son once more." He goes on to speak of his wife, who must certainly reciprocate his longing. Then: "All my endeavours are directed towards the firm establishment of this throne which the love of my people guarantees and restores to me; and towards handing it down to my son in due time, based upon an imperishable foundation. . . . Since a lasting peace is essential to the attainment of this important and sacred aim, there is nothing nearer to my heart than to remain at peace with all the powers."

Is this sublime, or is it ridiculous? Napoleon renounces war, and abandons his designs on Europe. He speaks truth when he says that he needs nothing more than France. The monarchs who had conquered him last year have formed a new alliance against him, and have declared him an outlaw. The sentence of outlawry has been signed by Emperor Francis, in the Austrian capital, with Marie Louise's express authorisation. She had left him after the last defeat; had thrown up the regency which she had sworn to carry on faithfully; had taken the boy with her; had thrown herself into another man's arms, and is still living with him: the Emperor knows these things. But now, instead of beginning the new era with a clear-cut severance from all that has overthrown and disappointed him, he begins by suing for the friendship of this old throne which had triumphed over his new one.

This is the ban, this is the outlawry, which will for the second time bring him to his doom.

XVII

The adventurer now becomes a rat-catcher, like the Pied Piper of Hamelin. Bourbon had been clever enough to invite the best talents to serve him; and as a result of this, when once the royalist national anthem had been sung, all went smoothly for him. Some of these men know not whether to go or to stay: they wait upon events. But Napoleon, who has always commanded, who has never canvassed for any one's services, places the flute of the tempter to his lips: he knows that now is the time for suggestion and smiles. The loyal few, he restores to their posts, with a shake of the hand. Maret, Davoust, and Caulaincourt, form part of his ministry.

He knows all that those who have proved ungrateful have been doing, and he judges them by their record. Officials, officers, and court dignitaries, again flock to his levees. A count of the old aristocracy comes likewise. Napoleon had called this man back from exile and had made him senator; but at the Bourbon restoration the count had gone over to the king. Now, as the Emperor draws near, the count casts his eyes heavenward and seems to imply that his actions were dictated by God's inscrutable will. The Emperor smiles. Not a word is exchanged. But the count comes no more to court. When, on the other hand, one of Marmont's generals, a man who had delivered a decisive speech in the war council before the marshal's defection, approaches Napoleon and begins to stammer out an explanation, the Emperor does not smile. He says, in an overbearing tone: "What do you want of me? Can you not see that I do not know you?"

Here is Oudinot: for twenty years he was Bonaparte's companion-in-arms; now he comes back to the Emperor. "You see, Oudinot? You were worshipped as a god by the Lorrainers; two hundred thousand peasants were ready, even last year, to go through fire and water for your sake. To-day I have to protect you against these same peasants!"

Here is Rapp. He has wavered longer than the rest, and even now comes hesitatingly to his master. "You've kept us waiting a long time! Did you really want to take up arms against me?"

Rapp is an Alsatian, half a German, and as such he is more a man of duty than a man of feeling: "My duty, Sire, constrained me."

"Diable! The soldiers would not have obeyed you; your Alsatians would have stoned you!"

But Rapp is nothing if not thorough: "You must admit, Sire, the position was a difficult one. You abdicate, you leave France, you advise us to serve the king, you come again. . . ."

"Were you often here? How did they treat you? At first, I suppose, they flattered you. Soon they'd have chucked you out of doors. That is what your fate would have been. . . . Have you read Chateaubriand's pamphlet? Is it true that I am a coward on the battle-field? They are always accusing me of ambition because they have nothing better to say. Does one get as fat as I, if one is constantly being spurred on by ambition? . . . Once again, General, we must serve France. Then we can be gathered to our fathers."

In such a debonair and lively manner does he play with this doughty and decorous old comrade. But Rapp holds his own: "You must admit, Sire, that you made a mistake in not concluding peace after Dresden. You treated as nonsensical my reports concerning German sentiment. . . ." The Emperor is quick with his repartee:

"You do not understand what such a peace would have meant!" Suddenly his tone changes into one more suitable to the camp than to this palace and to this hour; it is intimate and familiar, and goes home to Rapp's heart: "Or were you perhaps afraid of beginning a fresh war, you who for fifteen long years had acted as my adjutant? When you returned from Egypt you were nothing more than a soldier. I have made a man of you. To-day you can have whatever you like to ask for. . . . I shall never forget your conduct before Moscow. At Danzig you achieved the greatest that any man could achieve. Ney and you, you belong to the tiny legion of those who have strength of character! The Emperor embraces him, kisses him again and again. Then, pulling Rapp's moustache, he says:

"Eh? One of the braves of Egypt and Austerlitz—and you wanted to forsake me! You shall take command of the army on the Rhine, while I am dealing with the Prussians and the Russians. In two months, I hope you will be receiving my wife and my son in Strasburg. From to-day, you are my adjutant!"

"At your orders, Sire!"

Had the Emperor ever seen *Wallenstein's Death* performed on the German stage, as had, perhaps, that would-be murderer in Poland? He must have this fellow, Rapp, about him. The man is fundamentally honest, and is as brave as he is honourable; of all the Grand Army, he is the officer who was most frequently wounded. He only went over to the king from a sense of duty; he is not to be bought by the lure of promises. And yet, in a quarter of an hour, he is not only the Emperor's man once more, but has accepted the posts of army commander and adjutant, as of old. Fidelity, Napoleon realised it well, is what the Emperor most urgently needs.

Ney's case is a more difficult one. Remorse keeps Ney sleepless. With distraught countenance and extravagant words he addresses his master: "Perhaps you have heard, Sire, before I marched to Besançon, I said at the council of war—here, in the Tuileries, I promised the king—"

"Well, what did you promise?"

"To bring you in an iron cage, and place you before his throne—"

The Emperor stiffens. Then: "Foolishness! Such thoughts are unworthy of a soldier!"

"You are mistaken, Sire," exclaims the Marshal yet more excitedly; "allow me to finish. I said it, yes—but—I wanted to hide my real feelings—"

The Emperor is incensed. Ney quickly withdraws, and only after the lapse of two months takes command in the campaign. Thus near to madness had these iron warriors been brought through their struggle between duty and inclination, when the one great will which mastered them had been withdrawn. Berthier, who also rallied to Napoleon, had gone through the same experience.

"The donkey," exclaims the Emperor leniently, when talking of his old favourite. "He's a good fellow. I ask nothing of him than that he should present himself before me in the uniform of the royal guard!" But Berthier, since the Emperor's return, rushes all night through the rooms of his mansion, and at last throws himself headlong from a balcony, like Junot, to perish on the cobbles instead of dying in the battle-field.

Forwards! We have no time for loitering! Who else is there? Ah, Madame de Staël pops up again. This old opponent writes to him, admires his conduct, and promises that if he will restore the two million francs which France still owes her father, she will in future devote her literary gifts to the cause of France. The pity of it! Through making this stipulation, so splendid a woman must come down to history as beaten in the game! The Emperor mischievously replies that, to his great regret, he is not wealthy enough to fulfil her condition.

Who else is there? Marmont? Augereau? They are declared outlaws by the Emperor, because they sold the fatherland to the foreigner. And then, at long last, Talleyrand likewise! The lightning flashes that travel from Vienna to

Paris and from Paris to Vienna strike a deadly blow at this hostile friendship which has lasted for eighteen years. Each man thinks in his secret heart: "A pity that so fine a brain should be working for the other side!"

What about the second of the Dioscuri? Fouché is back again! He takes up his service as Minister of Police in the twofold capacity of working for and against his master. He says of the Emperor: "Well, he's here. We none of us exactly wished him back again; now we shall have to keep close watch on him. . . . The man has returned even madder than when he left. I give him three months!" Meanwhile, he corresponds with Metternich; but spies soon tell the Emperor, who angrily apostrophises him: "You are a traitor!" Lavalette, who is in waiting, hears the words through the half-open door. "Why do you consent to be my minister if you mean to betray me? I know that you are exchanging letters with Metternich through the intermediation of a bank official in Basle. I could have you hanged, and all the world would applaud my action." Fouché's answer has not been recorded!

The minister owed his present position to his radical outlook, for he had been a revolutionary in theory ever since Robespierre's time. The Emperor needed him in the cabinet as a decoy for the democrats. But Fouché not only betrayed his master to Metternich, he likewise betrayed Metternich to the radicals; he wanted to set up a republic—with Fouché at the head. Carnot, who was a more violent antagonist of the king than even the Emperor himself had been, now, for the first time since the days of the Directory, entered the ministry.

But, as spiritual leader, the Emperor wins over his whilom enemy, Benjamin Constant, a friend of Madame de Staël. This oldtime democrat, who had recently been thundering in the press against the brigand of Elba and comparing him to Attila and to Genghis Khan, is needed now that the Emperor proposes to govern through Chambers. Napoleon, therefore, invites Constant to an audience. The Emperor has not seen him for fifteen years. The interview, recorded by Constant, occupies four pages of print. We are shown, without periphrases, the last transformation of Napoleon, the statesman who was ever ready to adapt his course to the demands of practical politics.

"The nation again wishes for tribunes and assemblies. It has always wanted them, for it threw itself at my feet when I climbed to power. . . . I assumed less power than was actually conceded me. To-day, all is otherwise. The preference for constitutions, for elections, for speeches, is again to the fore. This is, however, the desire of a minority. The majority desires myself, alone. . . . I am not only the soldiers' Emperor; I am also the Emperor of the workers and peasants. . . . Thus, in spite of all, the people comes back to me. I treat the people severely, I never flatter the people; and yet the people cries: 'Long live the Emperor!' This is because there are common bonds between us. . . .

"It is otherwise with nobility. The nobles thronged my anterooms begging and receiving the posts they coveted. . . . But no common bond has ever existed between us. The horse submitted to the rider, it had been well trained; all the same, I felt it tremble beneath me. . . . Yes, I endeavoured to set up a world monarchy, and for this I needed unfettered power. Who, in my place, would not have wished to do likewise? Did not the world itself encourage me? Princes and subjects hastened to come beneath my sceptre's sway. . . . But if France is to be the whole of my dominions, then a constitution is better. . . .

"Tell me your ideas. Freedom of speech, free elections, responsible ministers, freedom of the press? . . . I am agreeable to all this. Especially the freedom of the press. To try and crush this any longer would be absurd. . . . I am the man of the people. If the people really wants freedom, I must give it. . . . I am no longer a conqueror; I can no longer be a conqueror. I know what is possible and what is impossible. My sole mission now is to set France on her feet once more and to give her a constitution adapted to the temperament of her people. . . .

"I do not hate freedom, although I gave it a wide berth when I met it on my way. I understand liberty; I was nourished on this idea. The labours of fifteen years have been destroyed; if I wished to begin all over again, I should need twenty years and should have to sacrifice two million men. . . . I want peace; I can get it only through victory. I will not fill you with false hopes; I foresee a terrible war. In order to win through, I must have the support of the people. The people will ask for freedom in exchange for its support. Very well, the people shall have freedom. . . . My situation is a new one for me. I am getting older. At forty-five one is no longer the man one was at thirty. The repose of a constitutional king would suit me excellently. And I am sure that this state of things would meet with the approval of my son."

Such were the basic ideas of Emperor Napoleon on his return from Elba; he was to become king of France. That his ideas are genuine and his intentions pure, is proved by the realism of his motives. We have not to do with a man who pretends to a change of heart; this is no hero who, in commune with his maker upon an island, has become a saint. Here we have the man himself, wishful to rule as circumstances permit; a man who has ever been mindful of public opinion. He recognises that he has to do with a new epoch. If he himself did not inaugurate such an epoch, at least, through his fall, he made its realisation possible. Napoleon feels that a land which has experienced the dictatorship of genius, can no longer revert to the dictatorship of inheritance. If the spirit of the revolution has become petrified into a single huge figure, a new structure must arise from its ruins, and the stone blocks that are used in the building must be so placed as to secure wider levels and a less tapering pinnacle. In very truth, the son of the revolution, even when he becomes a tyrant, cannot be succeeded by a king who reigns by God's grace. He can only be succeeded by democracy.

For this reason, the Emperor deals more severely with the émigrés than he was wont; he confiscates estates; he disbands the royal guard; and does at the end of his career what he should have done at the start, namely, he abolishes feudal titles, thus ridding himself of the old nobility whose false compliments had cost him so dear. By these decrees he recreates the revolutionary spirit, and makes it stronger than it has been since his coronation, eleven years earlier. He issues the following declaration to the civil authorities:

"I have returned to-day for the same reason which brought me back from Egypt: because things are not going well with the fatherland. . . . I do not want to carry on any more wars. We have to forget that we were masters of the world. . . . In those days, I pursued the aim of creating a great United States of Europe, and I was compelled to neglect many points of home policy which would have secured the freedom of the citizens of France. Now I shall work for no other object than for France's consolidation and tranquillity, for the protection of property, for the free interchange of ideas: the prince must be the first servitor of the State." Among the hearers are many who, but a year ago, amid the thunder crashes of the catastrophe, had listened to other words uttered by these selfsame lips: "I am the State." Nevertheless they pin their faith to his new constitution, whose elaboration is entrusted to Constant.

When the constitution is placed before them, they are alarmed. "Additional Act?" Are we once more to be cheated? The democrats pour forth a hail of criticism. Simultaneously, news comes from Vienna: the powers declare war on Napoleon; no harm shall come to France. A signal! For twenty years, so the saying runs through the land, we have desired peace. At last we have got it. Is it once more to come to an end?

"I cannot hide the fact from you any longer," says a councillor of State to the Emperor; "the women are your declared enemies, and these opponents are always dangerous in France." No one wants any more levies to be made. Instead of two hundred and fifty thousand men, only sixty thousand answer his call.

This decision of the powers is an expression of the mood of the princes, and not of the peoples they govern, for these, just like the French people, are eager for repose. The sentence of outlawry is not so much a political move as an insistence on a point of honour, and the expression of Emperor Francis' desire to exact moral vengeance. But it gnaws at the foundation of Napoleon's power. When he had first come back, France had been in his favour. Since, however, all the other States of Europe are against him, France will make no more sacrifices on his behalf. The funds, which had risen when he reached Paris, fall.

The Emperor is alarmed. An intimate, from whom he has asked news of the recruiting campaign, says to him: "Your Majesty will not be left unsupported." To which the Emperor replies in low tones: "I was almost afraid I should be!"

His friends find him less active than of yore; he is fatter, his features are lax, he needs many hot baths, and lies in them a long time; he takes a great deal of sleep. "He seemed full of cares," writes one of his circle. "The self-confidence of his speeches, his authoritative tone, had vanished."

Only four weeks ago, at his first advent, he appeared rejuvenated and lively. Why this relapse?

First and foremost, his wife's behaviour has shaken him. A semi-anonymous letter from Vienna, addressed to Lavalette, has fallen into his hands. Herein are described Marie Louise's scorn for the Emperor, her love for Neipperg; and a number of shameful details are added. The Emperor is surprised holding this letter, in his dimly lighted study, crouched over the fire, silent.

When Méneval, who was to have accompanied Marie Louise

on her return journey to Paris, comes back from Vienna, he finds the Emperor, in the very midst of these eventful weeks, lying on a sofa, sunk deep in reverie. For many hours that day, and for half the next, the secretary has to give his master a precise account of everything that is happening over there, of all he has observed. The Emperor spoke as though "overwhelmed by a calm sorrowfulness, and seemed so resigned that I was deeply moved. He was no longer confident of victory, and I felt that his belief in his good luck, which had sustained him during the march to Paris, had forsaken him." Méneval has to describe every trait and gesture of the little son. The Emperor, an ageing man, paces to and fro in the garden on this day in May, alone; he has to rely on a stranger's word to know what his boy is like, whether the child is growing up to resemble his father or his grandfather.

These things weigh him down. Tragically, the conflicts within him are renewed. Now that he wishes to be a democrat in response to the spirit of the time, now that his will-to-peace is great, the menace from without frustrates his attempts to establish democracy or maintain peace. If no one in Europe were to lift a finger in order to replace Louis on the throne, Napoleon might content himself with ruling within the boundaries of France, might introduce the freedoms he had promised. But the powers, which have no more lands to reclaim (since they have received back all that was ever taken from them, and now possess what they had had before the revolution), come forward as they had in '92, because the wind blowing from this stormy corner of Europe threatens their inherited calm, and because none of the monarchs can sleep sound o' nights so long as their Bourbon cousin is standing on the English shore of the Channel looking plaintively across the waters towards France, the land of his fathers.

Never had Napoleon taken up arms more reluctantly than he did when this war was forced upon him by the Vienna decree. Never had the rapidity and clear-sightedness of a dictator or

(From the "Corpus Imaginum" of the Photographic Society, Charlottenburg.)

Napoleon as Emperor in 1814. Painting by Horace Vernet. Tate Gallery, London.

the sympathy of public opinion been more necessary to him than in this terrible crisis. Just now, when every one wants peace, he is obliged to arm for war; just now, when he is to bestow liberties on the people, his actions are hampered at every turn. The struggle of the legitimists with this interloper (the upshot of which had been his own legitimisation), the struggle which had placed him on the throne, is resumed when, too late, he is cured of his longing to pose as legitimate monarch. Though he is reaching out towards liberty once more, he is now to sustain his final defeat.

Thus the great renewal gets no further than the Additional Act to the Constitutions of the Empire, which, as earlier with his great decrees, he leaves to the approval of the "sovereign people."

Nevertheless, the sixty-seven articles evolved out of Constant's head contain all the newer democratic elements; they are a great advance upon English constitutional law, and remain as a model for the whole of the subsequent century. No one henceforward can be imprisoned or banished without due form of law; religious belief and the press are to be free. The legislative body is changed into a Lower House, the Senate becomes an Upper House without the former privileges, all deliberations are open to the public, both Houses may initiate legislation and reject the budget, the ministers are to be responsible to parliament, the interpretation of the law devolves upon the Chambers.

A number of new laws, each a dagger in the dictator's heart! Yet he yields in everything save two points which he carries, after a lively debate against Constant: the hereditariness of the peerage, into which "after one or two successful battles," the nobility would again pour; and his right to confiscation, for "without this right I should be defenceless against the party factions. I am not an angel, but a man who cannot allow himself to be attacked without meting out punishment."

These two concessions to him create as bad an impression as the words "Additional Act" had done. Since he will allow no discussion on the matter, but only consents to the empty form of a plebiscite, as he had done in the days when he wished to become consul for life and subsequently emperor, the democrats begin to grumble, and no one is aware how greatly the nation is to be congratulated on this latest work of its leader. Instead of the four million votes he had received of yore, his constitution receives only just over one and a half million votes, for most of the citizens abstain.

A few venture to protest. Honest Carnot says: "Your Additional Act has not pleased the people; it will not meet with acceptance. Promise me that you will amend it. I must tell you the truth, for your and our salvation hangs upon your tolerance." His tone is upright, but wholly unprecedented. Since the days when Bonaparte was a lieutenant no one had ever spoken thus to him. He makes a gesture of annoyance, and Carnot continues: "This word alarms you, Sire? Yes, you must show tolerance in the face of the national will."

"The foe is at our gates," answers the veteran soldier. "First of all, help to chase him away. Then I shall have time to occupy myself with your liberal panaceas." Even though he profoundly recognises the demands of the new age, he finds it impossible to deliberate with representatives of the people.

Napoleon knows only how to command!

XVIII

On a bright spring morning, the plain is lively as on days of high festival. The Parisians are flocking in crowds to the Champ de Mai. The whole town has come forth to this revival of the Carlovingian folk assembly. The old troops are there, and the new. The platforms are gaily decorated with tricolours. Six hundred deputies and several hundred peers are waiting for the Emperor, who is to take the oath to the new constitution before starting on his campaign. It is the first time for two or three years that the people of the gay city have had a chance of glutting their lust for merrymaking. Under the king, all had been sober and staid.

Now the procession is coming forth from the town; from afar can be heard the fanfare of the trumpets, and every one is expecting the hero of the occasion, the warrior Napoleon, to be dressed as beseems the posture of affairs, seeing that within a few days he will be fighting for throne and country at the head of his troops. Rumour has run through Paris saying that he still wears his old green coat, in which people love best to see him.

But what is the pageant which unfolds itself?

First comes the guard of honour, followed by the eagles and the colours; then heralds and pages, clad in many-coloured costumes, as if in an allegorical picture; then the Emperor's coronation coach, drawn by eight horses. In it is seated a man picturesquely attired in white silk, almost overshadowed by a hat decked with huge ostrich plumes, and burdened by his vast coronation mantle; a solitary man, glittering with gold. Is this the Emperor?

The masses are dumbfounded, for they wanted to fraternise with their ruler returned from exile; they are stupefied by the spectacle of a Cæsar whose chill splendours seem to repel the cordiality they would fain exhibit. Painful indeed is the forlorn aspect of this middle-aged man, whose wife has not returned to him and whose son is far away, as he drives among the gaping crowds in his stately chariot.

When, after High Mass, the spokesman of the new Chambers confronts the Emperor, this citizen speaks in tones which ring athwart the plain: "Trusting your pledges, the deputies will sagaciously revise our laws, and harmonise them with the constitution"—the implication being that the representatives of the people are not yet satisfied, but want more than this Additional Act. Then the spokesman of the Chambers and the citizens expresses his hopes of victory, and wishes success to the eagles.

The Emperor has to hide his vexation. He announces the new constitution, and swears to observe it faithfully. Then the soldiers must acclaim the oath. But they can hardly recognise their master in this pompously attired ruler. They want the old green coat; their hero should be wearing the tricolour cockade, not gold and plumes. Their cheers lack enthusiasm. An eyewitness writes: "These were not the cheers of Austerlitz and Wagram. The Emperor could not fail to notice it."

A week later, when he opened both Houses with a speech from the throne, he was careful to avoid everything which had put people out of humour at the Champ de Mai. The Lower House promises to devote its energies to the defence of the nation; but goes on to say: "Even the will of the victorious ruler would not induce the nation to transcend the bounds of defence." The peers in the Upper House utter a like warning in their address, saying: "The French government will never be led away by the seductions of victory." Napoleon stands there constrained to silence, but trembling with wrath. He would like to sweep them all away, but dares not even give them the lie.

Among the new peers is Lucien. He has come to join his brother after all. A glance and a hand-clasp have reconciled the brothers. For the first time in his life he is styled prince and imperial highness. He is the Emperor's companion, delivers speeches, even gives lectures in the Institute, and receives large sums of money. Louis is ill, and does not come. Jerome is ready and willing. Hortense must replace the missing lady of the house, and her sons have once more become important to the man without a son. Napoleon appears on the balcony with his nephews, to show the crowd, to show France, that the Emperor still has heirs. Unseen, the spirit of irony contemplates this tragical conclusion to the history of his dynastic delusion.

Once he drives with Hortense to Malmaison, but goes alone

into the room where Josephine died, to come forth from it in silence.

Next day he sets out for the war, hoping it will be his last war. It is.

Carnot, to whom at this late hour he divulges his plan, strongly advises him to wait until the army has been reinforced. Neither the Russians nor the Austrians can arrive before the end of July. The English and the Prussians will not venture to attack until their allies have joined them. During these six weeks, Napoleon could double his forces, transform France into an armed camp, fortify Paris on the side whence the onslaught will come. The Emperor shakes his head:

"I know all that. But it is essential that I should win a brilliant victory without waiting so long!"

He knows what is at stake. It is his way to assume the offensive. But the master of figures would have done well to wait awhile, and collect his forces. "I must win a brilliant victory soon!" Is not that the thought of a beaten champion? Perhaps it is; but the gloomy vaticinations of the ruined Cæsar are fortified by the memories of General Bonaparte. Not since his youth has he ventured to do what he now proposes, to advance with a small army, without reserves, mobile, swift. Such, then, is his plan. He will not give his four opponents time to get together. The two that appear to be ready must be separately attacked and defeated. That is the picture which hovers before his mind. What Napoleon, the Emperor, now begins at Charleroi, when his prospective opponents are the Prussians and the English, Bonaparte, the unknown general, had begun at Millesimo, when his prospective opponents were the Austrians and the Piedmontese. His last battle is the parallel of his first.

But during these twenty years, all the commanders of Europe have learned the tactics of the new master of the art of war; and he, during these twenty years, has worn out his machinery. Moreover, swift though his movements are in the days before

Waterloo, he no longer possesses the old tempo. As in his recent campaigns, so now, anxious considerations hamper the boldness of his attack. Having taken Charleroi, he fails next day to make a mass onslaught on Blücher, sends Ney with half the army along the Brussels road against the English, only to learn with alarm in the afternoon that he is faced by the whole of the Prussian army. He sends to recall the marshal, writing: "The fate of France is in your hands." Ney, instead of continuing his advance, must envelop the Prussian enemy. Too late! Ney has become involved in the fight with Wellington at Quatre Bras, can spare only one army corps, and sends it to a place where it can be of no use. This makes it impossible for him to gain a victory over the English, and he is driven back.

Napoleon, this same day, fighting with only half his army at Ligny, secures a victory.

The last victory! Blücher falls from his wounded horse, and is reported killed. Gneisenau retains composure, prevents the retreat from degenerating into a rout, and sends to let his ally know that they can form a junction at Wavre the next day. With an inertia which we should wonder at did we not know that Napoleon is ailing and prematurely old, the Emperor makes no move on the day after his victory. Too late he sends Grouchy with thirty thousand men to follow up the Prussians, not believing that they can reorganise their forces speedily, or that after the heavy losses they have sustained they will be able to effect a junction with the English. Yesterday, he had dealt with the Prussians singly; to-morrow he will be able to defeat the English, now cut off from their allies. His seventy thousand men will suffice. He fails to allow for Gneisenau's imperturbability and for Blücher's impetuosity.

For the first time, he underrates an opponent. At Friedland, Aspern-Essling, and Laon, he was not beaten. Nor was he beaten in Russia. At Leipzig, and at Arcis-sur-Aube, he was defeated; but it was because he had only a small army with which to meet the onslaughts of vastly superior forces; those of three great powers in one case, and those of four in the other. Never, yet, had any isolated commander been able to say: "I have defeated Napoleon."

Now he thinks too much of his victory, and too little of his opponent. For the first time he fails to focus his lens accurately, with the result that one point escapes his reckoning. But it is not that he makes a wanton and ill-considered onslaught. Nor is the trouble on this occasion that family feeling makes him entrust leadership to inefficient hands. If he had kept Grouchy's force with him, his enemy would have scarcely outnumbered him. But the course of the decisive battle shows that this error in calculation was not the main cause of the French defeat.

The final cause, as any one can recognise who studies all the elements in Napoleon's fate, was the man's advancing years.

His activity was undermined by his ailments, and that is why, on the morning of the battle of Waterloo, he failed to attack promptly. In the middle of June, the sun is above the horizon by four. If the Prussians were able to march upon the roads that had been softened by the recent heavy rains, the French veterans could have done the same—for the Emperor's soldiers on this occasion were almost all of them tried men. But he waits till noon, that he may place his guns better when the ground becomes less sodden! At Jena, in October, in a Scotch mist, he had headed his troops, shouted to encourage them, attacking so early in the morning as to arouse many of his foes from their slumbers. To-day he waits till noon.

The loss of this half-day is to destroy him. He rides to an elevation bearing the fatal name of La Belle Alliance; he arranges his troops in three lines, rides along the front, shouts to his men in metallic phrases; he is going to break through the enemy and enter Brussels; he already has the proclamation to the Belgians in his pocket. He has only wasted half a day!

In the afternoon, when battle is already joined, news comes

that Bülow's corps is advancing. The Emperor turns pale, and sends Grouchy orders to come back. Will the orders reach him? If they do, will he be able to disengage himself from the enemy? Everything turns upon the fortune of the next hour. The English must be beaten before the Prussians can come to their aid. Napoleon delivers a great cavalry attack on the centre, but the English stand firm. Shall he use the old guard? Not yet! Not yet! Bülow is already beginning to fire. At all costs he must keep the line of retreat open, for otherwise there may be a catastrophe. But, in fact, the English forces are already half defeated. It is five o'clock, and the guard might have finished their defeat, for at this hour Wellington sent a message to his Prussian ally: "Unless your corps keeps marching, and attacks without respite, the battle will be lost." This would have been the moment for an attack by the old guard, but once more caution makes the Emperor hold his hand at the critical moment. He sees that a second Prussian corps is about to attack.

A dread decision! A brilliant gamester staking his last coins, but to-day he must not be beaten. At length, towards seven, he sends the last five thousand guardsmen, the veterans, to the attack. Now, it is only a forlorn hope. "Vive l'Empereur!"

This cry has shaken half Europe. Is it not a century old? In a decade it has gained a legendary force throughout the Continent. But what is imperishable? Even the eagles of Marengo are not imperishable. Is the mythical energy of this cry, Vive l'Empereur, to subside with the setting of to-day's sun? Yes, to-morrow it will be heard no more!

The second Prussian corps pours a deadly fire on the guard, which yields ground. The opposing force continues to grow; at eight, the third army corps appears on the scene, and a hundred and twenty thousand of the allies are now attacking half that number of Frenchmen. The battered French army takes to flight, and Bonaparte, in his last hour as a commander, is for the first time in his life commander of a routed army. After an hour on horseback in the open, exposed to the British fire, the Emperor rides into the centre of one of the two remaining French squares. When these, likewise, break up, he gallops across country protected only by mounted grenadiers. Though in bodily pain, he has to stay in the saddle until five in the morning, when he is able at length to secure a few hours rest in an old cart.

Is he discouraged?

By no means! What is Paris saying? This is the thought which continually drives him onward. He does not venture, as he had done last year, to assemble the guards in Laon or Soissons, or to betake himself to one of the fortresses. He thinks only of Paris, as the place from which more soldiers can be gathered. Calculations, as of old: "I can still mobilise a hundred and fifty thousand men; with the National Guard, there will be three hundred thousand in all. That will be enough to stop the advance of the enemy." The last orders he sends to Paris end with the words: "Courage! Firmness!"

Two days later, he is once more in the Elysée, which he had left so recently. Has the whole campaign been a dream? In nine days he has lost the empire which he had fought nine years to win.

XIX

Not lost yet!

In the cabinet and in the Chambers, opinions are divided. He sits in council with his brothers and his ministers; he is worn out, but there is no sign of collapse. What does he propose? To work hand in hand with the Chambers? Far from it; he proposes dictatorship. In this national crisis, he needs, for a short time, full freedom of movement. Some of the ministers point out to him that the Chambers no longer trust him. Then Lucien takes the floor, and with all the fire of a youth urges the Emperor to dissolve the Chambers, declare Paris in a state of siege, take all power into his hands, get together the remaining troops—thus alone, now, can France be saved!

He listens. Sixteen years have passed since that November day at Saint-Cloud when this very Lucien had made the same proposal, and, with a single speech, had snatched his brother from the abyss. Then Lucien had raised Napoleon higher than he had wished. The Emperor approves the plan, but does not instantly act on it. Instead, he listens while Davoust, the Minister for War, refuses to place the remnants of the armed forces at his disposal. While they are disputing, news comes from the Chamber of Deputies. It has declared itself in permanent session, will regard any attempt to dissolve it as high treason, and will impeach any one who may dare to try. "I can see only one man between us and peace," said old Lafayette from the rostrum. "If we rid ourselves of him, peace will be ours for the asking!"

Is this the cry of the people? Paris is perfectly calm, so it is nothing more than the cry of a liberated democracy. But it is also the cry of a society which loves change and bears adversity badly, for the House of Peers now passes a vote identical with that of the Chamber of Deputies. The Chambers demand that the Emperor shall appear before them. Why does he not go? Who would venture to oppose him openly? "I ought to have gone," he said subsequently, "but I was tired out. I could have dissolved them, but I lacked courage; I am only a man, after all. My memories of the Nineteenth Brumaire terrified me."

Now the Chambers send for the ministers. The Emperor replies that he has forbidden them to go. The Chambers rejoin that they will depose him unless the ministers come. He gives way. He sends Lucien and the ministers to the Chamber of Deputies, and they report that he has formed a commission to negotiate with the enemy. "The powers will not treat with him!" cry the Chambers. "They have outlawed him. He must abdicate. If he refuses, we shall depose him!"

While this is going on in the Chambers, the Emperor, much agitated, is walking to and fro in the garden with Constant. At length he is roused, and flames out:

"Not my own future, but that of France is at stake! Have they considered the consequences of my abdication? The army is grouped round me. Do they think they can fight the general dissolution with ideology? I could have understood it if I had been repelled when I landed three months ago. But to-day, when the foe is only a hundred miles from Paris, they cannot overthrow a government without suffering for it. A fortnight back, to repudiate me would have been a bold action. Now, I am part of what the enemy is attacking, a part of France which it is their business to defend. France will sacrifice itself if it sacrifices me! It is not liberty which would fain depose me, it is Waterloo—fear! . . . All I want now is to be the commander; but even if part of the troops were to fall away, I should promptly replace them by workmen, who can readily be moved to revolt."

At this moment, the two men in the garden hear shouts from the avenue, "Vive l'Empereur!" Whose are these last voices raised for Napoleon? The workers from Saint-Antoine; men whose troubles he had remembered in days of need, men who cared little about the suppression of liberty, for equality had made them free. There they were, peering through the railings which separated the son of the revolution from them just as it had separated the kings, but shouting through the bars of the cage into which he had shut himself: "Dictatorship! National Guard! Vive l'Empereur!"

"You see?" said Napoleon to Constant. "I never loaded those fellows with honours. What have they got to thank me for? I left them poor men, just as I had found them. Nothing but instinct leads them to me. If I liked, these rebellious Chambers would be dissolved within the hour. . . . I need merely say the word, and all the deputies who oppose me would be butchered! But for one man, the price is too high. Blood must not flow in Paris!"

This mood of renunciation, which is akin to justice, this refusal to employ brute force in his extremity, just as he had refused (to begin with) sixteen years earlier, resembles the mood of Brumaire. But what was then the prudence of a statesman who did not wish to tarnish the origins of his long career of power, is now a prudence which does not beseem the adventurer he is to-day. Nevertheless, his unwillingness to use the bayonets with which, to-day, he could again have cleared the Chambers, is one more sign of his recognition of the new epoch, which wants more freedom and less force.

Meanwhile, the Chamber of Deputies is in secret session. Lucien has presented the imperial message. The deputies are willing to discuss matters. Some of them speak, in civil terms, of the abdication as a sacrifice necessary for France. Honest Carnot mounts the rostrum, and, in this moment of disaster, is almost alone in espousing the cause of the Emperor whom almost alone he had openly attacked in the days when all others had been subservient to the man of the hour. But now Sieyès, too, speaks in favour of the Emperor, speaks like a Roman of old: "Napoleon has lost a battle. . . . Let us help him to drive the barbarians from our country, for no one else is equal to the task. If, when he has done it, he wants to play the despot, we can hang him. But to-day we must march with him shoulder to shoulder!"

Lafayette springs to the rostrum once more: "Have you forgotten where the bones of our sons and our brothers whiten? In Africa, on the Tagus, on the Vistula, amid the snows of Russia. Two million have been the victims of this one man who wanted to fight all Europe! Enough!" In the small hours, the Chamber demands Napoleon's abdication.

The Emperor hesitates. In the morning there is another cabinet council. Much agitated, he paces the room, uttering gibes about these Jacobins, foreseeing a new Directory. Then the commandant of the Palais Bourbon arrives with a message from the Chambers. He stammers when he attempts to discharge his commission, but at length manages to get the words out. If the Emperor does not abdicate, the Chambers will outlaw him. Savary and Caulaincourt come in. All present urge him to the step, for even Lucien has given up the game. The Emperor says:

"I have accustomed them to great victories, and now they do not know how to endure a single day of adversity. What will happen to France?" He adds in low tones: "I have done what I could."

After this epilogue of six words, which tells the whole story, at noon he dictates his declaration to the people. He is making the sacrifice, his political life is at an end, he proclaims his son emperor as Napoleon II., the Chambers must establish a regency. To whom does he dictate these words? Who among his intimates can hold the pen firmly enough to write them down?

Lucien! The brother who for years from the enemy coast had gazed enviously at this city and this throne; who, if he had been a little less of a poet, might long since have collected the malcontents around him; and who might even now come to the front, not indeed as a second Napoleon, but at least as a second Bonaparte—and that would be something. Lucien sits there, a man of forty now. He had been no less ambitious than the Emperor, but had had to content himself with the modest career of a virtuoso and a Mæcenas. For four whole weeks, now, he has been an imperial prince! Smiling inwardly, he pens his great brother's abdication; writes from dictation, still a mere hodman, but this time animated with a humorous sympathy which atones for the old discords.

For, in truth, it is the eternal recurrence of the similar. As before, come cries from the Chambers, "Outlaw him!" As before, five Directors, like those Bonaparte had once deposed, are appointed. They call themselves a provisional government.

But when they proceed to elect from among their own number one to function as president of the Directory, who is chosen to take over the authority from Napoleon's hands? Who, by his own vote, has decided his own choice as president?

Fouché.

But the Chamber has become less turbulent. Those who, yesterday, were thirsting for Napoleon's blood, to-day send a deputation to thank him for his abdication. To these polite gentlemen the Emperor says: "I fear things will turn out badly, now that there is no head. I trust France will never forget that my sole object in abdicating was to promote the welfare of the nation, and that I have abdicated in favour of my son. Only under my dynasty, will France remain free and happy."

At the very time when he is saying this, Fouché and the others are considering the possibility of having one of the Orleanist Bourbons, a member of the Brunswick family, or even the king of Saxony, as Napoleon's successor. Moreover, the five Directors are appointed to form a government, not a regency; and, in his decrees, Fouché often speaks of the nation, but never of Napoleon II. The Emperor notes all this, but holds his peace. Slowly his dream of a dynasty vanishes, the dream for whose realisation he has fought half a lifetime. It has become for ever unattainable. When Lavalette comes to see him in the evening, he is in a hot bath, has been there for several hours.

"Where am I going? Why not to America?"

"Because Moreau went there."

To the Emperor this answer seems surcharged with emotion, for he has serious thoughts of seeking an asylum in the United States, and he asks the government for a frigate. But the only answer is a request that he should leave Paris, for crowds are flocking round the Elysée, clamouring for a dictatorship. He burns a number of documents, and then betakes himself to Malmaison.

In the garden there, the garden that is full of memories of Josephine, he passes two whole days in a state of reverie. The few who remain faithful to him are there: his mother, Hortense, Caulaincourt, Lavalette, Lucien, even Joseph. But when the Emperor asks who will go with him, the answers are evasive. Letizia, indeed, will go gladly, but he thinks that at her age it would be dangerous. Lavalette has a daughter growing up, and his wife is expecting another child; perhaps he will follow later. Drouot, who shared the Elba exile, is wanted in France. The secretary had promised the day before to accompany Napoleon into exile, but now his mother, who is blind, has implored him not to leave her. "You are right; you must stay with your mother," says the Emperor, turning away.

Pauline, before the last campaign, had pressed her jewels on him; now Hortense offers him a diamond necklace; a quixotic return of imperial gifts, a gesture suitable to the strange turn in his fortunes. He tells Hortense she will have a million, but no one knows if it will ever be paid. Lucien and Eugene get money, and he gives little Léon something for his mother—still dealing in hundreds of thousands.

But he does all these things like a man in a dream. He does not say a word about the last few weeks, but talks only of old times, and chiefly of Josephine. "I have promised the minister to go away. I shall start to-night. I am weary of myself, of France, and of Paris. Make your preparations."

Whither away? Conjectures, deliberations. Spectral is the tone of the manifesto he now addresses to the army:

"Soldiers! . . . I am with you even though I am away. I know every corps. If any one wins a victory, I shall approve his courage. . . . Show, in days to come, that, before all, you serve your country, show it by obeying me; and show that I have earned your affection (if indeed I have earned it) by my ardent love for our common mother. One more storm, and the coalition will be shattered! Napoleon will know you by the blows that you deal out. Save the honour and the liberty of the French. Be what you have been for twenty years, and you will be unconquerable!"

The government suppresses the document, but could have published it without risk. No one could be more aloof, no living man could have become more completely a part of history, than this man who speaks of himself as if he were speaking of a stranger. He seems to be no longer present in the flesh.

Suddenly he is startled! The old sounds assail his ears. The noise of cannon shots reaches him from the plain of Saint-Denis; the foe is at the gates. Officers and soldiers, scarred and tattered, but hastily patched up, bring him the news, vague and dispersed like the sound of the firing. Instantly he returns to life. "In two detachments? You must attack and defeat them separately; first one and then the other." At night he elaborates a plan for the defence of Paris. Next morning it seems as if the familiar sounds had rejuvenated him, and he writes to the five Directors as General Bonaparte had written of old:

"I offer to place myself at the head of the army. At sight of me, the soldiers will recover their courage, hurl themselves on the foe, and punish him. I pledge you my word as general, soldier, and citizen that I will not retain the command an hour after the victory has been won. I vow to conquer, not for myself but for France."

It is impossible that after such words he should fail to conquer, unless he is slain in the first onslaught. In this mood of impending death, he writes his magnificent letter. Napoleon, in the garden, surrounded by his remaining officers, restlessly awaits the answer.

Fouché's great moment has come. To this ex-master of his, to the man whom he so cordially detests, he does not even vouchsafe a written answer. The Emperor, who is trembling with eagerness to take up arms, and who has never since he grew to full manhood had to wait for another man's permission, tears the response out of the returning messenger. It is curt: The Emperor is mistaken if he thinks the members of the government are such fools as to entertain his proposal; all they ask is that he should go away as soon as possible. Napoleon says bitterly: "I ought to have hanged him long ago. Now I must leave the job to the Bourbons."

Mufti; a rapid gathering together of necessaries; Hortense sews her necklace for him into a black silk belt. For a few minutes he entertains the thought of Corsica, with Lucien as governor of the island. His mother's eyes sparkle. But he knows that the scheme is impracticable. America is his last resource. The only thing lacking is the frigate for which he has been asking. All are aware that every hour increases the risk to his liberty. It is said that Wellington has demanded his surrender, and the number of the deputies in favour of his being handed over is steadily increasing. Lavalette urges him to start, but the Emperor is stubborn.

"I cannot leave without an order from the government to the captain."

"Why not, Sire? Have the anchor weighed, promise the crew money, send the captain ashore if he won't set sail. You may be sure that Fouché has already promised to hand you over to the allies."

"Drive to the Minister for the Navy!"

The councillor drives to Decrès', and finds him in bed. Decrès refers the messenger to Fouché, saying: "I can do nothing."

Fouché cannot be found. The councillor gets back to Malmaison at one in the morning. The Emperor is awakened, gets up, still thinks the United States will be best, but hesitates. "Over there, they will grant me land, or I will buy an estate and till it. I shall end where mankind began. I shall live upon the produce of my fields and my herds."

"But what if they propose to hand you over?" enquires the secretary.

"Then I shall go to Mexico. There I shall find patriots at whose head I can place myself."

"The leaders there might turn against you."

"All right; I shall leave them and go to Caracas. If I don't like it, I shall go on to Buenos Ayres or to California. I shall sail across the seas until I find a city of refuge where I can be safe from the persecutions of my fellows."

"But what if the English catch you, Sire?"

"I must risk that. A bad government, but a great nation, noble and generous. England will treat me properly. Besides, there is no choice. Am I to allow myself, like a ninny, to be taken prisoner here by Wellington, to be led in triumph through the streets of London like King John the Good of old? Since they have no use for my services here, I must go elsewhere. Ability will do the rest."

"Your Majesty was not made for flight."

"Flight! What are you talking about?" He looks at the secretary "questioningly and proudly."

"The English must certainly be on the watch for you already. Your end ought to be the worthiest possible."

"Suicide, like Hannibal? Leave that to weaklings and persons of disordered mind! Whatever fate may hold in store for me, I would never deliberately shorten my life by a single day."

"I did not mean that, Sire. But what if you were to hand over liberty and life to the enemies of France in order to save France? That is how Napoleon the Great should act."

"All very fine, but to whom am I to hand myself over? To Blücher? To Wellington? They have no plenipotentiary powers. They would simply take me prisoner, and do what they pleased with France and with me."

"The tsar, perhaps?"

"You do not know the Russians! Still, I will think the matter over. To sacrifice my own person would be easy enough. The question is, whether it would help France?"

Almost every element that goes to make the statesman seems to have been eliminated from this all-too-human dialogue. Here is an adventurer hankering after fresh voyages in every corner of the world. Here is the man without a country, the ocean traveller without any earth under his feet, always on board, always driven hither and thither, a bold pirate fearless of death. Ay, fearless of death! The dry manner in which, once again, he waves aside the idea of suicide, the sober realism of his outlook, this grasp at the flying moment, the old-time dauntlessness of the islesman—what unconquerable vital energy!

Now he is to start. The last person with whom the Emperor has a quiet talk is his mother. But a soldier rushes in; he will not let any hold him back: the soldier is Talma. The call of his heart and his love of the tragical have urged him to come for a great farewell; he feels he must be there. Later he is to represent this leave-taking between mother and son, in all its dignified simplicity, in a pathetic scene on the stage. Then the Emperor invites young General Gourgand, the scatter-brained idealist, into his dilapidated carriage. Bertrand and his wife, who had lived with him in Elba, and two others, accompany him. They drive to Rochefort, to the port where they hope to find a frigate. The pace is too slow for a fugitive. He still looks over his shoulder, listening for the call which shall summon him back at the eleventh hour. They meet two regiments marching northward. The men raise a cheer, and the Emperor discusses with the generals the possibility of overthrowing the government if he places himself at their head and marches on Paris. . . . Away again, at length the long drive is over, and he stands gazing at the Atlantic Ocean. Joseph is there, and urges Napoleon to charter a brig which is taking a cargo of spirits to America. The Emperor assumes the name of Muiron, his seventh name. This name calls up the vision of another coast, the Mediterranean with its many isles, and Corsica, and then Italy; and again he sees the young, small, lean general, with long hair falling on his shoulders and cold grey-blue eyes, and the bridge of Arcola where the fate of a man and a country hung in the balance; and he sees Lieutenant Muiron fling himself before the young general in the mêlée, he sees Muiron fall, and he knows that by this love-death the lieutenant's name will be immortalised. It would seem that once again a new epoch is opening before the genius of energy, and that across the seas, in new zones, on uninhabited prairies, the adventurer will swing himself into the saddle, will watch the increase of his herds; maybe, even, will travel to Mexico and become the leader of a band of rebels!

But God is wiser.

He sees to it that this great life shall have an epilogue such as no man has ever lived through before, an epilogue which shall fitly round off its tragical poesy. Once more the Almighty stifles the adventurous impulse in the soul of Napoleon; once more there are days of questioning, negotiation, vacillation—ten days before the final decision.

The Emperor crosses to a small island. They think of chartering two fishing smacks which the English will never dream of searching for Napoleon; but in the end he rejects the plan. There are two American ships available. Negotiations are entered into with a Danish sloop. Enthusiastic youths from the naval training school propose to carry him off in an advice-boat. Sixteen midshipmen will spirit him out of the harbour at dead of night. They sit packed together in the little room, feverishly discussing the plan with Las Cases, the Emperor's new confidant. The man to whom this madcap venture is proposed, talks over the situation coolly with his companions, asking each in turn for an opinion as to the best course. Most of them advise a return to the army, for there are still good prospects that the soldiers in the south will support him. He emphatically refuses:

"Nothing will induce me to light up a civil war. I will have no more to do with politics; I need repose; I shall go to America!"

But his self-respect makes him shrink from the thought of escaping in disguise.

News comes that the Bourbon has re-entered the land of his fathers, once more under the protection of allied troops. The path of escape seaward is now blocked by an English cruiser which bears the ominous name of "Bellerophon." The Emperor has missed his chance. Here are his thoughts: "A return to Paris is impossible. The port is blockaded. Shall I allow myself to be seized like a pirate, and taken in chains to London? England has been my foe for twenty years. Next to the French, the English nation is the greatest and the most distinguished in the world. Have I not been an Emperor? Has not, from of old, chivalry toward a fallen enemy aroused universal admiration? In Corsica, they knife any one who violates the rights of hospitality."

Making up his mind, he dictates the following letter to the prince regent:

"Your Royal Highness, Exposed to the factions which distract my country and to the enmity of the greatest powers of Europe, I have closed my political career, and I come, like Themistocles, to throw myself upon the hospitality of the British people. I put myself under the protection of their laws, and beg Your Royal Highness, as the most powerful, the most persistent, and the most generous of my enemies, to grant me this protection. Napoleon."

Eight lines, three words of respect, neither arrogance nor humility, almost courtly. There is, however, one word which embodies the pathos of the step he is taking, and assumes that his adversary will give moral guarantees; that in this century, after such a life, Napoleon will be as welcome a guest in the enemy land, as of old in Persia had been—Themistocles. It is overwhelming self-confidence, based upon historical parallels, which determines the last great step of his career, as, in youth, it had determined his first advances to Paoli. Now, this self-confidence will be his ruin.

Next day, Las Cases hands the letter to the captain of the "Bellerophon," and negotiates with Maitland for Napoleon's reception on board. Admiral Hotham, Maitland's immediate superior, was not a party to the negotiations, but had long since received orders to seize the fugitive if possible. In accordance with international law, this was quite in order, for England, with the other powers in Vienna, had decreed Napoleon's outlawry. But it is an undisputed fact that Captain Maitland, supreme on his own ship, guaranteed his guest's liberty, saying: "Napoleon will receive all proper attention in England. Our people are generous and democratic."

No record was taken at the time of the terms of the understanding in accordance with which the man who had been the master of Europe went on board one of his enemy's ships. Nevertheless, it was not an affair of hours, but, rather, of days; not the outcome of haste and desperation, but the logical conclusion of a long chain of reasoning. Napoleon's own experience of the last twenty years had shown him that verbal agreements are untrustworthy, whereas written agreements are comparatively reliable. Yet he takes this last step, one of profound historical significance, without any written document having been signed, sealed, and delivered. In truth, he cannot await an answer from London. He trusts, however, not in the mere word of a captain in the navy, but in the moral effect of what he is doing. That is why, just before going on board the "Bellerophon," he writes the above-quoted heroic lines, addressed to the ruler of the land in which he seeks hospitality, and the supreme commander of all its navies.

Then, in uniform, Napoleon boards the British vessel.

XX

Maitland stands on the quarter-deck. Napoleon raises his hat, a thing he has not always done to greet princes, and addresses the captain as follows: "I come to place myself under the protection of your king and your laws." The British naval officers are introduced to him, and he asks about the sea-fights in which they have been engaged. Then, with the detachment of a man discussing ancient history, he talks about the English navy and the French, says that the English sailors are cleaner and more efficient, and argues with his host about certain punishments customary in the navy after a fight. Then he passes to generalities:

"I really cannot understand why your ships have defeated our French vessels so easily. The best of them were ours to begin with. A French ship is stronger in every respect than an English vessel of the same type. It has more and heavier guns, a larger complement."

"I have already explained that to you, Sir. Our seamen have had more experience than yours."

Napoleon does not move an eyelash. The conversation remains strictly academic; they talk of the nautical science of their respective countries.

"If you had tried to escape in a French frigate," says Maitland, "you would have seen for yourself how well we can shoot."

No repining! Here stands a gamester who has lost the game. All that the Emperor troubles to dispute is Maitland's contention that two frigates with a few twenty-four pounders could not possibly have got the better of the "Bellerophon," which carried seventy-four heavy guns. The captain proves that it would have been impossible. Napoleon examines the ship's guns, praises what he sees, but has some criticisms to make here and there. Maitland declares afterwards, when alone with his own people, that he has been amazed by the extent of the Emperor's technical knowledge.

The ship puts out to sea.

Meanwhile, the legitimate ministers and kings are discussing their course. Not a single member of this circle proves great enough to advise a great gesture, before Europe and before history. Ten days after leaving the roads of Rochefort, the "Bellerophon" anchors in Plymouth harbour. It is a fine morning in the end of July, and the water is thronged with rowing boats full of people anxious to catch a glimpse of the caged lion. Since no decision has yet arrived from London, civilian visitors are not allowed on board. But it is a great time for the crew. They can see Napoleon every day, and he converses with any of them that are able to speak French. The gaping crowds in the boats are the thousands who for twenty years past have heard nothing but abuse and mockery of "Boney"; have seen numberless caricatures of him, depicted as a hideous monster. Now, they are all animated with the same curiosity; they all want to feast their eyes upon this dread spectre.

For the most part, Napoleon stays in his cabin. He does not want to become a raree-show. A few days' patience, and he will be able to go ashore, and live where he pleases. At length, however, feeling the need for fresh air, he comes up the gangway and mounts the poop. There he stands, the great defeated foe, in his old world-famous green coat; defenceless. Thousands of eyes instantly converge on him, so that it seems as if he must be consumed in their fire.

But the man with the simple, impenetrable countenance, who is thus pilloried, must radiate an aura of dignity and suffering, for an extraordinary thing happens. Thousands of heads are bared. As far as Napoleon's gaze can reach, on the boats, the ships, throughout the harbour, not a man remains covered. The greeting is universal, but for one exception. Only one man among all those onlookers keeps his three-cornered hat on his head. It seems as if the whole nation were willing to pay the Emperor the homage which a pettifogging captain withheld.

Such was the judgment of the British nation, which in this

tense moment cleared itself from all the contumely so soon to be heaped upon its name. The waiting lasted three days. On the fourth, British officers entered the Emperor's cabin, and laid before him a paper containing the government's decision. No direct answer had come from the prince regent.

The document was to the effect that it would not be consistent with the government's duties towards England and her allies to allow General Bonaparte any further opportunity of disturbing the peace of Europe, and it would therefore be necessary to restrain his liberty to "whatever extent may be necessary for securing that first and paramount object." St. Helena would be his place of residence, as it was healthy, and would admit of a smaller degree of restraint than might be necessary elsewhere. He could take with him three officers, a physician, and twelve servants.

Such was the reply of the modern Xerxes.

Napoleon, we are told, "laid the paper on the table, and, after a pause, began to protest in vigorous terms." He said:

"I am not a prisoner of war! . . . I came on board the 'Bellerophon' of my own free will, after previous negotiation with the commander. I threw myself on your protection, and claimed the rights of hospitality. The tricolour was still waving over Rochefort and Bordeaux. I might have gone back to the army; or might for years have lived secretly among the people, who were devoted to me.

"Instead, I came to this country as a private person. I asked the commander of one of your warships whether he was disposed to take me and my train to England. He told me he had orders to this effect from his government. If I have fallen into a trap, your government has acted dishonourably and has dishonoured your flag. . . . St. Helena will kill me in three months. I am used to riding twenty leagues a day. What can I do on a little rock at the world's end? I will not go! . . . If your government wishes to kill me, that can be done here. . . . I gave the prince regent an opportunity of performing the finest action of his life. I have been the greatest of his country's foes, and I paid you the highest compliment in the world by voluntarily entrusting myself to your protection. . . . What you are proposing will be an everlasting disgrace to the whole British nation!"

The most characteristic point in this protest, which he renews in writing, is the moral indignation with which it thrills. International law is but lightly touched upon, for what he claims is a hero's right. Such were the words spoken in the heat of the moment, in that small cabin, to the officers who had brought him notice of his doom, and who subsequently recorded them for posterity. Though spoken in haste, they have a historical ring and some of the sentences are modelled for imperishability. A soul has been wounded, a soul that is mourning, not so much on account of its own loss of freedom, as because the world fails to recognise greatness.

Thus, in the first moment of his doom, he recognises that which, a century later, cannot be more profoundly expressed by the great grandchildren of the men of those days, who have been brought up on contemplation of the legend of Napoleon's career. Themistocles feels that he has been betrayed. Once again, one of these legitimate princes has failed to seize the opportunity of performing the finest action of his life. A man void of imagination, a weakling in possession of brute force, he crushed the great and splendid thing which has fallen into his hands.

But from under the brutal pressure of this fist, the spirit of what he is crushing rises in a tenuous column. He upon whom the doom is enforced has acquired a power over himself, a power which sustains him in his powerlessness—stoicism. After the first outbreak, he bears the injustice with indomitable firmness, enduring for ten days the indignity of his position at Plymouth, and unruffled while England seizes his baggage and his money.

In due course, the Emperor and his companions were transferred to the "Northumberland," which set sail for St. Helena. It was on an August morning that, for the last time, Napoleon set eyes on the coast of France, looming through the mist. But what did he care about the coast? The centre of his interest lay many miles to the eastward—Paris, which he had wooed more hotly than all the rest of the world, Paris, which had rejected his suit.

By evening, he loses sight of Europe, which he has ruled. Darkling is the sea, which he has never been able to rule. He stands in the bows, not looking backwards, nor forwards either. As on the voyage to Egypt, he looks upwards towards the stars. He is seeking his own star.

A great saga is drawing to its close.

BOOK FIVE

THE ROCK

On Judgment Day, before God's throne,
There stood at last, Napoleon.
The Devil had his list begun
Of crimes the Bonapartes had done,
When God the Father, or God the Son,
Cut Satan short before God's throne:
"Don't bore us all to death with reading
A German professorial pleading!
If you're bold enough to face him,
In your kingdom you may place him."

—GOETHE.

I

THE sea spreads out into the vast distance. It is like a mirror of steel. The man on the rock, hands clasped behind, stares across the watery plain. He is lonely, so lonely.

One looking at him from a distance would see a fat man with short legs, a man of uncertain age. He is wearing a green coat, decorated with the star of the Legion of Honour; silk stockings; three-cornered hat in his hands. The head is large; the brownish hair makes a bush at the back; there is no sign of whitening. The short neck springs from powerful shoulders. The features are as if hewn out of stone, with a yellowish tint, like the marble of an ancient statue that has been darkened in the course of the ages; no wrinkles, but the classical profile is somewhat marred by the heaviness of the chin. The only beautiful features are the nose and the teeth. These last are perfect, and he has never lost a tooth. His hands, too, are beautiful. All through his campaigns he was scrupulous in his care for them; and, when correcting the letters and despatches he dictated, he generally used a pencil in order that he might avoid staining his fingers with ink.

The doctors have told us a good deal about his physical condition. "Pulse never more frequent than 62; bosom well padded, almost like a woman's, and with very little hair; partes viriles exiguitates insignis sicut pueri." He himself knows much about his body, he has studied his battle-field of his life in order that here, likewise, he may utilise his forces to the best advantage.

"I have never yet heard my own heart beating; it is almost as if I had none," he says, half seriously. Moderation, he assures us, is the secret of his amazing faculty for work. "Nature has bestowed on me two valuable gifts: the capacity for sleeping whenever I want to; and the incapacity for committing excesses in drinking and eating. . . . However little a man may eat, he always eats too much. One can get ill from over-eating, but never from under-eating." The alternation between campaigning and sedentary life enables him again and again to escape from the air of the study, and to fortify his constitution by long rides and drives. "Water, air, and cleanliness are my favourite medicines."

With a body thus steeled, he can drive without stopping from Tilsit to Dresden, nearly five hundred miles, and be quite fresh at the journey's end: can ride fifty miles from Vienna to Semmering, breakfast there, and be back at work in Schönbrunn the same evening; can gallop in five hours from Valladolid to Burgos, a distance of about eighty miles. After long rides and marches through Poland, he reaches Warsaw at midnight and receives the new authorities at seven next morning. These are the excesses he practises to restore the balance of his natural forces. After a long spell of sedentary life, he will start off on a ride of seven days, or will go out shooting for the whole day; after great exertions, he will keep his room for twenty-four hours. He believes that his energy has saved his life. He says to Metternich: "Sometimes death only comes from lack of energy. Yesterday, when I was thrown out of my carriage, I thought I was done for. But I had just time to say to myself that I would not die. Any one else in my place would have been killed."

His muscles are powerful, but his nerves are sensitive. Accustomed to command, he cannot endure anything in the nature of compulsion. If his coat is at all tight, he tears it off; the same with shoes that pinch him in the slightest. On these occasions, he will box his servants' ears. If he has to wear court dress, they watch out while they help him on with his coat. When his mind is busy (when is it not?) he will push away his breakfast, jump up from his chair, and stride about, talking, issuing orders. His handwriting is nothing more than

Napoleon as Emperor in 1815. Engraving by Robert Lefèvre, after a painting by Muneret.

a series of violent contractions of the hand which cannot keep up with the furious pace of his thoughts; a sort of involuntary shorthand, which in places has not been deciphered after a hundred years of study. He cannot endure the smell of paint or size; he always masks unpleasant odours by using eau-de-Cologne. If his nerves are utterly exhausted, he soothes them in a hot bath. When the war with England broke out, he worked continuously, with four secretaries, for three days and three nights, and then spent six hours in his bath dictating dispatches. This nervous irritability is the antithesis of his slow circulation. He thinks that, the constitution of his nerves being what it is, he would be in danger of going mad, "if it were not that my blood works so slowly."

But there is no evidence at all that his nervousness ever rose to the pitch of convulsions, that he suffered from epilepsy. This illness usually begins in childhood, and none of his school-mates have reported that he had fits. Never was any one's life more closely watched than Napoleon's; and the documents upon which the assertion that he was an epileptic is based are scanty, confused, and untrustworthy.

As long as his body remained healthy, he was able to endure all the tensions and shocks to which he was exposed. It was when he was approaching forty that he began to show the first symptoms of a stomach trouble which was in those days summarily diagnosed as cancerous. Beyond questions, the tendency to it was inherited. During the last three years of warfare, he was put out of action in decisive hours by paroxysms of gastric spasm. His courage and resolution were practically unimpaired; had it not been for these attacks, the history of his decline would have been different.

II

The soul which governed this body was driven forward by three fundamental powers:

Self-confidence, energy, imagination.

"I am not as other men; the laws of morality and convention cannot be applied to me." In these cold words, he emphasises the "I" with which he began his first political writing in the days of his youth. They are a plain acknowledgment of a fact, by a man of thirty to whom nothing is more alien than vanity. "I alone, because of my position, know what government is," he said when he was Consul. "I am persuaded that no one save myself could govern France at this moment. Were I to die, it would be a great misfortune for the nation." He utters such words seldom, and only when he is with an intimate; but these sayings show with what scientific aloofness he could contemplate the phenomenon, Napoleon. When, during the Russian disaster, he was asked who in spite of all would defend him in France, he replied: "My name."

His contemporaries and posterity have held this fundamental feeling to be ambition. That view is mistaken. Common ambition distinguishes itself from Napoleon's self-confidence as a restless, climbing animal does from a bird of prey whose free flight, by a law of nature, assumes wider and wider circles as it swings heavenwards. Napoleon's aspiration is neither restless nor envious: it is nothing but his natural disposition which, as Consul, he once charmingly explained to his friend Roederer:

"I have no ambition whatever; or if I have, then it is so inborn, so intimately knit up with my very life, that it is as the blood in my veins. It does not incite me to outstrip my associates. . . . I have never had to fight for or against it; it does not urge me to greater speed than is natural to me, it comes out only when circumstances and my ideas demand."

Already in the days when he was a general, ideas and circumstances forced upon him the conviction that he was the man predestined to rebuild France. It is nothing other than the conviction of his mission which makes him say to Roederer: "Circumstances have changed. I am now one of those who found States, not one of those who ruin States." Another time, he speaks of Corneille, but he means himself when he says: "Whence did this man acquire his antique greatness? From himself, from his soul? Very well. Do you know what that is called, My Lord Cardinal? It is called genius. Genius is a flame, which comes from heaven, but seldom finds a head ready to receive it. Corneille is a man whom the world has recognised." When his interlocutor observed that the poet had not seen the flame, so how could he recognise it, the Emperor answered scornfully: "Precisely for that reason I consider he is a great man!"

He thus, indirectly by anticipation, announces his own genius to the world, just as Goethe had announced his own.

The will-to-power, not as an endeavour or even as a question, but, rather, as simplicity, dwells within him close at hand. He calls interest the key to ordinary deeds; the will to govern the intellect, he describes as the strongest of all the passions: and the artistic urge of genius, he depicts in the following words: "I love power, yes, I love it, but after the manner of an artist: as a fiddler loves his fiddle in order to conjure from it tone, chords, harmonies."

That is why it is his nature to command. "Wherever I may be, I command, or else I keep silence." He might have added: "I negotiate," for he had spent a quarter of his time in negotiating. Even as a young general of twenty-seven, he aroused the respect of all who came in contact with him. He never learned to obey; but to command came to him naturally at the very outset, just as a calf stands and walks in the first hour of its life. Because this power of commanding comes so naturally, he never acquires the art of asking; because he can command as no other, he is denied the gift of being able to ask favours.

His self-confidence confers on him a natural dignity that amazes and angers the legitimist world, which believes dignity to be consonant only with heredity and culture. The friends of his youth stand embarrassed when they recognise him as their commander in the field and yet realise the solitude which his position as leader entails. All his companions-in-arms speak of him with spontaneous homage. One of his intimates writes: "When he speaks, every one listens, for he speaks as an expert; if he is silent, his silence is respected; and no one would venture to say that he was silent because of ill humour. We all felt that between him and us there lived a great thought which was wholly occupying his mind and forbade familiar accost." This statement is all the more surprising since it was made during a campaign, when tent life usually breaks down barriers. With absolute ingenuousness he once said, while playing and chatting with friends at Malmaison: "I have no sense of the ridiculous. Power is never ridiculous."

An adept at analysis, the greatest psychologist of his epoch, he knows all about his own qualities, and is therefore able, by degrees, to elaborate these instincts into principles. "The goodness of a king," he informs his brother Louis, King of Holland, "must always bear a regal stamp and must never be monkish. . . . The love which a king inspires should invariably be a manly love, wedded to reverence, fear, and esteem. If people speak of him as 'a good man,' his rule is a failure." This love and fear which he himself inspires has the greatest practical results.

Nevertheless, the dignity which holds people at a distance is not assumed, for a leading element in it is a bewildering naturalness, which grows with the years and with his successes. His unsophisticated and frank realism, the sterling simplicity of his character, shows itself in a hundred gestures and words, and in the freshness with which he repeatedly makes fun of his own ardency. He expresses this in a profound saying: "A truly great man will rise superior to the events which he himself has brought about." The greatest successes, whose fateful origin and consequences he fully grasps, he sums up to his intimates in a schoolboy's laugh. Many have reported this, for between the boisterous gaiety of a soldier and the most delicate curl of the lip are many shades of good humour; he possesses all.

On the eve of his coronation he exclaims: "Is the result not truly delightful, to be named brother by the kings?" Or he sends his ambassador to St. Petersburg with the words: "Our brother in Russia is fond of luxury and festivity. Very well, then, give him his fill of them!" Sometimes his simplicity of manner infringes etiquette, and the legitimists blanch: "When I was an insignificant lieutenant," he begins once at table with the kings in Dresden. General consternation! Every one gazes into his plate. Napoleon clears his throat: "When I had the honour of serving as lieutenant in the second artillery regiment at Valence . . ." Or he is sitting with the tsar in Tilsit, and, since he is ever eager to learn, he asks offhandedly across the table: "How much does your tax on sugar bring in yearly?" We are told that this question places all present in a state of grave embarrassment. Why? Because, as a big man of business, he calls money by its name; whereas the kings never mention it by name, though they are glad enough to reap the harvest!

Since he was not vain, he knew when he had made mistakes. His whole life long he was in the habit of saying that next day he might lose a battle; he frequently consulted his friends and his experts, and was inspired with the feeling of God-given necessity. How well Napoleon could bear to be told the truth, we can learn from Marmont—who, when he praises, is one of the most trustworthy of witnesses, for he wrote his memoirs long after the Emperor had publicly stigmatised him as a traitor. "Napoleon had a strong sense of justice, and would readily forgive an improper word or other sign of anger in one who had good grounds for complaint, provided of course he was alone with the offender. . . . He made kindly allowance for others' weaknesses and could never resist the appeal of well-grounded sorrow. One who chose time and place, could say anything to him. He was always willing to listen to the truth. Though it did not invariably influence him, there was no danger in uttering it."

He saw through the wiles of flatterers, and they gained nothing from him. Byzantine bombast, devoid of political value, infuriated him. "How could you depict the French eagle tearing the English leopard to pieces, at a time when I cannot safely send even a fishing-smack out to sea? Break up your moulds instantly, and never show me anything of the kind again!"

On the other hand, those who fearlessly speak the truth to him, impress him. He praises Chateaubriand, who has attacked him. In the days when he was Consul he was wont, after a sitting of the Council of State, to invite to dinner the man who had most vigorously opposed his wishes. In the Russian campaign, a captive general tells him some home truths about the burning of Moscow. Napoleon dismisses the prisoner in a rage; but presently has him recalled, and shakes the Russian's hand, saying: "You are a brave man!" Méhul plays a trick on the Emperor, producing his new opera as the work of an Italian composer, and thus earning approbation. Paisiello also plays a trick by introducing into one of his own compositions an aria by Cimarosa, a composer whose work Bonaparte cannot endure. The Consul applauds; and when afterwards told of the deception, he only laughs.

Madame de Staël has been a worry to him for fifteen years, voicing Europe's call for freedom. He suppresses her books, banishes her from Paris, continues to take measures against her even when he is in Russia, speaks of her as the dangerous driving-wheel which sets the salons in motion; but he pays this enemy the high compliment of dreading her, and acknowledges as much in many of his private letters.

In the Bavarian muster rolls, he comes across the name of a former regimental comrade, a declared royalist. He makes this man his military attaché. They have not met for fourteen years. Now, during the campaign, they meet, and the old companion introduces himself. The Emperor rides with him out of the press, dismounts, and sits down on a convenient stone; the other wishes to hold his horse. "Let be," says Napoleon; "that's not your business," and beckons a chasseur to take the bridle-rein. The Emperor promptly becomes reminiscent: "Do you remember how, at the lieutenants' mess in Besançon, you flung your table napkin down and shouted: 'I will not sit beside an officer who belongs to the Jacobin Club!' That is ancient history, and is of no consequence now." He beckons his attendant staff and points to his interlocutor, saying: "Look at this fellow. Ability of the old school. He and I worked at equations together." Then, coming down to practical matters: "Have you plenty of ammunition? What is your artillery like? How soon will you be ready?"

Unique, perhaps, in Napoleon's life, is the scene at Erfurt in the year of 1813, when von Müller, the Weimar chancellor, braves his anger. Two privy councillors have written letters in cipher. These have been seized at the outposts. The writers have been arrested. Müller has been sent for. The Emperor has stormed at him, threatening to burn Jena, to shoot the culprits. Müller breaks in impetuously: "No, Sire, you will not commit this abomination! You will not tarnish your record for all time by shedding innocent blood!" In his excitement, the German presses so close that the Emperor anticipates a personal attack, and lays his hand on his sword-hilt. Müller is dragged back by a companion. A pause. "You are a bold man, but I see that you are a good friend. Berthier shall look into the matter once more." The privy councillors are pardoned.

This scene, creditable to both participants, is another proof of Napoleon's invulnerable dignity. It is invulnerable, unless the arrow is poisoned. A sense of honour is the vulnerable point of self-confidence. "If the French people expects certain advantages from me," said Bonaparte when First Consul, "it must put up with my weaknesses, and the chief of these is that

I cannot endure an affront." It was he who said: "I am a man whom people may kill, but will not affront." Bourrienne tells us that from Bonaparte's earliest days he had no faith in law or morality, but always believed in honour. This compensated for his fundamental amoralism. The power exercised over him by his conception of honour distinguishes him absolutely from the condottieri of the Renaissance, with whom he ought never to have been compared. When he is Consul, betwixt night and morning he breaks off his intimacy with this very Bourrienne, who has been his private secretary for so long, because Bourrienne is involved in an unsavoury financial scandal. Years afterwards, he refuses to admit Bourrienne to the Legion of Honour, saying: "One who worships the golden calf may have money, but not honour." When a bill signed by King Jerome goes to protest, Napoleon writes: "Sell your diamonds, your silver plate, your furniture, your horses—anything to pay your debts. Honour comes first!"

He was so sensitive on this point that after his coronation he summoned to his presence a notary who had long before advised Josephine against marrying a person of doubtful character; Napoleon wished to rehabilitate himself in this man's mind. In exile at St. Helena, he remembered how his German teacher in Brienne had always treated him with contempt: "I should very much like to know whether Herr Bauer ever learned how I made good!"

He is a stickler for morality, just as he is for honour. "Nothing can be worse in a ruler than immorality. He makes it fashionable, and it poisons society." Napoleon does not say this merely because he has been warned by the example of the Bourbons and the Directors. He has an inborn sense of decency, which is part of his dignity. No one has ever recorded having heard Napoleon, the soldier, tell an obscene story. Nor did he ever listen to one complacently. When he becomes First Consul, he forbids Josephine to have anything more to do with friends of hers who are leading gay lives. Years afterwards, when the empress allows Tallien to visit her, Napoleon writes to reprimand his wife, saying: "I can see no excuses for Tallien. I know that some poor devil has married her with her eight bastards, and I despise her even more than I did before. She was an amiable cocotte; now she is nothing more than a common woman."

Talleyrand, who has had a liaison for many years, is told that he must marry his inamorata or quit Napoleon's service within twenty-four hours. Berthier is made a prince, but the same condition is imposed on him, Napoleon saying: "This passion of yours has lasted too long, and is becoming ridiculous. You are a man of fifty, but may live to be eighty, and these thirty years are left you for marriage." The revolution had encouraged nudity in mythological representations, but Napoleon wants nakedness to be draped. When, in one of the squares there is set up a fountain where there is a group of naiads with water spouting from their breasts, he has "these wet-nurses" removed as improper, and decrees that "the naiads were virgins." His own women friends must not make themselves conspicuous. He lavishes money on them; but if they are actresses, he does not allow his liaison to be used as a reason for promotion. On the other hand, like any bourgeois he boasts of sharing his wife's bedroom, saying: "It has a remarkable influence upon conjugal life, strengthens the man's influence, guarantees his faithfulness, promotes intimacy and good morals; a couple will never become estranged if they spend the whole night together. As long as Josephine and I kept this custom, she was familiar with all my thoughts."

One of the most sublime forms of his egotism is gratitude. This is not ordinary kindness, but the pride of a man who feels he is unique, and overwhelms with benefits any one who has ventured to be useful to him, lest he should possibly remain in the other's debt. That was the consideration which really underlay his frequently declared policy, that he would never make use of any party, lest he should incur obligations. We must not look upon these things in a romantic light. But it is an actual fact that he was not content to promote only the friends of his youth, his fellow-students at the military academy. As soon as he rose to power, he found for the priest who had been headmaster at Brienne a sinecure at Malmaison as librarian—without any books! The sometime school porter became lodge keeper at his country house. A young lady of noble birth to whom, in his lieutenant days, he had once paid court for a whole evening, and who sixteen years later applied for help to the Emperor, received what she wanted, together with a post for her brother, and a friendly letter. He remembered many of his former associates in his will. Years after his brief intimacy with "Giorgina," when he hears that she is in difficulties (though she has made no application to him), he provides her with a competency.

Hitherto we have been talking about money, or money's worth. But the nature of his gratitude is different when he loves, as in the case of Josephine. When we consider his relationships with her, we realise the truth of Marmont's tribute, which is all the more remarkable as coming from an enemy: "He had a grateful, kind, indeed affectionate, heart." At the time of the coronation, he says to Roederer: "What right have I to put away a good wife merely because I have become a greater man than I was when we married? . . . Before all, I am a just man." A little later, he writes to Josephine: "As far as I am concerned, I deem ingratitude the greatest weakness any one can have."

III

Napoleon's self-confidence, his self-esteem, his egotism, lies at the root of his wavering between revolution and legitimacy. Relying entirely upon himself, scorning all whose pride rests upon the accident of birth, he has nevertheless to take the egotism of others into account in so far as this egotism becomes embodied in achievement. And yet he is constitutionally incapable of suffering others to be on an equal footing with himself. For his own sake he has to choose the most capable to fill administrative and other positions, and yet he has to please the masses: he must stand for equality of all, and at the same time bear the individual in mind. These contradictions give rise to a tragical conflict.

Both the weapons he has chosen for his battle of life, namely, the spirit and the sword, he conceives of in a revolutionary sense. "Why is the French army the most dreaded in the world? Because the officers became émigrés; non-commissioned officers replaced them, and became generals. One can lead a people's army with non-commissioned officers, for they have risen from the people. For years, Napoleon refused to confer the grand cross of the Legion of Honour upon Metternich and Schwarzenberg. It was only after their gallant behaviour during the fire at Schwarzenberg's mansion, that the Emperor relented, and conferred the decoration. The orders which his brother, the king of Holland, distributed with so lavish a hand, Napoleon would not allow to be worn in Paris. He sends his brother the following memorandum for kings:

"How can one give this indelible mark of appreciation to a man one does not know, to a person who may before long prove to be a rogue? Learn to know those who gather round your throne! The wish to distribute decorations should not be gratified suddenly, as one can gratify a desire to go out for a day's shooting. Noteworthy achievements must come first. . . . You have as yet done nothing to deserve the honour of decorating others with your effigy. . . ."

His egotism makes him emphasise the advantage of the lack of any ancestry to an original or unusual person. When flatterers suggest that one of his Italian forebears should be canonised, he calls the suggestion an idiocy. Metternich lays before Napoleon an ancestral tree manufactured in Vienna from records of the Buonaparte family in Tuscany. The Emperor says: "Take these papers away!" In the official gazette, Napoleon has the following notice inserted: "To all questions as to when the house of Bonaparte began, the answer is simple: on the Eighteenth Brumaire. How can one show so little tact and good breeding for all one owes the Emperor as to stress the question of his ancestry?" Once he is so angry because some one has contradicted him in this matter of his genealogy that he exclaims: "I shall not suffer any one to insult me by treating me as if I were a king!"

Then come transitions in which the cleavage begins to show itself. "I shall be the Brutus of the kings and the Cæsar of the republic:" which saying is certainly ambiguous. "I know of no aristocracy but the rabble which I have allowed to escape; and of no rabble but the aristocracy which I have created:" here there is hardly any ambiguity. "Tacitus is praised because he made the tyrants fear the people—and that was a very bad thing for the people:" which is open to but one interpretation.

No one, in the presence of such a man, can be satisfied with the facile assertion that Napoleon only pretended to believe in the principles of freedom until he attained to power, and then promptly betrayed them. On the contrary, we have here to do with a spiritual struggle. This is the one problem with which the self-confident man had to wrestle; a problem he never solved.

"I am the man of the people: its pulse beats in unison with my own. . . . The aristocracy remains always aloof, and never forgives." Such utterances show us the original trend of his character. Inasmuch as he overcomes this trend, never becomes an ideologue, but gets the better of his inborn sympathies, he is a statesman of genius. Of course it is ridiculous when he, who only rewards merit, decorates his baby son's cradle with the grand cordon of the Legion of Honour; or again, when he has the deposed king of Spain, who addressed him as "cousin," informed through the intermediation of Talleyrand that the Emperor must be addressed as "Sire." These weaknesses are grotesque, and yet they are superficial; he himself recognises them and spurns them if the mood is upon him. When he is hesitating whether he shall send Eugene, or perhaps better still Talleyrand (a man sprung from the old noblesse), to prepare the ground for the "imperial diet" at Erfurt, he suddenly, in virile fashion, ceases to bother about the question: "After all, what does it matter to me whether I am criticised? I will show them that I do not care."

A more serious problem, both for him and for us, is when the origin and the laws of the right of succession to the throne come up for discussion. "It is false to call me a usurper; I have simply taken the unoccupied place which Louis could not keep for himself. Had I been Louis I should have hindered the revolution in spite of the amazing progress which has accrued to thought because of the change. . . . My strength is in my good luck; I am as new as the Empire." Yet, in spite of this somewhat confused reasoning, he ventures a step farther, and writes to Brother Louis: "I hold myself responsible for everything that has happened since Clovis' days down to the days of the Committee of Public Safety; and I shall consider everything that is deliberately said against the governments as an attack on myself."

Thus we see that his egotism reaches so paradoxical an intensity in the championship of legitimacy, and that he sails so near the serious acceptance of rule by divine right (which is otherwise only used by him as a political formula), that he makes himself responsible for the actions of those very kings whose dethronement has opened the way to his rise!

All his life he restlessly hovered round this question of status. At Kaunitz Castle, during the night after Austerlitz, while at every minute Austrian and Russian colours, captive generals, and dispatches from the beaten commanders, are being brought to him, he thrusts everything aside because the courier from Paris has entered the room. Then he does the same with all the tidings from the capital, in order to read a letter full of gossip from a lady, who tells how the Fronde of the Faubourg has sworn never to put in an appearance at court. He is furious: "Ah! so these people fancy that they are stronger than I? Very well, gentlemen of the old aristocracy, we shall see! We shall see!" This is on the evening after the battle of Austerlitz!

Here we see such hatred as that which a man gradually comes to feel for a woman who stubbornly resists his wooing. He must win over the spirit of tradition, cost what it may. One evening, not very long before the scene just described, he takes Roederer from the drawing-room into the billiard-room, begins knocking the balls about, and then says, apropos of nothing in particular:

"Your Senate has no feelings for the aristocratic, no esprit de corps in favour of the imperial system."

"Sire, it is devoted to your person."

"That is not what I want. It must be devoted to my mantle, no matter who wears it. The mantle ought to be enough to guarantee the safety of the wearer. This is the aristocratic spirit, which is lacking to you ideologues!"

The whole problem of hereditary succession is implicit in these considerations; it logically develops therefrom, leading to the second marriage, and thus to the tragical issue. There are only two things which Napoleon cannot create unaided: children and ancestors. He therefore asks the world of legitimate rulers to enter into an alliance with him, which will settle his difficulty as far as offspring is concerned, and will also provide his children with an ancestry. He is not really a man of the people, but a nobleman; and who can complain because he regards himself as such?

"I am in a peculiar position. The genealogists want to trace my pedigree back to the deluge, while there are some who describe me as sprung from the lower middle class. Truth lies between. The Bonapartes are a good Corsican family, not celebrated, but certainly better than these coxcombs who believe themselves entitled to humiliate us."

This is the tone of the sixteen-year-old lad, scion of the lesser territorial nobility, whom a handful of counts made fun of at the military academy and slighted at the boarding school in Paris. They are the very words which the young man had used in his letters and literary sketches when the noblesse of monarchical France had mortified him. Nothing can expunge the memory of his early mortifications. It may well be that, but for these never-to-be-forgotten affronts suffered at the hands of a few silly young marquises, his whole outlook upon the question of legitimacy would have been different; his court life, his marriage, his destiny, would have been different; and therewith the course of European history would have been other than it was.

His egotism finds expression in the struggle with France, just as it does in the struggle with the noblesse. He does not wholly belong to the high nobility, and therefore throughout life he remains critical of the pretensions of birth. In the same way, though formally he was a Frenchman, he was not French by blood, and he was therefore irritably critical of the French, just as he was irritably critical of the noblesse. He conquered both, but never felt perfectly secure in either of his conquests.

But he had more success with France than with the legitimists. Because he is not really a Frenchman, France never becomes his legitimate spouse; she remains his beloved mistress. He knows this; he wooes, gives himself, renounces; and from the perpetual uncertainty of his relationship to France, he derives the keenest joys of his life. "I have only one passion, only one mistress: France. I lie by her side. She has never been untrue to me; she pours out her blood for me, and lavishes her treasures upon me. If I need half a million men, she gives them!" When he chides his mistress, he does it as a jealous lover; he rules her "with an iron hand in a velvet glove"; he gratifies all her caprices; and he knows better than any one else how to allure her by the glamour of fame and fantasy. That is why she beams on him when he comes home victorious; that is why she gives him her children.

Yet lover and mistress remain critical of one another. Mutual jealousy persists. Neither of them ever forgets the wish to master the other. Hear his exclamation in the tone of a despotic lover: "I swear that I do everything for the sake of France alone! If I do not give her more liberty, it is because she does not need more!" He is standing in the middle of his drawing-room, scrutinising his guests sharply as he speaks to them with raised voice. Among intimates, he will often use harsher words: "Always the same old Gauls! The same frivolity, the same vanity! When, if ever, will these be replaced by a proper pride?"

The French, likewise, remain sceptical. Must they not, in confidential talks, say of this Italian the very thing that he once wrote to his brother Louis? "Since you ascended the throne, you have forgotten that you are a Frenchman, and have strained every nerve to persuade yourself that you are a Dutchman. The foreign environment tickles your fancy, but it is still foreign." Roederer writes of Napoleon: "He is making a mistake. They are by no means so enthusiastic about him as they were about Lafayette (who did nothing practical for them). At bottom, they merely admire and respect him because he is useful to them."

Such a liaison cannot fail to end tragically. The mistress discards her lover when he is no longer useful to her.

Tragical, too, is the ending of another embodiment of his egotism, its noblest incorporation. "I wish I could be my own posterity, and read what such a poet as Corneille would make me feel, do, and say." From boyhood's days down to the time of his exile, in the island where he was born and in the island where he died, his self-esteem is nourished on historical parallels. History, he said, was the only true philosophy. Had he not had his peculiar feeling for history, Napoleon's career would have been very different; nay, it would have been impossible.

His political calculations are fed from two sources, history and imagination; the first of these streams being intellectual, and the second passionate. It is history alone which gives him alighting places on his flight. In his own age he is unique; he travels alone; nowhere but in history can he find prototypes by whose example he can guide his impetuous progress. With Cæsar, the lieutenant begins to soar. At Rochefort, the Emperor ends the active phase of his existence by trusting too implicitly in the heroic example of Themistocles.

Between the opening and the close, we find numberless indications of the way in which his imagination remains at work, mirroring the great incidents of classical and modern history. Why is he opposed to Tacitus and Chateaubriand? Because they warn the people against tyrants. Why does he blame the assassins of Cæsar? Because he wishes to defend his own sentence upon the duke of Enghien. When he is First Consul, he actually thinks of writing a few chapters of Roman history, to prove "that Cæsar never wanted to become king, and that he was murdered because he wished to re-establish order by uniting all parties." He goes on to add that Cæsar had been killed in the Senate House, and that in the Senate were forty Pompeians, personal enemies of the dictator. Napoleon's unexpressed inference is that he must clean up the Senate, and he does so.

In the Roman style, he sketches the ideas for eight splendid bas-reliefs which, on triumphal arches, are to illustrate the doings of his reign; they are to be representations of fact, devoid of self-commendation, and only in a formal sense illustrations of historical egotism. He summons historiographers and imaginative writers from all civilised lands, and converses with them for hours, in order that, through their intermediation, he may win the approval of posterity. When his portrait seems to him too crudely lifelike, he says that Alexander never sat to Apelles; David must paint him "in a tranquil attitude, mounted upon a fiery steed." It pleases him to write army orders when he is sitting in Frederick the Great's study; at Sans Souci, to invite the biographer of the former master of the house to dine with him; in Lombardy, to visit the arch of Augustus, in Egypt, the pillar of Pompey, and on these monuments to inscribe the names of those who have recently fallen; in Madrid and Moscow, to study the environment and the habits of Philip and of Catherine. But his pleasure in these things is not purely æsthetic. The hours he devotes to them are heroical; they are Napoleon's true recompense; they are realisations of his earliest dreams.

With his own hand, he is continually writing his own history. The young general records his first victories in orders of the day; with each new campaign, and after every battle, he adds to the long series; and the work is done with the hand of an artist, is wrought with an eye to immortal fame. When he is offered the crown of Italy, he surveys his own deeds of little more than five years ago as if they had come down in legend: "When, a few years later, we learned on the banks of the Nile that our aims had come to naught, we were bitterly distressed at this evil turn of fortune; but, thanks to the courage of our armies, we were able to appear in Milan at a time when Italy believed us to be still on the shores of the Red Sea." Actually, in the interim, he had, before the eyes of all the world, trampled on the constitution of France, and even the meanest herd in the Apennines knew of his return from Egypt.

When he is carrying on a struggle with the pope he pens a long letter, and sends it to Eugene for the latter to copy, since ostensibly it is to be a letter from Eugene to the pope; therein Eugene is made to say that Napoleon can only be compared to Cyrus and Charlemagne.

At the height of his career, he says to his Austrian ambassador: "Don't you make any mistake, I am a Roman emperor, in the best line of the Cæsars. Chateaubriand has compared me with Tiberius, who could only travel from Rome to Capri. A pretty idea! Trajan, Aurelian—that would be another story. They were self-made men, who shook the world out of old ruts. Do you not see the resemblances between my regime and that of Diocletian? The net so widely spread; the Emperor's eyes everywhere; the civil authority omnipotent throughout an empire that is fundamentally warlike. . . . A man is born to be a Cæsar."

This is not a proclamation, not a political letter, not an attempt to seduce any one. The words are spoken lightly, in a drawing-room, without emotion and without ulterior aim, with all the simplicity of a man aware of his own strength.

After victories and successes, this historical feeling for his own personality becomes as objective as the attitude of the chessplayer towards the pieces on his board. We seem to be contemplating a man whose fondness for the game is the only thing which makes him want to win; and who, as soon as he has won, can converse dispassionately with his defeated opponent about the mistakes they have made and the artifices to which they have had recourse. When he is talking to enemy generals whom he has taken prisoner or with whom he is negotiating, he will say: "You ought to have done this, that, or the other. There, you were in an advantageous position. That would have been an excellent move."

Immediately after his victory at Wagram, he says to Count Bubna: "I am certain that you are damnably strong, for you can deliver shrewd blows. At what figure do you estimate my forces? . . . You appear to be uncommonly well informed! Would you care to have a look at my army? . . . No? Well, at least you had better study my position on this map. It was my own fault when I failed to win a victory at Aspern-Essling. I got the punishment I deserved."

Only with regard to one matter does this detachment fail him—Waterloo. In St. Helena, an English surgeon ventured to say that people in England would be glad to hear his opinion of Wellington. The remark was followed by an embarrassing silence.

Fame is the supreme goal of his egotism; substantially, it is the only goal. All his energies are directed towards this end: his consciousness of his uniqueness; his historic sense; his sense of honour; his dignity; the boy's dreams, the youth's plans, the man's deeds, the prisoner's unrest. Posterity is the great confused picture which fills his imagination; and the desire of his heart would seem to be rather the Latin "gloria" which thinks of future generations, than the French "gloire" which suns itself in the smile of contemporaries. He is animated by a daimonic being's eager wish for immortality, although he knows that he must share the fate of all mortal men. "Better never to have lived; than to exist, and pass without leaving a trace."

He modifies the coronation oath by swearing, not only to protect the realm and the happiness of France, but also to rule for the glory of his people. On one of the battle-fields of Henry IV in Normandy he has a column erected with the inscription: "Great men love the fame of those who resemble themselves." Frederick's sword is "more precious than all the treasures of the king of Prussia"; but it is not only when he is campaigning that his thoughts turn towards the future. When he is having houses built for the unemployed, his order to the minister to whom the task is entrusted ends with the phrase: "We must not pass out of the world without leaving traces that will commend us to the thoughts of posterity." At the close of his career as Emperor, he refuses to make peace on terms that will involve the renunciation of territories upon whose conquest part of his fame depends; and towards the end of his life he utters a melancholy parable, darkly significant, lonely as his own destiny:

"The love for glory is like the bridge which Satan tried to build across chaos in order to make his way into paradise. Glory is a connecting link between past and future, from which an abyss separates him. I leave to my son nothing but my name."

IV

Energy is the second element in Napoleon's make-up. How does this quality show itself?

First of all in calculation. Never a trace of the flash of genius; but, rather, continuous weighing, over-elaborating, discarding:

"I have known myself to argue with myself over the thoughts concerning a battle, and have contradicted myself. . . . When I have drawn-up a plan of battle I am the most pusillanimous of men. I magnify the dangers and the incidents, am in a terrible state of excitement even when I seem cheerful; I am then like a girl who is going to have a baby." This is the mood of an artist during the conception of his work. He once described these feelings to Roederer in even franker terms:

"I am always at work; I think a great deal. If I appeared to be ever ready and equal to any occasion, it is because I have thought over matters for long before I undertake to do the slightest thing; I have foreseen all eventualities. There exists no guardian angel who suddenly and mysteriously whispers in my ear what I have to do or to say. Everything is turned over in my mind, again and again, always, whether I am at table or at the theatre. At night, I wake up in order to work."

This constant deliberation builds up something within him which he names "the spirit of things:" the precision, which penetrates he touches; the thinking in numbers, to which he ascribes part of his success and for which he has to thank his mathematical training. There is nothing too small for this brain; for the sum total of millions of details is a plan whose scope is world embracing. If one of his officers writes to say that the Emperor's instructions have been carried out, Napoleon waives this general statement aside and demands details. Nothing is so small but he wants to know all about it and judge its importance for himself. He writes to Eugene, who is in Italy:

"How is it possible that you are distributing three million seven hundred and forty-seven thousand rations of meat? . . . I can calculate a similar gross total for dried vegetables, wine, salt, and spirits. But I want calculations according to corps. I am robbed of fifty per cent., even as much as seventy per cent. . . . How can you allow them to calculate for one million three hundred and seventy-one thousand rations of hay? I should have to provide twelve thousand horses to eat it, not counting the Istrians and Dalmatians! You know I have only seven thousand. . . . The office charges are insane! Frs. 118,000 for four months! That equals frs. 400,000 a year! Such a sum should suffice for the whole of Italy!"

This is but one example among many. Thousands of such letters, hailing from every corner of the military and civil administration, personally dictated, are to be found in the volumes of correspondence, and must sadly disappoint those who expect to find only ideas and temperament in the letters. He is the man who, in the midst of his wars in Italy, writes home that they must concoct a letter, nominally written by a German patriot and dealing with Austrian politics, and have it circulated throughout Germany; again, in the throes of a campaign, he has to write to Murat, King of Naples, detailing how the latter is to behave at balls or when he visits the theatre, whom he is to invite and whom to exclude from his invitations. While the preparations are being made for the Erfurt gathering, he suddenly remembers that some one must be there to introduce the actresses to the gallant grand dukes. He never demonstrates more forcibly the way he formulates destinies in figures than by the following incursion into social life: "Each household should have six children, seeing that, on the average, three are sure to die. Of the three who survive, two should replace the father and mother; the third will serve for an unforeseen emergency."

His precision of thought goes to such grotesque lengths!

A third means for expressing this energetic faculty is his

tempo. "Activity! Speed!" he writes with his own hand at the foot of an order. The king of Prussia has depicted this peculiarity with especial felicity: "We need but see him ride: he always gives his horse rein, and never troubles about what may be happening in his rear!" But Napoleon negotiated better than he rode, for he never negotiated until after long reflection. "Not a moment must be lost," is the slogan even when nothing presses for decision. The instinctive impetus of an overburdened but short life drives him forward; it seems as if he could not arrive quickly enough at the end of his career. He writes to Bernadotte, in the course of a campaign: "I have lost a whole day through you, and the fate of the world hangs upon one single day."

The drive he imposes upon himself has its reaction upon those who serve him. He drives them, not only in the field, but also in circumstances which ordinary governments would take months to decide. He demands a treaty with Russia from Talleyrand, saying it is to be drawn up and ready in a couple of hours. To explain the reasons for his second marriage, he wants a circular letter sent to all his ambassadors and consuls; this is to be drafted "in the course of the day." One night he is immersed in thoughts concerning the embellishment of Paris. Next morning he says to his Minister for Home Affairs: "I require that Paris shall have two million inhabitants by the end of ten years. I want to do something useful and great for the city. What do you suggest?"

"Provide the town with a good water-supply, Sire," and the minister expounds a plan whereby the Ourcq water can be conveyed to Paris.

"Your proposal is good. Summon G.; he must send five hundred men to La Vilette to-morrow, in order to start work on the canal."

Another of his weapons is memory. "I always know my position. I cannot remember a single Alexandrine, but I never forget a figure relating to my military situation." This is the productive memory. Although he pronounces them abominably, he retains the names of all the important places—important from his point of view—in all the countries where he has fought. The Postmaster General reports that the Emperor is able to mention, offhand, distances which he himself has to hunt up in works of reference. On his way back to Paris from the camp at Boulogne, Napoleon encounters a troop of soldiers who have lost their way, asks the number of their regiment, whence they set out, and when. He tells them their line of march! "Your battalion will be at H. this evening." At this time, two hundred thousand men were on the march close at hand!

His technique is to arrange things in his head "as in a wardrobe." He says: "When I wish to put any matter out of my mind, I close its drawer and open the drawer belonging to another. The contents of the drawers never get mixed, and they never worry me or weary me. Do I want to sleep? I close all the drawers, and then I am asleep."

Among the numerous heraldic emblems which might have tickled the fancy of an upstart—stars, tutelary deities, saints, beasts of prey—he finds none to please him. He chooses the bee, thus emphasising once more his opinion that a man of talent who aspires and works unceasingly, can achieve everything that can otherwise be achieved through what is vaguely spoken of as genius. He declares that genius is industry; meaning, of course, that genius is industry among other things. He says that work is his element, that for which he has been created. Had he left nothing behind him, had all his works perished, still his industry and his glory would have been an emblematic stimulus to the youth of countless generations after he had passed away.

Many witnesses testify to his amazing powers of continued work. Roederer, who was his close companion during the Consulate, writes as follows: "That which especially characterises him is the power and persistence of his attention. He can work for eighteen hours at a stretch, it may be at one piece of work, it may be at several in turn. I have never seen his mind flag. I have never seen his mind without a spring in it, not when he was physically tired, not when he was taking violent exercise, not even when he was angry. I have never seen him distracted from one affair by another, neglecting the matter in hand for one which he is about to work. Good or bad news from Egypt never interfered with his attention to the civil code, and the civil code never interfered with the steps it was necessary to take for the safety of Egypt. No one was ever more wholly immersed in what he was doing, nor did any one ever make a better distribution of his time among all the things he had to do. Never was any one more stubborn in rejecting the occupation or the thought which was not appropriate to the hour or the day; nor was any one ever more adroit in seizing an occupation or a thought when the right moment had come."

He robbed hundreds of his fellow workers of health and youth, because he demanded too much of them when he demanded from them what he exacted from himself. His private secretary would be sent for at a late hour, and would get to bed at four in the morning; at seven, the poor man would find new tasks ready for him, and would be told that they must be finished within two hours. When Napoleon and his secretary were together all day, one dictating and the other writing from dictation, at meal times the chief would order food for two, and would share with his subordinate at a corner of the work-table, just as he would have shared with his adjutant on a boundary stone. During the Consulate he would sometimes begin a sitting with his ministers at six in the evening and keep it up till five next morning. In the three months at Schönbrunn, his official correspondence comprised four hundred and thirty-five letters occupying four hundred folio pages of print. This was only his political and administrative correspondence; in addition he wrote a great many private letters, and delivered innumerable orders by word of mouth.

These are the main forms of his energy. It is with their aid that he enters upon his duel with the world, availing himself of their interplay, and speaking of his genius as a talent for combination. In his plans and orders, he is fond of the phrase "at the given moment." He is not hampered by any principle; is always willing to modify his scheme to suit the weather of destiny, to adapt his combinations to the slightest modifications of the situation. This man of iron will had a most supple intelligence. While forcing all those with whom he came in contact to bend before his resolves, he himself showed a wonderful elasticity in compliance with the will of circumstances.

"The weakness of a captain who, instead of forcing his way into port, preferred to let himself be chased on the open sea—this, and some of the trifling defects of our frigates, were the reasons why I failed to change the face of the world. Had Acre fallen, we should have made our way to Aleppo by forced marches, have enlisted Christians, Druses, and Armenians; have speedily reached the Euphrates: thence I should have gone to India, and should have stablished new institutions everywhere."

Whether these vaticinations were historically tenable, may remain an open question; but his belief that he could have done what he describes, bears witness to his realism. In this world of figures and magnitudes, for Napoleon everything depends upon the individual behaviour of the individual man at his post. Since the failure of any one individual may give the totality of circumstances a new trend, he is always ready to adapt the trend of his own intelligence to changing circumstances. But he does not himself attribute his successes to this, saying that they were due to his having been born at the right moment, and that under Louis XIV. he would only have become a marshal like Turenne.

Napoleon's energy is very little disturbed by the passions. His self-confidence and his sense of dignity made self-command easy to him, and, being habituated to surprise, he was always fully master of himself. "Since I am used to great events, they make no impression on me at the moment when they are reported; I feel the pain an hour later." This sometimes makes him appear more stoical than he might wish people to believe him. When Hortense's boy dies, he tells her to be composed, saying: "To live means to suffer; but the brave man is continually striving for self-mastery, and achieves it in the end."

Nevertheless, he sometimes loses his temper. The fierceness of his passion is then proportional to his pride, the irritability of his nerves, and the impatience of his creative will—the will of one who needed a thousand hands to complete his work. The stories about his threatening an ambassador with his fist, and similar outbursts of violence, are fabulous; but there is trustworthy evidence as to the terrible moment when Berthier had infuriated the First Consul by his tactlessness. Led on by Talleyrand as Mephistopheles, Berthier, in the Tuileries, had urged upon the Consul the need of assuming the title of king. Bonaparte's anger flashed from his eyes, his lips twitched, he seized the offender by the throat, and pushed him back against the wall, shouting: "Who put you up to raising my bile in this way? You will pay for it, if you dare to do anything of the kind again!"

Even amid his anger, his faculty for combination is at work, and he realises that the notion cannot have originated in the good Berthier's mind. In its psychical significance the scene is unique.

Often he is a rough, irritable soldier, who furiously lifts a badly closing window off its hinges and hurls it into the street; lashes a groom with his whip; when dictating a letter, utters curses against the addressee, which his secretary suppresses; even before the vicars-general speaks in an unseemly way, asking, "Which of you leads this blockhead of a bishop by the nose?"

One of these vicars-general, who has been absent from duty for a long time, returns, and comes to report.

"Where have you been, misérable?"

"At home, with my people."

"How dare you stay away so long when you know that your bishop is such a damned fool?"

More important are the occasions when he simulates anger to gain some political end. Occasionally he gives the show away afterwards. "You think I was in a rage?" he says in Warsaw. "You are making a mistake. While I have been here, my wrath has never exceeded bounds." One day he is playing with his little nephew and gossiping with the court ladies, in the best of humours. The English ambassador is announced. Instantly his face changes like an actor's, his features are convulsed, he turns pale, strides towards the Englishman and storms at him for a whole hour in the presence of numerous witnesses. He is genuinely angry with England and he is genuinely annoyed at being disturbed by this visit; but the wrathful mask, the scene he makes, the angry expressions he uses, are political expedients.

The frequency of such incidents made many people believe that Napoleon was a passionate man. Talleyrand has more insight: "He's a perfect devil. He humbugs us all, even about his passions, for he knows how to act them, though they are really there!"

Self-command and coldness are so dominant in him that he never takes the vengeance that might seem appropriate to his irritable sense of honour and to the extent of his power. He never punished rivals or traitors unjustly. He only banished those whom he had good reason for wishing out of the way; and it was a point of chivalry with him to leave beaten enemies, great or small, unmolested.

Here is a scene with the Badenese envoy. The envoy asks compensation for the duke of Brunswick. The Emperor angrily refuses: not because the duke is supposed to have incited Prussia to make war against France; but because, long before this, during the first campaign against France in 1792, he had issued the famous manifesto of Coblenz, in which he had said that in Paris he would not leave one stone standing on another. "What harm had this city done to him?" fiercely enquires the Emperor two decades later, the man who in those days had been Lieutenant Bonaparte. "This affront must be avenged!"

V

Napoleon's energy is most conspicuous in his role of conqueror. But in this case it finds a more spiritual expression than one would be led to anticipate from a soldier. "I have seldom drawn my sword; I won my battles with my eyes, not with my weapons." To gain a knowledge of his soul, it is not important to understand the new forms of his art of war; of importance is to understand the way in which his whole being vibrated before, during, and after a fight. In this, too, he is wholly original.

Even courage, that fundamental virtue of the soldier, assumes in Napoleon a form peculiar to himself. During his youthful days, and again during the last campaigns he displayed so much personal courage that he can venture to say, "no soldier is proof against cowardice"; but such moments of panic fear must be utilised against the foe. What he believes himself almost alone to possess is "two-o'clock-in-the-morning courage": courage in face of the unforeseen, the sudden; courage which demands presence of mind and power of determination. But he despises the "chivalrous" courage of the duel, which he crushingly describes as "cannibal courage."—"Since you have both fought at Marengo and Austerlitz you do not need to give any further proofs of your courage. Women are fickle, and so is good luck. Go back to your regiments and become comrades again."

The commander of armies clearly recognises the line of demarcation between humaneness and coldness. The same man who, in his study, could exclaim to Metternich: "Such a man as I does not care a snap of the fingers for the lives of a million men"; will say on the field of battle: "If the kings of the world could contemplate such a sight as this, they would hanker less after wars and conquests." Another time he writes to Josephine: "The earth is strewn with dead and bleeding men; this is the obverse of war; the heart is tortured at the sight of so many victims." Calculation and feeling are at cross purposes in this case, and he excuses himself for the duties imposed by his own craft: "He who cannot look upon a battle-ground dry-eyed, allows many men to be killed purposelessly." This is what he wants above all to avoid. For the great aim, Europe entrusts him with a million men: his lesser aim, the taking of this trench or that bridge, must be thriftily achieved, for "he who heedlessly allows ten men to be killed where at most two need have died, is answerable for the lives of eight men."

Since most of his wars are fought from political necessity, and are always conducted without hate, as soon as the fight is finished the foe ceases to exist. He writes from Schönbrunn: "I am appalled to learn that the eighteen thousand prisoners on the island of Lobau are suffering from hunger; this is inhuman and unpardonable. Have twenty thousand rations of bread sent there immediately; a similar amount of flour for the bake-houses." But when, after the truce, soldiers are still being killed by the embittered Tyrolese, he is furious, and orders that "at least six of the larger villages are to be plundered and burned, so that the mountain folk may not soon forget the vengeance that has been exacted."

War is for him an art, "the most noteworthy art, one which contains within itself all the other arts." Like a true artist, he declares that, in the long run, this art cannot be taught: "You fancy that because you have read Jomini you are fitted to be a leader in war? . . . I have fought in sixty fights, and I can assure you that I have learned nothing from any of them. Cæsar used the same tactics in his last battle as he had used in his first." In typical artist fashion, he contradicts himself in the definitions of those things in which he is a master. After the Spanish campaigns, he delivers the following lecture to one of his generals: "War is decided far more by the power of strategical calculation than by material forces." At another time he will maintain that it is the superior numbers or the moral courage of the troops which constitutes the deciding factor. Sometimes he even goes so far as to say that inspiration decides an issue: "The result of a battle hangs on a thread and is mostly the outcome of a sudden thought. One approaches the enemy according to a prearranged plan, one comes to blows, one fights for a while, the critical moment draws near, a spark of inspiration flames up—and a small reserve division does the rest!"

More logically, but not less as the artist, he speaks of the decisive moment which, after a couple of engagements, one can find out for oneself without any difficulty. "Such moments are not more than quarter hours. . . . In every battle a moment comes when the bravest of soldiers would like to turn tail: it needs but a trifle, but a plea, to put heart into him again." This power of suggestion has won him many a victory, for soldiers constitute the only mass to which he can speak with effect. The soldier understands him, because Napoleon is simple. The Emperor even describes war as "a simple art like everything that is beautiful." By this contention he seems to uphold the idea that war is the highest of all arts. "The military profession is a freemasonry . . . and I am the grand master of its lodge."

He draws this personal influence from the history of his own rise, which is known to every soldier. As a young general, he had learned to put up with his dependence on the civil authority; and as emperor he still commiserates his royal adversaries because their generals' activities are frustrated by civilian control. On the other hand, he knows the dangers of amateurishness, and writes to Joseph: "When the king himself commands, the soldier does not feel commanded. The army applauds him as when a queen is riding by. If one is not oneself a general, one must give the generals full power of command."

Because he is the only ruler in Europe who has risen from the ranks, from youth upwards he remains familiar with details, and always understands how things look to an officer on the fighting front. "There is nothing connected with the art of war which I cannot do with my own hand: power, siege engines, artillery." But he does not concern himself with these details unless it is necessary, and laughs at the romantic anecdote in a book where he is said, one night, to have taken over the duties of a sentry who had gone to sleep at his post: "That is a civilian's idea, the sort of thing a lawyer would think of, and was certainly not written by a soldier."

But he is a stickler for equality in the army, and in this matter remains true to the revolution until the very end of his career. No one is promoted unless his record in the service justifies the advancement. If Napoleon makes an exception in the case of his brothers, we must remember that after he has made them kings he continues to scold them as if they were subalterns. He writes to Jerome, commenting on a report from Silesia: "Besides, your letter is too clever for my taste. . . . What a man needs in war is precision, firmness, simplicity." When Joseph plays the prince in Boulogne, and vies with Marshal Soult in the splendour of his receptions, Napoleon scolds him. "In the army, no one must put the commander in the shade. On review days, it is the general and not the prince who must give a dinner. At a review, a royal colonel is a colonel and nothing more. Discipline can tolerate no exceptions. The army is a whole. Its commander is everything. Keep to your own regiment."

Nevertheless, a wounded commander-in-chief has become a private soldier. At Eylau, where there have been heavy losses, the Emperor forbids a famous surgeon to go out of his way in

Napoleon as Emperor in 1815. Woodcut, after a medal.

order to care for a wounded general: "Your business is to attend to all the wounded, and not to any one in particular." A German officer reports that after a fight Napoleon would often stand by the wounded and see that they were carefully lifted into the stretchers: "If this good fellow pulls through, there will be one victim the less."

In all the memoirs, we read how in camp the Emperor would foregather with his men at the bivouac fire, ask whether their food was being properly cooked, and laugh at their replies. When they confided all their troubles to him, and often said "thou" to him, this was not the assumed good fellowship of a condescending monarch, but a genuinely paternal relationship. If he calls them "my children," to them he is their "little corporal," meaning the comrade who takes the responsibility. "I have received your letter, dear comrade," he writes to a veteran grenadier who wishes to re-enter the service. "You need not speak to me of your deeds, for I know you to be the bravest grenadier in the army. It will be a pleasure to see you once more. The Minister for War will send you your orders."

He never confides his plans to any one; but when it is a question of rewarding merit, he calls in Everyman as adviser. After a fight, he often forms a circle, speaks to the officers, the non-commissioned officers, and the rankers individually, asking who were the most valiant, rewarding then and there, allotting eagles with his own hand. "The officers pointed out, the soldiers confirmed, the Emperor approved," relates Ségur as eyewitness.

It is true that Napoleon loves war, but as a fine art, just as he loves power. It is true that he laughs incredulously at a traveller who tells him a tale of a Chinese island where there are no weapons.

"What do you mean? But they must have weapons!"

"No, Sire."

"Pikes, anyhow; or bows and arrows?"

"Neither the one nor the other."

"Daggers!"

"Not even daggers."

"But how the devil do they fight there?"

"There has never been a war on the island."

"What, no war?"

It sounds to the traveller as if the very existence of such people under the sun outrages the Emperor. The thought stirs a soldier's bile!

All the same, he looked forward to the coming of peaceful days, not with an ardent desire for them perhaps, but with the seer's vision. He showed his superiority to all the modern commanders against whom he fought, in that he, the greatest soldier of the new times, declared the primacy of the spirit over the sword. When Canova made a statue of him in which he was shown with a threatening mien, he said contemptuously: "Does the man think I achieved my conquests with blows of my fist?" But, more than this, he himself defined a commander as something above and beyond a soldier. When First Consul, he said in the Council of State:

"In what does the commander's superiority consist? 'In his mental qualities: insight, calculation, decision, eloquence, knowledge of men.' But all these qualities are what make a man shine in civil life. . . . If bodily vigour and courage sufficed the commander, any brave private could be a leader of armies. Everywhere, crude force now yields ground to moral qualities. The man with the bayonet bows before the man who possesses exceptional knowledge and understanding. . . . I knew perfectly well what I was about when, as the head of the army, I bore the title of Member of the Institute; and the youngest drummer understood what I meant."

At a later date, he spoke more decisively.

"*War is an anachronism. Some day, victories will be won without cannon and without bayonets. . . . Whoever troubles the peace of Europe, wants civil war.*"

Remember that these are the words of Napoleon, the military commander.

VI

His energy is concentrated on human beings. Very rarely does he come into conflict with natural forces; and whenever he does so, he is beaten. But, in general, all he has to do is to compel men to conquer, for him, the mountains and the miles. Human beings are the material in working with which the energy and the imagination of this artist are destined to become weary; them he must overcome if he is to do his work at all. No mortal ever conquered more men than did Napoleon. He subjugated, not only armies and peoples, but something more: individuals, and the best of these.

To achieve his goal, he followed the road of contempt; and used as his means, glory and money. Self-confidence and experience had convinced him that every one acts only from self-interest; that some are driven to grasp at money through love of pleasure, or avarice, or clannishness; that others seek public recognition in order to gratify their vanity, their jealousy, or their ambition. Denying the force of ideal motives, Napoleon relied exclusively upon material means; and if the spur of ambition occasionally assumed the aspect of a desire for eternal glory, this occurred against his will, but the magic of his personality sometimes exercised a more puissant lure than the well-calculated material attractions offered by others. To quote Goethe: "Napoleon, who lived wholly for ideas, was nevertheless unable to grasp the nature of ideal motives; he repudiated the ideal, denied that there was any such thing, at the very time when he himself was eagerly trying to realise the ideal."

Yet to Napoleon the Mephistophelian conception of men was as alien as it was to Goethe. He said: "Most people bear within themselves the seeds of good and of evil, of courage and of cowardice. Thus is human nature created: upbringing and circumstance do the rest." Since, for twenty years, he needed this human nature, daily and in quantities of a hundred at a time, the subtlest knowledge of it was a primary condition of his success. Among all the materials which Napoleon bent to his uses, the human heart was the most familiar.

"I am a great friend of analysis. . . . 'Why' and 'How,' are such useful questions, that they cannot be uttered too often." Coldly and clearly as a nerve specialist, he controls all psychical symptoms, utilises every method for the attainment of such control, and trusts especially to physiognomy—for he knows his Lavater. He is fond of reproving people. "According as they react, I discover the pitch of their souls. If I strike brass with a glove, it gives back no tone: but if I strike with a hammer, it rings out." A person meeting Napoleon for the first time, is gripped by the magnetism of his glance.

By talking and questioning, he makes himself acquainted with the atlas of human types, an atlas he is ever enlarging. He questions so long that a stranger grows embarrassed, confused, and alarmed; he questions until his questions become ridiculous; but he must at all costs get the information he needs, even if he is not negotiating. In what way can the twenty minutes that a doctor sits at Napoleon's table in St. Helena be put to the best use by the ex-Emperor?

"How many patients suffering from ailments affecting the liver had you on board? How many cases of dysentery? What is the fee for a consultation in England? What is the pension awarded to an army surgeon? . . . What is death, or how would you define it? When does the soul quit the body? When does a body first receive a soul?"

Another means is monologue. One of his intimates declares that the right of the Emperor to hold forth in monologue was the only real pleasure his high estate awarded him! We have testimonies concerning other men of action: but who ever talked so much as Napoleon! Since he always faces the world alone, he must continually hold forth that he may convey his suggestions to the world. His conversations often lasted from five to eight hours, some of them ten or eleven hours; and during the greater part of them Napoleon took the floor. We must admit that this was more in accordance with the Italian manner than the Roman; Italian, too, were the rapidity of his utterance, and his foreign accent: but he gesticulated little; and only when much moved did he unclasp his hands—generally they were clasped behind his back, as if he wished to throw out his chest against the world.

Upon all who serve him, he lavishes money with oriental profusion. But as far as his personal expenditure is concerned, he is thrifty. During the Consulate he says: "A man who has been through so many wars will have acquired a little property whether he will or no. I have a private income of from frs. 80,000 to frs. 100,000, with a house in town and a country mansion. What more do I need? If I should get out of humour with France, or France with me, I should retire from public life without a qualm. . . . But every one round me is stealing; the ministers are weak. Some people must be laying by vast sums. . . . What is to be done about it? France is corrupt through and through. It has always been like that; as soon as a man becomes a minister, he builds himself a palace. . . . Do you know what they are trying to make me pay for my installation in the Tuileries? Two millions! . . . It must be cut down to eight hundred thousand. I am surrounded by a pack of scoundrels."

"Your great operations," answers Roederer, "must cost you much more than these domestic defalcations."

"All the more reason why I should watch over my personal expenditure."

This conversation tells us how the head of the State, a man of thirty, regards money. He needs nothing for himself, and complains of the venality and profusion of those by whom he is surrounded; acknowledges that he has himself made money out of the wars; rails at the tradesmen who want to charge two millions for the equipment of a palace, when, as far as his own taste is concerned, he sees no reason for spending anything at all. Amid the frightful corruption which is a heritage of the revolution, he fights with the army contractors and war profiteers; but as soon as, by drastic punishments, he has succeeded in putting an end to this scandal, he assigns preposterous incomes to his marshals, some of whom receive more than a million francs a year. As Consul, he rids the State of the thieves who are making away with the national property; and then, as Emperor, he burdens this same State with extortionate salaries.

Still, there are a few persons who make money thanks to their relationship with him, though without his aid. "When I have nothing left," he says to Talleyrand, "I shall turn to you. Tell me honestly, how much have you made out of me?"

"I am not a rich man, Sire, but all that I have is at your service."

Napoleon's way of dealing with men is modified by a hundred and one considerations. If we wish to study the variations of his technique, we must class his instruments in groups.

Generals and marshals are the easiest to keep dependent, for they have unceasing opportunities of winning military renown; and, since he pays them so liberally for their services, they grow more and more wealthy. By loading them with money, he gains two ends, spreading effulgence around himself, and keeping his most powerful officers in a state of dependence. It delights him to see these soldiers unused to money spending extravagantly, running into debt, and then turning to him for help in their difficulties. He leads them from profusion to want, and then back to profusion again. At the same time, he gives them little scope for originality, reserving important decisions for himself, so that even the commanders of armies rarely have a chance of proving themselves men of genius. He shrewdly regulates his public mention of them in his bulletins, both in respect of time and form, so that, through their vanity and jealousy, he can get his way with his generals.

The result is that their sentiments towards him are a mingling of hatred and love, whereby they are chained to his service more firmly than if the feeling had been one of pure affection. Perhaps only two of them are wholly devoted to him, Berthier and Duroc, whose love for him he compares with that of a child and a dog. Ney speaks of himself as a loaded musket which is fired when and where the Emperor orders. Napoleon, for his part, has a personal affection for those only who have risen with him, and in his memoirs he pays his tribute to them. He extols Desaix's mental balance. Moreau has "more instinct than genius"; whereas Lannes has "more courage than sense," though as time goes on he makes good in the latter respect. Kléber seeks glory only as a means of enjoyment. Masséna is not really courageous until he is under fire. Murat "has not a spark of intelligence, but what dash! He is a duffer and a hero." Napoleon cannot break away from these witnesses of his rise, although almost all of them have learned the weight of his anger. In his tent, after Wagram, Napoleon thunders at Marmont for having made a mess of things, and a quarter of an hour later appoints him marshal.

Sometimes the Emperor's misanthropy got the better of him. "In those moods, I begin to distrust even my companions-in-arms; that causes me intense suffering, and I do everything I can to rid myself of such horrible suspicions." Yet he really knew. Lannes' death touched him to the quick, but he never really uttered the moving farewell words which he publishes. Indeed, he confided to Metternich: "Lannes hated me. When I heard that, on being wounded, he had called out my name, I knew it was all up with him. He called on me as a dying atheist calls on God."

The remembrance of friendships formed in youth does not prevent him from scolding the most exalted of his marshals like schoolboys when he considers they have behaved foolishly or have been wanting in courage. He says to Junot: "Your conduct was unprecedented, extraordinarily indiscreet. . . . You have a strange notion of your military duties. I don't recognise you!" To a general in Lombardy: "Under your command, there has been very little honesty and a great deal of avarice; but I never knew until to-day that you were a coward. Leave the army, and never let me see your face again!" In Spain, one of his generals capitulated in the open field. Six months later, this man ventured to appear before Napoleon at a review. The Emperor stormed at him in full hearing of the troops; would not be appeased. The witnesses say that the scene lasted a whole hour. "A man may have to surrender a fortress. The fortune of war is uncertain, and defeat is always possible. Any one can be taken prisoner. The thing may happen to me to-morrow. But honour, before all! On the battle-field, a commander's business is to fight: and if he capitulates instead, he deserves to be shot. . . . A soldier must know how to die. Have we not all to face death? . . . As a subject, you committed a crime in capitulating; as a general, a stupid blunder; as a soldier, your action was cowardly; but as a Frenchman, your surrender was dishonourable!"

He alarmed the diplomats of his day by a frankness which none of them trusted. "Tact, and putting all the cards on the table, will do better service in diplomacy than cunning. The tricks of the diplomats of the old school are out of date; all their rogueries have been exposed long since. . . . Nothing betrays weakness more than the attempt to deceive."

Just before the renewal of the war with England, he tells the British envoy how many years it will take before France can face England at sea, but he explains how quickly he can increase his army to four hundred thousand. In Schönbrunn, he says to the Austrian negotiator: "That is my last word. If you defeat me, I shall propose more favourable terms; but if I gain the victory, I shall make them harder. What I want is peace."

He studies every shade of expression when he wishes to influence the envoys of foreign powers. We see this especially when he is adapting his demeanour towards the Austrians with an eye to the Habsburg traditions. He waits for the formal reception on his birthday, and then, faced by the semicircle of the diplomats, he stops in front of Metternich to say: "Well, Monsieur l'Ambassadeur, what does your emperor want? Would he like me to come to Vienna?" This is calculated to intimidate the Austrian envoy, and at the same time to advertise Napoleon's threatening attitude throughout Europe. But two days later, when Metternich comes to a private interview, the Emperor says: "To-day, we won't play at being Emperor of the French and Austrian envoy. There is no audience now, so we need not make any fine speeches."

Shortly before the conclusion of the first peace with Austria, he wishes to avoid meeting the defeated archduke in Schönbrunn, lest he should commit himself prematurely to peace terms. He therefore arranges that the meeting shall take place in a hunting lodge. "I shall spend only two hours there: one of them will be occupied in having dinner, and the other will be devoted to talk about the war and to mutual protestations of respect." When the First Consul receives Count Cobenzl, he has personally arranged the stage in the Tuileries; writing-table in the corner; no chairs, so that they will have to sit on the sofa; only one lamp, no lights in the chandelier, although it is late in the evening. When Talleyrand ushers in the Austrian, the room seems almost dark, and the Consul, on the farther side of it, is scarcely visible; the stranger is perplexed, and has to sit exactly where his host chooses.

He is even more subtle in his dealings with the princes. During the years of his supreme power, he ceases to pay them visits. In Tilsit, he becomes the host within two days; in Dresden, though he is the king of Saxony's guest, he plays the master. He avoids having anything to do with queens. When Queen Louise pathetically implores justice, he begs her to sit down. "Nothing interrupts a tragical scene more effectually than this. When people sit down, tragedy becomes comedy."

In his dealings with the peoples he was less happy, and his only tolerable successes were secured with the French and the Italians. During the Consulate, he said in the Council of State: "My policy is to rule in accordance with the will of the majority. This, I think, implies the recognition of the sovereignty of the people. I became a good Catholic when I wanted to finish the war in Vendée; in Egypt, I was a Turk; when I wished to win over the Italians, I was an ultramontane. If I reigned over the Jews, I should rebuild Solomon's temple. That is why I propose to talk about freedom in that part of San Domingo where the slaves have been liberated, while maintaining slavery in the other part of the island."

His policy was not very successful in the negro republic; he did better in Poland, which he tried to win over by festivities and phrases; and better still with the Jews. These had been granted equal rights by the revolution, and on the Rhine many of them were doing harm by the practice of usury. Napoleon, who knew their value as traders, did not have recourse to crude prohibitions. He bethought himself of Jewish laws and customs; summoned to Paris their highest council, the Sanhedrin, which had not met for centuries; left the decision to this body, and was able to arrange that the supreme Jewish authority should forbid usury as sinful. But in Spain he made a complete mess of things, overlooking the risks he was running, and advising Joseph to make himself agreeable to the whole nation "by instilling fear into the rabble."

The Germans puzzled Napoleon most of all. They had everything he lacked, and none of the things he had. He therefore, even in the midst of his successes, regarded them with a mixture of fear and admiration; they seemed to him uncanny.

When he went to Erfurt and wished to influence the German princes by the drama, he told the managing director not to stage any comedies. "No one understands comedies on this bank of the Rhine. Corneille's *Cinna* might be played, for therein great interests are portrayed; then a scene depicting royal clemency, which would certainly have a good effect." He went on to misquote *Cinna*. Rémusat, having put him right, said: "In this sacred office, to which God's grace has appointed the king, the past is justified, and the future is free. He who is advanced to this office, cannot be held culpable; whatever he does, he remains invulnerable."

"Splendid!" exclaims the Emperor, "especially for the Germans, who always cling to the same ideas, and are still talking about the death of the duke of Enghien! We must broaden their moral outlook. That will be good for people with melancholy ideas, the sort of persons with whom Germany is filled." It is as if he were talking about German music, of which he knows practically nothing; but really he is thinking of German philosophy. The one is as uncongenial to him as the other, for he is fond of Italian arias and the wisdom of Voltaire, but says that "Kant is an obscure writer." This misconception of his prevents him from foreseeing the possibility that so slow-moving a people may one day become inspired with a passionate enthusiasm.

Perhaps the reason for the misinterpretation lies in the impracticability of understanding the masses of a foreign nation. In northern Italy, he did indeed make headway, for he was a young man, his ideas were naïve, the yearning of the oppressed was still fresh in him; and he was the herald of the revolution. But the dictator could no longer bring a torch to foreign peoples. Nevertheless, he continued to watch the sentiments of the masses. "A ruler should reign for the masses, without asking whether he is pleasing Mr. So-and-So. . . . Men of mark look from above, and have no party ties; one who belongs to a party, is a slave." Such were his principles, but his actions told another story.

The masses, even in France, saw a man who made himself dreaded. They feared him for a decade, but became sceptical at his first failure. "A ruler should be dignified in his demeanour towards the people," says Napoleon. "But he must not flatter the crowd, which will then think itself cheated if he does not give it everything. You ask me why I make threatening speeches? I make them in order to avoid having to do the things I threaten!"

But this severity is, in the long run, out of keeping both with his own simplicity of nature and with the instincts of the crowd. He could not seduce the masses by the offer of fame and money, so he showed them symbols: crowns and coronation ceremonies; courts and splendour and princes: but the people felt the growing distance between them and their ruler, and were not deceived.

When the people of Paris learned that the Emperor, in his theatre, would no longer allow King Henry to say, "I tremble," but only, "I shudder," because, though a king (being only a man) may tremble, he may not admit it—the crowd must either feel angry or become derisive. But the crowd did not hear the words in which the Emperor instructed Talma how to play Cæsar:

"When Cæsar utters his long tirade against kingship, saying, 'for me, in whom the throne inspires nothing but contempt,' he does not mean a word of what he says. He only talks like that because he knows that his Romans are standing behind him, and wishes to persuade them that the throne is an abomination to him. In reality, it is already the goal of his desire. Consequently those words ought not to be spoken with conviction."

He wants to use religion, just as he uses the drama, that he may lull the masses to sleep. Here is what the newmade Consul says to the Council of State: "What I see in religion is, not the mystery of the incarnation, but social order. It associates with heaven an idea of equality, which prevents the poor from massacring the rich. Religion has the same sort of value as vaccination. It gratifies our taste for the miraculous, and protects us from quacks; for the priests are worth more than the Cagliostros, the Kants, and all the German dreamers. . . . Society cannot exist without inequality of property; but this latter cannot exist without religion. One who is dying of hunger when the man next him is feasting on dainties, can only be sustained by a belief in a higher power, and by the conviction that in another world there will be a different distribution of goods."

Though he knows all this, and though he takes kindly measures for the relief of the poor, he can never free his mind from thoughts of the rabble and the mob. When he turns from contemplating the princes to contemplating the masses, his contempt for his fellows diminishes, but not enough. The masses, like the princes, are to be used for his own ends. He says: "The men of intelligence who have changed the world, have never done so by influencing the leaders, but have always set the masses in motion. He who influences princes is only an intriguer, and his results are second rate; but he who moves the masses, changes the face of the earth." Democracy came between him and the people; and what he has to say about parliamentarism is not creative but critical:

"The republic is the political form which elevates the soul and contains the germ of great things: but, precisely because of its greatness, it will sooner or later perish; for it needs a unified authority to maintain its power, and this must lead either to despotism or to a patriciate. The latter is the worst of despotisms; Rome, Venice, England, and even France are instances. If the republic wishes to attain greatness, the central authority must be established upon a permanent parliamentary majority; . . . but this can be secured only by corruption, which is the cancer of the peoples, and a terrible weapon in the hands of the central authority. The liberals have discovered the expedient of constitutional monarchy. That is a mezzo termine, which has its advantages, but only when the popular assembly, whose business it is to bridle the monarchical authority, is elected by universal suffrage."

Napoleon recognised the existence of all the problems that confronted the nineteenth century; but he never understood the social problem, with which his own story began.

VII

Imagination, the third element of his personality, is the real driving force of his self-confidence and his energy. Continually at war with the calculating part of his nature, fantasy, in the end, brings this harbourer of opposites to destruction. The imaginative power, which links the poet to the statesman (enabling both unceasingly to dwell in the affective world of strangers as well as in their own), is also the source of his knowledge of men and his guide to the management of men. But always his energy interacts with other qualities. One who, for analytical purposes, would force the living whole of his character into the framework of a system, cannot avoid, from time to time, breaking threads that he may bind other threads together.

"I know not what I do, for everything depends on events. I have not a will of my own, but expect everything from their outcome. . . . The greater one is, the less can one have a will. One is always dependent upon events and circumstances." Such words, casually introduced into a letter from husband to wife, express the distantly visible forms of his fantasy; for only the imaginative man, not tied to systems and principles, trusts himself to the movements of the moments, allows his spirit to roam freely, and discovers his course as he goes. In this sense, his whole career is improvisation, though in the converse way from that in which most people improvise. He calculated little things in advance with great precision; whereas his worldwide designs were originated, transformed, improvised, in accordance with circumstances and developments. "One who has become familiar with affairs, despises all theories, and makes use of them only like the geometricians, not in order to move forward in a straight line, but merely to keep heading in the same direction."

This direction, this fundamental idea of the statesman, was, moreover, only possible in a man whose mind was simultaneously imaginative and mathematical. It is his most ardent vision and his coolest calculation; it is his political aim, his hope, his ambition: Europe. If this vision could be realised only by force of arms, that was because of the fierceness with which the first republic of Europe was again and again attacked by the European princes. We have seen how earnestly he strove for peace. No doubt he chose his means badly, his error being due to the time, the circumstances, and his own domineering character. But his mistakes as to method still leave undiminished the genius of the seer who looked forward towards an aim which was again to become an object of statesmanship a hundred years after his fall.

"There are in Europe more than thirty million Frenchmen, fifteen million Italians, thirty million Germans. . . . Out of each of these peoples, I wanted to make a united national whole. . . . That would have supplied the best chance of establishing a general unity of laws; a unity of principles and thoughts and feelings, of outlooks and interests. . . . Then it would have been possible to think of founding the United States of Europe after the model of the United States of America or of the Greek Amphictyonic League. . . . What perspectives of strength, greatness, and prosperity this opens up! . . . For France, unity has been wrought; in Spain, it has proved unattainable; to establish the Italian nation, I should have needed twenty years; to make the Germans a nation, would have required still more patience, and all I could do was to simplify their monstrous constitution. At the same time, I wanted to pave the way for the unification of the great interests of Europe, just as I had unified the parties in France. . . . The transient mutterings of the peoples troubled me little; they would have been reconciled to me by the result. . . . *Europe would soon have become one nation, and any who travelled in it would always have been in a common fatherland. . . . Sooner or later, this union will be brought about by the force of events. The first impetus has been given; and, after the fall and the disappearance of my system, it seems to me that the only way in which an equilibrium can be achieved in Europe is through a league of nations.*"

Here there is no talk of a dictatorial welding together of different stocks, or of an enthusiastic fraternisation. He speaks only of interests, and of a preliminary unification of these on a national and racial basis. The work of the nineteenth century was to inaugurate the preliminaries by the establishment of the nations. The twentieth century opens with the realisation of the Napoleonic idea.

VIII

The effects underlying his energy and his imagination are dominated by the clarity of his thought. Napoleon hated less, and loved more, than he would have been willing to admit. In this domain, we find the converse of what happens in the matter of his sympathies in war time, when a million men are coldly sacrificed, while one man wounded and bleeding touches him to the heart. Since his fantasy needs enormous masses, he is enraged when Joseph says: "I am the only person who cares for you." Napoleon rejoins: "Nothing of the sort. I need five hundred million men to love me." In these icy words glows the volcano which one of his school masters heard rumbling long ago.

Emotionally convinced of his mission to order the affairs of the nations, he deliberately rejects anything that may distract him from this aim, and nothing sustains him but his monomania. Even in the drama, he objects to the interweaving of love stories, saying: "Love is a passion which should only be the main theme of a tragedy, and never a subsidiary motif. . . . In the days of Racine, it was the whole content of a human life. That happens in a society where no great deeds are being done."

If love becomes intrusive, he annuls it. "I have no time to be bothered with feelings and to repent them like other men. . . . There are two motives to action: self-interest and fear. Believe me, love is a foolish blindness! . . . I love no one, not even my brothers—Joseph a little, from force of habit, and because he is the elder. I am fond of Duroc, too; he is serious and resolute; I believe the man has never shed tears in his life! . . . Let us leave sensibilities to women. Men should be firm of heart and strong of will, or else they should have nothing to do with war or governance." Another time: "The only friend I have is Daru; he is unfeeling and cold; that suits me." Last of all, in St. Helena: "A man of fifty has done with love. . . . I have an iron heart. I never really loved; perhaps Josephine, a little; but then I was only seven-and-twenty. I incline to the view of Gassion, who once said to me that he did not love life well enough to give it to another being."

Always half ashamed of his feelings; ever ready to make excuses for them; "perhaps," "a little." Yet this is the same man who said: "I am the slave of my way of feeling and acting, for I value the heart much more than the head." This very feeling is his fantasy.

One in whom egotism is supreme, will be more inclined to jealousy than to love. His first letters to Josephine show him devoured by jealousy. Years later, as Consul, when he is inspecting his new bridge in course of construction across the Seine, he has to step aside with his companions for a moment to let a carriage pass. In the carriage sits Hippolyte, his sometime rival. That was long ago; everything has been condoned; the man's name is never mentioned in his presence. But now, at a chance encounter in the street, Bonaparte grows pale and confused, and takes a little while to recover composure.

From time to time, he shows an involuntary kindliness. On one of the Italian battle-fields, he sees a dog howling over the dead body of its master. "The poor beast seemed to be asking for an avenger, or begging help. I was profoundly moved by the dog's suffering, and at that moment I should have been very much in the mood to grant quarter to an enemy. I understood why Achilles surrendered Hector's body to the weeping Priam. Such is man; so little can he count upon his moods. Impassively I had sent my soldiers into the battle; dry-eyed I had watched them marching past in an advance where thousands of them would meet their fate; then I was shaken to the depths by the howling of a dog."

Affectionate tones are to be heard in many of his letters. To Cambacérès: "I am so sorry to hear that you are not well. I hope it is only a passing trouble. If you did not take so much medicine, you would be better already. . . . But anyhow, you must do your utmost to get well, if only because of my friendship for you." To Corvisart: "Dear Doctor, I wish you would see to the arch-chancellor and to Lacépède: the former has been ailing for a week, and I am afraid he is in the hands of a quack; Lacépède's wife has been ill for some time. Give them the benefit of your advice, and cure them as soon as you can. You will save the life of a man of note, and one who is very dear to me."

Chénier, who has written against him for years, is assisted by him in poverty and given a secure position. Carnot, for ten years an enemy of the Emperor, is heavily in debt; Napoleon learns this, settles the debts, and refuses to hear of being given a note of hand; reckons up the pay which Carnot would have received as general in active service, makes this calculation the basis of a large pension; and when Carnot says he would like to do some work for his money, Napoleon commissions him to write a military treatise, lest his pensioner should have to undertake duties that might go against the grain.

During the Hundred Days, learning that some of the Bourbon princes are greatly distressed for lack of money, he sends them large sums anonymously. On one occasion his secretary is asleep, and he himself has nothing particular to do; he looks through a pile of begging letters, and writes in the margin of each the amount of an allowance which is to be given to the sender. Hundreds of officers whom, in fits of anger, he has sworn to have shot, remain at their posts—to forsake him in the end. When he orders Jerome to get a divorce, he is alarmed at his own harshness. After he has written to enforce his command with threats he sends a letter to his mother saying that she had better write to Jerome at once and get his sisters to write as well, "for if I have passed judgment on him, nothing can alter it, and his life will be spoiled."

From his few friends, he demands blind devotion. Never is the self-centred nature of Napoleon more plainly shown than in the words the exile speaks to Montholon, from whom he has been temporarily estranged: "I love you like a son, for I believe that you love me only; otherwise you could not love me at all. According to my way of feeling, it is not in our nature to love several persons at once. People deceive themselves in these matters; they cannot even love all their children with the same intensity. For my part, at any rate, I want to be the supreme object of affection in the case of those whom I love and honour with my confidence. I cannot bear partings. They stab me to the heart, for my disposition is too sensitive; spiritual poison affects the body more powerfully than arsenic."

Logically enough, he dislikes western views concerning the enlightenment of women. He always hankers after the East, and in this matter he is an oriental. "Nature intended women to be our slaves; and it is only because of our distorted outlooks that they venture to describe themselves as our rulers.

. . . For one who can influence us in a good direction, there are a hundred who will only lead us into follies. . . . What a mad idea to demand equality for women! They are our property, we are not theirs; for they give us children, but we do not give them any. They belong to us, just as a tree which bears fruit belongs to the gardener. . . . In this difference, there is nothing degrading; every one has his privileges, and every one his duties. You, ladies, have beauty, attractiveness; but also dependence."

IX

Throughout life, the imagination of this creator was troubled by the thought of the Creator. This ruler of men was greatly disturbed that there should be no one who ruled all men. It was not that he ever regarded himself as divine; he laughed at all mystical interpretations of his own power: but there was one great power which remained uncoercible—no matter whether it were called God, destiny, or death. How do self-confidence and fantasy escape from this snare?

First of all by the rejection of dogma. "My firm conviction is that Jesus . . . was put to death like any other fanatic who professed to be a prophet or a Messiah; there have been such persons at all times. For my part, I turn from the New Testament to the Old, and there I find one man of mark, Moses. . . . Besides, how could I accept a religion which would damn Socrates and Plato? . . . I cannot believe that there is a god who punishes and rewards, for I see honest folk unlucky, and rogues lucky. Look at Talleyrand; he is sure to die in his bed! . . . How could I have remained independent if I had been subject to the influence of a confessor to threaten me with the pains of hell? Think what powers a confessor who is a rascal can exercise! . . ."

In this matter he is consistent; from childhood, when he

would not go to Mass, until the end of his life, he rejected (for himself) all the religions. The man who, in his own life, would not recognise the existence of miracle, and ascribed everything that he was able to achieve to the working of the healthy human understanding, boldness, power of combination, knowledge of men, and imagination, could not possibly believe in the miracles recorded in the Bible. He was perfectly logical when he told one of his subordinates it was impossible that two million men could have quenched their thirst at the Wells of Moses.

Even more uncongenial to him is any dread of a great assize. He does not talk about morality; or at most, he does so with some political end in view. Only towards the last, on the island, he says once in an evening conversation with his intimates: "How happy should we be here if I could confide my troubles to God, and could expect from him happiness and salvation! Have I not a just claim to it? I, who have had so unusual a career, have never committed a crime, and need not fear to step before God's judgment seat and await his sentence. Never has the thought of committing a murder entered my mind."

For these reasons, he does not falter in the days of misfortune. Five years before the end, he expresses the hope that he will die without a confessor, but adds that no one can be certain what he will do in his last hours. In fact, this heart of steel was steadfast to the end.

Nevertheless, his ideas as to the nature of the creation developed, and just as the revolutionist became a legitimist, so the materialist became a theist. But these developments were not transformations; there was simply a broadening of the basis of his thought. Throughout life, he had a sense that things had come into existence by a natural process: "When out hunting, I had the deer cut open, and saw how like the beast's internal organs were to those of a human being. Man is merely a more perfect creature than a dog or a tree. The plan is the first link in a chain whose last link is mankind."

It should be remembered that the Emperor had not read Goethe's *Zur Morphologie*, or Lamarck's *Philosophie zoologique*. He had actually refused to receive Lamarck.

Still more remarkable are his deductions concerning psychophysical processes. In a Christmas discourse at St. Helena, he expresses his doubts as follows: "How can any one understand that God should sanction the caprices of a ruler who sends thousands of men into battle that they may die for him? . . . Where is the soul of a child; or that of a madman? . . . What are electricity, galvanism, magnetism? In these lies the great secret of nature. I am inclined to believe that man is a product of these fluids and of the atmosphere; the brain sucks them in and imparts life, and the soul is composed of them. After death, they return into the atmosphere, whence they are sucked up again by other brains." After giving utterance to these Goethean motifs, he is alarmed at his own temerity. Breaking off suddenly, he says, as a soldier among soldiers: "Oh, well, my dear Gourgaud, when we are dead, we are simply dead."

Side by side with this scepticism, there exists and expands a theism. To Laplace, who denies the existence of God, he says: "You should be more ready than any one else to admit that God exists, for you, more than most, have seen the wonders of creation. If we cannot actually see God with our own eyes, this is because he did not wish our understanding to reach so far." On another occasion: "We believe in God because everything around us testifies to his existence." In St. Helena: "I have never doubted the existence of God, for, even if my reason were incompetent to grasp him, still my inner feelings would convince me of his reality. My temperament has always been in harmony with this feeling."

How shall such a spirit come to terms with destiny? Since his self-esteem makes it impossible for him to believe that any man can have beaten him, he is forced to ascribe his defeat to fate. But this sense of the workings of destiny is present in his mind before the final overthrow; it accompanies him throughout life, and appears to be an equivalent for the reverence, devotion, and faith by which other men live. With the aid of his belief in destiny, Napoleon wages a heroic struggle. In his strongest moments, he feels that he wears armour of proof: "I have a soul of marble. The lightnings were unable to destroy it, but broke on it in vain." Once he expresses his defiance even more poetically: "Should the heavens fall down on us, we shall hold them off with the points of our lances!"

But these defiant moods are rare. In general, he is resigned to fate. There are hundreds of his sayings to bear witness to this. Here are three: "All that happens, is written; our hour is fixed, and no one can postpone it. . . . No one can escape his fate." To the duchess of Weimar: "Believe me, there is a providence which guides all. I am merely its instrument." To Johannes von Müller: "Fundamentally, all things are linked together, and are subject to the unsearchable guidance of an unseen hand. I have only become great through the influence of my star." In such tropes we see awareness of God and a sense of dependence welded into pride in his own mission. At these times, a prophetical effulgence seems to radiate from him, but is obscured again and again by the self-confidence of his iron energy.

Yet Napoleon was far from believing in his star as another man may believe in a god or a talisman. He could not bear to have the greatness of his deeds minimised by insistence on his good fortune. He was, therefore, far less superstitious than other men of his type. Louis brings him a valuable knife, but hesitates to give it to him; Napoleon snatches it from his brother's hand, saying: "Don't bother, it won't cut anything but bread!" He scolds Josephine because she consults fortune-tellers; but then, being curious, asks her to tell him all about the hocus-pocus. He wants to have the signing of the peace of Pressburg postponed for a few days, that it may take place after the reintroduction of the prerevolutionary calendar; but he does not order this, being content to use the unwonted phrase, "that would please me very much." Schwarzenberg's death, in 1820, is a great relief to him; for when a fire broke out in the Schwarzenberg mansion at the ball given in honour of Napoleon's second marriage, the Emperor had interpreted this as a bad omen for himself; now Schwarzenberg's death is a derivative for his own uneasy forebodings!

Apart from these trifles, in a life so packed with important happenings, we do not hear of a single day during twenty years on which he forms, postpones, or modifies a resolution on superstitious grounds. But he makes an adroit use of his "star" and his "destiny" for political or rhetorical purposes. Since he wishes to pose before Europe as the Man of Destiny, he tries to work upon suggestible minds like Alexander's by such turns of phrase as the following: "It is wise and politic to do what fate commands, and to march on the road along which we are led by the irresistible course of events." His mind is fond of playing with the kindred notions of destiny, circumstance, and chance; and while he regards destiny as involved in more or less obscurity, he believes himself able to calculate the chances of a coming battle with almost mathematical certainty. "In these matters one must be careful not to make a slip, for an overlooked fraction can modify the whole result. . . . To people of mediocre intelligence, chance will always remain a mystery; but to the clear-sighted, it becomes a reality."

Sometimes he lumps them all together—talents, destiny, and power,—and shows himself an energetic fatalist when he says: "Against attempts on my life, I trust in my luck, my good genius, and my guards."

In this virile spirit, he strides resolutely along betwixt life and death.

A modern tragedy depicts a man who wishes to die. Napoleon says that the portrait is well limned, but unnatural: "A man must wish to live, and must know how to die." That is why, from youth upwards, he opposes suicide; first, in an essay;

then, in an order of the day; then, with the reiterated argument that suicide is cowardice, especially in hours of misfortune. A careful study of the documents shows that the story of his having attempted suicide just before the first abdication is apocryphal. The leading memoirs make no reference to the matter, and such accounts as we have are at second hand and untrustworthy. There is no doubt that during his last battles Napoleon deliberately sought a soldier's death; but he never tried to poison himself.

Yet it was not only in those last days at Fontainebleau, and after Waterloo, that he suffered from tedium vitæ. The weariness recorded in the diary of the lad of sixteen, and in the letter which the man of thirty wrote from Cairo to his brother, were little in evidence during the most energetic years of febrile activity. Those who trouble to ask whether persons of genius are happy, will have to agree that this man of genius, who was not fitted by nature for happiness, enjoyed during the climax of his career, hours of content, and even sublime moments. But there were periods of doubt:

"For the tranquillity of France," says Bonaparte at Rousseau's tomb, "it would have been better if this man had never lived."

"Why, Citizen Consul?"

"He paved the way for the revolution."

"Surely you are not the man to deplore the revolution?"

"Time will show whether it would not have been better for the peace of the world if neither Rousseau nor I had lived."

Gradually these doubts fade. But what he never loses is the sense of daimonic loneliness, which increases as his soaring flight leads him to chillier altitudes. "There are times when life is hard to bear." Since the sea has always been unfriendly to him, there is only one place where he really feels at home—the desert, which to him is the image of the infinite. The desert is the sublime vacancy which expands before him when the myriad-faceted pictures of ordinary life sink from sight.

But never was Napoleon more perfectly freed from the tyranny of his thoughts, never was he happier, than when seated alone in his box at the theatre, watching a tragedy being enacted.

Nothing else could restore his inner peace of mind; for, since he loved less than most, he was doomed to a tragical loneliness, the price he had to pay for his egotism. "There is neither happiness nor unhappiness," he said. "The life of a happy man is a picture showing black stars on a silver background. The life of an unhappy man is a picture showing silver stars on a black background." But it is not these heroic images which best characterise the loneliness of a soul. Even more poignant voices reach us from the familiar arena of the daily struggle:

"Don't you understand, Caulaincourt, what is going on here? The folk I have got together want to enjoy themselves; the poor devils don't realise that a man has to fight before he can get the repose he longs for. What about myself? Have not I a palace, a wife, a child? Do I not weary myself to the utmost with every possible kind of tension? Do I not day by day give my life to my country?"

He gives his life to his work, for that is what he means when he talks of his country. A human note, gently plaintive, and fraught with the lofty irony of the finale, sounds when he says on the island:

"The whole time I was bearing the world on my shoulders. 'Tis rather a tiring job!"

X

A volcano made the island, which was flung up from beneath the waters thousands upon thousands of years ago. Forth from the midst of the sea, projects the gloomy mass of rock. Steep, black, and deeply furrowed are the walls of lava that run down from the heights into the waves. The chasm above the harbour looks like the gate of hell to one who first sees it from a ship; and the traveller fancies that these dark ramparts must have been built by the hands of demons. Nothing betrays the work of man but the cannon placed among the rocks. When the voyager lands, the ground crunches softly beneath his feet, for the soil is made of disintegrated lava. He is treading the road of death.

An extinct volcano in the Atlantic Ocean, two thousand miles from Europe and nearly a thousand from Africa, guarded by British guns—such is the rock of St. Helena, on which this limitless life might have ended like a tragedy of Æschylus. But, owing to the mendacity of a moralising century, the malice of English oligarchs, and the dry spitefulness of a colonial governor, the island becomes the stage for a tragi-comedy.

The diligence of a few farmers and the energy of the East India Company had made the place pleasant enough. Hundreds of frigates had, by degrees, brought garden mould, building stone, and timber. But since no one would stay long on the rock unless under compulsion, there were twelve hundred negro slaves and Chinese to serve the five hundred whites who dwelt there for a few years at a time.

No one can stay there. On this island, no one reaches the age of sixty, and very few live to be fifty; the climate is deadly. We are in sunless tropics, where the fierce heat of the equator is variegated with cloud bursts, and where within an hour a damp sultriness may give place to a cold downpour. The skin of those who, just before, were dripping with sweat, is suddenly chilled by the storming south-east trade wind, whose vapours are arrested by the rock. One who, after a burning day, ventures abroad in the evening, will pant for breath as he walks. Those who stay for a year, suffer from dysentery, giddiness and fever, vomiting and palpitation. Above all, they suffer from liver disease. Whenever England tried to station a squadron at St. Helena, the sailors died by hundreds; the ships had to put out to sea, and to keep under sail. The officials and the planters fall sick. Unless they have the luck to live in one of the four or five sites protected from the wind, they and their families are soon compelled to seek some healthier place of residence.

The inhabitants will tell you that one of the most unwholesome regions is a chilly tableland seventeen hundred feet above sea level; a lonely place, on the windy side of the island, made specially insalubrious by the persistence of fogs. There grow sparse gum trees, blighted by the trade wind, gnarled and twisted, leaning away from the prevailing blast. The St. Helenians call the region Deadwood. Here is Longwood. That is the place selected by England as the one in which the sick foe can most certainly be killed. It was not a temporary asylum, chosen hastily and in an emergency; it was not originally intended for the Emperor; it was made ready for him while he was living elsewhere on the island, in poor case, but still in fairly good health.

Till yesterday, Longwood had been a stable, built fifty years before, and only at the last moment transformed into a dwelling-house. Negroes, and the carpenters of the "Northumberland," fixed a wooden floor over the mud of the interior, neglecting to clear away the cattle dung. Soon after the Emperor's entry, the planks rotted and broke, the stinking damp soaked through the flooring, and he had to move into another room. For himself and his followers, a home has been made out of a cow-shed, a wash-house, and a stable. In his bedroom, a dark and narrow corner, the brown nankeen which covers the walls is stained with saltpetre; smells from the kitchen invade it. In this last point it resembles the lodging he had in a café thirty years ago when he was lieutenant in Valence. But in that earlier abode his books kept dry; here they are attacked by mould. The dining-room is lighted through a glass door; the drawing-room is furnished with a worm-eaten mahogany suite; the servants' quarters are flooded by the rain, for the roof here is made of roofing-felt.

The Emperor lives in two small rooms, each about fourteen feet by twelve, and ten feet high. The bedroom boasts a threadbare carpet, muslin curtains, a fire-place, painted wooden chairs, two small tables, a wash-hand-stand, and a sofa. The workroom has a bare table, under which two chairs are tucked; rough shelves closely packed with books, and an extra bed where he would rest sometimes in the daytime or which he would use on the nights when he was restless and sleepless. The bedroom contains some trophies rescued from his ruin; the little camp-bed he had used at Austerlitz, hung with green silk curtains; a silver lamp; and, on the wash-hand-stand, magnificent silver ewers and basins.

These rooms, and indeed the whole premises, swarm with rats, which kill the fowls, gnaw the leg of a sick horse, bite General Bertrand in the hand, and spring out of Napoleon's three-cornered hat as he takes it from the sideboard.

Who lives in the house besides the rats? Three counts and one baron with their families (all of them officers, and accustomed to court life), two valets, and the rest of the Emperor's staff with their dependents; nearly forty persons in all, when they first land. After six years, at the end of Napoleon's life, the number has been reduced by half.

Las Cases and his young son hold out for a year. Marquis and émigré, older than the Emperor, a sprig of the Faubourg, count of the empire, it was not until the Hundred Days that Las Cases became one of Napoleon's close associates. He was a man of the world, author of some works on geography; later he was to write his *Memorial of St. Helena,* which is said to have brought him thousands of pounds. He was shorter than the Emperor, and as lean as General Bonaparte had been. He was cultured, pleasant of temper, always ready to serve: certainly the most agreeable companion and secretary the prisoner had. He entertained the Emperor with witticisms the Parisians had made at Napoleon's expense, thereby unfolding the comic obverse of a tragic career. Las Cases taught the Emperor

English, thus widening the scope of the exile's reading. When the two men exchanged notes in English, the count would underscore the Emperor's mistakes. Las Cases, under various pretexts, finally abandoned the island, and left a vacant place which during the last years of the Emperor's life was never to be filled.

For Bertrand, sometime governor of Illyria, and devoted to the Emperor, is touchy, and is too proud to write from dictation; in other respects, he observes a faultless passivity, except when he shows fear of offending his wife. This lady, a beautiful creole, half-English with the head of a young lord, had been loath to share Napoleon's exile. At Plymouth, she had tried to throw herself overboard; she is miserable, thinks of Paris, and weeps over her youth; consorts much with the enemy. One day her place is empty at the Emperor's board. Napoleon says that his house is not an inn; Bertrand is aggrieved at the reproach, and does not put in an appearance next day. Then the Emperor is so unhappy that he cannot eat, and pushes his plate away, saying softly and with deep melancholy: "If, in Longwood, they are going to fail in their respect for me, my lot is bitterer than if it had happened in Paris."

Gourgaud is unbearable. The young general had been through the last campaigns as Napoleon's adjutant. His affection for his chief has made him accompany the Emperor to St. Helena; but he is quite unable to overcome his feelings of wonder at his self-sacrifice. After a few weeks' sojourn on the island he meets a charming lady, and writes in his diary: "O liberty, why am I a prisoner?" He is useful to the Emperor because of his erstwhile position on the general staff; he is conversant with the science of strategy, understands maps and mathematics. Not a day goes by, however, but Gourgaud is offended. Innate vanity and jealousy are increased a thousandfold by the narrowness of the circle; he becomes the incarnation of the grotesque, which, from the first day on the island, begins to encompass the Emperor about. Gourgaud has the temperament of a snarling dog; he cannot allow Las Cases to take precedence; Napoleon vainly tries to smooth the young man's ruffled plumes, and only by resorting to command is he able to prevent a duel. "You followed me here in order to comfort my life, so you are brothers. Am I no longer here to care for you? And are you not aware that the eyes of strangers are upon you?"

The Emperor learns patience upon the rock. He also learns considerateness, especially where Gourgaud is concerned. A dozen times and more, he speaks to the young man in fatherly fashion; tries to persuade him to bear with his companions; cajoles him with the promise of a wealthy and beautiful Corsican bride. Another time he sends the general to a little festivity in the town: "You will meet the Baroness Stürmer there, and see Lady Lowe. At your age, it is always agreeable to consort with pretty women. You will go to sleep filled with pleasant thoughts, and by to-morrow morning you'll feel fit for work once more. We'll talk over the Russian campaign. . . ." A voice from Tartarus! But next day Gourgaud again takes offence because in a picture of the group which has been painted by one of the valets, he appears in civilian dress. A few days later he reminds his master of an episode near Brienne: Gourgaud saved Napoleon's life by cutting down a Cossack who was about to attack the Emperor. The Emperor pretends to have forgotten; Gourgaud is outraged, saying that all Paris was buzzing with talk of the incident. Napoleon smiles: "You are a brave man, but amazingly childish."

Las Cases' servant steals a diamond cross belonging to Gourgaud; in order to secure peace, the Emperor has to put the cross in his own pocket, and, later, present it to Gourgaud with the assurance that he had taken it himself. Again, Gourgaud complains that he is short of money and has not enough to keep his mother in comfort. The Emperor writes: "General! We are here on a battle-field. He who runs away because he does not receive enough money, is a coward! . . . I do not owe you any thanks. If you had remained in France you would have been executed, for you had a command in the '15 campaign!" In rare moments only, does the rage in his heart find such vent. Napoleon does, indeed, tell Gourgaud that he is free to leave any day he pleases. But immediately afterwards the Emperor turns the conversation on to cannons, gun-carriages, and cartridges. Next day he says:

"My dear Gourgaud, how glum you look! Have a cold rub down; that'll do you good. One must curb one's imagination, otherwise one is liable to go mad; it is like the Danube: at the source of the river one can cross it in a bound. . . . When I die, I shall leave no family behind me but you. I am no longer wealthy, but I have a few million still. In addition you will inherit my writings. I know what I owe you. But, while we are here, I want my friends to cheer me, and not to make me sadder by pulling long faces. . . . Do you fancy that I have no terrible moments? At night I wake up and think of what I was and to what I have come."

When such poignant words are uttered at the table of this tiny court, all sit silent and tremble. Each one feels that from this room, this house, this island, an echo like a belated rock-fall from the volcano must surely find its way to Europe's shore. For a few days thereafter, intrigues are discontinued and enmities subside. But next week, over a trifle, the quarrels break out anew. Gourgaud can stand life on the island no more. He leaves at the end of two years. He makes friends with the English, and, when he bids farewell to Emperor and island, he sails away with letters of introduction from the governor who is the deadly foe of his master.

Count Montholon is the most loyal of the exile's companions. As a youngster of ten he had been instructed by Captain Buonaparte in mathematics. Later, he had served in two score battles under his master, and was much at the Emperor's court. Many decades after Napoleon's death, he proved his fidelity to

Napoleon at St. Helena. Watercolour painting, probably by a Japanese, with a marginal inscription in Chinese ideographs concerning the owner. Broadley collection.

the House of Bonaparte; for, just as now he offers up six years of his life to live with his exiled master on this rocky site, so, too, he devotes six further years to Napoleon's nephew, sharing the third Napoleon's captivity in a fortress. The only drawback in St. Helena is that the count's wife does not get on with Madame Bertrand. One day the countess declares in the hearing of all that the Bertrands' latest born is puny because the mother's milk is good for nothing.

Meanwhile Madame Bertrand is reckoning that her eldest is sure to be made grand marshal as soon as Napoleon II ascends the throne. How much jealousy rages in these breasts because, meanwhile, under Napoleon I, Bertrand remains "grand marshal," while Montholon superintends culinary affairs and Gourgaud attends to the Emperor's stable. Besides, none of them have enough to do. Their duties cannot occupy more than two hours of the endless day. At last things come to such a pass in this ramshackle palace that the members of the little court can only communicate with one another in writing. Even Countess Montholon and her children have in the end to forsake the Emperor and the island.

Who is really loyal, loyal in his heart of hearts?

Three servants. Marchand, the valet, who has attended the Emperor for the last four years; and two Corsicans who, in the hurry of departure, Napoleon had pressed into his service, thereby linking up the island of his birth with the island of his latter days. These servants never have any dealings with the English foe, who would gladly draw their secrets from them. Cipriani has a special reason for his reticence: as sergeant he had seized Capri from the governor of Capri who to-day is governor of St. Helena. Santini occasionally asks for a day off in order to go shooting. But his sport is soon stopped when the fact gets known that he intends to shoot "that monster, the governor," and then tc put a bullet through his own head.

The Emperor sternly forbids his man to contemplate any such deed, for who in Europe would not immediately cast suspicion on himself? But when the servant has withdrawn, the master thinks indulgently: "We Corsicans are all like that!"

XI

A lean, middle-aged man with restless movements, red-haired, freckled, with a large brown patch on the cheek; his throat is stringy; he has pale golden eyebrows shading eyes which can look no one in the face; he is clad in a British uniform—such is the governor of the prison.

He lives in a fine country house, in the most sheltered part of the island, with a garden which is the oldest and most luxuriant in St. Helena. When he pays his first visit to Longwood, the Emperor says: "Execrable! A real hang-dog face, like that of a Venetian sbirro. He glared at me with the eye of a hyena caught in a trap. Perhaps he is my executioner."

It was not Sir Hudson Lowe's position which made him seem so obnoxious to the prisoner, who was on excellent terms with two or three army officers and with the admiral. But Lowe had been an English Fouché on the small scale, had been chief of the spy service in Italy, and had taken over his present delicate task in Fouché's spirit. It was true that the peace of Europe depended on his watchfulness; and since, in Europe, people loved sleep more than greatness, one section of the public was hounding Lowe on to be brutal.

The English press was describing the prisoner in atrocious terms. One of the most noted of English journals pilloried him as the murderer of the Jaffa prisoners, described his sisters as whores, and spoke of Murat as a waiter; a special law was passed to make any attempt at freeing him a capital offence, with the proviso that the offender would be denied spiritual consolation on the way to execution; the prince regent was said to have "besmirched his name" by presenting some fowling-pieces to Napoleon. The honour of England is saved only by the Whigs; and by the formal protest of two members of the

House of Peers, the duke of Sussex and Lord Holland. Lady Holland ventures to send the Emperor books and fruit; another noblewoman, who in earlier days had wanted to raise a corps of amazons against him, now boldly espouses his cause in London; a great English lawyer writes twenty-one theses to prove that Napoleon's detention after peace has been signed is illegal; Thomas Moore and Lord Byron save England's credit before the tribunal of history. Germany's good fame is rescued by the fierce attacks upon Lowe in the German press, attacks that go on for years.

The governor is attacked because he has turned the whole island into a prison. He has issued regulations arranged in twenty-four paragraphs, informing the captains and crews of vessels that touch at St. Helena about all the things that are forbidden, under penalty; posters in the streets of Jamestown prohibit contact with the French; no one may approach Longwood without a written permit. Every movement of the prisoners is watched through a telescope; for six long years British officers keep their eyes riveted on the place of detention, but can rarely see anything more noteworthy than the lizards on the roof. Semaphores keep the governor informed as to all that is going on. They report: "General Bonaparte is out of bounds."—"He is accompanied."—"He is alone"—One flag was kept in reserve for a terrible emergency, to announce the news that General Bonaparte had vanished. This blue signal was never hoisted.

The "bounds" are a twelve-mile ring round Longwood, subsequently restricted to an eight-mile ring; at 9 p.m. (or, when the restrictions are increased, at sunset), a cordon of sentries at fifty paces' interval is posted. If Bertrand, who lives at Hutt's Gate (a small villa about a mile away), is summoned by the Emperor after nightfall, he is escorted to Longwood by two soldiers with fixed bayonets—these bayonets, so runs the order, "must point at the Frenchman's heart."

The Emperor, who has for thirty years been accustomed to

horseback exercise, may not go out of bounds unless accompanied by a British officer. He protests, "Not because I object to the red uniform more than another; after their baptism of fire, all soldiers are alike. But I refuse to do anything which involves the acknowledgement that I am a prisoner." When in high spirits, as he was sometimes in the early days of his captivity, he would defy the regulations. Once he gave the English officer the slip, rode across country with Gourgaud, burst into a private plantation, saying to the owner: "Don't let any one know that we have been here!" But during the latter part of his stay at St. Helena he kept within bounds, and, indeed, rarely left the grounds of Longwood. Sometimes he would order his horse for a ride; and then, when all was ready for the start, overwhelmed with bitterness at sight of the officer who was to accompany him, he would countermand the order and re-enter the house.

The result of this lack of outdoor exercise is that his health suffers more and more. The climate alone would have brought premature death, but confinement to the house quickens the pace of his maladies. For lack of movement, his legs swell. Furthermore, while Sir Hudson Lowe is giving dinner parties, for weeks at a time Napoleon cannot get even fresh water or milk. His stomach trouble grows much worse. The sick man would like a wider bed, but there is no room for one; he must content himself with rigging up a sofa beside his camp bed.

He and his companions have been deprived of their money. The letters he writes to France asking for funds are intercepted. Being positively in want, he has some of his silver plate put up to auction. When this is reported to the governor by semaphore, the inhabitants are forbidden to buy; Lowe himself purchases the articles at knock-down prices through an agent. Six months later, when the governor reads in the newspapers what Europe thinks of his conduct, he is greatly incensed, makes the regulations stricter than ever, supplies Longwood with uneatable meat and sour wine.

Like the villain in the folk-tale, Lowe is continually on the lookout for new ways of mortifying his prisoner. On the anniversary of Waterloo, he holds a great review close to Longwood. He invites "General Bonaparte" to Plantation House on the prince regent's birthday. Another invitation is "to meet the countess" (Lady Loudoun, wife of the governor general of India). When the mail brings him a new lampoon against Napoleon, the governor sends it to one of the Emperor's companions; but when a bust of the king of Rome, modelled by an admirer, arrives, he proposes to impound it, for documents may be hidden in its interior. He intercepts a letter from Napoleon to the prince regent, in which the prisoner begs for news of his wife and child; refuses to allow a Viennese traveller who has seen the little boy to visit Longwood; and when, through the kindly thought of a nurse and the loyalty of a valet, a lock of the boy's hair at length reaches the Emperor by devious channels, Lowe sends home a detailed report concerning the obvious dangers of a conspiracy to liberate the caged eagle.

To begin with, the gaoler sees the prisoner a few times. "Throw away that cup of coffee," says the Emperor after one of these interviews; "the man was near it." From the first, Lowe does his utmost to shorten Napoleon's life. When the Emperor's vital energies begin to flag, the governor deprives him of the services of the English surgeon in whom Napoleon has confidence because this man, O'Meara, has refused any information beyond medical bulletins. O'Meara is one of those on whom Lowe has to keep a wary eye. It is not enough to surround Longwood with spies; the whole island is beset with them; they watch all the officers; and when they have nothing better to do, they watch one another. Soon a network of intrigue envelops the little house, whose interior is hung with yet another network—that of the jealousies which of old had been so rife in the Tuileries.

In the third year of the captivity, O'Meara reports to London that the Emperor's liver trouble has been greatly aggravated by the climate, the dampness of his dwelling, the lack of exercise, and the vexations to which the prisoner is subjected. It is amazing that the illness does not advance with more rapid strides. This would happen, were it not for the energy with which the patient bears up, and were it not that his body has not been weakened by any excesses.—Since this report is shown to the British Minister for Foreign Affairs, and presumably to the prince regent as well, and since in spite of it the Emperor is kept for three years more at St. Helena instead of being sent to the Azores or some other suitable place, the bad faith of Napoleon's custodians may be taken as proved—and Lowe was a worthy interpreter of his instructions.

The man's animus, and the craftiness of his designs, are well shown by a passage in one of his reports. Lowe says he will arrange matters so that Napoleon will be able to resume horse exercise. Otherwise the prisoner might die of apoplexy, and that would be extremely inconvenient. Death from some lingering disorder would be better, for then the British doctors would have no difficulty in certifying that death was due to natural causes.

In the early days at St. Helena, the Emperor compiles a long official protest (it occupies twelve pages of print); it contains all his grounds of objection, and he has a private copy made upon silk, hoping that he will be able to smuggle it away to Europe. In this document he reiterates his refusal to allow himself to be addressed as "General Bonaparte," for that implies a disavowal of his position as popularly elected Consul and Emperor. He remarks that he had proposed, as a reasonable compromise, to name himself Duroc or Muiron, after one of his two dead adjutants; but that England had refused to concede to him this "privilege accorded to persons of sovereign rank." The governor had even attempted to address him as General "Buonaparte."

In this tragi-comical fashion, after bearing seven names,

he returns with the eighth, to the first name by which he had been known.

Soon there are actual hostilities. The lust of battle glows once more in the prisoner. He displays a vigour of hatred which in former days he had hardly ever shown in words, for then he had simply annihilated the objects of his wrath. Longwood, too, inaugurates a system of signals, though a less conspicuous one than that of the British, who use flags and semaphores. When the governor approaches, the Emperor, warned by his vedettes, hastens indoors, and tells his servants to say he is "not at home." Once, however, he is taken by surprise in the garden; Lowe bluntly tells him that his establishment is too costly, and asks him to cut down expenses. The soldier flames in the Emperor.

"How dare you talk to me of such matters? You are nothing but a gaoler. You have only commanded brigands and deserters. I know the name of every English general who has won distinction. All I have ever heard of you is that you were one of Blücher's quilldrivers, and a robber captain who never had the honour of commanding real soldiers.—Don't send me any more food! I will take meals with those brave fellows of your 35th, over there; not one of them will refuse to share his rations with an old fellow-soldier. You can dispose of my life as you please, but not of my heart. That is still as proud on this rock as it was when all Europe was awaiting my orders.—You would stick at nothing. You would poison me if you had the courage, or were sent orders to do so!"

Without a word, the governor turns on his heel, mounts his horse, and gallops away. The Emperor compares past and present. "In the Tuileries, I should have blushed at such a scene."

For ever, the governor remains on the watch, negotiates about details with the Emperor's companions, but does not see the living Napoleon again. One day, however, Lowe makes another attempt, persists in spite of a refusal to admit him, wants to see with his own eyes that "General Bonaparte" is still there. The servant announces this importunacy. Then the governor hears the Emperor shout through the door:

"Tell him he can bring his executioner's axe if he likes. But if he wants to enter my room, he must do so over my dead body. Give me my pistols!"

Lowe was able to satisfy himself as to the general's presence when Napoleon lay dead.

XII

The Emperor rises as late as possible, so that the day may seem shorter. He rings; Marchand enters; Napoleon asks about the weather, slips on his white morning gown, and retains his headgear—a red chequered Madras kerchief he has been wearing all night. The red kerchief seems to be a whimsical parody of the turban he once dreamed of donning! Cold douche and rub—but of eau-de-Cologne, alas, there is none! Then Dr. O'Meara pays a visit. He speaks Italian with the Emperor, and gossips over the ludicrous happenings on the island. Sometimes there is no sugar to sweeten the coffee. Has the mailship come to port with fresh newspapers? Nothing as yet. Gourgaud arrives and writes from dictation. Where were we? The pyramids? The Emperor paces to and fro in the narrow room; a map of Egypt lies spread on the table.

He breakfasts with Gourgaud since the young man chances to be there. The talk is of artillery fire, and means of defence against it. In the afternoon, lounging on the sofa in the bedroom, he reads. The old home on the other island was certainly more comfortable. A couple of bound volumes of the "Moniteur" pass the hours. If he wearies of reading, his book will sink on to his knees, and his gaze will wander to Isabey's portrait of wife and child. Nearby, on the white lacquered shelf, are two eagles, candlesticks, from Saint-Cloud. Between them is the marble bust of his son; and, hanging to the faded gilt frame of the mirror, four miniatures of the boy. There is also a picture of Josephine; and the gold watch of Rivoli, suspended by a chain made from the fair plaited hair of Marie Louise, hangs to the wall. There hangs also the silver alarum clock of Frederick the Great. Jetsam from the past, adorning his last, tiny bedroom!

He dressed for dinner in the old green coat; sported the decoration of the Legion of Honour; wore white silk stockings, and shoes with golden buckles. He was waited on at table by his Parisian servants in their rich liveries of green and gold. The table in his fusty dining-room was set with a dinner service of Sèvres depicting Napoleon's battles, branched candlesticks, glass globes crowned with eagles. Cipriani carved for His Majesty and served his master with great ceremony. Conversation was usually carried on in monosyllables; it concerned the cost of various things in Paris; the price of the throne and the sceptre. After dinner, the company would pass into the drawing-room for a reading of Corneille; the same plays over and over again; the Emperor read with too much feeling to read well. Sometimes his hearers would nod: "Madame, you are asleep!" or, "Gourgaud, wake up!"

"At your orders, Sire."

Occasionally he plays chess with Bertrand or reversi with Montholon. Then it is time to withdraw.

"What o'clock is it?"

"Eleven, Sire."

"Another victory over time. One day the less!"

Thus passed more than two thousand days and nights. His campaigns in Italy and Egypt and his coup d'état had taken half the time!

The best way of getting through the weary hours is by reading and dictating. For five-and-twenty years he had had no time for reading; in earlier days he had devoured and annotated a whole library of books. What is he reading to-day?

The things which the young man had not had an opportunity of reading. In those days, standing outside the closed portals of the world, he gathered materials from all sides, went to first-hand sources: a practically minded student. Now, standing on the further side of the portals of the world, which have now closed behind him, he surveys the material: a sceptical philosopher. In those days, he searched history; now, he searches the poets, and especially relishes those passages from the poets which apply to his own case. An epic lies behind him; in the epics of others, he tries to find his prototype.

First of all, the *Iliad*. He sometimes browses over this till midnight. "Now, at length, I understand Homer. He is, like Moses, a child of his epoch: poet, orator, historian, lawgiver, geographer, theologian. . . . I am specially struck by the rough manners of the heroes as compared with their lofty thoughts." Napoleon finds ease of heart in Homer. He cares less for the *Odyssey*. This seems to him no more than the story of an adventurer: he himself is more than that. Next in order of preference come Sophocles' *Œdipus*, a tragedy of banishment; Æschylus' *Agamemnon;* Milton's *Paradise Lost;* the Bible. Corneille and Racine depict, in the French style, the heroes of antiquity, who for thirty years have been his models: unending are his readings of *Cinna* and *Philoctète*. Ossian rises out of the roar of the Atlantic: this he reads in an Italian translation. In addition, the satirists of the social life of Europe: Molière, whom in the ardent years of conquest and success the Emperor had scorned; and Beaumarchais' *Figaro* and the *Barbier de Séville*. Finally, all the latest publications, whether memoirs or pamphlets, and, preferably, anything against himself.

The golden day for him was when the ship arrived with cases of books. In the course of his stay, he collected three thousand volumes; they were ranged on the bare damp shelves. Unfortunately, he reads so fast that a book hardly lasts him an hour, and the servant is kept busy carrying away armfuls of finished books which only a day before had been brought from the shelves. As soon as a book is read (or rejected) the Emperor flings it on to the floor.

In the early days on St. Helena, Napoleon's actions were performed at his erstwhile speed, a speed which was many times faster than that of any of his associates. He forgot that now it was expedient to go slower. The consequence was that the few duties the prisoner imposed upon himself came to an end too quickly.

When, on taking leave of the imperial guard, he had promised that, during his reign in Elba, he would record their deeds, this had only been thought of as a way out of the threatened idleness. In the days of his first exile, he had begun no such record. Now, during the first year of his second exile, he dictates the whole of his memoirs. This work too, like all else in his life, is begun on the inspiration of the moment. Some pamphlets have arrived. In one of them, his landing at Cannes in the year '15 is falsely described. He tells his doctor the true sequence of affairs; paces up and down, declaiming; motions to Montholon while continuing his tirade, and dictates, without a pause, the whole chapter dealing with his return from Elba. Separated from his archives by five thousand miles and more, lacking documents, from his unerring memory, and with an inspiration unsurpassed in the days of his greatest activity, he dictates the story of the Hundred Days. Then, suddenly, he breaks off. What's the use of it all?

Another day, the report of an incident in the Lower House excites him: he thereupon dictates for fourteen hours without a rest. Those who take down his words, collapse, and replace one another at the task. Napoleon laughs them to scorn, and continues his dictation. Or, again, he sends for Montholon in the middle of the night to pen his recollections of more recent times.

Since he loves above all to dwell on his early victories, his friends at first advise him: "Perhaps Your Majesty might set about describing the Italian and Egyptian campaigns, and the days of the Consulate?" Set about describing! No one seems to notice, and least of all the Emperor, that these events are being spoken of as one might speak of the Thirty Years' War. And just as, in those days, the man in whose heart and brain these things first took birth had projected his thoughts to the ends of the earth and had commanded his legions, so now, to the last instruments in his service, he communicates the details of his early campaigns, and in a few weeks describes how he conducted the wars from 1796 to 1799. Up and down, up and down, the Emperor paces, noticing nothing, wholly absorbed. Without, doors bang, people talk; the amanuensis is disturbed by these noises; not so Napoleon.

Las Cases, after taking down the description of the battle of Arcola, exclaims: "That's finer than the *Iliad!*" The Emperor makes a wry face, and laughingly rejoins: "Bah! You still fancy yourself at court! I shall rewrite that chapter twenty times ere I shall be satisfied." This expostulation is only a defence against flattery, for he has no intention of writing the chapter again; all he does is to make certain emendations when it is read over to him.

On the other hand, he dictates the events of Waterloo over and over again. Since, in spite of his historical objectivity, he cannot understand the result of this battle which undid him, he is always searching for new formulations. When, through the good offices of some sympathetic Englishmen, an opportunity occurs for smuggling documents to Europe, he works laboriously at the battle of Waterloo in order to dim England's glory in the eyes of the European continent. But, he avers: "this task always makes me sad."

In these memoirs, there are errors here and there. They are not due to lapses of memory, but to the author's desire to emphasise his own place in history. Such errors are not more serious than those to be found in Cæsar's works, are not serious errors at all. When he erroneously records that in his lieutenant days he received the gold medal from the academy of Lyons for his solution of a problem, and states that the money prize was of great use to his mother; when telling the story of his battles he ascribes to himself certain deeds which, in reality, had been performed by his generals (at Marengo, for instance); when he invents a treaty in which the tsar, before the Russian campaign, is made to propose the division of Europe we have inaccurate statements regarding the individuals concerned, but the broad facts are correct. It is true that, in accordance with his conception of the hero, he formally idealises the hero's deeds; but he seems to us to lose more than he gains thereby. Since he is describing the period of his rise to power, he cannot materially falsify the facts: the immeasurable consequences of his first victory were bound to give rise, on the one hand, to a certain boastfulness, and, on the other, to detraction. But these volumes, which deal for the most part with the exploits of the commander, furnish but little real knowledge of Napoleon. Where we have to seek for the true Napoleon is in the memoirs of those who had the privilege of recording his conversations in exile.

Soon, indeed, his pleasure in dictation evaporates. Though he had intended to dictate in a few weeks the campaign of 1800 which had lasted but that amount of time, he postpones this labour, and tells Gourgaud to collect material bearing upon the Russian campaign. Then the young general, who had himself participated in the campaign of 1812, sets to work to read—not a Russian work dealing with the campaign, but an English work dealing with the life of the Emperor who is there, three rooms away, and could probably furnish full particulars!

Napoleon, the movement of whose mind was from events to ideas, and very rarely from thought to deed, is still true to type. When he reads news from Paris, he dictates rejoinders which demonstrate his expertise, and he compiles financial schemes. From his rock, from his little room, he answers the sounds coming from the outer world, although the sounds are no summons and his answer dies away into the void. He often proposes to write a treatise on the art of war, but he gives the notion up, "for the generals who in days to come get beaten will blame me, and say they were following my principles. . . . I could instruct them, for I am a good teacher; but I cannot have my principles of warfare set down in print." He mistrusts every systematisation, for he is essentially a man who has learned by experience, by the unexpected. But if an isolated problem crops up in the course of a book he is dictating, then he deals with it in the precisest of terms. Thus, he makes Gourgaud calculate how much water a fire hose can deliver, for he wants to introduce the fire hose to combat the consequences of artillery fire.

Congenial society occasionally shortens the day. Or visitors come to see the Emperor. English travellers, men of learning, colonial magnates, are admitted to audience. On their return to Europe, they bear witness to his mental alertness. Napoleon himself desires such reports to be spread abroad, for they can do nothing but good to his cause now that Las Cases' diary has aroused fresh sympathy for his plight.

"Scatter your complaints throughout Europe! I myself do not complain." And he adds the orphic saying:

"I command, or else I hold my peace."

His visitors tell him interesting things. An English admiral, whose vessel had been lying off the coast during the battle of Waterloo, assures the Emperor that Wellington had already given orders to ship the English army because Blücher did not arrive. When his companions inform him of the enthusiasm with which the enemy officers were filled after their interview with the Emperor, he says, assuming the role of the revolutionary: "Of course, these people belong to us. They all come from England's third estate, and are the natural foes of their haughty aristocracy."

All the men in the services are on his side. English sailors, on shore leave for a day or two, will prowl round the place all night. At the first opportunity, they pounce upon him, stuttering incoherent words, presenting him with flowers. The Emperor claps them pleasantly on the shoulder. When the garrison is changed, he receives the members of the officers' corps, exactly as though they had been Frenchmen and he their army chief. They form a semicircle; he asks, "How many years' service; how many wounds? I was greatly pleased with the 53rd regiment. I shall always be delighted to hear of good strokes of luck coming in its way. You are sad, Admiral Bingham, that these brave soldiers are leaving you. To comfort your heart, My Lady must bear you a little Bingham!" The army men laugh. The admiral blushes. When, next day, the transport hoists sail, the men give the prisoner three hearty cheers. A few months later, all Europe is agog with the anecdote.

On another occasion, he sees a medal displayed on the chest of a captain, half raises it, and reads: Victory at Vittoria. The Emperor allows the decoration to slip from his fingers, and passes without a word to the next visitor.

Each of England's allies sends a commissioner to the island. They are there merely to gratify the curiosity of their sovereigns. The prisoner refuses them access to his presence, and, though they are here on this desolate rock with the sole purpose of seeing that he is in safe custody, during all the years of their sojourn they never clap eyes on him once. Here is a fresh focus of intrigue and boredom. The only one of the commissioners whom the Emperor allows his suite to make friends with is Monsieur le Marquis. This is the representative chosen by His Very Christian Majesty King Louis XVIII to keep watch on his formidable predecessor. The marquis sees that Napoleon gets all the most recent periodicals; the Emperor reciprocates by the loan of books. When tidings are brought announcing the assassination in France of a Bourbon duke, General Bonaparte sends his condolences to the marquis of the old nobility by the intermediation of Count Bertrand, who is also a sprig of the noblesse. A scene out of comic opera!

When the prisoner is in happy vein he seeks other pastimes. One evening he spends fluttering the pages of the official year-books of his reign, and says, like the bewitched tinker in the old folk-tale: "It was a fine empire. I ruled eighty-three million human beings; more than half the population of Europe!" He spends the whole of another evening with Las Cases chatting over old times. They laugh, the Emperor's spirits rise, he orders champagne to be brought, and before they realise it the hands of the clock point to eleven. Napoleon says delightedly: "How quickly the time has gone! What agreeable hours! My dear fellow, you are sending a happy man to bed."

Words which grip one perhaps more poignantly than any complaint could do.

He takes Montholon's seven-year-old child on his knee and recites La Fontaine's fable of the wolf and the lamb. The child has not fully understood, and makes a delicious muddle of lamb, wolf, and His Majesty. Another happy half hour in the Emperor's life! Again, he strolls up and down the room in the evening after dinner, humming an Italian aria, and laughing gleefully, for he has just read that King Louis always speaks of him as "Monsieur de Buonaparte." If he has a sleepless night, he makes Las Cases tell him anecdotes from the Faubourg; or he says to Gourgaud: "Let us exchange stories about love affairs. I never had enough time to spare for women. Otherwise they would have ruled my life for me." If he gets bored in his bath, he takes the opportunity of demonstrating to Gourgaud why the pressure of the water upon a floating body is equal to the weight of the body. On one occasion, in the drawing-room, he has his own height and that of his companions measured against the door.

Sometimes he will not dress or go out in the morning, putting off both until the afternoon. On one of these occasions, after an exceptionally torrid evening, he does not re-enter the house till midnight, and says that he has won a real victory by staying out so long. Another day he goes up the stair-ladder into his valet's garret, having been told that it is so nicely furnished. He is shown his own wardrobe, which is stowed away there, and is amazed to find what a lot of clothing he still possesses. He fingers the uniform he had worn as Consul (a gift from the city of Lyons), the spurs he had worn at Wagram, the cloak of the Marengo days. He makes no comment; goes down the stair-ladder in silence.

Amid these desperate attempts to kill time, does the prisoner come across no one whose situation moves him?

Yes, there is one. Of all the dwellers on this rock, the one whose lot touches the Emperor's heart most profoundly is a slave, a Malay who passes by the name Tobias, has been kidnapped, sold into slavery, and cast up on this remote island. Napoleon comes across him working in the garden, or meets him in the road, is never weary of studying him, and gives him a gold coin whenever he sees him. The Malay thanks him in broken English: "Good gentleman."

"Poor devil!" says the Emperor to his companion, obviously picturing himself in the position of this dusky piece of flotsam. "Snatched from his family, torn from his home, robbed of himself, sold into slavery! Was there ever a greater piece of wickedness? If a captain did it, he was a villain; but if the crew combined to seize poor Tobias, they were hardly responsible. Wickedness is always individual, never collective. Joseph's brethren could not make up their minds to kill him, but Judas betrayed his master."

After the next encounter with the Malay: "What a pitiful machine man is, after all! Not one bodily wrapping like another; not one soul that does differ from all the rest. Those who fail to recognise this, make a great many mistakes. Had Tobias been a Brutus, he would have hurled himself on death; an Æsop, and he would have been governor by now; a good Christian, and he would have blessed his chains. But he is only poor Tobias, so he is none of these things, merely bows his head in his simplicity and goes on with his daily task."

The two continue their walk: "Certainly it is a long way from poor Tobias to King Richard. But the deed which brought the fellow here is no less shameful, for this man had his family, his friends, his own life. What a crime to have condemned him to slave on this island until the day of his death!" Suddenly, Napoleon stops short, and eyes Las Cases quizzically:

"I read from your face that you are thinking he is not the only sufferer of the kind on this island." Las Cases nods assent, and the Emperor bursts out with a youth's ardour: "There is no warrant for such a comparison! True, the violence done to us is more refined in its cruelty, but, in compensation, we are more distinguished victims. . . . The world has its eyes fixed on us. We are the martyrs of an immortal cause! Millions weep for us, the fatherland sighs, the spirit of glory mourns. . . . Adversity, too, has its heroism and its fame. Had I died on the throne, surrounded by all the emblems of power, I should have remained a riddle to many. To-day the wrappings have been stripped from me; thanks to my misfortunes, every one can judge me in my nakedness."

Subsequently, the Emperor buys the slave, wishing to send him back to his own land and his own folk, but the governor forbids the repatriation: "It is plain to me that General Bonaparte is trying to win the hearts of the coloured population, in the hope of setting up a second negro empire, as in San Domingo."

Tobias, therefore, remains a captive; a slave in a far country, like the Emperor.

XIII

"I am very old to make a journey of two thousand leagues. Perhaps I should die on the way; but, never mind, I should die nearer you."

Thus writes his mother. The Emperor reads the letter again and again, when it is delivered to him a year after it was penned. The powers forbade the journey: who could tell, the old lady might concoct a plan for his escape! Letizia had been banished from France when the other members of her family were expelled. For the second time in her life, she is unable to go to her island home: the first time had been long ago when Corsica was in revolt; now, Europe stands in the way. She, therefore, goes to Rome, where the moral power of the pope upholds her; always making fresh attempts to secure her son's removal to a more healthy abiding place. Although the tsar is favourable to such a transfer, Habsburg and England are determined Napoleon shall die; so there is nothing more to be done. Neither mother nor any of the brothers and sisters is allowed to send money to the exile.

When the monarchs assemble in Aix-la-Chapelle for the congress, Letizia writes to the princes: "A mother, more bowed with grief than words can tell, has long been hoping that the meeting of your imperial and royal highnesses would give her back her life. It is impossible that the captivity of Emperor Napoleon should not come up for discussion. Your magnanimity, your power, and your memory of earlier events, will surely incline Your Imperial and Royal Majesties to work for the liberation of a prince for whom you once professed friendship. I pray to God and to you, for you are God's representatives on earth. Interests of State have their limits. Posterity, which confers immortality, admires a generous conqueror."

No answer.

Later the captive learns that his mother has been accused of fostering a conspiracy in Corsica. She is said to have provided money amounting to millions. The pope is ordered to send his secretary of State to see the old lady and to make enquiries. Letizia gives the emissary the following message: "Tell the pope, and may the monarchs mark my words: If I were so fortunate as to possess all these millions they have credited me with, I should certainly not spend them in buying champions for my son's cause. He has enough of them already. I would, rather, equip a fleet capable of rescuing him from the island where he is unjustly detained."

What a feeling of pride and elation fills the son's heart as he reads his mother's words! But he never hears of Letizia's bitter remark to an Austrian noble: "Why is my daughter-in-law amusing herself in Italy instead of joining her husband in St. Helena?"

Round what sun are the other planets turning? What an anticlimax!

Lucien and Joseph have gone to America, and are later joined by Jerome. They assume exotic titles. The Spanish revolutionaries have offered their ex-king the crown of Mexico. This piece of news excites the prisoner:

"Joseph will refuse. He is too fond of the pleasures of life to bother himself again with the burden of a crown—and yet, it would be a stroke of luck for England that the whole problem of Spanish America should be solved in this way. For if Joseph were to become king of Mexico a breach with France and Spain would be inevitable. For myself, his acquiescence would be weighty with consequences. He loves me and would use his position as a weapon to coerce England into treating me differently. Unfortunately, he is sure to refuse." Thus quickly and hopefully does Napoleon, in the first year of his captivity, toy with every fresh opportunity.

The other brothers and sisters retire into obscurity. Jerome alone lives to be an old man, and, in the days of the third Napoleon, appears once more at court. The Emperor receives few letters from his brothers and sisters. Caroline begs her mother to send some money. Letizia refuses: "All I have belongs to the Emperor, from whom I have received all I possess." To Lucien she writes: "When one is no longer king, one makes oneself a laughing-stock if one tries to live ostentatiously. Rings may adorn the fingers; but, if they fall off, the fingers still remain." Hortense and Pauline once more play comedy as they had done at Malmaison.

Other tidings give Napoleon food for thought. Bernadotte becomes king. And Désirée? At last Napoleon's early love wears a crown; she also lives to see the Second Empire. Countess Walewska, now a widow, marries a French nobleman. He approves the step, passes her situation in review, considers all he has done for her son, and then says complacently: "She is rich, and must have saved." The tactless Gourgaud makes answer: "Your Majesty paid Madame Walewska ten thousand francs a month." The Emperor blushes, and asks with embarrassment: "How do you know that?"

King Murat and Marshal Ney are both shot after court martial. Their master accepts their fate with soldierly fortitude. His only annoyance is that Murat should have been such a fool as to land in Calabria. He bears his brother-in-law no grudge. Even Marmont, who lives happily under the Bourbons, comes in for no more reproach than: "I am sorry for Marmont; I was really fond of him. He's not a bad fellow. They appealed to him through his feelings. He fancied he was to be saviour of his country, and behaved like a madman. He would have done better to shoot himself. . . . Human nature is weak."

And yet it is precisely Marmont who stifles every movement which might be of advantage to the exile. Murmurings against the Bourbon ruler spread throughout the land. But when, once more, the émigrés and the members of the new nobility are placed in great positions, notwithstanding their lack of qualifications for such posts, and a Richelieu is given high office in spite of his long absence from France and his ignorance of French affairs; when Lafayette, the veteran fighter for liberty, becomes leader of the proletariat and makes ready for a new revolution, gathering his forces in the clubs and even in the schools, and preparing among the troops "the men of the coming day," to clear out the Bourbons, who can only maintain their position by the aid of foreign armies; when the radical provinces, eager to flaunt the tricolour cockade, rally in support of Napoleon II—it is Marmont, Bonaparte's eldest comrade, who crushes the movement, and thereafter becomes minister.

The Emperor composedly reads that Louis XVIII. has dissolved the Chambers because many of the members favour Orleans or Napoleon. Executions for treason are the order of the day. But who is the most trusted associate of the Bourbon? A little nobody of a Corsican, whom Letizia once upon a time had made her private secretary—a sinecure job created to provide the man with a livelihood. Since all these events take place during the first year, the Emperor is filled with hope, and meditates upon the chances of a fresh revolution.

"What a cruel decree of fate that just at this moment I should be held prisoner! Who is there to set himself at the head of things? Who will be there to save thousands of the bravest from the scaffold?" He stays alone in his room until the morrow, when he speaks absently of Elba. Soon stranger ships heave in sight, the prisoner counts the shots. What is happening? The Emperor sends his friends to gather tidings; they hear nothing; but hope is strong. "What children we are, to be sure," he exclaims next day. "And I, instead of giving a good example, am no better than the rest of you. Were I in America, I should think of nothing but my garden."

Nevertheless, he would not have gone to America. He owns as much when he says: "If I were in America with Joseph, instead of suffering here, nobody would ever think of me, and my cause would be lost. I may have another fifteen years of life, but I am doomed to die here—unless France should summon me."

These hopes are not unfounded. England considers it wise to increase the garrison from two hundred men to three thousand, in order to keep guard on one individual, although the cost of the troops in St. Helena is £320,000 a year. Still, there are possibilities, for the soldiers are whole-heartedly on his side. On one occasion six officers were arrested. They had come from Rio de Janeiro, and had planned to get the Emperor away in a kind of submarine. Again, two captains, travellers to India on a ship which has touched at the island, make him proposals for an escape: Napoleon listens attentively, but decides not to accept. On a third occasion, Montholon breaks in on the Emperor while he is at work with Gourgaud to remind his master that the passport of a certain individual expires in an hour's time and a decision must be made. Montholon writes: "It had been proposed to take the Emperor to America for the sum of one million francs payable on landing. The Emperor's word would suffice. Unfortunately I may not divulge any more of the scheme, lest I expose the originator, for whose loyalty to the Emperor we must be eternally grateful. The Emperor listened to me, and considered all I had to say: he paced to and fro several times in silence, asked Gourgaud and myself for our opinions. He took no part in the discussion. In the end, he said: 'You must decline the offer.' "

There he stands, he has not been captive a year as yet, passably well in health, athirst for action, goaded by the pin-pricks of a mighty government and a puny governor. Before him opens out the possibility of escape, escape with the aid of English officers. The fact that risk is attached does not alarm one who is used to bold enterprises. There he is, dictating the story of his youth, when suddenly, at the end of his career, a friend makes proposals that are certainly not cobwebs of the brain. Napoleon is silent, he questions, he is silent again. Then: "You must decline the offer." Why?

Because France is once more in a state of unrest, and so he decides to stay where he is. He is so sure of a change of feeling among the people that, later, when a ship is sighted and signals to the station, the Emperor says: "Perhaps the vessel brings news of my recall. If the prince regent dies, the young queen will summon me to England. She was always against my being sent to St. Helena." When, on the outbreak of fresh revolts in Paris, his companions mention the possibility of France demanding his return, he concedes the point, adding:

"But what can they hope from my return? That I should again conduct wars? I am too old. That I should seek for fresh glories? I am sated with them. . . . It will be much better for my son that I should stay here. If Christ had not died upon the cross, he would not have become the Son of God. My martyrdom will give the crown back to my son, if he lives."

Napoleon's feeling for the dynasty is as deep as ever. His preoccupation with the thought of founding a line overpowers, in his maturer years, his impulse to action, to adventure, and even to win fame.

Though he is inspired with these lofty moods of hope and heroical renunciation, nevertheless despondency overwhelms him at times; then he becomes greatly depressed, and the most trifling upset in the household will seem an intolerable burden. When Bertrand stays away from dinner in a pet, the Emperor is out of sorts for days: "I know that I have fallen from my high estate, but that one of my nearest companions should rub it in is dreadful. . . ." He groans. Las Cases offers to intervene. "No, I forbid it. I had to say that much. But now all is forgotten and I shall behave as though I had noticed nothing." If travellers should wish to see him on such days, he refuses, saying: "Tell them, dead men do not receive visitors." Occasionally Napoleon broods alone for the whole evening, sends at last for one of his companions, says a word or two, and dismisses him.

A quarrel arises between Montholon and Gourgaud as to whose room shall be furnished first, the Emperor has to mediate, the countess weeps, the Emperor proposes a game of chess. Dinner. A reading from the Book of Esther. Sometimes these scenes verge on the grotesque: a cow has escaped, the Emperor shows his vexation, Gourgaud sits glum throughout dinner because he is responsible for the cow, and is feeling aggrieved by his master's anger. After dinner, the Emperor speaks of

Islam and his preferences for the Mohammedan faith, then passes to a discussion of the trinity; finally he withdraws, making painful attempts to conceal his angry mood and muttering between his teeth: "Moscow! Five hundred thousand men!"

Gourgaud, who has left him overnight in an agreeable state of excitement, finds him next day in a gloomy temper: "What sort of an education will they give my son? Will they teach him to loathe his father? Hateful thought!" When Las Cases, who has copied out the chapter on Waterloo, deplores that victory should have been snatched from the Emperor's grasp, Napoleon makes no reply, but says to Las Cases' son in a voice which seems to come from a great distance: "My lad, go and fetch *Iphigenia in Aulis;* that will do us good." Or he has Racine's *Andromache* read to him.

> I am come to the place where my son
> lies captive: for one moment only,
> allow my tears to flow with his!
> This is all that is left to me
> of Hector and of Troy. Permit me, Lord,
> to visit him once on every day. . . .

But the Emperor breaks in on the reading with the cry:

"Enough! Leave me; I would be alone!"

XIV

With the growing inactivity and boredom, the moods of this tortured heart become more and more agonising; this many-toned instrument can no longer be controlled; discords arise.

He has been an emperor! How can he cease to play the part to which the society of a handful of courtiers and the degrading mockery of the enemy constrain him? In order to protest against the use of the title of general and against the illegality of his captivity, he drives out, at first, in full imperial grandeur, his carriage drawn by six horses, and an equerry in uniform riding at each door. His companions appear before him in general's uniform or in court dress; no one opens conversation uninvited; when he takes his walks in the garden his suite does not approach till he gives a sign; visits are announced by an adjutant general, booted, and wearing a sword. When Gourgaud rises as Countess Montholon enters the room, he is reproved for this breach of etiquette.

Meanwhile he makes fun of the whole thing, mockingly calls Gourgaud "my grand master of the horse," or announces at table: "I have been anointed by the pope; thereby I have become a bishop, and have the power to consecrate you as priests." When he teases his friends about their all being in the "Dictionary of Weathercocks," whose pages he is at the moment fluttering, Gourgaud ventures to say that the Emperor himself deserves a place in it. "Oh; and pray why?"

"Because you first of all recognised the republic, Sire, and yet, later, you were the crown."

"You are right. Oh, well, the Empire was certainly the best of the republics!"

At the feast of Epiphany, he has a cake made for the children. Then he crowns little Napoléon Bertrand as king. When he is informed that there has been a complaint from the governor about the expenses of his household, and that, now that the price of meat has risen to forty sous, they must be more moderate in their consumption, he turns the matter off with a laugh, saying: "Parbleu! You might have answered that it costs us more than a crown."

Never before has so much self-control been forced on him. Impassively he reads Lowe's answer to a statement of grievances from Bertrand, who had said something about "the Emperor." The governor writes that he is not aware of the presence of any emperor on the island.—The prisoner asks Gourgaud to order his horse to be saddled. Gourgaud replies that he has not seen the animal for three days, since the blacksmith insists on being paid three napoleons before he will send it back. The Emperor masters his anger, and says nothing more at the time; but next day he bursts out at Gourgaud: "Why did you insult me by talking to me about the blacksmith's bill?" The day before, by a superhuman effort, he had managed to restrain his wrath, but by the torturing thoughts of the intervening hours his pride had been broken. The adjutant's sullen reply had disturbed the Emperor's equanimity quite as much as Austria's desertion had done in earlier years.

A soldier and a southron, he is choked sometimes by the passion for vengeance. On one occasion, when uneatable meat is served at dinner, he contents himself with the remark: "I should trouble little about myself, if I could only feel sure that some day our humiliations would be proclaimed to the world, so that those who are responsible for them would be covered with shame!"

With a sublimity of spirit which grows in him now, he tries to moderate the natural rebelliousness of his disposition: "I am living here under a weight, so to speak; a weight which compresses the spring, but does not break it. Resignation—that is the dominion of reason, the real triumph of the soul." This masterful man does his utmost to regulate his own conduct in accordance with the foregoing axiom. Subsequently he says: "Misfortune has its good side; it teaches us truths. . . . For the first time, I am able to contemplate history as a philosopher."

For the first time, too, he is able to contemplate the present with a tranquil mind. During the early weeks of his stay on the island, when he was out walking with a pretty young Englishwoman, he conversed with her agreeably about various topics: how the climate was bad for the complexion; Ossian; the plantations. At this moment some negro slaves carrying heavy boxes crossed the path, and the lady called to them imperiously: "Get out of the way!"

The Emperor interposed: "But, Madame, please remember that the men are carrying burdens!"

Collapse of lady! Yet Napoleon Bonaparte himself would

not have been so considerate in the days before he came to St. Helena.

In all matters now, except when he is playing the shadow emperor in pursuance of his feud with Lowe, Napoleon adopts a simplicity of life which outdoes that even of his poorest days as a lieutenant. When for some time there has been very little to eat, and the cook has had to eke things out with French beans, he eats them enthusiastically, praises the dish and the cooking.

"In Paris, I could get along with twelve francs a day. Dinner frs. 1.50; reading room; theatre in the evening, pit; I should hire a room for frs. 20 a month. I should only want one servant; and I should associate exclusively with people of like fortune. One can be happy in any station in life. When my mother sang lullabies over my cradle, there was not a word about what I was destined to become. I believe 'Monsieur Bonaparte' would have been quite as happy as 'Emperor Napoleon.' Everything in life is relative."

His doctor has a fainting fit. Coming to himself, he finds that he is being attended to, not by a servant, but by the Emperor in person. Napoleon has lifted him on to the bed, has unfastened the collar of his shirt, and is kneeling beside him, administering vinegar.—When Cipriani, the Corsican servant, is dying, the Emperor asks the doctor whether a visit from the master would stimulate the man's flagging forces.

"The excitement would kill him."

"Oh, well, I suppose I had better not go."

When playing reversi, he establishes a bank. For whose benefit? The money is to be used to buy the freedom of the most beautiful female slave on the island. One evening, his companions find him at work beside the lamp, slowly and carefully stitching the pages of a manuscript.

Sometimes, however, his dreams reawaken, and flutter against the bars of the cage. "I wish they would transfer me to a desert island, where I could have two thousand people of my own choice, with muskets [illegible]n. I should found a glorious colony, and should en[illegible]ys happily in that model land. There I should not find it necessary to be at grips all the time with antiquated ideas." Having said this apropos of nothing in particular, he passes on to the details of the scheme, dictating specifications—how much money and stores would be needed for the founding of his colony.

A chained sculptor, his plastic impulses must be content with such outlets in the world of imagination; but, side by side with these capriccios, he displays a heroic simplicity. One day, during the early weeks at St. Helena, he is out riding with Las Cases. "We came to a field that was being ploughed. The Emperor dismounted, and took the handles of the plough. With incredible speed, he drove a long and perfectly straight furrow. All this without saying a word until he had finished, when he told me to give the ploughman a napoleon. We remounted, and rode on our way."

XV

"No one but myself can be blamed for my fall. I have been my own greatest enemy, the cause of my own disastrous fate."

This admission, the profoundest of all those made by the exile shows that Napoleon has completely outgrown the cloudy Cæsarist fancies of his middle period. Had he been a believing Christian, the confession would have rounded off his atonement upon the rock. His sense of responsibility, however, is not directed towards God but only towards himself, and therefore the utterance represents a great man's final settlement of accounts with destiny. But, at the same time, it is a last outburst of defiance, for his self-overweening esteem made it impossible for him to admit that there were any greater forces in the world than his own. Napoleon alone could overthrow Napoleon.

The remark was not the outcome of transient depression.

During the closing years of his power, he had again and again spoken to his intimates about his faults and errors; now, upon the island, such admissions are frequent. Some of them are ardent, and some of them are cold; for even in these self-examinations there is an alternation between fantasy and realism. From time to time, we have the heartfelt cry of a penitent: "When I close my eyes, all my mistakes parade themselves before me, like figures in a nightmare." Or, again: "I wanted too much. . . . I strung the bow too tightly, and trusted too much in my good fortune."

But he will coldly reckon up the cases in which he has failed to understand men, coming at this late hour to views which the ablest observers had held while he was still on the throne. The reader who knows his story will require no comment on the remarks that follow.

"I considered Emperor Francis a good man; but he was only a blockhead, and in Metternich's hands he became an instrument for my destruction."—"I ought to have left Talleyrand at his post. What concern was it of mine that he was plundering the foreign chancelleries. I should have been content with having him closely watched. He served me well, as long as he could hope to make anything out of me. If I had kept him in office, I should still have been on the throne."—"If only that man Fulton, with his steamboat, had been right, I should have been master of the world. But those idiots of savants made fun of his invention, just as they make fun of electricity. All the same, gigantic powers are hidden in steam and electricity!"

He regrets that at Tilsit he had decided to maintain the Hohenzollern dynasty. He regrets having crossed the Memel too early; having crossed it in 1812, before he had settled matters in Spain. He regrets that, in defiance of Carnot's advice, he began the last campaign too early, and he regrets that at Waterloo he did not send the guard forward soon enough. Most of all, he regrets having, when his power was finally broken, entrusted himself to England, instead of to the tsar, or, better still, to the United States. Always, when he hears of crises in France, he regrets that he did not go to America.

"From that vantage ground I should have been able to guard France against humiliation from abroad, reaction from within; the dread of my return would have sufficed. In America I should have established the centre of a new French fatherland. Within a year, I should have had sixty thousand men grouped round me. . . . It would have been the most natural place of refuge—a land of vast expanses where a man can live in freedom. If I had had a fit of the blues, I should have mounted a horse, ridden hundreds of miles, enjoyed travel with the ease of a private individual, lost amid the crowd. In Europe I was too popular; bound up, in one way or another, with every nation. . . . As a fugitive, and disguised, I could certainly have escaped to the United States; but both expedients would have been undignified. I put my trust in the approach of danger, thinking that the nation would be forced to turn to me as its saviour; that is why I stayed as long as possible at Malmaison and in Rochefort. The destiny that brought me to St. Helena was the outcome of those feelings."

This is the most productive of his meditations. The other mistakes of his career had entailed such complicated consequences that it was impossible for him to trace what might have been had he acted otherwise. But the final resolve at Rochefort had, as its inevitable upshot, brought him to this rock. In that respect, therefore, his mind was continually busied with alternative possibilities. Although, when in fancy he roams across the American prairies, he sometimes pictures himself as founding new States there, and sometimes as galloping through the wilds, we may ascribe it to the infinite variety of human passions that he should at the same time justify his final blunder on patriotic grounds.

His critical faculty is most keenly at work when he is pondering his dynastic aspirations. In the last days of the Empire, he had confided his doubts to a few choice spirits; now, when it is too late, he freely acknowledges his error. "I was a softy where my family was concerned; by sticking to their point they could get anything out of me. What terrible mistakes I made there! If my brothers had communicated a common impulse to the masses I placed under their rule, we should have been able to make our way to the ends of the earth! . . . I was not so lucky as Genghis Khan, whose four sons vied with one another in their father's service. If I made any one king, he instantly regarded himself as king by divine right; the mere word was as infective as the plague. The new king was no longer my representative, but became a fresh enemy; instead of serving me, he wanted to make himself independent. I was the only stumbling block in his path. In the twinkling of an eye, they all became kings warranted genuine; under my protection, they all tasted the sweets of dominion. I alone bore the burden. Poor devils! Once I had been defeated, the enemy did not even bother to declare their formal deposition."

That was as far as his penitence reached. However self-critical he might be, Napoleon never uttered a word of regret for having assumed a crown, or for having wished to found a dynasty. On the contrary, again and again he returned to his basic social idea: "I was the natural mediator in this struggle between the revolution and the past; my empire was in the interests of the rulers as well as in that of the peoples. My aim was the social rebirth of Europe; fate interfered before I had completed my task." In line with his general conception of kingship, he deplores that the kings should have made an end of Murat. They would have done better to show the peoples that kings are above the law. Though the guillotining of King Louis had opened the road along which he himself had advanced to a throne, he condemned the act of regicide; not because he regarded the Bourbons as competent rulers, but because continuity seemed to him essential.

For he will never misunderstand Europe's historical condi-

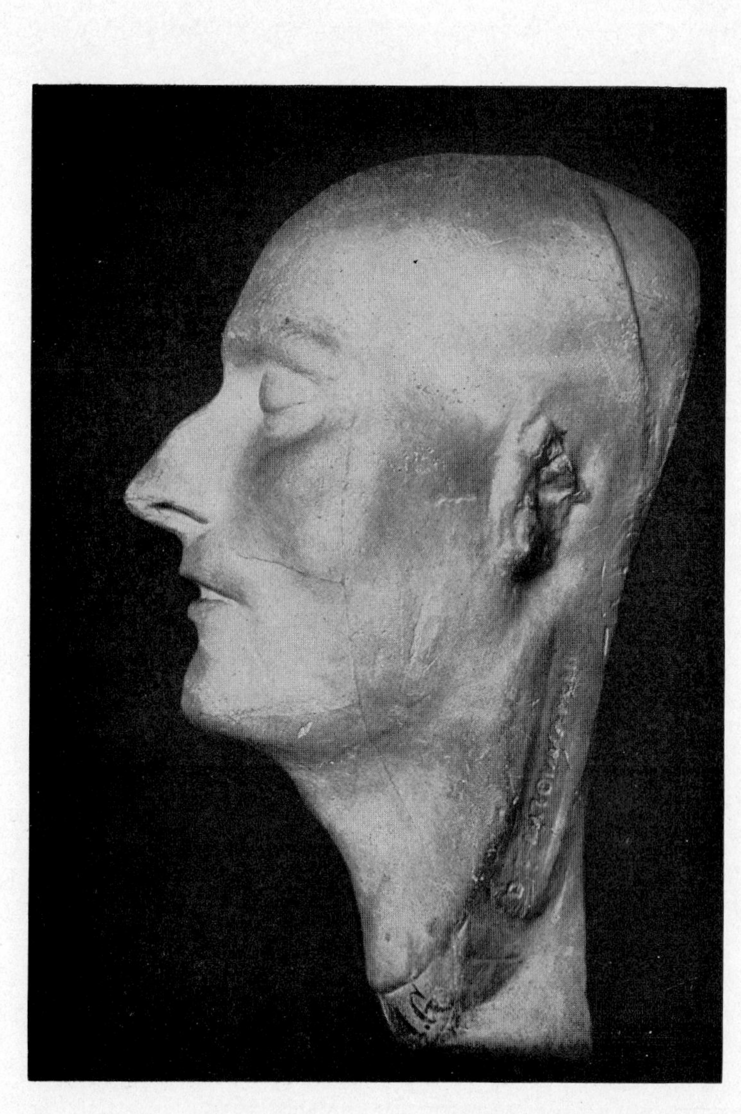

Death mask of Napoleon. By Dr. Antommarchi.

tions; he will never try to establish offhand in Europe that which he dreams of establishing in the promised land of America or in the utopian island of his fancy. He always sees what is, as an outgrowth of what has been; always transforms the extant, instead of destroying it; he never wants to build entirely anew. Consequently, he does not discard the old forms, but uses them as a foundation for his new buildings. With a passion for ordering and arranging, and with a hatred for destruction, he feels how much can be done when the basis is secure. "When I rose to power, people thought I was going to be a Washington. Words cost nothing! In America, the role would have suited me well enough; there would have been no merit in adopting it on the western side of the Atlantic. In France, I could only become a Washington as a king among kings."

That is the truth as he sees it. Since, at bottom, he despises the purple he has hung round his own shoulders, he would have been careful to avoid taking it to America, just as Washington had resisted the solicitations of his officers. By birth, he had been neither proletarian nor prince, but a member of a petty noble family which had fallen on evil days. Thus his position was an intermediate one, sandwiched between the classes. In his conversations with Englishmen about England, he displayed the naïveté of his class feeling, and his faith in the right of succession, for he closed an attack upon the British nobility in the following remarkable way:

"It is not a handful of nobles or rich men that makes a nation, but the mass of the people. True, as soon as the mob gains the upper hand it adopts an alias, and speaks of itself as the People; whereas, if it is conquered, a few poor wretches are hanged, and spoken of as robbers and rebels. 'Tis the way of the world: mob, robbers, rebels—or heroes. As the fortune of war may decide!"

After a reading of Voltaire's *La mort de César*, he remarks that in youth he had himself wanted to write a "Cæsar." One of his auditors, with a courtly double meaning, says that the Emperor has done so. Napoleon laughs the flatterer to scorn. "I? You poor babe! Yes, if I had been completely successful! But, in fact, Cæsar had no better luck than I have had—for he was assassinated!"

Closely associated with his self-criticism is his own estimate of his deeds. His historical sense, which is an integral part of his composition, leads him to an objective clarity in his contemplation of himself; perhaps an attitude of mind we may vainly seek for elsewhere in history before his day. Las Cases tells us that Napoleon talks of his career as if three hundred years lay behind him; and Countess Montholon movingly observes: "It seemed to me as if we found ourselves in another world, and I was listening to a Dialogue of the Dead."

He stubbornly defends his alleged crimes, the poisoning of the plague-stricken in Jaffa, the execution of the duke of Enghien. One day he is seized with the impulse to confide to an English physician the whole story of the Enghien episode; since, as Consul, he ran the risk of being murdered, a counterstroke was necessary. Another time he deliberately sets himself to the task of finding out what O'Meara really thinks of him. The Emperor knows the doctor to be whole-heartedly devoted to his person, but of independent character. They are sitting over a jug of porter, drinking together. Napoleon suddenly puts his question:

"What sort of a man did you think I was before you came to know me? Speak your mind frankly!"

O'Meara gives the description of an amoral chimera, a man capable of any crime to achieve his end.

"I expected as much!" exclaims the Emperor. "Probably many Frenchmen think the same. They'll be saying: 'Yes, he climbed to the top of the ladder of fame, by his own efforts; but in his climb he had to commit many atrocities.'" Thereupon he launches forth into vehement self-defence.

One night he summons Montholon in order to dictate the

thoughts which throng his sleepless brain. He sets down how he was ever inclined to peace, how before a battle and after a victory he always entered negotiations. Or he compares the two revolutions, adding: "Cromwell achieved his aim when he was in the full maturity of his age, and attained to the highest rung of the ladder through cunning and hypocrisy. But Napoleon came to the fore as a stripling, and his first steps are illuminated with deeds of glory. . . . Whose blood have I shed? Who can boast that in my place he would have acted differently? What epoch confronted with similar difficulties has ever come through with such blameless results? . . . I believe it to be without parallel in history that a plain man should have attained to such amazing power without committing a single crime. In face of death itself, I could make no other declaration."

Something now occurs which takes us wholly by surprise. Instead of, in the midst of this harangue, laying the blame for ill success on others, instead of allowing his inborn misanthropy to storm the heavens in resentment, he shows us that his days of exile have fostered his sense of justice. He who, for a lifetime, had declared that cupidity lay at the root of all men's endeavours, and had dealt with his fellows on that presupposition, now becomes a cautious analyst; the man of power becomes a philosopher; Napoleon becomes tolerant.

Now, he declares that mankind is prone to gratitude rather than to ingratitude; the only trouble is, people always expect more thanks than the deed is worth. Las Cases informs us that his greatest censure nowadays is expressed by silence. He defends even those who were faithless: Augereau, Berthier, were not equal to the magnitude of their positions; he excuses his brothers. From the altitude of these judgments, he surveys the wide perspective with a tolerant eye. We seem to be listening to the imprisoned Socrates when we read:

"It is difficult to give people their due. . . . Do they even know themselves? Those who forsook me would never have believed, in the days of their good fortune, that a time would come when they would deny me. . . . Our last trials were more than human nature could endure. As a matter of fact, I was left in the lurch rather than actually betrayed, just as Peter denied his master. . . . Perhaps they have already shed tears of repentance. Who ever had more friends and more adherents than I? Who has ever been more beloved? . . . My fate might have been far worse!"

XVI

The Emperor's companions keep diaries. He is well aware of this; he even has a look into one of them, but he reserves his thoughts. As a realist he calculates the monetary worth of these records, and he foretells what the writers will earn when they publish their books after his death; his only mistake is that he underestimates the amount. He bequeaths to each of his secretaries those portions of his writings which he has dictated to them severally. But he is correct in his estimate of the incalculable value the diaries will have for posterity in the study of himself.

Accustomed as he is to dictate, he shapes his sentences carefully even when conversing, so that his hearers may record his sayings with advantage. The value to future generations is thus enhanced, and these summaries of his thoughts raise him above his present wearisome existence. His passionate feeling for historical events drives him to this self-expression, no less than regard for those who shall come after.

Five days pass, sometimes, without his seeing anybody; he reads and he writes nothing. The future gives him no more food for thought. But during these periods of seclusion he surveys his life as a whole. Then his soul is shaken, and his lightning glance searches through and through his personality for a hundred hours at a stretch. Never has any man before him had to submit to such a scrutiny. The tension of his being is at these moments greater than at Austerlitz, more elemental than in the Council of State: he is a bound Prometheus, one who wishes to promote human happiness; and, shackled to the rock, he groans. Yet he is but a little man in an old green coat! The visions, the dreams, which for twenty years he was able and willing to conjure into reality, he now dissects into ideas. Thus, in the end, he becomes the severest commentator upon his own life story.

A book arrives. It is a collection of his manifestoes and decrees. He reads. Then he throws the volume aside, strides to and fro, and says to Las Cases:

"Every future historian will have to allow me my share. . . . Facts speak for themselves. I closed up the chasm of anarchy, and put an end to chaos. I cleansed the revolution from the filth it had accumulated, I ennobled the peoples, I stabilised the thrones. I encouraged all those who had talents, rewarded every merit, and widened the boundaries of fame and glory. . . . Could not historians protect me against many grave charges? . . . If I am accused of despotism, they can claim that dictatorship was necessary in the circumstances. Is it freedom I attacked? They can answer that anarchy was still threatening on our very threshold. Love of war? I was never the aggressor. Striving for world dominion? This arose accidentally, because of the conditions of the time. Too ambitious? Yes, true indeed. But my ambition was of the sublimest: to found the kingdom of reason, with full development and unrestricted enjoyment of all the human faculties. The historian may deplore that such ambition could not wholly attain its goal." After a momentary silence, he concludes: "There, my dear fellow, in a few words, you have my entire story."

Here he is on the defensive. But neither in such moods nor in any other do we ever hear him rave enthusiastically over his battles. In all the six years of his captivity, he does not seem, even once, to have sung the praises of General Bonaparte. If he is summing up what he achieved, he says:

"My fame does not rest upon my forty victorious battles, nor does it lie in the fact that I bent the monarchs to my will. Waterloo will wipe out the memory of so many victories; the last act makes one forget the first. What will never pass away, is my book of laws, the minutes of my Council of State, my correspondence with my ministers. . . . Through its simplicity my code of laws has had more effect than any civil codes before it; the schools I have set up, my methods of instruction, are creating a new generation; crime has decreased during my rule, whereas in England crime has become more prevalent. . . . *I wanted to found a European system, a European code of laws, a European court of appeal; there would have been but one people throughout Europe.*"

He reads in an English newspaper that Napoleon has hidden away vast treasures. He leaps to his feet, and dictates, to the man who happens to be his companion at the moment, these splendid sentences:

"Would you like to know about Napoleon's treasures? Yes, they are vast, but they are not hidden away. The harbours of Antwerp and Flushing, where there is room for the largest fleets in the world, harbours which are open all through the winter; the waterworks at Dunkirk, Havre, and Nice; the huge docks at Cherbourg; the port of Venice; the high roads from Antwerp to Amsterdam, from Mainz to Metz, and from Bordeaux to Bayonne; the passes over the Simplon, Mont Cenis, La Corniche, and Mont Genèvre, which open up the Alps in four directions, and excel all the constructions of the Romans. Then there are the roads from the Pyrenees to the Alps, from Parma to Spezia, and from Savona into Piedmont; the bridges across the Seine, and the bridges of Tours and of Lyons; . . . the Rhine-Rhone canal and the draining of the Pontine marshes; . . . the re-establishment of the Church destroyed by the revolution; the setting up of new industries; the new Louvre; warehouses, streets, the water supply of Paris, the quays along the Seine; . . . the revival of the weaving mills in Lyons; more than four hundred sugar factories; the repair and embellishment of the royal palaces at a cost of frs. 50,000,000, and the refurnishing of them out of Napoleon's private fortune at a cost of frs. 60,000,000; the redemption of the only remaining crown diamond, the Regent, which had been pawned to Jews in Berlin for frs. 3,000,000; the Napoleon Museum, where all the works of art had been obtained by purchase or by the peace treaties; many millions for the support of agriculture and horse breeding. . . . These are the treasures of Napoleon, which represent an expenditure of milliards, and will outlast the centuries! These are the monuments which defy calumny. . . . Moreover, history will record that they were all erected while long wars were being waged, and without loans being raised to pay for them!"

There he is in his little room, in the narrow house, on the rock in the midst of the sea, defending his work, and, with a regal gesture, shaking things together pell-mell—main roads, sugar factories, crown diamonds, and the Catholic Church! Foreseeing the criticisms of history, he is fully aware of the truth about himself; though a century will elapse before posterity will begin to see in him something more than the military commander whose fame (as he says) was dimmed by the failure at Waterloo.

One evening, after dinner, the question assumes a personal aspect. An inquisitive member of his circle has asked when he was happiest, and all present give their ideas. Napoleon tells them that he was made content by his marriage and when his son was born, "I cannot say happy, but content."

"When you were First Consul?"

"I was not yet sure enough of myself."

"At the coronation?"

"In Tilsit, I think. By that time I had learned the vicissitudes of fortune; Preussisch-Eylau had been a warning to me, and nevertheless I had won a victory there; I had dictated the terms of peace; the tsar and the king of Prussia were paying court to me. But no, I am wrong, that was not the best. The happiest days I ever knew were after my first victories in Italy, when the masses surrounded me, shouting: 'Evviva il liberatore!' I was only twenty-six, but I foresaw what I might become. It was as if I were being lifted up into the air, and the world were disappearing beneath my feet!"

With a sudden transition, he hums an Italian song, and then stands up, saying: "Ten o'clock. Time for bed."

How pale do these comparisons of happy moments seem in contrast with the fiery rhapsody of his deeds! It was in the work he did that was concentrated the life happiness of the man who enjoyed nothing but the completed action. He surveys his past; doubts this suggestion and that, saying that he was no more than "content," and finally hears again the first chorus of evvivas. In imagination he is again the youth soaring upwards; and in the evening of his life, spent in this tropical exile, the vision of fame floats once more before his eyes. That was what the disciple of the classical heroes had set out to win—fame!

Fame, whose lure he had felt for the first time on the island of his birth, still allures him on the island to which he had been banished. Moreover, he knows that it is the glamour of warlike fame which has made him most widely known among men. He asks whether there can be any one in Paris who has never heard of Napoleon; he does not really mean Paris, but the world. When Las Cases tells him how, in the remotest valleys of Wales, shepherds had asked for news of the First Consul, or how yellow men in China had spoken of him in the same breath with Tamerlane, then the Emperor Napoleon forgets the shame and the weariness of his life on the rock, and knows his happiest moments. If he is in such a mood, some trifling item in the newspaper may arouse a flight of fancy:

"Yes, the reaction is doomed! Nothing can destroy great principles; they will endure for ever in the light of the wonderful deeds we have done! The first stains have been washed out in the waters of glory, and now the principles are immortal. . . . Adorned with our laurels, acclaimed by the peoples, sanctified by treaties with the powers, they are breathed from all lips and hearkened to by all ears. . . . They will rule the world; will become the faith and the morality of all the peoples; and, say what you will, this new epoch is associated with my name. I lighted the torch; friends and foes alike will acclaim me the leading champion, the greatest representative of the new principles. After my death, for the nations I shall still be the sun of their rights; my name will be the war cry of their struggle, the slogan of their hopes!"

Still, these heroics about himself lack the right conclusion. Politically he overestimates the value of his martyrdom; it has not been able to save the dynasty: but he does not foresee the effect which this last act of the drama will have upon the hearts of men. A soldier's death looms before his eyes; he had sought it under fire on the last battle-fields; again and again he turns his own story over in his mind, in search of the romantic moment which would have been the most appropriate close; he often recurs to the subject in conversation. Like a playwright he looks for the fitting climax: "I ought to have died in Moscow. Till then my fame was undiminished. . . . If only heaven had sent me a bullet in the Kremlin! My dynasty would have been established; history would have compared me with Alexander and Cæsar. Whereas, as things have turned out, I am practically nothing." On another occasion he thinks that death shortly before attaining the goal, would have had even more effect on posterity: "Had I fallen at Borodino, my death would have been like Alexander's. A death at Waterloo would have been a good one. But perhaps Dresden would have been better. No, no, at Waterloo would have been best. The love of the people, their mourning!"

Once he summarises the whole as follows:

"Taking it all in all, what a ballad my life has been!"

XVII

Sunrise. A man stands at the door of a house where all the inmates are still asleep. He wears a white coat, red slippers, a broad-brimmed straw hat; he holds a spade in one hand, and rings a huge bell with the other, rousing the sleepers to work. A wall is to be raised, a ditch lengthened; land is to be reclaimed from the inroads of the sea; this is the scheme. Doors open, tent-flaps are flung back, and from all directions men flock to the master's side. They are armed with shovels, rakes, axes; and are eager to carry out the Emperor's commands.

He resembles the centenarian Faust.

The last year of his life has opened. He has made up his mind, come what may, to stay on this rock; and, since no one offers to make a verdant bower for him, he has decided, after yearlong feuds and resistance to his plans, to make a garden for himself. A half-circle of wall is to protect the growths from too much sun, from the trade wind, and from the watchful eye of the sentry. Cisterns are to store rain water; within the ramparts, earth is distributed for the flowers and the bushes; four-and-twenty large trees are planted; peaches, oranges, and, in front of his window, an oak. The trees have been imported from the Cape, and are brought to Longwood with the aid of the English artillery regiment—an old acquaintance of the Peninsular War. Chinese gardeners, Indian coolies, French servants, English stablemen, all help in the work; the doctor must take a hand too, with Montholon and Bertrand; and when the English officer on duty draws near, he sees the Emperor take a turf from his grand marshal's hands, fit it into its place on the bank, and pat it down carefully. But since Napoleon knows that transplanted soldiers must be especially well treated in foreign parts, he waters the square of grass assiduously.

The work goes on for seven months; and, when it is finished, the garden, so swiftly brought into being on the rock, is regarded as a wonder. The governor's daughter comes secretly to look at it. This is the last miracle wrought by Napoleon.

It is because he has become aware of the decline in his energies, that he has decided to beautify the place in which he is to pass the remainder of his days. He is overheard murmuring to himself Voltaire's line: "See Paris once more? I cannot hope for that." When his birthday comes round, he says it will be the last, gives the children presents; "at dinner, where we were all assembled, he beamed on us like a father in the family circle."

That autumn, he takes his last ride, a long one, going out of bounds for the first time after four years.

He seldom dictates now, but has a fancy to do so sometimes at night when sleep will not come; dictates comments on the battles of Turenne, Frederick, and Cæsar; literary criticism upon Voltaire's *Mahomet* and Virgil's *Æneid;* remarks on suicide, which he had condemned long ago when he had been a lieutenant. His best secretaries, Gourgaud and Las Cases, have left the island long since. For a quarter of an hour at a time, he will stand drumming with his fingers on the door of the veranda, watching the gulls, or gazing at the clouds; he no longer scrutinises the ships through the telescope; he is only waiting for death.

The news of a fresh conspiracy against the Bourbons, originating in the army and widely supported by civilians, no longer excites him. During the last six months of his life, he rejects two schemes of rescue. "It is written in the stars that I am to die here. In America I should be assassinated, or forgotten. Nothing but my martyrdom can save my dynasty. That is why I prefer to stay in St. Helena."

His mortal illness gains on him. The climate of the island is dangerous to persons whose livers are healthy when they first come; Napoleon, at thirty-five, had foretold that he would die of liver trouble like his father, and his liver complaint is greatly aggravated. He says that his stomach burns like fire; in some of the paroxysms, he rolls on the floor in agony. He complains of a pain in the gastric region, "like the stab of a penknife." He shivers with cold, though he is burning within; when hot compresses are applied, they can never be hot enough for him.

He watches his symptoms, and studies their meaning; will not take any medicine until its action has been explained to him. He says ruefully: "I have got so fond of my bed that I would not exchange it now for a throne. What a pitiful creature I have become! I, who hardly ever needed sleep, pass my days in lethargy. It seems a desperate resolve merely to open my eyes. Often enough, I used to dictate on different topics to four secretaries at once. In those days, I was Napoleon." His mood vacillates between heroic pathos and irony. When his valet reports that a comet is visible, the Emperor rejoins: "That was the sign before the death of Cæsar." But when his doctor declares that there is no comet to be seen, the sick man says: "Well, people die without comets!"

His medical attendant is a Corsican named Antommarchi. Owing to the quarrel with the governor, the prisoner had no doctor for a year after O'Meara's departure. At length Madame Letizia, after much effort, was able to arrange for the sending of this compatriot as his physician, together with two priests, a body servant, and a cook. Thus it is that, after years of silence, the Emperor hears trustworthy details about his mother. Once, during these last days, he says in simple words what she means to him: "All that I am and was, I owe to my mother; she taught me her own principles, and encouraged in me the habit of work."

Now there are five Corsicans round the lonely man. Only two of them are any good: the body servant and the cook. Of the two priests, one is a deaf old man, partially paralysed, and unable to articulate clearly; the other, fresh from the seminary, is ignorant and uncouth. Antommarchi, too, is a young man, inexperienced but pretentious. Still, the sight of these islanders, men of his own race, revives memories of his Corsican home. Hence, towards the close, feelings reawaken which in early life he had stifled because of his determination to be a Frenchman. Napoleon dies as he was born, an Italian.

He often talks Italian, now, or intersperses his French with strange locutions literally translated from his mother tongue. When he reads an attack made on him by a senator who declares that in the day of the Empire France had chosen her master from among a people whom the Romans did not consider good enough to use as slaves, Napoleon's comment is that it is a great compliment to the Corsicans, "for the Romans knew that this people could not be forced to serve. . . . Besides, Corsica, lying between France and Italy, was an appropriate birthplace for a man who was to rule both."

Then, suddenly, it is again his fatherland. "Ah, Doctor, where are the lovely skies of Corsica? If only I could have fled thither, the people would have received me with open arms, and would have become my family. Do you think that the allies could have mastered me in Corsica? You know our mountaineers, their courage and their pride! I am familiar with every ravine in the island, every stream!" He declares that he would fain have made much of this island (about which he never troubled after leaving it), would have signalised his love for it before all France. Only his misfortunes had prevented his carrying out these plans. He speaks of the spiritual greatness of the islanders, of their veneration for honour, of the blood feuds they hand down from generation to generation; he speaks of Paoli. "Everything is better there, the very smell of the ground. If my eyes were shut, I should recognise it; I have never come across it anywhere else. . . . No longer to own the house where one was born, to be homeless—this is to be without a fatherland!" Thus late, thus painfully, and thus indirectly, does this man without a fatherland make his great discovery; or thus late does he acknowledge his true feelings.

The Corsican doctor has no great sympathy with the Emperor; he does not credit Napoleon's sufferings; he believes them to be simulated for political ends, in the hope of a removal to Europe; and is absent during the worst paroxysms. Thus the political use the Emperor has made of his ailments works out its own revenge; for now, when he is really dying, his own compatriot regards his sufferings as spurious. There is ample record of these differences between doctor and patient. Napoleon wishes to get rid of Antommarchi, and asks Lowe to have him sent back to Europe. This is a new triumph for the governor, to whom the quarrel between the great Corsican and the little is useful ammunition. Only four weeks before the Emperor's death, his gaoler once more tries to force a way into his presence, and the consequent excitement is very bad for Napoleon.

The number of the faithful diminishes, as if to justify the misanthropist at the close of his life. Now, in the very last weeks, four of the servants and the old priest set sail for Europe; two others fall sick, and the last remaining members of his suite are meditating flight: Montholon is corresponding with the countess about the possibility of a substitute; Bertrand is about to yield to the continued solicitations of his family, and return to France. Montholon, to induce him to remain, has to assure him that when the Emperor talks of being seriously ill, this is not done merely to play upon Bertrand's sympathies. When Bertrand finally decides to remain, the invalid is greatly encouraged. The only one who never thought of leaving, was Marchand, the valet. The Emperor says to him: "If this goes on much longer, no one will be left here but you and me. But you will look after me till the end, and will then close my eyes for me."

What really cuts him to the heart is that the man who has been his close companion for so many years should now let long-hidden truths peep out. He has had an argument with Bertrand, who says: "It would have been the happiest day in my life if, after the deposition of the king, the Convention had raised the duke of Orleans to the throne." The Emperor makes no immediate rejoinder, but afterwards says bitterly:

"Bertrand, who owes everything to me, whom I made one of the grand officers of my empire!"

As his strength wanes, he looks round for something to lean on, and, for the first time in his life, he appeals to his relatives for help. Pauline is the dearest of them. Dictating a letter to her in the third person, he gives a bulletin of his condition, and ends as follows: "The Emperor earnestly hopes that Your Highness will acquaint influential Englishmen with his situation. He is dying on this dreadful rock, forsaken by all. His death struggle is terrible."

In the middle of April, three weeks before the end, behind locked doors, he dictates his will to Montholon. Then the amanuensis has to redictate the document to the Emperor, for it must be in his own handwriting, that it may be above suspicion. The Emperor sits writing for five hours, in a cold sweat. The testament is characterised alike by statesmanlike greatness and by human feelings; it represents, as it were, a survey of his whole life.

XVIII

He begins his testament by declaring that he dies in the apostolical and Roman religion, in the bosom of which he was born,—the faith which he re-established in France, which he always protected, although, in his innermost soul, he never accepted its teachings. Then his thoughts turn to the glory of a hero's grave, and, with a turn of phrase which shows that he regards himself as a Frenchman by choice rather than by birth, he writes: "It is my wish that my ashes shall be laid to rest on the bank of the Seine, in the midst of the French people, which I have loved so well."

Next come thoughts of his son, upon whom are lavished all the hopes a man can entertain concerning what will happen after his own death, and for whom he wishes to concentrate such rights as he may possess, such treasures as he may own, and such teachings as he may utter. He tells his "beloved wife" that he retains for her the most tender sentiments, and beseeches her to watch over their son, since the lad is being brought up as an Austrian prince. She is never to forget that the young Napoleon was born a Frenchman. She must never allow the boy to become a tool in the hands of the triumvirs who oppress the peoples of Europe—among whom the greatest oppressor is the child's own grandfather.

Then comes a last thrust at the enemy: "I am dying before my time, murdered by the English oligarchy and its hired assassins." But, in the challenging tone of a tribune, he adds: "The English people will not be slow to avenge me." He closes this part of his will by declaring that he had been defeated "through the treachery of Marmont, Augereau, Talleyrand, and Lafayette." Though he adds, "I forgive them," behind this mask of Christian charity the warrior's steel glitters in the words: "May the France that is yet unborn forgive them as I do."

Now, quite in the patrician style, he thanks his beloved mother and his brothers and sisters for the interest they have continued to feel in him. "I pardon Louis for the libel he published in 1820: it is full of false assertions and falsified documents." Then come the actual bequests.

The main substance of what he has to leave consists of his savings out of the civil list during fourteen years, together with all the furniture, plate, etc., he had himself bought for his palaces; and also his Italian property. He estimates it as amounting to more than frs. 200,000,000, and points out that, as far as he is aware, no law has deprived him of it. Half of it is bequeathed to the surviving officers and men who had fought in the glorious campaigns from 1792 to 1815, in sums proportional to their rates of pay on active service; the other half is to go to the provincial towns and communes that had suffered in the two invasions. His aim, in these provisions, is to put the Bourbon government in the wrong for laying an embargo, at the time of his abdication, upon all his money and securities. These clauses in his will are to promote a Napoleonic sentiment among soldiers and civilians alike; his secret hope being that his testament will exercise an influence in favour of his dynasty, like Cæsar's will when disclosed to the Roman populace by Mark Antony.

Now comes legacies to ninety-seven specified individuals. The list was drawn up in the course of ten days. "His mind is continually at work discovering new objects for his liberality; day after day he recalls the names of additional old servants whom he wants to remember in his will." The bequests are to come from a special property of frs. 20,000,000, of whose ownership he feels more secure than of the great imperial treasure. Frs. 6,000,000 had been deposited in hard cash on leaving Paris in 1815.

Who are the legatees?

Montholon is to have frs. 2,000,000; Bertrand and the valet Marchand, about half a million each. The valet is the only one whom Napoleon honours with the name of friend, and he adds: "It is my wish that he should marry the widow, sister, or daughter of an officer of my old guard." Marchand, Bertrand, and Montholon are to be the executors, and all three of them have to affix their seals to each page of the will. Thus the last document penned by Napoleon's hand bears four seals: the Emperor's eagle volant, the arms of the two counts of the old noblesse, and the plain monogram of the man of the people in whom the Emperor showed supreme confidence by appointing him one of his executors. "The services he has rendered me are those of a friend."

Every one of the servants on St. Helena receives a competence; so do the three surgeons Larrey, Percy, and Emmery. Of Larrey, Napoleon adds: "He is the most virtuous man I have ever known." Similar large sums, frs. 100,000 in most instances, are left to various generals who had been closely associated with him, to his secretaries, to two authors, the Elba guards, and the children of generals killed in battle. The stablemen, the valets, the orderly officers, the huntsmen, a house-porter, a librarian, the children or grandchildren of old family friends in Corsica; the children or grandchildren of his nurse (if in need, despite previous benefactions); the children or grandchildren of his sometime tutor in Auxonne; those of the general in command at Toulon under whom he had had his first experience of active service; those of the deputy who had helped him to get his plans put in force against Toulon; those of Muiron, "our aide-de-camp, killed at our side at Arcola, covering us with his body"—all are remembered. The next item to the Muiron bequest is a legacy "to the subaltern officer Cantillon," who had been acquitted of the charge of attempting to assassinate Wellington. "Cantillon had as much right to assassinate that oligarch, as the latter had to send me to perish upon the rock of St. Helena. Wellington, who proposed this outrage, attempted to justify himself by pleading the interest of Great Britain. Cantillon, if he had really assassinated that lord, would have excused himself, and have been justified, by the same motives, the interest of France."

This revolutionary outcry about Cantillon concludes the list of legatees. In the instructions to the executors, the following items are enumerated: the malachite furniture from Russia; the golden table service (which was presented to him by the town of Paris); a small farm on the island of Elba which had been purchased with Pauline's money; a store of quicksilver at Venice, reckoned to be worth frs. 5,000,000; gold and jewels in a hiding-place at Malmaison; and so on, the fantastic inventory of a monarch and an adventurer.

To his mother, he leaves his silver night-lamp which has lighted many a sleepless night during his sojourn on St. Helena; each brother and sister receives a special bequest; Joseph and Lucien, as if no cloud had ever shadowed his relations with them, are mentioned calmly one after the other, each receiving "an embroidered mantle, vest, and small-clothes," though the living Napoleon had given a crown to one and offered a crown to the other.

But the principal legatee of Napoleon is his son. First of all, the boy is to have all his "arms, field-beds, saddles, spurs, snuff-boxes, orders, books, body linen, which I have been accustomed to wear and use. . . . It is my wish that this slight bequest may be dear to him, as recalling to him the memory of a father of whom the universe will discourse to him." Amid the inventories, which mention such items as two pairs of night-drawers and two pillow-cases, there flash out such entries as the following: "My sword, the one I wore at Austerlitz; . . . my gold travelling box, the one I made use of on the morning of Ulm, of Austerlitz, of Jena, of Eylau, of Friedland, of the island of Lobau, of Borodino, and of Montmirail; . . . four boxes found on the table of Louis XVIII. in the Tuileries on March 20, 1815; . . . my alarm-clock, it is the alarm-clock of Frederick II. which I took at Potsdam (in box No. III); . . . a blue cloak (that which I had at Marengo); . . . a consular sword; . . . a grand collar of the Legion of Honour." Each list of items finishes with a charge to one or other of his confidants to take care of the articles named, "and to convey them to my son when he shall attain the age of sixteen years."

Here is another entry: "Marchand shall preserve my hair, and cause a bracelet to be made of it, with a gold clasp, to be sent to the empress Marie Louise, to my mother, and to each of my brothers, sisters, nephews, nieces, the cardinal, and one of larger size to my son."

Various persons and places are named in which his son is likely to be interested. "I wish my executors to make a collection of engravings, pictures, books, and medals which may give my son sound ideas, and destroy the erroneous ideas which the policy of a foreign land may have tried to impress on him. I want him to be able to see things as they really were. . . . My memory will be the glory of his life. . . . I do not expect my son to benefit by my mother's will, for he is likely to be wealthier than her other children, but I hope that she will leave him some such precious legacy as her own portrait and my father's, or some trinkets which he will know have come down to him from his grandparents."

It may seem as if his life were ending with very simple thoughts, since he makes this touching reference to his parents; but in the next clause the abyss yawns. Those who are about his son, Bertrand's children perhaps, or Montholon's, are "to see to it that he resumes the name of Napoleon as soon as he comes of age, and is able to do so without inconvenience."

After this sedulous care for the legitimate heir, there follows, at the very last, a clause of a few lines, §37, in which Napoleon writes: "I should not complain if little Léon were to enter the civil service, should he be so disposed. I should like Alexandre Walewski to serve France in the army." The writer could not foresee that, some decades after the death of his legitimate son, Léon was to end his ne'er-do-well life in America as the husband of a cook; but that Count Walewski was to attain high distinction, as a diplomat under Louis Philippe, and as minister of State and senator during the second empire. By his talent and good looks, Marie's son was to show that he had, in very truth, been a love child.

But there is a second testament for the legitimate heir. Two weeks before his death, towards three in the morning, the Emperor sends for Montholon, who has been tending him faithfully for the last few weeks: "When I entered the room, I found him sitting up, and the fire glancing in his eyes made me fear a fresh attack of fever. He perceived my uneasiness, and said kindly: 'I am not worse, but my mind has been roused by discussing with Bertrand what my executors ought to say to my son when they see him . . . it is better, therefore, that I should, in a few words, give you a summary of the counsels which I bequeath to my son. Write:' "

There follow twelve printed pages, containing the Emperor's political testament. Not a word about war, but a great many words about peace; and, as regards Europe, we find almost all the leading thoughts of the century which opened with his rise to power. We are given a glimpse of a fancied second reign. He tells us how he would govern, loftily criticising his own previous work. He looks forward to new political forms, and, with a seer's vision, contemplates the twentieth century. From the rock, he issues an appeal for the union of Europe, a manifesto on behalf of an understanding among the peoples to promote liberty, equality, civilisation, talent, and commerce. All these thoughts form themselves in the mind of the dying Napoleon during one of the last restless nights of his illness:

"My son should not think of avenging my death; he should profit by it. . . . The aim of all his efforts should be, to reign by peace: if he should recommence my wars out of pure love of imitation and without any absolute necessity, he would be a mere ape. To do my work over again would be to suppose that I had done nothing; . . . the same thing is not done twice in a century. *I was obliged to daunt Europe by arms; in the present day, the way is to convince her reason.* . . . I have implanted new ideas in France and in Europe; they cannot retrograde: let my son bring into blossom all that I have sown. . . .

"It is possible that the English, in order to efface the remembrance of their persecutions, will favour my son's return to France; but in order to live in a good understanding with England it is necessary, at any cost, to favour her commercial interests: this necessity leads to one of these two consequences —war with England, or a sharing of the commerce of the world with her. This second condition is the only one possible in the present day; questions of foreign policy will, in France, for a long time, take precedence of questions of home policy. I bequeath to my son sufficient strength and sympathy to enable him to continue my work with the sole aid of a lofty and conciliatory diplomacy. . . .

"Let not my son ever mount the throne by the aid of foreign influence; his aim should not be to fulfil a desire to reign, but to deserve the approbation of posterity. Let him cherish an intimacy with my family, whenever it shall be in his power. My mother resembles the great women of classical antiquity. . . . The French nation, when it is not taken the wrong way, is more easily governed than any other; its prompt and easy comprehension is unequalled; it immediately discerns who labours for, and who against it; but then it is necessary always to speak to its senses, otherwise its uneasy spite gnaws, it ferments and explodes. . . .

"Let him despise all parties; let him only see the mass. Excepting those who have betrayed their country, he should forget the previous conduct of all men, and reward talent, merit, and services, wherever he finds them. . . .

"France is the country where the chiefs of parties have the least influence: to rest for support on them, is to build on sand. Great things can only be done in France by having the support of the masses. . . .

"I relied on the whole mass of the people without exception; I set the example of a government which favoured the interests of all. . . . To divide the interests of a nation is . . . to engender civil war. A thing indivisible by nature cannot be divided; it can only be mutilated. I attach no importance to the constitution; but its fundamental principle should be universal suffrage.

"The nobility I created will not be a buttress to my son. . . .

"My dictatorship was indispensable, and the proof of this is that I was always offered more power than I wanted. . . . It will not be the same with my son: his power will be disputed; he must anticipate every desire for liberty. . . . The aim of a sovereign is not only to reign, but to diffuse instruction, morality, and wellbeing. Anything false is an untrustworthy prop. . . .

"The French people is animated by two equally powerful passions, which seem opposed, but which, nevertheless, are derived from one and the same feeling, namely, love of liberty and love of distinction. A government can only satisfy these two wants by the most exact justice. . . . In order to govern, it is not necessary to pursue a more or less perfect theory, but to build with the materials which are under one's hand; to submit to necessities, and profit by them. . . .

"The liberty of the press ought to become, in the hands of the government, a powerful auxiliary in diffusing, through all the most distant corners of the Empire, sound doctrines and good principles. To leave it to itself would be to fall asleep beside a danger. . . . Under pain of death, nowadays, one must either direct or hinder everything.

"My son ought to be a man of new ideas, and of the cause which I have made triumphant everywhere: . . . to reunite Europe in the bonds of an indissoluble federation. . . .

"Europe is moving towards an inevitable transformation: to endeavour to retard this progress, would be to waste strength in a useless struggle; to favour it, is to strengthen the hopes and wishes of all. . . .

"My son's position will not be free from immense difficulties. *Let him do by general consent what circumstances forced me to work for by force of arms.* If I had remained victorious over Russia in 1812, the problem of peace would have been solved for a hundred years to come. I cut the Gordian knot of nations; at the present day it must be untied. . . . It is no longer in the north that great questions will be decided, but in the Mediterranean; on the shores of the Mediterranean, there is enough to content all the ambitions of the different powers, and the happiness of civilised nations may be purchased with fragments of barbarous lands. *Let the kings listen to reason; Europe will no longer provide matter for maintaining international hatreds.* Prejudices are dispersing; interests are widening and becoming fused; trading routes are being multiplied. No longer can any one nation monopolise commerce. . . .

"All that you say to my son, or all that he learns, will be of little use to him, unless he has in the depths of his heart that sacred fire and love of good which alone can achieve great things.

"I hope, however, that he will be worthy of his destiny.

"If they refuse you permission to go to Vienna . . ."

The document suddenly breaks off; Napoleon's powers have flagged; like the utterance of an oracle, the soothsaying ends in the middle of a sentence. But what this man on his deathbed designed for the instruction of his poor little son, can serve to instruct Europe a century after it was written. The political problems of our own day, however we may attempt to solve them, are in truth solved here by the sovereignty of genius.

XIX

After this brilliant outpouring, the productive spring dries up. Agreeable visions float before his mind. It seems as if fate intends him to enjoy the euthanasia. The day after writing his political testament, he lies free from pain and care, surrounded by the mist-wreaths of hope:

"When I am dead, each of you will have the sweet consolation of returning to Europe. You will see again, the one his relatives, the other his friends; but for my part, I shall meet my brave warriors in the Elysian Fields. Yes," he continued, raising his voice, "Kléber, Desaix, Bessières, Duroc, Ney, Murat, Masséna, Berthier; all will come to meet me: they will talk to me of the deeds we did together. I shall recount to them the later events of my life. When they see me, they will be inspired with their old enthusiasm, their old passion for glory. We shall talk of our battles to the Scipios, to Hannibal, Cæsar, and Frederick. What a delight that will be. If only people here on earth are not terrified at seeing so many soldiers put their heads together!"

Such is the dying man's flight of fancy. In all the thousands of his recorded utterances, there is none that shows the naïveté of his mind more plainly than this reverie. He looks into a world peopled by the shades of the heroes, sees his generals there in familiar converse with those of ancient Rome, enters an idyllic paradise in which they talk of big guns. While Napoleon is speaking, the English doctor (whose ministrations the Emperor has at length consented to accept) enters the room.

At this moment, the music of flutes, to which he has, in fancy, been listening, breaks off; once more he hears the rattle of the drums. The statesman recurs to the present. Without transition, he passes into a new register, after his manner, and makes a formal oration which embodies what he wishes to be the official view of his death:

"Come nearer, Bertrand, and translate what I say word for word to this gentleman. My death is the results of injuries worthy of the hands that have inflicted them. I surrendered to the British people, that I might settle down at a British fireside. In defiance of international law, I was loaded with chains. . . . England overpersuaded the princes, and the world saw an unprecedented sight. Four great powers hurled themselves upon one solitary man. How shamefully you have treated me on this rock! There is no possible mortification to which you have not subjected me! . . . With cold calculation, you have slowly done me to death! The vile governor has been the executioner appointed by your ministers! I end like the proud republic of Venice! I bequeath the shame of my death to the royal family of England!"

After this outburst, he sinks back upon his pillows. The doctor stands there dumbfounded, and Napoleon's companions are in little better case. What was it? An epilogue; a protest; a commination? Pure politics! In the evening, he has an account of Hannibal's campaigns read aloud to him.

Next day, April 21st, a fortnight before the end, he sends for the Corsican abbate. Since this man's coming, Napoleon has had Mass read every Sunday, but otherwise has had nothing to do with the priest. Now he says:

"Do you know what a 'chapelle ardente' is? Have you ever

officiated at one before? Never? Well, now you will officiate at mine." Details follow. "After my death, you will set up your altar at my bedside, and will say Mass with the usual ceremonies until I am under ground."

In the evening, the priest spends nearly an hour with him. Since, we are told, Vignali was not dressed for the occasion, he can only have conversed with Napoleon, and cannot have confessed him. Napoleon has not communicated for forty years, and does not do so now.

The sick man is much wasted; for several weeks he has not been shaved; his face is sunken and dusky. Now he has his bed carried into the drawing-room, for he finds the bedroom too confined. He is racked by terrible attacks of gastric spasm. In the intervals of calm, he continues to speak of persons to whom he wishes to leave legacies. Sometimes he dozes and dreams. In these dreams, women appear to him; Marie Louise is not one of them: "I saw my good Josephine, but she would not put her arms round me. . . . She was unchanged, loving as always. She said we should soon meet to part no more. She assured me— Did you see her too?" Just like the dream about his generals; from the paradise of children, from the land of faëry.

When he feels better, he has the latest newspapers read aloud. An attack on him in one of them excites him, and he has his will brought to him. Breaking the seals he has laboriously affixed, without saying a word he writes with tremulous hand:

"I had the duke of Enghien arrested and brought to trial because this trial was necessary for the safety, the interest, and the honour of the French people, at a time when the count of Artois, according to his own admission, was maintaining sixty assassins in Paris."

Like two ghosts, they face one another; the dead Bourbon and the dying Bonaparte.

On the 27th., he asks for the will once more, and laboriously reseals it. He has inventories made of the contents of his boxes and cupboards; valuable documents are put into envelopes, on which he writes the inscriptions. All this is done in the intervals between attacks of vomiting. His companions have to affix their seals, and every one of them must verify a written record of the packets. So great is his mistrust of England.

Is there anything still to do? Various articles which have not yet been dealt with are lying on the counterpane. "I am very weak; there is not much time left; we must finish things off." What is that? Hortense's diamond necklace, which used to gleam from her neck on festal occasions in the Tuileries, and was sewn into his waistband the day he left Malmaison. This he gives to Marchand. There is a plain golden snuff-box. Toilsomely, with the point of a penknife, he scratches his initial N on the lid, and gives the box to the doctor, saying:

"I expressly demand that a post-mortem shall be made, and, in especial, that the stomach shall be examined. I believe that I am dying of the same illness as my father. Ask Louis to send you the report about that, and compare it with what you find at the autopsy. Then you may at least be able to spare my son this horrible illness. Tell him how he can guard against it, and how he can be saved from the dread of it which has so afflicted me."

For six years he has been blaming the climate of the rock for his liver trouble; only a few days ago he had charged England with killing him in the unwholesome prison-house. By ordering a post-mortem examination, he is risking the collapse of this theory; indeed, that is what he expects. All is done for his son's safety. He hopes that the lad can be saved from the family disorder.

Is everything ready? Can we start? Wait a moment! There is still lacking an official address to the authorities. He dictates the following letter:

"Monsieur le Gouverneur! Emperor Napoleōn died on the ——, after a long and painful illness. I have the honour to inform you of the fact. . . . Please let me know what arrangements your government has made for the conveyance of his body to Europe, and also in respect of the members of his suite."

"Count Montholon, you will sign that."

Napoleon had dictated sixty thousand political letters. Perhaps this one, the formal report of his own death with the date left open, is the most remarkable of them all; for who would have expected that destiny would leave so much time and so much tranquillity of mind in face of approaching death to a man who had faced sudden death on sixty battle-fields? The lines above quoted seem rather a grotesque close to his domineering career, and we feel a hope that this gruesome epistle will not be his last.

It is not the last. On the 29th., after a feverish night, he dictates the drafts of two communications. One deals with the utilisation of Versailles; the other with a reorganisation of the National Guard. But these are not addressed, as they would have been before his abdication, to the Minister for Public Works and to the Minister for War. He dictates the superscriptions: "First Dream"; and "Second Dream." Then he says: "I feel so wonderfully well now; I could go for a thirty-mile ride." Next day, he becomes icy cold and sinks into a delirium, which lasts five days till the end.

But Napoleon Bonaparte's vital energies do not subside so easily. During these five days, there is a lucid interval, and he seizes the opportunity for issuing orders and making declarations:

"When I lose consciousness, you must on no account admit an English doctor. . . . You will remain true to my memory, and will not do anything that might harm it. All my laws and all my actions were based upon the strictest principles. Unfortunately, the circumstances were so grave that I could not be lenient, and had to postpone many good things. Then came the disasters. I could not string the bow more tightly; . . .

that was why France never secured the liberal institutions I had intended to introduce. But the country credits me with my good intentions; it loves my name and my victories. You will do the same! Be true to our principles and to our fame!"

His thoughts are still circling round his work. With the mournful glance of a dying sculptor, he sees before him nothing but a fragment; and with his last breath he tells those around him what he had designed to fashion.

Next day, his mind is wandering once more amid memories of youth and of Corsica. But still, from time to time, there revives the wish to be useful to his son. His fantasy creates possessions on the island, and the faithful Marchand takes down from dictation these mind-wanderings that are so precise in their details:

"I leave to my son my house in Ajaccio with its outbuildings; two houses adjacent to the saltpits with their gardens; and all my estates in the Ajaccio district. These will bring him an income of frs. 50,000. I bequeath. . . ."

This is Napoleon's last command. He has won and lost half the world; but in his dying visions he sees the Corsican home of his ancestors, together with the son to whom he had intended to leave half the world as heirloom. The strains mingle; to keep his son from want, he bequeaths the lad a house which he does not own. Then his mind turns back from his kin. He is once more the soldier, on his first campaign, in Italy. Around him flit the wraiths of his earliest comrades. He shouts:

"Desaix! Masséna! Victory is ours! Quick! Forward! We have them. . . ."

Next day the abbate goes to him unsummoned. Beneath a layman's dress, the priest carries something he seeks to hide. He demands to be left alone with the dying man. After a while he comes out, saying: "I have given him extreme unction. Owing to the condition of the stomach, no other sacrament was possible."

A terrible last night. Towards morning, when he is murmuring in delirium, Montholon hears the words:

"France! . . . Armée! . . . Tête d' armée. . . . Joséphine!"

This is Napoleon's last utterance.

Next moment, with amazing energy, he springs out of bed, overpowering Montholon, who is alone with him. The two fall to the floor, and he grips Montholon so fiercely that the count cannot even cry for help. Archambaud, who is in the next room, hears the noise, comes in, and releases Montholon. No one knows what enemy the Emperor was trying to strangle in this last fight.

The rest of the day he lies breathing quietly. By signs he seems to ask for water, but since he can no longer swallow they must be content with holding a sponge moistened with vinegar to his lips. Mist and rain drive fiercely round the house. A count of the old noblesse and a man of the people watch by the camp-bed of Austerlitz.

At five o'clock, the rage of the south-east trade wind is redoubled, and two trees of the latest planting are uprooted.

At this moment, the man on the bed is in the throes of a prolonged rigor. There is no sign of pain; his eyes are widely opened, staring into vacancy; the death-rattle is in his throat. As the tropical sun sinks into the sea the Emperor's heart stops beating.

XX

On the study table, in the garish light of noon, lies the naked corpse of Napoleon. Five English surgeons, three English army officers, and the three Frenchmen, surround the extemporized post-mortem table, where Antommarchi is performing the autopsy. The Corsican doctor has removed the liver and incised it. He holds up the organ for the others' inspection, and demonstrates, as if to a class of students. "You see, gentlemen, how this ulcerated part of the stomach has become adherent to the liver. What are we to infer? That the climate of St. Helena has intensified the gastric disorder, and has thus brought about the Emperor's premature death."

A vote is taken: England against France. The majority declare the viscera to be healthy, while the Corsican is ostentatiously thrusting his finger through the perforated wall of the stomach. Medical report.

The Emperor's body was embalmed, and at the lying-in-state was covered with the gold-embroidered cloak of Marengo. The whole garrison, by its own wish, marched past. All who saw the body testify to the calm and serenity of the features. In mysterious fashion, his face, which, since the days of the coronation, had tended to assume the robust maturity of the Roman emperors, had now returned to the delicacy of youth.

The British authorities refused to allow the shipment to Europe. The grave was dug in a secluded valley, beside a spring shaded by two weeping willows. He was accorded the honours of a British general; salvos of artillery and musketry were fired over the grave, what time there fluttered in the breeze the colours on which were emblazoned the names of the English victories in Spain. The governor was present, and declared that he had forgiven the Emperor.

Six stone slabs from gun emplacements cover the tomb. A seventh was needed for the artillery officer's grave; but, since it was not available at the moment, three glazed tiles were taken from the cooking-stove of a new house. The governor would not allow the inscription "Napoleon" to be placed on the tomb, but insisted upon "Napoleon Bonaparte." There was, therefore, no inscription. The furniture of Longwood was sold by auction; the house was bought by a farmer, who turned the place into a mill; the two rooms in which the Emperor had lived for six years were restored to their former uses, becoming a byre and a pig-sty.

One thing only did England do in honour of the dead: a sentry was posted at the grave. For nineteen years, the guard was relieved at the proper intervals; then the dead Emperor was brought home to Paris.

Without waiting for this, all the others return to Europe. The governor was publicly horsewhipped in London by Las Cases' son; he died in obscurity. Bathurst, who, as Minister for War and Plantations, had been responsible for the treatment of Napoleon, ultimately killed himself in an access of melancholia. All England was writing and talking about the barbarous treatment of the great exile.

The Corsican doctor goes to Italy. Lucien refuses to see him. In Parma, Marie Louise also shuts her door against him, but he sees her in her box at the theatre. In Rome, Antommarchi visits Letizia Bonaparte, and for three days she makes him tell her all his news. He leaves the silver lamp with her, and sails back to Corsica. Letizia sits by the fireside, weeping over the fate of her second son, Napolione.

She has still fifteen years to live. She outlives Elise; outlives Pauline, who dies with a mirror in her hands; outlives several of her grandchildren, and three popes. She is half paralysed, and has become blind. But she sits there facing her son's bust, her spirit unbroken, mourning her dead.

Like a princess, she welcomes to her palace all those who have remained faithful to the Emperor. Her servants are the last persons in Europe to wear his colours; her carriage is the last to bear his escutcheon. She has news at times from Vienna and her grandson, but the young man is not allowed to visit her. When he is one-and-twenty, he dies. Now, Marie Louise writes to her. She does not answer the letter. At last she is told that she may return home, but she refuses to go, since the same right is not accorded to her children.

Nine years after the Emperor's death, the Bourbon dynasty is overthrown, and the Orleans monarchy is established. The new king knows how strong the Bonapartists are, and he orders that the statue of Napoleon, which fifteen years before had been removed, shall be replaced on the Vendôme column. When

Marie j'ai reçu votre lettre du
15 les sentiments qu'elle contient
me touchent vivement et sont digne
de votre belle âme et de la bonté
de votre cœur. Lorsque vous
aurez arrangé vos affaires si vous
allez aux eaux de Lucques ou de
Pise je vous verrai avec
un grand et vif intérêt ainsi que
votre fils pour qui mes sentiments
seront toujours invariables. Portez
vous bien n'ayez point de chagrin
pensez à moi avec plaisir et
ne doutez jamais de mes sentiments
le 16 avril.

N

Letter to Countess Walewska

Jerome brings his bed-ridden mother these tidings, she has a renewal of health and is able to leave her bed. For the first time after a long interval she makes her way into the drawing-room, and her blind eyes turn towards the bust. She says in a toneless voice:

"Once again the Emperor is in Paris."

ENVOY

To write the history of a man, or the history of an epoch, these are two distinct undertakings, differing both in name and technique. Vain has been the attempt to combine them. Plutarch renounced the one, and Carlyle renounced the other; that is why both these masters were able to achieve their respective tasks. It would be fair to say that Plutarch's example has found no imitators; no one, after Plutarch, has made it his specific task to write the history of great minds upon a strictly historical foundation.

Such a work does not come within the domain of the historian, seeing that the search for truth demands other talents than those requisite for the art of portrayal. Artists have sometimes dramatised historical figures with a free hand; sometimes they have produced one of those horrible mishmashes which pass by the name of "historical novel"—of which Goethe, like Napoleon, said that they confuse everything.

The attempt is especially difficult when, not works, but deeds, are the milestones along the road of life. Cæsar, Frederick, and Napoleon, only became great powers through their victories in the battlefield; and yet their battles tend, more and more, to become unmeaning for posterity. Nowadays, it is only in military academies that Pharsalia, Rossbach, and Austerlitz, have a historical significance. Not one of the three great generals I have named would mean any more to us than Crassus, Seydlitz, or Masséna, had they, too, been nothing more than military commanders; it is the political genius of Cæsar, Frederick, and Napoleon, that makes these men supreme. In his highest embodiment, the statesman shapes all our destinies. Where genius and character intersect, is the focus for the searcher of the soul.

In this book, I have tried to write the inner history of Napoleon. Since his personality finds expression in every step of his political career, his ideas as founder of States and as legislator, his attitudes towards revolution and legitimacy, towards the social order and the problem of Europe—are valuable means of portrayal. Irrelevant was the course of the battles; irrelevant the contemporary position of the European States, in so far as this was manifested only in coalitions or antagonisms as mutable as the weather.

Every difference of opinion with his brothers or his wife, every hour of gloom or elation, his outbursts of wrath and his accesses of pallor, tricks or acts of kindness towards friend or foe, every word to his generals or to women (as reported in letters or authentic conversations), seemed more important than the order of battle at Marengo, the items of the peace of Lunéville, or the details of the Continental System. What we have all learned about him at school and the university has here been restricted to a minimum; but there has been a broad demonstration of the things that are lacking amid such everyday knowledge. Yet we have not been concerned only with that Napoleon intime who is so favourite a topic with French writers; but, rather, with the Napoleonic figure as a whole, in public career and in private life, as representative of all mankind. Affairs of State and love affairs that happened on the same day, have been referred to on the same page: they derive from the same source; they determine one another; and a study of the imbroglio of the human heart will often give us more information concerning great plans than all the calculations of the tactician.

Napoleon's personality, which has no more to do with the nation for which or against which he was fighting than it has to do with morality, has not been treated here as miraculous, nor yet as split up into abstract concepts. In the episodes of his life I have tried to grasp the innermost moods (of which his rise was a natural and logical outcome), and to trace his movement towards the climax of St. Helena. To examine this man's inner life; to explain his resolves and his refrainings, his deeds and his sufferings, his fancies and his calculations, as issuing from the moods of his heart—the disclosure of this *great chain of affects,* was at once the means and the end of the portrayal.

That is why there was no place in my record for portraits of the generals. Nothing could be admitted to this one volume which did not throw light upon the history of the one interior.

If we wish to give a picture of a life so full as this man's, we must perforce follow his tempo; the writer, therefore, is bound to the words of the person being described, and can never let that person speak too much. For, in truth, a man always explains himself better than any one else can do it for him; even when he is mistaken, or when he is lying, he reveals himself to those who come afterwards, to those who know the truth. But the author must forget that he, too, knows the end. Only if, from moment to moment, he describes the feelings as they must have been experienced by one without foresight into the completed destiny, will he be able to generate that tension which, in actual life, made the sequence of events vibrant with passion.

Thus with his own sympathy, he forces the heart of the man to reveal its sympathy. In the present work, the spirit of dispassionate analysis is shown once only, towards the end. We cannot study the motor engine till it stops running.

Such a portrayal, which brings us into close proximity with its object, may give the impression of being a work of pure fancy. If, by its method of treatment, it is to be sharply differentiated from an imaginative creation, it must throughout cling to the framework of historical truth. One who believes that there is a logical succession of happenings in which there is no room for chance, will guard against retouching any detail; he will never bend a date or an incident to fit a preconceived purpose, even though, for stylistic purposes, he may think fit at times to leave one or the other unmentioned.

In this book, all the data are recorded facts, except the soliloquies. To it there might well be applied Goethe's judgment upon Bourrienne's *Memoirs:* "All the nimbus, all the illusion, with which journalists and historians and poets have surrounded Napoleon, vanishes before the awe-inspiring realism of this book: but the hero is by no means diminished thereby; he grows. We learn from this what a splendid thing truth is, when any one has the courage to speak it." Napoleon's life is a great epic, written by the hand of fate; its full meaning will not reveal itself to one who gives rein to imagination, but only to him who gives himself up to the amor fati.

Thus, likewise, for the reader of these pages should be reconstructed the tragedy which once only in a millennium a mortal man has created out of his life. What a man can attain through self-confidence and courage, through passion and imagination, through industry and will, he attained. To-day, in the age of the revolutions which once again are opening every path to the man of supreme ability, the ardent youth of Europe can find as an example and a warning no greater man than the one who, of all men of the West, made and suffered the most violent commotions.

AUTHOR'S ACKNOWLEDGMENTS

The author wishes to thank Monsieur Edouard Driault, editor of the "Revue des Etudes Napoléoniennes," Versailles, and Herr F. M. Kircheisen, for kindly help in supplying material for the illustrations; and to make due acknowledgments to Professor Pariset of Strasburg and Herr Kurt Wildhagen of Heidelberg, for advice during the preparation of the book.

INDEX

Abdication. *See* Demand, He drafts and He signs
Aboukir, 131, 135, 232, 240
Bay, 126, 135
Academy, 6
on Board, 119
Achilles, 598
ACHMED, 131
Acknowledgement of Democracy, 513
Acre, 132, 133, 134, 135, 242, 265, 397, 574
Adaptation to Circumstances, 574
Adda, 66, 113
Additional Act, 514, 517, 518, 519
Adige, 70, 77
Admiral. *See* Emperor and Admiral
Admiralty, 372
ADOLPHUS. See GUSTAVUS ADOLPHUS
Adrianople, 133
Adriatic, 90
Advancement of Relatives, 224
Adventurer once more, 419
ÆNEID, 655
ÆSCHYLUS, 607, 622
ÆSOP, 629
A-flicker with Excitement, 384
Africa, 11, 117, 232, 528
Again attacked, 237
Against the Grain, 157
Again Unity of Command, 82
Agamemnon, 622
Aix, 140, 479, 497
Aix-la-Chapelle, 238, 631
Aim. *See* True
Ajaccio, 18, 24, 27, 139, 251, 481, 485, 673
Alarm. *See* Emperor's
Aleppo, 133, 574
Alessandria, 72
ALEXANDER THE GREAT (of Macedon), 11, 115, 117, 119, 121, 127, 229, 232, 238, 242, 259, 324, 359, 361, 370, 565, 653
ALEXANDER I, Tsar of Russia, 232, 240, 252, 253, 270, 271, 292, 308, 311, 312, 314, 315, 316, 317, 318, 320, 334, 373, 374, 375, 376, 378, 385, 386, 391, 397, 406, 409, 411, 433, 437, 443, 467, 604. *See also* TSAR ALEXANDER, *also* What is ALEXANDER Thinking?
as Prototype, 11
ALEXANDRINE, 571
Allah is Allah, 122
Alliance, La Belle, 523
All young France is ready, 472
Alps, 40, 55, 63, 179, 289, 455, 497, 650
Alsace, 207
ALVINTZY, 60
America, 109, 171, 473, 530, 533, 537, 632, 634, 635, 643, 645, 655. *See* He should, *also* United States
Ambitions. *See* BERNADOTTE'S Great
America, Spanish, 632
American Marriage. *See* JEROME'S
Amours, 202
Amphictyonic League, 595
Amsterdam, 650
Anachronism. *See* War
Ancients. *See* Council of Ancients
Ancona, 89, 90, 284
Andalusia, 329
Andromache, 460, 637
and Astyanax, 460
An everlasting Disgrace, 542
Anger. *See* Genuine
Angleterre, Hôtel de l', in Warsaw, 418
ANGOULÈME, Duchess of, 489
An Idyll renewed, 486
ANNA, Grand Duchess, 349
Annexations, 89
Another Family Council, 348
Ansbach, 252
Antibes, 57, 498
Antiquity. *See* Heroes of
ANTOINETTE, MARIE, 219
ANTOMMARCHI, 656, 658, 674, 676
ANTONY. *See* MARK ANTONY
Antwerp, 650
Anxieties. *See* JOSEPHINE'S
Any Crown You like, 300
APELLES, 565

Apennines, 55, 64, 566
Apollo, Salle, 155
Apostolical Emperor, 370
ARCHAMBAUD, 674
ARCHDUKE CHARLES. *See* CHARLES
Arcis-sur-Aube, 463, 522
Arcola, 64, 65, 76, 77, 78, 112, 137, 158, 536, 624
ARISTOTLE, 229
Arm the Peasants, 464
Army. *See* Tatterdemalion
  Grand. *See* Grand Army
  in the East, 116
  of Waly, 40, 50, 56
  of Liberators, 61
  of the Interior, 45
  of the Rhine, 40, 41, 86, 87, 114, 120
ARNAULT, 93
ARRIAN, 119
Artillery Fire, 532
ARTOIS, Count of (afterwards Charles X), 490, 501, 670
"As General Bonaparte," 433
Asia, 11, 41, 128, 188, 229, 232, 237, 244, 282
Asia Minor, 11
Asiatic Conquests. *See* Dreams of
Aside. *See* Naïve
Aspern-Essling, 337, 341, 419, 522, 567
A Son! 260
Assassination. *See* Attempted
Astorga, 331, 363, 377
Asturia, 299
Astyanasc, 460, 488
At Headquarters, 92
Athens, 63, 69
Atlantic Fleet, 372
Attacked. *See* Again
Attempted Assassination, 159
Attempted Rising, 24
Attempt on His Life, 193. *See also* I intended
At the masked Ball, 347
ATTILA, 86, 90, 511
Audience of Kings, 309
Auerstädt, 255
AUGEREAU, 60, 75, 81, 92, 101, 114, 133, 448, 462, 463, 468, 510, 647, 660
AUGUSTUS, 194, 228, 272, 566
AURELIAN, 566
Austerlitz, 243, 244, 245, 251, 252, 253, 255, 270, 274, 318, 334, 381, 386, 387, 395, 439, 461, 500, 509, 520, 561, 562, 577, 609, 649, 663, 674, 679. *See also* Eve of Austerlitz
Austria, 40, 87, 118, 179, 183, 238, 244, 251, 258, 259, 274, 308, 314, 315, 318, 333, 369, 370, 375, 380, 382, 383, 410, 419, 430, 435, 439, 440, 451, 455, 459, 462, 639
  Felix, 369
Auxonne, 14, 56, 662
Avignon, 497
Awaiting the Signature, 473
Azores, 494, 618
Aztecs and Incas, 307

Back Room at Saint-Cloud, 155
Back to Europe, 308
Back to Paris, 525
Baden, 206, 246, 279, 493
Bad News from Spain, 399
Bag of Gold, 153
BAGRATION, 389, 394
Ball. *See* At the Ball
Ballad. *See* What a Ballad
Baltic, 273, 420
Banishment, 29
Bank of England, 380
Bank of France, 454
Barbier de Séville, 622
BARCLAY DE TOLLY, 389, 390, 394, 395, 399
BARON VOM STEIN, 406
BARRAS, 38, 43, 44, 47, 50, 80, 109, 115, 142, 146, 147, 152, 153
Bar-sur-Aube, 462
Basle, 38, 511
Bassora, 132
Bastia, 480
Bastille, 16, 217
BATHURST, 676
Battalion, Holy, 242
Battle, Death in. *See* He seeks
  of Jena, 255
  of the Nations, 446
BAUDIN, 141
BAUER, 556
BAUSSET, 344
Bautzen, 434, 439, 445
  "Messenger," 445
Bavaria, 127, 183, 241, 246, 279, 334, 430, 446, 493
Bayonne, 308, 312, 650
BEAUHARNAIS. *See* EUGENE, *also* HORTENSE, *also* JOSEPHINE
  Vicomte de, 47
BEAULIEU, 60
BEAUMARCHAIS, 622
BEETHOVEN, 231
Belated Blessing, 226
Belgium, 30, 89, 453, 458
Belle Alliance, 523

"Bellerophon," 537, 538, 539, 540, 541
Benevento, 494
BENJAMIN CONSTANT, 512. *See also* CONSTANT
Beresina, 415, 416
Berlin, 256, 257, 258, 274, 290, 308, 334, 400, 405, 445, 446, 651
BERNADOTTE (afterwards CROWN PRINCE, then King, of Sweden), 118, 144, 145, 148, 149, 153, 161, 198, 246, 281, 365, 366, 386, 406, 429, 436, 438, 443, 445, 446, 448, 452, 462, 467, 571, 633
  Désirée. *See* DÉSIRÉE
  triumphans, 305
Bernadotte's Ambitions, 386
Bernard. *See* Great St. Bernard
BERTHIER (afterwards Prince of Neuchâtel), 60, 72, 81, 92, 100, 120, 148, 149, 219, 246, 256, 335, 336, 351, 368, 388, 398, 411, 461, 462, 464, 468, 471, 473, 474, 495, 510, 555, 557, 575, 587, 647, 668
BERTHOLLET, 120, 129, 138
BERTRAND, 481, 484, 535, 609, 610, 613, 615, 621, 636, 638, 654, 658, 659, 661, 664, 669
  Madame, 10, 613, 627
  Napoléon, 638
Besançon, 501, 509, 555
BESSIÈRES, 668
Betray. *See* Old Friends
Bible, 120, 122, 601, 622
Big Guns, 13
BINGHAM, 627
Birchen Staff. *See* Leaning
Blenheim, 127
Blessing. *See* Belated
Blindness. *See* Brotherly Blindness
Blindness to its Dangers, 212
Bloodhound, A, 187
BLÜCHER, 443, 444, 445, 455, 457, 459, 460, 461, 462, 467, 522, 534, 619, 626
Blunder. *See* Consequences of a
Body of Steel, 548
Bohemia, 447
Bois (de Boulogne), 38
Bologna, 75, 99, 476
BONAPARTE. *See* As General Monsieur
  and Europe, 184
  and the Sphinx, 121
  Caroline. *See* CAROLINE
  CARLO, 298, 305
  Elise. *See* ELISE
  Jerome. *See* JEROME
BONAPARTE,
  Joseph. *See* JOSEPH
  La Pagerie. *See* JOSEPHINE
  Letizia. *See* LETIZIA
  Louis. *See* LOUIS
  Lucien. *See* LUCIEN
  Napoleon Francis. *See* NAPOLEON FRANCIS
  Pauline. See PAULINE
Bon, Cape, 137
"Boney," 540
Bordeaux, 464, 541, 650
BORGHESI, 199, 200, 485. *See also* PAULINE
Born to rule. *See* Man born to rule
Borodino, 399, 653, 663
Bosnia, 90
Bosphorus, 41, 259, 273, 282
Boulogne, 234, 235, 238, 572, 580
Boulogne, Bois de. *See* Bois
BOURBON, Duke of, 490
  Palais, 529
Bourbons—never! 469
Bourbons' Return, 489
BOURRIENNE, 25, 37, 58, 91, 107, 118, 119, 124, 127, 148, 156, 161, 179, 204, 438, 556, 681
Breach between the Brothers, 197
Brescia, 74
Breslau, 268, 425
Brienne, 6, 9, 48, 457, 556, 558, 611
Brieg, 269
Broil with Prussia, 252
Broils. *See* Family
Brooding Lad, 8
Brother Lucien. *See* Sire
Brotherly Blindness, 456
Brotherly Hate, 304
Brothers. *See* Dangerous
Brothers and Sisters, 198
Brothers, The. *See* Breach between
BRUIX, 234, 235
Brumaire, 528. *See also* Eighteenth, *also* Nineteenth
BRUNSWICK, 253, 255, 408, 576
Brussels, 523
BRUTUS, 64, 85, 149, 343, 560, 629
BRUYÈRE. *See* La Bruyère
BUBNA, 341, 430, 567
Bucharest, 269
Buenos Ayres, 534
BUFFON, 10
Bulletin from Russia. *See* Last
BÜLOW, 524
Bukovina, 384
Bureau of Public Opinion, 380, 381
Burgos, 548
Burgundy, 125

BUONAPARTE. *See* BONAPARTE
Burning Street, 403
But Talleyrand is indispensable, 313
BYRON, 231, 615

Cadets School, 9, 133
Cadiz, 388, 420
CADOUDAL, 438
CÆSAR, 24, 85, 121, 182, 186, 195, 212, 277, 285, 322, 326, 371, 378, 421, 463, 519, 521, 560, 565, 566, 567, 578, 592, 624, 645, 646, 653, 655, 656, 661, 668, 679. *See also* Christ
Cromwell, and Bonaparte, 195
Cæsar's Chariot, 519
Death, 326
Cæsars, 566
CAGLIOSTRO, 593
Cairo, 121, 122, 131, 132, 135, 136, 185, 264, 267, 286, 396, 476, 605
Cajoleries, 272
Calabria, 633
Calculation, 569
and Imagination, 117
Calculations. *See* I am the Man and Yearnings
Caldiero, 76
California, 534
CAMBACÉRÈS, 598
CAMILLA, 139
Campaign. *See* Excitement of
Campaigns of Napoleon the Great, 380
CAMPBELL, 479, 504
Campo Formio, 104, 109
Candour to Opponents, 341
Canino, 485
Cannes, 433, 497, 498, 503, 623
CANOVA, 248, 582
CANTILLON, 662
Cape Bon, 137
Cape (of Good Hope), 89, 103, 258, 372, 654
Capets, 414
Capitol, 64, 85, 105
Capri, 566, 613
Capua, 383
Caracas, 534
Care for the Children, 173
CARLO BONAPARTE, 298, 305
CARLYLE, 679
CARNOT, 57, 71, 82, 114, 214, 407, 511, 518, 521, 528, 598, 642
CARNOT'S Advice, 521
CAROLINE BONAPARTE (afterwards wife of MURAT), 198, 224, 247, 260, 266, 352, 364, 428, 429, 451, 475, 485, 632
Carpet, The, 305
Carrée, Fort, 34
Carthage, 10
CASES. *See* LAS CASES
Cassel, 394, 452
Castiglione, 75, 463
Castille, 331
Catalonia, 312
CATHERINE THE GREAT, 566
Cattaro, 273, 307
COULAINCOURT, 375, 376, 377, 401, 411, 417, 418, 432, 434, 446, 457, 458, 464, 465, 467, 468, 471, 472, 507, 529, 531, 606
Cause. *See* Espouse my
Cave. *See* Imagination
Chains. *See* In Chains, *also* Strike
Chamber of Deputies, 526, 528. *See also* Lower House
Chambers, 153, 186, 195, 455, 496, 511, 517, 519, 525, 526, 527, 528, 529, 530, 634. *See also* General
Chambers of Commerce, 176, 379
Chambers take the Initiative, 526
Champaubert, 460
CHAMPAGNY, 311, 343
Champ de Mai, 506, 518, 520
Champion of the Family, 172
Chance. *See* Circumstances
Chance missed, 235
Channel, 115, 516
Chapelle ardente, 669
Characterisation. *See* German
Chariot. *See* Cæsar's
CHARLEMAGNE, 226, 227, 238, 242, 245, 258, 259, 283, 284, 285, 359, 566
Charlemagne, 248
Charleroi, 521, 522
Charles XII, 393
CHARLES AUGUSTUS, 255
CHARLES, Austrian Archduke, 60, 88, 338, 351
CHARLES, Hippolyte, 73, 123. *See also* HIPPOLYTE
Charlottenburg, 258
CHATEAUBRIAND, 277, 508, 554, 565, 566
Châtillon, 458, 461, 492
CHÉNIER, 114, 195, 598
Cherbourg, 650
Chess. *See* Game
Chessplayer, 567
Childlessness. *See* Tragedy of
Children. *See* Care, *also* Name your
China, 11, 652
Chinese Island where there are no Weapons, 581, 582

Christ, 86, 184, 321, 322, 338, 636. *See also* Jesus
and Cæsar, 322
Christianity, 319, 322
CIMAROSA, 554
Cinna, 591, 622,
CIPRIANI, 613, 621, 640
Circumstances and Chance, 604
Cis-alpine Republic, 82, 105, 182
CITERNI, 277
City. *See* Rome, *also* The Eternal
Civil Code, 170
CLARKE, 80
CLARY. *See* DÉSIRÉE, *also* JULIE
Cleaning up the Mess, 176
Clear the Hall, 160
CLEOPATRA, 128
Cleves, 247
Climax of the Scene, 302
CLOVIS, 561
Coblenz, 577
Coburg, 273
Cockade. *See* Red
Code, Civil, 170
Code Napoléon, 170, 171, 172, 173, 280, 286, 371
Coffee and Sugar, 398
COLLI, 60
Colours. *See* Kissing
Command. *See* Again, *also* Last, *also* Unity
Commander. *See* Statesman
Commander of the Forces, 45
Comédie Française, 410
Commercial Warfare, 361
Committee of Public Safety, 40, 42, 47, 561
Companions, 610. *See also* Fate
Company at Morfontaine, 452
Comparison with Napoleon, 407
Compiègne, 351, 352
Concerning the Germans, 591
Concordat, 284, 372, 429, 430
CONDÉ, 206, 207, 490, 500
Confederation of the Rhine, 246, 279, 287, 341, 373, 382, 388, 420, 424, 425, 433, 443, 445, 447
Confessions, 214
Confidants conspire, 331
Congress. *See* Tidings
Conquests. *See* Dreams and Plans
CONSALVI, 185
Consequences. *See* Political
Consequences of a Blunder, 208
Consequences of Marmont's Desertion, 471
Conservatoire, 98
Considerations, 639
Conspiracy, 148
CONSTANT, Benjamin, 195, 511, 512, 514, 517, 527
Constant (Napoleon's Valet), 267
CONSTANTINE (Roman Emperor), 284
(Russian Grand Duke), 405
Constantinople, 133, 242, 273, 282, 284
Consul, First, 166, 174, 175, 183, 185, 186, 187, 190, 201, 203, 204, 205, 206, 207, 210, 225, 232, 280, 373, 379, 381, 498, 550, 554, 555, 556, 565, 575, 582, 586, 597, 605, 629, 646, 651, 652
for Life, 186, 187, 213
Consuls, 154, 155, 160, 161, 165
Contempt for his Fellows, 583
Content. *See* Form without
Continent, 109, 114, 116, 183, 214, 244, 246, 248, 258, 282, 361, 367, 524
Continental System, 258, 680
Contradictions of Monarchy, 423
Convention, 26, 27, 28, 31, 33, 35, 42, 43, 44, 45, 658
Conversation. *See* Memorable
Conversation with Rapp, 508
Conversation with Wieland, 320
Corfu, 89, 90, 103, 473
CORIOLANUS, 23
CORNEILLE, 218, 276, 551, 564, 591, 621, 622
Corniche, 650
Corsica, 1-49, 85, 95, 96, 113, 117, 138, 199, 251, 338, 476, 480, 483, 484, 496, 505, 533, 535, 537, 631, 657, 662, 673, 676
again, 138
Corsica comes to St. Helena, 656
Corsica's Struggle, 4
Corsican Election, 23
Corsicans, 294
Corso, 73
Corte, 16, 251
Cortes, 453
CORVISART, 475, 598
Cossaria, 86
Council. *See* Another Family
Council of Ancients, 149, 150, 155, 156, 160
of Five Hundred, 149, 150, 151, 153, 155, 157, 158, 159
of State, 166, 169, 170, 192, 194, 195, 207, 224, 230, 279, 332, 360, 414, 423, 554, 582, 590, 592, 649, 650
Councils, 146, 147, 153, 154, 156, 159, 188

Counterplot. *See* Plot
Counterstroke. *See* Stroke
Countess. *See* Polish, *also* Walewska
Cracow, 430
CRASSUS, 679
Creation, 193
Crete, 11
CRŒSUS, 458
CROMWELL, 195, 463, 647
Coup d'Etat. *See* Plans
Courage, 577. *See also* Returning
Court. *See* Little Court, *also* Plebeians at Court
Court Dress. *See* Mummy in
Courtship, 351
Crises, 75
Criticism of the French, 215
Crowd. *See* Tuckets
Crown. *See* Any
Curse of Legitimacy, 422
CYRUS, 566

Dagger in the Dictator's Heart, 517
Daily Life, 621
Daimonic Loneliness, 605
Dalmatia, 436
Damascus, 132, 133, 146
Danaids, 414
Danger and Discouragement, 77
Dangerous Brothers, 438
Dangers. *See* Blindness to
Dangers of Distance, 340
Danube, 259, 308, 337, 341, 419, 612
Danzig, 376, 388, 432, 509
DARU, 238, 323, 325, 410, 415, 418, 444, 597
Dauphiné, 20, 497
DAVID, 565
DAVOUST, 219, 255, 390, 394, 403, 507, 526
Days, Hundred, 599, 609, 623
Deadly Climate, 608
Deadwood, 608
Death, 674. *See also* Waiting
Deathbed. *See* Justifies.
Death in Battle. *See* He seeks
DECRÈS, 229, 533
Defeat, 448. *See also* First
  at Waterloo, 524
Defence. *See* Napoleon's
Defenceless, 540
Delta, 130
Demand for Abdication, 527
Democracy. *See* Acknowledgment
  Fiction of, 188
Denmark, 493
Deputies in secret Session, 528
DESAIX, 120, 132, 179, 587, 668, 673. *See also* Quai
Deserter, 25
DÉSIRÉE CLARY (afterwards Wife of Bernadotte), 30, 44, 46, 145, 452, 633
Destiny, 603. *See also* Follow, *also* Sense, *also* To Destiny
  Man of, 604
Destruction of the Fleet, 126
Devotion to Josephine, 99
Dialogue of the Dead, 646
Diarists, 648
Dictator. *See* Dagger
Dictatorship, 195
Dictionary of Weathercocks, 638
Die Standing. *See* I will
"Diet, Imperial" at Erfurt, 561
Dignity, 552. *See also* Imperial
Dijon, 178
DIOGENES, 324
Dilemma. *See* Tragical
DIOCLETIAN, 567
Dioscuri, 511
Diplomat, 88
Diplomats. *See* Hectoring
Directors, 48, 49, 50, 57, 65, 66, 67, 72, 79, 80, 81, 82, 84, 85, 87, 88, 89, 97, 101, 104, 106, 108, 109, 114, 115, 116, 118, 127, 139, 146, 147, 151, 152, 154, 165, 284, 529, 532, 556
Directory, 51, 106, 114, 127, 140, 153, 175, 276, 379, 511, 528, 530
Disastrous Inertia, 435
Discours sur l'origine et les fondements de l'inégalité parmi les hommes, 11
Discoveries. *See* Explorations
Disgruntled Kings, 363
Disillusionment. *See* Victory
Disquiet. *See* Growing
Distance. *See* Dangers of
Divine Right. *See* Rulers
Divorce, 345. *See also* Marriage and
Dniester, 259
Domingo, 590, 630
Don Quixote. *See* Quixote
Don't you know me?, 499
Dover, 137
Dramas, Family. *See* Opening
Dream, first, 672
Dream, second, 672
Dream, trivial. *See* Life
Dreams and Mathematics, 131
  of Asiatic Conquests, 41
Dresden, 335, 386, 388, 434, 438,

444, 492, 508, 548, 553, 589, 590, 653
DRIAULT, 683
Driven out, 533
DROUOT, 481, 495, 531
Drums of the Revolution, 15
Drum-Taps, 166
Druses, 132
Düben Castle, 445, 462, 470
Düben Heath, 445
Duchâtel, 203
DUCOS, 146, 147, 150, 151, 153, 155, 159
Dunkirk, 115, 650
DUROC, 260, 261, 262, 415, 434, 435, 587, 597, 618, 668
Dvina, 390
Dynastic Snare, 301
Dynasty. *See* Spanish

Eagle Volant, 230
East, the, 90, 91. *See also* Army in the East, *also* Lure of the East, *also* Messengers from the East
East India Company, 607
Eckmühl, 500
Egypt, 10, 11, 103, 115, 116, 117, 119, 122, 123, 124, 126, 127, 128, 130, 131, 136, 137, 138, 140, 141, 204, 210, 239, 242, 272, 372, 411, 413, 495, 498, 514, 543, 566, 573, 620, 621
Egyptian Plan, 116
Eighteen-hour Day, 174
Eighteenth Brumaire, 150, 179, 196, 197, 338, 365, 494, 502, 560. *See also* Nineteenth Brumaire, *also Brumaire*
Eighty-five Francs, 21
Elba, 184, 473, 475, 476, 477, 479, 481, 482, 483, 484, 485, 489, 491, 492, 493, 494, 496, 504, 511, 513, 531, 535, 623, 634, 661, 662
Elbe, 258, 273, 286, 308, 374, 447
Electoral Colleges of the Empire, 505
ELISE, Bonaparte (afterwards Grand Duchess of Tuscany), 92, 96, 198, 247, 248, 364, 451, 452, 475, 676
EL KEBIR, 128
Elysée, 466, 471, 525, 530
Elysian Fields, 668
EMMERY, 661
Emperor. *See also* Apostolical, I am, Return, Self-crowned
  and Admiral, 234
  and his Mother, 495
Emperor,
  and the Slave, 630
  drives a Plough, 641
  of the East, 242
  of Rome, 283
  of the West, 283, 285, 290
Emperors. *See* Two Emperors
Emperor's Alarm, 414
Emperor scores over the Poet, 321
Emperor's Onslaught, 324
Empire. *See also* Holy Roman Empire, Turkish Empire
End of Everything, 125
Energy in narrow Bounds, 481
ENGHIEN, 206, 207, 208, 210, 214, 281, 332, 565, 591, 646, 670. *See also* Kidnapping
England, 33, 91, 103, 105, 109, 114, 116, 127, 183, 207, 212, 233, 235, 237, 239, 240, 244, 247, 248, 258, 259, 282, 285, 306, 307, 312, 328, 333, 359, 361, 362, 363, 365, 373, 374, 377, 379, 380, 382, 390, 396, 420, 430, 436, 451, 459, 475, 490, 492, 503, 538, 541, 542, 584, 588, 593, 607, 614, 624, 626, 631, 632, 634, 635, 650, 669, 671, 675, 676
England's Enmity, 232
Enmities. *See* Intrigues
Enmity. *See* England's
Epilogue, 675
Equality at the Front, 581
Equality, not Liberty, 168
Erfurt, 255, 308, 309, 313, 315, 317, 318, 322, 326, 342, 350, 374, 392, 450, 555, 561, 591
  "Imperial Diet," 561
Eroica, 231
"Espouse my Cause," 294
Essling. *See* Aspern-Essling
Essonne, 465
Eternal City. *See also* Rome, The Eternal
Ettenheim, 206
Etiquette and Parody, 638
EUGENE DE BEAUHARNAIS (afterwards Viceroy of Italy), 47, 93, 118, 128, 143, 204, 222, 224, 246, 248, 249, 284, 285, 298, 299, 300, 331, 336, 348, 349, 382, 389, 402, 412, 417, 531, 561, 566, 569
Euphrates, 574
Europe, 11, 51, 64, 69, 85, 87, 88, 100, 104, 105, 109, 123, 137, 183, 205, 211, 217, 218, 239, 240, 244, 245, 246, 251, 258, 282, 287, 314, 318, 329, 334, 359, 362, 364, 365, 366.

368, 374, 375, 376, 377, 378, 383, 384, 396, 399, 430, 440, 447, 455, 473, 480, 483, 484, 492, 496, 498, 521, 524, 528, 538, 543, 554, 580, 582, 589, 595, 596, 612, 624, 625, 626, 631, 643, 644, 645, 650, 658, 665, 667, 668, 676, 680, 682. *See also* Back to, Bonaparte and, Farewell, Partition, United, and United States of
Europe is a Mole-hill, 91, 121, 378
Europe too small, 296
European System, 650
Eve of Austerlitz, 241
Everyman, 581
Everything is crashing round me, 453
Evil. *See* Prophet of
Examination of a Prisoner, 393
Excommunication and Victory, 338
Execrated by the Mob, 479
Execration. *See* Public
Excitement of the Campaign, 461
Explorations and Discoveries, 130
Extinct Volcano, 607
Eylau, 265, 311, 500, 580, 651, 663

Faithful grow weary, 658
Faithful Servants, 613
False to his own Principles, 279
Falsifications, 625
Fame, 568
  still lures him, 652
Family. *See* Champion
  Bequests, 662
  Broils, 428
  Council. *See* Another
Family Dramas. *See* Opening
  Man. *See* Genius and
  Troubles. *See* More
Fantastic Schemes, 283
Fantasy and Number again, 359
Farewell Europe, 543
Farewell to the Guard, 477
Fatal War, 373
Fate of old Companions, 633
Father. *See* Our
Fatherland. *See* Without
Faubourg. *See* Faubourg Saint-Germain
  Saint-Antoine, 527
  Saint-Germain, 218, 466, 562, 609, 628
Faust, 654
Felix Austria, 369
FERDINAND, 453
Ferrajo, 481
Ferrara, 99
Fertility. *See* Habsburg Fertility
FESCH, 20, 23, 27, 30, 95, 199, 226, 284, 352, 353, 371
Fiction of Democracy, 188
Figaro, 622
Fighting. *See* Street
Finckenstein, 266, 267, 268, 270, 339
Finisterre, 384
Fire!, 402
First Consul. *See* Consul, First
  Defeat, 337
  Dream, 672
  "I," 16
  Overtures for Peace, 87
  Place is occupied, 20
  Sword, 9
  triumphal Entry, 68
  Victory, 33
Five Hundred. *See* Council
Fleet. *See also* Destruction Through
Fleet sets sail, 118
Flight homewards, 136
Florence, 427
Flushing, 650
Foe. *See* Overestimating
"Follow your Destiny," 496
FONTAINE, LA, 628
Fontainebleau, 281, 465, 466, 467, 468, 471, 473, 474, 486, 504, 605
Foolish Speech, 156
Fop and the Husband, 73
Forces. *See* Commander
Forebodings. *See* Gloomy
Foreign Office, 103. *See also* Ministry for Foreign Affairs
Forgotten!, 376
Former Fellow-student, 555
Form without Content, 216
Fort Càrrée, 34
Fortress. *See* Invincible
Fortuné, 73, 74
"Fortune is a Strumpet," 400
Fortune of War, 457
Fortune's Wheel. *See* Turn of
FOUCHÉ, 177, 182, 186, 187, 197, 230, 231, 269, 277, 331, 332, 333, 340, 345, 365, 377, 378, 379, 436, 437, 443, 451, 473, 474, 475, 511, 530, 532, 533, 614
FOUCHÉ's Rise, 530
FOUCHÉ, TALLEYRAND and, 182
Four Teeth, 394
Fourth-act Moods, 432
Fourth Name, 217
Fowler, 81
Fox, 232
FOY, 277
France, passim. *See also* All young,

History, In southern, and King of
greets him, 141
is his Mistress, 563
FRANCIS, Emperor of Holy Roman Empire and of Austria, etc., 73, 87, 104, 109, 180, 181, 239, 240, 243, 252, 312, 350, 369, 370, 386, 398, 422, 430, 434, 436, 437, 439, 443, 445, 446, 505, 506, 515, 642
King of Rome, 488. *See also* NAPOLEON FRANCIS
Frankfort, 382, 455, 456
FREDERICK THE GREAT, 8, 10, 24, 111, 112, 175, 208, 251, 253, 255, 257, 259, 274, 277, 329, 463, 566, 568, 621, 655, 663, 668, 679
Frederick's Sword, 257
FREDERICK WILLIAM III, 251, 252, 383, 425, 437, 443
Fréjus, 140, 480. *See also* Landing
French. *See* Criticism of
are easy to rule, 666
remain sceptical, 564
Frenzied Energy, 72
Friedland, 270, 331, 500, 522, 663
Friends betray him. *See* Old
Friendship. *See* Last
Fridericus Rex, 251
Friuli, 75
Fronde, 562
Fruitless Wooing, 316
Fulfilment. *See* Tragedy of
FULTON, 235, 642
Further Peace Proposals, 180

Galicia, 259, 375
Gambler. *See* Great
Game of Chess, 443
Ganges, 242, 308, 359, 373
Gaoler, 617. *See* also Lowe
Garda, 73
Garden. *See* Kingdom
Gardener, 654
Gassion, 597
General against People, 43
and King, 580
and the Chambers, 151
Bonaparte. *See* As General Bonaparte
grows dangerous, 65
Generals. *See* Sons of the People
GENGHIS KHAN, 511, 644
Genius and Family Man, 213
German. *See* Homage
Genoa, 12, 33, 34, 82, 96, 117, 139, 184, 239, 504
Genoese Senate, 72
Genuine Anger, 575
GEORGE III, 236
George, Mademoiselle (Giorgina), 202, 203, 558
German. *See also* Homage, Two Germans, and Unconquerable
Characterisation, 111
Genius. *See* Homage
Opinions. *See* Other
Germans. *See* Concerning
German Spirit, 425
German Women. *See* Two German Women
Germany, 87, 90, 109, 171, 184, 206, 244, 285, 286, 308, 309, 319, 333, 335, 359, 382, 407, 410, 420, 425, 427, 429, 430, 436, 440, 443, 570
Gibraltar, 307
Giorgina, 202, 203, 258
Giuliano, San, 180
GLENDOWER, 273
Gloom, 37. *See also* Hours
Gloomy Forebodings, 459
GNEISENAU, 522
Goblet, golden, 181
God protect France, 503
protect the King, 502
"God's Image on Earth," 277
GOETHE, 1, 53, 163, 256, 322, 323, 324, 325, 326, 327, 357, 421, 449, 545, 551, 583, 602, 679, 681. *See also* How is
Goethean Motifs, 602
Goethe is imperturbable, 327
Goethe's Epilogue, 449
GOHIER, 142, 146, 147, 149, 152, 153
Golden Goblet, 181
Good-night, Bourrienne, 161
Gospel and Republic, 86
Gospels, 86
GOURGAND, 535, 602, 610, 611, 612, 613, 616, 620, 621, 625, 626, 628, 633, 635, 636, 637, 638, 639, 655
Gourgand's Petulance, 611
Government. *See* Tottering
grows uneasy, 80
Grand Army, 424
Grape-shot. *See* Why not use
Gratitude, 558
GRASSINI, 100, 192
Graz, 364, 427
Great Ambitions, 66
Great Britain, 662. *See also* England
Great Gambler, 442
Great Nation, 103, 109, 147
Great Pyramid, 11
Great St. Bernard, 178, 179

Greece, 319
GREGORY VII, 371
Grenoble, 498, 499, 500, 504
Grosbois, 389
Grouchy, 522, 523, 524
Growing Disquiet, 297
Grumble. *See* Peasants
Guadarrama, 330
Guard, National. *See* National Guard
Guard. *See* Farewell
Gumbinnen, 387
Guns. *See* Big
GUSTAVUS ADOLPHUS, 365

Hamburg, 233, 381
Hamelin, 507
Hammerfest, 359
Hampered Energies, 523
HANNIBAL, 55, 178, 189, 534, 668, 669
  modern, 178
Hanover, 374
Hansa Towns, 374, 439
Harassing Restrictions, 616
HARDENBERG, 383
Hat, 441
Hate. *See* Brotherly
HATZFELD, 256
Havre, 650
HAYDN, 193
Headquarters, 92
Head Shepherd, 285
Heart. *See* Sluggishness
He cheers up, 476
Hector, 598, 637
Hectoring the Diplomats, 104
He drafts an Abdication, 470
He dreams of India, 127
HEGEL, 450
Heir. *See* Hunt for, *also* Search for
  at last, 353
Helena. *See* St. Helena
HENRY IV, 568, 592
Herald's College, 6
Herat, 236
Hereditary Titles, 280
Heroes. *See* Rebels
  of Antiquity, 229
Hero's Return, 141
Herr Goethe. *See* How
He seeks Death in Battle, 463
  should have gone to America, 643
  signs the Abdication, 474
  threatens Paris, 100
  threatens Rome, 284
Hesitations, 444
Hindustan, 268. *See also* India
HIPPOLYTE, 73, 93, 123, 142, 204, 597
His Dealings with the Masses, 592
  Feeling for History, 565
  first Sword, 9
  Generals love and hate him, 587
  little Son, 368
  social Philosophy, 593
  Son's Heritage, 663
  Son's Portrait, 488
  Successors steal his Property, 475
  unfailing Memory, 175
History and France, 64
History of Bonaparte, 380
HOCHE, 114
Hofburg, 351, 369, 370
Hohenlinden, 206
HOHENLOHE, 253
Hohenstaufen, 336
Hohenzollern, 258, 408, 642
Holland, 116, 139, 183, 246, 247, 280, 287, 307, 371, 427, 428, 447, 453, 552, 559
HOLLAND, 615
Holy Battalion, 242
  Father, 340, 370
  Legion, 412
  Moscow, 402
  Roman Empire, 89
  Russia, 404
Homage to German Genius, 318
Homely Monarch, 483
HOMER, 119, 622
Honour, 556. *See also* Legion of, *also* Policy and
Hope. *See* Stirrings
Hopeless, 14
HORTENSE DE BEAUHARNAIS (afterwards Wife of Louis Bonaparte), 47, 71, 143, 198, 202, 204, 222, 224, 247, 249, 298, 301, 428, 474, 486, 503, 520, 531, 533, 575, 633, 671
Hostilities, 619
Hôtel de l'Angleterre in Warsaw, 418
HOTHAM, 538
HOTSPUR, 273
Hours of Gloom, 637
House of Peers, 526. *See also* Upper House
"How is Herr Goethe?", 421
How many of you are there?, 440
Human Heart. *See* Sluggishness
Humaneness, 578
Hundred Days, 599, 609, 623
Hungary, 87, 341
Hunt for an Heir, 129
Husband. *See* Fop
Hutt's Gate, 615

"I." *See* First
Iago, 315
"I alone have Money," 380
I am a Roman Emperor, 566
"I am the Man of Calculations," 392
"I am the State," 455
Ideals and Looting, 62
Idyll. *See* An Idyll Secret
I have lost all Hope, 71
"I intended to kill you," 342
Iliad, 622, 624
Illuminates, 343
Illyria, 438, 439, 610
Imagination, 594. *See also* Calculation
Imagination in its Cave, 12
"Imperial Diet" at Erfurt, 561
Imperial Dignity, 211
Imperialists. *See* Rival
Imperturbable. *See* Goethe is
Improvisation, 210
I must not stay here, 114
Inca State, 11
Incas. *See* Aztecs
Indies, 89
In Chains, 615
Incorruptible. *See* Letizia is
Increasing Tension, 146
India, 10, 11, 91, 127, 131, 137, 236, 258, 259, 268, 283, 359, 373, 617
Indus, 132
In Favour of the Working Classes, 191
Inertia. *See* Disastrous Inertia
Influence. *See* Stein's
In Motley, 480
Inner Man, 303
Inquisition, 328, 331
In Pawn to the Old World, 506
In southern France, 30
Institute, 98, 114, 120, 129, 135, 147, 192, 520, 582
Interior. *See* Army
In the Elysian Fields, 668
In the travelling Carriage, 335
Intrigues. *See* Island of
and Enmities, 612
Invalides, 484
Invincible Fortress, 133
Invitation to Paris, 326
Inward Reserves, 482
Ionian Islands, 90, 91, 273
Iphigenia in Aulis, 637
Ireland, 372
Iron Age, 510
Isabey, 227, 620
Islam, 637
Island, The. *See* Corsica
This. *See* This Island
of Intrigues, 27
Isola Bella, 100
Israel, 56
Issus, 242
Isthmus of Suez, 116, 131
Istria, 436
Italia unità, 62
Italian Temperament. *See* Understands
Italy, 3, 40, 55, 56, 58, 59, 62, 63, 70, 75, 81, 82, 83, 89, 90, 93, 94, 96, 105, 106, 107, 136, 138, 139, 150, 178, 183, 210, 239, 240, 244, 246, 283, 284, 285, 287, 291, 298, 300, 336, 379, 412, 419, 436, 447, 453, 458, 472, 473, 481, 489, 535, 569, 591, 621, 632, 652, 676. *See also* Army, *also* Eugene
Viceroy of. *See* Eugene
I will die standing, 447

Jacobin Club, 23, 27, 145, 153, 303, 555
Jacobins, 25, 26
Jaffa, 132, 614, 646
Prisoners, 132
Jamestown, 615
Janina, 90
Jealousy, 76
Jena, 255, 256, 319, 323, 381, 500, 523, 555, 663. *See also* Battle of
Jerome Bonaparte (afterwards King of Westphalia), 37, 125, 198, 248, 268, 287, 288, 294, 364, 382, 389, 394, 428, 430, 438, 452, 467, 474, 476, 520, 556, 580, 599, 632, 677
Jerome makes himself ridiculous, 288
Jerome's American Marriage, 248
Jesus Christ, 371, 372, 600. *See also* Christ
Johannes von Müller, 319, 321, 323, 603
John (author of Revelation). *See* St. John
John the Good, 534
Jomini, 578
Joseph I, King of Spain, 308, 330. *See also* Joseph Bonaparte
Joseph (son of Jacob), 629
Joseph Bonaparte (afterwards King of Naples, then King of Spain), 8, 13, 23, 27, 30, 38, 39, 45, 46, 72, 73, 92, 124, 144, 149,

198, 206, 207, 216, 222, 223, 224, 228, 246, 247, 268, 295, 300, 301, 302, 303, 308, 316, 330, 362, 364, 365, 428, 437, 438, 444, 452, 453, 456, 458, 459, 460, 461, 464, 465, 466, 531, 535, 579, 580, 590, 596, 597, 632, 634, 662
Joseph makes Difficulties, 330
JOSEPHINE DE BEAUHARNAIS (afterwards Empress), 47, 48, 49, 50, 51, 58, 70, 72, 74, 75, 76, 78, 79, 92, 93, 94, 95, 99, 100, 109, 113, 114, 115, 118, 123, 124, 141, 143, 144, 145, 146, 149, 153, 161, 172, 193, 197, 199, 202, 203, 208, 213, 214, 216, 217, 218, 222, 226, 227, 234, 239, 246, 247, 257, 260, 264, 267, 275, 289, 290, 291, 296, 298, 301, 303, 316, 344, 345, 347, 353, 354, 367, 368, 452, 474, 485, 521, 531, 556, 557, 558, 578, 597, 603, 621, 670. *See also* Devotion
Josephine cometh not, 70
Josephine's Anxieties, 203
  Infidelity, 124
  Plan of Campaign, 142
  Swoon, 344
JOSEPHINE (Giorgina), 203, 558
JOURDAN, 149
Joyful Days for Letizia, 484
JUDAS, 629
JULIE CLARY (afterwards Wife of Joseph Bonaparte), 44, 301
JUNOT, 33, 35, 36, 73, 123, 124, 438, 588
Jupiter, 229, 370
Justifies himself on his Deathbed, 670

Kandahar, 268
KANT, 591, 593
Katzbach, 444
KAUNITZ, 243, 561
Kaunitz Castle, 561
KEBIR, EL, 128
KELLERMANN, 66, 67, 72
Key of St. Peter, 96
Kidnapping of Enghien, 206
Kill you. *See* I Intended
King of Rome, 382
Kingdom in a Garden, 6
  of Westphalia, 287
Kingdoms. *See* New
King Lear upon the Heath, 397
King Log and King Stork, 247
King of France, 431
Kings. *See* Audience of, *also* Disgruntled
KIRCHEISEN, 683
Kissing the Colours, 478
Kléber, 120, 134, 137, 141, 587, 668
Königsberg, 387, 423, 425
KOLLER, 480
Koran, 119, 122, 123, 128
Kovno, 387
Knights of Malta, 103
Kremlin, 400, 401, 402, 403, 409, 410, 653
KUTUSOFF, 399, 400

La Belle Alliance, 523
LA BRUYÈRE, 74
Lacépède, 598
La Corniche, 650
Lady hesitates, 48
Lagoons, 89
LAFAYETTE, 526, 528, 564, 633, 660
LA FONTAINE, 628
LAMARCK, 602
La Mure, 498
Landing at Fréjus, 140
LANNES, 72, 112, 149, 219, 333, 337, 338, 587
Laon, 462, 468, 522, 525
LA PAGERIE, 115. *See also* JOSEPHINE.
LAPIE, 416, 417
LAPLACE, 114, 120, 169, 602
La Rothière, 457
LARREY, 661
La Scala, 100, 182
LAS CASES, 536, 538, 609, 610, 611, 624, 626, 628, 630, 636, 637, 641, 646, 647, 652, 655, 676
Last Bulletin from Russia, 417
  Command, 673
  Gifts, 671
  Letter, 405
  Offers of Friendship, 254
  Touches, 149
  Will and Testament, 659
LAVALETTE, 454, 511, 515, 530, 531, 533
LAVATER, 584
La Vendée. *See* Vendée
La Vilette, 571
Lavishness. *See* Oriental
Leads a retired Life, 113
Leaning on a birchen Staff, 412
Lear. *See* King Lear
LEBRUN, 296
LECLERC, 93, 148
LEFÈVRE, 470
Legality. *See* Semblances
Legatees. *See* Ninety-seven
Leghorn, 96, 486, 493, 494

Legion of Honour, 192, 211, 212, 279, 348, 491, 501, 547, 556, 559, 560, 621, 663
Legions. *See* Many
Legitimacy. *See* Curse
Legitimist Weaknesses, 561
Leipzig, 370, 446, 448, 449, 450, 454, 522
Lemberg, 387
LEO, 86
Leoben, 88, 90, 93, 104
LÉON, 290, 299, 457, 486, 531, 664
LESSEPS, 131
LETIZIA BONAPARTE ("Madame Mère"), 4, 5, 16, 29, 30, 92, 94, 95, 199, 202, 225, 250, 331, 345, 427, 428, 451, 474, 483, 485, 486, 496, 631, 632, 634, 656, 676. *See also* Joyful Days
at the Fireside, 451
implores, 631
is full of Trouble, 427
is incorruptible, 250
Letter to Louis of Bourbon, 189
with an open Date, 672
Letters on Corsica, 15, 19
Levant, 420
Liberation. *See* Price of, *also* War of
Liberators. *See* Army
Liberty. *See* Equality
Lieutenant Reads, 10
Life at Montebello, 96
"Life is a trivial Dream," 39
Life, retired. *See* Leads
Ligny, 522
Lilliput, 483
Limping Mephistopheles, 379. *See also* TALLEYRAND
Lion, Advice of. *See* That is
Lion of St. Mark, 96, 239
Lisbon, 248
Lithuania, 387, 410
Little Court, 93
Little Mother Russia, 398
Lobau, 578, 663
Lodi, 65, 66, 158, 331, 337
Log. *See* King Log
Loire, 473
Lombardy, 40, 55, 62, 65, 68, 69, 75, 83, 89, 178, 284, 289, 391, 566, 588
London, 205, 334, 361, 362, 492, 538, 615, 617
Loneliness, 38. *See also* Daimonic
Lonely Man, 263
Longwood, 608, 610, 614, 615, 616, 617, 619, 675
Looting. *See* Ideals
Loudon, 617
LOUIS XIV, 302, 312, 327, 574. *See also* Roi Soleil
LOUIS XVI, 22, 44, 221, 644
LOUIS XVIII. *See* Louis of Bourbon
Louis of Bourbon, Count of Provence (afterwards Louis XVIII), 96, 189, 209, 466, 490, 491, 501, 502, 516, 561, 627, 628, 634, 660, 663. *See also* Letter to, and Louis XVIII
LOUIS BONAPARTE (afterwards King of Holland), 21, 33, 38, 77, 198, 202, 222, 223, 224, 246, 247, 267, 268, 303, 307, 308, 363, 364, 427, 428, 451, 452, 520, 552, 561, 564, 603, 671
LOUIS FERDINAND, 253
LOUIS PHILIPPE, 664
LOUISE, MARIE. *See* MARIE LOUISE
Louise, Queen of Prussia, 254, 257, 258, 267, 274, 275, 590
Louvre, 83, 650
Love Letter from the Battle-field, 74
Love of Frankness, 554
LOWE, SIR HUDSON, 614, 615, 616, 617, 618, 619, 620, 638, 640, 658
Lady, 611
Lowe's Animus, 618
Lower House, 517, 520, 623. *See also* Chamber of Deputies
Lucca, 184
LUCIEN BONAPARTE (Archdeacon), 23
LUCIEN BONAPARTE (Napoleon's Brother, afterwards Prince of Canino), 27, 38, 39, 96, 144, 146, 147, 149, 150, 151, 153, 155, 158, 159, 160, 196, 197, 198, 201, 202, 222, 225, 249, 251, 266, 291-306, 427, 452, 475, 485, 520, 525, 526, 529, 531, 533, 632, 662, 676
Lucien as Rival, 196
Lucien's Portrait of Napoleon, 291
Luck. *See* Stroke of
Lunéville, 182, 680
Lure of the East, 90
Lutheranism, 285
Lutheran Terminology, 285
Lützen, 433, 439, 500
Lyons, 21, 22, 81, 141, 481, 500, 504, 625, 629, 650, 651
Academy, 21, 22

MACDONALD, 396, 448, 462, 470, 471, 472, 473

Macedonia, 90
Machiavelli, 10
Madame Mère, 225, 345, 459. *See also* Letizia
Madeleine, 269
Madras, 620
Madrid, 197, 286, 308, 327, 330, 333, 400, 405, 408, 438, 566
MAECENAS, 529
Maggiore, 100
Magon, 235
MAHOMET, 310. *See also* MOHAMMED.
Mahomet, 309, 655
Mai. *See* Champ
Main, 382
MAITLAND, 538, 539
Mainz, 112, 376, 433, 442, 450, 451, 650
Malay. *See* Tobias
Malet, 413
Malmaison, 124, 204, 237, 346, 347, 353, 474, 485, 520, 530, 531, 533, 552, 558, 633, 643, 662, 671. *See also* Reveries
Malta, 103, 118, 362
Maltese, 122
Mamelukes, 121, 132, 135
Mameluke, The, 335, 416. See also RUSTAM
Man. *See* Inner, *also* Lonely, *also* Only the strong
  born to rule, 98
  of Destiny, 604
  of Figures, 570
Manœuvres. *See* Poet's
Mantua, 40, 73, 75, 78, 139, 206, 292, 305
Many Legions, 387
MARCHAND, 613, 620, 658, 661, 663, 671, 673
Marchfeld, 338
Marching to Victory, 239
March of the Thousand, 498
Marengo, 173, 179, 180, 182, 232, 240, 245, 337, 359, 419, 461, 524, 577, 625, 629, 663, 675, 680
Maret, 413, 455, 457, 458, 459, 474, 493, 507
Marianne (the French Republic), 216
MARIA THERESA, 464
MARIE, 263, 476, 664. *See also* WALEWSKA
MARIE ANTOINETTE, 219, 349, 351
MARIE LOUISE, 351, 352, 354, 369, 370, 386, 387, 432, 464, 475, 476, 477, 487, 505, 506, 515, 621, 663, 670, 676
Marie Louise's Treason, 505
Marie, ou les peines d'amour, 364
Marie's Posy Ring, 270
MARK. *See* ST. MARK
MARK ANTONY, 661
MARMONT, 33, 36, 66, 70, 77, 125, 136, 148, 149, 150, 220, 363, 399, 433, 445, 446, 449, 462, 463, 464, 465, 467, 468, 470, 471, 472, 499, 507, 510, 553, 558, 587, 633, 634, 660
Marmont's Desertion, Consequences of, 471
  Treason, 468
Marne, 464
Marriage. *See* Jerome's, *also* Reasons for, *also* Undermined
  and Divorce, 171
Marseilles, 27, 29, 30, 500
Martinique, 46, 47, 372
Martyrdom. *See* Price
Masked Ball. *See* At the
Masséna, 60, 61, 72, 81, 91, 139, 147, 281, 362, 363, 375, 500, 587, 668, 673, 679
Mathematician and Seer, 56
Mathematics. *See* Dreams and
MAUBREUIL, 466
Maundy Thursday, 500
Mecklenburg, 273
Mediterranean, 91, 103, 115, 117, 121, 137, 138, 339, 476, 480, 483, 486, 535
  Fleet, 372
Medicis, 427
MÉHUL, 554
Melas, 179
Member of the Institute, 582
Memel, 270, 273, 373, 388, 389, 391, 419, 642
Memoirs, 623
Memoirs (Bourrienne's), 681
Memorable Conversation, 439
Memorial of St. Helena, 609
Memory, 572
  unfailing, 175
Méneval, 204, 205, 221, 302, 346, 350, 396, 515
Mephistopheles, 314, 575
  the limping, 379. *See also* TALLEYRAND
"Mercure de France," 277
MERVELDT, 446, 447
MESSALINA, 306
Mess, Cleaning up the, 176
Messenger. *See* Third
Messengers from the East, 268
Messiah, 600

METTERNICH, 271, 307, 312, 318, 347, 353, 369, 375, 383, 385, 423, 430, 436, 438, 439, 440, 441, 442, 443, 455, 493, 504, 511, 548, 559, 578, 587, 589, 642. *See also* News for
Metz, 650
Mexico, 307, 534, 536, 632
Midilli, 20
Milan, 64, 67, 69, 70, 72, 73, 75, 76, 78, 80, 93, 94, 97, 105, 118, 139, 181, 210, 218, 230, 347, 378, 400, 405, 566
Millesimo, 521
MILTON, 622
Ministry for Foreign Affairs, 101. *See also* Foreign Office
for War, 372. *See also* War Office
Minsk, 387
Mio dolce Amor, 49
MIRABEAU, 10, 18, 20
Miscalculation, 79
Mob. *See* Execrated
Modena, 75, 76
Modern Hannibal, 178
Mohammed, 122. *See also* Mahomet
Mohammedanism, 122
Moldavia, 259, 375
Mole-hill. *See* Europe.
MOLIÈRE, 622
Monarch. *See* Homely
Monarchy. *See* Contradictions
Money, 586. *See also* I alone
MONGE, 120, 138
"Moniteur," 33, 79, 205, 428, 500, 620
Mont Cenis, 650
Monsieur Bonaparte, 640
Montebello, 93, 94, 95, 96, 97, 100, 105, 113. *See also* Life at
Montereau, 460
MONTESQUIEN, 10, 120, 279, 457
Monteverde, 100
Mont Genèvre, 650
MONTHOLON, 599, 612, 613, 621, 623, 628, 635, 636, 646, 654, 658, 659, 661, 664, 672, 674
Madame, 638, 646
Montmirail, 500, 663
MONTMORENCY, 279
Moodiness, 281
Moods. *See* Fourth-act
MOORE, 615
Moravia, 242
MOREAU, 114, 133, 148, 167, 178, 205, 438, 443, 444, 530, 587
More Family Troubles, 364
More Peace Proposals, 236
Morfontaine, 330, 452, 457
Mort de César, 645
MORTIER, 464, 471, 472
Moscow, 286, 373, 393, 395, 396, 397, 398, 399, 400, 401, 402, 404, 405, 409, 410, 413, 419, 440, 455, 476, 489, 500, 509, 554, 566, 637, 653
Moskva, 399, 403, 500
Moselle, 26
MOSES, 56, 130, 600, 601, 622
Wells of, 130, 601
Mother. *See* Emperor and his
Mother Letizia, 94
Mother Russia, 398
Mother's Life comes first, 354
Motley, 480
MOULIN, 139, 146, 147, 148, 152, 153
MUIRON, 77, 535, 536, 618, 662
"Muiron," 137
MÜLLER, JOHANNES, 319, 321, 323, 603
(Chancellor, Weimar), 555
Mummy in Court Dress, 231
Munich, 205
MURAT (afterwards King of Naples), 43, 44, 48, 72, 92, 135, 148, 149, 160, 198, 219, 222, 224, 247, 248, 281, 308, 330, 331, 336, 349, 364, 366, 388, 390, 395, 402, 411, 412, 417, 421, 428, 429, 450, 451, 475, 494, 570, 587, 614, 633, 644, 668
and Bernadotte, 429
Murder. *See* Slow
Mure, 498
Muscovy, 392, 401. *See also* Russia
Mutable Many, 355
My Cause. *See* Espouse
"My Game is going awry," 445
"My Sceptre is from God," 371
"My Star is setting," 434
Mystifications, 204
My Strength is builded on a Rock, 223

Naïve Aside, 228
Name your Children after me, 243
Naples, 82, 183, 246, 300, 308, 336, 412, 421, 494, 570
King of. *See* Joseph, *also* Murat
NAPOLEON I, passim. *See also*, Comparison, Lucien's Portrait, Resume the Name, St. Napoleon
II, 529, 530, 613, 634. *See also* NAPOLEON FRANCIS
III, 613
and Maitland, 538

NAPOLEON I, passim,
  and the Royalists, 190
  FRANCIS, King of Rome ("Napoleon II"), 382, 488, 660. *See also* Napoleon II, Rome, King of
Napoleonic Idea, 596
Napoleon Museum, 651
Napoleon's Defence, 209
Napoleon the Conqueror, 257
Napoleon's Treasure, 651
Napoleon II, 529
NAPOLIONE, 5, 19, 216, 676
NARBONNOE, 279
Nation, Great. *See* Great Nation
National Assembly, 18
  Guard, 17, 23, 24, 42, 44, 57, 177, 414, 420, 424, 454, 457, 458, 465, 481, 525
Natural Philosophy, 601
NECKER, 110
NEIPPERG, 488, 515
NELSON, 118, 119, 126, 240
NERO, 277
NESSELRODE, 379, 465
NEY, 219, 423, 445, 470, 471, 472, 500, 501, 509, 510, 522, 587, 633, 668
Ney's Remorse, 509
New Testament, 600
New Kingdoms, 246
  Programme, 502
News for Metternich, 504
Nice, 30, 33, 34, 51, 57, 139, 433, 650
Niemer. *See* Memel
Nile, 121, 126, 130, 131, 135, 141, 360, 566
Nineteenth Brumaire, 295, 304, 479. *See also* Eighteenth Brumaire, *also* Brumaire
Ninety-seven Legatees, 661
Niobe, 346, 474
NOAILLES, 279
Nobles' School, 6
Normandy, 568
"Northumberland," 543, 608
No Sea Legs, 233
"Not one Polish Village," 377
Notre Dame, 185, 227, 230, 242, 338, 452, 456, 500
Not so lucky as Genghis Khan, 644
No Tragedies!, 298
Norway, 386
Novels, 396
Number again. *See* Fantasy
Nuremberg, 252, 450
Oder, 258, 382, 431
Odyssey, 622
Œdipus, 310
Œdipus, 622
Offers of Friendship. *See* Last
Old Companions. *See* Fate of
  Friends betray him, 462
  Home, 139
  Régime, 218
  Tempo and the New, 522
  Testament, 600
Oldenburg, 374, 375, 377
O'MEARA, 617, 620, 646, 656
Omens. *See* Russian
On Foot into Warsaw, 418
"Only the strong Man is good," 22
Onslaught. *See* Emperor's
On the Alert, 494
  the Banks of the Seine, 465
  the "Bellerophon," 539
Opening of the Family Dramas, 199
Operations Department, 40
Opinion, Bureau of Public, 380, 381
Opinions. *See* Other, *also* Two
Opponents. *See* Candour to
Orangerie, 155
Orbits of the Satellites, 632
Orestes, 309
"Orient," 118, 121
Oriental Devices, 128
Oriental Lavishness, 112
ORLEANS, 634, 658, 676
Ossian, 37, 119, 622, 639
Ostende, 175
Osterode, 266
Othello, 71
Other German Opinions, 450
OUDINOT, 462, 470, 507, 508
Our Father of Blessed Memory, 222
Ourcq, 191, 571
Outbreak of War, 253
Outlaw him, 158
Overestimating the Foe, 389
Over my dead Body, 620
Overtures. *See* First
OWEN GLENDOWER, 273

PAGERIE. *See* JOSEPHINE
PAISIELLO, 554
Palais Bourbon, 529
Palazzo Serbelloni, 69, 70, 80
PAOLI, 4, 5, 15, 16, 18, 19, 20, 24, 25, 27, 28, 29, 36, 95, 538, 657
Papal States, 84, 285, 371
Paradise Lost, 622
Parcae, 432
Paris, passim. *See also* Back to, He threatens, Invitation to, Putsch

in, Rising in, Road to, Tsar in, What is
Pariset, 683
Parma, 300, 475, 650, 676
Parody. *See* Etiquette
Partition of Europe, 273
Patriotic Society, 20
Paul et Virginie, 37
Tsar of Russia, 230, 232
Pauline Bonaparte (afterwards Princess Borghese), 92, 95, 198, 247, 248, 298, 303, 364, 485, 488, 495, 531, 633, 659, 662, 676
Pause in the Advance, 390
Pavia, 178
Peace. *See* First Overtures
Policy, 183 [More
Proposals. *See* Further, *also* with Rome, 185
Peasants. *See* Arm
begin to grumble, 382
Peninsular War, 362, 654
People. *See* General
needs a Chief, 106
People's Commissary for War, 36
Percy, 661
Peretti, 20
Persia, 268
Peter. *See* St. Peter
Petersburg. *See* St. Petersburg
Petroffsky Palace, 403
Pharsalia, 679
Phélippeaux, 133
Philip II, 327, 328, 331, 566
Philippe. *See* Louis Philippe
Philoctète, 622
Philosophie Zoologique, 602
Pianosa, 481
Pichegru, 205, 206, 207
Picture of Philip II, 328
Piedmont, 58, 184, 650
Pied Piper, 507
Pin. *See* Scarab
Pisa, 484
Pius, VI, 85
VII, 226, 227, 370, 371, 429
Place occupied. *See* First Place
Plan. *See* Egyptian
Plans for a Coup d'Etat, 147
for a Rescue, 635
for World Conquest, 372
Plantation House, 617
Plato, 10
Plebeians at Court, 219
Plot and Counterplot, 205
Plough. *See* Emperor drives
Plutarch, 6, 7, 19, 21, 34, 64, 69, 97, 119, 188, 212, 213, 679
Plymouth, 540, 542, 610
Po, 58, 65, 75, 127
Poet. *See* Emperor scores
Poet's Manœuvres, 325
Poland, 258, 259, 273, 285, 329, 375, 383, 385, 387, 401, 420, 433, 435, 447, 486, 492, 548, 590
Polish War, Second, 387
Poisoning the Plague-stricken, 134
Policy and Honour, 293
towards the Peoples, 590
Polish Countess, 261
Village. *See* Not one
Political Consequences, 194
Programme, 102
Testament, 665
Politics on the Stage, 310
Pomerania, 365, 429, 438
Pompey, 566
Pontine Marshes, 650
Pope. *See* Gregory VII, *also* Leo, Pius VI, Pius VII, Short Way with
Porte, 103
Porto Ferrajo, 481
Portrait. *See* His Son's
of Napoleon. *See* Lucien's
Portugal, 183, 362
Posen, 260, 387
Posy Ring. *See* Marie's
Potsdam, 256, 319, 321, 663
"Pourvou que cela doure," 199, 225, 451
Poverty, 7
Prague, 435, 437, 440, 442, 443
Preamble, 660
Pressburg, 244, 603
Preussisch-Eylau. *See* Eylau
Priam, 598
Price of Liberation, 83
of Martyrdom, 636
Princes. *See* Servile
Princess. *See* Which
Principles. *See* False to
Prison, 34. *See also* Socrates
Prisoner. *See* Examination
Programme. *See* New, *also* Political
Prometheus, 649
bound, 649
Promised Land, 56, 59, 63, 178
Property. *See* His Successors
Prophet, 122
of Evil, 311
Protestantism, 285
Provence, 382, 478
Count of, 189. *See also* Louis of Bourbon
Province. *See* This Island

Prussia, 8, 171, 183, 212, 251, 252, 253, 256, 257, 273, 274, 276, 286, 308, 333, 334, 383, 408, 424, 425, 429, 430, 433, 435, 439, 493, 568, 571, 576, 651. *See also* Broil with, *also* Louise, Queen of Prussia
vacillates, 383
Psychologist, 584
Public Execration, 28
Opinion, Bureau of, 380, 381
Pultava, 393
Pultusk, 265
Putsch in Paris, 413
Pygmies, 436
Pyramid, 11
Pyrenees, 362, 455, 650

Quai Desaix, 191
Quatre Bras, 522
Queen of Prussia. *See* Louise
QUERELLE, 206
QUIXOTE, 328

Racine, 597, 622, 637
RADZIWILL, 279
RAPP, 204, 256, 342, 388, 389, 398, 411, 508, 509. *See also* Conversation
Rastatt, 112, 118
RAYNAL, 10, 11
RAYNEVAL, 418
Reading, 622
Reasons for the Marriage, 50
Rebels or Heroes, 645
Rebuffs. *See* Two Rebuffs
RÉCAMIER, 38
Red Cockade, 17
Sea, 116, 566
Regent Diamond, 651
Reggio, 359
Régime. *See* Old
Reichenbach, 435
Relatives. *See* Advancement of, *also* Untrustworthy
RÉMUSAT, 214, 215, 278, 591
Republic, 10
Rescue. *See* Plans
Reserves. *See* Inward
Restoration, 313
Resume the Name of Napoleon, 664
Resurrexit, 677
Retired Life. *See* Leads
Retrospect, 646
Return of the Emperor, 497
Returning Courage, 454
Reyanche!, 264
Revelation of St. John the Divine, 1
Revenges. *See* Time's
Reveries at Malmaison, 531
Reverse, 18
Revolution. *See* Drums
Revolutionary Traits, 559
Revolution is at an End, 177
"Revue des Etudes Napoléoniennes," 683
Rex. *See* Fridericus
Rheims, 113
Rhine, 89, 118, 150, 178, 206, 207, 238, 253, 308, 373, 382, 388, 420, 424, 425, 433, 443, 445, 447, 450, 452, 453, 455, 458, 591. *See also* Army of, Confederation
-Rhone Canal, 650
Rhodes, 24
Rhone, 30
Rhythm of the Epoch, 426
RICHARD, 630
RICHELIEU, 101, 633
Ridiculous. *See* Jerome makes
Ring, Posy. *See* Marie's
Rio de Janeiro, 635
Rising. *See* Attempted
in Paris, 42
Rival. *See* Lucien as
Imperialists, 374
Riviera, 72, 496
Rivoli, 337, 378, 389, 462, 621
Road to Paris, 503
Robbers, 381
ROBESPIERRE, Joseph, 32, 35
Maximilien, 25, 30, 34, 35, 47, 498, 511
Rochefort, 535, 540, 541, 565, 643
Rock, The. *See* St. Helena
ROEDERER, 149, 169, 174, 181, 201, 213, 219, 453, 550, 558, 562, 564, 569, 572, 585
Roi Soleil, 227, 288, 327, 455. *See also* Louis XIV
Romagna, 99
Roman, 19. *See also* Holy
ROMANZOFF, 316, 333
Rome, 63, 82, 85, 86, 99, 185, 212, 225, 226, 245, 283, 285, 292, 336, 337, 338, 340, 371, 372, 382, 393, 459, 465, 467, 469, 475, 478, 485, 486, 488, 566, 593, 631, 676. *See also* He threatens, Peace with, The Eternal, Understanding
Rome, King of, 382, 459, 465, 467, 469, 488, 617. *See also* Napoleon II, *also* Napoleon Francis
Rosbach, 679
Rosetta, 130, 147

Rothière. *See* La Rothière
ROUSSEAU, 8, 11, 21, 111, 166, 229, 605
Royalists. *See* Napoleon and
Rubicon, 85, 389
RUDOLF (of Habsburg), 370
Rulers by divine Right, 437
Ruling from afar, 269
Russia, 183, 211, 239, 251, 258, 259, 311, 314, 318, 359, 360, 373, 375, 379, 380, 382, 383, 386, 387, 396, 397, 398, 404, 412, 418, 419, 420, 423, 430, 432, 433, 439, 441, 443, 459, 522, 528, 553, 554, 571, 662, 667. *See also* Muscovy, *also* Last Bulletin
Russian Omens, 265
RUSTAM, 135, 266, 292, 339, 396. *See also* Mameluke

Saale, 446
Saalfeld, 253
Saint-Antoine, 218, 527
St. Bernard, Great, 178, 179
Saint-Cloud, 147, 153, 154, 160, 189, 220, 221, 295, 432, 526, 620. *See also* Back Room
Saint-Denis, 532
STE. GENEVIÈVE, 456
Saint-Germain, 218, 466
St. Helena, 13, 473, 541, 543, 545-677. *See also* Corsica comes
St. John, Church of, in Moscow, 410
ST. JOHN THE DIVINE, 1
ST. LOUIS, 501
ST. MARK, 96
ST. NAPOLEON, 339, 484
ST. PETER, 96, 648
St. Petersburg, 333, 349, 375, 376, 395, 396, 401, 404, 405, 409, 410, 553
St. Sophia, 270, 385
Salamanca, 399, 414
SALICETI, 26, 27, 31, 35, 37, 65, 66, 80, 95
Salle Apollo, 155
Salzburg, 240
San Domingo, 590, 630
San Giuliano, 180
Sanhedrin, 590
Sans Souci, 257, 566. *See also* Visions in
SANTINI, 613
Saragossa, 333
Sardinia, 40, 59, 60, 65
  King of, 59, 60
Satan, 568
Satellites. *See* Orbits
Savants. *See* To the
SAVARY, 461, 529
Savona, 370, 650
Saxony, 325, 433, 443, 447, 493
Scala, La, 100, 182
Scarab Pin, 367
Scene with Lucien. *See* Climax
Scepticism, 600
Sceptre. *See* My Sceptre
SCHARNHORST, 253, 383, 437
SCHELLING, 450
Schemes. *See* Fantastic Schemes, *also* Worldwide Schemes
SCHERER, 136
SCHILLER, 416
SCHLEIERMACHER, 437
Schönbrunn, 336, 337, 338, 339, 340, 342, 345, 353, 430, 486, 548, 573, 578, 588, 589
SCHWARZENBERG, 348, 559
Schweidnitz, 269
SCHWARZENBERG, 367, 396, 443, 444, 461, 462, 468, 604
SCIPIO, 64, 189, 668
Scion of the lesser Nobility, 562
Scrivia, 180
Scutari, 90
Sea Legs. *See* No
Search for an Heir, 201
Second Dream, 672
  Polish War, 387
  Wife, 369
Secret Idyll, 267
  Session. *See* Deputies
Seeks Death. *See* He seeks Death
Seer. *See* Mathematician
SÉGUR, 175, 227, 402
Seine, 465, 650, 659
Self-confidence, 551
  Criticism, 642
  Crowned Emperor, 227
SELIM, 474
Semblances of Legality, 154
Semmering, 548
Senate, 90, 186, 198, 201, 210, 214, 296, 297, 353, 423, 445, 467, 468, 469, 484, 518, 562, 565. *See also* Genoese
  House (Roman), 565
Sense of Destiny, 360
Sensitive Nerves, 549
Serbelloni, Palace, 69, 70, 80
Serbia, 375
Servants. *See* Faithful
Servile Princes, 317
Sèvres, 621
Seydlitz, 679
She lays Siege, 143

Shepherd, Head, 285
Shiraz, 132
Short Way with the Pope, 336
Shot at Dawn, 207
SHUVALOFF, 480
Sicily, 118, 119, 372, 429
Siege of Torclon, 31
Sièrra de Guadarrama, 330
SIEYÈS, 139, 144, 146, 147, 148, 149, 151, 152, 153, 155, 159, 168, 528
Signature. *See* Awaiting
Silesia, 259, 382, 383, 435, 443, 444
Simple Tastes, 221
Simplicity, 553
Simplon, 650
"Simply Dead," 602
Simulated Wrath, 576
"Sire, your Brother Lucien," 292
Sisters. *See* Brothers and
Slow Murder, 669
Sluggishness of the human Heart, 487
Smelting Works, 485
Smolensk, 387, 390, 395, 39C, 397, 411, 412, 500
Snare. *See* Dynastic
SOCRATES, 647
Soissons, 525
Sombre Thoughts, 366
Son! *See* A Son!, *also* His little
Sons of the People as Generals, 60
Son's Portrait. *See* His
SOPHOCLES, 622
Sorrows of Werther, 120. *See also* *Werther*
SOUCHET, 472
SOULT, 325, 330, 472, 580
Southern France. *See* In southern
Spain, 116, 171, 183, 259, 300, 306, 307, 308, 312, 328, 329, 330, 333, 336, 359, 362, 363, 368, 375, 379, 382, 383, 390, 399, 420, 421, 427, 433, 437, 444, 447, 468, 560, 590, 595, 642, 675. *See also* Bad News
Spanish America, 632
Spanish Dynasty, 306
Sparta, 21, 63, 69
Spezia, 650
Sphinx, 121. *See also* Bonaparte
Spirit and Sword, 167
STAËL, 110, 198, 207, 216, 231, 277, 320, 429, 510, 511, 554
Stage. *See* Politics on the
Management, 589
STANISLAS, 419
STAPS, 342, 343, 344
State. *See* I am
State,
Prisoner, 415, 416
Statesman and Commander, 181
Stein, 258, 333, 393, 406, 407, 408, 409, 437, 451, 493, 505
Stein's decisive Influence, 604
Stickler for Morality, 557
Stirrings of Hope, 634
Stock Exchange, 176, 269
Stockholm, 282
Stork. *See* King Log
Storming Pace, 220
Storming the Habsburg Fortress, 352
Story of Waterloo, 624
Strasburg, 372, 509
Street. *See* Burning
Fighting, 44
"Strike off my Chains!", 35
Stroke and Counterstroke, 375
Stroke of Luck, 424
Strong Man. *See* Only the
Struggle against Venality, 84
Struggles in Vienna, 492
Strumpet. *See* Fortune
"Stupidest Thing in my Life!," 329
Stürmer, 611
Styria, 86
Subordinates. *See* Treatment
Successors steal his Property, 475
Such is my Will, 69
Suez, 116, 131, 147
Sugar. *See* Coffee
Surinam, 372
SUSSEX, 615
SUVAROFF, 405
Sweden, 365, 386, 430
Swiftly westward, 420
Switzerland, 10, 139, 171, 183, 246
Sword. *See* First Frederick's Spirit
Sympathetic, 598
Syria, 119, 131, 132
System. *See* Continental European

TACITUS, 277, 319, 320, 321, 560, 565
Tagus, 308, 528
TAMERLANE, 652
Talk. *See* Tea
Talking and Questioning, 585
TALLEYRAND (afterwards Prince of Benevento), 100, 101, 102, 103, 108, 109, 110, 113, 116, 133, 147, 148, 152, 153, 177, 182, 185, 205, 206, 208, 219, 230, 231, 240, 244, 246, 253, 291, 295, 303, 311, 312, 313, 314, 315, 316, 317, 318, 323, 331, 332, 333, 338, 349, 374, 378, 379, 406, 431, 453, 459,

465, 466, 467, 468, 473, 474, 475, 494, 510, 557, 560, 561, 571, 575, 576, 586, 589, 600, 642, 660
and Fouché, 182
as Internationalist, 315
indispensable, 313
is a Traitor, 312
rules, 467
smiles, 333
TALLIEN, 38, 47, 71, 75, 557
TALMA, 218, 309, 502, 535, 592
Taranto, 233
TASSO, 457
Tastes. *See* Simple
Tatterdemalion Army, 57
Taxis. *See* Thurn
Tea and Talk, 314
Teeth. *See* Four
Tempo, 571. *See also* Old
Terminology. *See* Lutheran
Terror, 46, 167
Testament, Napoleon's,
New, 600
Old, 600
"That is the Advice of a Lion," 410
Théatre Français, 191, 390
The Eternal City, 286. *See also* Rome
"The Mother's Life comes first!", 354
The People need a Chief, 106
Themistocles, 537, 542, 565
Thinking. *See* What is Alexander
Thinking Things over, 491
Third Messenger, 404
Thirteenth Vendémiaire, 44, 50
Thirty Years' War, 624
This Island, this Province, 95
"This War will last three Years," 395
Thoughts. *See* Sombre
Thousand. *See* March
Three Years. *See* This War
Thrift, 278
Through the Enemy's Fleet, 137
Thurn and Taxis, 314
TIBERIUS, 566
Tidings from the Congress, 493
Tiflis, 269
Tilsit, 270, 274, 282, 308, 315, 375, 380, 383, 384, 385, 390, 404, 406, 548, 553, 589, 642, 651
Threatens Rome. *See* He threatens
Three Cheers, 627
Fundamental Powers, 550
"Time is Everything," 32, 60
Time's Revenges, 408
Tippoo Sahib, 127
Tiring Job, 606
Tirol. *See* Tyrol
Titles. *See* Hereditary
Tobias, the Malay, 629, 630
"To Destiny!", 51
TOLLY. *See* Barclay de Tolly
TOLSTOY, 312, 404
"Too far, Sire," 388
Too small. *See* Europe
To Rochefort, 535
Tortona, 72
To the Savants, 97
Tottering Government, 145
Toulon, 6, 30, 31, 32, 33, 36, 57, 72, 115, 118, 128, 137, 139, 140, 460, 476, 662. *See also* Siege of
Tours, 650
Trafalgar, 240, 252
Tragedies. *See* No Tragedies
Tragedy of Childlessness, 200
of Fulfilment, 282
Tragical Dilemma, 516
TRAJAN, 566
Transitional Characteristics, 560
Travelling Carriage, 335
Treason. *See* Marie Louise's Treason, *also* Marmont's Treason
Treatment of Subordinates, 588
Treviso, 370
Trianon, 249, 346
Tribunate, 214
Triest, 89
Trinity, 122
Triumphal Entry. *See* First
Triumvirs, 154
TRONCHET, 169, 174, 194
Troubles thicken, 515
Troy, 637
TRUCHSESS, 480
True Aim, 299
Tsar Alexander, 271. *See also* Alexander
breaks away, 334
in Paris, 466
Tuckets for the Crowd, 105
Tugendhund, 383
Turks. *See* Victory
TURENNE, 279, 574, 655
Turn of Fortune's Wheel, 40
Turkey, 41, 90, 333, 375
Turkish Empire, 90, 91, 103
Tuscany, 66, 82, 427, 475, 487, 559
Two Emperors, 244
German Women, 256
Hundred and Fifty Men, 458
Opinions, 275
Rebuffs, 46
Tyrol, 40, 75, 333

Udine, 102
Ulm, 239, 500, 663
Unconquerable German, 343
Undermined Marriage, 115
Understanding with Rome, 85
Understands the Italian Temperament, 63
Under the Stars, 120
Unfailing Memory, 175
Unfeeling, 597
Unflagging Industry, 573
United Europe, 82, 378, 667
United States of America, 100, 390, 530, 533, 595, 643
of Europe, 245, 359, 378, 496, 514, 595, 596
Unity of Command, 67
Untrustworthy Relatives, 144
Upper House, 517, 520

Vacillations, 536
Valençay, 312
Valence, 9, 14, 21, 24, 141, 553, 608
Valladolid, 331, 340, 548
Varennes, 22
Vatican, 84, 85, 95, 185, 337
State Papers, 371
Venality. *See* Struggle
Vendée, 31, 36, 41, 189, 205, 590
Vendémiaire, Thirteenth, 44, 50
Vendôme Column, 676
Venice, 72, 82, 89, 90, 100, 117, 239, 240, 241, 593, 650, 662, 669
Venetian Sbirro, 614
Verona, 73, 240
Versailles, 6, 672
Viceroy of Italy. *See* Eugene
Victory. *See* Excommunication and, First Victory, Marching to
and Disillusionment, 78
over the Turks, 135
Vienna, 40, 86, 88, 96, 103, 118, 133, 286, 317, 334, 336, 348, 349, 351, 369, 386, 387, 400, 405, 430, 431, 439, 443, 459, 460, 488, 489, 492, 493, 494, 504, 511, 514, 515, 516, 538, 548, 559, 589, 668, 676
Vilette, 571
Vilna, 387, 390, 391, 392, 393, 397, 413, 419
VIGNALI, 670
Vincennes, 206
VINCENT, 316, 329
VIRGIL, 655
VISCONTI, 92
Visions in Sans Souci, 259
Visitors, 262
Vistula, 265, 382, 393, 431, 528
Vitebsk, 395
Vittoria, 437, 627
Vive l'Empereur, 399, 414, 448, 468, 477, 478, 499, 500, 524, 527
le Roi, 478
"Voilà un homme!", 323
Volant. *See* Eagle
Volga, 390
VOLTAIRE, 8, 10, 120, 166, 229, 259, 309, 320, 321, 591, 645, 655
Volcano. *See* Extinct

Wagram, 338, 340, 381, 461, 500, 520, 567, 587, 629
Waiting for Death, 655
Walewska, 260, 264, 267, 289, 338, 339, 342, 349, 353, 418, 457, 476, 486, 633
again, 339
WALEWSKI, 664
Wallachia, 375
Wallenstein, 417
Wallenstein's Death, 509
War. *See* Fatal, Fortune of, Outbreak, Peninsular, This
as an Art, 579
Office, 40, 41. *See also* Ministry for War
of Liberation, 287
Warfare. *See* Commercial
War is an Anachronism, 582
Warnings, 520
Warsaw, 259, 260, 375, 376, 418, 419, 421, 439, 548, 576. *See also* On Foot
WASHINGTON, 645
Waterloo, 523, 524, 527, 567, 605, 617, 624, 626, 637, 642, 650, 651, 653
See also Defeat, Story
Wavre, 522
We have to forget, 514
We must be content, 501
"We need him in the Army," 36
Weathercocks, Dictionary of, 638
Weimar, 255, 256, 318, 320, 325, 330, 421, 449, 493, 603
Wellington, 362, 368, 399, 437, 491, 522, 524, 533, 534, 567, 626, 662
Wells of Moses, 130, 601
Werther, 119, 323, 324. *See also* Sorrows
Weser, 374
West Indies, 51, 313
Westminster, 13
Westphalia, 252, 287. *See also* Kingdom of
Westward. *See* Swiftly

What a Ballad my Life has been, 653
is Alexander thinking?, 385
is Paris saying?, 276
Where is Ney?, 500
is the Enemy?, 391
Which Princess?, 349
Whither to go, 534
Why not use Grape-shot?, 26
WIELAND, 320, 321, 322, 323
Wife. *See* Josephine, His second, Marie Louise
WILDHAGEN, 683
Will. *See* Last
Without a Fatherland, 057
Women. *See* Two German
are Slaves, 599
Wooing. *See also* Courtship, Fruitless
Words overheard, 415
Working Classes. *See* In Favour of
World Conquest. *See* Plans
Worldwide Schemes, 103
Wrath. *See* Simulated
WURMSER, 60, 73, 75, 78
Würtemberg, 246, 326

Xerxes, 541
Xerxes' Answer, 541

Yearnings and Calculations, 346
YORCK, 245, 424
"You are frightfully young!", 289
"You must!", 411
Young France is ready, 472
Your Brother Lucien. *See* Sire
"Your holiness being infallible," 430

Zante, 90
Zeus thunders, 332
Zur Morphologie, 602